Enterprising Images

Enterprising Images

The Goodridge Brothers,
African American Photographers,
1847–1922

John Vincent Jezierski

Wayne State University Press • Detroit

Great Lakes Books

A complete listing of the books in this series can be found at the back of this volume.

Philip P. Mason, Editor
Department of History, Wayne State University

Dr. Charles K. Hyde, Associate Editor
Department of History, Wayne State University

Library of Congress Cataloging-in-Publication Data

Jezierski, John Vincent.
    Enterprising images : the Goodridge brothers, African American photographers / John Vincent Jezierski.
        p.   cm. — (Great Lakes books)
    Includes bibliographical references and index.
    ISBN 0-8143-2451-7 (alk. paper)
    1. Goodridge, Glenalvin J., 1829-1867. 2. Goodridge, Wallace L., 1840-1922. 3. Goodridge, William O., 1846-1890. 4. Afro-American photographers—Michigan—Saginaw Biography. 5. Photography—Michigan—History—19th century. I. Title. II. Series.
TR139.J48 2000
770'.92'273—dc21
    [B]   99-39386

For Diane

and in memory of

my parents and maternal grandparents

Contents

Foreword

People have long known the Goodridge Brothers as photographers in antebellum York, Pennsylvania, and of Michigan's Saginaw valley during the white pine era—especially its public buildings, train yards, rivers jammed with logs, banking grounds, logging camps, champion loads of logs. Their work illustrates books, articles, and museum exhibits throughout the state. Thanks to a much copied 1879 New Year's photo, many also have been aware that the brothers were black. But there are no known Goodridge family diaries, letters, or even account books. And so, far too many of us have assumed that the brothers would remain among the hidden stories of our past.

Then John Jezierski began looking more carefully at the images and searching for the people behind them. He eventually assembled more than a thousand photographs covering seventy-five years of one family's work as professional photographers. Much as a historian annotates a diary, he annotated the photographs—mining newspapers, public records, and the landscape for clues that would broaden our understanding of the images. In the newspapers of York, Pennsylvania, and Saginaw, Michigan, he found advertisements and an occasional article mentioning the family. He found records of land sales and court cases, births, marriages, and deaths. And he continued to find more photographs—portraits, scenic views, floods, fires, picnics, women's clubs, parties, cityscapes, and the family.

The result expands our knowledge on several levels. First there is the family. In 1827, William C. Goodridge, the free son of a slave woman and a white man, married Evalina Wallace. Three of their sons became the Goodridge Brothers. William and Evalina were entrepreneurs who owned a business block in York, Pennsylvania, and a railway freight service when their oldest son, Glenalvin, began offering the citizens of York the chance to have their images captured by means of the new scientific marvel called daguerreotypes. The year was 1847. Photography was only eight years old, but Glenalvin had started the most significant, prolific, and enduring African American photographic establishment in North America.

The family's business successes and failures give us a glimpse into the lives of middle-class northern blacks. The Goodridges' Pennsylvania success occurred against the backdrop of slavery just across the border, and it was surely a more fragile success than that of their white neighbors. The brothers' Michigan triumphs placed Wallace in a leadership position as Michigan's black community sought a stronger voice in state politics. Wallace and William O. Goodridge's Saginaw studio sold photographs to national newspapers such as the *New York Daily Graphic*. Their work appeared in the U.S. Department of Agriculture's exhibit at the 1889 Universal Exposition in Paris. They were the photographers of choice for major Saginaw business and civic events. Yet they also saw the percentage of blacks working as laborers in their town nearly double, from 38 percent in 1879 to 68 percent in 1900.

As important as the social context for the Goodridge Brothers Studio is the story told here of photography as a business enterprise. Much has been written about technological change in photography—from daguerreotypes to ambrotypes to tin types, cartes de visite, cabinet cards, stereographs, panoramas, and more. But when these changes are seen through the eyes of a business struggling to keep one step ahead of the competition, a different image appears. For photographers in the late nineteenth and early twentieth centuries, technological change—especially Kodak's introduction of the personal camera in 1887—must have seemed every bit as challenging as that presented to late-twentieth-century businesses by the personal computer.

The Goodridge brothers survived change. They survived personal tragedy, fire, and foreclosure. Through their photographs and Jezierski's work, they have survived time as well. They will not again be relegated solely to the role of illustrators of others' lives. In this book, and in a traveling exhibit now under preparation by the Michigan Historical Museum, they take center stage. And they and Jezierski challenge us to discover other hard-to-find stories that can enrich our understanding of the world that came before ours.

Sandra Sageser Clark
Michigan Historical Center

Preface

From the very first days following announcements of its discovery, photography has been the subject of a multitude of works written from every conceivable perspective. Some have analyzed its development as science, others as art. Most major photographers have found biographers. We have even begun to understand photography's role as media in defining our lives. *Enterprising Images* is part of that tradition. At the same time, it also considers photography from a somewhat different perspective—as an opportunity for both the photographer and the researcher.

Glenalvin, Wallace, and William Goodridge were among only a few African Americans who were able to experiment with photography soon after the technology first became available. Wallace, the last of the brothers, continued to work actively as a photographer until his death in 1922. That opportunity to share and, in fact, to help shape their profession for the better part of its first century was made possible largely through the enterprise and energy of their parents, William and Evalina Goodridge. As members of southeastern Pennsylvania's small but increasingly influential antebellum African American elite, the Goodridges early on established the solid personal, financial, and professional foundations that enabled their sons to pursue photography with such considerable success.

Opportunity, on occasion, also exacted its cost. Not only did the elder Goodridge ultimately lose his fortune as a result of commitments to those less fortunate than he, but even the persistent perception of the family's financial promise

and position led to son Glenalvin's arrest, trial, imprisonment, and premature death from a scheme designed by a young woman of York to profit at the expense of the family's reputation. Some years later the career of the youngest and most artistic of the three Goodridge brothers, William, also was cut short by a darkroom accident that led to his death in 1890 when he was only forty-four. With the same energy and enterprise that his parents earlier had demonstrated in York, Wallace maintained but also built on the momentum that his partnership with Glenalvin and William had generated until his own death three-quarters of a century after the Goodridge studio had first opened its doors on the top floor of the family business block in York.

The studio's evolution may have ended with Wallace's death, but its history persists in the photographs that the Goodridge brothers have left to us. And it is those photographs which present yet another opportunity. More than two decades ago this book began as something of a mystery. In 1972 as I undertook to prepare a series of lectures for a course in the history of Michigan, I encountered regularly a group of photographs that were used to illustrate the extent and impact of the pine lumber boom in Michigan during the second half of the nineteenth century. A bit of investigation revealed that many of the lumber-era photographs (and numerous others) had been created at the time by the "Goodridge Bros." studio in East Saginaw and that the Goodridges were African Americans. Unfortunately, other than the photographs themselves, a few bits of documentary evidence, and local tradition, none of the documents that might make a history of the studio possible were extant. Perhaps the Goodridges and their work always would remain a mystery and a local tradition.

Two discrete but related events then made it possible to begin the process of documenting the tradition and thereby comprehending the Goodridge mystique. In 1974, I encountered Michael Lesy's *Wisconsin Death Trip.* Lesy had created an extraordinary historical synthesis of the town of Black River Falls in Jackson County, Wisconsin, at the turn of the century by juxtaposing photographs created at the time by local photographer Charles Van Schaick and selections from area newspapers and institutions. As Lesy described the process, his book became "an exercise in historical actuality . . . as much an exercise of history as it is an experiment of alchemy. Its primary intention is to make you experience the pages now before you as a flexible mirror that if turned one way can reflect the odor of the air that surrounded me as I wrote this; if turned another, can project your anticipations of next Monday; if turned again, can transmit the sound of breathing in the deep winter air of a room eighty years ago, and if turned once again, this time backward on itself, can fuse all three images, and so can focus who once I was, what you might yet be, and what may have happened, all upon a single point of your imagination, and transform them like light focused by a lens on paper, from a lower form of energy to a higher."[1] In other words, to Lesy and his readers Van Schaick's photographs were not to be mere illustrations of Black River Falls—"eye candy," as one author has recently described the all too common use of historical photographs[2]—but were to serve instead as the essential documents from which both author and readers had and would create their understanding of Black River Falls, Wisconsin. Why not

then with the Goodridge photographs the same for York, Pennsylvania, and Saginaw, Michigan?

Lesy had provided the inspiration, and a few years later Ronald Paulson, during a National Endowment for the Humanities summer seminar at Yale University in 1976 titled "Verbal and Visual Texts," added the second essential element, the analytical tools necessary for reading photographs as historical documents. The two, inspiration and technique, would come together in a tentative fashion for the first time in the winter of 1982 when the Saginaw Art Museum and I organized an exhibition titled "The Goodridge Brothers: Saginaw's Pioneer Photographers." The exhibition brought to light more than three hundred Goodridge photographs in both public and private collections that have served as the documentary core of the research, but as many and more have been added to the known Goodridge oeuvre since. Several years of research followed, including a search of the available public documents and in particular a close reading of York and Saginaw newspapers for the time, that made it possible to establish a correspondence between the visual and verbal texts for the Goodridge brothers and their work.

The process and its result have been much like working a jigsaw puzzle with hundreds, even thousands of seemingly unrelated pieces slowly but ultimately becoming pattern and form. It soon became clear, nonetheless, that the photographs, organized according to their format and analyzed according to their subject matter, were more than capable of revealing their essence. The result is a mystery with some questions still unanswered and a puzzle to which some pieces certainly may yet be added, but which reveals the exceptional talent and enterprise of the Goodridge family and photography studio.

Acknowledgments

During the past two decades many individuals and institutions have been most generous in their assistance to this project. In 1981 Robert Struthers, Director of the Saginaw Art Museum, learned of my interest in the Goodridge family and studio and suggested that an exhibition of their photographs could serve as a solid beginning for my research. With the help of curator Martha W. Ross and support from the Michigan Council for the Arts, the Museum presented "The Goodridge Brothers: Saginaw's Pioneer Photographers" during January and February 1982. The exhibition identified a core of more than three hundred photographs that became the basis for my research. Financial assistance from the National Endowment for the Humanities during the summer of 1983 and regular travel grants and occasional release time from the Saginaw Valley State University Foundation made the research possible.

Because there is no single archive that holds a majority of the Goodridge oeuvre this project would have been impossible without the cooperation of several institutional and individual collectors. The institutions include the Breckenridge (Michigan) United Methodist Church, Citizens Bank of Saginaw, the Clarke Historical Library at Central Michigan University, the Eddy Local History and Genealogical Collection of Hoyt Public Library in Saginaw, the Ella Sharp Museum of Jackson, Michigan, the Frankenmuth Historical Association, the Historical Society of Saginaw County, the Historical Society of York County, the Michigan Historical Museum, the Midland (Michigan) Historical Society, the Oblate Sisters of Providence of Baltimore, Maryland, the Still Picture Branch of the National Archives and Records Administration, the Prints and Photographs Division in the Library of Congress, *The Saginaw News,* St. John's Episcopal Church of Saginaw, and the State Archives of Michigan. The individual collectors who deserve my considerable thanks include Derrick Joshua Beard, Julie Beffrey, Val Roy Berryman, Marsha and Dennis Burkett, James Devers, William A. Frassanito, William H. Granlund, Marilyn A. and Nicholas M. Graver, Granville W. Hurley, the William H. Kain family, Ross J. Kelbaugh, William Oberschmidt, Beverly S. Osborne Pearson, Frank M. Polasky, the Eugene Schreyer family, Barbara and Michael Slasinski, Beth Cordes Thompson, David V. Tinder, Thomas F. Trombley, William Wegner, and Lloyd C. Wright.

After the photographs themselves the most important sources of information about the Goodridge family and studio are the York and Saginaw newspapers for the period 1820 to 1920. Without the able assistance of the interlibrary loan and reference librarians at Hoyt Public Library in Saginaw and the Wickes Library at Saginaw Valley State University, most of what we have come to know about the Goodridges would remain hidden in the thousands of pages of those newspapers. Also many persons with the specialized knowledge that made it possible to interpret the photographs and to understand the world of the Goodridge family generously shared their knowledge with me. Among them are James D. Abajian, Anthony Barboza, Mary Jo Blackport, Charles L. Blockson, Arnold Bransdorfer, Martin F. Bryan, Sister M.

Reparata Clarke, O.S.P., Dawn I. Coates, Larry Coulouris, David J. Corrigan, John Cumming, John C. Curry, Eleanor S. Darcy, William Culp Darrah, Earle D. DeGuise, Jeannine A. Disviscour, Douglas Doughty, Robert L. Drapkin, M.D., Harold E. Evans, William A. Falkenberg, Harold M. Foehl, Lila Fourhman-Shaull, Patricia Gillis, William H. Granlund, Mary Hedberg, Charles Hoover, Matt Isenberg, Ross J. Kelbaugh, Hideki Kihata, Nancy Knight, Allen Koenigsberg, Lorri D. Lea, Maria Quinlan Leiby, June Lloyd, Anna Mae Maday, Forrest B. Meek, Tom Mudd, Jack Naylor, Mary Neuchterlein, William Oberschmidt, Richard Oestreicher, Maura H. Overland, Bruce Reinhold, Master Gary Reynolds, Linda A. Ries, Floyd and Marian Rinhart, Ralph K. Roberts, Karen Rousseau, Candace Main Rush, Thomas Scaefer, Sandy L. Schwan, Georg R. Sheets, Michael F. Slasinski, R. Grant Smith, Sherrill Smith, David V. Tinder, T. K. Treadwell, Donald and Carol Walderzak, Leonard Walle, W. Leslie Whittaker, Deborah Willis-Kennedy, Sergeant Arthur Windt, Lloyd C. Wright, R. Lee Weaver, and Henry Van der Kalk, M.D.

Since this project began several persons who were important to its completion in many essential ways have died, and each of them deserves my special recognition. Mrs. Virginia E. Buettner (Aunty) regularly provided her warm hospitality for our many research trips to Pennsylvania, Maryland, and Washington, D.C. Mr. William C. Darrah gave a clear and patient instruction in the history of early photography. From the beginning Mr. Harold M. Foehl recognized the significance of the Goodridge studio and provided substantial encouragement. Mrs. Catherine Grey Hurley, a Goodridge descendent, supplied both information and her enthusiasm to the project. Mrs. Emily A. and Mr. William H. Kain not only shared the hospitality of their home in York but also introduced me to the highways and byways of York's historical development. Mr. Norman D. Osborne helped me with his considerable knowledge of Saginaw's early African American community. Mr. John Putz patiently answered my many questions about early Saginaw Valley history. Dr. Roosevelt S. Ruffin's pioneering research on Saginaw Valley African

Americans created a solid foundation for all future research on the subject. Dr. Johnie D. Smith helped me to find answers to many specific questions regarding Michigan's African American history. Mr. Ralph W. Stoebel, many years ago, began my education as a Michigan and Saginaw Valley historian. And Mr. Robert A. Weinstein often shared with me his expertise in the history of early photographic processes. I hope this work in some small way reflects their patience and confidence in me.

Several of my colleagues suffered through early drafts of the inital chapters of the manuscript and yet somehow remained friends. They include Tom Hearron and John Willertz of Saginaw Valley State University and Deborah Willis-Kennedy at the Smithsonian Institution. More recently Eric Petersen, also at Saginaw Valley State University, read the entire manuscript and made important suggestions regarding its historical continuity. And David V. Tinder, the dean of Michigan photo historians, who also read the entire manuscript, more than once, saved me from several important errors and inconsistencies. Any that remain are, of course, my responsibility.

Saun L. Strobel almost magically converted early typescript into text and spent many hours patiently introducing me to the wonders of word processing.

A summary version of chapters 1 and 2 appeared as "'Dangerous Opportunity': Glenalvn J. Goodridge and Early Photography in York, Pennsylvania" in the special "History of Photography in Pennsylvania" issue of *Pennsylvania History* in spring 1997, and the Photographic Historical Society provided an opportunity to introduce the Goodridge Studio to many colleagues at PhotoHistory X at the George Eastman House in Rochester, New York, in October 1997.

For many years now Wayne State University Press has patiently and confidently stood by this project. Arthur B. Evans has guided its development thoughtfully for several years. Kathryn Wildfong has proved to be a most effective editorial manager. And Alice Nigoghosian has supervised both design and production most efficiently. One of the Press's best decisions, to my mind, was its choice of Jonathan Lawrence as copy editor. He understood implicitly from the very beginning what it was I have attempted to do in this book and used his editorial pen effectively but appropriately. I am most grateful to all the staff at Wayne State University Press for their assistance.

Simultaneously with publication of *Enterprising Images* the Michigan Historical Center in Lansing is creating an exhibition devoted to the Goodridge family and photography studio to open at the Center in the summer of 2000. It has been most exciting to work with the Center's director, Sandra S. Clark, and staff members Susan Cooper Finney, JoAnn Fristche, Larry Griffin, and Maria Quinlan Leiby and to see, through their eyes, the Goodridges and their work once again from yet another perspective. Grants from the Charles J. Strosacker Foundation and the Rollin M. Gerstacker Foundation have assisted both publication and exhibition of *Enterprising Images.*

Most important to the success of this project has been the understanding and support of my family, Diane, Nathan, and Caroline. They have shared with me the occasional "Eureka!" after cranking microfilm for hours but also the frustrations that inevitably come with twenty years of effort. For that they all know how grateful I am. In fact, this project has outlived two of the family's cats, Miss Kitty and Addie, who together with our third cat, Clara, would have liked to pose for Glenalvin, as had their compatriot many years before in York!

1

William C. Goodridge: Family Foundations, 1806–1865

BALTIMORE IN 1806 was a busy and prosperous port city. During the quarter century since Independence, local merchants and politicians had worked to establish the town as the primary Chesapeake entrepôt for the Atlantic and Caribbean trade. Their success was apparent in the reports of ship arrivals and departures at the harbor printed in the columns of the *[Baltimore] American and Commercial Daily Advertiser.* For example, the Tuesday, December 23, issue listed more than two dozen substantial vessels recently arrived from or bound for major European, Caribbean, African, and South American ports with cargoes as ordinary as cod and herring or as exotic as Java sugar and Turkey opium. Baltimore, indeed, was a city that could anticipate a most flourishing and positive future. That same day, December 23, 1806, William C. Goodridge, a young mulatto child whose prospects were much less apparent or promising, also was born in the city.[1]

The origins of the Goodridge family are hidden by the absence of records documenting the lives of individual slaves in colonial America. According to tradition, the family began before the mid-eighteenth century on one of the plantations of Charles Carroll of Carrollton in Maryland. Sometime after 1785 a slave woman whose name is not known bore a daughter whose name most likely was either Emily or Mary. During 1806 this young woman became pregnant, either on the Carroll plantation or in Baltimore, where she had been

sent to live with a new master that year. Her child, born on December 23, 1806, was William C. Goodridge.[2] Carroll family records corroborate the tradition, at least in part. In 1766 and 1772 children named Emilia and Mary were born to Carroll slaves, and as late as 1819 freed persons named Emily and Mary were living at Carroll's Doughoregan Manor in Anne Arundel County near Baltimore. Analysis of the Carroll plantation records also has revealed unusually stable family and slave community development there during the second half of the eighteenth century, especially as the number of Africans imported to the tidewater declined. William's mother very likely, therefore, was the daughter of either of these Carroll slaves, Emilia or Mary. The same names, Emily and Mary, later were chosen by William and his wife, Evalina, for their own daughters and were regularly utilized by family members thereafter. There is, however, no record of the sale of a slave named Emily or Mary by the Carrolls in or before 1806.[3] The records also do not reveal the name of William's father.

Various explanations have been advanced to explain Goodridge's paternity. Early York historians I. H. Betz and G. R. Prowell, who had access to Goodridge family history from relatives in York, wrote that William's mother was sold by the Carrolls in 1805 or 1806 to a prominent but unnamed Baltimore physician who, by implication, may have been William's father. Some years later Goodridge relatives suggested that William's father was a Carroll and that in fact it was his mother's pregnancy that led to her being sold to the Baltimore physician. "Carroll" and "Carrollton" were names that later were used by Goodridge family members and may even have been the source of William C. Goodridge's middle initial.[4]

The origins of the Goodridge surname also are unknown. And it is not even clear that William was named William at birth. Both names may have been adopted later. The name William C. Goodridge does not appear in any record until 1824, when William established and advertised his first business in York.[5] The assumption is that William took or was given the name of his master, the Baltimore physician. Yet Maryland and Baltimore medical records have failed to yield a "Dr. Goodridge," and although the names "Goodridge" and "Goodrich" do appear in both the Maryland and Pennsylvania censuses before 1830, when William was first counted in the Pennsylvania census, it has not been possible to establish a familial connection between William and any of these Goodridges or Goodriches. It is possible, therefore, that William created his own name when he gained his freedom and did not adopt that of his father or former master.[6] Throughout the nineteenth century the family name appeared both as "Goodridge" and "Goodrich," with the latter more common before 1860 than after. Perhaps young William had taken the name in anticipation of or as a prediction of his successful future.

———◦-◦———

William Goodridge lived with his mother in Baltimore until 1811. During that year the Baltimore physician indentured William to the Reverend Michael Dunn, who operated a tannery about fifty miles to the north across the Mason-Dixon Line in York, Pennsylvania. After the passage of "An Act for the Gradual Abolition of Slavery" in Pennsylvania in 1780, two intermediary semi-free statuses continued to affect the children of the then freed slaves. Under the provisions of the 1725 act "For the Regulation of Negroes," Pennsylvania justices of the peace had the authority to indenture children of free African Americans until age twenty-four if males or twenty-one if females. The 1780 emancipation act had limited the term of the indenture to seven years, but it became common practice to hold the children of female servants until they were twenty-four no matter their gender or length of indenture.[7] By 1769 an apprenticeship system had developed from the indentures and was legalized as an additional option. According to the most recent analysis of the system: "In contrast to indentureship where no trade need be taught, the apprentice—usually a child—was bound out until maturity, with his consent together with that of the parent or guardian, to be taught an art or occupation. The master on his part had to teach the occupation specified in the contract and give the apprentice food, clothing, shelter, and a certain amount of schooling and instruction. At the expiration of the contract the master was obliged to give the apprentice gifts of clothing or a sum of money."[8]

The two statuses appear to have merged by the time William was sent north to York in 1811, for although called an indenture the terms of the contract described an apprenticeship. William was to live with the Reverend Dunn, who would supervise his religious and secular education, train him as a tanner, and provide him with his freedom, a Bible, and suit of clothing when William had attained the age of twenty-one.[9] The contract ultimately served as one of the foundation stones upon which William Goodridge built his success, and marked him as one of "an extremely small number of free Afro-American children [who] were bound out in apprenticeship programs for specific trades. These apprenticeships usually lasted until the children were between the ages of eighteen and twenty-one years. Provisions were made for clothing, room and board, and in some cases, instruction in reading and writing. Some of those free Afro-American children who completed the program, eventually [like Goodridge] established their own businesses."[10] The contract also hints at the nature of William's paternity. Because his father may have been a Carroll or at the very least a prominent Baltimore physician and not a slave, an effort obviously was made to secure William's future with training in the semi-free status possible in Pennsylvania—an option unavailable for him in Maryland.

Nothing is known of young William Goodridge or his master, the Reverend Dunn, for more than a decade after William left Baltimore for York. Presumably William grew to manhood as he acquired some of the skills that would eventually serve him so well. Indeed, he long maintained a connection with his first trade. As late as 1852 the then well-established businessman advertised that he would pay "the highest cash prices for GLUE PIECES AND COW TALES [sic] . . . in large or small quantities."[11]

The indenture/apprenticeship ended five years early when Dunn's business failed. The tanner, nonetheless, honored his commitment and in 1822 William, then only sixteen, was a free man. The relationship between Dunn and Goodridge did continue. In 1836 Goodridge was listed as a creditor of Margaret Dunn, the tanner's daughter, in the disposition of an estate to which she was an heir.[12] And one York correspondent later reported that "in after years, when the former apprentice [Goodridge] had become a rich merchant, his former guardian [Dunn] had a hard time in traveling around the country on horseback ministering to the sinful . . . and was frequently, for months at a time, a guest of his former ward, who was a man of appreciation and accorded hearty hospitality to the good old minister."[13]

During his first year of freedom, William left York and lived for a time in the nearby town of Marietta, Pennsylvania, on the east bank of the Susquehanna River. There he became a barber, the profession that served as the basis for his later success and one that was open to young, free African Americans during the early nineteenth century. Goodridge also may have traveled to New York City and even worked for a time as a barber in Philadelphia, but he most certainly visited Maryland regularly, for he met Evalina (known also as Emily after their marriage) Wallace there between 1822 and 1826 and married her in 1827.[14]

Little is known of Evalina Wallace Goodridge. The 1820 and 1830 Maryland censuses list several Wallaces who were African Americans, but it has not been possible to connect Evalina with any one of them directly. Evalina's mother was Letitia Wal-

lace, and although no Letitia is enumerated by the Maryland census, a "Hetty" Wallace is listed as living in the Eleventh Ward in Baltimore in 1820 and is the best candidate of several.[15] A brief obituary printed at Mrs. Goodridge's death in 1852, as well as the 1850 census, which was the first national census to specify individuals other than heads of families, do reveal the following basic biographical data. Evalina was born in Maryland, most likely in July or August 1807. Her first child, a son named Glenalvin, was born in York in 1829. Before her death on October 31, 1852, Evalina bore several children, only six of whom survived their mother. She was remembered in later years as a wife who had "assisted her husband materially in his business at York."[16] The narrative of William C. Goodridge's success and the subsequent accomplishments of his and Evalina's children, however, testify to her full partnership and not mere assistance in this enterprise.

The decision to return to York was a fortunate one for Goodridge, as his success mirrored that of his adopted home. York had been chartered as a town by the Pennsylvania proprietors in 1741, the first so established west of the Susquehanna River. Slow but steady growth had resulted "in a town of about 1,800 people, with some 300 homes," when the Second Continental Congress convened at York in September 1777. York's location on the main east-west and north-south transportation routes resulted in rapid expansion during the decades following Independence. By 1820 York's population had nearly doubled, to 3,545, and it served as the economic and administrative center for York County's 38,759 citizens. As its most recent historian has concluded, "By 1825 York Borough had been formally incorporated; its new municipal services were firmly in place; its churches and industries had long since settled in; it had survived natural and manmade disasters and bred artistic triumphs; and it had clear connections with the outside world. York was ready for the future," a future that certainly included William C. Goodridge.[17]

Although no business records or correspondence exists to document the evolution of Goodridge's personal and financial growth, other evidence does make it possible to reconstruct the chronology of his success. Goodridge regularly advertised his varied business activities in each of the York newspapers and, beginning in 1827, bought, sold, and rented substantial real estate in York. Analysis of these records reveals that Goodridge's business activities can be organized into three stages of development. Between 1824 and 1841 William Goodridge the barber used his shop as the basis for expansion into a variety of business ventures, although retail sales remained the focus throughout this initial period. From 1842 until approximately 1857 his retail success permitted Goodridge to expand his real estate holdings, construct a large business block at the center of York, and operate a railway freight service throughout southeastern Pennsylvania. This economic success established William as one of York's most respected but also most visible leaders of the town's more than three hundred African American residents by 1840. In addition, William and Evalina's sons and daughters enjoyed personal, educational, and economic opportunities available to few young men or women anywhere in antebellum America. After 1857, however, for reasons often of his own design but also circumstances both local and national that were beyond his control, Goodridge's carefully crafted network of business enterprises collapsed, he was forced to sell his property to pay his debts, and he turned once again to barbering on a full-time basis until he left York in 1865. As a result, William and Evalina's children, following her death in 1852 and his misfortunes after 1857, migrated west to Minnesota and Michigan, where they found success but certainly not at the same level that their parents had achieved earlier in Pennsylvania. There is no evidence that William Goodridge owned property or practiced his craft in Minneapolis, where he settled with his daughter Emily Goodridge Grey and her family in 1865.

The evolution of the Goodridge enterprise reflects somewhat the development and demise of the African American elite described by Carl Douglass Oblinger in "New Freedoms, Old Miseries." According to Oblinger, in southeastern Pennsylvania during the early 1800s a "black elite" emerged which, "on the strength of its ties to a paternalistic class of whites, derived its power as the results [sic] of steady white patronage, and began to establish institutions of control over the entire black population." This leadership class "embraced an ideal that aped the white elite and promoted a sense of stewardship over the black community as their standard for behavior." Their control was challenged but never threatened by the appearance, during the 1830s, of an African American middle class which sought to develop "all-black institutions for its base." In the end, Oblinger concluded, the elite and the structure it had created were "in economic trouble." By 1860 "it [the elite] had neither the resources . . . nor the will and desire . . . to invest in businesses and expand job opportunities for blacks." It was, "in short, dependent on a pre-industrial class system incapable of adapting to the needs of a rapidly expanding industrializing economy." Racism from without, but its own paternalistic ideology as well, became the bases for its demise.[18]

—◆—

Precisely why William Goodridge choose to return to York in 1824 is unknown. Presumably during his ten-year apprenticeship to the Reverend Dunn, Goodridge had made friends in York. Perhaps during his year's absence from York the future entrepreneur had begun to establish the network of business connections that would serve him so well in the future. For the center of that network he had chosen York, located as it was at the juncture of important transportation and communication routes. But Goodridge also may have used his first year of independence to seek in Baltimore or from the Carroll family the modest capital that would allow him to ensure that independence. Whatever his motives or York's attractions, the results of William's decision were almost immediate.

In October 1824, after less that a year in the employ of barber Israel Williams, eighteen-year-old William Goodridge bought out his employer and opened his own shop in a small one-and-a-half-story building located at the northwest corner of Centre Square. Within two years he was selling candies, cosmetics, and toys from the barbershop as well. During 1830 Goodridge also began to manufacture his own treatment for baldness, which he labeled "Oil of Celsus." By 1836 the potion had become "Oil of Celsus and Balm of Minerva" (see figure 1.1), which Goodridge at first marketed locally and then distributed on a wholesale basis through agents in thirteen cities from New York and Washington to Pittsburgh and Columbus, Ohio. One application of the oil was guaranteed to retain, even restore, "a beautiful head of hair."[19]

The 1836 advertisement certainly was not Goodridge's first, but it is important for what it reveals about Goodridge the entrepreneur by this point in his career. The ad is large, two columns wide and half a column long, more than twice the size of any other. It appears at the top center of the page and is headed by a large and very energetic woodcut. The illustration is unique, made specifically for this advertisement, and signals very early in his career William Goodridge's appreciation for the impact of visual communication. It was an understanding that he would impress upon his sons even before they had begun to explore careers in photography. The woodcut prominently features the Goodridge name on a signboard across a substantial building in the left background. To the right, William, dressed as a gentleman in frock coat and breeches, and indistinguishable from his customers except for his full head of curly hair, stands on a platform surrounded by the bald citizens of York—men and women both—who literally implore his assistance to remedy their disorder. With left hand on his hip, Goodridge uses his right to apply a generous dose of the oil and balm to the partially bald head of a most satisfied-looking York

OIL OF CELSUS,
AND BALM OF MINERVA,
FOR THE PRESERVATION, GROWTH AND RESTORATION OF THE
HUMAN HAIR,
BY WILLIAM GOODRIDGE, PERFUMER,
YORK, PENNSYLVANIA.

So many remedies for the restoration of the Human Hair having been offered to the public, (too many of which having proved insufficient for the consummation of their design,) that to offer another invention now, with a hope of obtaining the confidence of the people, would seem an undertaking almost too formidable to venture upon. But experience is an apt and faithful teacher, and a constant and most successful use of the Oil of Celsus and Balm of Minerva, for fourteen years past, enables the undersigned to recommend it with the utmost confidence.

Nearly all diseases of the hair can be traced to two primary causes, producing in most cases similar effects, but which require remedies materially different in their characters. The Oil of Celsus and Balm of Minerva are composed of ingredients different in their natures, and different in their manner of operation, each being intended for different diseases.

The Oil is intended for hair that is dry, scurfy and harsh. It prevents the hair from falling off by sickness, or any other cause. By an early use of it, baldness will be checked, and in a short time, a fine vigorous crop of hair is restored to the head. It has an exquisite perfume, and may be used as a perfume for hair, whether diseased or not. It imparts to the hair a gloss and liveliness of colour, disposes it to curl, promotes the growth and prevents it from falling off. These effects are more strikingly produced after sickness, and may with confidence be recommended to the ladies as well for the qualities enumerated, as the healthy and vigorous appearance which it invariably imparts to the hair. The hair of children is much improved by the use of this oil, as it has a tendency to remove scurf and keep the skin moist, which nourishes and promotes the growth of the hair.

In describing the virtues of this oil, it is sufficient to say:—that it nourishes the hair by keeping it continually moist, stimulates the pores of the head in a peculiar manner, and thereby contributes the growth of the hair. It prevents the change of colour in cases of sickness, surprise, fear, grief and vexation of mind.

The Balm of Minerva is intended for that kind of hair which has a superabundance of moisture. This kind of hair wears a greasy appearance, and in most instances is very oppressive to the head, frequently producing violent headache, &c. The Balm is peculiarly adapted to reduce the moisture, and relieve the head from the disagreeable sensations which generally accompany this kind of hair. The Balm cleanses the head from pimples and humour, and relieves itching of the head, and removes dandruff from the hair.

The proprietor asserts that the ingredients of the Oil and Balm, are extracted solely from vegetable substances. They will not in one instance injure, either the hair or the head, and will upon trial establish their reputation for curing the different diseases of the hair for which they are intended. He possesses numerous certificates from gentlemen and ladies of respectability, testifying to the permanent efficacy of the Oil and Balm.

The inside wrapper of each bottle of Balm and Oil contains a treatise on the human hair, describing the growth and an enumeration of the diseases to which it is subject with proper directions for the application of the Oil of Celsus and balm of Minerva. It also contains a number of approved certificates.

CERTIFICATES.

I hereby certify that one of my children born entirely bald, in which situation it remained six months, has by application of one bottle of W. Goodridge's Oil of Celsus, a beautiful head of hair.

P. K. ZACHARIAS.

Clear Spring, Md. August 19th, 1834.

We do hereby certify that we have used the Oil of Celsus, and have found it of infinite value, in the promotion of the growth of the hair. We would recommend it to the public as an indispensable article in the preservation as well as the growth of the hair.

REV. MR. OSWALD,   DANIEL SCHRIVER,
HENRY SCHRIVER,   T. N. HALLER,
JOHN TRUETT,   WM. B. SNODGRASS, Jr.
JOHN KOLB,   A. DEMUTH,
GEORGE W. LOUCKS,   HENRY NESS.
York, Pa.

AGENTS:

Philadelphia—ISAAC THOMPSON, Drug and Chemical store, N. W. corner of Market and Second street. P. WILLIAMSON, Drug and Chemical store, corner of Almond and Second street. JAMES GLENN, No. 33, South, 5th street. JOSEPH SMALLWOOD, No. 583, Race street. Mr. LEWIS, Hairdresser, Basement Mrs. YOHE's Hotel. JOSHUA P. B. EBIR, corner 11th, and Market streets.

New York—SILAS CARLE, and NEPHEW, Drug and Chemical store, 199 Water, corner of Fulton street. RUSHTON and ASPINWALL, Druggists, No. 84, William street.

Baltimore—R. H. COLEMAN & Co. Chemists, No. 135, Market street.
Washington City—W. GUNTON, Druggist, corner of 9th street, Penn. Avenue.
Columbia, Pa.—S. H. & E. GOHEEN, Druggists.
Lancaster—BENJAMIN SIMMONS, Hairdresser, Centre Square.
Harrisburg—J. W REMBERGER, Druggist.
Gettysburg—SAMUEL BUEHLER, Druggist.
Carlisle—JOHN PECK, Hairdresser.
Mountpleasant, West. co, Pa.—SAMUEL BRECKNELL, Druggist.
Pittsburg—MEDARA, Druggist, corner of Front and Market street.
Hagerstown, Md.—WILLIAM BROWN, Hairdresser.
Columbus, Ohio.—HERANCOURT & DRIESBACH.
York. November 1st. 1836.

Figure 1.1. William C. Goodridge, newspaper advertisement, *York Gazette*, November 1, 1836.

matron. To the left, with the Goodridge signboard above his head, draped in his classical robes, stands Aulus Cornelius Celsus, who, with an approving smile, endorses Goodridge's action and the product that bears his name. A first-century Roman encyclopedist best known for his *De medicina,* Celsus was cited even in the nineteenth century as an authority on nutrition, pharmacology, and mental illness. Minerva, of course, was the Roman goddess of wisdom. Goodridge's identification of his product with Celsus and Minerva was not uncommon, but it does suggest that the Reverend Dunn's efforts to educate his young apprentice had been successful.[20]

Beyond its size and location in the *Gazette,* its carefully crafted design, and obvious classical illusions, the ad also is significant for what it discloses about Goodridge's position in York and the region little more than a decade after his establishment there. The ad includes several testimonials from satisfied Yorkers who "certify that we have used the Oil of Celsus, and have found it of infinite value, in the promotion of the growth of the hair." Five of the ten (Oswald, Truett, Kolb, Loucks, and Ness) can be identified. Each was a white professional or craftsman who would have been known to and respected by his neighbors in York. The network of agents who marketed Goodridge's "Oil of Celsus" included twelve druggists and pharmacists and six barbers or hairdressers. The latter likely were African Americans. Among them were Joseph Smallwood of Philadelphia, no doubt a relative of the York Smallwoods with whom the Goodridge family would soon intermarry, and Benjamin Simmons, Goodridge's tonsorial colleague from Lancaster. Celsus's enthusiastic supporters and the makeup of the network of agents suggest that the young entrepreneur already enjoyed the patronage of York's substantial citizenry and was an integral part—if not a leader—of the small group of African Americans in southeastern Pennsylvania that had established itself as Oblinger's "black elite" by 1830.[21]

Much of Goodridge's early and rapid success was due to his skill as an entrepreneur. Throughout the 1830s he continually experimented with a variety of ventures, building on his success but also absorbing the failures. During the decade Goodridge advertised an ever more varied stock of cosmetics and homemade confections at what he and Evalina had now begun to call their "Jewelry and Variety Store." In the summer of 1832 Goodridge proudly announced to the York community that he had expanded his barbershop to include a "Bathing Establishment" in "a perfectly private situation" where patrons were supplied with "pure water, either cold or hot, as they may desire it." Whether the bathhouse venture succeeded or was a failure is unknown, for the newspaper ads ceased in October 1832 and never reappeared. Almost immediately, however, Goodridge then began to advertise his willingness to lend money "On all kinds of Pledges and securities." This was a business scheme which he continued quietly for several years and which ultimately may have contributed to his financial difficulties in 1857.[22]

During 1838 and 1839, perhaps in response to the hard times caused by the Panic of 1837, Goodridge, like many York businessmen, dramatically reduced his advertisements in the local newssheets. In fact, during that two-year period the volume of all newspaper advertising in York fell by 25 to 40 percent, and by the final months of 1838 Goodridge ads would disappear until the end of the following year. While it is certain that the Panic of 1837 did affect Goodridge's efforts to expand his holdings in York at least temporarily, it also may have prompted him to act even more boldly.

In February 1840 the *York Democratic Press* again advertised Goodridge's "Oil of Celsus and Balm of Minerva" for sale at his "Comb, Jewelry and Variety Store" in York, but noted that it now also was available at his new "Barber and Hair Dressing" establishment at No. 24 South Seventh Street in Philadelphia.[23] The Philadelphia shop lasted only about a year, for during the summer of 1840 Goodridge had decided to concentrate his efforts in York once again. William now announced to prospective York employers that he had opened an "Intelligence Office" in his "Variety Store, opposite the Market House." He had launched an employment agency that proposed to match the skills of "apprentices, servants, or boys or girls . . . wishing places" with "Housekeepers" and "Gentlemen" requiring such services. The "Intelligence Office" operated throughout the summer and into the autumn of 1840, and Goodridge regularly advertised the skills of specific clients. Once again it is not clear whether the agency was a success, as the ads ran out in October 1840 and the office apparently went the way of other Goodridge ventures at this time.[24] As the holiday season approached, however, Goodridge unveiled yet another scheme. From Christmas Eve until the New Year, "Sundays excepted," a Christmas tree was to be exhibited at the Goodridge home on East Philadelphia Street. Tickets were available at the Goodridge store.[25] William most likely sought to capitalize on the German ancestry of his neighbors. For a selection of Goodridge newspaper advertisements at this time, see figures 1.2a–d.

Exactly what his York neighbors thought of this young African American entrepreneur who in little more than a decade had firmly established himself in his adopted community is difficult to determine precisely. The barbershop and several of the commercial schemes are remembered in York as successful and innovative, but it is clear that William's race also was obvious. For example, during the difficult times brought by the Panic of 1837 scores of York merchants and businessmen regularly drafted petitions to the York burgesses seeking tax relief and other assistance. In spite of his apparent success, neither William Goodridge nor any of his African American colleagues are included as petitioners. Furthermore, Goodridge was not invited to join any of the local service or social organizations in York, such as the "Horsethief Detecting Society," which counted among its membership the most important but also not-so-important York citizens during the 1830s.[26]

While Goodridge's race may have limited his success in York at this time, it did not prevent it. In fact, race may indirectly have advanced it. Although he was rapidly becoming an entrepreneur with a variety of interests and investments, William Goodridge was primarily a barber. Given

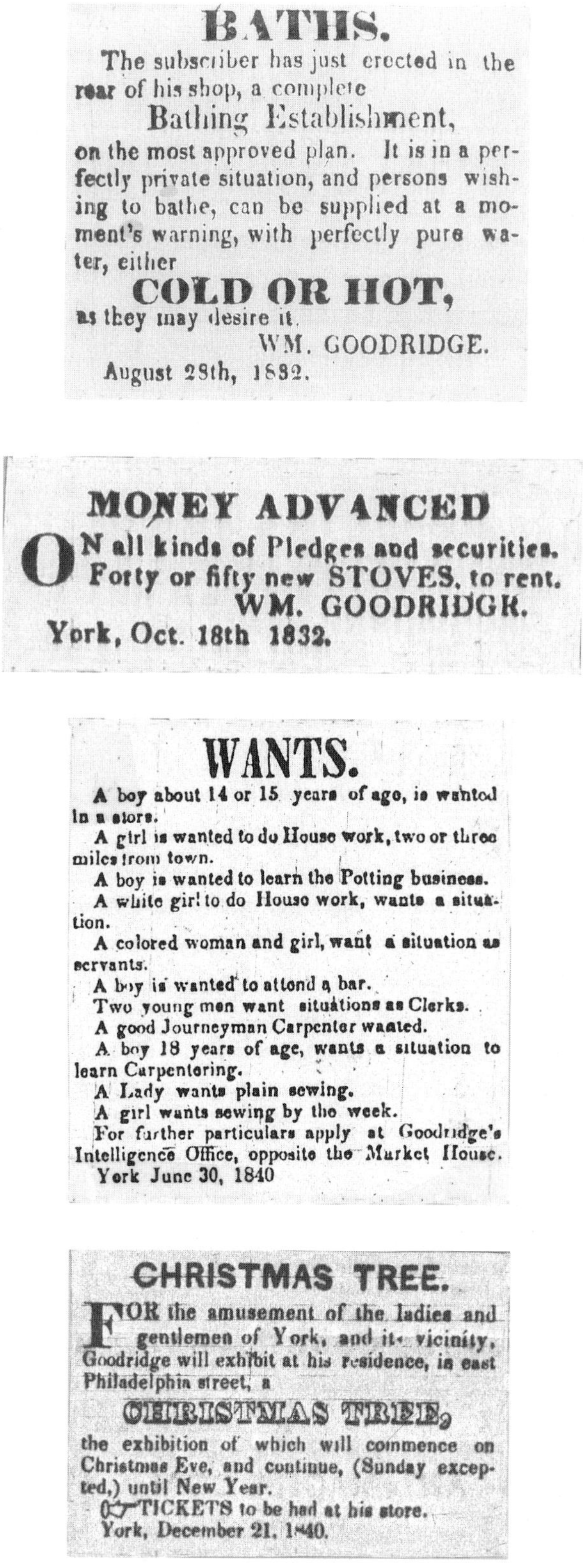

BATHS.

The subscriber has just erected in the rear of his shop, a complete Bathing Establishment, on the most approved plan. It is in a perfectly private situation, and persons wishing to bathe, can be supplied at a moment's warning, with perfectly pure water, either **COLD OR HOT,** as they may desire it.

WM. GOODRIDGE.

August 28th, 1832.

MONEY ADVANCED

ON all kinds of Pledges and securities. Forty or fifty new STOVES, to rent.

WM. GOODRIDGE.

York, Oct. 18th 1832.

WANTS.

A boy about 14 or 15 years of age, is wanted in a store.

A girl is wanted to do House work, two or three miles from town.

A boy is wanted to learn the Potting business.

A white girl to do House work, wants a situation.

A colored woman and girl, want a situation as servants.

A boy is wanted to attend a bar.

Two young men want situations as Clerks.

A good Journeyman Carpenter wanted.

A boy 18 years of age, wants a situation to learn Carpentering.

A Lady wants plain sewing.

A girl wants sewing by the week.

For further particulars apply at Goodridge's Intelligence Office, opposite the Market House.

York June 30, 1840

CHRISTMAS TREE.

FOR the amusement of the ladies and gentlemen of York, and its vicinity, Goodridge will exhibit at his residence, in east Philadelphia street, a **CHRISTMAS TREE,** the exhibition of which will commence on Christmas Eve, and continue, (Sunday excepted,) until New Year.

TICKETS to be had at his store.

York, December 21, 1840.

Figures 1.2a–d. William C. Goodridge, newspaper advertisements. *From top: York Gazette,* August 28, 1832, October 18, 1832, and June 30, 1840. *Bottom: York Democratic Press,* December 21, 1840.

the nature of this service-oriented occupation and the opportunity for his customers to relax while in his hands, William may have gathered information from them regarding investments and real estate acquisitions. This, in turn, gained their confidence and respect and later provided the occasion to conclude real estate acquisitions or business deals with them. Ira Berlin has written that "unlike many of the trades at which free Negroes worked, barbering was not physically burdensome. The diversity of the trade and the moderate physical demands allowed the hard-working free Negroes to give full rein to their ambition." And Ruth Ellen Johnson has concluded that "Many of their White clients were leading citizens and powerful businessmen of the community. Thus, these contacts gave the Afro-American barber the opportunity to be informed on business or community affairs that might affect his business."[27] The records of Goodridge's real estate transactions, for example, reveal that during the 1840s and 1850s he regularly bought from and sold property to several of York's leading citizens. During this initial phase of his development as an entrepreneur, therefore, with both its successes and failures, Goodridge was able, in spite of his race, to establish a firm economic base in York.

It is possible to measure this early success in a variety of specific ways. Since his return to York in 1824, Goodridge had married, become a father, and purchased the barbershop that would become the basis for his other business ventures. By 1830, according to the census, the Goodridge household included nine persons. All were African Americans, but other than their gender, age, and status the census does not identify the nine as individuals. Analysis of the data reveals that among the nine were William, Evalina, and their one-year-old son, Glenalvin. The other six members of the household included two females, one under ten and the other under twenty-four years of age, who were either members of the extended Goodridge-Wallace family or household servants, and four males, three of whom were under twenty-four and one of whom was under thirty-six years of age. The three were "Free Colored Males" no doubt employed in the Goodridge barbershop. The one male aged twenty-four to thirty-six is identified as a "Slave."[28]

Goodridge was one of only three African Americans in York County (two in York Borough and one in Spring Garden Township) who owned slaves. For Pennsylvania as a whole the census counted fifty slaves owned by twenty-three free African Americans. Goodridge's ownership was, therefore, unusual but not unique. According to Carter G. Woodson, under whose direction the list was compiled, the "census records show that the majority of the Negro owners of slaves were such from the point of view of philanthropy." Either it was a convenient way to emancipate one's children or spouse, often in the South, or more often, in the North, "benevolent Negroes . . . purchased slaves to make their lot easier by granting them their freedom for a nominal sum, or by permitting them to work it out on liberal terms."[29] Because the Goodridge slave is not identified by name, it is impossible to determine if he was a Goodridge relative or employee. Given that Goodridge was indentured as a child and subsequently gained his freedom and as a result the experience that became the basis for his own success, he may have employed a similar system, as Woodson suggests, to assist other African Americans to gain their freedom. Thereafter his open opposition to slavery and considerable involvement as an agent in the Underground Railroad argues against Goodridge's ownership of a slave as a business venture.

The 1840 census, which lists no Goodridge "slave" and which does not include a male individual between thirty-six and fifty-five, does reveal, however, that the Goodridge household had grown to sixteen persons, five of whom were employed in "Manufactures and Trades." By counting William, Evalina, and even their eldest son, Glenalvin, who was only eleven at the time, among the five, at the very least then two and possibly three individuals are left who can be considered live-in employees at the Goodridge barbershop, a practice common at the time. The 1850 census later identified four barbers in Goodridge's employ residing in the household. From a modest beginning in 1824, therefore,

Family Foundations, 1806–1865

Figure 1.3. William and Evalina Goodridge residence, 125 East Philadelphia Street, York. Before remodeling ca. 1897. Photographer unknown. Prints and Photographs Division, Library of Congress.

The buildings were embellished with gardens and an orchard. With an address only two blocks north and east of Centre Square, the Goodridge family had located early and strategically at the heart of York. During 1832 and 1835 they also increased their initial holdings through the purchase of several rental properties. A house and lot on Water Street for $300 were added in 1832, and four houses with lots for $1,000 followed in 1835. Records for the period listed the taxable value of the Goodridges' real estate as $1,450 in 1837 and almost twice that, $2,582, in 1843.[32] It is not clear, however, that the Goodridges owned their shop locations before 1840, but it is evident that as their business activity increased the space required did so as well. The barbershop began in a small building at the northwest corner of Centre Square, and remained at that location (after 1847 in the Goodridges' own building) until 1861. By 1830 the rapidly developing jewelry, toy, and confectionery trade which had begun in the barbershop was moved to its own location, probably under Evalina's supervision, next door on the Square.[33]

the shop had expanded to include at least three barber chairs before 1840.[30] During the same decade William also had climbed to the middle of the list of retailers licensed by the county to sell imported merchandise after having begun in 1826 in the very last position, thirty-third of thirty-three licensees.[31] Moreover, by 1840 William and Evalina already had purchased the first of several parcels of real estate in York that together were valued at over $25,000 a decade later.

In 1827, the year he and Evalina married, the young barber had made his first acquisition. For $1,000 he purchased a two-and-a-half-story brick townhouse on Philadelphia Street that remained the Goodridge family home until it, with other Goodridge properties, was sold by the sheriff to pay Goodridge's debts in 1858. The home, which stands today though modified somewhat in the facade and third story (see figure 1.3), contained a basement and attic as well as at least eight rooms on the two main floors. Outbuildings, including a stable, were located to the rear.

The February 26, 1842, issue of the *York Democratic Press* announced that "Goodridge & Co." had begun to operate a railroad freight service, the "Reliance Line of Burthen Cars," between York and Philadelphia. On the same route, the line also would serve Wrightsville, Cumberland, and Lancaster. At the peak of its operations Goodridge's rail service was made up of thirteen freight cars that hauled "all variety of goods" at a rate of "Forty Cents Per Hundred [lbs.]."[34] The Goodridge line did not carry passengers, nor did William operate his own engines, either horse-drawn or steam-powered. As was customary at this time in Pennsylvania, the state or, more often, a private corporation provided the tracks and engines that hauled the cars of private freight operators like Goodridge. In his case it was the Baltimore & Susquehanna Railroad that provided Goodridge with tracks and engine. Furthermore, it was to the

Baltimore & Susquehanna depot in York that Goodridge directed his customers to deposit or receive their freight. At the Philadelphia end of the line Goodridge offered his customers a choice. The warehouses of both Joseph S. Lewis & Co. on Broad Street and Thomas Borbridge at the corner of Broad and Arch Streets were available to serve them. Goodridge may have initiated these contacts during the year that his barbershop was opened in Philadelphia. Borbridge, in particular, had a residence on Seventh and Vine not far from the location of the Goodridge shop. Both Borbridge and Lewis were respected merchants in Philadelphia, and their cooperation with Goodridge in this venture indicates the level of his achievement at that time. Philadelphia also may have been the source for the name "Reliance Line." During 1839 the "Reliance Transportation Company" there advertised a "Line of Portable Boats" that carried freight and passengers between Philadelphia and Pittsburgh on Pennsylvania's system of canals, inclined planes, and railroads.[35]

The line of "Burthen Cars" operated through at least May 1851, when Goodridge's newspaper advertisements for them ended. However, the freight cars may have continued to run as late as 1859, but without the public attention that the advertisements drew to them. The available evidence suggests that the line was successful. The "Forty Cents Per Hundred" rate remained in effect through 1851, with the exception of April 1842 to June 1843, when Goodridge reduced it to "35 Cents Per Hundred." After March 1845 he then advertised service "at the Lowest Rates" without any indication of what they might be. In addition, the line does not appear to have had much competition from York to Philadelphia. Henry Kauffelt's "York and Baltimore Transportation Line" did compete with Goodridge for freight to Columbia on the Susquehanna River, but it then turned south and followed the river toward Baltimore, leaving the line from York to Philadelphia open to "Goodridge & Co." Although the records are not extant, one York historian wrote in 1912 that Goodridge "did a large business in hauling goods for individuals and business men in York. Some of his manifests

Figure 1.4. William C. Goodridge, newspaper advertisement, *York Democratic Press*, March 17, 1843.

are before us at this writing and bear the dates of 1847 and also their conductors. The names of prominent citizens of the time of over 60 years ago are found upon them, bearing the list of articles hauled for them."[36]

In 1843, the year following its organization, "Goodridge & Co." expanded the operations of the "Reliance Line" dramatically. Goodridge now offered his services as a commission agent in the sale of "Grain, Cattle, Horses, Hogs, Hides, . . . Flour, and all other kinds of Country produce and Merchandize." He proposed to serve customers "at a very small charge" within a network of twenty-four cities and towns from Philadelphia to York to Pittsburgh and from Hagerstown, Maryland, to Harrisburg (see figure 1.4). In addition to the York (Goodridge) and Philadelphia (Borbridge) depots, the "York and Philadelphia Reliance Line," as this expanded service came to be known, added a third major depot at the offices of Shearer & McCumsey in Lancaster. For "Twenty-Five Cents Per Load" the line also provided drayage to and from the depots in each of the communities served. On his own Goodridge also offered an express or "Small Packages" service from York "to any part of the City of Philadelphia."[37]

More so than his marketing scheme for "Oil of Celsus and Balm of Minerva" in the 1830s, but certainly based upon the experience and contacts he gained there, the network of cities and towns that Goodridge created for the "Reliance Line" between 1843 and 1847 testifies to his ability and success as an entrepreneur. Not only would the line serve more than two dozen cities and towns on both sides of the Mason-Dixon Line, but each required an agent or at the very least a deputy to ensure effective pickup and delivery. Furthermore, the day-to-day management of the entire system was much greater than anything Goodridge had attempted thus far.

An analysis of Goodridge's newspaper advertising at this time reveals that the enlarged "Reliance Line" operated simultaneously with the original "Burthen Cars," which were confined to the York-Philadelphia run, until September 1847, when the ads for the expanded line ceased. Although the "Burthen Cars" continued to operate until at least May 1851, the volume of Goodridge's newspaper advertising for all his business ventures between 1847 and 1850 was slashed. "Goodridge & Co." had not, however, come upon hard times. Instead, William and Evalina Goodridge's energy and resources in 1847 were directed toward yet another new project, the construction of Centre Hall, Goodridge's business block in York.

After their initial purchase of residential and rental properties, William and Evalina acquired their first commercial real estate in 1843. That year, for $2,600, they purchased from Colonel John Hough a choice 1,800-square-foot lot near the northwest corner of Centre Square. The deed does not identify a building on the lot at the time of purchase, yet the Goodridge barbershop and variety store had been located at that site since at least 1827.[38] Because there are no records indicating that the Goodridges owned a building or land at the location before the purchase from Hough, it is likely that they had rented the shop and the land

until either the resources or the opportunity became available to purchase the property. The Goodridges clearly did have plans for the parcel, as they and Hough had agreed the year before the purchase that the barber-entrepreneur had "the privilege and the right of using the brick wall adjoining the above property whenever he . . . wishes to build against it."[39] The Goodridges did not choose to exercise their option until 1847. Perhaps their attention and resources were demanded by the "Reliance Line" which had expanded so rapidly at this time. Or, their acquisition of an additional property on Centre Square had tied up their capital for a time.

On April 1, 1845, William and Evalina, for an undisclosed sum, purchased from John Hartmann "a three-story brick house, a two story brick building and a warehouse" with lot on the southwest corner of Centre Square. Less than a year earlier Hartmann had purchased the property from the estate of Thomas McGrath.[40] The Goodridges purchased the property as an investment and for its income potential. By 1846 they began to describe the building as "China Hall," perhaps after a well-known ceramics and crockery emporium in Philadelphia, although there is no evidence that the Goodridges ever included a china shop among their various business ventures. The barbershop and variety store remained at their original location across the Square but during the construction of Centre Hall in 1847 may have been moved into China Hall temporarily. Beginning in October 1846 Goodridge advertised the corner room on the second floor "immediately above China Hall, on the southwest corner of Market Square" for rent. In September 1847 he rented the "Oyster-cellar under China Hall, on Centre Square" to William Butler for a restaurant. And, between April 1847 and February 1848, the third story was occupied by two different daguerreotypists, one of whom was eldest son Glenalvin Goodridge. Whether William found a tenant for "the Back-Building" that he regularly advertised is unknown. Goodridge also used space in the "Hall" for the expanded version of the "Reliance Line." Shortly after the line's operations were scaled back in September 1847, William and Eveli-

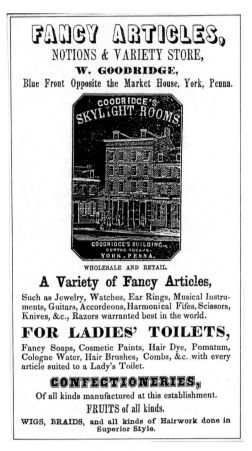

FANCY ARTICLES,
NOTIONS & VARIETY STORE,
W. GOODRIDGE,
Blue Front Opposite the Market House, York, Penna.

COODRIDGE'S
SKYLIGHT ROOMS

GOODRIDGE'S BUILDING.
CENTRE SQUARE.
YORK. PENNA.

WHOLESALE AND RETAIL.

A Variety of Fancy Articles,

Such as Jewelry, Watches, Ear Rings, Musical Instruments, Guitars, Accordeons, Harmonical Fifes, Scissors, Knives, &c., Razors warranted best in the world.

FOR LADIES' TOILETS,

Fancy Soaps, Cosmetic Paints, Hair Dye, Pomatum, Cologne Water, Hair Brushes, Combs, &c. with every article suited to a Lady's Toilet.

CONFECTIONERIES,

Of all kinds manufactured at this establishment.

FRUITS of all kinds.

WIGS, BRAIDS, and all kinds of Hairwork done in Superior Style.

Figure 1.5. William C. Goodridge, advertisement, *York Gazette and Business Directory*, 1856, p. 73. The Historical Society of York County, Pa.

na sold the entire China Hall property, in February 1848, to David and Daniel Rupp for $8,500 and invested what was likely a handsome profit in their most ambitious and best-known York venture, Centre Hall.[41]

During 1847, on the lot they earlier had purchased from Hough, the Goodridges began construction of Centre Hall, their business block. At the time the five-story building, at the very center of York, was remarkable for its size—York's tallest—but more so because it had been built by York's most affluent and best-known African Americans. The Goodridges had engaged the services of master carpenter John Louis Kuehn, who completed the building at a cost of $6,000.[42] See figure 1.5 for a view of Centre Hall as it appeared in 1856. Into the first floor the Goodridges moved their various family enterprises, including the barbershop

and jewelry-confectionery-toy store. The remainder of the building was rented to a variety of tenants. From the beginning the basement was occupied either by an "Oyster and Eating House" or later by Sellak's "New Lager Bier Saloon." During 1857 and 1858 Jacoby and Schall's dress goods shop, at the "Sign of the Big Window," shared the first floor with the Goodridge shops. Second-story tenants included a tailor, the Farmer's Mutual Fire Insurance Co., and the operations of the *York Democratic Press*. Rental to the latter may have given rise to the belief that Goodridge was responsible for the introduction of daily newspapers to York. The *Democratic Press* was printed and published at this time by Oliver Stuck. While Goodridge was a regular advertiser and sold the paper in his shop, there is no evidence that his connection to the paper was a more formal one. The third story Goodridge regularly rented as storage space. The fourth, however, had been constructed with an especially high ceiling, at least ten feet, and Goodridge leased it to the Worth Infantry Band, which used it as a practice and concert space for more than twenty years. It was reported years later that "Hundreds of people collected on the street [in front of the Goodridge building] on summer evenings to listen to the music discoursed by this trained band of musicians under the skilled leadership of Captain Filby." The topmost floor was somewhat smaller than the others but had two dormers and a skylight that provided an abundance of natural light. It was reserved for the photography studio operated by Glenalvin, William and Evalina's eldest son.[43]

In addition to their substantial holdings of commercial real estate at this time, the Goodridges began to speculate once again in residential properties. In 1849 and 1850, for $1,170, they purchased five lots in the Hay's Addition, which had been annexed to York after the War of 1812. During 1854 the lots were subdivided and sold separately for a total of $2,750, a tidy profit of $1,580. Between 1848 and 1854 the Goodridges also added to the Philadelphia Street property with the purchase of four parcels of land adjacent to the family home at a total cost of $1,890.[44] The records of these real estate transactions confirm that leaders of the white community acknowledged the Goodridges as members of the African American elite in York and in effect supported and subsidized their position as "elite" by engaging in such contracts with them. William Matson, Henry Small, Langley Meads, Jacob Stair, and John Stahle were among York's most substantial and respected citizens at the time.

During the decade Goodridge continued to add to his holdings so that by 1858, the year of his bankruptcy, he owned a major business block, a substantial townhouse, and at least eighteen other parcels of property, including six houses that he rented to York residents. The total value of the properties exceeded $25,000.[45] Two of the parcels may have been purchased as philanthropies. One York church historian has written that while "There are no records to prove that Goodridge and his family were members of the African Methodist Church . . . he did buy the property next to the Church, probably for use as a parsonage, and also owned the Lancastrian School Building which became home to York's 'colored' school."[46]

Goodridge's real estate speculations during the 1850s also extended far beyond the York city limits and even Pennsylvania's boundaries. The August 26, 1853, issue of Frederick Douglass's *Rochester (New York) North Star* reported that "Several distinguished persons have visited Canada West during the past week, among them were Wm. Whipper and Wm. Goodridge, Esqrs. of Pa. Robert Jackson, Esq. of Brooklyn, N.Y., Charles Redmond of Mass., John Langston, Esq. of Ohio, and Rev. A. R. Green of Pittsburgh, Pa. These gentlemen and many others profess to be delighted with our adopted country so much so that we know of several who have bought land in Canada upon which to settle hereafter."[47] This certainly was a distinguished company. William Whipper, Goodridge's counterpart from the neighboring town of Columbia, only a few miles from York, and opposite Wrightsville on the east bank of the Susquehanna River, was a partner in Smith and Whipper there. The business was described as "the most extensive business [owned by] colored men,

Figure 1.6. "William C. Goodridge," [carte de visite?], before 1862. Glenalvin J. Goodridge, York, Pa. Printed in *York Gazette*, November 24, 1907.

north of Mason and Dixon's line in this country." "Exclusive of lumber trucks, [they operate] some twenty-two of the finest freight cars upon the road . . . transporting continually every description of merchandise. They have also at present, in store four thousand tons of coal, and upwards of two million five hundred thousand feet of lumber in their depository, forming an area of about one hundred and fifty by five hundred feet."[48] Charles Redmond was a son of the wealthy and influential Redmonds of Salem, Massachusetts, and an active abolitionist. In 1840 he had been selected by the American Anti-Slavery Society to be one of its delegates to the World Anti-Slavery Convention in London.[49] Whether Goodridge purchased property in Canada is not known. The fact that he and Whipper as "gentlemen" headed this list of distinguished and wealthy African American leaders, however, demonstrates beyond doubt that William C. Goodridge was of the elite and that his position and influence had come to extend far beyond the limits of his adopted home town. Figure 1.6 is the only known life image of William C. Goodridge. It is a later copy of a photograph made during the early 1850s by Glenalvin.

The fifteen years from 1842 to 1857 were the most successful of Goodridge's life in York. His business ventures flourished. The 1850 census counted seven employees not family members living in the Goodridge home. His real estate holdings were substantial. Centre Hall had become the envy of Goodridge's York business competitors.[50] The large Goodridge family—the 1850 census identified six Goodridge children—lived in a comfortable home on fashionable East Philadelphia Street and enjoyed advantages and opportunities not readily available to other young people in York. For example, eldest son Glenalvin worked as a schoolteacher and by 1850 already had established what would become one of York's earliest and most important photography studios. Youngest daughter Mary was enrolled in St. Francis Academy at Baltimore in 1855 and 1856. Since its foundation by Mother Mary Elizabeth Lange in 1829, the academy had been a boarding and finishing school for young African American women. For tuition and fees totaling $325 per year, the Oblate Sisters of Providence taught Mary Goodridge art and needlework, French and German, and the deportment expected of any genteel young lady.[51] Figure 1.7 is a carte de visite portrait of the St. Francis alumna made by her brother Wallace at the family's East Saginaw studio in 1865 or 1866 that Mary sent to her former teachers in Baltimore. Also it was at this time that family members, but especially Mr. Goodridge, for many years members of the Bethel Church of God, joined the New Jerusalem Church, founded on the teachings of Emmanuel Swedenborg and then popular with many free-thinking Americans.[52]

By 1855 William C. Goodridge, the now fifty-year-old barber, had become a most successful entrepreneur who had established a network of important business and personal relationships that extended from Maryland, through Pennsylvania and New York, into New England and Canada. While Goodridge still was not listed with his white

Figure 1.7. "Mary Goodridge Nichols," carte de visite, 1865 or 1866. Albumen image, 2⅜ x 3 ⅜ inches, ivory bristol board mount, 2 x 4 ⅛ inches. Goodridge Brothers Studio, East Saginaw, Mich. Archives of Oblate Sisters of Providence, Baltimore, Maryland.

neighbors or business colleagues in any of the petitions, memorials, or membership rosters that were published in the York newspapers at the time, his position at the head of the African American community was acknowledged by them with the respect it deserved. As one commentator on his life later observed, Goodridge had a reputation in York for being "scrupulously honest in his dealings. He gave thorough attention to his business and exercised tact with his customers, who had utmost confidence in his integrity. He had the universal respect of the community."[53]

In spite of their success, the Goodridges' life was not without its tragedies. Ten-year-old Albertus, the family's second-eldest son and third child, died in 1846. Six years later, on October 31, 1852,

Figure 1.8. "[Evalina Wallace Goodridge?]," before 1851, sixth-plate daguerreotype. Glenalvin J. Goodridge, York, Pa. Collection of Marsha and Dennis Burkett.

William's beloved Evalina left him a widower after twenty-six years of their extraordinarily successful partnership. Figure 1.8, a daguerreotype made of an unidentified African American woman by Glenalvin during the late 1840s, his first years as a professional photographer, may be a portrait of his mother, Evalina Wallace Goodridge. The cause of her death was not disclosed, but three of William and Evalina's children already had or would die of a heart ailment that may have been hereditary.[54] William's sorrow was lightened somewhat when eldest daughter Emily married Ralph Toyer Grey of Baltimore in 1855 and then by the birth of his first grandchild and namesake, William Toyer Grey, the following year. But it was a short-lived joy when Emily and young William headed west to join husband and father Ralph, who had gone on ahead to St. Anthony, Minnesota Territory, where he worked as a barber at the Jarret House Hotel. The same year, 1857, daughter Susan was stricken with the heart condition that would leave her an invalid and from which she would die four years later.[55]

The final period of William Goodridge's residence in York began, therefore, with personal loss and separation. It ended with the complete collapse of the enterprise he and Evalina had worked so long and so hard to create. Between 1857 and his own departure from York in 1865, the several tragedies that had befallen the Goodridge family would be extended to William's business affairs as well. A notice printed in the January 4, 1859, issue of the *York Gazette* announced that York County sheriff Samuel Forscht "sold on Friday, last [December 31, 1858], the estate of William Goodridge, to P. A. and S. Small." The record of the sale indicates that the sheriff sold twenty Goodridge properties to three individuals for a total of $11,479.88, including costs. Philip A. Small, a wealthy York hardware merchant, purchased seventeen of the twenty parcels, including Centre Hall and the Goodridge residence on East Philadelphia Street. Small paid only $3,200 for Centre Hall, which had been built at a cost of $6,000 in 1847. The sheriff used $2,700 of the sale price to pay a mortgage on the building. The sale price of the family home was $1,330, and Small paid only an additional $5,938 for fifteen other Goodridge properties, either houses or lots. David Rupp, to whom the Goodridges had sold China Hall in 1848, purchased one parcel for $495, and a Jason H. Schlosser of York acquired the other for $705. Goodridge was represented by attorney John L. Evans of the firm Evans and Mayer in the proceeding.[56]

Unlike the Panic of 1837, which caused severe economic hardship for most Yorkers and reduced business activity dramatically, the post–Crimean War Panic of 1857 had little affect on business in York. Between 1850 and 1860 the city's population continued to grow at the healthy rate of 23 percent for the decade, from 7,000 to more than 8,600 inhabitants. York historian Georg R. Sheets, in fact, has characterized the decade as "a continuation of . . . [previous] commercial advancement." He has appropriately attributed the borough's growing prosperity—even during the late 1850s, when most other northern industrial communities suffered a severe economic depression—to its "strong trade relationships with the South," its location on "a central trade route between North and South," and "particularly [its] close ties with neighboring Maryland (especially the city of Baltimore) and its lucrative trade with other Southern states."[57] William Goodridge was the exception to this pattern of continuing prosperity.

For several months after the sheriff's sale Goodridge continued to occupy his Centre Hall shops, though on a rental basis. Newspaper advertisements suggest that the confectionery-variety store remained opened into December 1859 and that the Goodridge barbershop did not vacate the "Sign of the Blue Front" at Centre Hall until the end of January 1861. Although the Philadelphia Street residence also had been sold in December 1858, the family did continue to occupy it for a time.[58] During March 1861, however, Goodridge announced that "The Barber Shop, and Confectionery . . . will be removed on the first of April next, from its present location in Centre Square to North George Street, in the house occupied by Emanuel Beck, third door from the South West corner of George and Philadelphia streets." Beck was a shoemaker and had been a Goodridge neighbor for several years. Whether Beck's George Street address served both families as shop and residence is unknown.[59]

The move was a successful one and gave Goodridge the opportunity to regain a bit of the stability that his barbering had always provided. By June 1862, in fact, he was thanking his "old customers and the public in general for the very flattering encouragement he has received at their hands and hopes by strict attention to his business and a desire to do his work in a satisfactory manner, to merit a continuance of public patronage."

To demonstrate that his difficulties had not dulled his wit, he also treated them to the following poem:

> I'll shave your beard when'er you come,
> And my towels so clear and clean,
> For I'm prepared, from morn till night,
> With razors sharp and very keen.

The advertisement also referred to "His workmen [who] understand how to shave smoothly and to cut hair in the latest style," suggesting that Goodridge continued to employ other barbers in his shop after having been forced to give up Centre Hall and may even have taken over the location from shoemaker Beck.[60] In January 1864, however, John Adam Gardner, "a native of Frankfort, Germany," informed Yorkers that "he has become the proprietor of William Goodridge's well known Barber and Hair Dressing Establishment in North George St." William had moved once again, this time to 49 North Duke Street, where his son Glenalvin and family had been living since purchasing the townhouse from wife and daughter-in-law Rhoda Grey Goodridge's parents, Hamilton and Jane Grey, in 1853. Goodridge's "Shaving and Hair Cutting Saloon," the last of his business ventures in York, remained there until the summer of 1865, when William and Glenalvin and his family left York and headed west to East Saginaw, Michigan, and Minneapolis.[61]

If most York businesses weathered or were unaffected by the Panic of 1857, why then had William Goodridge failed at this time? One historian has suggested that Goodridge's fate was part of a larger pattern. "Whatever progress the Northern Afro-American businessmen made, especially in the fields of catering and barbering, was greatly reduced between 1830 and 1860," writes Ruth Ellen Johnson. "During this period, almost five million White European immigrants came to America. These immigrants reinforced the racial prejudices already existing in America by refusing to work with persons of color. . . . The immigrants who had entrepreneurial experiences immediately became competitive with Afro-Americans in business."

And, Johnson concludes, "Although White Americans did not have much interest in personal service businesses, the new White immigrants took control in certain areas of personal service, which Afro-Americans had dominated," including barbering.[62]

Johnson's hypothesis may explain John Adam Gardner's takeover of the Goodridge barbershop on North George Street in 1864, but the origins of William's fate are to be found at least a decade earlier with Evalina's death in 1852. Through the quarter century of their partnership, Evalina Goodridge had served as willing and equal associate in her husband's multitude of business ventures. The Christmas tree scheme of December 1840, for example, would have been impossible without her approbation, and her dominion over the family confectionery-jewelry-variety store was widely recognized. She also jointly owned many of the Goodridge properties with William. But most important was the fact that her realism served to temper his often overly optimistic entrepreneurial schemes. With her death he lost both his partner and the person who defined the boundaries of his enthusiasm.[63]

After 1852 Goodridge continued to speculate in real estate, but he also began to gamble on the success of his friends and neighbors. One of his sons later remembered that his father "was worth about $200,000, but endorsed notes too freely, one being for $40,000, and was consequently wrecked in the financial crash of 1857, from which he never recovered." There can be little doubt that the entrepreneur was the most important philanthropist and financial guarantor within the African American community in antebellum York, yet the value of Goodridge's holdings and his commitments to others may have appreciated over time in his son's memory.[64]

William and Evalina rarely had incurred significant debt. The only record of a judgment against the Goodridges before 1852 occurred in December 1847, when a lien in the amount of $2,515 was placed against their property by the York Bank. It was quickly redeemed, however, with the sale of China Hall the following February.[65] Between August 1856 and December 1858, however, ten judgments were filed against William Goodridge, all of which he lost, both for his own debts and those of others that he had guaranteed. The largest was for $2,000, the smallest only $23.87. Together the judgments amounted to a bit more than $5,100, hardly the $40,000 his son later remembered. Nonetheless, because Goodridge was unable to pay the entire amount his properties were auctioned by the sheriff and the proceeds distributed to his creditors.[66]

William's grief at Evalina's death and the uncharacteristic financial decisions that may have reflected his state of mind at the time were the occasion for Goodridge's economic downfall in 1858, but during the decade he also had become involved in events of even greater consequence that almost certainly distracted his attention from its usual focus on his business affairs. By 1850 Goodridge had become an active opponent of slavery and during the decade worked with other abolitionists in Pennsylvania and the North to destroy the institution.

Although Goodridge earlier had owned a slave and may have used such ownership as a means of assisting slaves to gain their freedom, he rarely made his political views public. Only two bits of evidence from before 1850 signal his persuasion, and both are carefully camouflaged within a deluge of his business advertisements. In December 1840, an ad for "More New Goods at Goodridge's Jewelry Store," which listed "A Splendid Assortment" of everything from figs and prunes to dolls and German silver spoons, also noted that Goodridge stocked "Harrison Song Books" and "Anti Slavery Almanacks for 1841." The excitement of the Whigs' national party convention held in nearby Harrisburg in December 1839, the resulting nomination of William Henry Harrison and John Tyler, and the ensuing "Tippecanoe and Tyler too" campaign that had given the Whigs their first presidential victory, coupled with his anticipation of the inauguration, may have emboldened Goodridge to declare his political position.[67]

Although he never had the opportunity to vote for the party, William remained a Whig. During 1846, in the midst of President James K. Polk's expansion of the Mexican War with his directing General Winfield Scott to move against Mexico City by way of Veracruz, Goodridge published one of his most ingenious advertisements opposing the Democratic leader's decision. The ad took the form of a poem titled "PEACE WITH MEXICO!" and couched its biting political satire in the language of commerce. Goodridge may have added to his intended irony by publishing the poetic ad in York's *Democratic Press*. He wrote:

> Just now's the time for girls and boys,
> To buy of GOODRIDGE one cent toys.
> A little chicken with a man's head,
> Or troops of soldiers made of lead.
> Come on ye boys and just see
> The MEXICANS from Monterey,
> Women and men both made of Candy.
> So that a child can eat quite handy.
> He's also got small barking dogs,
> And little boys a riding frogs.
> Prunes and Raisins every day,
> Just from the Isle of Malaga.[68]

The poem may be interpreted to mean that the Democrats were "children," that their generals were "barnyard fowl" (both Zachary Taylor and Winfield Scott wore cockaded hats that made them look like roosters), that their troops were "toy soldiers" who would "eat quite handy . . . Mexicans from Monterey . . . made of candy" (Taylor had recently led American forces toward Monterey and Buena Vista), and that the Democratic leaders (President Polk in particular) were "barking dogs" leading a party of "little boys a riding frogs"! Or, it simply may have been an advertisement for Goodridge's usual stock of goods.

According to his descendants, though, William Goodridge's opposition to slavery and the Democrats' efforts to spread it westward was much more than poetic. One later wrote that her great-grandfather "left York and went West when the Government offered a reward of $500 for him, for his activities in the underground in helping free the slaves." Others described him to York's early historians as "an admirable conversationalist," "of

great presence," and "a man of rare intelligence" who read "the Liberator, the Anti-Slavery Standard, Bailey's New Era, the New York Tribune and other papers relating to the slavery question." They remembered him as "an active anti-slavery man" who "was familiarly acquainted with William Lloyd Garrison, Wendell Phillips, Gerrit Smith and most of the abolitionists of his time." His "wealth, work, and intelligence" put him in "high standing with those who were the leading spirits in anti-slavery," including Frederick Douglass, with whom he shared a lifelong friendship. He even "was well acquainted with John Brown." One person noted that his activities prompted "Southern men" to attempt "to kidnap him, but [that they] did not succeed."[69]

The historians of the movement have not quite agreed with William's descendants. Charles Blockson, for example, in *The Underground Railroad in Pennsylvania*, states that York County's "most important and brilliant agent [in the Underground Railroad] was William C. Goodridge, the black barber and businessman of York City," but this importance did not translate into inclusion in Blockson's more general and highly respected accounts of the Underground Railroad. And William Still, whose 1873 *The Underground Railroad* was a very detailed and personal account of his own and others' experiences at the time, does not mention his friend, business associate, and presumably compatriot William C. Goodridge.[70]

R. C. Smedley, however, who in the decades immediately following the conclusion of the Civil War focused his research specifically on southeastern Pennsylvania, characterized Goodridge as "an active and valuable agent" in the Underground Railroad at York. He explained his method of operation as follows:

> Whenever he [Goodridge] received information that "baggage" was on the road that it was necessary to hurry through, he sent word to Columbia the day before it was expected to arrive. Cato Jourdon, colored, who drove a team which hauled cars over the bridge, brought all "baggage" safely across, where the agents had another trusty colored man to receive it. The fugitives were then taken through Black's hotel yard to another portion of the town, and concealed overnight; when

Wm. Wright, of that place, generally took them in charge and sent some to Daniel Gibbons, and some direct to Philadelphia, in the false end of a box car, owned by Stephen Smith and William Whipper, colored men and lumber merchants of Columbia. They got off at the head of the "plane," near Philadelphia, where an agent was in waiting to receive them.[71]

The Philadelphia "agent" doubtless was William Still, a member of the Pennsylvania Anti-Slavery Society, and who with Whipper, Smith, and Wright was among Goodridge's closest friends and business associates at this time.

Details of two violent incidents and William Goodridge's involvement in them demonstrate the intensity of his opposition to slavery and the extent of his participation in the Underground Railroad. On September 11, 1851, Edward Gorsuch, a Maryland slave owner, was killed and his son severely injured during a confrontation known as the "Christiana Riot." Gorsuch, acting on warrants issued under the recently enacted 1850 Fugitive Slave Law, had come to Christiana, Pennsylvania, a hamlet outside of Coatesville between Lancaster and Philadelphia. He correctly believed that two of his runaway slaves were hiding at the home of the former fugitive William Parker in Christiana. Forewarned of Gorsuch's objective, Parker and his neighbors, some black and some white, had organized to resist. As a result of the "Riot," forty-one (thirty-six black and five white) participants were charged with treason. Charges against most of the defendants were dropped. The others were acquitted by a jury that deliberated only fifteen minutes. William Parker and the two fugitive slaves, Alexander Pinckney and Abraham Johnson, escaped to Canada.[72]

According to Betz, Goodridge's special freight cars "were used to convey several of the fugitive blacks, who took part in the Christiana riot, in Lancaster County, in 1851. These men were forwarded to Canada." Neither Betz nor the most recent accounts of the event identify Parker as one of the fugitives using the Goodridge line.[73] However, it is clear that Parker knew Goodridge as early as 1839, that the two collaborated in the activities of the Underground Railroad thereafter, and that

Parker may have turned to Goodridge to assist in his escape or that of his associates in 1851 as he had a decade earlier.

During the summer of 1839 or 1840, William Parker had fled the plantation of Major William Brogdon in Anne Arundel County, Maryland. From Baltimore Parker then escaped north to York. In an 1866 interview Parker described his experience in York: "We walked on a long distance before we lost the sounds; but about four o'clock the same morning, entered York, where we remained during the day. . . . Once in York, we thought we would be safe, but . . . our ideas of security were materially lessened when we met a friend during the day, who advised us to proceed further, as we were not out of imminent danger. . . . According to this advice we started that night for Columbia."[74] Although Parker did not name William Goodridge as the "friend" in York who had assisted him, Goodridge's position in the community and especially his connections in Columbia and Lancaster County point to him as the most logical candidate. In fact, it was at the Goodridge home on East Philadelphia Street that Parker likely had "remained during the day." According to Betz, "There was [at the Goodridge home] a movable trap-door in the kitchen floor, covered by carpet, which allowed the fugitive to find ingress into a cavern, which was filled by straw. . . . One of Mr. Goodridge's sons described this hiding place some years ago. When the house was remodeled . . . the hiding place was found just as he described it."[75]

From York Parker made his way to Columbia and then on to Christiana, where by 1850 his home had become "a center and meeting place for the black people of the neighborhood." With five or six other free African Americans Parker formed "an organization for mutual protection against slaveholders and kidnappers, and had resolved to prevent any of our brethren being taken back into slavery, at the risk of our own lives." It was this organization that led to Parker's involvement in the "Christiana Riot," and one that no doubt regularly used Goodridge's "Reliance Line," whose tracks to Philadelphia and freedom passed close by Christiana.[76]

Eight years after the "Christiana Riot," Goodridge was more directly involved in a second incident that created an even greater national excitement and by which he may have drawn attention to himself and his family in York. Under the cover of darkness during the evening of October 16, 1859, the abolitionist John Brown and nineteen followers, including five free African Americans, occupied the federal arsenal at Harpers Ferry, Virginia. Historians continue to debate Brown's intentions, but by the morning of October 18 a force of federal marines under the command of Lieutenant Colonel Robert E. Lee had stormed the arsenal, killed ten of Brown's men, and captured the abolitionist leader. Brown was convicted of treason and conspiracy to incite insurrection on October 31 and hanged at Charlestown, Virginia, a month later.

Five of Brown's men escaped capture, although the hunt was widespread. Emotion for and against ran high both in the South and the North. Within a fortnight of the event most newspapers in major cities and small towns published the details, including the *York Democratic Press,* which reported "the startling news of the negro and abolitionist insurrection at Harper's Ferry."[77] Little did most Yorkers know the role that their city had played in assisting the escape of Osborne Perry Anderson, one of John Brown's most trusted lieutenants (see figure 1.9).

Two years after having made his escape to Canada, Anderson published some of the details. "At night," he wrote, "I set out and reached York, where a good Samaritan gave me oil, wine and raiment. From York I wended my way to the Pennsylvania railroad. I took the train at night, at a convenient station, and went to Philadelphia, where great kindness was extended to me; and from there I came to Canada, without mishap or incident of importance." Jean Libby, Anderson's most recent biographer, believes that the "'Good Samaritan' whom he [Anderson] did not name was William C. Goodridge." Further, she argues that Anderson's escape was possible only "because he connected with the Underground Railroad for fugitive slaves"—Anderson's "Pennsylvania railroad,"

Figure 1.9. "Osborne Perry Anderson," ca. 1861. Photographer unknown. Prints and Photographs Division, Library of Congress.

otherwise known as Goodridge's "Reliance Line."[78]

According to Betz, "one of the colored men who escaped from Harper's Ferry after that disastrous failure came to York and arrived by night at the Philadelphia street house and produced great fear and consternation in the Goodridge family." By that time, Betz wrote, the Goodridge home was "watched day and night." Yet, "through some means," Goodridge "hid . . . Anderson in the third story of his building in Centre Square [see figure 1.10], under the stairway in a closet for several weeks, until the excitement subsided. When it was considered safe he was sent away on a Goodridge car."[79] Ironically, Goodridge had hidden Anderson in Centre Hall on the floor immediately above the offices of the *York Democratic Press* that had reported the "startling news of the . . . insurrection at Harper's Ferry."

For many years William Goodridge's descendants attributed his seeming clandestine departure from York in 1863 for Michigan and then Minnesota to the success of these antislavery efforts. When son William O. Goodridge died in East Saginaw in 1890, surviving son Wallace L. Goodridge recalled for a local newspaper reporter that their father was "a noted abolitionist . . . [who] owned what was known as Goodridge's York & Pennsylvania line, his possession being the equipment of a railroad 100 miles in length, which he operated about fifteen years. He used to transport fugitive slaves over his line, and for so doing rewards were offered for his capture if brought into Baltimore." Other family members who had continued to reside in or who had returned to York to live at the turn of the century provided York historians George R. Prowell and I. H. Betz with information that allowed Prowell to conclude that "when the Confederates approached York in 1863 the family departed" and Betz to write that "rewards were offered to those who would kidnap him [Goodridge] and spirit him to the south, where dire punishment was in store for him." But Goodridge, suggested Betz, was a man who managed to avoid "all pitfalls that were laid for him," at least until the summer of 1863, when "the invasion of Pennsylvania [and the battle at Gettysburg] . . . led the whole family to hurriedly leave the place. . . . The reason for this step . . . [being] their underground record, which they rightly supposed would lead to their personal harm at the hands of the invaders."[80]

Subsequent historians sustained the belief that there was a direct connection between the Underground Railroad, the Confederate occupation of York and Battle of Gettysburg in 1863, and the family's flight west. For example, in a 1980 general overview of Saginaw's development, Stuart D. Gross wrote that William C. Goodridge "worked in the underground railroad which spirited slaves to freedom in northern states and Canada. He was so well known for his activities against slavery that a price was placed on his head by irate Southern slave owners. When the Army of Virginia approached York in 1863," Gross concluded, "the family fled." In documenting Wallace Goodridge's 1972 induction into the "Saginaw Hall of Fame," the organization noted that he and "his brothers . . . arrived in Saginaw in 1862. The family had fled

Figure 1.10. "Northwest Angle of Centre Square, York," ca. 1904. Photographer unknown. Prints and Photographs Division, Library of Congress.

Pennsylvania after the invasion of southern troops. The father and some of the other children went to Minnesota. Their flight from Pennsylvania was made necessary because of the father's activity in operation of the Underground Railroad." In his popular 1981 history of York, Sheets echoed Gross's and the Hall of Fame's conclusions. More recently, however, Sheets has concluded correctly that while the story "makes a neat, almost romantic, tale . . . bits and pieces of information seem to refute [it]."[81]

As part of his strategy for an offensive thrust into the North for the summer of 1863, General Robert E. Lee crossed the Mason-Dixon Line into Pennsylvania intending to capture Harrisburg and Philadelphia. The result instead was the defeat at Gettysburg. Following his original plan, Lee ordered a regiment under the command of General Jubal Early "to take York and move across the Susquehanna toward Philadelphia." On Sunday, June 28, approximately nine thousand Confederate troops occupied York. By Tuesday, after "requisitioning" supplies and destroying telegraph lines and railroad switches, Early's men had marched west out of York to join Lee near Gettysburg.[82]

The Confederate invasion and occupation may have given the Goodridges cause to consider their situation in York for a time, but it was not the catalyst that drove family members from their home and forced them to relocate in Michigan and Minnesota. By June 1863 three of the Goodridge children already had left York. Emily had settled with her family in Minneapolis in 1857, and Mary and Wallace were living in East Saginaw. Glenalvin and his wife and children could not have left York at that time even though they may have wished to do so, for Glenalvin had been imprisoned in the Eastern State Penitentiary in Philadelphia since February 1863 and would not be released until December 1864. During 1863 and 1864 William C. Goodridge and his youngest son, William O. Goodridge, remained in York, where the elder Goodridge continued his barbering trade and father and son undertook a Herculean effort to obtain a pardon for Glenalvin. According to the terms of the document signed by Governor Andrew G. Curtin on December 13, 1864, Glenalvin had promised "if pardoned to leave the State . . . [and as] he is a man of good education and a good teacher . . . [he] may be useful in that capacity elsewhere."[83]

During the spring or summer of 1865, William C. Goodridge traveled west with Glenalvin and his family to East Saginaw, where they joined Mary, Wallace, and young William O. Goodridge. Mr. Goodridge returned to his barbershop in York for a time, but by the end of 1865 he had settled in Minneapolis with Emily and her family. He regularly visited his children and grandchildren in East Saginaw, but there is no record that he ever returned to York. He died in Minneapolis on January 15, 1873.[84]

2

Glenalvin J. Goodridge: Early Photography in York, 1847–1865

A T SOME TIME DURING 1829, the second year of their marriage, William and Evalina Goodridge celebrated the birth of their first child, Glenalvin J. Goodridge.[1] Glen, as he came to be known, grew up in the midst of his parents' expanding business ventures and presumably was involved with their development. Little, however, is known of his first two decades. The 1830 census notes his presence as the only male under ten years of age in a household of nine individuals. By the 1840 count he had become one of five males aged ten to twenty-four years in a household that had increased to sixteen persons. Given his future career and his father's philanthropies, it seems certain that Glen Goodridge attended school during the late 1830s and into the 1840s, but no evidence exists to corroborate his attendance in York or elsewhere. Like many eldest sons, Goodridge doubtless also spent vacations and after school employed in various family enterprises. But it was only in the 1850 census that the then twenty-one-year-old Goodridge was recorded independently for the first time. His occupation was listed as "teacher."[2]

Young Goodridge's success as an educator impressed at least one visitor to York, who reported in 1848 that

> There is a good school here [York], taught by Mr. G. J. Goodridge, who is also clerk for his father, and quite a young man, but one of excellent deportment and highly exemplary character. The pupils under the charge of Mr. Goodridge, were examined on several of the minor branches, and promise well for future usefulness; and should Mr. G. who is a very intelligent and well-quali-

fied gentleman, but persevere and keep pace with the march of improvement and reform, he may prove a most useful instrumentality in rearing up the young of York for positions of future usefulness.[3]

"M.R.D.," the correspondent, added that "Mr. Goodridge, in addition to other qualifications, is a Daguerreotypist, and keeps a fine gallery at his father's dwellings, where he has his private study, and operates at leisure hours." By the late 1840s, therefore, Glen had embarked on complementary careers as teacher and photographer. While we can never know whether he ever became "a most useful instrumentality in rearing up the young of York for positions of future usefulness," it is possible to follow his development as a photographer.

When Glenalvin Goodridge began to work as a daguerreotypist in 1847, he joined hundreds of other men and women in the United States who, since photography's introduction in 1839, had abandoned earlier careers or chosen, like Glen, to share existing ones with photography. Goodridge, however, was one of only five or six African Americans who at present are known to have worked as photographers before 1850. The studio that Goodridge established in York in 1847 was preceded by those of Jules Lion in New Orleans, John B. Bailey and Edward M. Bannister in Boston, and Augustus Washington in Hartford. J. P. Ball, who also opened his first studio in 1847, in Cincinnati, is much better known. Yet none of the studios established by Goodridge's predecessors and contemporaries lasted as long as or are represented by as large a group of extant photographs as the

Goodridge studio, which after 1863 continued to operate in Saginaw, Michigan, until 1922.[4]

⊹

G. J. Goodridge was not York's first photographer, but he was the community's first native son to establish a studio that operated for more than a few weeks or months. Previously another native son, William Wagner, a well-known engraver, chief burgess of York, and cashier of the community's second chartered bank, had also tried his hand for a time as a daguerreotypist. For approximately six months during 1845 Wagner had run an ad in the York newspapers stating that he had "purchased one of VOIGTLANDER'S CELEBRATED INSTRUMENTS" and was "prepared to take Daguerreotype Likenesses, in the most perfect style of execution." Like many other early daguerreotypists, however, Wagner soon abandoned his camera in pursuit of other opportunities.[5]

According to the *Democratic Press,* photographs were made in York as early as 1842 when the daguerreotypists John C. Stinson and Blanchard P. Paige visited "for a few days" in March and rented rooms above F. B. Cooke's jewelry store on South George Street. Stinson and Paige were followed by a succession of itinerant photographers—an almost permanent fixture in towns and small cities like York during the 1840s—who continued to visit on a regular basis until after 1850. On occasion studios from the not too distant metropolises, Philadelphia and Baltimore, also advertised for York's photo business.[6] One itinerant daguerreotypist, however, became much more important than the others.

The April 6, 1847, issue of the *Democratic Press* printed a notice that "Mr. Joseph Reinhart, Daguerreotypist, from Virginia, is now in York, and expects to remain for a few weeks." Reinhart had rented a room from William Goodridge in the third story of China Hall, "where he is now prepared to take Family Groups, Single Faces, Dead Persons, Scenery and Copy Portraits, in a style unsurpassed by any other artist in the country, on superior Plates, *gilded and colored to nature,* and put up in

beautiful cases, at reasonable prices." Reinhart invited Yorkers to view his portraits of "the Hon. Daniel Webster" and "the celebrated Capt. Walker, commander of a company of Texas Rangers" and hero of the recent Mexican War, that he had made during a recent trip to Philadelphia. With the exception of such an occasional excursion "to fulfill an engagement," Reinhart remained in York at China Hall consistently until the end of June 1847. According to the *Democratic Press,* the daguerreotypist was "a pupil of the celebrated [Montgomery P.] Simons of Philadelphia . . . [and] reflects great credit upon his teacher" by imparting his skills to his own students. Like many of the itinerants who had preceded him, Reinhart had offered "Instructions in Daguerrotyping at reasonable prices." One of those who had heeded his call was the local schoolteacher, Glenalvin J. Goodridge.[7] On July 27, less than a month after Reinhart's ads ended their run in the *Democratic Press* and he had vacated the third story of China Hall, "Goodridge's Daguerrian Rooms" purchased their first ad in the same newspaper and Glenalvin occupied his mentor's former studio.

The Simons-Reinhart-Goodridge connection is further sustained by the fact that Glenalvin even patterned this first advertisement after Reinhart's and offered to photograph "Family Groups, Single Portraits, Dead Persons and Scenery [with] Copies made from Paintings, Daguerreotypes and Pictures of all kinds" (see figure 2.1a). During his initial year as a daguerreotypist, Glenalvin maintained close ties with Reinhart and Simons. Within a month of opening his studio he traveled to Philadelphia to visit Reinhart and in the interim turned his "rooms" over to Simons, who was visiting York for a time. The *Democratic Press* reported on August 31, 1847, that

Mr. Simmons [sic], the celebrated Daguerretypist [sic] of Philadelphia, has arrived in this place and taken the rooms formerly occupied by G. J. Goodridge. We were shown one or two portraits taken by this artist, which far surpasses anything of the kind for brilliancy, artistical effect and depth of tone that has ever been in this place. Persons wishing their likenesses taken correctly and

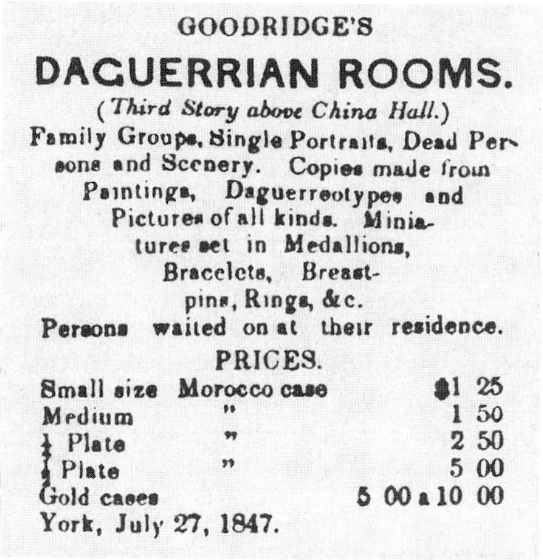

GOODRIDGE'S

DAGUERRIAN ROOMS.

(*Third Story above China Hall.*)

Family Groups, Single Portraits, Dead Persons and Scenery. Copies made from Paintings, Daguerreotypes and Pictures of all kinds. Miniatures set in Medallions, Bracelets, Breastpins, Rings, &c.

Persons waited on at their residence.

PRICES.

Small size Morocco case		$1	25
Medium	"	1	50
¼ Plate	"	2	50
¼ Plate	"	5	00
Gold cases		5 00 a 10	00

York, July 27, 1847.

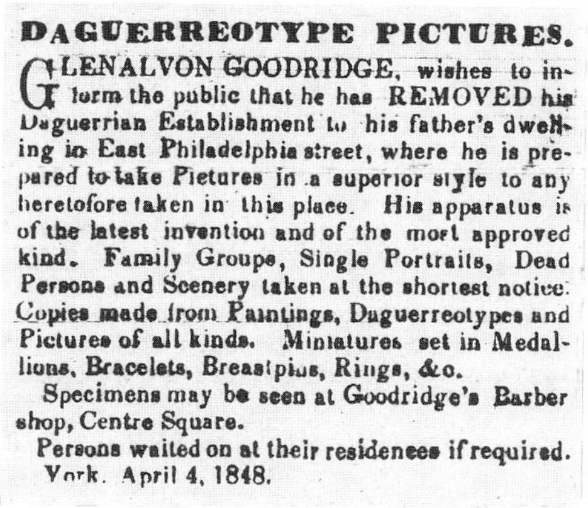

DAGUERREOTYPE PICTURES.

GLENALVON GOODRIDGE, wishes to inform the public that he has REMOVED his Daguerrian Establishment to his father's dwelling in East Philadelphia street, where he is prepared to take Pictures in a superior style to any heretofore taken in this place. His apparatus is of the latest invention and of the most approved kind. Family Groups, Single Portraits, Dead Persons and Scenery taken at the shortest notice. Copies made from Paintings, Daguerreotypes and Pictures of all kinds. Miniatures set in Medallions, Bracelets, Breastpins, Rings, &c.

Specimens may be seen at Goodridge's Barber shop, Centre Square.

Persons waited on at their residences if required.

York. April 4, 1848.

Figures 2.1a–b. Glenalvin J. Goodridge, newspaper advertisements, *York Democratic Press: left,* July 27, 1847; *right,* April 4, 1848.

in a superior manner, should embrace the present opportunity and have them taken immediately. We understand he remains here for a short time only.[8]

The following summer Glenalvin again traveled to Philadelphia, where he presumably sharpened his skills under Reinhart's and Simons's tutelage. The *Democratic Press* reported that this Philadelphia sojourn had been "attended with the utmost flattering success" and that Glenalvin was "now prepared to take Daguerreotype portraits superior to any ever taken in this place."[9]

It often has been assumed on the basis of his multitude of accomplishments that Glenalvin's father was responsible for introducing him to photography. Recent accounts of the family's activities in York have, for example, described William Goodridge as "a photographer" and "involved in photography for many years."[10] In spite of Mr. Goodridge's wide-ranging interests and early appreciation for and use of "visuals" (see the discussion of figure 1.1), there is no contemporary evidence to support such assertions. During the late 1850s, when Glenalvin's studio faced stiff competition and his success began to falter, he did issue coupons in the form of "Daguerrian Dollars" that were intended to stimulate business by reducing prices. One form of the coupon "issued" by the fictitious "Farmers & Mechanics Bank of York" identified "G. J. Goodridge [as] Pres't" and a "W. Goodridge [as]

Cashier and Operator" (see figure 2.15a). "W. Goodridge" may have been father William, but more likely was brother Wallace, who was sixteen at the time and already had joined his brother as a cameraman or "operator" in the studio.

On the basis of the newspaper advertisements and reports of visitors to York, it also is clear that before 1851 photography for Glenalvin Goodridge was not a full-time activity. Teaching continued to be his primary occupation. Goodridge's initial advertisement, the "China Hall" ad, ran in the *Democratic Press* for only six months, until January 25, 1848. A second appeared in the same newspaper three months later, on April 4, and lasted for more than two years, ending on August 21, 1850. In it Goodridge announced that he had "REMOVED his Daguerrian Establishment [from China Hall] to his father's dwelling on East Philadelphia street, where he is prepared to take Pictures in a superior style to any heretofore taken in this place" (see figure 2.1b). The move corresponded to William and Evalina Goodridge's sale of China Hall in February 1848. Nonetheless, had Glenalvin required the studio space, he certainly could have continued to rent it from China Hall's new owners, David and Daniel Rupp. Instead, as "M.R.D." had noted during a visit to York in November 1848, Glenalvin "keeps a fine gallery at his father's dwellings, where he has his private study, and operates at leisure hours."[11]

The fact that Goodridge continued to teach did not mean that he was not a serious or a successful daguerreotypist. During photography's initial decade such a practice was common. Furthermore, Goodridge's advertised prices suggest that he was more than an itinerant interested in quick profit. Up to $15 for a gold-cased, half-plate daguerreotype portrait was more than twice that advertised by any of his itinerant predecessors or contemporaries in York. According to one recent account of photography's early development, this placed Goodridge among those who had begun "to transform the nature and organization of photography from an experimental practice into an integrated business system managed by dedicated and respected individuals."[12] In that respect Glenalvin shared excellent company. Mathew Brady made it clear that he was "unwilling to abandon any artistic ground to the producers of inferior work." He had "no fear in appealing to an enlightened public as to their choice between pictures of the size, price and quality which will fairly remunerate men of talent, science, and application, and those which can be made by the meanest tyro. I wish to vindicate true art," Brady concluded, "and leave the community to decide whether it is best to encourage real excellence or its opposite; to preserve and perfect an art, or to permit it to degenerate by inferiority of materials which must correspond with the meanness of the price."[13]

The quality of the photo images that survive from Glenalvin's earliest years in the profession also are a measure of the level of his talent and intent at this time. Figures 2.2–2.6 demonstrate that by 1851 Goodridge, although not yet a full-fledged professional, was more than a competent portrait photographer. He had, in fact, mastered what have been described as "the basic essentials needed in portrait taking—lighting, posing, and the mechanical requisites of daguerreotyping procedures." His portraits also compare well with Montgomery Simons's known work and demonstrate the degree of affiliation between master and student. For example, in figure 2.2, made in 1851 or earlier, Glenalvin's subject is dressed in a boldly patterned plaid dress with white collar. A Simons portrait

Figure 2.2. "Unidentified Woman," before 1851, sixth-plate daguerreotype. Glenalvin J. Goodridge, York, Pa. The Historical Society of York County, Pa.

from circa 1847 presents a young woman in a very nearly identical frock. The young man in figure 2.3 is distinguished in his black silk vest, which brilliantly reflects the light that Glenalvin used to capture this image in or shortly before 1851. Simons created a similar portrait of a dashing young Philadelphia gentleman also in a black silk vest using identical lighting technique only the year before.[14] The standard poses—right arm on books and left resting in lap—and attention to details such as the cameo in figure 2.2 similarly compare favorably with any of Glenalvin's better-known contemporaries. But figure 2.4 suggests that the young photographer, perhaps because of his experience in the classroom, had already established an easy studio style to which children agreeably responded. Although his sisters might not have agreed, the young fellow in figure 2.4 found Glenalvin's technique sufficiently relaxing to produce at least the beginnings of a smile. And his use of light to highlight the parted hair and hands and arms of Clara and Amanda Hay in figure 2.5 not only provides the structure in the portrait but em-

Figure 2.3. "Unidentified Young Man," before 1851, sixth-plate daguerreotype. Glenalvin J. Goodridge, York, Pa. The Historical Society of York County, Pa.

Figure 2.4. "Three Unidentified Children," before 1851, sixth-plate daguerreotype. Glenalvin J. Goodridge, York, Pa. The Historical Society of York County, Pa.

Figure 2.5 (right). "Clara Maria and Amanda Hay," before 1851, sixth-plate daguerreotype. Glenalvin J. Goodridge, York, Pa. Private Collection.

Figure 2.6 (left). "Unidentified Young Man, Postmortem," before 1851, sixth-plate daguerreotype. Glenalvin J. Goodridge, York, Pa. Derrick Joshua Beard.

Figure 2.7. "Unidentified Mulatto Man with Horse," before 1851, quarter-plate daguerreotype. Glenalvin J. Goodridge, York, Pa. William A. Frassanito Collection.

phasizes the tender relationship between these sisters. Both girls were daughters of General George Hay (see figure 2.13) and Susan Demuth Hay of York.

Glenalvin would also follow Reinhart's lead, as his initial advertisement indicated, and transported his camera from the studio to record much more solemn events (see figure 2.6). By 1850 post-mortem photographs were "a common aspect of American culture, a part of the mourning and memorialization process . . . [and] make up the largest group of nineteenth-century American genre photographs . . . [although] they are largely unseen, and unknown" today.[15]

Without doubt, however, the most intriguing image to survive from these earliest years is figure 2.7.

The young man bears a striking resemblance, especially the aquiline nose and high forehead, to his father, William C. Goodridge (see figure 1.6). The age, perhaps thirty years, is appropriate. The dress, including the pocket watch, is suggestive of his status. The family home on East Philadelphia Street included a stable. And the Goodridges, both in York and East Saginaw, were known horse fanciers. A self-portrait in terms of the subject "releasing the shutter" would have been technically possible although difficult at this time. Was it then the father, Mr. Goodridge, or perhaps the young studio apprentice and brother, Wallace, who made this portrait of Glenalvin and his favorite steed?

On June 10, 1851, Glenalvin J. Goodridge married Rhoda Cornelia Grey. The sixteen-year-old bride was the daughter of Hamilton and Jane Grey.[16] Originally from Maryland, the Greys had lived for a time in Harrisburg before settling in York, probably in the mid-1840s. The 1850 census does not list Rhoda's brother Hamilton W. Grey, who already may have been living in Minnesota Territory. Hamilton W. and Rhoda were cousins of Ralph Toyer Grey of Baltimore, who would marry Glenalvin's sister Emily in 1855. Emily, in fact, traveled west to join her husband in 1857 with Hamilton W., who had returned east that year to marry Mary Smallwood, a Goodridge neighbor in York. The elder Hamilton Grey is listed by the census as a "laborer," but one who owned $1,800 in real estate. An April 1850 ad in the *York Gazette* announced the opening of a "New Livery Stable" owned by Hamilton Grey and operating at "Mr. Erb's Stage Stable, in this Borough," which accounts for his substantial real estate listing in the census. Glenalvin and Rhoda's marriage, therefore, was not only a personal union but also helped to reinforce the already well-established bonds among three of York's most important African American families. According to Oblinger, the result of such marriage patterns in York and other southeastern Pennsylvania communities by the 1840s was that "elite black families had been extended to become 'clans.' The children and grandchildren of the original elite black families had intermarried . . . [with] the upwardly-mobile black middling group in a bewildering arrays of patterns."[17]

Glenalvin's prospective marriage was the occasion, but not the only reason, for his decision in January 1851 to devote more of his energy and talent to photography. While he would continue to do some teaching during the 1850s, photography offered the possibility for greater financial gain. The "Daguerrian Gallery" had by then been operating successfully from China Hall and the family home on East Philadelphia Street for more than three years, and still the York newspapers carried no advertisements from full-time resident competitors. Opportunity, therefore, existed. The late

1840s and the decade of the 1850s also were a prosperous time for many Americans and, as a result, photography generally underwent significant expansion. Glenalvin decided to be a part of that trend. For most Americans in the 1840s, photography, especially the daguerreotype, represented simultaneously the cutting edge of practical technological development, akin to the railroad and the reaper, and an almost magical transformation of reality. A number of factors—Glenalvin's career as an educator, the family's broadly based religious convictions, but most certainly its entrepreneurial sensibility—may have made the profession, for a time at least, irresistible.[18]

This second phase of Glenalvin's career as a photographer began with a new studio in the fifth story of his parents' business block, Centre Hall. Near the northwest corner of George and Main Streets on Centre Square, the new studio was at the crossroads of York County's economic, social, and political activity. No photographer, itinerant or resident, who located in York before 1860 was ever more than a block from the Square. The fifth and uppermost story of Centre Hall provided an abundance of natural light, necessary for quality daguerreotypes, through two large gables and a skylight (see figure 2.8). In fact, with the move to Centre Hall Glenalvin began to designate his studio as Goodridge's "Skylight Rooms" or "Extra Sky Light Gallery" rather than simply Goodridge's "Daguerrian Rooms." A later ad described it as a complex of four rooms that included a "Sky Light Operating Room, Ladies' Private Room, and two large Work Rooms," all supplied with water and gas. The Goodridge "Extra Sky Light Gallery" was not as large or as lavish as Mathew Brady's new facility at 359 Broadway in New York City, with its three floors and multitude of rooms, some with "ceiling-to-floor mirrors" and walls "covered with green velvet, satin, and gold paper," which Glenalvin certainly visited during his 1853 trip to New York City, but it was York's largest and most opulent at the time. To his new studio Glenalvin invited "the Ladies and Gentlemen of York and its vicinity," where "in clear and cloudy weather" he would "take likenesses in a few seconds with per-

Figure 2.8. "Centre Hall at Centre Square, York, Pa.," before 1900, stereograph. Silver print, 6⅛ x 3¾₆ inches, yellow bristol board mount, 6⅞ x 3¾₆ inches. Von Neida & Coombs Photographers, York, Pa. The Historical Society of York County, Pa.

fect natural expressions."[19] Yorkers responded enthusiastically.

Through at least 1853 Goodridge faced no serious competition in York from other than an occasional itinerant photographer. As a result his confidence soared, and this was reflected in the self-assurance of his newspaper advertisements from early in the decade. For example, figures 2.9a and b are whimsical, almost playful "commercials" in comparison to the earlier more straightforward and businesslike newspaper notices announcing the opening of the "Daguerrian Gallery." This novelty ad, like his father's earlier "Celsus and Minerva" woodcut, was a unique design created specifically for the Goodridge studio. Like its predecessor, it relied on the "visual" action for its im-

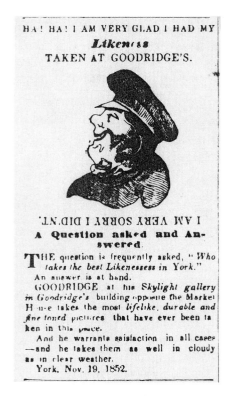

Figures 2.9a–b. Glenalvin J. Goodridge, newspaper advertisements, *York Democratic Press: left,* "Glad," November 19, 1852; *right,* "Sorry," November 19, 1852.

pact. The ad demonstrates that the son, like the father, clearly understood that much of the message was the medium.

At the same time, Glenalvin's confidence did not compromise his commitment to quality, and as a result he continued to attract the patronage of York's elite. In 1853 Robert J. Fisher, the president judge of the Nineteenth Judicial District, which included York and Adams Counties, married Mary Sophia Caldwell of Northbridge, Massachusetts. Fisher, a widower with six children, was the area's most respected jurist, serving the district court from 1851 to 1881. To celebrate his marriage, Judge Fisher commissioned Glenalvin to make a daguerreotype portrait of his new wife and two of his youngest children, most likely Anne Helen and Robert Jones Fisher, accompanied to the studio by their trusted canine friend (see figure 2.10). Ironically, ten years later it was Justice Fisher who would preside at Glenalvin's trial and sentence him to five years in the Eastern State Penitentiary.[20]

By 1853 Glenalvin's photography also began to achieve national and local recognition. In January the prestigious photographer's magazine *Humphrey's Journal* reported that "G. J. Goodridge, of York, Pa., has pleasant rooms, with every convenience for producing the finest Daguerreotypes." Later that fall the same journal noted that Goodridge "has just visited New York, and supplied himself with all that is desirable for the ladies of York."[21] Shortly after this New York visit the *York Gazette* reported that Glenalvin's photography had won its first award, a "second premium" for a "case of Daguerreotypes" at the 1853 York Agricultural Society Fair. The "first" went to Dr. Washington Barr of Harrisburg. Barr was a native of Harrisburg who, like the Goodridge family, also operated a variety store and photography studio, which was quite successful in the capital city during the 1850s.[22]

Obviously, photography for Glenalvin rapidly had become significantly more than a leisure activity. Yet at the same time, in true Goodridge family fashion, the *Gazette*'s premium lists for the 1853 fair also reveal that Glenalvin's interests, like his father's, were quite diverse. Besides his prize for the

Figure 2.10. "Robert Jones, Mary Caldwell, and Anne Helen Fisher," 1853, sixth-plate daguerreotype. Glenalvin J. Goodridge, York, Pa. The Historical Society of York County, Pa.

"case of Daguerreotypes" the newspaper reported that Glenalvin also received "diplomas" for a "Coffee Mill" and "Can of extract of coffee" (an early form of "instant") and that he had entered in the fair as a curiosity "One double chicken, with one head only."[23]

This professional success had a positive impact on family life for the young Goodridges. Between 1853 and 1857 Glenalvin and Rhoda became the parents of a daughter, Emily, and two sons, William H. and Ralph J. In April 1853 they also moved from the family home on East Philadelphia Street to their own residence just around the corner on North Duke Street, which they had purchased from Rhoda's parents. Within two years they added five additional parcels of real estate to this initial purchase.[24]

During 1853 Glenalvin's first significant competition established himself strategically next to the post office only a few doors from the Goodridge studio in Centre Hall. Although York County, with a population of more than fifty-seven thousand in 1850, could support several resident photographers comfortably, J. T. Williams was a formidable competitor. Little is known of Williams's background or professional life as a photographer, but he apparently had moved to York from Baltimore, where the 1851 city directory listed him as a daguerreotypist located at 211 West Baltimore Street. The 1850 Census of Agriculture and Manufacturing for Baltimore included the following about him: "$1,000 invested, 250 plates on hand, 2 male employees, $100 average monthly labor cost, [and] 3,000 likenesses produced annually."[25] By the summer of 1853, however, he had left Baltimore for York, and in his initial newspaper advertisement Williams proclaimed to Yorkers that with "an experience of twelve years," he "has been at the business longer than any one else in this part of the country, and understands it better." Furthermore his studio was "fitted up with the most POWERFUL INSTRUMENTS, [and] Large Sky-Light," enabling him "to produce DAGUERROTYPES OF THE BEST QUALITY, *with clear eyes, and colored in natural colors.*" In an obvious swipe at Glenalvin, who likely continued to devote at least some time to teaching, Williams declared that he was "the only one in York who devotes his entire attention to the art." In fact, such had already been the response to his studio's opening "as to require the engagement of an experienced assistant."[26]

Williams's ad was not all rhetoric. Although Washington Barr again won the diploma for "best specimens of Daguerreotypes" at the York County Fair in 1854, Williams also received a diploma for "a beautiful group of 61 Daguerreotype likenesses of the Young ladies of Professor Hay's College on one plate." A few weeks later Williams won a second diploma for "large and handsome DAGUERROTYPE GROUPS," this time at the Lancaster County Fair. There were no prizes listed for Glenalvin Goodridge at any fair that year. The Hay's College commission that won Williams his prize was exactly the sort of business that no photographer could stand to lose and remain successful. By the spring of 1855 Williams not only was crediting himself with the area's "Best Likenesses" but also was reminding potential customers that "a Committee appointed by the York Bank, after careful examination awarded to Williams, ONE PREMIUM OF $20.00, ONE PREMIUM OF $10.00, [and] ONE PREMIUM OF $5.00, for Best Daguerreotypes of York." In April 1855 the *York Gazette* editorialized that Williams's work "cannot be surpassed."[27]

Goodridge, of course, responded to the challenge. The novelty ads (for example, figures 2.9a and b) which he had begun in 1852 continued to November 1855, but during 1853 they often appeared in association with other Goodridge family advertisements in the newspapers. For example, during much of 1854 they were part of a group that included notices for valentines at the family jewelry store, Glenalvin's coffee extract, and "new goods" at the confectionery. The ads were grouped all one atop another in a single newspaper column, with the novelty ads at the very top of the column. It was as if the gallery were literally supported by and gained strength through association with the family's already successful ventures. The visual impact of a column of Goodridge advertisements would not escape the notice of Yorkers and continued the pattern the family had established early on of utilizing such marketing strategies.[28]

Even more important, however, was the fact that during the summer of 1855 Glenalvin introduced the people of York to the very latest, most up-to-date photographic technique, the collodian positive or ambrotype. While the quality of the daguerreotype could never be challenged, the cost, time, and talent usually necessary to create that quality would by the mid-1850s begin to give way to the glass collodian negative, which could be used to create a multitude of acceptable paper prints, ultimately in a variety of photographic formats, often at a fraction of the cost, time, and talent required for the unique daguerreotype.[29]

The collodian positive or ambrotype was a stage in the evolution of photography midway between the positive and negative processes in that it employed elements of each. The Englishman F. Scott Archer, who in 1851 introduced the collodian negative, suggested at about the same time that an underexposed and weaker version of the collodian negative could be backed with black (painted glass, paper, metal, or cloth) to create a positive image. A variation of the process that came to be known as the ambrotype was patented in the United States by James A. Cutting of Boston in July 1854. Cutting's method was an excellent one in that it sealed the image protectively between two plates of glass. His patent specified balsam of fir as the sealant. That and Cutting's attempt to license the process for between $100 and $1,000 (depending upon the size of the population the photographer served) gave rise to many variations of the Cutting ambrotype. Montgomery Simons, for example, evaded the patent requirements by using *"any varnish* except balsam of fir" to cement his plates of glass. Many ambrotypes were made simply by using a single piece of glass with the black backing of the case serving to reveal and at the same time to protect the image. Like daguerreotypes, ambrotypes were matted and cased. And like daguerreotypes, ambrotypes were one-of-a-kind images, but on glass, not a silvered copper plate. In addition to being much less expensive and technically less complex, the ambrotype image did not temporarily disappear (as did the metallic daguerreotype) if not held at the correct angle to the light.[30]

Although ambrotypes were made well into the 1880s, perhaps because of the Cutting patent but probably more so because of the rapid and widespread popularity and ease of using the collodian negative to make photographs on paper, the process never was very popular in large cities. Many of the very best ambrotypists, as a result, were more modest local and regional photographers. Glenalvin Goodridge was one of them.[31]

That the introduction of the ambrotype carried Glenalvin to the zenith of his professional success as a photographer in York in 1855 and 1856 is clear from an editorial in the same newspaper which six months earlier had suggested to Yorkers that J. T. Williams "cannot be surpassed." The *Gazette* now reported that

> We had an opportunity, a few days ago, of examining some very fine specimens of AMBROTYPES, which is the name given to a recent and very important improvement of Daguerrean pictures. The Ambrotype is decidedly superior to the Daguerreotype, Callotype, or Talbotype. It has the advantage of being without the peculiar glare of Daguerreotypes which renders it necessary that the picture, to be seen, be held in a particular light or at a particular angle. The Ambrotype is like a fine, rich toned steel engraving; and, like such an engraving, presents its lights and shades at any angle of light. The specimens we saw were by Mr. GLENALVON GOODRIDGE, who is constantly vigilant in the wonderful photographic art—to his great credit he is never content to remain a single step in the rear of its progress.

The editorialist also revealed that Goodridge was the first York photographer to introduce his customers to the enchantment of the stereoscopic view. "We consider," he wrote, "Goodridge's ambrotype pictures, with the stereoscopic application, the very perfection of the art—the relief being, in very truth, so *life-like,* that the beholder finds it difficult to persuade himself that he is looking upon a plain surface."[32]

Goodridge may have purchased a license from Cutting for 1855 and 1856 that granted him the exclusive right to make Cutting's ambrotypes in York County. Some of his ambrotypes surviving from this period bear the imprint "Patent July 4th and 11th, 1854" (see figure 2.13, in the lower right corner of the mat). The dates are those of the Cutting patent.[33] In a full-page advertisement in the 1856 York city directory (figure 2.11), Glenalvin proclaimed his "exclusive right" to the ambrotype "for York county" and included a number of testimonials extolling its excellence, reminiscent of the earlier editorial in the *Gazette*. Introduction of the ambrotype as well was the occasion for Glenalvin to enlarge his aspirations for the studio. No longer could it simply be "Goodridge's Daguerrian

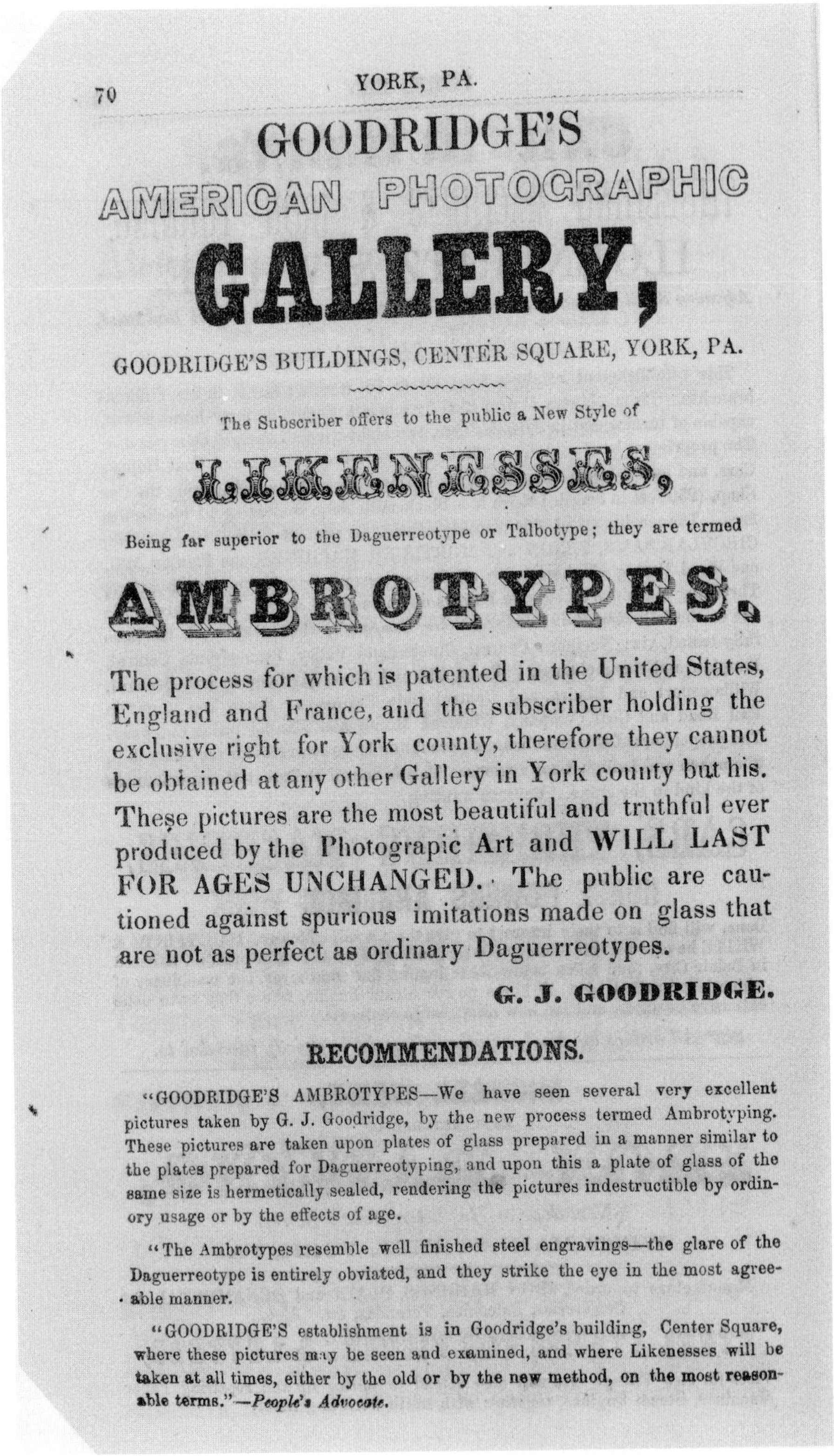

70 YORK, PA.

GOODRIDGE'S

AMERICAN PHOTOGRAPHIC

GALLERY,

GOODRIDGE'S BUILDINGS, CENTER SQUARE, YORK, PA.

The Subscriber offers to the public a New Style of

LIKENESSES,

Being far superior to the Daguerreotype or Talbotype; they are termed

AMBROTYPES.

The process for which is patented in the United States, England and France, and the subscriber holding the exclusive right for York county, therefore they cannot be obtained at any other Gallery in York county but his. These pictures are the most beautiful and truthful ever produced by the Photograpic Art and WILL LAST FOR AGES UNCHANGED. The public are cautioned against spurious imitations made on glass that are not as perfect as ordinary Daguerreotypes.

G. J. GOODRIDGE.

RECOMMENDATIONS.

"GOODRIDGE'S AMBROTYPES—We have seen several very excellent pictures taken by G. J. Goodridge, by the new process termed Ambrotyping. These pictures are taken upon plates of glass prepared in a manner similar to the plates prepared for Daguerreotyping, and upon this a plate of glass of the same size is hermetically sealed, rendering the pictures indestructible by ordinory usage or by the effects of age.

"The Ambrotypes resemble well finished steel engravings—the glare of the Daguerreotype is entirely obviated, and they strike the eye in the most agreeable manner.

"GOODRIDGE'S establishment is in Goodridge's building, Center Square, where these pictures may be seen and examined, and where Likenesses will be taken at all times, either by the old or by the new method, on the most reasonable terms."—*People's Advocate.*

Figure 2.11. Glenalvin J. Goodridge, advertisement, *York City Directory, 1856*, p. 70. The Historical Society of York County, Pa.

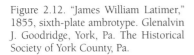

Figure 2.12. "James William Latimer," 1855, sixth-plate ambrotype. Glenalvin J. Goodridge, York, Pa. The Historical Society of York County, Pa.

Rooms" or even the "Extra Sky Light Gallery," as it had become with the move to Centre Hall in 1851. Henceforth it was to be "Goodridge's American Photographic Gallery."[34]

The consequences of the decision to meet Williams's competitive challenge through expansion and growth can be measured in a variety of ways. On the positive side it is clear that, for a time at least, perhaps because of their novelty and exclusivity, Goodridge's ambrotypes captured the attention of York's citizens. The glowing endorsement of the *Gazette* editorial in 1855 was

echoed by the judges at the 1856 York County Fair, who awarded Glenalvin the premium that year for "the best Ambrotypes."[35] Without any doubt, the ambrotypes that survive from these years include Glenalvin's very best work and validate the testimonials, editorials, and premiums. The clarity and directness, as well as his ability to distill the essence of the character of both James William Latimer in figure 2.12 and General George Hay in figure 2.13, manifest much more than simple technical competence on the part of the photographer. The lighting in each, but especially the

Figure 2.13. "George Hay," 1855 or after, sixth-plate ambrotype. Glenalvin J. Goodridge, York, Pa. Private Collection.

Figure 2.14. "Cat," 1855 or after, sixth-plate ambrotype. Glenalvin J. Goodridge, York, Pa. Ross J. Kelbaugh Collection.

selective focus and reduced depth of field in the portrait of young Latimer, further accentuates Glenalvin's empathy with the personality of each of his subjects. In 1874 James Latimer would marry Anne Helen Fisher, the young girl in figure 2.10, and later served as a justice in the York County District Court from 1886 to 1896. General Hay, born in 1809, was prominent in the Pennsylvania State Militia as a young man and attained the rank of major general during his Civil War service. When not in the military, from which he retired in 1863, he worked as a successful cabinetmaker and undertaker in York. He died in 1879.[36]

To be sure, however, the most captivating of Glenalvin's ambrotypes is figure 2.14. Not only because few such ambrotypes exist—most are portraits of human subjects—but because Glenalvin was able to capture the very instant at which he attracted his subject's curiosity, it remains the most enchanting example of his work.

Glenalvin's professional success at this time also is reflected in his more private dealings. Between December 1854 and March 1859 Glenalvin and Rhoda Goodridge added six parcels of real estate to their initial 1853 acquisition from Rhoda's parents. The properties included two one-and-a-half-story frame weatherboarded houses with lot and improvements, two two-story frame weatherboarded houses and accompanying one-story back buildings with lot and improvements, a double frame weatherboarded stable and lot, and a lot of vacant land. All the properties were near or in the "Goodridge-Grey" residential block bounded by East Philadelphia Street on the south, North Duke and North Queen Streets on the west and east, respectively, and a public alley running between Duke and Queen on the north. Although neither the census nor existing directories specify, it is likely that the younger Goodridges resided in one of the two-story houses on North Queen Street at this time.[37]

As apparent as is Glenalvin's success during the 1850s, it also is manifestly clear that by 1858 he had passed the pinnacle of his accomplishment as a photographer in York. Perhaps because his affairs were so closely integrated with his father's, whether in business or even in the family's opposition to slavery, their fates were similarly linked. As William C. Goodridge began to lose his considerable holdings after 1857, so also his son inevitably was swept up in that financial collapse. Only two months following the *Gazette*'s announcement that the sheriff had sold William's property, the *Democratic Press* published a similar notice regarding Glenalvin and Rhoda's real estate. They had defaulted on a note held by the York Bank, apparently a loan to purchase their additional properties. The bank sued and won a judgment against them, and the sheriff auctioned their holdings to satisfy the judgment. The note had been co-signed by Rhoda's parents and a neighbor, Jacob Quickell, a local carpenter. From the sale of the younger Goodridge's property, the court also awarded both cosigners the amount they had lost. The same newspaper notice that announced the sheriff's sale of Glenalvin's real estate also announced the impending sale of Hamilton and Jane Grey's two-story brick home and the land on which it was situated.[38]

Although there may have been a general Goodridge-Grey family economic collapse at this time, for whatever reason, there were also circumstances specific to Glenalvin's situation that precip-

itated and intensified his and Rhoda's difficulties. In spite of the innovations he had introduced and the expansion he had effected, Glenalvin never completely overcame J. T. Williams's competitive challenge. In fact, the very same judges who had awarded Goodridge the premium for "best Ambrotypes" at the 1856 York County Fair conferred on Williams a diploma for "View of York and Harrisburg." The language of the award is not precise and the use of the term "view" was yet to be standardized, but it is possible that Williams's diploma was for stereoscopic photographs on paper, which had only recently begun a two-decade period of extraordinary popularity in the United States and which is what the term "view" at that time was coming to mean.[39] The *York Gazette* had raved about Goodridge's "ambrotype pictures, with the stereoscopic application," but none are known to exist, and Glenalvin did not include them in his advertising even in the rather elaborate 1856 York city directory presentation (see figure 2.11). William C. Darrah also has concluded that while the ambrotype flourished briefly between 1854 and 1860 "as a cheap competitor of the daguerreotype," only "a few stereo ambrotypes were [ever] produced."[40]

It may be then that Goodridge's decision to specialize in ambrotypes in 1855 was a mistake, or at least had resulted only in fleeting success. Although the ambrotype had provided an inexpensive but viable alternative to the daguerreotype during the early 1850s, it in turn was eclipsed by the even less expensive but more durable tintype (collodian positive on metal) and literal deluge of cheap paper portraits, the carte de visite, by the end of the decade.[41] There is no evidence that Glenalvin adjusted in a timely fashion to compensate for the technical advances made in the profession soon after 1855. No tintype or photograph on paper in any form produced by the Goodridge studio in York before 1860 is known to exist at the present time.

Sometime after 1856, J. T. Williams left York. Perhaps he returned to Baltimore or even headed a bit further north to Harrisburg and reestablished his studio there. In his place, however, Goodridge

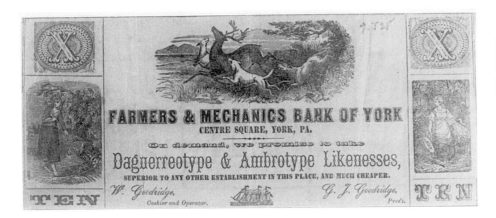

Figure 2.15a. "Advertising Note, $10," 1855 or after, 7⅝ x 3⅛ inches. Glenalvin J. Goodridge, York, Pa. The Historical Society of York County, Pa.

Figure 2.15b. "Advertising Note, $20," 1855 or after, 7⁷⁄₁₆ x 3¹⁄₁₆ inches. Glenalvin J. Goodridge, York, Pa. Collection of Nicholas M. and Marilyn A. Graver.

now faced stiff competition from Henry Barratt, an English-born daguerreotypist who earlier had worked in Philadelphia but who, during the summer of 1857, established the "Sunbeam Gallery" in the Hartmann Building on the southeast corner of Centre Square. Barratt boasted of thirteen years' experience and advertised "Melainotypes" (tintypes) as a more durable and less expensive alternative to Glenalvin's ambrotypes. The following year Barratt's challenge was buttressed when another Philadelphia transplant, Charles Evans, who had operated his own "Sun Beam" gallery there until 1856, and his partner, a Mr. Seiling, advertised the opening of the "Premium Skylight Gallery" in Williams's former studio next to the post office.[42]

Evans and Seiling appear to have been what later would be characterized as "the 'cancer of the profession,' . . . so-called 'cheap-johns,' commercial photographers who used the declining cost of

materials and processing to sell photographs at dramatically reduced prices." According to Sarah Greenough's recent analysis, "When they could attract and maintain a steady, high volume of business through creative promotional schemes and advertising, these unscrupulous professionals forced more established businesses to lower their prices, and thus cut their margin of profit, or risk losing all their clients." Such may have been Glenalvin's fate, for Evans and Seiling advertised price cuts of 40 percent for standard-sized ambrotypes and of up to 60 percent (from $6.00 to $2.50) for "large sized pictures, in fine gilded frames." Glenalvin's ads no longer specified prices, but earlier he had not been known for the lowest prices in town.[43]

These challenges obviously succeeded, as both the 1858 and 1859 York County Fairs recognized their merit with premiums and diplomas.

Evans and Seiling were cited first for an "extensive exhibition of superior hallotypes, ambrotypes and photographs" and then for "Best display of ambrotypes and daguerreotypes," while Barratt's award was for "very superior specimens of drawings and colored photographs." Glenalvin received not even a mention.[44]

That his early success with the introduction of the ambrotype and even his having outlasted Williams were now being mortally threatened is indicated by Glenalvin's printing and circulating facsimile banknotes drawn on the "Farmers & Mechanics Bank of York, Centre Square, York, Pa." The notes were issued in two denominations, $10 and $20 (see figures 2.15a and b). Bearers could redeem them at Goodridge's American Photographic Gallery toward "Daguerreotype & Ambrotype Likenesses, SUPERIOR TO ANY OTHER ESTABLISHMENT IN THIS PLACE, AND MUCH CHEAPER." William C. Goodridge had issued similar notes earlier in the decade in $10 denominations but drawn on the "York County Deposit Bank" and entitling customers at the family jewelry, variety, and confectionery store to a 10 percent premium on their purchases there. Once again the son had followed the father in adopting this very visual advertising scheme. But as Alan Trachtenberg has pointed out, such notes were a common "gimmick [that] some daguerreotypists used in the hard times of the 1840s" and which signaled the poor circumstances that Glenalvin faced by 1858.[45]

The studio's $10 and $20 coupons are identical in design and differ only in denomination and in the fact that while G. J. Goodridge is listed as "Pres't" on both, "W. Goodridge" (presumably his younger brother Wallace) is identified as "Cashier and Operator" on the $10 and a "W. H. Wood" is given the same designation on the $20. Both Wallace and Wood obviously functioned as Glenalvin's assistants while learning the basics of the profession under his direction, and Wallace ultimately succeeded his brother as senior partner in the Goodridge studio. There is no record of a W. H. Wood working as a photographer in York or the area thereafter. An African American named William Wood, however, is listed in the 1863 York city directory as a "machinist" who lived on South Newberry near Market, and may well have been the young man who was the studio's "Cashier and Operator" earlier.[46]

If Glenalvin had, indeed, purchased a license for the exclusive right to make Cutting's ambrotypes in York County during 1855 and 1856, the fee could have been as high as $1,000. With such an investment and facing so considerable a challenge without the financial support that his now bankrupt father otherwise might have provided, Goodridge may have been unable to meet his financial obligations by 1859. As a result the York Bank brought and won its suit, the sheriff sold his property, and Glenalvin turned once again to teaching to provide for his family.

During August 1859, "Mifflin," a correspondent for the *Weekly Anglo-African,* had reported following a visit to York in July that "Mr. G. J. Goodridge, does an excellent business as an ambrotypist." Only a month later, however, the same correspondent, writing from Baltimore, noted that "Our schools have opened [and] Mr. G. J. Goodridge, of York, Pa., is now occupying Mr. Wm. T. Dixon's former position" as teacher. Precisely why Goodridge choose to teach in Baltimore rather than in York is not clear. Perhaps it was the Goodridge-Grey family connections in Baltimore that drew him there; or, following the personal economic disaster of the previous year, a change of scene was welcome. In any case, 1859 brought an end to Glenalvin J. Goodridge's most successful years as a photographer in York.[47]

<hr />

Glenalvin worked as a teacher in Baltimore only for a year and by the summer of 1860 was back in York, where he taught at "the Colored High School" during the following year. Whether he was able, with Wallace's assistance and that of his youngest brother, William, who was fourteen in 1860, to continue to operate "Goodridge's American Photographic Gallery" on even a part-time basis in the fifth story of Centre Hall after its sale to Philip A. Small is not known. No newspaper advertisements were purchased for the studio during 1859 and 1860, and the York County Fair awarded no diplomas or premiums during those years to the Goodridges for their photography.[48]

During the winter of 1860–61, however, Glenalvin and Wallace developed a plan of action to reestablish the gallery on a firm financial basis once again. Their father always had believed in taking advantage of an opportunity when it presented itself, and the sons decided to follow the example. In the spring of 1861 Henry Barratt vacated his "Sunbeam Gallery" in the Hartmann Building across the square from Centre Hall, and the Goodridges moved their "American Photographic Gallery" into Hartmann's in its place. In fact, the *York Gazette* later reported in its account of the city's Fourth of July festivities that while the parade was forming, "a photographic view was taken of the line by Glenalvin Goodridge, from his gallery in Hartmann's building." According to the reporter, who also had "seen the negative plate," it "is about 4 by 3 inches, and although the figures are extremely small, we were able with the aid of a magnifying glass, to recognize a number of them quite plainly. The photograph is considerably larger than the negative, and will be on exhibition this week."[49]

The notice is significant because it reveals that the Goodridge studio had relocated and was headed for success once again. Of even greater consequence, however, is the information that Glenalvin and Wallace had abandoned their earlier reliance on daguerreotypes and ambrotypes and had begun to create collodian negatives and then used them to print enlarged paper photographs. In addition, the reported 4 x 3 negative was the standard size for the production of stereoscopic views on paper then becoming very popular, and the photograph of the Fourth of July parade also could have been marketed in this format. A 1985 letter to the author from William C. Darrah confirms that during the early 1860s the Goodridges were making paper stereos, although none is presently known to exist. Mr. Darrah wrote that during 1967, in a town near York, he had acquired two stereographs of York from "Goodridge's American Photographic Gallery,

Centre Square." The views were on "pale yellow mounts, [with] black imprint." The first was a "Residential street, horse and carriage at curb. No driver; no people in scene." He suggested that it may have been "taken on Sunday without traffic; appears to be looking eastward." The second was "a business block, rather distant view, building fronts mostly three stories high, others two. *Could be Market Street, but if so, looking eastward (street is nearly level).*" Mr. Darrah believed that the views were made in the "early 1860s, about 1862, not later." Both have since been lost. Nonetheless, it is clear that photography again was becoming more attractive to Glenalvin than teaching.[50]

This success in York by the spring of 1861 convinced Glenalvin and Wallace to gamble once again on the future by dramatically expanding the size of their operation and opening a branch of the "American Photographic Gallery" in Columbia, a town about twelve miles from York on the east bank of the Susquehanna River on the main road to Lancaster. It was an excellent move. The local newspaper, the *Columbia Spy,* welcomed the expansion with an enthusiastic and laudatory editorial:

> Goodridge, the well known Photographer of York, has taken the gallery opposite the Spy office, formerly occupied by Jolley, and offers his services to the citizens of Columbia. Goodridge has a reputation as a photographic artist. He has been familiar with the business in all its progressive stages, from the infancy of daguerreotyping to its present high perfection, and his experience has not been wasted. He is known as the best operator in York, where he has long been established, and his pictures invariably give satisfaction. He will now give the citizens of Columbia an opportunity to test his quality. He has first class apparatus, and can turn out pictures from the minutest medallion to life size.[51]

In his advertisements for the Colombia studio, Glenalvin promised "Ambrotype and Melainotype Likenesses [with] Satisfaction warranted in all cases, or no charge."[52]

During the remainder of 1861 and into the next summer it appeared that the gamble would pay off, that renewed success at both studios in

York and Columbia was within their grasp. Then disaster struck. On August 28, 1862, Glenalvin J. Goodridge was indicted on two counts by a York County grand jury. The first was for rape and the second for assault with intent to commit rape. Glenalvin pleaded innocent to both counts the day the indictment was issued, and a trial was set before the Court of Oyer and Terminer in York for November 5. Justice Robert J. Fisher presided. The prosecution was conducted by District Attorney William C. Chapman. Glenalvin's lawyers were Vincent K. Keesey and John Gibson, both of York. The indictment, signed by grand jury foreman Daniel A. Stillinger, a local tailor, charged that on March 30, 1862, Glenalvin J. Goodridge "did feloniously have unlawful carnal knowledge of a certain Mary E. Smith forcibly and against [her] . . . will . . . [and] against the peace and dignity of the Commonwealth of Pennsylvania." It further charged that Goodridge "did make an assault . . . [on] her the said Mary E. Smith [and] did beat round and ill-treat [her], with an intent forcibly and against the will of the said Mary E. Smith."[53]

In support of its case the prosecution called only four witnesses, Smith and three of her friends. Mary Smith testified that "last spring, can't say the day or time, I should think the 30th of March," she and "another girl [Susan Kemerer]" went to Goodridge's gallery in the Hartmann Building "to have my likeness taken." When they were finished, "he [Glenalvin] said he had some frames upstairs." We went up and "when I got to the head of the stairs he got me by the arms and forced me into the room . . . [and] had connexion with me there." According to Smith, "He took us a story higher than the daguerrean room. . . . I screamed and he put his hand over my mouth. He got on top of my person. He had such connexion with me then. I struggled and resisted. He left me up and said don't you dare to say anything. . . . When I went down in the rooms below I was crying. I told the girl I was with what he had done, and that I was going to sue him. . . . I never went back there again."

Prosecutor Chapman, presumably in anticipation of the defense's case or to answer testimony taken as depositions earlier, then asked Smith a series of questions which in retrospect appear directed more to establishing the innocence of the alleged victim than the guilt of the defendant. To his questions Smith responded that she "was never at Goodridges but that once," that she "hadn't any idea Goodridge was rich," that she "didn't say to Celia Smith [a defense witness] that I was going to make a fortune out of this case and then I needn't work any more," and that "I am no soldier's friend."

Chapman then led her testimony in a different direction, focusing more on Wallace Goodridge than the defendant. In response to the district attorney's questions, Smith stated that "There was a boy there [at the studio] when I went there[,] a colored boy." But she was adamant that she was never at the studio "when Wallace was there," that "I don't know Wallace Goodridge if I should see him," and that I "don't know whether he is in town or not." She swore that she "did not ask Celia Smith whether if I went with Wallace I would get in the family [way]," that "I never was up with him," and that "He never spoke to me about anything of that kind." Smith insisted that she did not "give her [Celia] my bonnet and go upstairs and [that] Wallace followed, and when I came down had 37½ cents and gave her 10 cents of it. . . . I did not say that I had connexion with Wallace" and "didn't say to Celia that I believed I was in the family way because I hadn't my changes."

As Smith neared the end of her testimony, Chapman had her review the timing of the alleged assault. She was quite certain it had taken place on a Monday because "I was in Church the day before," but then changed the date of the alleged assault from March 30 to March 25 because two of her friends "Kitty Anderson and Lizzie Hoffman was up at the same time, [and] they said it was the 25th of March." She was positive, however, that "Glenal. Goodridge did it," and finished her testimony by stating clearly that "This is the man that committed the outrage upon me."

Smith's friends corroborated parts of her story but contradicted others and added little new or significant evidence. Her companion on the visit to the studio, Susan Kemerer, stated that it was Glenalvin Goodridge who "asked her [Mary] to go up stairs to look at some cases" but that "as he took hold of her she hollered, [and] when she hollered I got scared and ran down." Susan remembered that "Mary was crying when she came down, [but] I couldn't tell that she said he had connexion with her." She had seen "him take hold of her arm," but because she had come downstairs "I didn't see him pull her." She concluded her testimony by stating that she "knew the Goodridges before," that "I know Wallace," that "I don't think they [Glenalvin and Wallace] look alike," and that she did not "remember whether Wallace was there or not." But she was certain that Glenalvin "was the man that went up with Mary and took hold of her arm." Elizabeth Hoffman and Kitty Anderson remembered being in Goodridge's gallery on a Tuesday—March 25, they thought, because Elizabeth "had holiday then." Elizabeth did not know the Goodridge family, but there "were two of them" at the studio. One was Wallace, whom she "did know," but she did not know "which one was talking with Mary Smith." She "hadn't seen Wallace Goodridge lately, [and] don't know whether he is in town or not. He had whiskers then." Kitty recalled "three of the Goodridges there [at the studio]," but could not remember which was which, although she thought Glenalvin had whiskers, and was older than his brothers. With that District Attorney Chapman concluded the case for the prosecution.

Glenalvin's lawyer, Vincent Keesey, opened for the defense and called twice as many witnesses to the stand as had the prosecution. Keesey's first witness was Celia Smith, an acquaintance of but not related to Mary Smith. Celia stated that she "became acquainted with Mary Smith when the 87th Rej. was in York," that "there was a great many soldiers always about her [Mary's] house," and that "she asked me to help her wash for them [the soldiers]." According to Celia, Mary had "offered me six dollars not to appear against her, and if that wasn't enough, if I wasn't satisfied with that, she [Celia] would get half that she [Mary] got from Goodridges." Mary wanted Celia to "go to Phila. or

Baltimore and if she [Celia] hadn't a bonnet fit to go she [Mary] would lend me her new bonnet." Celia testified that Mary had "said that people told her she would get a fortune from Goodridge."

Keesey then elicited from Celia Smith an account of the events at the Goodridge studio on March 25 that was dramatically different than that presented earlier by Mary Smith:

> No person was there but Wallace and William and Mary and her sister and myself. She [Mary] was talking to Wallace in the back place behind the curtains. He asked her something and she said yes. She then came to me and asked me if she would stay with Wallace whether she would get in the family way. I said she would have [to] enquire of those that knew more about it than I did. She gave me her new bonnet to hold. Mary went out first and Wallace after her. But where they went I don't know. After they came back she came first and she showed me three [coins] that she had got from Wallace, and she said she had staid with Wallace and that was the first time she had staid with any person. I met her in South St. near her home afterwards, she asked if Wallace Goodridge was at home. She said she thought she was in the family way as she hadn't her courses. She said people told her that she wouldn't have to live out [leave York], that Goodridge would keep her.

Under further questioning by Keesey, designed to discredit Mary Smith's character, Celia Smith stated that she "went to Goodridges gallery pretty often" but "was not on intimate terms with him and his family." At least once "Mary was with me . . . and she paid for the likenesses." On one of these visits Celia also had seen "the likenesses of several females naked, [but] I never had my likeness taken so," implying that Mary Smith indeed may have. She admitted that she had been subpoenaed to testify by the Goodridges and that she "saw Goodridge two or three times and talked over what I knew before he subpoenaed [me]." She concluded her testimony by sticking to her story that "Wallace was talking to Mary behind the screen. She said yes, didn't hear what he said. They were not gone a half an hour. Will Goodridge was there. I waited till Mary came back and went away with her. A week afterwards I met Mary. She had one silver quarter. She gave me ten cents of it."

Keesey then produced a series of defense witnesses who corroborated Celia Smith's testimony. Mary Houcke and Sarah Fry both swore that "Glenalvin was not there" but that "Wallace and William were" and that they both saw Mary Smith "coming down the stairs" about fifteen minutes after Wallace. Young William Goodridge, who was only sixteen years old in 1862 and who assured the court that he knew "the nature of an oath," testified that he had seen Mary Smith "at my brother's gallery eight or nine times" before but that on this occasion she came "on Monday . . . in March with Susan Kemerer . . . and Celia Smith," and that "through the keyhole" he "saw Wallace and Mary Smith go up[stairs]" and that he thought "Wallace went up first." Mary Simmes stated that she had a conversation with Mary Smith about whether "Glenalvin was well off, whether he owned any property or not," and that she "saw her [Smith] one evening with a soldier."

Keesey's final witnesses—Hamilton and Jane Grey, William Sutton (a ferryman on the Susquehanna at Columbia), and P. A. Gottwalt (a photographer in Columbia)—all testified respecting Glenalvin's regular habit of traveling to Columbia each Monday to work in his studio there.

District Attorney Chapman called six witnesses to the stand—including Joseph Smith, Mary's father—in rebuttal, but none added anything of substance to the prosecution's case. Martin McCreary, a clerk who may have worked in the Hartmann Building, did testify, for reasons unknown, that he had "looked through the keyhole in the door of Glenalvin Goodridge's room. Couldn't see the face of the person in the passage unless stooping. Could not see any of the steps of the stairs, could see any one going up." With that both prosecution and defense rested their cases.[54]

Neither case was conclusive. The prosecution, in its line of questioning, had raised rather than resolved questions about Mary Smith's character and motivation. And the defense, by failing to produce Wallace Goodridge as a witness to support his brother's innocence, equally left substantive ques-

tions regarding both Goodridges' relationship to Mary Smith without answers and, therefore, subject to the judgment of the jury.

The case was turned over to a jury of twelve "free[,] honest and lawful men of York County" the same day, November 5, that testimony was concluded. The jurors were identified as John W. Wilson, Henry F. Gable, Felix C. Herbert, John B. Trone, George W. Welsh, Nathaniel D. Anderson, Simon Leib, Henry Winter, Ambler Jones, Alexander Thompson, John R. Moore, and Henry Hammond. Eleven of the twelve were residents of rural York County. Only George W. Welsh, a butcher, lived in York Borough and, unlike the majority of his fellow jurors, presumably had day-to-day dealings with York's African American residents, the vast majority of whom lived in the borough. That the jurors were troubled by Glenalvin's race as well as by the quality of the evidence presented by both prosecution and defense is reflected in the fact that the York Gazette reported the unusual situation of the jury's deliberating "an entire night and the greater part of the next day" before reaching its "guilty" verdict.[55]

As a result the defense twice moved for a new trial. The first motion was made on November 8, the day following the jury's verdict. Glenalvin's lawyers argued for a new trial on grounds that, first, "the finding of the jury is against the law and the evidence . . . because . . . information could not be found which was material for the defendant's defense & because he can procure it before the next Court" (presumably Wallace's testimony); second, that "under objection [the court] allowed the District Attorney to ask defendant's witness (Celia Smith), if defendant had ever exhibited to her obscene daguerreotypes" (thereby prejudicing the jury against the defendant); third, that "the Court refused to permit defendant's counsel to show by witness for the purpose of proving general bad Character, that prosecutrix (Mary E. Smith) was seen by the witness in the evening with a person on the street with his hand under her Clothes at an indecent place"; and finally, that "the Court [mis]charged the jury as follows—When the defendant caught hold of Mary E. Smith prosecutrix it is for you to say what his intentions were[,] did he intend committing robbery? did he intend committing an assault and battery upon her? or did he intend doing something else? If he did as there are two counts in this indictment, one for rape, the other for assault with intent to commit a rape, you should convict of the one or the other."

A panel of three justices, including trial judge Fisher and associate judges Adam Ebaugh and David Fahs, heard the motion. Justices Fisher and Ebaugh denied it, while Fahs was in favor. Fisher was the area's most respected jurist and would serve as president judge of the state's Nineteenth Judicial District between 1851 and 1881. Ebaugh was a prominent member of the local Democratic Party, and Fahs had only recently been appointed to serve out the term of the deceased justice John Reiman.[56]

Two months later, on January 17, 1863, the second motion was presented to the same panel of judges. It argued first that Glenalvin was prepared to prove that on March 25, 1862, the day "on which the offence charged was said to have been Committed, he . . . did not leave his daguerian room while the prosecutrix and Susan Kemerer were in said room, and that Wallace Goodridge took the likeness referred to in the testimony of the prosecutrix, and not the Defendant." The second part of the motion argued the technicality that the alleged victim, Mary Smith, in her testimony before Justice White on July 30, 1862, had identified the day of the alleged assault as June 30, 1862, but that the resulting indictment had specified it as being March 30, 1862, and, therefore, the defendant "could not . . . be prepared to meet and contradict the testamony [sic] as to any other time." Again, by the same vote as the previous November, the justices denied the motion for a new trial.[57]

Exactly a month later, on February 17, Justice Fisher sentenced Glenalvin

to undergo an imprisonment in the Eastern Penetentiary [sic] in the City of Philadelphia in separate and solitary confinement at labor in the Cells and work house yards of said Prison for and during the term of Five years (to commence from this 17 day of February A.D. 1863) and during said imprisonment that he be sustained upon wholesome food of a coarse quality sufficient for the healthful support of life and that he be furnished with clothing suited to his situation at the discretion of the inspectors of the said Penetentiary [and] Pay a fine of one dollar to the Sheriff of York County for the use of said County, Pay the Costs of Prosecution and stand committed until the sentence be complied with.[58]

That Justice Fisher was troubled by the prosecution's case against Glenalvin as well as by the length and difficulty of the jury's deliberations in reaching its verdict is clear from the leniency of the sentence he imposed. Glenalvin's five-year sentence for rape, even as punishment for a first offense, was one-third that received by another resident of York—a white man named Thomas McCauley—found guilty of the same crime in the same court only six months before. McCauley was sentenced to serve fifteen years in the Eastern State Penitentiary under the same conditions as Glenalvin. Another York resident, tried at the same time as McCauley but found guilty of burglary, was sentenced to only five years, the same as Glenalvin. A glance at the "Descriptive Register" of the Eastern State Penitentiary listing prisoners admitted at the same time as Glenalvin also calls attention to the lightness of Judge Fisher's sentence. For example, a twenty-two-year-old white laborer convicted of postal theft was sentenced to four years, while a nineteen-year-old white first-time offender was ordered to serve nine years for larceny, both crimes and sentences hardly comparable to Glenalvin's. If anything, at this time and in this place, Glenalvin's race should have added several years to his sentence. It did not. It may, however, have been responsible for his conviction.[59]

In the end, when the indictments had been read, the evidence presented, the deliberations concluded, the verdict reached, the motions made, and the sentence imposed, the key question remained unanswered. If, indeed, Glenalvin were innocent, and, as the second motion for a new trial specified, "Wallace Goodridge took the likeness referred to in the testimony of the prosecutrix [Mary Smith]," and then, in effect, it was he and not Glenalvin who had "had connexion" with Mary, either with or without her consent, where was Wallace?

During the summer of 1862 Wallace had left York and joined his younger sister Mary Goodridge Nicholas (Nichols), who sometime earlier had settled in East Saginaw. Wallace never was known to have commented either privately or publicly on the trial or his brother's fate. Yet action he later took on behalf of his brother, his solicitude for Glenalvin's widow and fatherless children, and his own failure as a father to accept his illegitimate son who may have been born as a result of a liaison between himself and Mary E. Smith all point to a considerable degree of guilt on Wallace's part in this whole affair.

Without the evidence, however, one is left only to speculate about the possible course of events. It is likely that Wallace and Mary Smith did have a sexual relationship, that Mary became pregnant, that as a result Wallace left York for East Saginaw, that Mary, with no other option apparent, accused Glenalvin of rape both to explain the imminent birth of her mulatto child but also to obtain as much as possible from the Goodridge family as compensation for Wallace's desertion. Perhaps she never believed her accusation would result in a trial. That certainly would explain her own confusion and the disorganized nature of the prosecution. Perhaps the family knew the truth and placed its trust in that truth and in the justice system which it believed also would recognize Glenalvin's innocence. That certainly would explain the failure to bring Wallace back to York at the time of the trial to vindicate his brother but at the same time to face his own culpability. Once the authorities and the legal system, however, became aware of Smith's accusation, its ultimate determination was removed from the hands of both accuser and accused. Given the fact that the nation continued to be bitterly divided by a second year of civil war and that York was a border town, split politically, with loyalties that looked both to North and South, that certainly would explain the protracted jury deliberations respecting an African American male accused of raping a white woman of even doubtful character and the subsequent lenient sentence which,

nonetheless, sealed Glenalvin's fate and which became the turning point in the development of this African American family.

Although the sentence was for five years and Glenalvin served only one year, nine months, and twenty-four days of the total, that time, in effect, became the rest of his life. Records of the Eastern State Penitentiary in Philadelphia note that Glenalvin J. Goodridge was admitted on February 19, 1863, that he was a mulatto, with black hair and eyes, who was five feet, seven and one-quarter inches tall and had a ten-inch foot. He was listed as married, sober, and literate, and his occupation was given as "barber." His mental and physical condition were listed as "good" and he had been vaccinated for smallpox, but he did have a "Small spot in nose from Chicken Pox" and suffered from erysipelas (or St. Anthony's Fire), an infectious, bacterial skin disease characterized by redness, swelling, fever, pain, and lymphadenopathy. When he was discharged on December 15, 1864, Glenalvin's mental health continued to be described as "good," but his physical condition had deteriorated to "delicate." In fact, during his almost twenty-two months in prison he had contracted tuberculosis, from which he would die on November 14, 1867. Although it ultimately would cause his death, the tuberculosis also became the occasion for his release from the Eastern State Penitentiary.[60]

Almost as soon as Glenalvin was transported to Philadelphia in February 1863, his father, with the assistance of attorneys Gibson and Keesey, initiated a vigorous campaign to obtain a gubernatorial pardon for his son. Although the effort may have been interrupted for a time during the occupation of York by General Jubal Early's nine thousand Confederate troops late in June 1863, and then by the events at nearby Gettysburg during the first week of July, William Goodridge's determination in his struggle was no less than that of the thousands in blue and gray who fought and died that same summer.

Goodridge launched his campaign for a pardon on two fronts. Beginning in the fall of 1863 he circulated a petition among York's leading citizens. By the following winter he had gathered a total of

107 signatures. There can be little doubt that in amassing this extraordinary litany of the most influential religious, economic, legal, and political leaders—both Republicans and Democrats—in the community, Goodridge employed every bit of the persuasive power that earlier had been the foundation for his own success. Most likely he also cashed in the very last favors that might still have been owed to him in the community that had been his home for more than half a century.

The petition, drafted with the assistance of Gibson and Keesey, was addressed to Pennsylvania's first Republican governor, Andrew C. Curtin, who had been swept into office with Abraham Lincoln in 1860, ending a half century of Democratic domination in the state. The document took aim at the very heart of the prosecution's case and hinted at the special circumstances that existed in York at the time:

> The undersigned citizens of York, Pennsylvania respectfully represent[:]
>
> That Glenalvin J. Goodridge (colored) was convicted of the crime of Rape on Mary Smith (white girl) in the Court of Oyer and Terminer . . . for York County in November 1862.
>
> That on the 17th of February 1863 he was sentenced to the Eastern Penitentiary for five years.
>
> That in the opinion of your petitioners the evidence of the Commonwealth in itself was unsatisfactory, that there should have been no conviction.
>
> The evidence of the Commonwealth was in effect, that the defendant about twelve o'clock in the day time, in a building in Centre Square of York committed the crime.
>
> No complaint thereof was made until about three months thereafter.
>
> The evidence given on the part of the defendant contradicted the prosecutrix in this, that it proved the defendant was not in York on the day she fixed to wit 25 of March 1862, but in Columbia, Lancaster County. In addition her character for chastity was impeached.
>
> Further your petitioners believe that no conviction for rape would or could have taken place un-

der the evidence, if the defendant had been a white man.

> The jury had retired to the jury room in charge of a constable and remained there some twenty hours before they returned into court with their verdict of guilty.
>
> We therefore ask . . .[61]

Mr. Goodridge's second front was even more impressive in that he prevailed upon nine of York's most influential citizens, seven of whom had participated in the trial as either lawyers or jurists, to address personal letters to Governor Curtin spelling out their own thinking about the trial and the circumstances that may have influenced its outcome. A first group of six letters was addressed to Governor Curtin during a two-week period in February 1864 and delivered to the executive office in Harrisburg by Mr. Goodridge himself. The Goodridge lawyers, Keesey and Gibson, led off. Their letter duplicated the argument presented in the petition to the governor but added the interesting fact that "information at the time of the trial"—it did not specify what or by whom—"was mislaid and could not be found," suggesting, at least, a miscarriage of justice. David Fahs, one of the three judges who had reviewed both motions for a new trial and who had voted in favor on both occasions, wrote that "the evidence was not sufficiently strong to warrant his conviction" and that Glenalvin "never would have been convicted if he had been a white man." William Chapman, district attorney of York County and prosecutor at Glenalvin's trial, informed the governor that "I have no hesitation in expressing my doubts whether the same evidence would have convicted any white man in the County of the offence charged" and concluded that "I do not think, on a review of the case, that the exercise of the executive clemency in his favor would be improper." Justice T. K. White, who had issued the original warrant for Glenalvin's arrest in 1862, wrote two years later that even at the time of the warrant "I had my misgivings with regard to the validity of the charge." He also noted that "the girl bore a rather bad character and her veracity even on oath was strongly questioned and

I am of opinion the trial would never have resulted in a conviction but for the prejudice so well known to exist against a person of his color." David E. Small, one of York's leading entrepreneurs and a business associate of Mr. Goodridge over the years, tried to focus on the human side of the tragedy. Small wrote that Glenalvin had "always conducted himself properly in our community," that he knew "the character of the girl . . . to be dishonest," and that with "the state of feeling against coloured persons here during the 2 previous years, it was not a difficult thing for a York County jury to render such a very severe verdict." Small also presented the governor with a proposal that likely came from Mr. Goodridge. If the governor, he wrote, "will give this case a favourable consideration," Mr. Goodridge "assures me, and I am sure it will be so, that his son & family will remove to the west where his brothers now are, immediately after his release."[62]

Governor Curtin might have seized the opportunity to right an obvious miscarriage of justice in February 1864 except for the fact that one final letter among this first group gave him reason to hesitate. The letter, from Justice Fisher, stated that "In deciding the case I acted according to the best of my ability and judgment and so I think did the other judges. I have no reason to regret my agency in the matter for I think I did what was right. I have heard," he continued, "that some persons here say 'Had he been a white man he would not have been convicted' [and] perhaps they have so written to the Governor. For myself I cannot say so. If the jury believed the evidence a conviction was inevitable." As a result of Fisher's letter, Governor Curtin chose not to pardon Glenalvin at that time.[63]

William Goodridge, however, refused to be deterred. In June, William Hay, senior partner in York's oldest and most prestigious law firm, Cochran and Hay, renewed the campaign and wrote Governor Curtin that he "was present at the trial of Goodridge and heard much of the evidence on the part of the Commonwealth." It was his judgment that "the conviction of Goodridge was improper," and he wanted the governor to know

that "the friends of G. J. Goodridge" were "desirous of having him pardoned." Curtin still refused to act, but William Goodridge refused to concede. By the fall of 1864 his persistence apparently had convinced Justice Fisher to soften his original position, and Goodridge prevailed upon one of the area's most influential Republicans to convey this information to the governor.[64]

Near the end of November, Dr. Charles H. Bressler, York's most respected physician and dentist but also one of the founding members of the Republican Party in that part of the state, wrote to his friend and political ally Governor Curtin. Dr. Bressler informed the governor that "Goodridge's father called on me the other evening and requested me remind you of his son's case. He says," Bressler wrote, "that Judge Fisher will give you a satisfactory letter if you drop him a line as he [Fisher] admits that he [Glenalvin] would not have been convicted if he had been a white man (or as much as admits it)." He also reminded Curtin that "the petition," which the governor had received several months before, was "signed by David Small Esq. Chief Burgess, Dr. Pents, and many of the hardest *Democrats* of the place [York]." He concluded, on the same theme of the earlier correspondents, that "There is not a man in our party [the Republicans] but is satisfied that he never would have been convicted if he had been a white man," but then Bressler also added, "and if *he had been a democrat!*"[65]

Bressler's letter apparently had convinced the governor to contact Judge Fisher, for on December 10 Fisher answered Curtin that "Your letter in relation to the case of Glenalvin G. [*sic*] Goodridge (a mulatto man) reached this place when I was not at home or it would have received an earlier reply." Fisher did not alter his original position regarding "the merits of the case," but admitted that there now were extenuating circumstances. He conceded to Curtin that "I understand that his health is failing. As he has a large family and promises if pardoned to leave the State, perhaps it would be as well to release him. He is a man of good education and a good teacher and may be useful in that capacity elsewhere. He formerly taught our colored school."[66]

Fisher was unwilling to admit that either he or the judicial system had failed to dispense the justice to which Glenalvin was entitled. Instead he settled on Glenalvin's flawless reputation, his likely death from tuberculosis, and the fact that he and his family would be "elsewhere" as the crutches to support his recommendation. Whatever the merit of Fisher's argument, it was the goad that Curtin needed finally to take action. On December 13, 1864, the governor "fully pardoned" Glenalvin of "the Crime whereof he is convicted," but only on the condition that "he promises if pardoned to leave the State." Two days later, Glenalvin J. Goodridge, in "delicate" health, was discharged from the Eastern State Penitentiary.[67]

The pardon did result in Glenalvin's release from prison, but it did not exonerate him from the guilt or shame associated with the crime. In fact, the conditions for the release, although originally suggested by Mr. Goodridge and then imposed by the governor as the price for his freedom, in a sense abridged that freedom by denying to Glenalvin and his family the opportunity to return to or to remain in their home. The pardon, and in particular the arguments presented by Glenalvin's defenders, consistently called attention to the two facts that ultimately convinced the governor to act but which also were originally and ultimately responsible for Glenalvin's plight, his race and York County's politics at that time. Actually the two were separate but closely related parts of the same circumstance.

For nearly two decades after 1854, York County was the political exception to most of Pennsylvania. Whereas the newly organized Republican Party swept state elections beginning in 1855 and continued to dominate state and local elective offices through the 1870s, York Borough and County remained under the control of a Democratic majority. In fact, during elections held in York in the midst of the Civil War the Democrats extended their control over most local offices. A recent analysis of York politics at the time has argued that Yorkers "consistently supported the Democracy [Democratic Party] in the 1840s and 1850s at a time when Democrats became identified with the pro-slavery movement. They continued to vote Democratic because of trade links to the South through the slave state of Maryland, the perception that the Republicans continued to stress a strong centralized government and the notion that the Democracy was the only true national party. Some Democrats believed the Republicans would never gain support in the South, so a vote for the Republicans was a vote for splitting the union." As a result, the study has concluded, "many in York County were ambivalent toward the issue behind the war—the slavery question."[68]

This attitude is best summarized by A. B. Farquhar, a York businessman and Democrat but certainly not one of the community leaders who had added his name to support the Goodridge pardon. He wrote in retrospect regarding Yorkers at the time: "The beginnings of the events which developed into the Civil War did not much move us. York was distinctively Northern but not bitterly anti-Southern. The community felt that slavery was wrong in principle. At the same time, being acquainted with many slave owners, we also knew that slavery was better in practice than in theory and that the planter who was cruel to his Negroes was a rare exception."[69] As a result, the Goodridges, as African American Republicans, and in particular Glenalvin, suffered on both accounts.

⸺◆⸺

The trial with all its attendant circumstances became the pivotal event in Goodridge family history. It marked an end to the family's half century of success in York but then became the occasion for renewed achievement once again in East Saginaw. It confirmed William C. Goodridge's role as an effective leader among southeastern Pennsylvania's African American elite, but at the same time signaled the passing of his generation's leadership on to the next. It ended prematurely a most promising career in photography, but stimulated a commitment by Glenalvin's brothers that carried the Goodridge studio's success far beyond anything he might have dreamt only a few years before.

Without a doubt, however, it was the intensity of this tragedy which became the cement binding the members of this family to each other that served as its strength for the remainder of the nineteenth century and well into the next.

Understandably, references to Glenalvin's trial, conviction, and pardon disappeared even more completely and more rapidly from York's collective memory than did the members of the Goodridge family who had remained in York during the weeks following his release from the Eastern State Penitentiary. No reference to it to this point has appeared in any document left by or in literature describing Goodridge family members.[70] For decades thereafter York instead was distracted by yet another community tragedy—the borough's invasion, occupation, and controversial surrender to Confederate forces at the end of June 1863.[71]

Few York residents noticed, therefore, when sometime during the spring or early summer of 1865, as promised, Glenalvin and Rhoda and their children left York and joined sister Mary and brothers William and Wallace who, more than two years before, had reestablished both the family and then the Goodridge photography studio in East Saginaw. William C. Goodridge most certainly accompanied his gravely ill eldest son and family on their difficult journey to Michigan. Yet even as late as May 1865 he also continued to operate and advertise his "Shaving and Hair Cutting Saloon" at 49 North Duke Street, only "about 10 Doors from the Railroad Station."[72]

Precisely when William C. Goodridge left York for the last time is not known. He was a regular visitor to East Saginaw during the final years of the 1860s and, in fact, accompanied Glenalvin on a trip from East Saginaw to Minneapolis in May 1867. Shortly thereafter, on November 14, Glenalvin died of the tuberculosis that had become his Eastern State Penitentiary legacy. Perhaps it was then that Mr. Goodridge decided to settle in Minneapolis with his daughter Emily Goodridge Grey and her family. When he died there on January 15, 1873, his death certificate noted that he was seventy years old, had suffered from dropsy, had worked as a merchant, and had by then been living in Minneapolis for eight years.[73]

A generation later, in 1891, Glen J. Goodridge, Glenalvin and Rhoda's youngest son, returned to York from Saginaw with his mother and reestablished a Goodridge family presence there once again. Like his grandfather before him, Glen Goodridge also opened a barbershop on North Duke Street, only a few doors down from William C. Goodridge's location in 1865. He married Virginia E. Brown. His mother, Glenalvin's widow, remarried when she returned to York. Her new spouse was Abraham Rayno. The Raynos (also Reyno or Reno), originally from Pennsylvania, were African Americans who were among the first settlers in East Saginaw and were operating a barbershop there by 1860. Rhoda Grey Goodridge Rayno died in 1903, Glen J. Goodridge in 1928. Both are buried in the Lebanon Cemetery, North York.[74]

3

Wallace L. and William O. Goodridge: East Saginaw Origins, 1863–1872

THE TRAGIC CIRCUMSTANCES that resulted in the Goodridge family's financial difficulties, the closure of both the York and the Columbia, Pennsylvania, branches of Glenalvin's "American Photographic Gallery," and the migration of family members to Michigan and Minnesota between 1862 and 1865 have been described in detail elsewhere. What is not quite so clear, however, is why Mary, Wallace, William, and ultimately Glenalvin Goodridge all chose East Saginaw as their new home at this time. There is no evidence that any family member resided in the community or had visited before 1862. Emily Goodridge Grey, who traveled between York and St. Anthony, Minnesota, to join her husband there in 1857, did not include a stop at East Saginaw or Saginaw City on her journey. In fact, the first record of a Goodridge presence in Saginaw appeared only in August 1863, when the *Weekly Enterprise* printed a list of letters awaiting recipients at the East Saginaw post office that included the names of Mary and William O. Goodridge.[1]

During the 1860s the Saginaw Valley did offer great opportunity to settlers headed west. No reports extolling this potential, however, were published by the York newspapers to guide migrants in that direction. Such information could have come to York from any of the almost twenty thousand inhabitants of Saginaw County at the time, yet no personal or professional contact between any of them and the Goodridge family can be confirmed. For example, Saginaw photographers Henry N. Eastman and William A. Armstrong, both professional contemporaries of the Goodridge brothers,

were born in Pennsylvania, but no evidence exists linking any of them before all had settled in the Saginaw Valley. Furthermore, among the several African American families listed as residents of East Saginaw and Saginaw City in the 1860 and 1870 censuses only two included members who were born in Pennsylvania, and neither can be traced to York County.[2]

Two additional possibilities exist which may explain the decision to settle in East Saginaw. Shortly after her arrival in East Saginaw, Mary Goodridge, William C. Goodridge's second daughter and the photographers' sister, married John L. Nicholas (Nichols), an East Saginaw barber. Although Nicholas's origins are unknown, Mary Goodridge may have met him before 1863 and subsequently joined him in Michigan, a pattern earlier established by her sister Emily and brother-in-law Ralph Toyer Grey in Minnesota.[3] Brothers Wallace, William, and Glenalvin then followed her to East Saginaw. It also is possible that the family was familiar with the area as a result of Mr. Goodridge's political activism, first as a Whig, then a Republican, and always as an opponent of slavery. During the spring of 1842 James G. Birney and his family settled in Lower Saginaw (later Bay City), Michigan. Originally a slave owner but converted to the abolitionist cause by Theodore Weld, Birney became executive secretary of the American Anti-Slavery Society in 1837. Twice nominated for president by the Liberty Party, he garnered only seven thousand votes in 1840 but raised the total to sixty thousand four years later. Stung by the magnitude of his initial defeat, Birney "retired" to the Saginaw Valley to speculate in land and raise Durham cattle. He could not resist the lure of local politics, however, and was instrumental in the organization of both Bay City and Bay County. Birney remained a vocal opponent of slavery until his death as the result of a fall from a horse while on a trip east in November 1857. Eldest son James took over both his father's holdings and political causes, serving as Republican governor Austin Blair's lieutenant for a time in 1861 before accepting an appointment as circuit judge and returning to Bay City. Given Goodridge's earlier travels to Canada (as reported by Frederick Douglass) and especially his contacts within the abolitionist community, it certainly is likely that the Goodridges and Birneys would have met at some point. It also seems that the one family's successful "retirement" to the Saginaw Valley during the 1840s may well have served as a precedent for another family's seeking similar "retirement" in the face of its own defeats twenty years later.[4]

While any of the above possibilities might explain the Goodridge's decision to relocate in East Saginaw, none does so with certainty. Whatever their motive may have been, the decision was a timely and fortuitous one.

——◆——

In 1863, East Saginaw and Saginaw City (united as Saginaw in 1889) were at the threshold of an economic boom and period of extraordinary expansion that would exceed even the predictions made by Alexis de Tocqueville following his 1831 visit to the Saginaw Valley. De Tocqueville believed that the valley's future was certain. "In but few years," he wrote, "these impenetrable forests will have fallen. The noise of civilization and of industry will break the silence of the Saginaw. Its echo will be silent. Embankments will imprison its sides, and its waters, which today flow unknown and quiet through nameless wilds, will be thrown back in their flow by the prows of ships." The achievement of this clearly evident potential, however, would be realized only gradually. With its extensive system of rivers and abundant resources,

the valley had long been home to a large and varied Native American population. Their presence, in turn, had attracted two centuries of competition among French, English, and American adventurers, missionaries, and fur traders. In the years immediately following the War of 1812, which resolved English and American differences over the Great Lakes, much was expected in the valley as a result of the Saginaw Treaty and Cession from the Natives in 1819 and the construction of Fort Saginaw in 1822. But by the summer of Tocqueville's visit the fort had already been abandoned for most of a decade and relatively few resolute pioneers had taken advantage of the government's offer of the all but free land. Tocqueville reported only "thirty people" and fewer dwellings "half lost among the leaves." The decade-long depression following the Panic of 1837 further curtailed these modest achievements as well as a variety of attempts to intensify the valley's rate of development. Nevertheless, by midcentury Tocqueville's "thirty" had increased to more than two thousand, with nearly half those in Saginaw City, the county seat since organization in 1835. Improved economic conditions during the 1850s brought increased settlement, investments in roads, mills, and farms, and the incorporation of the village of East Saginaw in 1855 by a group of New York investors.[5] Though separated by a river, the two communities henceforth were united in their determination to consume the vast resources that surrounded them.

The process already was well under way when the Goodridges began to arrive in East Saginaw. The county's population would more than triple, from 12,000 to 39,000, between the 1860 and 1870 censuses. East Saginaw grew from 3,000 to 11,000 residents, and Saginaw City, with 1,700 citizens in 1860 and almost 7,500 in 1870, was expanding even more rapidly. During the 1880s, the decade of peak growth, the county surpassed 60,000, with East Saginaw accounting for more than 20,000 and Saginaw City over 11,000 of that total. Much of this increase was stimulated by an even more rapid expansion in the pine lumber industry.[6]

For centuries Michigan forests had sheltered and supplied the native peoples, yielded number-

Figure 3.1. "East Saginaw, Washington Street, Looking North from Genesee Street, About 1860." Copy from daguerreotype original. [Henry N. Eastman, Photographer ?], East Saginaw, Mich. Eddy Local History and Genealogical Collection, Hoyt Public Library.

less pelts to French and English competitors, and more recently thwarted the efforts of expansive American pioneers. During the middle of the nineteenth century, however, the pine forests were discovered as a valuable resource. By the end of the century they were gone. In Saginaw County alone, twenty-four mills were cutting 60 million board feet of pine lumber in 1857. In 1880 ninety mills were sawing 850 million feet annually. During 1863 the Saginaw mills employed more than three thousand men. In forest lumber camps throughout the valley and on boom company river drives, these mill hands were joined by nearly as many "shanty boys" and "river rats." The timber they cut and processed each year was the basis for the wealth of the celebrated lumber barons, and the

wages they earned fueled the valley's rapid expansion and development for a generation after 1860.[7]

In 1863 there was little in either of the Saginaws that these laborers and barons could not buy if they decided to spend. Dozens of tradesmen and professionals catered to a wide variety of needs and tastes. What was not available locally could be brought by steamer from Detroit. The service sector of the economy, in fact, was growing even more rapidly than the general population. An 1856 directory listed only 28 "professionals and tradesmen" in East Saginaw; by 1863 their number had increased to 142. And although in 1860 East Saginaw looked very much like a frontier town, with one-story structures and muddy streets (see figure 3.1), the process that would transform it and Saginaw City across the river into a metropolitan center of some regional importance during the second half of the century had already begun. The Goodridges' decision to make East Saginaw their home enabled them to record the process.[8]

An unknown itinerant or perhaps an enthusiastic local amateur made the Saginaw Valley's first photographs sometime during the 1840s. Yet as late as 1856 no photographer was listed among the "professionals and tradesmen" in either Saginaw City or East Saginaw. The following year, however, Henry N. Eastman established Saginaw's first photography studio. Eastman remained in East Saginaw through 1865. From his rooms above the grocers Sanborn and Tucker in the Corliss Block on Genesee Street, Eastman advertised ambrotypes and melainotypes (tintypes). He also printed "BROMO ELODISED COLODIAN PICTURES" (wet-plate negatives) on various media, including "Niello paper or Patent Leather," which were "as natural as life and far better looking than the original," for "as low as FIFTY CENTS." He admonished those customers who might hesitate, in one of his trademark poetic efforts, that "Of those, for whom, you fond emotions cherish, Secure the shadow, ere the substance perish."[9] During most of four years, Hank Eastman had Saginaw to himself. Apparently he prospered. By 1860, marriage, three children, a housemaid, and property valued at more than $1,200 made him an established, though not necessarily prominent, member of the community.

During the summer of 1860 Eastman's monopoly was broken by two competitors, H. W. Boozer of Ionia, Michigan, who lasted only the year before moving on to Grand Rapids, and T. S. Mahan of Cleveland, Ohio, who proved to be more of a challenge. Mahan declared that he had "the largest SKY-LIGHT in the county" and "in fact the only good light in the city." This, he claimed, enabled him to make "Pictures in all the various styles known in the art, many of which were never before offered to the citizens" of Saginaw. Eastman objected to Mahan's claim of "the *only Sky-Light* in the City," since he had been "working with an *ex-cellent Sky-Light* ever since I commenced business here." Furthermore, Eastman stated that "*taking Pictures* and not '*blowing*' " was his trade and invited everyone to inspect his work. To stimulate their interest he noted that he had "on hand a very good assortment of JEWELRY and all persons purchasing a Picture for $1.00 or upwards, will be entitled to draw a handsome Prize."[10]

By June 1861 Mahan had moved on, but his place was taken by William J. Driggs, recently of New York City. Driggs advertised "a NORTHERN LIGHT" which was "indispensable to a perfect Picture," cameras that were "bought in New York," and the talent to create a "handsome Picture from a homely copy." In the spirit of the times, he also offered to "make Pictures [of those] who have enlisted for the War to defend the flag or our country . . . at half the usual price."[11] Eastman's response was once again to "bring out that old Masheen [*sic*] of ours . . . [and to] grind out a little Poetry":

Saginaw Folks, attention!
While we whisper in your ear,
Where you can find the treasure
Which friends will find most dear.

'Tis of our life-like Pictures
We wish to hint to all,
And hope you will delay not
In giving us a call.

We take all kinds of Pictures,
On Iron Plates and Glass
So if you want a likeness,
Be sure you do not pass.

In Lockets, Rings and Breast Pins
In Keys, and Seals and Cases,
We are ready to convert at will,
The semblance of your faces.
And when you've time to spare,
Just drop in one and all
For if you do not wish to buy
We'll thank you for a call.[12]

Fortunately, by the end of 1862 Eastman's business talent outshone his humble verse. Not only had he moved to a "LARGE SKY-LIGHT GALLERY–Over the Post Office, on Washington st.," but he also had taken on a partner. James T. Randall, a native of Connecticut, was twenty-six when he joined Eastman and "had considerable experience in the best Galleries in New York City." Eastman claimed that "competent Judges" had determined that the partners "make the best PHOTOGRAPHS, CARTE DE VISITES, AMBROTYPES, &C., of any Gallery in the State." The expansion also allowed them to offer a variety of services and photographic supplies, including copies, enlargements, albums, cases, and frames, as well as to introduce "VIEWS OF BUILDINGS, MACHINERY, VESSELS &C. &C.," the first known in the Saginaw Valley.[13]

The partnership lasted until April 1864. Exactly what caused the split is not clear. Eastman did announce that his "GREAT TEMPLE OF ART" had "BEEN undergoing a Change," that he had "dissolved his Copartnership with Mr. Randall and has engaged the services of Mr. J. C. MORE [sic], from New York, to attend to the Photographing Department." That was the last Saginaw heard from Hank Eastman. He did continue to work in East Saginaw until at least January 26, 1865, when it was reported that his studio was among the businesses destroyed by a fire that swept through the block on the southeast corner of Washington and Genesee Streets.[14]

William Driggs, Eastman's other competitor, closed his studio during 1864, but three new ones opened—William Roberts from Detroit and Maylor and Hutchinson, a team of daguerreotypists, located in East Saginaw, and J. M. Clark, who had been making daguerreotypes in Syracuse, New York, since 1840, settled in Saginaw City—but none of them appears to have been directly responsible for Eastman's exit.[15] Following the dissolution of their partnership, Randall established his own studio at 325 Genesee, where he became the most financially successful of Saginaw's early photographers. By 1870 he and his wife, Sophia, had a son and daughter, owned property valued at more than $23,000, and had taken on two apprentices in the studio, Hiram Hadstate and Lysander Miller, as well as employing Joseph Brown as a "photographic operator."[16] (See figure 3.2 a–d for examples of work by these early Saginaw photographers.) It was in this highly competitive and ever-changing photographic marketplace of the Saginaws during the 1860s that the Goodridge brothers decided to reestablish their studio.

—◆—

The exact date that the Goodridge photography studio reopened at its new location in East Saginaw is not known. Wallace Goodridge later celebrated July 1863 as the firm's Saginaw anniversary, but it is unlikely that he or either of his brothers was making photographs regularly or on a commercial basis at their new location much before the summer of 1864. Wallace, in fact, remembered in a 1902 interview that during his first years in Saginaw, 1862 and 1863, he had worked as a barber for the S. G. Clay shop in the Bancroft Hotel.[17] Young William O. Goodridge had joined his brother Wallace and sister Mary in East Saginaw by late summer 1863. During 1864, perhaps in anticipation of their brother's release from prison later that year, Wallace and William decided to reopen the Goodridge photography studio, but on a reorganized basis. In York Glenalvin had founded and then operated "Goodridge's American Photographic Gallery" on his own. By 1860 first Wallace and then the younger William would have joined their elder brother as assistants in his studio there. The East Saginaw studio, on the other hand, from its organization in 1864 clearly was a joint effort among the three brothers. There can be little doubt that the partnership arrangement was designed to support Glenalvin and his family. This pattern of shared responsibility was a Goodridge family hallmark that had been initiated decades earlier by their father in York, and one which the Goodridge brothers and sisters sustained long after his death.

For their new photography studio the three Goodridge brothers rented room on the third floor of the Crouse Block at the northeast corner of

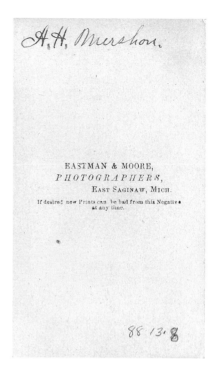

Figure 3.2a. "A. H. Mershon," 1864, carte de visite. Albumen image, 2³⁄₁₆ x 3⅜ inches, ivory bristol board mount, 2⅜ x 4¹⁄₁₆ inches. Eastman & Moore, Photographers, East Saginaw, Mich. Historical Society of Saginaw County, Inc.

Figure 3.2b. Verso of figure 3.2a.

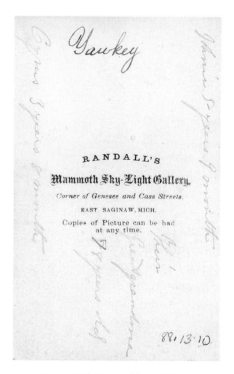

Figure 3.2c. "Yawkey Family," after April 1864, carte de visite. Albumen image, 2⁵⁄₁₆ x 3⅜ inches, ivory bristol board mount, 2½ x 4 inches. James T. Randall, Photographer, East Saginaw, Mich. Historical Society of Saginaw County, Inc.

Figure 3.2d. Verso of figure 3.2c.

Figure 3.3. "Crouse Block," 1864 or after, carte de visite. Albumen image, 3¾ x 2⁵⁄₁₆ inches, ivory bristol board mount with gold trim, 4 x 2⁷⁄₁₆ inches. Goodridge Brothers Studio, East Saginaw. Mich. Eddy Local History and Genealogical Collection, Hoyt Public Library. Notice the man (one of the Goodridge brothers) in the window second from the right in the third story of the Crouse Block below the signboard advertising the studio.

Washington and Genesee Avenues (see figure 3.3). The choice was a perfect one. The building was little more than a year old, was prominently located at the city's busiest intersection, and included a number of other tenants, such as Dunk's Drug Store and the Woodard Grocery Store, which would have brought large numbers of potential customers to the studio's door. The third (topmost) story, with its large skylights and northeasterly location, provided not only the excellent natural light necessary to photography at the time but also a means to advertise the studio's existence. No photographer had occupied the location previously, and while the other East Saginaw studios (Eastman, Randall, Roberts, and Maylor and Hutchinson) all were within a block or two of the Genesee-Washington intersection, none now was quite at the center of things as were the Goodridges.

In spite of their excellent new location, Wallace and William began quietly in the summer of 1864.

No directory listing or newspaper advertisement appeared for the studio that year, and, in fact, it is only possible to document its early existence indirectly. The earliest extant Goodridge photographs from East Saginaw, both tintypes and cartes de visite, bear tax stamps (see figure 3.4a–b) mandated by Congress beginning on August 1, 1864, to raise revenue for the war. According to William C. Darrah, the method of canceling the stamps provides a rough estimate of the date of the photograph in that the "law [originally] required that the stamp be cancelled with the initials of the photographer and date of sale." Before the end of the year many photographers ignored the regulation or "simply cancelled with an X or a few strokes by pen or pencil, a practice that was immediately accepted without complaint by the Treasury Department." Note that figure 3.4a is cancelled "Goodr. Bros.," the earlier (summer 1864) form, while figure 3.4b, made during the final months of 1864, is not. According to Kathleen Fuller, during

Figure 3.4a. "Carte de Visite with 2 Cent Revenue Stamp," summer 1864, 2⁷⁄₁₆ x 4 inches. Goodridge Brothers Studio, East Saginaw, Mich. Collection of Dave Tinder.

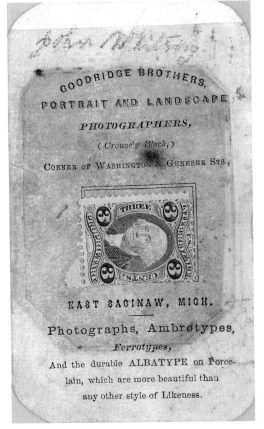

Figure 3.4b. "Verso of Tintype Paper Cover with 3 Cent Revenue Stamp," fall 1864, 2⁷⁄₁₆ x 4¹⁄₁₆ inches. Goodridge Brothers Studio, East Saginaw, Mich. Collection of Dave Tinder.

the initial months the tax was in effect, perhaps August to October 1864, photographers complied with the requirement to cancel the stamp with name or initials and date of sale. Thereafter, because the ink from the full cancellation often damaged the photograph beneath it in a stack of duplicates or multiple images, most photographers used the minimum cancellation possible or none at all.[18]

The Goodridges' first East Saginaw newspaper advertisement, which appeared in January 1865, warned potential customers that "THE GREAT RUSH NOW, IS AT GOODRIDGE BRO.'S PHOTOGRAPHY GALLERY." Yet, in spite of "Pictures of all sizes from the little Gem, to the life-size Photograph, in India ink or in Water Colors . . . [and] Rooms . . . gotten up expressly for this Business, . . . [which] cannot be excelled in its advantages between this city and New York," the "great Rush" appears to have been more

imaginary than real. Competition remained strong. Although Eastman and then Maylor and Hutchinson had left by or during 1865, Randall and Roberts in East Saginaw and Clark in Saginaw City were well established. Furthermore, by the end of 1865 additional new studios would have opened in each of the communities. In East Saginaw, Meade and Merrill (possibly an offshoot of the famous Meade Bros. of New York) offered a complete line of photographs, including "AMBROTYPES, . . . Letter Pictures, . . . [and] VIEWS OF PUBLIC BUILDINGS AND PRIVATE RESIDENCES." At Saginaw City, W. A. Armstrong, who also had migrated to Michigan from Pennsylvania, opened a "Fine Art Gallery" that remained a most important studio in the valley even after he had moved to Chicago in 1873.[19]

While the Goodridges' early advertisements offered "Pictures of every description," few from the period before the summer of 1866 are known to exist, and those include none of the cased photographs (either daguerreotypes or ambrotypes) that had been Glenalvin's specialty in York. In addition, by the spring of 1865 four years of Civil War had weakened both the national and local economies, and the postwar boom that would stimulate Michigan's resource-based economy was at least a year away. Consequently, during its first years in East Saginaw the new Goodridge studio was only modestly successful.[20] Moreover, it had become clear by the first weeks of 1867 that the tuberculosis which Glenalvin had contracted as a result of his almost two years in the Eastern State Penitentiary soon would end his life.

Early in May 1867, William C. Goodridge and Glenalvin left East Saginaw and traveled by train across the state to Ludington (originally Pere Marquette) on Lake Michigan, the western terminus of the Flint & Pere Marquette Railroad. They crossed Lake Michigan to Milwaukee on one of the new steamers operated by the railroad. In Milwaukee, on May 17, father and son met Dr. Hannibal H. Kimball of Minneapolis. Together the trio traveled by train and riverboat to Prairie du Chien on the Mississippi. There they boarded a steamer and arrived in St. Paul on May 20. Less than six months later, on November 14, thirty-eight-year-old Glenalvin J. Goodridge died of tuberculosis in Minneapolis at the home of his sister Emily and her husband, Ralph Toyer Grey. Exactly why Glenalvin, who certainly must have understood the gravity of his illness and sensed the imminence of his death that spring, chose to leave his wife and children in East Saginaw and traveled with his father to Minneapolis at this time is not clear. A possible reason, however, is revealed in the details of a lawsuit decided by the Saginaw County Circuit Court two years later.[21]

On May 1, 1869, Glenalvin's widow, Rhoda C. Goodridge, sued the Massachusetts Life Insurance Company for failing to honor her spouse's life insurance policy. The suit argued that on June 20, 1867, Glenalvin had purchased a $3,000 policy from the company through its East Saginaw agent, Henry Plessner. The Goodridge lawyer, D. W.

Perkins, claimed that all premiums had been paid, that Glenalvin had met the travel and hazardous occupation restrictions in the policy, that he had died on November 14, 1867, that proof of death had been furnished to the company on January 15, 1868, and that the company had refused payment. The suit asked originally for $5,000 and later increased the amount to $10,000. In December 1869 the court denied Rhoda Goodridge's suit and found in favor of the Massachusetts Life Insurance Company, awarding the company $87.44 in costs, which were charged to Mrs. Goodridge. The full amount of the costs was paid only in August 1871 after the company had filed a writ of *fieri facias* demanding that the sheriff collect the outstanding costs.

The court, in its decision, had accepted the argument presented by the company's East Saginaw attorneys, Augustine S. Gaylord and Benton Hanchett, that the insurance policy was void because it had been purchased under fraudulent circumstances. According to the attorneys, Glenalvin already was critically ill with tuberculosis in the spring of 1867, and a substitute (possibly Wallace or William) was sent in June 1867 in Glenalvin's place to the company's medical examiner in East Saginaw, Dr. William K. Wheat, who unknowingly certified Glenalvin's health. Furthermore, the policy application specifically denied that Glenalvin had or ever did have tuberculosis or a persistent cough and claimed, in fact, that he was in excellent health. When Glenalvin died of tuberculosis only five months later the company became suspicious, suspended payment, and began its investigation into the circumstances of Glenalvin's death.

In October and November 1869, at the request of the company and the order of the court, depositions were taken in Minneapolis from Glenalvin's father, his brother-in-law Ralph Toyer Grey, and Dr. Hannibal H. Kimball, who had attended Glenalvin at his death. Mr. Goodridge testified that Glenalvin had traveled with him from East Saginaw to Minneapolis "between the latter part of May and the 10th of June 1867," that Glenalvin "was free from any disease at the time I first saw him in 1867," that he had "a slight cough but I do not know how long it continued," and that he and Glenalvin had conversed "very frequently on the subject of his health, but I do not remember what he [Glenalvin] said." Ralph Toyer Grey avowed that he first saw Glenalvin in St. Paul in May 1867 and then "almost every day for several months before his death." He remembered that Glenalvin "had no cough" but did tell him that he was "suffering from neuralgia" and "thought he would recover." Dr. Kimball had traveled with William and Glenalvin Goodridge from Milwaukee to St. Paul, arriving there on May 18 or 19, 1867. Shortly thereafter, he recalled, at the request of both father and son, he had examined Glenalvin. He found "his constitution broken down and very much debilitated." The doctor noted that his examination also had revealed that Glenalvin's "lungs [were] badly diseased and both full of tubercles." It was Dr. Kimball's judgment that Glenalvin had contracted the disease "one year at least" before his death and that his health had been "quite feeble during all that time."[22]

The court, in denying Rhoda Goodridge's suit, assigned no specific guilt for the fraudulent application or physical examination. The company, however, suspected Glenalvin's widow and had attacked her character. In a July 1869 deposition, its investigator, Thomas E. Morris of East Saginaw, testified that he had "some acquaintance with the Plaintiff [Rhoda Goodridge] in this case and with her pecuniary responsibility and that he has made inquiry within the past two weeks as to the pecuniary responsibility of the Plaintiff of such persons in the City of East Saginaw where said Plaintiff resides as deponent believed would be able to give him any information upon the subject and was informed by such persons that the Plaintiff is irresponsible and from his own knowledge and the information desired as aforesaid the deponent avers that said Plaintiff is irresponsible."[23] Morris did not identify the sources of this information, so it is impossible to assess its accuracy.

In any case, it is clear that the court's decision was an appropriate one. Two specific items of evidence confirm that Glenalvin's and/or his family's action was fraudulent. As early as December 1864, Glenalvin's discharge report from the Eastern State Penitentiary and then the later testimony from Dr. Kimball both reveal that by the spring of 1867 Glenalvin had been gravely ill for more than a year. And furthermore, as all the various depositions made clear, in June 1867, when Glenalvin supposedly was visiting the office of Dr. Wheat in East Saginaw to undergo the physical examination required by the insurance company, he already had arrived in or was en route to Minneapolis with his father. However cursory that examination may have been, the healthy individual whom Dr. Wheat had examined could not have been Glenalvin.

Only the issue of motive and the source of the scheme, therefore, remain. The family's long-standing tradition for mutual support and common action makes it unlikely that Rhoda Goodridge acted without their support or at least tacit compliance. The complex circumstances of Glenalvin's trial and imprisonment, with its mortal consequences, further suggest that the ruse may have been conceived as a means of compensating Glenalvin and his immediate family for the perceived failure of the York County judicial process. Given Wallace Goodridge's role in that affair—in particular, his almost certain involvement with Mary Smith, his absence from York during his brother's trial, and the resulting burden of guilt and responsibility that he certainly carried—it is likely that Wallace developed and then attempted to carry out the scheme. Had Glenalvin survived a year or more after purchasing the insurance policy, the plan might have succeeded. His death within months, however, alerted the insurance company, and its investigation exposed the plan. Rhoda Goodridge, her children, and the rest of the Goodridge family were fortunate in that the Massachusetts Life Insurance Company chose not to prosecute the widow for fraud. Perhaps the company was aware of the circumstances that led to Glenalvin's death. The court record does not state whether the company's understanding extended to the point of returning the premiums paid to it for the now voided life insurance policy.

Glenalvin's trial, imprisonment, and death, followed almost immediately by the mess resulting from the abortive life insurance scheme, made the 1860s, already a decade of extraordinary national upheaval, one of intense personal grief for the entire Goodridge family. Rhoda Goodridge's pain was heightened by the fact that in addition to Glenalvin, three of her four children also died during the same decade, possibly from the tuberculosis that killed their father. According to the 1860 census, Rhoda and Glenalvin were the parents of three children, William H., who was seven; Ralph J., five; and Emily, three. Glen J., their fourth and youngest child, was born shortly after in 1860 or 1861. In October 1868, William H., the eldest, died of a "chill fever" in East Saginaw. Ralph and Emily disappeared from the records at about the same time, and although it is impossible to confirm, they likely died from the same cause, complications resulting from tuberculosis. After 1868 only Glen J. Goodridge is listed as his father's heir.[24]

Glenalvin's death also necessitated reorganization of the studio partnership. From its inception in York during the summer of 1847 as "Goodridge's Daguerrian Rooms" through its development as the "Extra Sky Light Gallery" and ultimately "Goodridge's American Photographic Gallery," the York studio clearly was Glenalvin's creation and under his immediate direction. By the late 1850s, first Wallace and then William had joined their brother in his studio and, in fact, it was their assistance that made it possible to open the branch studio in Columbia during the spring of 1861. After the family relocated to East Saginaw and the studio began to function once again, it became clear that Glenalvin's health limited his participation but not his influence in studio operations. Goodridge advertisements during the 1860s, for example, strongly emphasized portraits, especially the ambrotypes which were Glenalvin's specialty, and the studio's prize-winning entries in the 1866 and 1867 Saginaw County Agricultural Fairs were limited to daguerreotypes and ambrotypes. By the 1868 fair and thereafter, however, Goodridge entries would include only photographs on paper. In East Saginaw the studio also had begun as and remained a joint venture, as its

name "Goodridge Brothers" clearly indicated. Beginning in 1868 and until William's death in 1890, the Saginaw city directories identified the "Goodridge Bros." only as "Wallace L. and William O. Goodridge, photographers." Glenalvin never again was listed there with his brothers.[25]

In 1868 William O. Goodridge was twenty-two years old. Born on May 28, 1846, in York, he was the youngest of William and Evalina's surviving children. Only six when his mother died, William was raised by his sisters Emily, Susan, and Mary. There are no records of his attending school, but with his talent and the family's commitment to education there can be no doubt that he did. His education also included working with his brothers in "Goodridge's American Photographic Gallery" in York, sharing their expertise and developing his own considerable talent as an artist and photographer. His position in the studio, both in York and East Saginaw, nonetheless remained secondary until 1868. He had achieved sufficient security by 1867, however, to marry Alice Guin Hayner. The bride was eighteen years old, had been born in Louisville, Kentucky, and was attended by her mother, Mrs. Martha Hayner. William's best man was Robert Campbell, a native of Virginia, whose masonry business had made him the wealthiest African American resident of the Saginaw Valley other than the lumberman William Q. Atwood. The newlyweds lived on their own in a series of rental properties until 1874. The early years of the partnership in the studio apparently served William well. The 1870 census listed him as a "Photographer" and recorded the value of his property as $1,400. Tragically, Alice died before the couple's seventh wedding anniversary in January 1874. There were no children, and William later remarried.[26]

According to his obituary, Wallace L. Goodridge was born in York on September 4, 1840. He was the second of William and Evalina's surviving sons. The 1850 census noted that he was "at school" that year. With his brothers and sisters, Wallace was enrolled in York's school for African American children. The school was located on West Philadelphia Street in the former Lancastrian

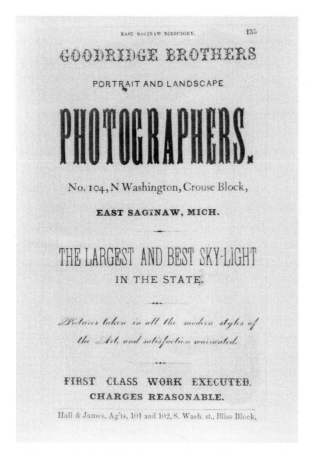

Figure 3.5. "Goodridge Brothers Studio Advertisement," *East Saginaw Directory*, 1866, p. 135. Eddy Local History and Genealogical Collection, Hoyt Public Library.

School Building that was owned by William C. Goodridge and which he had donated for the school. For at least three or four of his student years Wallace's teacher was his brother Glenalvin, and that relationship continued through the 1850s as Wallace followed his elder brother into "Goodridge's American Photographic Gallery." By 1860 the census was identifying him as an "Ambrotypist," and it was in that capacity that he maintained the gallery in York while Glenalvin taught school in Baltimore during 1859 and 1860. His flight to East Saginaw in 1862 resulted in relocation of the studio there by 1864. For whatever the reasons—his difficulties in York, a sense of responsibility for Glenalvin's family, or devotion to his craft—Wallace chose not to marry until 1889, when he was forty-nine years old.[27]

As early as the summer of 1866, even before (but perhaps because of) Glenalvin's imminent death, the Goodridge brothers signaled that they were prepared to invest the effort and resources necessary to establish their studio as equal or superior to any competitor in the Saginaw Valley. Starting with the 1866 edition and continuing until after 1872, the Goodridges regularly purchased the largest single full-page advertisements in the Saginaw city directories. In the 1866 ad (see figure 3.5) they pointed to their versatility as "PORTRAIT AND LANDSCAPE" photographers, touted their "CHARGES REASONABLE," claimed "THE LARGEST AND BEST SKYLIGHT IN THE STATE," and did so in large, clear, bold type. The 1869 directory ad (see figure 3.6a) then announced a major redesign and expansion of the studio. In only a few short years it had now become a "PHOTOGRAPHIC PALACE" that was "The Largest and Most Magnificent Gallery in Northern Michigan." That same spring the *Saginaw Daily Enterprise* reported the expansion and noted that the "Goodridge Bro.'s [new] photographic palace is modeled after Gurney & Sons's gallery in New York," that "The only Sarony Posing apparatus and Williard's [*sic*] improved Camera in this State [are] at Goodridge's," and that to celebrate the "grand opening" of their redesigned "PHOTOGRAPHIC PALACE," "Pictures for half price" would be made on Thursday, May 11. In the 1872 edition of the directory (see figure 3.6b) the brothers also touted their "REMBRANDT, BERLIN AND. . . NEW AMERICAN PORTRAITS," while simultaneously announcing a new series of "Michigan Views."[28]

The ads, reminiscent of their father's in the York newspapers, were impressive for their size. Other East Saginaw photographers, such as Randall and Roberts and, after 1871, Daniel Angell, were content with simple, one-line listings in the directories or an occasional notice in one of the newspapers. Only Armstrong, in Saginaw City, matched the size of Goodridge directory ads, and then in only a single edition, 1867, adding that "MRS. ARMSTRONG will always be in attendance to assist ladies in arranging their toilet, thereby doing away with one great annoyance in Photography."[29] While the Goodridges' commercial notices no doubt exaggerated somewhat developments in the

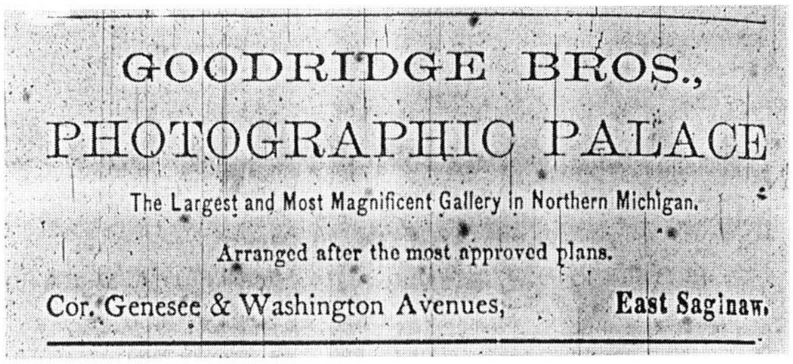

Figure 3.6a. "Goodridge Brothers Studio Advertisement,"
East Saginaw Directory, 1869, p. 132. Eddy Local History
and Genealogical Collection, Hoyt Public Library.

Figure 3.6b. "Goodridge Brothers Studio Advertisement,"
East Saginaw Directory, 1872, p. xlvii. Eddy Local History
and Genealogical Collection, Hoyt Public Library

third story of the Crouse Block, they also provide a means to document the studio's early evolution and the brothers' growth professionally.

During the late 1850s and through the 1860s, Jeremiah Gurney of New York City was Mathew Brady's most intense competitor and was best-known among photographers for his opposition to the Cutting ambrotype patent. The general public knew of him because of a political controversy that had resulted in 1865 from Gurney's having gained the exclusive right to photograph the assassinated President Lincoln who lay in state at New York's City Hall on April 24 and 25. New York mayor C. Godfrey Gunther was a "Peace Democrat" opposed to continuation of the war. Apparently he had chosen Gurney for his similar political views. The resulting photographs were seized by Secretary of War Edwin M. Stanton, and all were destroyed but one.[30] Whether the Goodridges shared Gurney's views on the war is unknown. They did, however, find the Gurney studio an attractive model. The December 1858 issue of the *American Journal of Photography* described it as follows:

GURNEY has just opened, at No. 707 Broadway, a sort of *Photographic palace* which he has erected for the purposes of his business, and with a special view to its requirements. Discarding the practice of sending customers up three or four flights of stairs to an operating room which the sun can get at, he receives them in the ground-floor—shows them his pictures, cases and so forth, takes their orders and passes them forward to his main gallery, on the floor above, from which they enter upon a ladies dressing room on one side, and an operating room on the other. This latter apartment is provided with side-lights and roof-lights, so that in the event of his having a customer more "wrinkly" than usual—in which case the roof-lights, are insufficient—GURNEY usually smoothes down the creases with side-light, and somewhat rejuvenates him by the process. When the operating rooms below are full, which would seem to be a common occurrence at this establishment, there are others on the next floor, which are, however, mainly devoted to the artists, who are there, in great force, to finish the photographs. These are taken of all sizes, from the "locket miniature" to the "life," sometimes containing only the face, at others giving the bust also, and not uncommonly the whole form, of the size of life.[31]

There is no indication that the Goodridge "PHOTOGRAPHIC PALACE" occupied any more than part of the third floor of the Crouse Block in 1869. Nonetheless, the arrangement of their "rooms," the provisions for lighting, and the variety of photographic services available certainly followed Gurney's example.

Without doubt, however, the most flamboyant and often imitated of North America's photographers in the decades following the Civil War was Napoleon Sarony. Born in Quebec in 1821, Sarony was moderately successful as a lithography artist, first with Currier and Ives and then during the 1850s on his own in New York City. Between 1858 and 1866 he traveled and studied art in Europe, working for a time in England with his brother Oliver, a photographer of some note. In 1866 he returned to the United States and opened a gallery at 630 Broadway in New York City. During the next three decades the name "Sarony" became almost synonymous with photography to most Americans. The general public avidly collected his portraits of the world's celebrities. According to his biographer, "Sarony photographed virtually every actor and actress working on the New York stage. Indeed, Sarony photographed everybody who was anybody (and thousands who simply wanted to be somebody) whether they were in the theatre or not. His portraits of actors and actresses tended to attract others to his studio, mainly firstnighters and society women, but also figures from government, the military, and the business world."[32] His colleagues sought to duplicate Sarony's popularity and financial success by emulating both his technique and purchasing the posing apparatus he marketed. Among them were the Goodridges. According to William Welling, quoting Edward L. Wilson, editor of the *Philadelphia Photographer:*

> A sitter's head, back, arms, sides, "and in fact the whole person were at perfect rest and repose" in the Sarony device. "We were comfortable and could keep still an hour in its most pleasant embrace," Wilson said. "The sensation is almost indescribable. It must be experienced to be fully realized." Sarony customarily made eight poses on a single plate, which prompted Wilson to observe that "those who have four positions of the same person, will notice the changes in position that can be rapidly made in using Mr. Sarony's machine. With the old arrangement it would be almost impossible to secure eight positions before the film became dry and horny." Sarony made his prints "entirely in the shade," Wilson said, and the tone of the prints he characterized as "peculiar to Mr. Sarony's paper."[33]

Close examination of figures 3.7a and b will reveal the base of the Goodridges' Sarony posing apparatus behind the left foot of the subject in 3.7a and behind and to the right of the subject in 3.7b. To the modern eye the pose in each of the illustrations appears rigid, even awkward. But as Wilson pointed out, use of the apparatus, at least until the introduction of the new and faster gelatin dry-plate process of the 1870s, extended the flexibility of both the subject and the photographer.

The Goodridge advertisements not only were impressive for their size and the claims they made, but obviously they also were accurate. Whether Wallace or William was able to travel to New York City from East Saginaw and call on their better-known colleagues there, as Glenalvin had done earlier from York, is not known. More likely their information came from articles in professional photography journals like *Humphrey's* or the new *Philadelphia Photographer,* both of which were then popular and influential. Whatever their source, it is clear that of all Saginaw Valley photographers it was the Goodridge brothers who were most carefully attuned to the latest developments in the profession at this time.

Goodridge advertisements also confirm that portrait photography, whether influenced by Gurney or Sarony, remained the most significant component of the studio's success during the early years in East Saginaw. Glenalvin had established the pattern in York, and the brothers continued it thereafter. Although no examples are known to exist at present, contemporary evidence confirms that the Goodridges maintained Glenalvin's earlier success, for a time at least, with both daguerreotypes and ambrotypes. For example, a February 1865 advertisement in the *Saginaw Weekly Enterprise* described the studio as a "Photograph and Ambrotype Gallery."[34] By the 1860s, however, each of these earlier processes had been eclipsed by the less expensive and technically complex tintype and carte de visite.

Tintypes (also known as ferrotypes and melainotypes) were collodian positives made on black enameled tinplate. Like daguerreotypes and ambrotypes, they were unique images. The rapidity of the whole process (usually little more than a minute), their modest cost (between twenty-five

Figure 3.7a. "Unidentified Man," 1864–72, carte de visite. Albumen image, 2⅛ x 3¹¹⁄₁₆ inches, ivory bristol board mount with gold trim, 2⁷⁄₁₆ x 3¹⁵⁄₁₆ inches. Goodridge Brothers Studio, East Saginaw, Mich. Collection of Dave Tinder.

Figure 3.7b. "Unidentified Man," 1864–72, carte de visite. Albumen image, 2⅛ x 3¾ inches, ivory bristol board mount with gold trim, 2⁷⁄₁₆ x 4 inches. Goodridge Brothers Studio, East Saginaw, Mich. Collection of Dave Tinder.

and fifty cents), and their durability (the metal plate was cased only in paper and could be sent through the mail) made them dramatically different from their more fragile and expensive predecessors. These qualities, in spite of acknowledged technical inferiority to either the daguerreotype or ambrotype, made tintypes especially popular in the United States during the late 1850s and into the 1860s. Soldiers on both sides in the Civil War regularly chose tintypes as a means of sending their memory to loved ones back home. It is likely that Glenalvin and his brothers made tintypes in York (the process was patented in the United States in 1855 by Hamilton Smith), but no examples are known to exist. Tintype portraits, however, were a staple of the East Saginaw studio from its beginning and retained their importance through the 1870s.[35]

Goodridge tintypes from the 1860s demonstrate that the studio easily was able to reestab-

lish the quality for which Glenalvin had been so well known in York. All the surviving examples are portraits. Tintype landscapes were made, but rarely, and none by the Goodridges are known to exist. The portraits are in all the usual sizes, from the half-inch-square "gem," always only the head of the subject, to the standard "card" size of 2⅜ x 3⅞ inches. The latter included a variety of poses. The vignetted head (see figure 3.8a), where the oval mat of the paper case was used to frame the head and shoulders of the seated subject, was popular. But the full-length portrait (see figure 3.8b), utilizing the Sarony posing apparatus, was most common. The subjects were a cross section of the Saginaw populace. Shop girls and shanty boys, mill owners and matrons, all at one time or another seem to have stopped by the third-floor studio in the Crouse Block. The brothers, however, had a particular affinity for their youngest customers.

Figure 3.8a. "Unidentified Male," 1864–72, tintype vignette with paper cover. Image 1⁷⁄₁₆ x 1¹⁵⁄₁₆ inches, cover 2⁷⁄₁₆ x 4¹⁄₁₆ inches. Goodridge Brothers Studio, East Saginaw, Mich. Collection of Dave Tinder.

Figure 3.8b. "Unidentified Young Man," 1864–72, tintype with paper cover. Image 1⁹⁄₁₆ x 2¾ inches, hand-colored, cover 2⅜ x 3⅞ inches. Goodridge Brothers Studio, East Saginaw, Mich. Collection of John V. Jezierski.

Figure 3.8c. "Unidentified Young Boy," 1864–72, tintype with paper cover. Image 1⁹⁄₁₆ x 2¾ inches, cover 2⅜ x 3⅞ inches. Goodridge Brothers Studio, East Saginaw, Mich. Collection of John V. Jezierski.

Figure 3.8d. "Unidentified Young Girl," 1864–72, tintype with paper cover. Image 1⅛ x 1⅞ inches, hand-colored, cover 2⁷⁄₁₆ x 3¹³⁄₁₆ inches, Goodridge Brothers Studio, East Saginaw, Mich. Collection of William Wegner.

Exposure times that lasted anywhere from a few seconds to a minute caused photographers at the time to request that "Mothers . . . bring their children in the fore part of the day, to ensure a good Likeness," and the Goodridges made a similar request.[36]

Their success with young subjects is obvious from an examination of the results. The pride of the young fellow in figure 3.8b shows in his best and probably only suit (even though the jacket arms are a bit too short), in the sheen of his highly polished shoes, in the brilliant white of his shirt, and especially in the jaunty angle of what must have been his favorite hat. The studio technician, perhaps one of the brothers or an assistant, chose as well to enhance the impact of the outfit by adding a rosy tint to the cheeks and highlighting the prominent watch chain and pinkie ring with gold. The rigidity of the youth in figure 3.8c, as he appears almost to be backing away from a threatening camera, is tempered somewhat by the forward thrust of his left foot and the photographer's decision to direct the light from above and the subject's right side. As a result, the large forehead and full cheeks that surround frowning lips are gently framed by the smoothness of freshly combed hair and the edge of delicate white collar emerging above the coat. The bright curves formed by the reflections of the straw hat and the lines of the boot fasteners also temper an otherwise unyielding subject. Figures 3.8d and 3.9a confirm that the Goodridge brothers were able to win and hold the interest of their very youngest customers with most pleasing results.

The paper cases which were used to protect both the tintype and anyone who might be cut by the sharp metal edge also served a variety of other functions. Presumably chosen in consultation between photographer and customer, the case served to frame the image (as in figures 3.8 a–d). It also bore the tax stamp as mandated by Congress in 1864. The back of the paper case in figure 3.9b reveals a three-cent tax stamp, without cancellation. Note that a specially framed location has been printed for the stamp and that the three-cent tax meant the photograph sold for between twenty-six

and fifty cents. In addition, the case served to advertise the studio's location (the Crouse Block) and the photographer's wares (for example, ALBATYPE). Some cases (figure 3.9c) came with front covers that not only protected the photographic image but also projected the photographer's. On occasion the case also could communicate both the photographer's and the customer's sense of humor. The caricature of the stamp affixed to the back of the paper case in figure 3.9d likely was a humorous parody of the 1864–66 revenue stamp which all photographers were known to oppose.[37] Some attacks were more direct. The texts on the effects of tobacco and Patrick the Irishman need no explanation.

Although the Goodridges continued to make tintype portraits well into the 1870s, during the later 1860s the studio's most popular and successful portrait format became the carte de visite. Unlike daguerreotypes, ambrotypes, or even tintypes, all of which were positive, and therefore unique, images (copies could be had only by making a new photograph), cartes de visite were photographs printed on albumenized paper from collodian glass negatives. Hypothetically, an unlimited number of identical paper photographs could be printed from a single negative. Photo historians dispute their specific origin, although most agree with Darrah that "the Frenchman A. A. Disderi introduced the name, the format, and method for producing multiple images, as many as ten, on a single glass plate, in November 1854."[38] The procedure was rapid. Exposure times varied but were usually less than thirty seconds and rarely more. The cost was modest, normally less than twenty cents per carte, although some small-town photographers advertised prices of $1.50 or even less per dozen. The prints were portable yet durable. The albumenized print was a standard-sized 2⅛ x 3½ inches and mounted on a slightly larger 2½ x 4 inch card of bristol board. And, the photographer could manipulate both the negative and the resulting print in a variety of ways to produce the most pleasing image.

Darrah suggests further that the rapid and worldwide popularity of the carte de visite was due to the combination of a variety of circum-

Figure 3.9a. "Two Unidentified Infants," 1864–72, tintype with paper cover. Image 1⅞₆ x 2¾ inches, cover 2⅜ x 3⅞ inches. Goodridge Brothers Studio, East Saginaw, Mich. Collection of Dave Tinder.

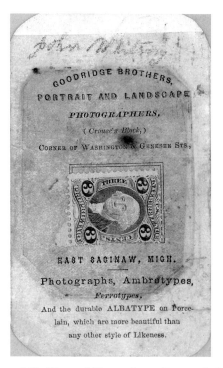

Figure 3.9b. "Verso of Tintype Paper Cover with 3 Cent Revenue Stamp," fall 1864, 2⁷⁄₁₆ x 4¹⁄₁₆ inches. Goodridge Brothers Studio, East Saginaw, Mich. Collection of Dave Tinder.

Figure 3.9c. "'Artists,' Tintype Paper Cover, Front," 1864–72, 2⁷⁄₁₆ x 3¹³⁄₁₆ inches. Goodridge Brothers Studio, East Saginaw, Mich. Collection of William Wegner.

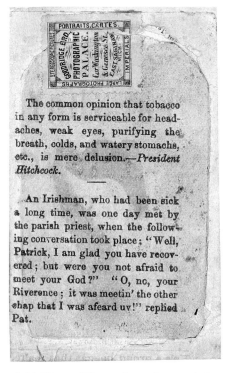

Figure 3.9d. "Verso of Tintype Paper Cover with 'Stamp,'" 1864–72, 2⅜ x 3⅞ inches. Goodridge Brothers Studio, East Saginaw, Mich. Collection of Dave Tinder.

stances. In August 1860 an American daguerreo-typist, J. E. Mayall, who had settled in England, published a "Royal Album" of carte de visite photographs of Queen Victoria, Prince Albert, and their children. Sixty thousand of Mayall's "Royal Album" and an unknown number of pirated copies were sold in Britain, the colonies, and the United States within the year. Collecting photo portraits of royalty became the pastime even of royalty. Darrah noted that "One of the Queen's [Victoria] ladies in waiting, Eleanor Stanley, recorded on November 20, 1860, her part in acquiring portraits: 'I have been writing to all the fine ladies in London, for their or their husband's photographs, for the Queen; . . . I believe Miss Skerrett is right when she says "the Queen could be bought and sold for a Photograph"!'" But it was not only royalty who were photographed and collected the results. "Within weeks," Darrah concluded, "the well-to-do, merchants, clergymen, soldiers, writers, the great and the near-great joined the ranks of the photographed. Now for a few cents anyone could have his likeness taken and, what was more persuasive, could have a dozen or more copies that could be placed in envelopes and mailed to distant relatives and friends." At the same time, he added, in the United States the outbreak of the Civil War and the subsequent westward migration of thousands of settlers "created a demand for ordinary portraits. The family album became a treasured possession linking scattered relatives and friends."[39]

The Goodridge brothers helped to fill many family albums with literally thousands of carte de visite portraits, if those that have survived for more than a century now are any indication of the original number.[40] Carte de visite portraits were made concurrently with tintypes from the first months the studio opened in 1864. Figure 3.10a is an excellent example of a Civil War carte, with the verso (figure 3.10b) displaying a two-cent tax stamp hand-canceled "Goodr. Bro." The Sarony posing apparatus (see figure 3.11c) continued to "relax" portrait customers facing the Goodridge lens. And Saginaw's youth (see figure 3.10c) remained fasci-

nated with the brothers' technique. At the same time, collodian glass negatives and albumenized paper prints offered the photographer technical options for the carte portrait that the tintype did not.

During the 1860s the vignetted head was especially popular. Figure 3.10a is an example of the technique. The subject was photographed in a seated pose. When the negative was printed, the background and torso were masked in such a way "so as to show only the head and shoulders seemingly clouded off."[41] The Goodridges also were especially fond of the "Rembrandt" effect which they featured in the 1872 directory ad (see figure 3.6b). A series of reflectors were used to concentrate and direct the natural light from the skylights onto the face of the subject. Against a dark background the result was a dramatic contrast between light and shadow, usually emphasizing strong features and cloaking weak ones, with a most positive effect, as in figure 3.11a. The process was perfected by the New York City photographer William Kurtz in 1870 and widely imitated, certainly in East Saginaw. The technique, however, was not without its hazards. The strong light and the typically larger head size of the carte portrait also could accentuate undesirable features such as moles, pockmarks, scars, and wrinkles. The photographer or an artist assistant removed them by retouching. The procedure had been applied to the positives of the 1840s and 1850s, and during the 1860s it was commonly employed to rework the collodian glass negatives used to print cartes de visite. By the late 1870s, in fact, mechanical devices such as the Getchell & Hyatt stippling and hatching machine, which was attached to a sewing machine treadle, simplified the process. According to Darrah, the most common techniques involved drawing "a thin line . . . to sharpen the border between neck or face and background. Often the face on the lighted side blended into the background. Commonly the hairline on the forehead was strengthened or the blonde hair itself separated from the background. Occasionally the mouth, eyes, or ears were touched up."[42] Figure 3.11b demonstrates the technique. Note the lines defining the face and

Figure 3.10a. "Unidentified Soldier," 1864, carte de visite. Albumen image, 2⅛ x 3⅜ inches, ivory bristol board mount with gold trim, 2⁷⁄₁₆ x 4 inches. Goodridge Brothers Studio, East Saginaw, Mich. Collection of Dave Tinder.

Figure 3.10b. "Verso of Carte de Visite with 2 Cent Revenue Stamp," 1864, 2⁷⁄₁₆ x 4 inches. Goodridge Brothers Studio, East Saginaw, Mich. Collection of Dave Tinder.

Figure 3.10c. "Brothers," 1864–72, carte de visite. Albumen image, 2¼ x 3¹³⁄₁₆ inches, ivory bristol board mount, 2½ x 4⅛ inches. Goodridge Brothers Studio, East Saginaw, Mich. Collection of John V. Jezierski.

chin and the shading added to the mouth, eyes, and brows. About 1870 many photographers, including the Goodridges (see figure 3.6b), began to advertise carte de visite portraits with a "Berlin" finish. Here (see figure 3.11c) retouching techniques were extended to the entire figure, not simply the face of the subject.

In the cartes de visite, photographers also paid much greater attention to backgrounds and accessories. Painted scenery on panels or rolls of up to twenty scenes as well as papier-mâché and cardboard columns, fences, or fireplaces could be ordered from supply houses like L. W. Seavy of New York City, who after 1865 became the world's largest, with customers even among the exacting photographers of Paris. Whether the Goodridge brothers purchased the painted scenes and elaborate accessories included in figures 3.10c and 3.11d from a supplier like L. W. Seavy or created their own, as many photographers in smaller towns and cities did, is not known.[43]

During the peak years of their popularity, cartes de visite photographs also were made of all

Figure 3.11a. "Unidentified Woman," 1864–72, carte de visite. Albumen image, 2¹¹⁄₁₆ x 1⅞ inches, tan bristol board mount, 2½ x 4³⁄₁₆ inches. Goodridge Brothers Studio, East Saginaw, Mich. Collection of William Oberschmidt.

Figure 3.11b. "Unidentified Young Man," 1864–72, carte de visite. Albumen image 2³⁄₁₆ x 4³⁄₁₆ inches, ivory bristol board mount, 2½ x 4³⁄₁₆ inches. Goodridge Brothers Studio, East Saginaw, Mich. Collection of William Oberschmidt.

Figure 3.11c. "Unidentified Man," 1870–72, carte de visite. Albumen image, 2⅛ x 3¾ inches, hand-colored, tan bristol board mount with gold trim, 2½ x 4³⁄₁₆ inches. Goodridge Brothers Studio, East Saginaw, Mich. Collection of Dave Tinder.

Figure 3.11d. "Unidentified Woman," 1870–72, carte de visite. Albumen image 2³⁄₁₆ x 3⅝ inches, tan bristol board mount, 2½ x 4³⁄₁₆ inches. Goodridge Brothers Studio, East Saginaw, Mich. Collection of William Oberschmidt.

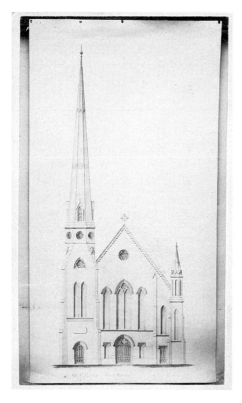

Figure 3.12a. "Jefferson Avenue Methodist Church," 1867–68, carte de visite. Albumen image, 2¼ x 3¹³⁄₁₆ inches, ivory bristol board mount, 2⁷⁄₁₆ x 4 inches. Goodridge Brothers Studio, East Saginaw, Mich. Eddy Local History and Genealogical Collection, Hoyt Public Library.

Figure 3.12b. "The 'Old Academy,'" 1871, carte de visite. Albumen image, 2¼ x 3⅞ inches, ivory bristol board mount, 2⁷⁄₁₆ x 4 inches. Goodridge Brothers Studio, East Saginaw, Mich. Eddy Local History and Genealogical Collection, Hoyt Public Library.

possible subjects. Darrah has identified more than sixty topical categories that included everything from advertising to zoology. Yet together these non-portrait cartes, he estimates, accounted for less than 1 percent of all cartes de visite made. It is intriguing, therefore, to learn that the Goodridge studio created substantial numbers of non-portrait cartes. All of the survivors are of East Saginaw and date from the period 1864 to 1872, the years that the studio was located in the Crouse Block. With few exceptions, these cartes include street scenes and views of the river, commercial and public architecture, and an occasional local disaster or copy of a popular print.[44] Together they constitute an informal "city view album," although there is no evidence in the form of a serial numbering system, advertising, or album that they were so intended by the photographers. A recent analysis has concluded, however, that mid-nineteenth-century

"city view albums" were created to suggest "a solid basis for future growth through the building by building, street by street documentation of a city's development."[45] As a group the Goodridge cartes of East Saginaw certainly fulfilled such a function.

In the Goodridge "album," carte de visite photographs of significant buildings were most common. Jefferson Avenue Methodist Church (figure 3.12a), for example, originally was organized in 1852 under the pastorate of Rev. A. C. Shaw. For fifteen years church members worshiped in a small building at the corner or Washington and German Streets. On May 27, 1867, the cornerstone was laid for the structure illustrated. After little more than a year's construction, the impressive example of gothic architecture was dedicated on December 27, 1868. The photograph emphasizes the magnificent 162-foot spire, which was destroyed during a storm on August 9, 1896, and may well have been

Figure 3.12c. "Bancroft House Hotel," 1867, carte de visite. Albumen image, 3¹¹⁄₁₆ x 2⅛ inches, ivory bristol board mount with gold trim, 4 x 2½ inches. Goodridge Brothers Studio, East Saginaw, Mich. Eddy Local History and Genealogical Collection, Hoyt Public Library.

made by the Goodridges to celebrate the 1868 dedication.[46] One of the community's most beloved buildings was the "Old Academy" (figure 3.12b). Not only was it East Saginaw's first permanent schoolhouse when it opened in the summer of 1852, but even after it was destroyed by fire in 1871 the "Old Academy" continued to serve as a symbol of the town's commitment to public education.[47] The Goodridge carte may have been issued as a memento following the 1871 fire. If created before 1871, it doubtless became a keepsake thereafter. The clarity of the fence pickets and window mullions and the sharpness of the angles of the neoclassic architecture of the building demonstrate the potential of the non-portrait carte when created by a talented photographer. The Bancroft House (figure 3.12c) was not East Saginaw's first hotel, but when it opened in September 1859 it certainly was the city's largest and most pretentious and remained so for years to come. Built by Jesse Hoyt and named for historian and statesman George Bancroft, the four stories of rooms, suites, parlors, and "culinary apartments" were considered "equal to those of any hotel East or West."[48]

Street scenes and views of the river included in the Goodridge "album" reveal that the develop-ment Alexis de Tocqueville had foreseen in 1831 did materialize, and in a single generation. The possibilities for the future were even greater. Figure 3.13a, with its prominent Grant-Colfax banner, suggests that many East Saginaw residents and the photographers as well were Republican partisans in 1868. It documents more strongly, however, as you look east along Genesee Avenue from the bridge, the booming development that the recent-ly incorporated city was experiencing. Business block after business block, and most were of brick, stand solidly facing each other across the avenue to the horizon. The horse-drawn railcar in the fore-ground was operated by the Saginaw River Bridge Company, which had built the span in 1864 and charged a toll for its use.[49] Figures 3.13b and 3.13c demonstrate the extent to which the Saginaw Riv-er was the industrial lifeblood of the communities on both its banks. Figure 3.13b was made from the roof of the Bancroft House looking west and some-what south upriver. On the west bank are sawmills and docks owned by George Davenport and the Grant and Saylor Company. The east riverbank, hidden by the rooftops of various commercial buildings, literally is covered by drying lumber awaiting shipment from Jesse Hoyt's dock. The

Figure 3.13a. "Genesee Street Bridge, Looking East," 1868, carte de visite. Albumen image 3⅜ x 2⅛ inches, ivory bristol board mount with gold trim, 3¹⁵⁄₁₆ x 2⅞ inches. Goodridge Brothers Studio, East Saginaw, Mich. Eddy Local History and Genealogical Collection, Hoyt Public Library.

Figure 3.13b. "Saginaw River, Looking Southwest," 1868–72, carte de visite. Albumen image, 3¹¹⁄₁₆ x 2⅛ inches, ivory bristol board mount with gold trim, 3¹⁵⁄₁₆ x 2⁷⁄₁₆ inches. Goodridge Brothers Studio, East Saginaw, Mich. Eddy Local History and Genealogical Collection, Hoyt Public Library.

Figure 3.13c. "Saginaw River, East Bank, and Steam Vessel *Huron*," 1866–67, carte de visite. Albumen image, 3¹³⁄₁₆ x 2¼ inches, ivory bristol board mount, 3¹⁵⁄₁₆ x 2⁷⁄₁₆ inches. Goodridge Brothers Studio, East Saginaw, Mich. Historical Society of Saginaw County, Inc.

steam vessel *Huron* in figure 3.13c was one of several operating on the Saginaw River in the 1860s that carried passengers and cargo from the Saginaws to a variety of Great Lakes ports. Built at Newport (Marine City), Michigan, in 1852 by John L. Wolverton for Samuel and Eber Ward of Detroit, the *Huron* was a 384-ton wood-hull, paddle-wheel steamer, 165 feet long and 23 feet, 6 inches at the beam. The Wards sold the *Huron* in 1857 to Albert E. Goodrich (no relation to the photographers) and General C. Drew of Chicago. Goodrich made her the first of the Goodrich Line, which in later years was an important Lake Michigan shipping company. After 1861 the *Huron,* too small for the Goodrich Line, was sold several times. During 1866–67 she was owned by Alexander English and Darius Cole of East Saginaw. She was dismantled in South Haven in 1877 after having settled to the bottom of the Black River there.[50] Note the rafts of logs in the foreground awaiting saws at the river's mills that would transform them into lumber for Hoyt's and other docks.

In their "album" the Goodridges looked to a prosperous future but also implied that success was based on solid foundations in the past and the ability to overcome any present disaster. To rapidly expanding nineteenth-century communities, especially those like East Saginaw which were built literally on sawdust, fire was a constant danger. In July 1854 and May 1861 major fires temporarily checked East Saginaw's expansion and caused thousands of dollars' damage. Neither, however, was as destructive or expensive as the fire that occurred on January 26, 1865. The fire broke out in Gravier's wholesale liquor store on Genesee opposite the Crouse Block. It spread west along Genesee to Water Street and north along Washington to the Koehler Block, where it burned itself out. More than twenty shops and offices, valued at over $125,000, were destroyed, including the post office, although its contents were saved. Hank Eastman's "Great Temple of Art" was among the casualties.[51] Perhaps because of this loss to their competitor and colleague, the Goodridge brothers, the morning following the fire, stood before their studio in the Crouse Block and recorded the results

for their neighbors. Figure 3.14a shows the ruins of the Hess Block and adjoining buildings at the northwest corner of Genesee and Washington.

By the end of the 1860s not only had East Saginaw been around long enough to have survived the effects of three major fires, but it also had begun to acquire a history that its residents wished to remember. Figure 3.14b was the Goodridge contribution to that collective memory. The carte is a copy of a drawing by an anonymous artist showing the village of Buena Vista as organized by Curtis Emerson in 1849. The little community was located near what would be the eastern terminus of the Bristol Street bridge and soon absorbed by East Saginaw just to its north. Emerson had come to Michigan in 1836 from his native Vermont. In 1846 he settled in Saginaw City. With no immediate success there, he moved across the river the following year and purchased the land and mill pictured. The mill had been built in 1836 by Harvey Williams of Saginaw City to cut lumber for local residents. Emerson expanded its operations and in 1848 shipped the first recorded cargo of clear pine lumber from the Saginaw Valley to C. P. Williams & Company of Albany, presumably helping to stimulate interest in Saginaw Valley pine and the subsequent lumber boom. The mill was dismantled in 1854 and its ruins burned in 1866. Long before that, the idealized Native Americans in the right foreground had been supplanted by pioneers like Emerson who measured progress in terms of steam power, board feet, and technological development.

The drawing includes the steamer *Buena Vista.* According to Saginaw County historian James Cooke Mills:

> In 1847, at a suggestion of Captain Mowry, who had navigated the upper Ohio River and knew the requirements of navigation in shallow waters, James Fraser, Daniel H. Fitzhugh, Curtis Emerson, and Captain Mowry formed a company to build a steamboat for use on the Saginaw River. The keel of the vessel was laid at the mill of Emerson & Eldridge, and that summer Messrs. Fraser and Fitzhugh went to Pittsburg and contracted for the engines. The steamboat was com-

Figure 3.14a. "Ruins of Hess Block," January 1865, carte de visite. Albumen image 3¹³⁄₁₆ x 2⁵⁄₁₆ inches, ivory bristol board mount, 3¹⁵⁄₁₆ x 2⁷⁄₁₆ inches. Goodridge Brothers Studio, East Saginaw, Mich. Historical Society of Saginaw County Inc.

Figure 3.14b. "Buena Vista in 1849," 1868–72, carte de visite. Albumen image, 3⅝ x 2⅛ inches, ivory bristol board mount with gold trim, 3¹⁵⁄₁₆ x 2⁷⁄₁₆ inches. Goodridge Brothers Studio, East Saginaw, Mich. Eddy Local History and Genealogical Collection, Hoyt Public Library.

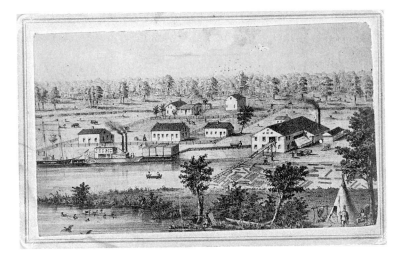

Figure 3.14c. "'Halls of Montezumez [sic],' Curtis Emerson Residence," after 1880. Silver print, 9¾ x 8 inches. Goodridge Brothers Studio, East Saginaw, Mich. Collection of Beffrey Family.

pleted in 1848 with oak timber and other materials furnished by Mr. Fitzhugh, and was given the name *Buena Vista*. It was a queer looking craft, having a large stern wheel with two engines placed in the stern, and the boiler at the bow, the steam being conveyed to the engines by cast iron pipes placed under the upper deck. Although a slow and awkward vessel the *Buena Vista* filled very well the purposes for which she was built, and did a goodly amount of business, both as a tug and packet, in navigating the upper streams. The early residents looked upon her as a marvel of speed and convenience, despite the fact that her movements were somewhat asthmatic and noisy; and she was a favorite means of communication between the settlements on the river.[52]

The schooner astern the *Buena Vista* was the 122-ton *Tuscola*. Little is known of her origins or fate.[53]

In 1850, not far from his mill, Emerson constructed a residence which he named the "Halls of Montezumez [sic]" in honor of his hero, General Zachary Taylor, and the Mexican War. According to Mills, Emerson made the "Halls" his "bachelor home and . . . the scene of many rollicking assemblies during which his conviviality and profanity attained a local celebrity."[54] The Goodridge files contained a photo of Emerson's "Halls" long after its heyday had passed (see figure 3.14c).

City view albums, whether remembering the past or predicting the future, were restricted in their effect by the limitations of lens, film, and perspective. This was especially true in the case of small-format cartes de visite. Many photographers, particularly in the West and Midwest, turned to the multiplate panorama as a solution. As early as 1845 the Langenheim brothers of Philadelphia created eight sets of a five-part daguerreotype of Niagara Falls and sent copies to President Polk, Daguerre, and Queen Victoria. International response to the feat helped to establish them as leaders in American photography.[55] Between 1850 and 1853 at least eight multiplate daguerreian panoramas were made of San Francisco alone. And, in 1878, Edward Muybridge created a 360-degree (17 feet, 4 inches), mammoth plate (14½ x 20½ inches) photographic behemoth of the same city.

Similar though smaller examples exist for almost all nineteenth-century American towns. According to their most recent historian:

> Multi-plate panoramic city views had a purpose similar to . . . urban albums. Conceived as a means of breaking the confining borders of the individual photographic view, they were designed to celebrate urban growth and prosperity. Their narrative function was implicit: a less prosperous past was implied by a grandiose present. In form and presentation, the photographic panoramas echoed their painted counterparts and underscored the continuing efforts to transform photography into a narrative medium. Too long to be taken in at a single glance, these panoramic views had to be scanned from left to right like a line of text or a painting moving on rollers. Subtle differences in the shadows from section to section of the panorama hinted at the passage of time. These long images invited the viewer to become a kind of pedestrian stroller. Even as static images, they suggested a kind of movement that the single photographic print could not.[56]

No doubt the Goodridges had a similar narrative function in mind when they created a series of multiplate panoramas of East Saginaw (figure 3.15a–c). The three that have survived are unique in that they are constructed of two cartes de visite hinged with linen tape and designed to open and to close like a billfold, alternately revealing and then concealing their photographic contents. Certainly figure 3.15a (compare it with figure 3.21) and, presumably, the others as well were cropped from larger negatives, thereby accentuating further their purposeful "construction." Two of the three are concerned with the city's struggle against the onslaught of an almost annual spring flood. Figure 3.15a was made from the roof of the Bancroft House looking west and north across the river as it overran its banks and spilled into Carrollton. Notice how effectively the photographer uses the partially opened Genesee swing bridge to emphasize the sweep of the constructed panorama. The vantage point for figure 3.15b was the roof of the Everett House, a three-story hotel built at the corner of Genesee and Franklin in 1864, and thereafter a favorite Goodridge photographic roost. The immediate concern of these two mini-panoramas (each is approximately 8¼ x 2½ inches) was the 1870 flood as the Saginaw River ran over its banks and into the businesses and residences that lined its course. But by focusing in 3.15b on the steepled firehouse immediately to the left of center, First Congregational Church in the distance, and the commercial blocks between the two, as well as the Genesee swing bridge and lumber mills in 3.15a, the photos also testify to the persistence of these structures and to man's success in the struggle against nature. Figure 3.15c completes the trio, although it ignores the flood, metaphorically "turns its back" to the river, and calls our attention instead to the rapid and expansive growth that East Saginaw had experienced in less than a generation. For this panoramic construction Wallace, or more likely William, used the roof of the Goodridge studio in the Crouse Block. The view is to the north and east looking out across what was East Saginaw's most densely populated, most rapidly growing, and most desirable residential neighborhood at the time. The sea of solid two-story frame houses which completely fills the horizontal axis of the photograph is anchored and thereby defined by the only multi-storied structure visible against the line of trees in the distance. When originally built in 1867 at a cost of $28,000, the "Carroll street [school] building . . . [was a] commodious and elegant structure. It accommodates one intermediate and three primary grades, 320 pupils and five teachers." In 1871, shortly before figure 3.15c was made, a select committee of the East Saginaw Board of Education voted to honor General Isaac Crary—who, with John D. Pierce, is credited with the establishment of Michigan's public school system a half century before—by naming its newest building for him.[57]

Taken together, the three cartes-panoramas not only highlight persistence and progress and thereby fulfill the predictive and narrative functions of panoramas as described by Sandweiss above, but when joined end-to-end or stood in a circular Stonehenge-like fashion also constitute a nearly complete 360-degree perspective of East Saginaw as viewed from its node at the intersection of Washington and Genesee. One can only imagine the wonder experienced by Goodridge studio visitors and customers who were able to view or even purchase this miniature marvel. It made them, in fact, almost the equals of their countrymen in Philadelphia and San Francisco who were dazzled by the larger but no less dramatic views of Niagara and the Golden Gate created by the Langenheims and Muybridge. And, no doubt, they could feel quite confident, knowledgeable, and self-assured when the "great panorama of the United States from 1776" visited the Academy of Music in June 1876. They already were familiar with its local counterpart![58]

Figure 3.15a also apparently was made on the occasion of a visit to East Saginaw by Goodridge sister Emily Goodridge Grey. The verso contains a note in Goodridge handwriting stating that "this is a view on the other side of the river of the Salt Works where [sic] Emily went to see. This view was taken from the top of the Bancroft House."

During the early 1870s the Goodridges, like most of their contemporaries, also experimented with variants of the carte de visite. The "Carte Victoria" was to be an intermediate (3 x 5 inch) option between the smaller carte de visite and the recently introduced 4½ x 6½ inch cabinet card which had begun to capture the portrait market. The Goodridges found the "Victoria" format more appropriate for city views. Figure 3.16a, for example, successfully records the impact of an 1871 snowstorm on Genesee Avenue. They also used the larger carte to make their first photographs beyond the limits of the studio, the city, and the immediate vicinity of the river. A caption on the verso of figure 3.16b documents "Opening the State Road at Clare Station, Dec. 4, 1870." The "Victoria" format never became very popular, and the Goodridges used it rarely.[59]

In addition to portraits, cityscapes, and carte de visite panoramas, as well as the occasional "Carte Victoria," the Goodridges also included subjects of much greater consequence in their carte de visite inventory. During 1865, the end of the Civil War and the assassination of Abraham Lincoln shortly thereafter created an enormous demand for photographs of the martyred president. Like most of their pro-

Figure 3.15a. "Saginaw River in Flood, to West," April 1870, carte de visite panorama. Albumen image, 8⅛ x 2¼ inches, beige bristol board mount, hinged, 8⁷⁄₁₆ x 2½ inches. Goodridge Brothers Studio, East Saginaw, Mich. Collection of Beffrey Family.

Figure 3.15b. "East Saginaw, to South," April 1870, carte de visite panorama. Albumen image, 8⅛ x 2¼ inches, beige bristol board mount, hinged, 8⁷⁄₁₆ x 2½ inches. Goodridge Brothers Studio, East Saginaw, Mich. Collection of Beffrey Family.

Figure 3.15c. "East Saginaw, to Northeast," 1871, carte de visite panorama. Albumen image, 7¾ x 2¹⁄₁₆, ivory bristol board mount with gold trim, hinged, 7¹³⁄₁₆ x 2⁷⁄₁₆ inches. Goodridge Brothers Studio, East Saginaw, Mich. Historical Society of Saginaw County, Inc.

Figure 3.16a. "Genesee Street, East from Bridge, 20 Inches of Snow," January 16, 1871, carte victoria. Albumen image, 4¹³⁄₁₆ x 2⅞ inches, ivory bristol board mount, 5 x 3¼ inches. Goodridge Brothers Studio, East Saginaw, Mich. Collection of Beffrey Family.

Figure 3.16b. "Opening the State Road at Clare Station," December 4, 1870, carte victoria. Albumen image, 4¹³⁄₁₆ x 2¹⁵⁄₁₆ inches, tan bristol board mount, 5 x 3¼ inches. Goodridge Brothers Studio, East Saginaw, Mich. Collection of Beffrey Family.

fessional colleagues, the Goodridge brothers met the demand for Lincoln portraits with a carte pirated from an unidentified source. The Goodridge Lincoln carte (see figure 3.17) is actually a "hybrid" photograph of the president that had been widely circulated before his death. The Goodridges probably owned a copy and used it as their source. In the carte the head of the well-known "Cooper Union" portrait of Lincoln by Mathew Brady had been grafted onto the body of an equally well known engraving of Henry Clay. According to one source, Clay's body also had served a similar function for John C. Frémont during the 1856 presidential campaign. In some versions of the Lincoln portrait a beard has

been added. The Goodridges retained the original "beardless" Cooper Union version, although the head has been reversed to match the right-to-left direction of Clay's body.[60]

Much like the paper cases that protected tintypes, the bristol board cards upon which carte de visite photographs were mounted provide a wealth of information about the photographers who created them. For example, when the carte verso bears a tax stamp, as does figure 3.10b, it becomes a convenient means for dating the image (summer 1864) and an indication of its cost (twenty-five cents or less). However, because cartes de visite were popular to the end of the century and be-

Figure 3.17. "President Abraham Lincoln," 1865, carte de visite. Albumen image, 2⅛ x 3¾ inches, ivory bristol board mount with gold trim, 2⁷⁄₁₆ x 4 inches. Goodridge Brothers Studio, East Saginaw, Mich. Collection of Dave Tinder.

was used to cancel the revenue stamp.⁶¹ The Goodridge brothers used a rubber-stamped imprint in violet or blue ink (see figure 3.18a) regularly through the end of the century, but no example of it as a revenue stamp cancellation exists.

Similar to the rubber stamp, although it was printed on the mount either at the studio or a local print shop, was the "Artists" in oval design (see figure 3.18b). The tendency for most photographers was to use the title "Artist" during the early years of the profession or the initial years of a studio's establishment as a means of securing professional legitimacy.⁶² Hank Eastman, for example, had described his studio as a "Great Temple of Art." The Goodridges followed a similar pattern even after mass-produced commercial imprints became available (see figure 3.18c). As the decade progressed and the studio achieved a successful stability, the title "Artists" was replaced by the more straightforward designation "Portrait and Landscape Photographers." At the same time, Goodridge imprints became more ornate and ever larger, eventually covering the entire card. The imprint in figure 3.18d was favored for carte de visite portraits in the mid-1860s. Simultaneously, a similarly ornate "Portrait and Landscape" design with a place for the photographer or customer to enumerate a collection (see figure 3.19a) was used exclusively for cartes de visite city views. The imprint in figure 3.19b was a local design, while the bilateral ovoid area for the imprint with ornate groundwork in figure 3.19c was a most popular style nationally after 1865. Lincoln's assassination and the design's resemblance to funeral drapery may account for its popularity. By 1870 all photographers would have adopted the very largest designs. The "FIRST QUALITY, BERLIN FINISH" imprint in figure 3.19d was the Goodridge choice. In 1871 the Goodridge brothers also joined more than one thousand of their colleagues nationwide in using the National Photographic Association (NPA) logo as part of their imprint (see figure 3.20).

The NPA was founded at a gathering of the nation's leading photographers in April 1868 at the Cooper Institute in New York City. The immediate purpose of the group was opposition to the exten-

cause their popularity coincided with the establishment of the large photo supply houses, carte de visite mounts and, in particular, the standardized imprints the photographers could order printed on the verso provide important clues to the development of the profession and the individual studio.

According to Darrah, the earliest form of photographer identification found on American cartes were small stamplike labels pasted on the verso. The Goodridges used such labels (see figure 3.9d) on tintypes and stereo views, but none exists on a Goodridge carte de visite. During the early 1860s, blind stamps or imprints impressed without ink on the front of the mount were common. After 1872 blind stamps were used often on the board mounts of large Goodridge photographs, but no carte de visite mount bears one. During the 1860s, especially after the August 1864 stamp tax, a rubber-stamped imprint giving the name and the location of the studio was common. Often the rubber stamp

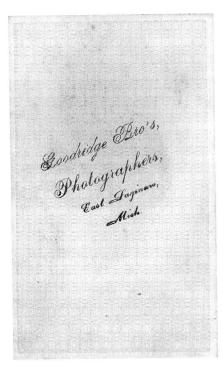

Figure 3.18a. "Studio Imprint, Rubber Stamp, Violet Ink," 1864–72, verso of carte de visite, 2⅞ x 4 inches. Goodridge Brothers Studio, East Saginaw, Mich. Collection of Dave Tinder.

Figure 3.18b. "Studio Imprint, 'Artists,'" 1864–72, verso of carte de visite, 2⅜ x 4 inches. Goodridge Brothers Studio, East Saginaw, Mich. Collection of Dave Tinder.

Figure 3.18c. "Studio Imprint, 'Artists,'" 1864–72, verso of carte de visite, 2⁷⁄₁₆ x 3¹⁵⁄₁₆ inches. Goodridge Brothers Studio, East Saginaw, Mich. Historical Society of Saginaw County, Inc.

Figure 3.18d. "Studio Imprint, 'American Photographic Gallery,'" 1864–72, verso of carte de visite, 2⅜ x 4 inches. Goodridge Brothers Studio, East Saginaw, Mich. Collection of Dave Tinder.

Figure 3.19a. "Studio Imprint, 'Portrait and Landscape' with Space for 'No.,'" 1864–72, verso of carte de visite, 2⅞ x 4 inches. Goodridge Brothers Studio, East Saginaw, Mich. Collection of Beffrey Family.

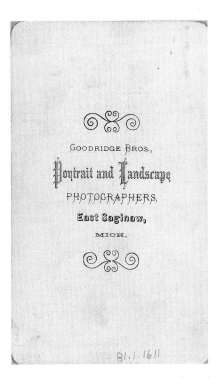

Figure 3.19b. "Studio Imprint, 'Portrait and Landscape' Local," 1864–72, verso of carte de visite, 2½ x 4³⁄₁₆ inches. Goodridge Brothers Studio, East Saginaw, Mich. Historical Society of Saginaw County, Inc.

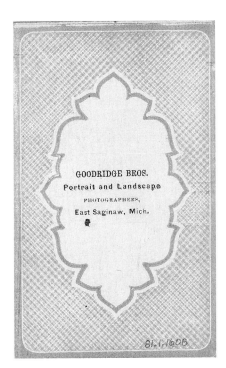

Figure 3.19c. "Studio Imprint, 'Portrait and Landscape' National," 1865–72, verso of carte de visite, 2⁷⁄₁₆ x 4 inches. Goodridge Brothers Studio, East Saginaw, Mich. Historical Society of Saginaw County, Inc.

Figure 3.19d. "Studio Imprint, 'First Quality, Berlin Finish,'" 1870–72, verso of carte de visite, 2½ x 4³⁄₁₆ inches. Goodridge Brothers Studio, East Saginaw, Mich. Collection of William Oberschmidt.

Figure 3.20. "Studio Imprint, 'National Photographic Association,'" 1871, verso of carte de visite, 4⅟₁₆ x 2⁷⁄₁₆ inches. Goodridge Brothers Studio, East Saginaw, Mich. Collection of John V. Jezierski.

sion of the Cutting bromide patent, issued in 1854, which would have required photographers to pay a licensing fee to the patent holders for use of basic photographic chemicals. After the commissioner of patents denied the extension in July 1868, the NPA continued to serve photographers until 1880, when it was succeeded by the Photographers' Association of America. At its annual conventions, the first in Boston in 1869, and in the pages of the *Philadelphia Photographer,* its "official journal," the NPA promoted the profession through competitions, the dissemination of technical information, and legislative lobbying. For example, on July 7, 1870, Congress passed a new copyright law that for the first time extended protection to photographers' negatives.[63] Among the benefits of association membership was the right to display the NPA logo, as the Goodridge brothers did in figure 3.20. Although they were members, there is no evidence that the Goodridges attended NPA conventions or entered their photographs in the fraternal competitions before 1880.

Through the 1860s, tintypes and cartes de visite, both portraits and city views, were the staple of the Goodridge photo business in East Saginaw. Toward the end of the decade, however, the brothers began to use new formats and to adopt a style that would remain the hallmark of the studio into the next century.

Larger-format (5½ x 7½ inch) collodian glass negatives were the source of the carte de visite panoramas that the Goodridges made of the 1870 flood (see figure 3.15a–c). Full-size prints from the same negatives also were mounted on bristol board, trimmed in gold, and sold as "Imperials" (see figure 3.21). Few such large prints survive from before 1872. Their apparent popularity and the studio's improved technical capability after 1872, however, would make them a regular Goodridge feature. During the late 1860s a new portrait format, the cabinet card, also began to challenge the popularity of the carte de visite. The larger-sized print, 4 x 5½ inches, and mount, 4¼ x 6½ inches, was first introduced in England in 1866. Samples were sent to Edward L. Wilson the same year. In an article in the influential *Philadelphia Photographer,* Wilson described the cabinet as "something like a carte de visite enlarged." According to Robert Taft, it was much more. "The new size," he wrote, "as far as portraiture was concerned, marked a turning point in the annals of the profession. Photographers had, in effect, to begin anew, for the much larger size gave greater opportunity for the portrait artist with respect to posing, lighting, background, and accessories. Flaws which were not particularly obvious in the small card sizes now became conspicuous, so that greater skill in the mechanical routine of making portraits was required."[64] But, Darrah notes, "in the United States, the cabinet portrait gained popularity slowly. Pre-1873 cabinet cards are surpris-

Figure 3.21. "Saginaw River in Flood, to West," April 1870. Albumen image, 7⁷⁄₁₆ x 5⅜ inches, ivory bristol board mount with gold trim, 9¹⁵⁄₁₆ x 8 inches. Goodridge Brothers Studio, East Saginaw, Mich. Eddy Local History and Genealogical Collection, Hoyt Public Library.

ingly scarce. By 1876 about a third of the studio portrait business in the United States was cabinet, two-thirds carte de visite. By 1880 it was roughly half and half, although in the large cities the cabinet portrait was more popular. By 1890 the carte de visite had declined drastically, amounted to less than a tenth of the portrait trade."[65] The Goodridges followed the pattern. Pre-1872 cabinet cards are rare (see figure 3.22), but as the style gained favor and the quality improved after 1872, cabinets supplanted cartes in Saginaw Valley albums. Likely the new cabinet cards were the "AMERICAN PORTRAITS" that the studio featured in its 1872 directory ad (see figure 3.6b).

The same advertisement also informed customers that the brothers were "publishers of MICHIGAN VIEWS." Ultimately, both for the success of the studio and the Goodridges' place in history, the various series of stereo views that they began to issue regularly by 1870 are of the greatest significance.

Figure 3.22. "Unidentified Woman," 1870–72, cabinet card. Albumen image, 4⁵⁄₁₆ x 5¹³⁄₁₆ inches, black bristol board mount with gold trim, 4¼ x 6½ inches. Goodridge Brothers Studio, East Saginaw, Mich. Collection of Dave Tinder.

The principles of stereo (bifocal) vision had been known long before the invention of photography. In 1838 the English scientist Sir Charles Wheatstone had created a viewing instrument that he called a "stereoscope." Although the result was a three-dimensional image, Wheatstone's scope was a reflecting viewer suited to the laboratory and not to small photographs. As early as 1842 the French daguerreotypist Antoine Francoise Claudet attempted to create stereo photographs for Wheatstone's reflecting stereoscope, but without great success. The amount of light necessary to reflect the image often washed out the result. In 1850 Wheatstone's countryman Sir William Brewster solved the problem with a closed, lenticular stereoscope that allowed the viewer to control the amount of light admitted and to adjust the focus. In time for the Great Exposition of 1851, which was photographed extensively in stereo, Brewster's scope made stereo daguerreotypes and the paper stereograph practicable and popular. In 1854 the London Stereoscopic Company was organized to mass-produce views and soon advertised a trade list of more than 100,000 titles. By 1852 D. Appleton Company of New York was selling European-made stereos, and two years later the Langenheim brothers of Philadelphia began the first commercial production of stereographs on glass and paper in the United States. During the 1850s the Langenheims were joined by Edward Anthony, William Notman, and Delos Barnum, among others, as major producers and distributors of stereographs in North America. "By the end of 1860," Darrah has concluded, "no fewer than two hundred American photographers were producing them on glass and paper."[66]

That same year, the impetus in the development and interest in the stereograph as a form of photograph shifted from England to the United States, where it remained through the century. The occasion was the introduction of the handheld stereoscope in 1859 by Oliver Wendell Holmes and its improvement soon thereafter by Holmes's friend and fellow Bostonian Joseph L. Bates, who added a sliding card holder to adjust the focus and a hood to shield the eyes from extraneous light.

Additionally, Holmes published a series of essays in the *Atlantic Monthly* in 1859, 1861, and 1863 that promoted the stereograph as more than mere photography. A recent analysis concludes that Holmes "saw outdoor view photography as an agent of modernization and a necessary part of American life, uniting a rapidly dispersing nation, providing its citizens with access to the vast and steadily increasing body of information in modern systems of knowledge, drawing together and shrinking the globe into its orderly frame, and affording a means of leisurely, intellectual analysis of these new phenomena outside the press of events."[67]

Americans enthusiastically agreed. Darrah estimates that in North America alone between 1850 and 1935 more than two thousand photographers created at least five million different stereo views. Many were made by local professionals who might take a few views of an event to sell for souvenirs, or who produced stereo series of regional and local interest that included tourist attractions, disasters, occupations, and town views. Most, however, were published by large producers like E. & H. T. Anthony and B. W. Kilburn in the nineteenth or Underwood & Underwood and the Keystone View Company in the twentieth century, who sent their own photographers into the field or purchased stereos from local studios. Stereographs remained popular in the United States from their introduction in 1851 to the end of their commercial production in 1939. The peak years of popularity lasted from 1865 to 1878, with a later revival stimulated by the Underwoods and Keystone after 1881.[68] Goodridge success with stereographs corresponds to the years of the format's national popularity, although 1872, the year the original Crouse Block studio was destroyed by fire, divides their career into two distinct stereo production periods in East Saginaw.

None are known at present, but Glenalvin and his brothers did create daguerreotype, ambrotype, and paper stereographs at Goodridge's American Photographic Gallery in York before 1863. The first views to appear in East Saginaw, however, were made before the Goodridges arrived, probably as a result of the Eastman and Randall partnership. Their January 1, 1863, ad in the *Saginaw Weekly Enterprise* offered "VIEWS OF BUILD-INGS, MACHINERY, VESSELS, &C." It is likely that Randall brought the technique from New York City, where he had worked before joining Eastman. Valley residents who might have been interested in other than local views also could purchase stereographs from E. & H. T. Anthony, who regularly advertised "a large assortment of STEREOSCOPES & STEREOSCOPIC VIEWS" in East Saginaw newspapers. For the price of a stamp the Anthonys would send their "Catalogue . . . to any address."[69] In 1865 Meade and Merrill had "VIEWS OF PUBLIC BUILDINGS" for sale, and from 1866 to 1870 Armstrong advertised a large inventory of "Stereoscopic Views" at his "Fine Art Gallery" in Saginaw City.[70] It is not clear if Armstrong was selling his own views of the valley or simply distributing those made by other studios or acquired from national supply houses like Anthony's. In any case, no Eastman and Randall, Meade and Merrill, or Armstrong stereographs of the Saginaw Valley are known to exist at the present time. Examples of stereo views of Saginaw made by Leonard W. Gradt for the period before 1872 are extant. Gradt was born in Prussia about 1842, served in the Seventh Michigan Cavalry in 1865, and worked as a photographer in Saginaw City on and off between 1866 and 1884.[71]

Their ad in the 1872 East Saginaw Directory (see figure 3.6b) was the first commercial notice promoting Goodridge stereographs. The "Michigan Views" which it featured were an ambitious and ultimately very successful series of stereos that the studio had begun to create and publish that very year (they will be described in detail in the following chapter). By 1872, however, the Goodridge brothers already had been making various series of stereographs for at least four years, and possibly longer, under the collective title "Saginaw Valley Views." The series were restricted largely to East Saginaw, although it is clear that subject matter throughout the region also had begun to attract the brothers' attention. The "Saginaw Valley Views" were popular with Saginaw residents. This success served as a stimulus for the Goodridges to undertake the more ambitious series of "Michigan Views" in 1872.

The "Saginaw Valley Views" contain what appear to be at least four identifiable series. Each is grouped by subject matter. Some individual stereos bear a series number, but the total number of "Saginaw Valley Views" created is not known and the extant examples with numbers reveal no logical pattern. Thirty-three views have been identified, and sixteen bear numbers. The first of the "Valley" series is a diverse group of twelve stereos. Its subject matter is much like the carte de visite city views which the Goodridges were making simultaneously—street and river views and examples of significant public and private structures. Figures 3.23a and 3.23b are typical of this earliest Goodridge series, with the focus on purely local subjects. Figure 3.23a documents the initial stages of paving Genesee Street during late summer 1868. James S. Webber had recorded in his diary on October 21, 1868: "The Nicholson pavement is finished today; it was commenced at Franklin Street running west to the foot of Genesee Street across two blocks, then north on Water and Washington Streets to Tuscola, being one block north and south of Genesee Street. The cost of the pavement, including curb-stones, was $30,000; sand taken from Cass Street and the bayou."[72] Its companion, figure 3.23b, commemorates the completion of the new First Congregational Church building at the corner of Jefferson and Hayden Streets that same summer. Leeson's *History of Saginaw County* noted that construction began "in the autumn of 1866," that the structure "was dedicated Sunday, June 14, 1868," and that the "cost of the ground, building and furnishing was $66,472.82." He described the style as "composite, being a combination of all [architectural] orders." He was especially impressed by the building's size, which the stereo accentuates, and the interior decor, observing that "the auditorium will seat 1,000 persons comfortably, and is finished in oil and varnished pine, and finely upholstered."[73]

Both stereos illustrated were made by using a single camera to create two similar negatives consecutively, which were then printed as a single stereograph. Because of the time lapse, sometimes slight and sometimes great, in making two nega-

Figure 3.23a. "Laying Nicholson Pavement, Genesee Street East from Washington," summer 1868, stereograph. Albumen image, 5⅝ x 2¹³⁄₁₆ inches, yellow bristol board mount, 6¼ x 3¼ inches. Goodridge Brothers Studio, East Saginaw, Mich. Eddy Local History and Genealogical Collection, Hoyt Public Library.

Figure 3.23b. "First Congregational Church," summer 1868, stereograph. Albumen image, 5⅝ x 2¹³⁄₁₆ inches, yellow bristol board mount, 6¼ x 3¼ inches. Goodridge Brothers Studio, East Saginaw, Mich. Eddy Local History and Genealogical Collection, Hoyt Public Library.

tives with the same camera, interesting differences often occurred between the two. Notice in figure 3.23a that the two individuals in the foreground of the left half of the stereo are missing from the right. There is also a slight change of position in the right arm of the workman in the white shirt in the left foreground of both halves of the stereo. In figure 3.23b, count the men standing by the door in the base of the tower of the new First Congregational Church building.

Before stereoscopic cameras became available commercially in 1854, or to avoid their cost later, some photographers used two single-lens cameras to create almost simultaneous negatives which then were printed as a stereograph. Even after the invention of the stereoscopic camera, a photographer also might use two single-lens cameras and separate them by as much as three feet to achieve

an especially dramatic binocular effect. Their extant stereographs do not reveal if the Goodridges ever used either of these two-camera techniques. By the 1860s most photographers who made more than a few stereographs were using stereoscopic cameras. Because of the great variety of models available and because studios often modified them to suit their own needs, it is difficult to assign a particular stereograph to a specific type of stereoscopic camera. A typical model, according to Darrah, "had two lenses mounted 2½" apart (the average distance, center to center, between human eyes). A thin septum separates the two lenses from the lens board to the film plane. It is like two cameras with a single common back, each lens forming an image equivalent to what would be seen by one eye. Both images are recorded on a single plate or film separated by a dividing line formed by the septum.[74] Figure 4.10 reveals that as late as the end of the 1870s or the early 1880s the Goodridge studio included just such a "typical" stereoscopic camera in its equipment inventory.

An analysis of the extant photographs, however, suggests that the Goodridges, like most studios at the time, actually employed a variety of techniques to produce stereographs with their stereoscopic cameras. In the first the photographer exposed two glass negatives, approximately 3½ x 3½ inches each, simultaneously in the camera, thereby creating the basis for the desired duplicate image. Once developed, the negatives were then reversed, left to right and right to left, and the stereo print made. The reversal was necessary to correct the lateral inversion of the negatives made in the stereoscopic camera. The Goodridges used this technique rarely. More common was a second option that utilized a single piece of glass, as large as 5 x 8 inches, for the negative. To make the stereoscopic print from the single negative, the photographer or technician employed a transposing frame that facilitated the necessary reversal of the negative from left to right and right to left in the printing process. The frame included a slide and mask mechanism that allowed the photographer to print the left half of the negative while masking the right on the right side of the stereograph, and vice versa. Most of the stereos in the various "Valley" series and a significant number made after 1872 were produced by this technique and resulted in a stereograph that was a single 3½ x 7 print. The two halves of Goodridge stereographs made in this manner, although a single print, almost always are separated by a thin black line or septum that had resulted from "light leakage" between the two negatives or two halves of the single negative during the printing process.

The Goodridges also used a third method to make stereographs with their stereoscopic camera. A single 3½ x 7 negative was exposed to make a single 3½ x 7 print. The print was then cut into two halves and the halves reversed, left to right and right to left, and then pasted on the mounting board to create the stereograph. As a result of the division after printing, no dark septum from "light

leakage" is visible in the stereograph. Instead, a close look reveals that the stereograph actually is two nearly identical photographs mounted side-by-side on the bristol board card.[75] Only two of the thirty-three known "Saginaw Valley Views" were made utilizing this single negative/divided print technique. As we will see in the next chapter, the Goodridge brothers reserved this technique, which resulted in the most visually impressive stereographs but which also was the most labor intensive, for their premier series of "Michigan Views" which they sought to market statewide and nationally.

An excellent example of a stereograph made by the stereoscopic camera (two negatives, single print, or single negative, transposing frame technique—notice the dark line or septum separating the two halves) is figure 3.24a. The view is striking in stereo. The plain snow-covered foreground (actually Genesee Street), the strong parallel lines of the fence and gate, the delicate tracery of the dormant tree branches, and the mass of the structures, both house and church, result in a dramatic vision of "hyperspace," the term photographers used to describe the illusion of depth in stereographs.[76] The stereo was made specifically for James Webber, whose home on the east side of Jefferson Street between Genesee and German is shown. The church building, First Baptist, had been completed in 1868, and with its neighbors on Jefferson, the Methodist (figure 3.12a) and First Congregational (figure 3.23b), formed an impressive trio in that part of the city. The photographer's primary subject, however, was the Webber home.

James S. Webber was born in Maine and had lived for a time in New York. In 1836 he and his family migrated to a farm in Livingston County, Michigan, just over the line from the town of Milford. Webber prospered and in 1853 moved his family to East Saginaw. For six hundred dollars he and his son William L., twenty-eight at the time, purchased the entire block bounded by Genesee, Jefferson, and German Streets from Norman L. Little. The elder Webber opened a grocery and provisions store on Genesee near Water Street, and his son became attorney and counsel, first to the Flint

Figure 3.24a. "First Baptist Church and J. S. Webber Home from Genesee Street," 1868–72, stereograph. Albumen image, 5½ x 2⅝ inches, yellow bristol board mount, 6¹⁵⁄₁₆ x 3⁷⁄₁₆ inches. Goodridge Brothers Studio, East Saginaw, Mich. Historical Society of Saginaw County, Inc.

Figure 3.24b. "James S. Webber," 1876, stereograph. Albumen image, 6¼ x 3⁷⁄₁₆ inches, black bristol board mount, 6¹⁵⁄₁₆ x 3¹⁵⁄₁₆ inches. Goodridge Brothers Studio, East Saginaw, Mich. Collection of Dave Tinder.

& Pere Marquette Railway Company and soon thereafter to Jesse Hoyt of New York, who had extensive holdings throughout the valley and state.[77] In addition to business, the Webbers were interested in photography. James Webber, in fact, collected Goodridge stereographs. Eleven of the thirty-three extant "Saginaw Valley Views" bear Webber's initials as well as dates and descriptions in the same handwriting. In 1876 the Goodridges honored this interest by making of and for James Webber their only known portrait stereograph (see figure 3.24b).[78]

The second series of "Saginaw Valley Views" is the largest of the four, containing thirteen stereos, although gaps in the serial numbering system suggest that it may have included fifteen or even twen-

ty individual stereographs. Unlike the first series of fairly diverse city, river, and architectural views, the second was devoted to a single event, the spring 1870 flood. Darrah reports that such series were commonly turned out by local photographers "who produced a few views when some unusual event—flood, fire, train-wreck, parade, or such— created a transitory market for souvenirs. In some instances the negatives, or rights to them, were sold to large-volume publishers."[79] The April 1870 flood was such an opportunity for the Goodridge brothers. The Saginaw River regularly overran its banks. In fact, an abundant flow of water each spring was necessary for the river drives that brought timber from lumber camps and banking grounds throughout the valley to the sawmills

Figure 3.25a. "Saginaw River, High Water, South of Genesee Street Bridge," April 1870, stereograph. Albumen image, 5⅝ x 2¹³/₁₆ inches, yellow bristol board mount, 6¼ x 3¼ inches. Goodridge Brothers Studio, East Saginaw, Mich. Eddy Local History and Genealogical Collection, Hoyt Public Library.

Figure 3.25b. "Genesee Street and Franklin, High Water," April 1870, stereograph. Albumen image, 5½ x 2⅝ inches, yellow bristol board mount, 6¹⁵/₁₆ x 3⁷/₁₆ inches. Goodridge Brothers Studio, East Saginaw, Mich. Eddy Local History and Genealogical Collection, Hoyt Public Library.

along the river. The spring rains during 1870, however, were much too generous. The log drive was disrupted, and for more than a week homes and businesses for blocks beyond the river were inundated. Figure 3.25a reveals the chaos caused by the high water as thousands of logs rushed helter-skelter past the mills that normally would have been cutting them into lumber. In figure 3.25b one of the Goodridges held the other as he made this view up Genesee Street across Franklin from their studio window in the third story of the Crouse Block. Notice the barrel barricade across Genesee and the planks used to cross puddles and mud. William Street (figure 3.26a), a block away across Franklin Street, needed more than plank walks. Although four blocks from the river, it was water-

covered almost to the Methodist Episcopal Church on Jefferson. Apparently the series was popular, for when more than twenty-five inches of rain fell between March 9 and March 20 the following year the flooding returned, and so did the Goodridges with a second Saginaw flood series. The *Saginaw Daily Courier* reported under the headline "High Water Views" that "During the siege of high water, the enterprising firm of Goodridge Bros. Photographers, took a number of photographic views of various parts of the city and river. These views have been placed on cards and are for sale. They are an interesting study and will doubtless be valuable in times to come as an illustrated reminder of the great freshet of 1871, the likes of which may probably never occur again."[80] As figure 3.26b

Figure 3.26a. "Franklin and William Streets, High Water," April 1870, stereograph. Albumen image, 5½ x 2⅝ inches, yellow bristol board mount, 6¹⁵⁄₁₆ x 3⁷⁄₁₆ inches. Goodridge Brothers Studio, East Saginaw, Mich. Eddy Local History and Genealogical Collection, Hoyt Public Library.

Figure 3.26b. "South Cass Street during Flood," March 1871, stereograph. Albumen image, 5½ x 2⅝ inches, yellow bristol board mount, 6¹⁵⁄₁₆ x 3⁷⁄₁₆ inches. Goodridge Brothers Studio, East Saginaw, Mich. Historical Society of Saginaw County, Inc.

clearly shows, the flooding in 1871 was even more extensive than the year before. The *Courier* noted that in most places the water was eleven inches above the peak it had reached in 1870.[81]

The final of the four "Saginaw Valley Views" series took the brothers away from city views and flooded streets to the streams and forests of the Saginaw Valley. Although the series is the smallest, containing only six known views, it was especially important. Probably it was made about the same time, the fall of 1870, that the Goodridges were experimenting with scenic "Cartes Victoria" (see figure 3.16b, "Opening the State Road at Clare Station"). Unlike the "Victorias," which soon were abandoned, the creation of this small series of stereographs established a pattern that the studio

would repeat regularly and with great success after 1872. The subjects were the lumber camps and banking grounds located along the route of the Flint & Pere Marquette Railroad through Midland and Clare Counties. Internal evidence (railroad tracks, the river, and terrain) suggests that the locations of these early views were the banking ground near Averill on the Tittabawassee River in Midland County (see figure 3.27a) and further along the route of the railroad in Clare County on the Tobacco River between the towns of Clare and Farwell (see figure 3.27b). Both locations, but especially the banking ground at Averill and the P. Glynn & Co. lumber camp in Midland County, were favorite destinations for the Goodridges and their cameras after 1872. The Flint & Pere Mar-

Figure 3.27a. "Banking Ground, Tittabawassee River at Averill's Station," 1868–69, stereograph. Albumen image, 5½ x 2¹¹⁄₁₆ inches, yellow bristol board mount, 6¹³⁄₁₆ x 3⁷⁄₁₆ inches. Goodridge Brothers Studio, East Saginaw, Mich. Collection of Dave Tinder.

Figure 3.27b. "Tobacco River, Clare County," 1868–69, stereograph. Albumen image, 5½ x 2⅝ inches, yellow bristol board mount, 6¾ x 3⁷⁄₁₆ inches. Goodridge Brothers Studio, East Saginaw, Mich. Collection of Dave Tinder.

quette route defined their itinerary and, as we will see in the next chapter, the brothers traveled it regularly. Tracklaying for the line had begun in East Saginaw in August 1859. In December 1868 it was complete to Averill and by 1870 had been extended beyond Clare to Farwell.[82]

Both stereos illustrated are examples of the single negative/transposing frame printing technique that the Goodridges used regularly at this time, with the resulting dark septum separating the two images. Each also reveals characteristics that Goodridge stereographs shared with the genre generally but which also came to typify the Goodridge style: a clearly defined horizon, often broken by the silhouettes of large trees; a strategically overhanging tree branch, in these illustrations from up-

per right; and the texture created by the rail fence, rough ground, and the precariously piled logs at the banking ground. These all enhanced the dramatic illusion of stereo vision. The Goodridges also regularly used roads, railway tracks, and the river to divide the middle and foreground in their views. Additionally, the trees and overhanging banks reflected in the water intensified the depth of the view, as in figure 3.27b. The individual seated on the riverbank in figure 3.27a was a device that most photographers used to represent the scale of the photograph. In the Goodridge oeuvre such individuals also were utilized to dramatize the interaction between people and nature.

Like the paper covers of the tintypes and the bristol board mounts of their cartes de visite, the

Figure 3.28a. "Verso of Stereograph Mount with Advertising 'Stamp,'" April 1870, stereograph mount, 6¼ x 3¼ inches. Goodridge Brothers Studio, East Saginaw, Mich. Eddy Local History and Genealogical Collection, Hoyt Public Library.

Figure 3.28b. "Verso of Stereograph Mount with Advertising Label," March 1871, stereograph mount, 6 ¹⁵/₁₆ x 3⁷/₁₆ inches. Goodridge Brothers Studio, East Saginaw, Mich. Historical Society of Saginaw County, Inc.

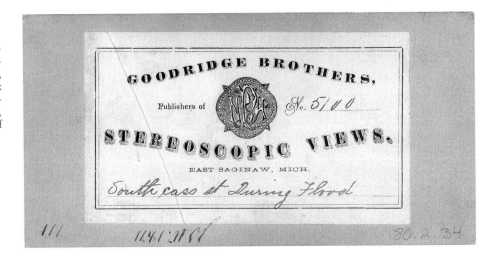

versos and mounts of the "Saginaw Valley Views" series reveal significant information about the Goodridges and the development of their studio. All mounts in the various "Valley" series are 3½ x 7 inches or smaller and are a characteristic yellow-gold color with black lettering. The name, general studio location, and an occasional series number accompany the image. Although the versos of most are blank, one displays the small stamplike label more common on earlier tintypes and cartes de visite (see figure 3.28a). Only the versos of the 1871 flood series among the "Saginaw Valley Views" bear a printed label (see figure 3.28b). Each of the labels is 2¾ by 5 inches, includes space for a series number and description of the view, and

prominently displays the National Photographic Association logo. The labels also reveal that the Goodridge brothers described themselves as "Publishers of STEREOSCOPIC VIEWS," meaning that they distributed their own stereo photographs and also on occasion purchased the rights to and distributed views made by other photographers. According to Darrah, "This was general practice until 1900. When the photographer was himself the publisher, marketing was relatively simple. Views were sold at his studio and by agents or outlets, such as opticians' and art shops. Many photographer-publishers were also able to engage in extensive mail order business."[83] It has not been possible to attribute a "Saginaw Valley View" published by the Goodridges to a photographer who did not work at the Goodridge studio. G. F. Lewis, a stationer in East Saginaw, and Andres and Adams, who sold furniture and general household items in Saginaw City, both advertised "A Choice Assortment" of photograph albums but did not mention a stock of stereographs for sale.[84] Only W. A. Armstrong in 1867, and then the same Armstrong and his partner Harrison N. Rudd in 1870, advertised "STEREOSCOPIC VIEWS" for sale at their "Fine Art Gallery" and "New Picture Establishment" in Saginaw City. Because they also kept an inventory of "Celebrities, [and] Cheap Pictures of all kinds," it is clear that Armstrong and Rudd were publishers and distributors of stereographs and photographs made by other photographers.[85] Whether the Goodridge views were among them is not known. Goodridge stereo views, however, are found in collections throughout Michigan and the United States, and it is likely that the Goodridges, like many of their contemporaries, sold stereographs by mail order. Yet no evidence exists to document the practice.

By 1872 the various series of "Saginaw Valley Views" were an increasingly larger component of the Goodridge studio's annual production. In the decade after 1872 stereographs became its most important type of photograph. Until at least 1890 the Goodridge brothers and stereo views were nearly synonymous to residents of the valley and the region. Several circumstances and events that occurred during the late 1860s may explain this development.

Darrah has described the years 1868–78 as "the grand flowering of stereo views" in the United States. For the period he has identified more than 1,650 photographers, nearly half of whom regularly made stereographs. The result was a "remarkable variety and volume of views" used for "amusement and information" as well as "for instruction and advertising and as mementos."[86] Although the New York firm of E. & H. T. Anthony and Saginaw City's W. A. Armstrong regularly advertised mail-order stereo views, and the photographer Leonard W. Gradt produced a few before 1870, no Saginaw studio is listed by Darrah as publishing significant

numbers of stereos until the Goodridges introduced their "Saginaw Valley Views" series. Its popularity caused them to concentrate even more heavily on producing stereographs for this expanding local market. By the late 1860s the Goodridge studio also was only one of at least five that were well established in East Saginaw and Saginaw City.[87] Each advertised portrait photography in all of its possible forms, but of the five only the Goodridges actively promoted its own stereographs. Apparently they turned to the stereo view to provide them with that bit of difference from their competitors that often meant success. Furthermore, their father regularly had introduced new products in his various business enterprises in York, and, following his example, the brothers may have recognized the stereograph as a commodity with great commercial potential and actively promoted it. Their introduction of the "Saginaw Valley Views," especially the final series on lumber camps and the banking grounds, also corresponded to a period of rapid growth in the Michigan lumber industry. A ready market for such series was provided by the hundreds of "shanty boys" and "river rats" who regularly visited the Saginaws from the forest camps, as well as the local mill hands and residents. The stereo views also were a fine complement to the tintypes and carte de visite portraits that most no doubt sat for at one studio or another.

—◦—

Although Glenalvin died shortly after he and his brothers had reestablished their studio in East Saginaw, he had left them with a solid foundation upon which to build their future success. No records exist that make it possible to document this process precisely, yet a variety of indicators suggest that by 1872 Wallace and William, with Glenalvin's inspiration, had made the Goodridge studio the equal of any in the Saginaw Valley. In the years that followed, their success and subsequent significance only increased.

As early as 1866, during a visit to East Saginaw, Horace Greeley, the celebrated founder and editor of the *New York Tribune,* chose the

Goodridge studio to make the photograph commemorating his visit.[88] The portrait does not exist to confirm whether Greeley chose the Goodridges for the quality of their work, as a gesture designed to promote the studio, or because of the Goodridges' race and political views. Each may have contributed to Greeley's decision, although in 1866 race and politics were of paramount importance. Greeley only recently had broken with President Andrew Johnson over Reconstruction and the Fourteenth Amendment, moving closer to the Radical Republicans.[89] Although the Goodridges did not advertise their political views at the time, both earlier in Pennsylvania and later in Michigan family members openly advocated abolitionist and civil rights positions. Given William C. Goodridge's role in the Underground Railroad, it also is likely that the family was well known to Greeley, an avowed opponent of slavery. At the same time, the quality of Goodridge portraiture was recognized by the "Fine Arts" judges of the first annual Saginaw County Agricultural Society Fair that summer. And, Darrah has noted that the popularity of celebrity portraits in the United States fluctuated, with two peak periods, 1860–66 and 1875–85. The earlier period conformed closely to the European fad, with "statesmen, military, clerical, literary and theatrical figures," and "at least 600 American photographers [are] . . . known to have issued such portraits."[90] Although a copy is not extant, the Goodridge portrait of Greeley may have been among them.

Six years after Greeley's visit, however, a decision to publish a series of Goodridge photographs based quite clearly on the quality of their work can be confirmed with certainty. On October 17, 1872, the *Saginaw Weekly Enterprise,* under the headline "PICTURES," reported that the "Goodridge Brothers have orders from Boston parties for photographic views of notable business blocks and private residences in this part of the valley, which are to be used in a forthcoming illustrated work. Among the residences to be given are those of Messrs. Estabrook, Corning, Sears, Bundy, Judd, Potter, Wood, Ballard, Weber, Robinson, Derby, Horr, and Wilkin of this city; and Messrs. Gould, Green,

Jerome, Barnard, Burrows, and others of Saginaw City."[91] Whether the work ever was published and which "views" it may have included is not known. The notice does indicate, however, that by 1872 the Goodridge reputation for quality already extended far beyond the valley.

Beginning with 1866, it also is possible to gauge Goodridge success on an annual basis. That year the Saginaw County Agricultural Society held the first of its annual fairs. Among a multitude of entries was a selection of "Fine Arts" that included photography. Although J. T. Randall won the award for "best photographs" and the Goodridges garnered a second, the brothers' "daguerreotypes and ambrotypes" were judged to be better than those that Randall had entered. In addition, one of the Goodridges, most likely young William, received a premium for "2d best pastelle painting." The next year Randall and the Goodridges were joined by their Saginaw City competitor, W. A. Armstrong. According to fair records, "Wallace Goodridge, East Saginaw [entered] a collection of plain and colored photographs; photographs in porcelain; one porcelain lamp shade; photographic curiosities; [and a] collection of ambrotypes [and] daguerreotypes." Although for the second time in as many years Randall won the prize for "Best photograph" (the second went to Armstrong), the Goodridges were awarded a first for "Best ambrotype" and followed that with firsts for "Best large plain photograph," "Best large photograph in India ink," "Best large photograph in water colors," "Best card photograph," "Best pictures on porcelain," and "Best collection of miscellaneous photographs." This deluge of awards may be due to the fact that by 1867 William's talent as an artist had begun to influence the studio's work. In addition, Wallace may simply have overpowered the competition by the sheer size of his entry. The following year, 1868, the Goodridge photographs won all prizes awarded. There is no record of the entries.[92]

By 1869 Saginaw photographers could also choose a second venue in which to enter their best work. In August the Saginaw Horticultural Society held its first annual "GALA" in Saginaw City, "combining the beautiful of art with the most charming productions of nature, and mingling with these the rarest attractions in the way of music." The "Horticultural Fair" was to be an exhibition of gardening, the work of local artists, and a variety of "crafts." Representing their Saginaw City location, Armstrong and his new partner, Harrison W. Rudd, submitted an impressive entry that included "one landscape, in oil, 8 x 10; one photograph in oil, 14 x 17; one portrait in crayon and ink, 18 x 22; three portraits in crayon and ink, 20 x 24; one frame of 15 photographs, one frame of eight photographs, four frame card photographs, one half plate ambrotype, and one 4 x 4 plate ambrotype." Mrs. G. W. Deitz of East Saginaw, a member of the Saginaw City Horticultural Society's executive committee, entered a "Photograph in oil." The Goodridge studio was not represented. Armstrong and Rudd were awarded all the premiums. The Goodridges apparently had reserved their year's best work for the annual Saginaw County Agricultural Society Fair held the following month. They split the awards with Armstrong and Rudd, who had made a strong entry as well. The Goodridges received firsts for "Best sample plain photograph," "Best large photograph in water colors," "Best pictures on porcelain," and "Best assortment of curiosities." Armstrong and Rudd won for "Best large photograph in India ink," "Best card photograph," "Best collection miscellaneous photographs," and "Best crayon drawing." Although both J. T. Randall and William Roberts continued to operate studios in East Saginaw, neither entered photographs in the fair after 1867. As the longest-established studios in the city, neither may have felt the need for the exposure the fair provided their work. The annual Saginaw City Horticultural Fair did not meet a second year, nor did Armstrong and Rudd enter the Agricultural Society Fair in 1870. Rudd left the partnership that year. As a result, the Goodridges' only competition was a Mrs. J. L. Glynn, who won premiums for a "crayon head," "Photograph in India ink," and "Photograph in water colors."[93]

Intense competition among photographers for awards at major international and national exhibitions was as old as the profession. Smaller annual city or county fairs, such as those held in East Saginaw and Saginaw City, have been characterized as little more than "a chance to solicit patronage."[94] To a point that accurately describes the level of competition in the Saginaws, as the valley's studios shared equally in the available "firsts" and "premiums." A newspaper description of the entries and prizes for the 1871 fair under "PHOTOGRAPHS," for example, was as much an advertisement as a report of the event:

> The Messrs. Goodridge Bro's of this city, had a splendid display as regards both quantity and quality. Their presence at the exhibition shows them to be men of enterprise, and speaks well for them. Among the many noticeable articles entered by these gentlemen is something new called photo pastell. In this a child's head, is one of the most beautiful pieces of workmanship it has ever been our lot to look upon. They had a fine display of Rembrandt and plain card photographs, photographs on silk, and one photograph on a watch crystal. This collection attracted much attention, and they took five 1st prizes in photographs and water colors. The only other exhibition was Armstrong of Saginaw City who had a fine display in which was a specimen of brake leaves, on card; used for mottoes, the one on exhibition read "God is Love," and was a gem. Mr. Armstrong was awarded a number of 1st prizes, among them one for best work in India ink.[95]

A later listing of specific premiums awarded, however, revealed that the competition, at least in 1871, was indeed as intense as at the larger national exhibitions. The newspaper noted that "A protest having been entered against the award of the Committee in regard to Rembrandt photographs, water color photographs, Pastell painting and large plain photographs, the publication of this portion of the list will be withheld until the protest is heard and decided by the Executive Committee."[96] The protest likely was filed by the Goodridges, as the disputed entries were those described by the earlier newspaper account. No decision by the committee was later reported. In 1872, at the next year's fair, all premiums were awarded to the Goodridge brothers. No protest was filed that year.[97]

What little is known with any certainty of the financial situation of the Goodridge family and the studio during its first decade in East Saginaw can be determined from the reports filed following fires that destroyed the Goodridge home in 1869 and studio in 1872. According to the reporter: "About ten o'clock Friday night [January 1, 1869] a house adjoining the Grant block, Washington street, was discovered to be on fire, and was nearly consumed before the engine got to work. . . . The house was occupied by Mrs. R. C. Gooderich [sic], a colored widow, and her brothers-in-law, the Gooderich Bros. . . . The whole family was absent at the time of the fire, at the emancipation celebration, so that almost nothing could be saved."[98] The loss was only partially covered by insurance and is estimated to have been several thousand dollars. It certainly exceeded $10,000 and may have amounted to as much as $15,000. More than half the total was "one of the finest libraries in the city, consisting of 1,250 volumes, nearly all works of standard authors, which was entirely destroyed." Its value was estimated at $8,200. Other personal property destroyed included "some very valuable hair work, a knitting and sewing machine and confectioner's tools, besides household furniture, wearing apparel and jewelry belonging to various members of the household," which was insured for $2,300 but probably worth twice as much. No value was placed on "about 1,000 negatives, a camera and other photographic apparatus," although the lost negatives doubtless included invaluable family photographs and numerous examples of Glenalvin's work in York from 1847 to 1863 and from the Goodridge brothers' earliest years in East Saginaw.[99]

The fire may have prompted Wallace to invest in additional insurance. In January 1872 he was listed as the owner of a $2,000 policy issued by the New York Life Insurance Company. While the policy was a much smaller one than Dr. Henry C. Potter's for $20,000, it was as large as or larger than those of dozens of Wallace's East Saginaw neighbors on the company's list of policyholders. No other Saginaw photographers were listed.[100] Later that year Wallace probably wished that he had insured the studio and its contents as well.

On Tuesday, October 22, 1872, almost four years after fire had destroyed the Goodridge home, a second conflagration swept through the Crouse Block at the northeast corner of Washington and Genesee Streets, reducing the block to rubble and devouring all the businesses that occupied it, including the Goodridge brothers' third-floor studio. A close examination of figure 3.29 reveals the rubble and smoke damage to the adjoining building from the blaze. The fire broke out about 6 p.m. in the Woodard grocery store on the first floor of the Washington Street side of the Crouse Block. Oil spilled accidentally by Mr. Woodard seeped through the floor and onto a hot stove in the Neptune Restaurant below. Woodard, who was badly burned, saw a flash and almost instantly the fire, fueled by the oil, spread throughout the building. So quickly did the fire spread that most occupants were fortunate to escape with their lives. For a time the fire, fanned by a strong west wind, threatened the entire block bounded by Washington, Genesee, Franklin, and Tuscola Streets, which included the Everett House Hotel and other property valued in the tens of thousands of dollars. The loss of the Crouse Block and its contents amounted to more than $100,000. First reports estimated the Goodridge brothers' loss as total and in the amount of $15,000. The following day, however, the brothers, who were in the studio when the fire broke out, indicated that they had been able to save five cameras and some photographic equipment but, once again, lost everything else, including "a fine piano" and all of their negatives. They calculated their loss at $3,800, saving only $500 in cameras and equipment. Unfortunately, they carried no insurance on the studio or its contents.[101]

Jesse Hoyt, who owned the Crouse Block, replaced it the following spring with an even more impressive structure. His agent offered first choice in the new building to Crouse Block occupants. The Goodridge brothers declined, taking temporary quarters within a week of the fire at a Washington Street location. On November 10, 1872, the *Saginaw Daily Courier* reported that "The foundation for the new photograph gallery of the Goodridge Bro's who were burned out in [the]

Figure 3.29. "Genesee Street East from Bancroft House Hotel, Note Rubble from Crouse Block Fire," October 1872, stereograph. Albumen image, 6¼ x 3⅜ inches, green bristol board mount, 7 x 3¹⁵⁄₁₆ inches. Goodridge Brothers Studio, East Saginaw, Mich. Collection of Dave Tinder.

Crouse block, was laid yesterday. The new gallery will be located on Washington street [in the 200 block south], nearly opposite Smith's Opera House."[102]

The "fine piano" destroyed in the studio fire had been the focal point of a lawsuit that involved its seizure, a Goodridge countersuit, and Wallace's arrest for perjury. The newspaper account and court records of the case are fragmentary but reveal that in July 1870 Justice of the Peace George A. Flanders rendered separate judgments against Wallace L. and William O. Goodridge. The suit against Wallace, for reasons the record no longer includes, was brought by George Lane of East Saginaw. At the same time, a Mrs. Jardine, again for reasons unknown, had sued William O. Goodridge. In each case Justice Flanders found for the plaintiffs, awarding Lane $45.02 damages and $2.50 costs and Mrs. Jardine $9.00 damages and costs. The Goodridges paid neither judgment when due. As a result, Deputy Sheriff T. Daily Mower, on December 20, 1870, seized "One Emerson's Piano with legs and cover," valued at $350, against the unpaid judgments. Four days later the Goodridge attorney, Lorenzo L. Durand, filed a Writ of Replevin claiming that Mower had seized a piano that actually had been the property of William C. Goodridge since at least 1862, a fact attested to by both Wallace L. and William O. Goodridge. Justice Jabez G. Sutherland granted the writ when Goodridge

friends Abraham Reyno and William A. Dutton provided security for the replevin bond. Although County Coroner and Notary Public George Mauer reported to the court on December 30, 1870, that he had delivered the writ to Mower two days earlier, the piano was not released to the Goodridge family. On January 10, 1871, William C. Goodridge, who was visiting his sons at the time, in a Plea of Replevin brought suit against Mower in the amount of $1,000 damages for his failure to return the piano. The piano eventually was returned, but only after the Goodridges had paid the judgments against them. Justice Sutherland later denied the suit for damages and in July 1871 charged William C. Goodridge $44.24 in costs. By the time William O. Goodridge paid the county clerk on September 29, 1871, the total costs had been increased to $52.[103]

The case, however, did not end with payment of the judgments or return of the piano. In July 1871 the firm of Perkins and Morehouse accused Wallace Goodridge of perjury. It is important to note that Perkins had represented Rhoda Goodridge in her 1869 lawsuit against the Massachusetts Life Insurance Company and more recently had defended Deputy Sheriff Mower in the Goodridge piano damages suit. Wallace was arrested and charged but released. Nevertheless, under the headline "A Case of Alleged Perjury," the *Saginaw Daily Courier* reported that the "examination of

Wallace Goodrich of the firm Goodrich Brothers, charged with perjury, is now in progress before Justice Miller." Wallace, for the first and only time in his life, was prompted to respond to the editor of the *Courier* regarding the "late special allusions to myself" in the "local columns of your paper." Wallace explained to the *Courier's* readers that the firm of Perkins and Morehouse, well-known "collecting agents," had attempted to collect from him a disputed claim. Failing in this, they decided—Wallace implied it was because of his race—"to experiment upon me." Wallace reported that Morehouse came to him with the disputed claim and demanded immediate payment. If Wallace did not pay, Morehouse threatened to accuse him of perjury "in a matter where I had justified my pecuniary responsibility under oath to become surety for the stay of an execution in a matter of a nine dollar judgement" (Justice of the Peace Flanders's decision in Mrs. Jardine versus William O. Goodridge in July 1870). Wallace refused to pay Morehouse's claim. Morehouse then tried to pressure Wallace by contacting "Mr. Reyno, a colored friend of mine and desired him to impress upon me the necessity of adjusting said claims to avoid said criminal prosecution." Wallace was steadfast in his refusal and, therefore, was accused and tried but acquitted of perjury before Justice Hezekiah Miller in July 1871. Wallace noted that the *Courier* had reported the accusation of perjury and his arrest but not his acquittal. Furthermore, "Mr. Morehouse is now under arrest, and awaiting his examination, upon the charge of attempting to extort money and to compel the payment of an alleged claim under the threats of accusing me of a crime, which by our statutes is made a prison offense, yet the fact of his arrest is carefully suppressed from your columns, while exaggerated statements in relation to my arrest, have been fully published without stint or reservation. [And] in the case of my discharge, you are made to say that it was on technical grounds, when in fact the proof by their own showing did not make out a case."[104] The outcome of the charges against Morehouse is not known.

That the original judgments against Wallace and William, the dispute over the seizure of their "fine piano," and Wallace's subsequent trial for perjury arose from the possible poor financial condition of the photography studio is unlikely. Only the next year, within days of the Crouse Block fire which had completely destroyed their uninsured studio and all but "$500 in cameras and equipment," the Goodridges began construction of a new, larger, and most up-to-date facility on South Washington Street. Whether the suits and accusations were prompted by the family's race, as Wallace implied, we will consider below.

The new studio was the first real estate owned by Goodridge family members in East Saginaw. Unlike their father and brother Glenalvin in York, Wallace and William did not acquire substantial residential or commercial properties in the Saginaw Valley. Before 1872 the local directories always listed family members as "boarders" at one location or another. After the construction of the new studio, at least until 1890, it appears that rooms adjoining the studio served the family as a residence. The 1870 census, in fact, does not record the Goodridges as owners of any real estate. Among the approximately sixty African American families living in East Saginaw and Saginaw City in 1870, twenty-four owned real estate. Some, like Henry Bundy, a salt block worker, owned as little as $250. Others, like William Q. Atwood, a lumberman with $85,000 in real estate, were among the valley's wealthiest residents.[105] Precisely why the Goodridges did not follow the family's earlier pattern and acquire substantial real estate holdings in East Saginaw is not clear. The bankruptcies in 1859 and Glenalvin's trial and conviction shortly thereafter likely left them without capital. Also, there may have been a reluctance to invest until the family was more certain of its decision to settle permanently in East Saginaw and the future of the studio was secure. Still, ownership of no real estate at all before 1872 was very much unlike the earlier generation of York Goodridges. The census does note, however, that between them Wallace and William owned approximately $3,000 in personal estate, most of which no doubt was cameras and studio equipment. The 1869 Emancipation Day fire truly had reduced family fortunes.[106]

In 1872 the Goodridge brothers certainly were not wealthy. Almost half of Saginaw's African American families owned more real property than they did. Their studio had begun to earn a reputation beyond the Saginaw Valley, but the competition remained intense. Glenalvin's death and two destructive fires within little more than five years had checked the studio's steady growth somewhat and swept away many of the family's physical connections with its own past. Yet the Goodridges' decision to build a new studio in November 1872 is a clear signal that their progress had been satisfactory and that they expected much from the future. The choice to remain in East Saginaw also suggests that the Goodridges found both the living conditions and opportunity available to African Americans there sufficient if not always acceptable.

＊＊＊

Shortly before the Goodridges settled in East Saginaw, the 1860 census had listed less than forty "Blacks and Mulattos" among a total population of more than four thousand in East Saginaw and Saginaw City. Mr. J. J. Richardson, who later lived in Bay City, may have been Saginaw's first African American resident. The *Michigan Manual of Freedmen's Progress* noted that Richardson had settled in Saginaw in 1855, "when there was only one other colored family in the valley."[107] By 1860, however, four families—the Jacksons, the Reynos, the Joneses, and the Walkers—and several married and single adults were well established in the Saginaws. Virginia was the most common state of origin, producing five of the eight parents in the four families, although other states, both North and South, were represented as well. Some families, like the Reynos, had moved regularly, having lived in Pennsylvania, Illinois, and Canada before settling in Michigan. Others, like the Joneses and Walkers, had moved directly from Virginia to Michigan, the Walkers as early as 1852. The census reveals that of the fifteen employed adults, eight were either barbers or cooks. Five adults owned real estate and eight personal property, with James L. Campbell, a barber, listing $2,300. Residential patterns are not known, although all but the Walker family—Mr.

Walker was a barber in Saginaw City—lived in East Saginaw.[108] During the years of civil war and for the remainder of the decade this original core of families and individuals developed into a cohesive and vibrant community that provided the foundation for and helped to stimulate the success of its members, including the Goodridge brothers.

Between 1860 and 1870 the Saginaws' African American population increased sixfold, more rapidly than the total population, to approximately 270 citizens, with two-thirds choosing East Saginaw and the remainder Saginaw City as home. The results of the recent war were reflected in the fact that Canada overtook Virginia as the most common place of birth, especially among the young and recent arrivals. And states of the Deep South, such as North Carolina and Alabama, for the first time contributed to the increase as well. Almost without exception, African Americans in the Saginaws were members of families or extended households that included relatives, boarders, and apprentices. The few exceptions usually were live-in servants. The majority of adults continued to be employed in the service sector as barbers, cooks, laundresses, or waiters, but a significant number also were craftsmen who worked as carpenters, machinists, masons, and plasterers. Reflecting the rapid growth in the lumber and related industries, several also were employed in the lumber mills and salt blocks as firemen, boilers, and salt packers. Figure 3.30, a group portrait of the crew of the Warner & Eastman lumber mill, located on the east bank of the river between Hoyt and Emerson Streets, includes three African Americans who were employed in the Saginaw lumber mills at the time. The age and common employer suggest that they likely were Allen Doholey, Henry Brown, and Archibald Robins, all members of the same Saginaw household. More than a dozen heads of families, including some of the craftsmen and barbers, two brothers who were photographers, and William Atwood, a wealthy lumberman, owned and operated their own businesses. Significant holdings of real and personal estate were not uncommon, with seventeen families listing at least $1,000 in combined assets. At-

Figure 3.30. "Mill Hands of Warner & Eastman," circa 1870. Albumen image, 8 $^{11}/_{16}$ x 5½ inches, beige mount board , 9 $^{15}/_{16}$ x 7$^{11}/_{16}$ inches. [Goodridge Brothers Studio], East Saginaw, Mich. Collection of John V. Jezierski.

wood's total of $103,600, however, was almost ten times the value of Robert Campbell's $11,200, which was a distant second. The census also reveals that by 1870 African American families resided and owned real estate in each of East Saginaw's six wards, with the exception of the First Ward, where the only African American resident was Maggie Cokely, a housemaid. A similar pattern existed in Saginaw City, where the Third Ward was the only one of the six that did not include an African American resident. An expanding local and regional economy with opportunity for all may explain the absence of a pattern of residential segregation that would begin to appear by the end of the century when the lumber boom had run its course.[109]

Soon after their arrival in East Saginaw, the Goodridges were already active and influential members of the African American community. In February 1866 the newly organized Colored Debating Society chose Glenalvin Goodridge as its recording secretary and younger brother William as corresponding secretary. Three years later, in January 1869, Wallace Goodridge was made "President of the evening" that celebrated the fifth anniversary of Emancipation. No doubt he organized much of the day's elaborate entertainment, and multitalented William O. Goodridge led a small orchestra that provided dance music "till an early hour in the morning."[110]

The Goodridges not only assumed or were elected to positions that required leadership and responsibility, but also were associated regularly with the small group that was emerging as the economic and social elite within the African American community. Fellow Debating Society officers included the barber Lewis Reyno and Washington Foote, a plasterer who, like the Goodridges, had migrated to East Saginaw from York. William Atwood, one of Michigan's wealthiest and most influential African American citizens, was treasurer. Robert Campbell, a mason whose real estate holdings had increased fivefold since 1860, was William O. Goodridge's best man at his 1867 wedding. And Abraham Reyno, another of East Saginaw's well-established barbers, had provided the security for the replevin bond that freed the Goodridge piano.[111]

One aspect of life in East Saginaw that did not attract Goodridge attention or participation at this time was organized religion. Bethel A.M.E. was founded in 1867 and Zion Baptist Church a year later. In spite of the fact that each had an enthusiastic and supportive membership, there is no record that the Goodridges were among them. In York the family had supported the African Methodist Church and were longtime members of the Bethel Church of God, later leaving it for the New Jerusalem Church, which was founded on the teachings of Emanuel Swedenborg and popular at the time among free-thinking Americans. Only in later years, after Wallace's marriage in 1889, are there references to the new Mrs. Goodridge's (and more rarely to Wallace's) participation at events sponsored by Zion Baptist.[112]

Although African Americans were only a small segment of the total population, less than three hundred of almost nineteen thousand residents, race often became a key issue for them in the Saginaws during the first decade that the Goodridges lived there. Racial references to African Americans and even racially motivated action were common and at times could be quite subtle. In 1915 the *Michigan Manual of Freedmen's Progress,* looking back over the previous half century, concluded that in most "instances when the term 'Negro' is used in news matters, it refers to the criminal Negro and not to that vast bulk of black people who are making good and pursuing the even tenure of their way. . . . On the other hand, when many of the newspapers mention anything commendable about a black man, his racial character is not mentioned . . . therefore the effect and result has been a seemingly growing hostility to colored people." The East Saginaw newspapers were typical in this respect. When reporting the ar-

rest of James Watson of Saginaw City for "a quarrel" that he had in East Saginaw, Watson became "A Naughty Negro." Similarly, Frank Lawrence was characterized as "one of the negroes arrested for the larceny of the coat and money" when his case was reported.[113]

In general, African Americans and their organizations and institutions, such as the Amateur Dramatic Association, were regularly characterized as "colored." This was true for African American women whatever their status might be. Rhoda Goodridge, for example, was identified as "a colored widow." References to African American males, however, often were adjusted to suit their economic or social standing. A young male without any status, like Hall Quicksett, was "a colored boy in the employ of Messrs. Barnard & Blinder" who "met with an accident, by which he lost a portion of this third finger and injured the others, on his right." But "colored" was a term that was used only rarely in the newspapers to describe wealthy African Americans like William Atwood. And the Goodridge brothers, perhaps because they already were so well known throughout the valley, almost always were simply "The Goodridge Brothers," or "These well-known photographers," or "Goodridge Bros. Photographers."[114]

Still, an analysis of attitudes toward race in East Saginaw newspapers during the 1860s and 1870s has concluded that

the local press faithfully reports those items critical to the minority population. There is little opportunity for editorializing and the papers are devoid of blatant outcries against the freedmen or one sided accusations even in cases of black-white confrontations. There are subtle illustrations, however, that reveal the existence of the anticipated dual society of nineteenth century America. The fact that there was a Colored Debating Society, a Colored Amateur Dramatic Association, [and] a black organization called the Mental and Moral Improvement Society of East Saginaw give testimony, at least, to a psychological separateness between the races. In the periodicals, the attitude is apparent in the depiction of the *rare colored man* who has earned the general approval of the citizenry due to his exceptional talent.[115]

And in fact the Goodridges are an excellent example of this more subtle sort of racism. Although the Goodridge brothers invariably avoided any racial epithets, they could not escape completely their depiction as that *"rare colored man"* of "exceptional talent." A *Saginaw Daily Courier* description of the Goodridge entry in the 1871 Saginaw County Agricultural Society Fair, for example, noted that it was "a splendid display as regards both quantity and quality." The reporter then could not help but to add, as an afterthought, that "Their presence at the exhibition shows them to be men of enterprise, and speaks well for them."[116] No other entrants were so characterized.

Two events of great consequence to the Goodridge family during their first decade in East Saginaw also suggest that more substantive racially motivated action may have been directed against them. The fire that destroyed the Goodridge home the night of January 1, 1869, broke out while the entire family, and most of the African American community, had gathered to celebrate the anniversary of the Emancipation Proclamation. As the historian of Saginaw's African American community has concluded: "One can but speculate as to the origin of the disaster to the Goodridge family occurring on the day of the function. Whether disgruntled individuals sought to disrupt the event by destroying the possessions of the 'President of the evening, Mr. Goodrich,' or if carelessness was the cause of the fire cannot be determined. Local press coverage gives no overt indication of racial tension or conflicts that might have culminated in misfortune."[117]

There is no record of an investigation into the cause of the fire, nor do the newspaper accounts that described the evening's celebration, the fire, or the subsequent insurance settlement report on a possible origin for the fire. The absence of even any speculation as to cause in the extended accounts of the tragedy is noteworthy considering that coverage of other East Saginaw fires invariably reports the cause, when determined, and the course of those fires in great detail. For example, the accounts of the Crouse Block fire that destroyed the Goodridge studio three years later describe the cause and spread of that fire in minute detail. Ob-

viously, the 1872 fire, which destroyed an entire business block, including several professional and commercial establishments, and threatened to spread, if unchecked, through the very heart of the city, deserved the attention it received. But the timing of the Emancipation Day celebration fire, which the newspaper account itself commented upon, was also sufficiently coincidental to have prompted at least some public speculation as to its cause.[118]

A second event in which race prompted action was Wallace's 1871 trial for perjury. In his letter to the editor of the *Saginaw Daily Courier* in July 1871 Wallace wrote that both the allegation and the newspaper's report of it were motivated by his race. He correctly pointed out that the newspaper had not bothered to report that his accuser, H. L. Morehouse, had been arrested for extortion, and furthermore that the only published account of the "collection scheme" which had resulted in the accusation of perjury appeared only in Goodridge's own letter to the newspaper. Wallace also argued that it was his race that had prompted Morehouse to target him initially.[119] Furthermore, Morehouse's partner in the scheme was the lawyer D. W. Perkins, who had represented Deputy Sheriff Mower in the Goodridge suit over the seizure of the piano. Specific details that Morehouse had regarding Wallace's testimony in the case obviously had come from Perkins. Earlier Perkins had represented Glenalvin's widow, Rhoda Goodridge, in her unsuccessful suit against the Massachusetts Life Insurance Company. While there is no evidence that Wallace was involved substantively in that case, the Goodridges were a close-knit family and it is likely that Perkins had confidential information about the principals in the failed insurance scheme that enabled Morehouse to focus on Wallace. If Perkins and Morehouse did have such information, Wallace never acknowledged the fact. He did believe that their action against him, with or without such information, was based on his race and said so in his letter to the *Courier*.

In the decade between 1863 and 1872 both East Saginaw and the Goodridge brothers studio established there came of age. The beginnings of each had been modest. Fires, floods, and the misfortune of a postwar economy, even the untimely death of an eldest brother, had presented constant obstacles. Yet by 1872 the youthful resilience of the city and the brothers who had adopted it as their home was apparent. During the 1860s portrait photography, in all its various forms, established their reputation. That success provided the confidence to experiment with carte de visite series and panoramas, carte victoria landscapes, and the early stereo series, the "Saginaw Valley Views." Successful yet again, Wallace and William Goodridge settled on the stereo series as the means to ensure their continued good fortune and to document the development of their new home.

4

The Stereo Series: Prosperity and Professional Recognition, 1872–1890

ALEXIS DE TOCQUEVILLE'S 1831 VISION of the future for the Saginaw Valley was more than fulfilled during the decades after 1872. The rapid population growth that had begun by 1860 continued. In 1880 nearly sixty thousand residents made Saginaw County their home, with at least one of every three living in East Saginaw. The annual growth rate would have slowed somewhat by the 1890 census, which counted a population of little more than eighty-two thousand in the county and forty-six thousand in the recently united cities of East Saginaw and Saginaw City. Consolidation of the two had been mandated by the state legislature on June 28, 1889, in an attempt to end decades of costly competition and useless duplication by the adjacent communities.[1] Success for the union, however, remained in the future.

Although the rate of growth had slowed somewhat by 1890, Saginaw's total population still was nearly seven times greater than it had been only thirty years earlier. A continuing influx of immigrants and a healthy birthrate fueled the growth. According to the 1890 census, for example, approximately 40 percent of Saginaw's population was immigrants, with the greatest numbers coming from Canada (42 percent) and Germany (39 percent). Average family size in 1880 is estimated to have been almost five persons.[2]

This rapid growth, as well as its recent slowing, was tied closely to the fortunes of the pine lumber industry in the valley. The boom years were 1870 to 1890. Flanked by relatively brief but bitter depressions that began in 1873 and 1884, 1882 was the peak year of production, when over one

billion board feet of pine lumber and almost 300 million shingles were cut by more than eighty mills along the Saginaw River. By 1890 the annual cut had been reduced to little more than 700 million board feet, and in 1896 it plunged to 316 million, less than in 1866. The pine was gone. In 1900 fewer than forty mills remained along the entire Saginaw River, and they, like the timber they had cut, soon disappeared.[3]

During the decades of peak production, however, the pine lumber boom had transformed both East Saginaw and Saginaw City. Before the end of the century, as figures 4.1a and b clearly demonstrate, East Saginaw's main intersection, Genesee and Washington, no longer was crossed by muddy ruts, outlined with wooden sidewalks, or surrounded by buildings with false-fronted second stories (see figure 3.1). Jesse Hoyt, as promised, had replaced the Crouse Block with an imposing structure, the Bancroft House continued to be the area's most celebrated hostelry, and solid three- and four-story business blocks and fashionable residences now lined Washington Avenue. By 1890 the consolidated cities could boast of 12 banks, 82 physicians, 57 real estate agents, 25 tailors, 5 decorators, 11 wallpaper shops, 183 grocers, 6 pawnbrokers, 56 hotels in addition to the Bancroft, 35 insurance agents representing 9 accident, 13 life, and 107 different fire insurance companies, a detective agency, 11 newspapers, 2 electricians, and an incredible 215 saloons. City directories rarely listed all residents and businesses, yet in 1872 the same communities had counted only 5 banks, 19 grocers, 3 insurance agents, 16 hotels, 5 newspa-

Figure 4.1a. "Northeast Corner Genesee and Washington," ca. 1885, copy from glass negative, 7⁷⁄₁₆ x 3⁷⁄₁₆ inches. Goodridge Brothers Studio, East Saginaw, Mich. Collection of Beffrey Family.

Figure 4.1b. "Washington Avenue, Saginaw, Mich.," 1906–7, Detroit Publishing Company Postcard No. 11914, 3¼ x 5¼ inches. Negative by Goodridge Brothers Studio, Saginaw, Mich. Collection of John V. Jezierski.

pers, 1 real estate agent, and only 100 saloons between them.[4] Their riverine location had made Saginaw Valley residents reluctant to invest in railroads—as late as 1886 Mills reports that 414 steamers and 1,088 other vessels docked at Saginaw River ports—but by 1890 eight different railroad companies, including the first, the Flint & Pere Marquette, and the most recent, the Cincinnati, Saginaw & Mackinaw, served the city's transportation needs. Property, both public and private, was protected by a force of 46 police officers and patrolmen, up from East Saginaw's 17 in 1873, and, after 1874, by a professional fire department operating from hosehouses located strategically throughout the two cities.[5] Growth and progress were everywhere evident.

Lumber boom prosperity and its accompanying growth provided a ready market for the tintype, carte de visite, and cabinet portraits that

Saginaw photographers continued to turn out in the thousands. The volatility of a local economy based on the prospects of a single commodity like pine lumber, however, made competition among the valley's photographers during the 1870s and 1880s even more intense. For example, during 1883, a depressed year for the lumber trade, Duncan J. McIntyre, known for slashing his prices, initiated a price war in the local newspapers by offering cabinet portraits for $3.00 per dozen. Most Saginaw studios—including the Goodridge brothers, who found it necessary to advertise only rarely during the 1880s—were forced to respond. In April 1883 the *Saginaw Evening Express* noted that "If you want any photographs prepare to get them now. There is a war among the artists. Like the railroads they are cutting prices. One of them put down the price of cabinet photos to $3 per dozen and this is followed by Angell and Beals with a reduction to $2.50 per dozen." As late as October the following year the *Saginaw Evening*

Figure 4.2a. "Verso of Carte de Visite Mount," 1870–74, 4⁷⁄₁₆ x 2½ inches. William A. Armstrong, Saginaw City, Mich. Collection of John V. Jezierski

News observed that the continuing price war made it "likely people can get pictures for almost nothing." By the time competing advertisements ended their newspaper runs in December 1884, C. W. Burdick, whose studio had opened only a few months earlier, had reduced prices to $2.00 for a dozen cabinet portraits.[6]

During the 1880s revolutionary changes in lens and camera design, as well as the introduction of gelatin-based film—all combined in George Eastman's Kodak, introduced in 1888—transformed photography forever. Henceforth Eastman's simple technology allowed ever-growing numbers of amateurs to make their own "snapshots." The era of inexpensive tintype, carte de visite, and cabinet portraits ended abruptly as photo studios hurried to adjust, not all successfully, to this technological revolution. William von Glazer, "A first-class Scientific Photographer," was among the first and certainly not the last Saginaw photographer to adapt by offering "instructions to amateurs in all branches of this art, from plain to the Most Artistic Photography."[7]

Intense competition and increasingly rapid change took a heavy toll on Saginaw's professional photographers. In 1872 five studios, including the Goodridge brothers, operated in East Saginaw and Saginaw City. During 1874, however, William A. Armstrong left Saginaw City to establish what soon became a successful studio in Chicago. For a time Mrs. Armstrong, herself a successful photographer and artist, maintained the studio, but by 1877 she had left to join her husband in Chicago (see figures 4.2a–c for examples of the Armstrongs' work). During 1875 both James T. Randall and William Roberts, who had opened their studios as early as 1860 and 1864, respectively, in East Saginaw, retired. Of

Figure 4.2b. "Mrs. William A. Armstrong." [William A. Armstrong?], Saginaw City, Mich. Mills, *History of Saginaw County,* 1:386.

Figure 4.2c. "Taylor House Hotel," 1865–74, carte de visite. Albumen image, 3⅜ x 2³⁄₁₆ inches, ivory bristol board mount with gold trim, 3¹⁵⁄₁₆ x 2⁷⁄₁₆ inches. William A. Armstrong, Saginaw City, Mich. Eddy Local History and Genealogical Collection, Hoyt Public Library.

these original Goodridge contemporaries, there-fore, only Daniel Angell, Jr., lasted through the 1880s, retiring in 1889. By 1890, however, the Goodridge studio would have been joined by nine new establishments. But of those nine, four—Beekmann, Cornish, Glover, and Pausch—would have opened their doors only in 1890. Among the others, Krupp and Dolmage had begun in 1889, Lyon in 1887, Crouch in 1883, and only McIntyre went back as far as 1881. Furthermore, between the five original studios that were operating in 1872 and the nine newcomers in 1890, at least twenty-four other photography establishments would have opened and closed their shutters in East Saginaw and Saginaw City. Most, like Fred Billings and William F. Kidney, lasted only a year or two, while others—Dan W. Smith and John T. Butterworth, for example—were in business for a decade or more. By 1890, remarkably, of the many Saginaw studios that had been established either before or after 1872, it was only the Goodridge brothers' that remained. See figures 4.3a–d for fine examples of the work of two long-term Goodridge contemporaries from this period.[8]

——◆——

The 1872 fire that destroyed the Goodridge brothers' Crouse Block studio was both a disaster and an opportunity to begin anew. In a symbolic and also a real sense, the fire broke the final links that remained for Wallace and William with their brother Glenalvin and the origins of the studio in York. News reports of the fire noted that the Goodridges were able to save only five cameras and some instruments, "losing everything else" and "nearly all their worldly possessions."[9] Obviously, their entire inventory of negatives and supplies as well as backdrops and props would have to be re-placed and rebuilt. In making these necessary de-cisions about their future, Wallace and William not only had to choose new equipment but also final-ly decided to abandon both daguerreotypes and ambrotypes. Although these early forms of photo-graph were less popular each year, they had served to maintain the studio's continuity with Glenalvin

and the past, and the decision was a difficult one. Furthermore, although they continued to make tintype portraits, paper cartes and cabinets now were much more popular. Most important was their decision to commit substantial effort and re-sources to new stereo series and ultimately larger-format photographs that might be successful in a regional or even national market. Building the new studio, therefore, forced Wallace and William to face their future without too many connections to the past.

Within days of the fire, the *Saginaw Daily Courier* announced that the Goodridge brothers had occupied temporary quarters and "will be in business again on Washington Street, in the early part of the coming week."[10] Exactly where "on Washington Street" this temporary studio was lo-cated or for how many days, weeks, or months the brothers occupied it is not known. No extant ad-vertisement or photograph specifies its location. No Goodridge family member or friend is listed in the 1872 East Saginaw directory as living or work-ing along Washington. And it is unlikely that the Goodridge studio moved in, even on a temporary basis, with any of its competitors. For a time, then, the brothers likely rented rooms in one of any number of available business blocks on Washing-ton until work on their new and permanent studio building had been completed.

In November 1872 the *Courier* reported that on Saturday the ninth "the foundation for the new photograph gallery of Goodridge Bro's . . . was laid." The future studio was to be built of brick, be fifteen by sixty-six feet, and one story, as figure 4.4 makes clear, so that "all work will be done on the ground floor, thus affording them the advantage of a north side, as well as sky light."[11] The site was in the middle of the east side of the 200 block of South Washington between German (later Franklin) and William Streets. Little more than a block south of the city center (Genesee and Wash-ington), the location was an excellent choice. The studio was in the same block as Charles Lee's orig-inal Academy of Music and directly opposite the very popular Smith's Opera House. In addition to the pedestrian traffic that the Academy and Opera

Figure 4.3a. "Verso of Photograph Mount," 1871–80, 4 x 8¼ inches. Daniel Angell, Jr., East Saginaw, Mich. Collection of John V. Jezierski.

Figure 4.3b. "Unidentified Woman," 1871–80. Albumen image, 3¾ x 7⅜, ivory bristol board mount with gold trim, 4 x 8¼ inches. Daniel Angell, Jr., East Saginaw, Mich. Collection of John V. Jezierski

Figure 4.3c. "Unidentified Boy," 1879–89, carte de visite. Albumen image, 2⅜ x 4 inches, beige bristol board mount, 2½ x 4⅛ inches. Dan W. Smith, Saginaw City, Mich. Collection of John V. Jezierski.

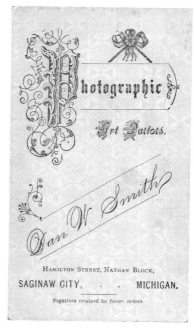

Figure 4.3d. "Verso of Carte de Visite Mount," 1879–89, 2½ x 4⅛ inches. Dan W. Smith, Saginaw City, Mich. Collection of John V. Jezierski.

Figure 4.4. "Goodridge Brothers Studio, 221 South Washington," 1873–83, copy of original, 5 x 6¼ inches. Goodridge Brothers Studio, East Saginaw, Mich. Eddy Local History and Genealogical Collection, Hoyt Public Library.

House attracted, passengers on the East Saginaw and Saline Street Railway also passed by the studio on their way up and down Washington. Furthermore, the studio was located along the axis of the city's future development. In 1873 East Saginaw annexed Salina, and South Washington became the artery that joined the two. When the new Academy of Music opened in 1884 on the southeast corner of Washington and William Streets, it was only a few steps from the Goodridge front door. Continued growth along South Washington kept the Goodridge studio in the center of things at least through the end of the century.

Although the *Courier* notice reporting the start of studio construction implied that the structure soon would be completed, the exact date that Wallace and William first occupied their new studio is not known. The site (specifically, the center one-third or twenty feet of the sixty feet of Lot 3 in Block 33 of Hoyt's original Plat of East Saginaw) did not officially become Goodridge property until April 20, 1874, when they purchased it for $2,000 from Mrs. Eliza Allison of Buena Vista. Following the original survey of the plat in 1850, the entire lot was sold for $1 to Daniel C. Curtis, who almost immediately resold it for $500 to William and Rhoda Brach. The property changed hands several times through the 1860s with its value ever increasing, reflecting East Saginaw's rapid growth at the time, until it was purchased by Clarence W. White of East Saginaw in 1868. Shortly before 1874 White subdivided the sixty-foot lot into three twenty-foot sections. White sold the center section to Eliza Allison for $2,000 on April 1, 1874, and she, in turn, sold it for the exact same amount to Wallace and William Goodridge less than three weeks later. The brothers had paid $500 as down payment or as part of an earlier land contract, and Mrs. Allison granted them a $1,500 mortgage. By August 1880 this initial mortgage would have been paid in full. Before his death in 1922, however, Wallace would again mortgage the property at least

Figure 4.5. "Goodridge Brothers Studio, 218–220 South Washington," 1884, copy of original stereograph, 7¹¹⁄₁₆ x 4¹¹⁄₁₆ inches. Goodridge Brothers Studio, East Saginaw, Mich. Historical Society of Saginaw County, Inc.

five times, perhaps reflecting the vagaries of his own and the studio's financial condition. In September 1874, less than six months after purchasing the property, Wallace and William mortgaged it a second time, now for $1,100, to their sister-in-law and Glenalvin's widow, Rhoda C. Goodridge. The mortgage was repaid by July 1880 when Rhoda had become Mrs. Rhoda C. Nicholas of Grand Rapids, Michigan.[12]

Construction of the studio, which began in November 1872, probably was not completed until the spring of 1874 when the Goodridges finally purchased the lot from Mrs. Allison. Whether they had leased the site earlier, had purchased it on a land contract, or were able to begin construction without owning the property is not known. Furthermore, the second mortgage from sister-in-law Rhoda suggests that the brothers may have needed capital to outfit the new facility. In any case, the transition from their original Crouse Block studio to the new South Washington location may have lasted up to eighteen months but was completed by early summer 1874.

From completion until 1887, although the studio continued to occupy its original location, the address changed three times. Until 1881–82 it was identified as 221 and 221–223 South Wash-

ington Avenue. In 1883 the address was changed to 218–220 South Washington, which it remained until 1887. That year it became 220 South Washington, which is the present address of the site.[13] Inconsistent street numbering, including even- and odd- numbered addresses on the same side of the street, was common in rapidly expanding nineteenth-century communities like East Saginaw. The system was standardized with consolidation in 1889.

The changes in address, to some extent, also correspond to the evolution of the physical structure that was the Goodridge brothers' studio. The original fifteen- by sixty-six-foot studio building, numbered 221 South Washington, was a freestanding structure with the family's residence adjoining along the south wall (see figure 4.4). Both Wallace and William listed 221 South Washington as their residential address until 1881. During 1881 and 1882 both then resided at 223 South Washington, most likely a separate address for the residence adjoining the studio building. By the summer of 1880 the original mortgages on this phase of the studio's development had been paid in full. Shortly thereafter, however, an October 22, 1881, report in the *Saginaw Evening Express* noted that the "Goodridge Bros. are enlarging their gallery and finishing it up in a style to surpass any other . . . in the state of Michigan."[14] A new mortgage, this one for $1,000, was taken out on the property in May 1882 to pay for the expansion. Figure 4.5 shows the enlarged gallery, probably in the spring of 1884. The newly expanded Academy of Music, whose advertisements appear on the billboards to the left of the studio, had reopened only in December 1884. And during the same year, the fire department also had acquired horse-drawn hose carts like the one in the photograph. Notice Wallace standing in the studio doorway behind the driver of the hose cart. The expanded studio, now 218 and 220 South Washington, continued to include the family residence. Both Wallace and William would list 220 South Washington as their home address until 1890. Notice that the edge of the roof of the family residence is visible along the right side of the studio addition. Shortly after this photograph (figure 4.5) was made, the original studio reception room was moved into the new and larger addition. For a time, 1887 to 1890, the front of 218 South Washington was taken over by Madame Mary A. Nichols, the Goodridge brothers' sister, who operated a hairdressing and manicure salon. The mortgage which financed this addition was paid off in November 1889. By the following spring the *Detroit Plain Dealer* reported yet another expansion when it noted that the "Goodridge Bro's will break ground for their new store building next week."[15] In spite of William's untimely death only weeks later, on August 18, 1890, Wallace completed this final phase of the studio's physical development within the next year. Figure 4.6 shows a dapper Wallace standing in the doorway of the studio at 220 South Washington with its totally reconstructed and very elaborate facade several years later, most likely about 1910. The peak of the roof of the original family residence remains visible behind and to the left of the building front bearing the name "GOODRIDGE BROS." The original studio building at 218 South Washington, much reduced in size, had either been converted into or replaced by a rental property occupied by a "24 HR SANDWICH CAFE." A mortgage for $1,300, paid off in 1908, had financed this final phase of expansion and reconstruction.

Figure 4.6. "Goodridge Brothers Studio, 220 South Washington," 1910, enlarged from original postcard. Goodridge Brothers Studio, Saginaw Mich. Hurley Family Collection.

As figures 4.4 and 4.5 make very clear, the availability of natural light, especially from the north or northwest, was particularly important in studio design through the 1880s. The large windows across the front of both studios and the single-story, freestanding construction of the building itself, allowing for large and effective sky- or roof lighting, provided as much natural illumination as possible. By the 1890s, however, the development of efficient artificial light sources eliminated the need for skylights at the very time that studios like the Goodridge brothers' (see figure 4.6) came to be overshadowed by multistoried neighbors.

The Goodridges' 1872 design for their new facility not only made best advantage of the available natural light but also was modeled, according to the *Courier* reporter, "after Sarony [of] N.Y.," which allowed the brothers to "claim great advantage over all operators [photographers] in the valley."[16] Precisely what, if anything at all, was meant by "after Sarony" is not clear. Napoleon Sarony was the most celebrated portrait photographer of the day, and in

Figure 4.7a. "Little Bo Peep," 1873–90, cabinet card. Albumen image, 4⅛ x 6⅛ inches, beige bristol board mount, 4¼ x 6½ inches. Goodridge Brothers Studio, East Saginaw, Mich. Clarke Historical Library, Central Michigan University.

Figure 4.7b. "Six Unidentified Women and Parasol," 1887–90, cabinet card. Albumen image, 4⅛ x 5⅞ inches, beige bristol board mount, 4¼ x 6⅝ inches. Goodridge Brothers Studio, East Saginaw, Mich. Clarke Historical Library, Central Michigan University.

their advertisements many provincial imitators claimed to emulate his style. Sarony reportedly never objected. According to his biographer, "Sarony's contemporaries thought of him as 'the father of artistic photography in America.' 'It was he,' one of his admirers wrote, 'who took our beloved science out of the rut and placed it on the pedestal of art.'" The widespread fame of Sarony's technique was based on the fact that he had "introduced painted backgrounds and interesting accessories into his pictures and, more importantly, photographed a new and exciting variety of poses, gestures and impressions at a time when most portrait photography in America tended toward a dull and lifeless sameness." As his friend and competitor Benjamin J. Falk concluded, "More than all others, he [Sarony] had the great gift of seizing what was characteristic and picturesque in his subjects with the quick intuition belonging to the successful photographer, and of making these features predominant in his pictures."[17]

During the 1870s the Goodridges had regularly utilized Sarony's "posing apparatus" (see figures 3.7a–b), so we might conclude that his portrait technique also became the model for the new studio, as the brothers claimed. Figure 4.7a makes abundantly clear, however, that the consequences of adopting a mentor's technique were not always positive. The inappropriate props and costume result not only in a pose that is obviously artificial but also in an atmosphere that even for an 1870s portrait is clearly contrived. A similar setting, but with more effective use of accessories and dramatic posing, as in figure 4.7b, could, on the other hand, capture what was most "characteristic and picturesque" in the subject, as Sarony so often did and which the Goodridges successfully demonstrate in this portrait.

The necessity of replacing props and backdrops lost in the 1872 fire, as well as the desire to duplicate some of Sarony's celebrated technique, also led Wallace and William to create what be-

Figure 4.8a. "Three Unidentified Women and Rustic Steps," 1873–84, tintype, 2½ x 3½ inches. Goodridge Brothers Studio, East Saginaw, Mich. Collection of John V. Jezierski.

Figure 4.8b. "Unidentified Man and Rustic Steps," 1873–84, cabinet card. Albumen image, 4⅟₁₆ x 5¹¹⁄₁₆ inches, ivory bristol board mount with gold trim, 4¼ x 6½ inches. Goodridge Brothers Studio, East Saginaw, Mich. Collection of John V. Jezierski.

came their most distinctive studio accessory. Figures 4.8a and b present their subjects posed on a set of rustic steps. From 1872 to 1890 these steps served as the brothers' favorite prop for individual and group portraits. No other Saginaw Valley studio, at least as revealed by the extant photographs, used such or even a similar device. And while Darrah notes that "Artificial rustic fences, gates and doorways . . . became standard studio equipment in the 1870s," he includes in his catalogue only a single example of a prop similar to the Goodridge steps—a rustic wooden fence used by the Hughes Brothers studio of Blanchard, Iowa, during the 1880s.[18] The stairs, interestingly, were not only an effective means of posing and organizing subjects, even after reduced film exposure times made such posing apparatuses unnecessary during the 1880s, but at the same time they also became the rustic emblem of a studio that had come of age in the midst of Michigan's white pine forests.

❖

In their new and expanded studio, the Goodridge brothers continued their already successful portrait business and also increased dra-

matically the number and scope of the stereo series they had tested earlier. In addition, they undertook several important private, corporate, and public commissions for larger-format photographs. Although something of a division of labor between Wallace and William is evident before 1872, with the new studio each took on responsibility for specific elements of its operation. Wallace, the senior partner, managed the studio's day-to-day business and conducted portrait sittings. William, with less of a head for business but a growing reputation as an artist, focused his talent on the stereo series and special commissions. An 1887 account of the studio's success in the *Cleveland Gazette* noted as much when it reported that "Besides the portraits they do an extensive view business, keeping a man taking views all the time, Wallace L. has charge of the portrait and William O. the view department."[19]

Figure 4.9a. "Three Isabella County 'Shanty Boys,'" 1878–81, paper-covered tintype, 1¹³⁄₁₆ x 3 inches. J. H. Freeney, Mt. Pleasant, Mich. Collection of Dave Tinder.

Figure 4.9b. "Verso of Tintype Paper Cover," 1878–81, 2⁷⁄₁₆ x 3¹⁵⁄₁₆ inches. J. H. Freeney, Mt. Pleasant, Mich. Collection of Dave Tinder.

The new studio and the business it generated also required that the brothers employ a staff which included studio technicians and an occasional assistant or associate photographer. The absence of any Goodridge business records makes it impossible to determine the exact size or composition of the staff in any given year. Yet there is evidence that between 1872 and 1890 the Goodridges employed family members and local residents in the studio and that Wallace and William had hired as assistants several young men who were seeking to become successful professionals like themselves.

John H. Freeney of Camden, New Jersey, was probably the first and ultimately the most successful of the Goodridge protégés. Freeney was a young African American who had migrated to Michigan in 1868 and was employed as a barber in Clare the same year. Before 1872 he would have moved to East Saginaw, where he came to work in the Goodridge studio. Exactly for how long and in what capacity Freeney was with Wallace and William is not known, but as late as 1875 he still was listed as a photographer and barber in East

Saginaw. He may have joined the Goodridges during their final months in the Crouse Block studio and then stayed on through the transition to South Washington. By 1876, however, he had established his own barbershop on Main Street in Mount Pleasant, and then two years later he added a photography studio. One of the few extant photographs bearing Freeney's name is a paper-framed tintype of three young Isabella County shanty boys imprinted "J. H. FREENEY, Photographer, Main Street, Mt. Pleasant, Mich." (see figures 4.9a–b). Whether Freeney was successful as a photographer is not known, but by 1882 he had joined the ranks of Michigan's timber entrepreneurs. He reportedly owned a mill sawing eight million shingles that year and had invested in substantial tracts of pinelands. His biography in the *Michigan Manual of Freedmen's Progress* noted that Freeney at one time also had "three lumber camps, ten teams, four yoke of oxen and 100 men employed." He is remembered as the "founder and sole owner of the village of Wise [now Loomis] containing about 400 inhabitants and located on a branch of railroad running from East Saginaw to Mt. Pleasant, with two daily mails and a flourishing condition." The *Cleveland Gazette* reported that Freeney also owned "large real estate possessions in East Saginaw," including a shingle mill, a salt block, and a charcoal-manufacturing facility. He lived at 2414 South Washington until 1889, after which there is no record of his activity. Freeney maintained his

Figure 4.10. "Wallace L. Goodridge, James H. Morris, Arthur W. Brown, William O. Goodridge," 1883, cabinet card. Albumen image, 4⁷⁄₁₆ x 5½, beige bristol board mount, 4⁷⁄₁₆ x 6⁵⁄₁₆ inches. Goodridge Brothers Studio, East Saginaw, Mich. Collection of Beverly S. Osborne Pearson.

connection to the Goodridge family after leaving the studio by employing Maurice Nicholas, a Goodridge nephew, as "his right bower . . . who acts in the capacity of chief bookkeeper."[20]

Freeney was not the only young African American photographer who worked for a time with the Goodridge brothers. The 1880 census recorded that two young men also boarded with the Goodridge family that year and were employed in the studio as assistants. Little is known of the

first, James H. Morris, other than that he was a single, twenty-one-year-old mulatto who was born in Ohio and that his parents were from Virginia. However, as figure 4.10, an extraordinary portrait of the Goodridges and their studio staff made in or shortly before 1883, confirms, Morris, who is standing behind and to the left of Wallace, served as the latter's assistant "operator." With his left arm resting casually on the retouching stand and a pencil in hand, Morris proclaims his expertise in sup-

Figure 4.11a. "Champion Loads," 1888–95, copy of original, 6⅜ x 3⅞ inches. Arthur W. Brown, Gaylord, Mich. Collection of Otsego County Historical Museum.

Figure 4.11b. "Banking Ground," 1888–95, copy of original, 6⅜ x 3⅞ inches. Arthur W. Brown, Gaylord, Mich. Collection of Otsego County Historical Museum.

port of Wallace's portrait photography. Opposite, his colleague and counterpart, Arthur William Brown, behind and a bit to William's right, with hand on his hip but elbow resting possessively on the stereo camera, defines his position as "Asst. View Photographer." Brown also was a single, twenty-one-year-old mulatto but had been born in Canada to a father from Delaware and a mother who was an Irish immigrant. He assisted William in the field until 1882, but left during that year to establish his own studio in Clare. The Clare venture apparently failed, for Brown returned to East Saginaw by late 1883 and then worked with William until at least 1887. He left once again in 1888 and this time opened a studio to the north in

Gaylord that remained successful until 1895. There Brown not only made the usual studio portraits but, with Gaylord as his base, traveled throughout Otsego County documenting the peak years of that area's participation in Michigan's pine lumber boom. As figures 4.11a and b demonstrate, Brown had been one of the Goodridges' most talented assistants. There is no evidence, however, that Brown's Otsego County lumber photographs were made into stereo views, were published by the Goodridge studio under their label, or, unfortunately, ever reached more than a local audience. During 1896–97 Brown moved to Marshall, Michigan, where he operated a studio in partnership with John H. Schultz.[21]

According to a published account of the studio's operations in 1887, the brothers also gave "employment to a number of [other] skilled hands," but little is known of their origin or tenure in the studio. For example, a William Edwards, who may have had a studio at 350 North Gay Street in Baltimore in 1878, was employed by the Goodridges as a photographer in 1886. And in 1890, shortly before William's death, the *Detroit Plain Dealer* reported that "George W. Watson, of Clio, will learn photography under [the] Goodridge Bro's." Whether Watson completed his training and began a career is not known. From time to time Wallace and William also included younger family members as assistants in the studio. During 1877 Joseph H. Gray, a relative of Goodridge brother-in-law Ralph Toyer Grey of Minneapolis (sister Emily's husband) was employed by the Goodridges as their "general agent for Michigan." Most likely Gray marketed Goodridge stereo series statewide. According to his biography, Gray was born in Minneapolis in 1859, educated in York, Pennsylvania, from the time he was six years old, and came out to Michigan fresh from school in 1877. After a year with Wallace and William he worked as a sports reporter in Mt. Pleasant, Michigan, for the *Philadelphia Record,* and then as a ticket agent both for the East Saginaw Trotting Association and a local baseball club, either the Uniques or the Continentals, who played in East Saginaw at the time. In that capacity Gray claimed the title of "Lightning Ticket Seller," having sold 2,347 tickets in only one hour. In 1884 he was appointed treasurer of the new Academy of Music, becoming its assistant manager in 1886. On May 14, 1882, he had married Miss Nellie McGee. Gray ended his career in East Saginaw as a letter carrier for the Saginaw Post Office (see figure 4.12 for his portrait at that time). Between 1884 and 1891 Wallace and William also employed their nephew Glen J. Goodridge in the studio. Glen was Glenalvin and Rhoda's son and had come west with the family in 1863. Twenty-four years old in 1884, Glen apparently had not inherited his father's talent for or interest in photography. Although he worked with his uncles for seven years,

Figure 4.12. "Joseph H. Gray," 1877–84,[cabinet card?] copy of original. [Goodridge Bothers Studio, East Saginaw, Mich.?] 1896 Saginaw County Atlas.

in 1891 he returned to York, where he opened once again a Goodridge barbershop and not a photography studio.[22]

Under Wallace's close supervision, the Goodridge studio, from its new location in the 200 block of South Washington, continued its decades-long tradition of the highest-quality portrait photography. After 1872 Wallace no longer made daguerreotype and ambrotype portraits, for which the studio earlier had been so well known. Tintypes, however, continued to be a popular option with customers almost to the end of the century. Figure 4.13a is a very straightforward but especially sensitive tintype portrait of a young bride made shortly after 1872. The pose is designed to highlight the contrast between a solid and sensible gown and the much more delicate lace collar and dainty flowers that frame her ample features. Notice, as well, that the right hand, not the left, bears the wedding ring and is positioned on the chair

Figure 4.13a. "Bridal Portrait," 1873–80, paper-covered tintype, 2⅛ x 3½ inches. Goodridge Brothers Studio, East Saginaw, Mich. Collection of John V. Jezierski.

Figure 4.13b. "Woman and Rustic Steps," 1880s, tintype, 2⅜ x 3½ inches. Goodridge Brothers Studio, East Saginaw, Mich. Collection of John V. Jezierski.

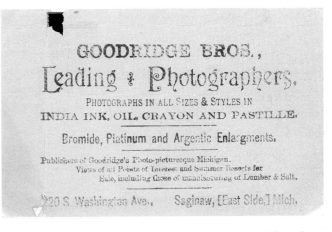

Figure 4.14b. "Verso of Tintype Paper Cover," blue ink stamp, 3⅛ x 5 inches. Goodridge Brothers Studio, Saginaw, Mich. Collection of John V. Jezierski.

Figure 4.14a. "Three Women, Umbrella, and Rustic Steps," 1889–90, paper-covered tintype, 2⅜ x 3⅜ inches. Goodridge Brothers Studio, Saginaw, Mich. Collection of John V. Jezierski.

back so that the ring, slightly touched with gold, is clearly visible. According to the verso of the paper case, the photograph was made at the Goodridges' "New Ground Floor Establishment, Washington Ave., East Saginaw, Mich." This may have been the temporary studio that the brothers occupied immediately after the Crouse Block fire but before construction of the studio in the 200 block of South Washington was completed.

Like the bride in figure 4.13a, the subject of figure 4.13b appears also to have chosen a tintype portrait for its aura of substance and stability. Her firm grip on the rail of the rustic steps and proximity to the massive pillar at her left anchor this subject solidly to the studio floor. The sense of stability she seeks is enhanced by the contrast between the light background and the dark shape of her body. Her drop-earrings, the tight curls of her coiffed hairdo, and the ruffled hat provide just the right finishing touch. The style of both dress and hat indicate that this portrait may have been made in the mid- to late 1880s.[23] Figures 4.14a and b suggest that an occasional tintype was made as late as 1889 or 1890, by which time the folding paper case itself was something of a marketing novelty. The fun that the subjects are having also makes the tintype very much of a frivolous and not a formal experience—photography had lost its mystery by that time. The address on the verso (figure 4.14b), listing the studio at "220 S. Washington Ave., Saginaw East Side, Mich.," suggests that this tintype was made during or near to 1889 when the names of East Saginaw and Saginaw City disappeared into that of the consolidated "Saginaw."

Throughout the 1870s and 1880s, carte de visite portraits also continued to maintain their popularity in East Saginaw. Darrah, in fact, describes this era in the evolution of the carte de visite as one of "routine studio portraiture, practiced from 1865 to about 1905, with steadily diminishing use of the . . . format after 1880 until 1905, thereafter rarely to 1915, [and] very rarely to 1925."[24] Many Goodridge customers (see figure 4.15a) continued to believe that the most simple and direct pose, enhanced by carefully directed "Rembrandt" lighting, produced the best carte por-

trait. Others, however (as in figure 4.15b), relied upon the addition of a sometimes distracting array of backdrop and props for not always positive results. Darrah notes that a wide variety of such studio accessories—"Potted plants, vases, cut flowers, books on a table, straw or buffalo skins on the floor . . . became standard studio equipment in the 1870s. . . . Whether one reacts favorably or abhorrently, is amused or disturbed," he concluded, "the fact remains: portraits made with these accessories were admired by those who produced them and those who purchased them."[25] After 1876 Wallace also made some of the studio's best portraits of children and infants.[26] Figures 4.15c–d demonstrate the intriguing results of combining the most up-to-date photographic technology and Wallace's ever-improving portrait technique. By 1879, through the use of dry-plate film and electronic lighting, which the Saginaw Morning Herald reported was being used in East Saginaw, it had become possible to reduce exposure time to at most a few seconds.[27] Wallace obviously used those seconds most effectively in creating these charming portraits.

From their earliest days in the Crouse Block studio, the Goodridges, like many of their Saginaw Valley colleagues, had advertised postmortem photography (see figure 4.16a). Glenalvin had made at least one postmortem daguerreotype in York before 1850 (see figure 2.6). During the nineteenth and early twentieth centuries such photographs "were a common aspect of American culture, a part of the mourning and memorializing process," writes Dr. Stanley B. Burns. "Surviving families were proud of these images and hung them in their homes, sent copies to friends and relatives, wore them as lockets or carried them as pocket mirrors. Nineteenth-century Americans knew how to respond to these images. Today," Burns concludes, "there is no culturally normative response to postmortem photographs."[28] "Mourning cartes," as Darrah describes them, were of many types, from obituary notices to photographs of family burial plots.[29] Most common, however, were portraits of the deceased such as figure 4.16b. This unique example of the genre, made by the Goodridge broth-

Figure 4.15a. "Unidentified Young Man," 1883–87, carte de visite. Albumen image, 2¼ x 3⁹⁄₁₆ inches, black bristol board mount, 2½ x 4⁷⁄₁₆ inches. Goodridge Brothers Studio, East Saginaw, Mich. Historical Society of Saginaw County, Inc.

Figure 4.15b. "Unidentified Woman," 1883–87, carte de visite. Albumen image, 2⁵⁄₁₆ x 3¾ inches, black bristol board mount, 2⁷⁄₁₆ x 4⁷⁄₁₆ inches. Goodridge Brothers Studio, East Saginaw, Mich. Collection of Dave Tinder.

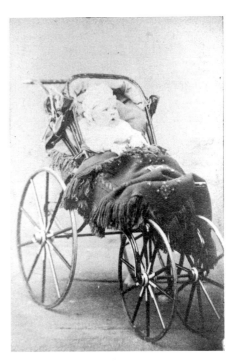

Figure 4.15c. "Girl with Doll," 1883–87, copy of original. Goodridge Brothers Studio, East Saginaw, Mich. Historical Society of Saginaw County, Inc.

Figure 4.15d. "Baby in Buggy," 1880s, copy of original. Goodridge Brothers Studio, East Saginaw, Mich. Historical Society of Saginaw County, Inc.

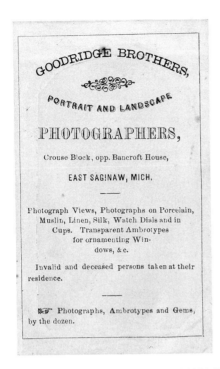

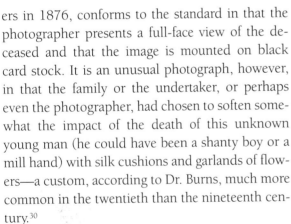

Figure 4.16a. "Verso of Tintype Paper Cover," 1864–72, 2⅜ x 3⅛ inches. Goodridge Brothers Studio, East Saginaw, Mich. Collection of Dave Tinder.

Figure 4.16b. "Male Postmortem," 1876–87, carte de visite. Albumen image, 2³⁄₁₆ x 3⁷⁄₁₆ inches, black bristol board mount, 2½ x 4³⁄₁₆ inches. Goodridge Brothers Studio, East Saginaw, Mich. Collection of John V. Jezierski.

ers in 1876, conforms to the standard in that the photographer presents a full-face view of the deceased and that the image is mounted on black card stock. It is an unusual photograph, however, in that the family or the undertaker, or perhaps even the photographer, had chosen to soften somewhat the impact of the death of this unknown young man (he could have been a shanty boy or a mill hand) with silk cushions and garlands of flowers—a custom, according to Dr. Burns, much more common in the twentieth than the nineteenth century.[30]

Unlike their 1860s counterparts, the Goodridges' later carte de visite mounts provide little direct information about the studio and its development. Figures 4.17a and b make clear that Wallace and William, at least through the 1870s, continued their membership in the National Photographic Association and that the South Washington address did indeed change from 221 to 218 and 220. Other than that there is little variation in post-1872 carte de visite imprints. The absence of

significant change in the Goodridge carte imprint after 1872, however, is important for two reasons. First, it implies that during the 1870s and 1880s the studio had reached a reasonable level of stability in its development. In fact, the combination of gothic and block-style letters used in the name and the three-word title, "Goodridge Bros. PHOTGRAPHERS" (see 4.17b), had become the studio's emblem or trademark and was used regularly on its various types of photographs between 1872 and 1890. Second, as Darrah suggests, there is a definite correlation between the popularity of the carte de visite and the rate at which photographers changed their imprints on the mounts. He has concluded that by "1885 the card mounts and types of imprints changed little as the format is slowly displaced by other types of images."[31]

Wallace made cartes de visite at least until 1890, and perhaps even after, although I have not been able to attribute an extant carte de visite to the period after 1890. At the Goodridge studio, cartes de visite, both portraits and city views, were

Figure 4.17a. "Verso of Carte de Visite Mount, National Photographic Association," 1873–83, 4⅗₆ x 2½ inches. Goodridge Brothers Studio, East Saginaw, Mich. Collection of Dave Tinder.

Figure 4.17b. "Verso of Carte de Visite Mount," 1883–87, 4⅗₆ x 2½ inches. Goodridge Brothers Studio, East Saginaw, Mich. Collection of Dave Tinder.

most popular from 1865 to 1880. Interesting, however, is the fact that all extant post-1872 cartes de visite are portraits. As we will see, by 1872 the success of the Goodridges' "Saginaw Valley Views" stereo series caused the studio to abandon the smaller carte city view in favor of the more dramatic stereograph. At the same time, carte de visite portraits slowly but inevitably lost the commanding popularity they had gained in the 1860s and 1870s to the larger and more impressive cabinet card portrait which would dominate after 1880.

The cabinet card first appeared in England in 1866 and in the United States soon thereafter. Its larger size—4 x 5½ image and 4½ x 6½ card mount, almost three times the size of the carte de visite—led many American photographers to applaud its introduction. Most saw it as an answer to the slumping portrait business following years of prosperity during the Civil War. As Darrah has pointed out, however, "pre-1873 cabinet cards are surprisingly scarce" and it would not be until after 1880 that they overtook the carte de visite in popularity.[32]

While shifts in style and taste might ultimately explain the cabinet card's surpassing the carte de visite portrait, it was the popularity of Napoleon Sarony's celebrity portraits with the American public that catapulted the cabinet card to its position of widespread popularity by 1880. As we already have seen (figure 3.22), Wallace had begun to experiment with cabinet card portraits during the

late 1860s. However, it would be only after the new South Washington studio was modeled "after Sarony [of] N.Y."[33] that Wallace began to create large numbers of cabinet portraits, and then it was not until the 1880s that Goodridge cabinets eclipsed the studio's already successful cartes de visite.

From the first weeks they had occupied the new studio, it was clear that Wallace, like Sarony, made the cabinet portrait his specialty. Whether he ever had visited New York City to observe Sarony at work is not known. Wallace did travel to his former home, York, several times, and Glenalvin had visited New York City from there more than once before 1863, so it is possible that Wallace did continue on to New York City from York. More likely Wallace simply viewed examples of Sarony's work. Directly and indirectly, however, Sarony's influence on Wallace is apparent in the cabinet portraits the latter made after 1872.

Each of the subjects in figures 4.18a–d demonstrates Wallace's success in using the camera, like his mentor Sarony, to distill essential character. Figure 4.18a is a portrait of Mrs. Peter Wunder of Frankenmuth, Michigan. Her husband worked as a teamster for Lorenz Hubinger, manager of the Star of the West Milling Company. The young Mrs. Wunder was only seventeen years old when this portrait was made, perhaps to commemorate her wedding. Although it is a portrait typical for its time in terms of pose and props—

Figure 4.18a. "Mrs. Peter Wunder," 1874, cabinet card. Albumen image, 4¹⁄₁₆ x 5½ inches, ivory bristol board mount with gold trim, 4³⁄₁₆ x 6 inches. Goodridge Brothers Studio, East Saginaw, Mich. Collection of William Oberschmidt.

Figure 4.18b. "Postman," 1873–79, unmounted cabinet card. Image 4 x 5¹⁵⁄₁₆ inches. Goodridge Brothers Studio, East Saginaw, Mich. Collection of Beffrey Family.

Figure 4.18c. "Sisters," 1873 to 1880s, cabinet card. Albumen image, 4 x 5½ inches, ivory bristol board mount, 4³⁄₁₆ x 6⁹⁄₁₆ inches. Goodridge Brothers Studio, East Saginaw, Mich. Collection of John V. Jezierski.

Figure 4.18d. "Brothers," 1873–82, cabinet card. Albumen image, 4¹⁄₁₆ x 5⁹⁄₁₆ inches, black bristol board mount, 4¼ x 6⁹⁄₁₆ inches. Goodridge Brothers Studio, East Saginaw, Mich. Collection of John V. Jezierski.

Figure 4.19a. "Woman in Hat," 1887–89, cabinet car. Albumen image, 4⅛ x 5⅞ inches, beige bristol board mount, 4¼ x 6½ inches. Goodridge Brothers Studio, East Saginaw, Mich. Clarke Historical Library, Central Michigan University.

Figure 4.19b. "Woman in Lace Collar," 1887–89, cabinet card. Albumen image, 4¹/₁₆ x 5⅞ inches, beige bristol board mount, 4⅛ x 6½ inches. Goodridge Brothers Studio, East Saginaw, Mich. Collection of Dave Tinder.

thousands like it still exist in family albums and antique shop sale boxes—through Wallace's lens we are able to observe the pleasing conjunction of youthful femininity and womanly competence in the young Mrs. Wunder. Wallace's use of lighting to brighten the curves made by the row of her buttons and the ruffles of her hem emphasize her femininity. A bit of retouching accentuates a sensible hairdo and square shoulders but also directs our view to her not large but powerful and capable hands.

Pride in a newly acquired position, a recent promotion, or perhaps the satisfaction that follows some years of successful employment is evident in Wallace's portrait of the postman in figure 4.18b. The jaunty tilt of his hat, a carefully brushed uniform and shiny brass buttons, as well as the gleam of a well-polished shoe, even the hint of a smile under an enormous load of packages, all signal a strong sense of duty in the subject of this portrait. Post offices had operated in Saginaw City since 1831 and East Saginaw from 1851. The precise

date of this photograph, however, is impossible to determine except that the presence of the rustic step and use of the Sarony posing device (its base is visible directly behind the postman) suggests that this portrait was made shortly after 1872.[34]

Youthful innocence and casual elegance might well describe what Wallace saw in the subjects of his portraits in figures 4.18c and d. Their very best lace dresses and prominently displayed chains and lockets cannot disguise the vulnerability of the young sisters (figure 4.18c) as they stare into the camera for what was probably their first-ever photograph. Yet the result is a positive one. It is clear from the awkward turn of a small foot, slightly parted lips, the gentle roll of a small fist and interlocked fingers, but most of all from the natural way in which the sisters are drawn to each other that Wallace had managed to capture forever the fascination they felt with the whole process. The three brothers (figure 4.18d), on the other hand, especially the eldest, seem to have been through it all before. In spite of the artificiality of the pose, with crossed legs, bent knees and elbows, and dapper hats and frock coats, there is a relaxed air to the portrait that achieves the level of elegance the subjects must have sought in coming to the Goodridge studio.

The cabinet card, because of its increased size, often allowed the photographer to include an extraordinary and sometimes distracting array of props in the portrait. At the same time, he also could choose to reduce these accessories to the bare minimum or to eliminate such props completely. Figures 4.19a, with its single prop and muted background, and 4.19b, with only the assistance of reflected lighting and the vignetting printing technique, demonstrate Wallace's ability to present character in its purest and most direct form, without any distractions at all.

In December 1878, or early in the new year, the Goodridge studio published a pair of cabinet-sized portraits (figures 4.20b and c) that are unique in the Goodridge oeuvre and most interesting for a variety of reasons. The portraits were published as advertising cards for the Singer Manufacturing Co. of East Saginaw (see figure 4.20a) and are the only examples of this sort of work by the Goodridges, although the practice was a common one between 1860 and 1890. Darrah notes that "Many types of businesses and professional enterprises used the services of photographers for promotional purposes. The most common were hotels and resorts, tourist attractions, schools and colleges, retail stores, factories, and real estate offered for sale." He adds, "Another common promotion use . . . was as premiums, being given free or at slight cost, with purchase of goods."[35] No doubt the Singer Company had the latter practice in mind when it commissioned the Goodridge studio to create portraits of the celebrated American actress Effie Ellsler as premiums for its customers.

Ellsler and her company played East Saginaw's old Academy of Music on December 20 with such success that the performance was held over an additional night. At the time of her 1878 visit, Ellsler was yet to achieve the national renown that would come in 1880 and 1881 from her role as the miller's daughter in *Hazel Kirke,* with a record 486 consecutive performances at the Madison Square Theatre in New York City. Nonetheless, Ellsler already was well known to Saginaw audiences as a result of her first starring role in the 1872 production of *Virginius* in Detroit. Through the 1870s she continued to appear regularly in that city but more often in nearby Cleveland, where her father managed the Euclid Avenue Opera House that Cleveland industrialist Marcus A. Hanna had built especially for Ellsler. In March 1878 her father brought a company to East Saginaw for *Catherine of Russia* that included the famous Fanny Janauschek. His success then prompted Ellsler to schedule a return engagement for November, but this time with his daughter Effie. Academy of Music manager Samuel G. Clay began to advertise the Ellsler engagement on October 20, 1878. By the twenty-fourth, however, it was clear that the Ellsler visit had been canceled for November and Henrietta Chanfrau in *A Woman of the People* booked as the replacement. A notice in the October 27 *Saginaw Daily Courier* reported that the "yellow fever epidemic in the south played such havoc with theatrical dates there that several rearrangements have been necessary. Manager Clay has ascertained that Miss Effie Ellsler, who was announced for two nights and a matinee early in November, will not be able to fulfill her engagement until later, and Mrs. Chanfrau will precede her." Chanfrau, who had achieved considerable fame in the 1860s and had recently revived her career by starring in the drama *Parted* in 1876 in New York City, was well received by East Saginaw audiences. Yet it was Ellsler's December performances in *Heroine in Rags* and *La Cigale, the Grasshopper* that became the theatrical event of the season. The *Courier* reported on December 20 that the "Effie Ellsler company are guests at the Everett [House]" and, in spite of "severe illness and a cold" that had curtailed an earlier performance in Bay City, gave her East Saginaw effort its unqualified approval. The reviewer, under the headline "EFFIE ELLSER," wrote:

> The name, we are sure, is enough to ensure a full house. Even though this charming little actress has only been in this locality for a few days her

Figure 4.20a. "Verso of Singer Sewing Machine Advertising Card," 1878–79, cabinet card, 4¼ x 6½ inches. Goodridge Brothers Studio, East Saginaw, Mich. Ella Sharp Museum.

Figure 4.20b. "Effie Ellsler," 1878–79, cabinet card. Albumen image, 4⅛ x 5½ inches, ivory bristol board mount, 4¼ x 6½ inches. Goodridge Brothers Studio, East Saginaw, Mich. Ella Sharp Museum.

Figure 4.20c. "Effie Ellsler as 'La Cigale,'" 1878–79, cabinet card. Albumen image, 4⅛ x 5½ inches, ivory bristol board mount, 4¼ x 6½ inches. Goodridge Brothers Studio, East Saginaw, Mich. Ella Sharp Museum.

Figure 4.20d. "Unidentified Woman," 1879–80, cabinet card. Albumen image, 3¹⁵⁄₁₆ x 5½ inches, ivory bristol board mount with gold trim, 4¼ x 6½ inches. Goodridge Brothers Studio, East Saginaw, Mich. Collection of William Oberschmidt.

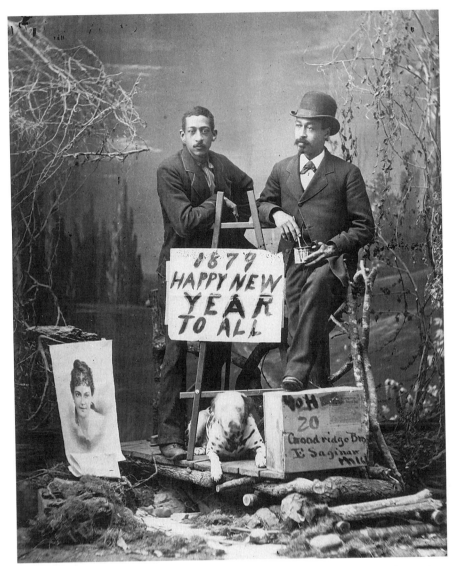

Figure 4.21a. "William O. and Wallace L. Goodridge" 1879, copy of original. Goodridge Brothers Studio, East Saginaw, Mich. Bosch-Devers Collection.

admirers and friends are numerous, and never has a Saginaw audience been so completely taken by storm, as on Thursday and Friday evenings at the academy of music by this versatile and lovely actress, supported as she is by the best stock company in the country. And now our people are to have the pleasure of seeing and listening to the coming favorite. Remember, this evening at the opera house. "A Heroine in Rags," Effie Ellsler. You who fail to see her will regret it.

An additional attraction for the Saginaw audience was the "local boy made good" story. The *Courier* noted that "Mr. Frank Weston, the leading man in Miss Effie Ellsler's company, is not a stranger in the valley, we are informed having about ten years ago tallied lumber on the river for a livelihood. . . . The young gentleman has the talent of the true artist and enjoys the confidence of his manager, Mr. John A. Ellsler, in such degree that Miss Effie is under his special protection during her present tour."[36]

Before the end of her East Saginaw engagement Ellsler visited the Goodridge studio, where the brothers made the portraits that later were used by the Singer Company on its advertising cards. Figure

Figure 4.21b. "William O. and Wallace L. Goodridge," 1879, copy of original. Goodridge Brothers Studio, East Saginaw, Mich. Bosch-Devers Collection.

4.20b was done in the "Rembrandt" style that the Goodridges especially favored at the time. The portrait also demonstrates the successful collaboration that Wallace and William had achieved. Wallace was responsible for the original portrait and the enlarged print most likely made with a solar camera (see figures 4.21a and b). William then "enhanced" the print with colored pastels and/or India ink. Darrah described the technique as follows:

> There were various other methods of "improving" a portrait. . . . The most striking was the pencil, pen, or crayon portrait. . . . The "artist" carefully traced

the features of the face, lined the hair and shaded by stipling as needed with a pen or medium hard graphite pencil. The silver image was then removed by chemical treatment. This could be done to a print or to a negative from which multiple prints could be obtained. . . . The charcoal portrait was made in the same manner but only on enlarged prints. . . . The surface was sprayed with protective thin varnish. . . . The crayon portrait was . . . sometimes colored over by pastel or wax crayons. It was therefore a reworked print.[37]

Throughout the 1860s at the Saginaw Agricultural Society Fair, at the 1875 State Fair held in

East Saginaw, and as recently as October 1878 the Goodridge brothers had accumulated a series of premiums and awards for portraits created by the very process Darrah described.[38] In an 1871 description of photographs entered at the Agricultural Society Fair that year, the reporter, in fact, noted that "Among the many noticeable articles entered by these gentlemen [the Goodridge brothers] . . . was something new called photo pastell [sic]. In this a child's head, is one of the most beautiful pieces of workmanship it has even [sic] been our lot to look upon."[39] For a similar portrait in charcoal of William O. Goodridge, Jr., the photographer's son, see figure 7.4.

Exactly how many versions or copies of the Ellsler "enhanced Rembrandt" portrait the Goodridges produced is not known. Two survive, figures 4.20b and 4.21a and b. That it was popular when they created the portrait is clear from the fact that at least one East Saginaw resident, perhaps an aspiring actress, used it as the model for her own portrait (see figure 4.20d).

In the second "Singer" portrait of Ellsler (see figure 4.20c), the Goodridges, taking their cue from mentor Sarony, have dressed her as La Cigale from the lead in the French farce by the same name, which Ellsler had performed in East Saginaw the evening of December 20, 1878. Here, not only by using costume but by combining it effectively with lighting, props, and posture, Wallace was able to capture the essence of her talent for Saginaw Valley Ellsler enthusiasts. One of the most interesting elements of the photograph, however, is the plank footbridge with rustic handrail that Wallace used to pose Ellsler. The prop appears in only one other Goodridge photograph (see figures 4.21a and b), and in that one it is Wallace and William who are now standing on Effie's rustic wooden bridge, with the pastel portrait of their favorite actress appropriately and prominently placed on the rustic bridge to their left.

Wallace and William Goodridge were among Effie Ellsler's most ardent East Saginaw admirers. They also recognized an opportunity to promote their studio when it presented itself. While there is no record of their attendance at the Ellsler performances in 1878, the family's interest in and support for local productions and the Ellsler portraits the studio created can leave little doubt that the brothers were at the Academy of Music for at least one of her performances. In addition, shortly before the New Year, once Ellsler had completed her East Saginaw engagement, Wallace and William invited her celebrated memory to join them in a New Year's photo greeting that was destined to become their photographic emblem. Ironically, this best-known of all Goodridge images may not have been made either by Wallace or by William. Certainly the brothers organized the shot and chose the props and accessories carefully, but exactly who controlled the exposure by using the lens cap or working a manual drop shutter on the camera (an effective between-the-lens or focal-plane shutter that would have allowed a mechanical release did not become available until later in the 1880s) is not clear.[40] It may have been either of the Goodridge assistants, James H. Morris or Arthur William Brown, who were working at the studio by 1880. In any case, it required at least two exposures to achieve the effect the Goodridges desired (see figures 4.21a and b). The first, in which Wallace is wearing one of his favorite hats and holding the brush and paint used to address the greeting, was ruined when the Goodridge dalmatian, who often showed his spots in Goodridge shots, moved his head. In the second and successful version, Wallace removed his hat, placed the brush and paint can on a wooden shipping crate addressed to the studio, and changed his pose from a three-quarter profile to full face. William also had shifted a bit, dropping his left arm and right shoulder, and tilting his head only slightly to confront the camera directly. Notice, however, that what has not changed in either version is the plank bridge with rustic rail that the brothers used in only one other photograph, Ellsler in the La Cigale portrait made only days before, as well as the mammoth plate portrait of Effie herself. The portrait, which unfortunately appears more clearly in the first but unsuccessful version of the photo greeting, is the 20 x 24 inch pastel "enhanced Rembrandt" that also

Figure 4.22a. "Home on Sheridan Avenue," 1889–90, cabinet card. Albumen image, 5⁵⁄₁₆ x 3⁷⁄₈ inches, ivory bristol board mount, 6½ x 4¼ inches. Goodridge Brothers Studio, East Saginaw, Mich. Collection of William Oberschmidt.

Figure 4.22b. "Brand & Hardin Roller Mills," 1882, cabinet card. Albumen image, 5¾ x 4⅛ inches, beige bristol board mount, 6⁹⁄₁₆ x 4⁵⁄₁₆ inches. Goodridge Brothers Studio, East Saginaw, Mich. Collection of Dave Tinder.

was used to create the Singer Company advertising card in figure 4.20b. The association that Wallace and William sought with Ellsler's recent celebrated sojourn in East Saginaw by the use of the bridge and inclusion of her portrait in their photo greeting is patently clear.

On rare occasions William Goodridge used the cabinet card to create city views. Unlike the carte de visite views, which sometimes included sweeping panoramas of the river or city scape, the cabinet views were of specific structures and probably were made for the owners or tenants and not intended for sale to the general public. Figure 4.22a is a rather poor photograph—note the util-

ity pole—of a beautiful example of classic Italianate residential architecture. The verso records that it was "the home on Sheridan Ave." Its exact location, however, is unknown. No doubt the photograph was made for the proud owners posed on the front step with their canine friend. The cabinet view of the Brand & Hardin Company's mill (figure 4.22b) no doubt was made for the owners J. F. Brand and A. C. Hardin, who may be among the figures near the door, shortly after they had built their new roller mill in 1882. The impressive mansard-roofed structure was located in Saginaw City at Mackinaw and Niagara Streets. Mills notes that a grist mill had been built at the site during

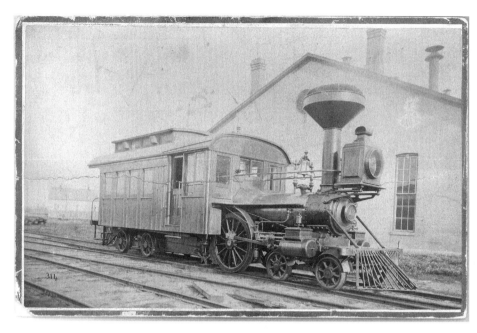

Figure 4.23. "F. & P. M. Railway, Superintendent's Engine, No. 43," 1874–90, cabinet card. Albumen image, 6⁷⁄₁₆ x 4 inches, ivory bristol board mount with gold trim, 6⅞ x 4¼ inches. Goodridge Brothers Studio, East Saginaw, Mich. Collection of John V. Jezierski.

the 1850s by the late Daniel Hardin and was "the oldest milling concern in the Saginaw Valley, and probably in this section of Michigan." J. F. Brand had taken over the business in April 1878 and was soon joined by A. C. Hardin. The partners then sold the original grist mill to John H. Shackleton, who moved the structure to Mackinaw and Lyon Streets, and replaced it with the new roller mill. Subsequently Brand and Hardin added a feed mill and elevators, which made their business "the foremost one in the milling trade of [the] Saginaw Valley."[41] For the photograph, William had located his camera on the slight rise to the north and west of the mill where Gratiot and Mackinaw Streets joined Michigan Avenue. The perspective enabled him to isolate the new structure at one of the busiest points along the river as the view across the water to the south and east demonstrates. The smokestacks in the distance are those of the Michigan Lumber Company and the Gebhardt and Estabrook lumber mills.

Without doubt the most interesting of the few extant Goodridge cabinet views that are not portraits is figure 4.23. "Superintendent's Engine, No.

43," originally christened "The Peckanese" but soon thereafter nicknamed "The Peggy," was built in 1874 as the official business car for Superintendent Sanford Keeler of the Flint & Pere Marquette Railroad. In that capacity "The Peggy" conveyed Keeler on his inspections of the road throughout Michigan and perhaps even farther afield. It was on such an inspection of the Flint & Pere Marquette's Lake Branch by Superintendent of Roadway and Structures George M. Brown in March 1893 that "No. 43" was wrecked. She later was dismantled by order of W. H. Baldwin, general manager of the railroad.

Keeler, Brown, and a group of East Saginaw businessmen that included William B. Mershon, the Morley brothers Jack and George, and Eben Briggs, among others, were avid trout fishermen. As a result "The Peggy" often was called on for other than official service. According to Brown, when "the Railroad Company and many of our sportsmen friends received notice of an assignment of trout fry, they were turned over to me to distribute with this car because we could stop anywhere, at all the small brooks tributary to the streams in

Clare, Osceola, the Sauble, Little Manistee and Manistee Rivers, also the North Branch of the Tobacco River and the Cedar River east of Harrison."[42] Mershon later remembered that after 1884:

> We used to get from Sanford Keeler, the genial Superintendent of the Pere Marquette Railroad, his business car, "The Peggy," and all of us being hard at work six days of the week, there was only Sunday for our fishing trips. With Frank Hatswell to drive the engine, we would get aboard it at Saginaw before daylight. Jack Morley, always a tinkerer and an inventor, had what was then a novelty—a kerosene heater or stove that was very smokey and smelly, but with it after we were under way, he would make a great big pot of strong coffee. We had an ample supply of lunch in baskets and boxes, so that our Sunday morning breakfast was just at the crack of day as the Peggy was speeding west towards Farwell. We had a clear track, for there was no Sunday traffic. A side track ran down to the little flouring mill that stood at the dam on Farwell Lake, so the Peggy would be run in there, and we were on hand for quite early Sunday morning fishing. . . . Tired but happy we would be home shortly after dusk. . . .
>
> After that we began going farther with the Peggy. Grayling was still very plentiful on the Little Manistee. W. D. Wing & Bro. were operating a lumber plant at Wingleton, four miles west of Baldwin in Lake County. . . . We would go up on the regular train, sometimes with the Peggy. If we had the Peggy it was generally for a day's trip only to Kinne Creek, where by that time trout were plentiful.[43]

Kinney Creek is a small stream, less than five miles long. It flows from Wingleton Lake, across the right-of-way of the former Flint & Pere Marquette Railroad to join the Pere Marquette River north of Big Star Lake in southwestern Lake County little more than twenty miles east of Ludington on Lake Michigan.

A wonderful account of a magical trip on "The Peggy" was published as recently as 1962 by G. Forsberg Macliver. As a young girl Miss Macliver lived in North Bradley, a small town along the route of the Flint & Pere Marquette in Midland County between Sanford and Coleman. She later wrote:

Peggy probably means a girl's name to you but to us, before the turn of the century, it suggested travel and far away places we had never seen.

The Peggy was a short passenger coach with an engine attached, which passed through town fairly often. We were told that it was a pay-car carrying money with which to pay employees. At other times it carried railroad executives on short trips. When it stopped at our station we had glimpses of a small parlor car with very comfortable looking chairs. All of us dreamed of riding on the Peggy.

One summer day the girls of our Sunday school class were invited to the home of Sara Whitmore, our teacher, for an afternoon party. She lived about a mile west and a bit north. After a very pleasant time, we started walking home along the railroad track. Of course, we had to keep a look out for trains. Finally someone said, "Here it comes." As we scurried off to let pass the freight train, the most numerous in those days.

But it was not a freight train. It was the Peggy! It had overtaken us beside the switch where trains entered the side track to await other trains. The Peggy stopped for that very purpose. The conductor of the Peggy said to us, "Girls, would you like a ride?" Would we!

He helped us aboard with ceremony and suddenly we were in the very coach that we had longed to see and ride. The fat revolving chairs were upholstered in bright colored plush; the carpet was green Brussels with gay flowers in it. As there were only six chairs the older girls held the younger ones. Sadie held me. All of us were thrilled to find ourselves in that parlor-on-wheels. The very unexpectedness made it an adventure.

The Peggy moved slowly. We had time to look out from the height of the coach upon familiar scenes. After a ride of about a third of a mile, we arrived at the other switch and the end of our journey. The conductor helped us off and we thanked him before we hurried in different directions to tell our exciting news at home. The party had taken on a special glamour with the ride in the Peggy. Best of all, to the younger ones of us, it proved that dreams do come true.[44]

During the 1880s, according to at least one report, the Goodridge brothers had been appointed "special photographers" to the Flint & Pere

Marquette Railroad.[45] It is likely, therefore, that William, in his many excursions as the railroad photographer, also rode "The Peggy" to photograph along the Flint & Pere Marquette and incidentally to make the several stereo series of the forests and lumber camps for which the Goodridge studio became so well known.

Like the carte de visite mounts favored by the Goodridge studio during the 1870s and 1880s, those chosen for cabinet card portraits and views reveal little direct information about the studio's development. Most card stock used for Goodridge cabinet mounts was cut to a standard 4½ x 6½ inches, was ivory or beige—black was the most common exception—and had rounded corners (see figures 4.18a–d). Only two examples of a cabinet mount with notched edges (see, for example, figure 4.22a) are presently known for the period. This style was popular during the late 1880s and through the 1890s. The majority of extant Goodridge cabinets bear the studio name, using its by then emblematic lettering in gold across the bottom front of the card (as in figures 4.18a and c). The next most popular option was to print the studio name, again using the characteristic lettering but in black, on the verso of the mount (see figure 4.24a). The imprint almost always was expanded to include the studio's South Washington address. During the mid-1870s, when the Goodridges contracted with East Saginaw printer William T. Rich to produce their carte, cabinet, and stereo mounts, a black card stock with gold lettering (figure 4.24b) on the verso was very common. Rich, however, reversed the styles of lettering in the imprint, using the gothic for the title "Photographers" and block letters for the Goodridge name. On rare occasions—only three examples are known—the Goodridges employed a blue ink stamp similar to that used on 1860s cartes de visite (see figure 3.18a) to imprint cabinet cards. This usage, however, came at the very end of the 1880s and likely continued through the 1890s. Notice that the stamp in figure 4.24c specifies "Saginaw, East Side," suggesting that it was used at or near the time that the adjacent cities of East Saginaw and Saginaw City were consolidated into a single jurisdiction. The least common Goodridge cabinet imprint—two examples are extant—was the most elaborate (see figure 4.24d). Precisely why the Goodridges and their customers favored the simplest imprints at the very time that other Saginaw studios—Angell, for example (see figure 4.3a)—had created, and national styles dictated, much greater embellishment, is not clear. A possible explanation is the division of responsibility between Wallace and William. Perhaps the more businesslike and studio-bound Wallace chose the simple but memorable imprint for the cabinet portraits that he created there. The precise dynamics of the brothers' partnership are impossible to reconstruct, and its impact on such a decision, therefore, is purely conjecture.

——◆——

The move to the South Washington studio was a significant opportunity for William, the youngest of the three Goodridge brothers. In York he had run errands for Glenalvin and Wallace and had begun to learn the basics of professional photography. His apprenticeship continued in East Saginaw, although Glenalvin's illness probably meant ever-increasing responsibility. Glenalvin's death in 1867 accelerated William's advancement in the firm, and it is clear that by 1868 he shared full partnership with Wallace as one of the two surviving Goodridge brothers.

In York Glenalvin had experimented with stereo daguerreotypes and the more common paper stereographs during the 1850s, the initial decade of their popularity. At the time, however, perhaps because of intense local competition or his continuing success with portraits, Glenalvin did not choose to create significant numbers of stereo views, and at present none are known to be extant from the studio's York period. Shortly after reestablishing their business in East Saginaw, the brothers began to produce a series of stereo views in an attempt to distinguish their new studio from its already successful competition. There is no evidence that young William O. Goodridge was wholly responsible for the "Saginaw Valley Views" (see fig-

Figure 4.24a. "Verso of Cabinet Card Mount," 1887–89, 4⅛ x 6½ inches, Goodridge Brothers Studio, East Saginaw, Mich. Collection of Dave Tinder.

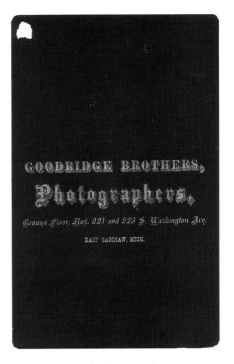

Figure 4.24b. "Verso of Cabinet Card Mount," 1873–82, 4¼ x 6⁹⁄₁₆ inches. Goodridge Brothers Studio, East Saginaw, Mich. Collection of John V. Jezierski.

Figure 4.24c. "Verso of Cabinet Card Mount," 1889–90, 4¼ x 6½ inches, Goodridge Brothers Studio, Saginaw, Mich. Collection of William Oberschmidt.

Figure 4.24d. Verso of Cabinet Card Mount," 1883–87, 4⁷⁄₁₆ x 6⁹⁄₁₆ inches. Goodridge Brothers Studio, East Saginaw, Mich. Collection of Dave Tinder.

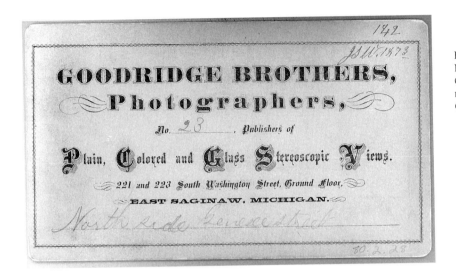

Figure 4.25a. "Verso of Stereograph Mount," 1873–82, 7¹⁵⁄₁₆ x 4 inches. Goodridge Brothers Studio, East Saginaw, Mich. Historical Society of Saginaw County, Inc.

Figure 4.25b. "Looking East from Saginaw River, South Side of Genesee St.," 1873, stereograph. Albumen image, 6¼ x 3⅜ inches, green bristol board mount, 7¹⁵⁄₁₆ x 4 inches. Goodridge Brothers Studio, East Saginaw, Mich. Historical Society of Saginaw County, Inc.

Figure 4.25c. "Looking East from Saginaw River, North Side of Genesee St.," 1873, stereograph. Albumen image, 6¼ x 3⅜ inches, green bristol board mount, 7 x 3¹⁵⁄₁₆ inches. Goodridge Brothers Studio, East Saginaw, Mich. Historical Society of Saginaw County, Inc.

ures 3.23 through 3.28) series that attracted so much attention before 1872 and helped to establish the reputation of the Goodridge studio in the Saginaw Valley. Yet because he is known to have had such responsibility with the move to the South Washington studio after 1872, and because the production of stereo views by the Goodridge brothers ceased abruptly with William's death in 1890, it is evident that he was the stereo specialist from the very first years in East Saginaw. Figure 4.10 specifically identifies William as the studio's "View [i.e., stereograph] Photographer," with Arthur W. Brown as his assistant.

The division of responsibility between Wallace and William after 1867 was a successful one for the brothers. It allowed the Goodridges, unlike almost all of their Saginaw Valley competitors, to succeed not only with studio portraits but also with stereo views made in the field. We might also assume that such a clear division of labor and the opportunity to work independently of each other could only promote the personal dynamics of the brothers' successful partnership. Consequently, between 1872 and 1890, building on the earlier success of the "Saginaw Valley Views," William created three groups of stereo series that became the basis for much of the studio's financial and professional success before and even after his death in 1890. Each of the new groups contained at least two and sometimes several topical series of stereo views. The series were published simultaneously or at the very least overlapped each other by several years. For example, the first new group, the "Michigan Views," appeared in 1873 and continued to be published until 1880. The "Saginaws and Tributaries," the second group of series, was issued initially in 1874 and also continued to be published until at least 1880. That year the most popular views from the first two groups of series were incorporated into a third, "Picturesque Michigan," which became the Goodridge studio's best-known and most successful group of stereo views.

Within weeks of the October 1872 Crouse Block fire, William had begun to create the first of the new groups of stereo series that he and Wallace

earlier had advertised as the "Michigan Views" (see figure 3.6b). Although he may have been making photographs for the series during the spring and summer of 1872, the studio fire interrupted the process and forced him to postpone the series introduction until later in 1873.

The "Michigan Views" were a large and diverse group of stereos. An original inventory does not exist, but the more than forty extant views can be grouped, on the basis of subject matter and technical characteristics, into four series—city views, fires, the river, and interiors. Initially the "Michigan Views" were much like the earlier "Saginaw Valley Views" in that streetscapes, architecture, and local disasters predominate. Improved photographic technology and the early success of the series, however, soon enabled William to expand its subject matter dramatically. The most immediately obvious difference from the "Saginaw Valley Views" was in size. "Saginaw Valley Views" were usually 5½ x 2⅞ inches and mounted on creamy yellow card stock that was 7 x 3½. "Michigan Views" always were at least 6¼ x 3½, often larger, with various colored mounts that were a minimum of 6⅞ x 3⅞ inches. In addition, the first two "Michigan Views" series, city views and fires, were mounted on card stock that bore a fancy label (see figure 4.25a) that identified them as "Plain, Colored and Glass Stereoscopic Views." Later series in the "Michigan Views" group were mounted on plain card stock or simply labeled "GOODRIDGE BROS., Photographers." The series labeled "Plain, Colored and Glass" also were distinctive in that they were made using the single negative/transposing frame technique, hence the dual images are separated by the thin, dark septum resulting from the printing process. The subsequent "Michigan Views" series, the river and interiors, were made by creating a single dual negative, cutting and reversing the resulting dual print, and pasting the reversed prints to the mounting board.[46] Although "Colored" and "Glass" views were advertised, none are known to exist, and only "Plain" (paper) stereos from the series are extant.

The popularity of the "Michigan Views" with Saginaw residents was immediate and lasting. As late as 1878 the local newspapers reported that "very fine" views of "Genesee and Washington avenue" were available at the Goodridge "gallery."[47] James S. Webber, who continued to collect Goodridge stereo views and wrote the captions identifying figures 4.25b and c, noted on the verso of each that they had been made in 1873 and were numbers "141" and "142," respectively, in his obviously growing collection.

Figure 4.25b is a ground-level view of the south side of Genesee Avenue looking east from Water Street. Visible are the Buena Vista, Irving, and Bliss Blocks, with the original four-story Bancroft House at the southwest corner of Genesee and Washington. The tracks on Genesee are those of the Saginaw City Street Railway Company, which had been organized by David H. Jerome, George L. Burrows, and S. S. Perkins in 1863 to facilitate travel by residents of Saginaw City to the Potter Street terminus of the Flint & Pere Marquette Railroad.[48] The corresponding north side of Genesee from the same vantage point is presented in figure 4.25c. The Exchange, Crystal, and Hess Blocks are visible between Water Street and Washington, and in the distance it is possible to make out the steeple of St. Paul's Episcopal Church, which had been constructed at the northeast corner of Warren and Lapeer Streets in 1864. Of greatest interest, however, is the vacant northeast corner of Genesee and Washington, the former location of the Crouse Block and the original Goodridge studio, before construction of the new Hoyt Block had begun. A close examination of the stereo reveals the blackened wall of the Stevens, Pool and Co. store that was adjacent to the Crouse building in the 200 block along Genesee Avenue.

Some years later, William made a similar view of Genesee Avenue (figure 4.26a) showing both the north and south sides simultaneously by moving his vantage point up onto the Genesee Avenue bridge. Relatively little had changed. The street railway continued to operate, and St. Paul's and all of the business blocks are in place. R. Boyd & Co. had moved into the Exchange Block, the new Hoyt building (which replaced the Crouse Block) had

long since been completed, and the first telephone lines were strung. A rare proof of the stereo (figure 4.26b) reveals William's shadow along the base of the photograph as he stood on the bridge with the sun to his back to make the negative that was used to print the stereo view.

As popular as William's city views were, it was his stereographs of two major East Saginaw fires, little more than three weeks apart in the spring of 1873, that brought the early "Michigan Views" widespread attention. The May 27 edition of the *Daily Courier* reported to Saginaw residents the details of a "most disastrous fire [that] had . . . visited our city." The May 26 Jackson Hall conflagration was a tragedy from a variety of perspectives. Within minutes of arriving at the blaze, one of the firemen, Edward Pringle, was killed by a falling stone windowsill that crushed him and injured two of his fellows. While such a death was not uncommon, it was made worse by the belief that "the cause [of the fire] can only be ascribed to the devilish work of the incendiary [arsonist], against whom scarcely any of our business blocks are safe." The *Courier* also noted that while the alarm had been given by a passing citizen at about "2 o'clock A.M. of yesterday," it was fifty minutes "before there was a stream [of water] doing service on the burning building." The delay, newly appointed fire chief C. A. Dolliver admitted, was due to his own lack of experience, the absence, "without leave," of fire company foreman Wilson on a fishing trip, and "the illness from small-pox of two of the most efficient men on the force." In addition, the hose cart driver had mistakenly deposited the nozzle rather than the intake end of the hose at the pump on the dock at the river so that before the mistake could be rectified several minutes had passed and the fire spread. Had the night not been nearly still, with "scarcely a breath of wind," the loss could have been even much greater. As it was, the fire was confined to the Jackson Hall, Gage, and Smith Blocks in the center of the east side of the 100 block of South Washington directly opposite the Bancroft House. The Goodridge stereo view of the ruins (figure 4.27a), made the afternoon following the fire, shows the three destroyed

Figure 4.26a. "Genesee Avenue, Looking East from Bridge," 1880s, stereograph. Albumen image, 6¾ x 3⁷⁄₁₆ inches, orange bristol board mount, 7 x 3¹⁵⁄₁₆ inches. Goodridge Brothers Studio, East Saginaw, Mich. Collection of Dave Tinder.

Figure 4.26b. "Genesee Avenue, Looking East from Bridge," 1880s, copy from original stereograph negative, 7⅜ x 9 ½ inches. Goodridge Brothers Studio, East Saginaw, Mich. Bosch-Devers Collection.

and parties for almost a decade. Frederick Douglass, for example, had lectured to Saginaw citizens there on the evening of January 31, 1868.[50] It is no wonder, therefore, that the *Courier* reported that the day following the fire the "Goodridge Bro's have taken some very fine stereoscopic views of the burned district."[51]

William had not sold out his stock of Jackson Hall stereos when little more than three weeks later, on June 20, a second and potentially more dangerous fire broke out at the Mead, Lee & Co. planing mill at the corner of Franklin and Hayden Streets, only a block from the Goodridge studio. According to the *Courier* report, the fire began on the second floor of the mill amid wood shavings from the planers in the area above the boiler room. Because the employees were on their lunch break at the time and because of the age and combustible nature of the building, the fire had spread rapidly by the time the alarm could be given. When Chief Dolliver and the East Saginaw engine arrived, the mill and adjoining structures, as well as more than 1.5 million feet of lumber stored nearby and even the tons of sawdust that had been used as fill in the low areas surrounding the mill property, were in flames. The fire continued to spread, destroying at least thirteen houses in the area, damaging more than eight others, and even threatening the First Congregational Church across Cass at Hayden. For a time the heat from the fire was so intense, as the *Courier* reporter noted, that "one could not ap-

structures, the rubble that crushed fireman Pringle, and the damage to the adjoining buildings. At least eleven businesses were a complete loss, with more the $65,000 worth of property destroyed.[49] In addition, Jackson Hall, where the fire had been set, had been one of East Saginaw's most popular public meeting places for lectures, concerts, dances,

Figure 4.27a. "Ruins of Jackson Hall Block," May 1873, stereograph. Albumen image, 6¼ x 3⅜ inches, black bristol board mount, 6¹⁵⁄₁₆ x 3¹⁵⁄₁₆ inches. Goodridge Brothers Studio, East Saginaw, Mich. Historical Society of Saginaw County, Inc.

Figure 4.27b. "Burning of Mead & Lee Planing Mill," June 20, 1873, stereograph. Albumen image, 6³⁄₁₆ x 3⅜ inches, green bristol board mount, 7 x 3¹⁵⁄₁₆ inches. Goodridge Brothers Studio, East Saginaw, Mich. Historical Society of Saginaw County, Inc.

Figure 4.27c. "Ruins of Engine Room, Mead & Lee Planing Mill," June 21, 1873, stereograph. Albumen image, 6¼ x 3⅜ inches, green bristol board mount, 6¹⁵⁄₁₆ x 3¹⁵⁄₁₆ inches. Goodridge Brothers Studio, East Saginaw, Mich. Historical Society of Saginaw County, Inc.

proach within a block without danger of being scorched." This time, however, prompt and effective action by Chief Dolliver and his men, as well as the assistance of fire departments from South Saginaw and Saginaw City—units were even rushed from Bay City and Flint by the Flint & Pere Marquette Railroad—limited the extent of the fire to the four blocks bounded by Washington, William (now Janes), Cass, and Millard. Nevertheless, the fire destroyed property worth at least $75,000. And, for a time at least, it also was feared that it had taken the lives of five children in the residences destroyed. Fortunately, the report proved to be only a rumor. The *Courier* concluded its account of the fire by reporting that "An illustration of Saginaw enterprise was noticeable when the air was full of smoke, and the heat the most intense, in a representative of Goodridge Bro's. stationed on Smith's Opera House, taking photographic views of the scene."[52]

According to James Webber's captions and numbering system, William Goodridge made a series of at least six stereo views of the fire and its aftermath. As figure 4.27b demonstrates, and the *Courier* reported, William had rushed with his camera to the top of Smith's Opera House, which was directly opposite the Goodridge studio in the 200 block of South Washington and which gave him an excellent vantage point on the conflagration. This first view in the series effectively captures the tense excitement during the initial stages of the fire as the crowd continued to gather to estimate the fire's potential for destruction. Soon after this view was made, in fact, each of the structures visible at the southeast corner of Washington and William was either destroyed or damaged as the fire spread. The day following the fire, while owners and residents evaluated the extent of their losses, William continued to create his pictorial record of the disaster. James Webber described figure 4.27c as "Ruins of Engine Room," but the photograph demonstrates William's artistic ability as well. Not only does the contrast between the dull, flat sky and the still smoldering rubble present a most dramatic stereoscopic view, but the counterpoint created by the contrasting textures

and shapes of twisted metal and rough brick turn tragedy into art.

The resulting series of views became a centerpiece of Webber's collection and most certainly was purchased by those who had suffered losses to the fire or who perhaps wished to identify themselves among the crowd that had gathered. When the series was available for purchase within days of the fire itself, the *Courier* concluded that the "Goodridge Bros., have completed some fine specimens of work in the way of photographic scenes of the recent fire. They are something entirely new in the art, as we understand it, and are as near perfect as work of this kind can be done."[53]

The Mead, Lee & Co. fire series placed the Goodridge studio firmly in the midst of a tradition of stereo photography that Darrah has described as one of "local operators . . . who produced a few views when some unusual event . . . created a transitory market for souvenirs . . ." and then sold "the negatives, or rights to them . . . to large-volume publishers."[54] There is no evidence that Wallace and William sold the rights to the series, or even reason to believe that the mill fire would attract attention much beyond the limits of the valley. It is clear, however, that the treatment of the subject matter, the quality of the photography, and the series' almost immediate availability did indeed impress the *Courier* and its readers throughout the Saginaw Valley. The initial sets of "Plain, Colored and Glass Stereoscopic Views" (the city views and the 1873 fires) provided a solid foundation for the "Michigan Views." William soon built on it.

Enterprising local photographers like the Goodridge brothers also used to their advantage the almost annual spring floods that visited the Saginaw Valley. In 1876 William created a series of at least ten stereo views of the year's flood which he added to the studio's already considerable inventory of "Michigan Views." An anonymous collector—perhaps an associate or acquaintance of James Webber—purchased the series from the Goodridges, catalogued it with his or her personal numbering system, and composed a descriptive caption indicating the location and vantage point of each view on the reverse of the mount.

The series began with an establishing shot, figure 4.28a, a general view of the river identified by our collector as "No. 1020: Looking South from East Side." The view was made from the roof of the Bancroft House, one of William's favorite vantage points. Visible in the foreground are the rooftops of the Union and Excelsior Blocks and Mrs. Rierdon's small hotel at the corner of German and Water Streets. Across the way, along the right middle-ground of the view, is Jesse Hoyt's Power Block and mill with thousands of feet of recently sawed and drying lumber awaiting shipment. In the distance, along the east bank of the river, are the Charles Lee and Warner & Eastman mills. In midstream are the pillars for the Emerson Street railroad bridge that the Michigan Central had begun to construct in order to connect its main line with that of the Jackson, Lansing & Saginaw Railroad (which the Central had acquired in 1871) on the west bank of the river. Just beyond the proposed bridge is the new A. W. Wright & Company mill at the foot of Throop Street, one of the largest mills in the valley at the time. Its sizable lumber dock can be seen extending into the river. West of the mill is its bayou, which has overrun its banks as a result of the flood. In the distance and upstream is the skyline of Saginaw City.[55] Dramatic in its own right, the stereo view may have been part of an even more spectacular photograph that the *Saginaw Daily Courier* singled out that same spring. Under the headline "Fine Photographic View," the newspaper reported that the "Goodridge Bros., the enterprising photographers on Washington avenue, have taken photographic views showing the entire river front of East Saginaw at high water. Carrollton and Saginaw City also appear in the distance. The picture is forty-three inches long, and every family in the city should have one."[56] The panorama is not known to exist at the present time.

Among the series' more specific views of the flood in East Saginaw is figure 4.28b, "No. 1021: Looking South over the bayou towards Hoyt School from about the corner of Franklin and Millard." Possibly because the location was only two blocks from the studio, Wallace had walked over, and he and his homburg are featured prominently in the center of the view. The series also contains a rather rare Goodridge photograph made in Saginaw City on the west bank of the river. Figure 4.28c is identified as the "Jackson & Lansing RR Depot" located along Water (now Niagara) Street between Van Buren and Adams. The line had been absorbed by the Michigan Central in 1871. Some years later it was reported that the Goodridge studio had done contract work for most of the area's railroads. The Michigan Central was among them.[57]

The 1876 flood series is an excellent example of the quality work that William was producing by the mid-1870s. Each of the views in the series was created using a stereo negative and then cutting and transposing the resulting print. The mounts are a plain beige and, at 7 x 3$^{15}/_{16}$ inches, among the largest the studio used. Each of the views is clear, well composed, and when viewed through the stereoscope would result in a dramatic three-dimensional image of the scene.

The Saginaw River, with its seemingly annual inundations of East Saginaw, also allowed William to expand the subject matter of the "Michigan Views." "Mayflower Mill & Elevator" (figure 4.29a) is a rather straightforward yet effective stereograph. By sandwiching the buildings, the vessels, and the dock with its pilings between the two layers of flat, cloudless sky and smooth, glassy water, William was able to achieve the effect he desired. The mill, located along the east riverbank between Fitzhugh and Carroll Streets, was constructed by Norman Little in partnership with James M. and Jesse Hoyt in 1851. Its six millstones and steam power gave it a capacity of more than 150 barrels of flour per day and a reputation as one of the best-equipped flour mills in the country. It continued to operate until 1892. The vessels are the nearly new steam tug *Tom Dowling*, which had been built at Cleveland in 1873, and the two-masted schooner *Robert Howlett*, built at Grand Haven, Michigan, in 1870. The *Tom Dowling*, among other duties, towed rafts of logs to the mills along the river. The *Robert Howlett* continued in service as a general cargo vessel until 1904.[58]

More than once William also followed the course of the Tittabawassee River, a main branch

Figure 4.28a. "Looking South from East Side," 1876, stereograph. Albumen image, 6¾ x 3³/₁₆ inches, beige bristol board mount, 7 x 3¹⁵/₁₆ inches. Goodridge Brothers Studio, East Saginaw, Mich. Clarke Historical Library, Central Michigan University.

Figure 4.28b. "Looking South over the Bayou towards Hoyt School from about the Corner of Franklin and Willard," 1876, stereograph. Albumen image, 6¾ x 3³/₁₆ inches, beige bristol board mount, 7 x 3¹⁵/₁₆ inches. Goodridge Brothers Studio, East Saginaw, Mich. Clarke Historical Library, Central Michigan University.

Figure 4.28c. "Jackson & Lansing R.R. Depot," 1876, stereograph. Albumen image, 6¾ x 3³/₁₆ inches, beige bristol board mount, 7 x 3¹⁵/₁₆ inches. Goodridge Brothers Studio, East Saginaw, Mich. Clarke Historical Library, Central Michigan University.

461.–Mayflower Mill&Elevator,E.Saginaw,Mich.

Figure 4.29a. "Mayflower Mill & Elevator," 1881–82, stereograph. Albumen image, 6¹¹⁄₁₆ x 3½ inches, orange bristol board mount, 7 x 3¹⁵⁄₁₆ inches. Goodridge Brothers Studio, East Saginaw, Mich. Clarke Historical Library, Central Michigan University.

Figure 4.29b. "Banking Ground, Averill," 1881, stereograph. Albumen image, 6¹³⁄₁₆ x 3½ inches, orange bristol board mount, 7 x 3¹⁵⁄₁₆ inches. Goodridge Brothers Studio, East Saginaw, Mich. Collection of Dave Tinder.

Figure 4.29c. "Moonlight, Tittabawassee River," 1881–82, stereograph. Albumen image, 6⅝ x 3⅝ inches, orange bristol board mount, 7 x 3¹⁵⁄₁₆ inches. Goodridge Brothers Studio, East Saginaw, Mich. Clarke Historical Library, Central Michigan University.

of the Saginaw system, upstream to the town of Averill's Station (now Averill) on the main line of the Flint & Pere Marquette Railroad. At a bend in the river there, area lumbermen and the railroad had established an especially large banking ground where all stored the winter's cut of logs until the spring thaw enabled them to ride the floodwaters to the mills at Saginaw City and East Saginaw.[59] William had visited Averill's Station in 1868 or 1869, soon after the town and banking ground were established, to photograph it for the "Saginaw Valley Views" series (see figure 3.27a). He continued to make regular trips there on the Flint & Pere Marquette until shortly before his death. Figure 4.29b is impossible to date precisely, but most likely was made in March 1881. The *Saginaw Daily Courier* reported on March 25 that "Goodridge Bros., artists, recently sketched the 'rollway' at Averill, and have them now on exhibition at their place on Washington avenue. They are receiving numerous orders for them."[60] And the *Midland Republican,* the same month, commented on the large inventory of timber then at the banking ground:

> We have been at Averill—went there Monday last. Of course we looked over the big "log pile." Mr. John Stratton very kindly piloted us about and gave some interesting facts. The log bank is about three-quarters of a mile long, reaches halfway across the Tittabawassee, 6 or 8 rods, and way down into the mud at the bottom of the river, and high above the river with plenty of bad places to fall into. There are several logs there, but 18,000,000 feet is probably a large estimate. It was quite interesting to note the different marks of the logs. Here are some of them: JAKE, JAR, JIM, LOW, $14, 5½, P 2 E, 4E (in a diamond), besides a mark in the shape of a snowshoe with the letter E in the center; and another with two nicely executed keys crossed. These marks are quite deep and distinct, being struck on with a steel instrument.[61]

William's stereo certainly captures the magnitude of the piled logs. In addition, his use of the brush in the foreground and the large skeletal tree to the right, with the river flowing off through it to the horizon as the boundary of the banked timber, emphasizes the immensity of the banking ground

and makes this an excellent stereograph in the viewer.

William, on occasion, also used the river to experiment with photographic technique. The December 16, 1873, issue of the *Daily Courier* announced to East Saginaw residents that the Goodridge studio was exhibiting "two new styles of Photograph." One was "a beautiful Rembrandt photo *representing* a moonlight scene" that was "gotten up in good style and speak[s] well for the above firm."[62] Although the photograph (figure 4.29c) was titled "Moonlight, Tittabawassee River," in actuality the moonlight was sunlight. William, like many other photographers at the time, manipulated both the negative and the resulting print to "*represent* a moonlight scene." An article in the November 1880 issue of *Photographic Times* titled "Photography by Moonlight," which included an illustration of a stereo view similar to figure 4.29c, explained the technicalities of the process. "The method indicated," it declared, "is that by which the finest French 'moonlight views' are taken, the image of the sun, unless in exceptional instances, being made to do duty for that of the moon." Even a cursory examination of William's view reveals that the intensity of the "moonlight" is much too strong to be an "exceptional instance." Instead, the location and setting for the view provide the conditions that made William's "representation" possible. The scene was the sorting pens of the Tittabawassee Boom Company near its headquarters on the west side of the State Road (Gratiot) bridge from which the view was made. A few hundred yards above the bridge the river bends to the west, providing just the right conditions to create the image, which, according to the *Photographic Times,* included water, trees, and the morning sun.[63] Whether William read the *Photographic Times* article published some years after having made his "moonlight" view is not known. If he did there would be little he could have learned from it.

Almost all of the "Michigan Views" were exterior shots—cityscapes, landscapes, floods, and fires. But striking examples of stereo views of interiors do exist from the late 1870s and demonstrate

Figure 4.30a. "St. Paul's Episcopal Church," 1879, stereograph. Albumen image, 6⁹⁄₁₆ x 3⁵⁄₁₆ inches, orange bristol board mount, 7 x 3¹⁵⁄₁₆ inches. Goodridge Brothers Studio, East Saginaw, Mich. Historical Society of Saginaw County, Inc.

Figure 4.30b. "Greenhouse, Brady Hill Cemetery," 1879, stereograph. Albumen image, 6⁹⁄₁₆ x 3⁵⁄₁₆ inches, orange bristol board mount, 7 x 3¹⁵⁄₁₆ inches. Goodridge Brothers Studio, East Saginaw, Mich. Collection of Dave Tinder.

Figure 4.30c. "Victorian Parlor," 1881 or 1882, stereograph. Albumen image, 6⅝ x 3⁵⁄₁₆ inches, yellow bristol board mount, 7 x 3¹⁵⁄₁₆ inches. Goodridge Brothers Studio, East Saginaw, Mich. Collection of Dave Tinder.

William's success with this technique. The views were made using natural light, although sources of artificial lighting were available to the Goodridges well before the end of the decade.

On April 16, 1879, the *Saginaw Morning Herald* reported that on the previous day, Easter Tuesday, the Goodridge brothers had made a "photograph of the Easter decorations in St. Paul's Church."[64] Figure 4.30a was the result of William's effort. By locating his camera in the choir loft, William was able to use the shape of the roof and window vaulting and the parallel but contrasting lines of the roof panels to present the impression of an almost cathedral-like massiveness in the modest structure. Notice, as well, that William used the natural light pouring through the sanctuary windows both to create the material object, the photograph, and to enhance the spiritual nature of the subject matter. The light that makes the photograph possible also bathes the altar and Easter decorations in its radiance. And, from its midst, the banner proclaiming the Easter message, that "Christ is Risen," appears to rise.

Perhaps it was that same spring that William visited the greenhouse at Brady Hill Cemetery and made the view in figure 4.30b. The location, originally about twenty-two acres at the southwest corner of Jefferson Avenue and Brewster Street (now Holland), was being used as a public cemetery as early as 1855, when Alfred M. Hoyt donated the land to then Buena Vista Township for that purpose. In 1882 the township made it officially a part of East Saginaw.[65] The greenhouse, located on the grounds, supplied plants—geraniums appear to have been the most popular—for the cemetery's formal plantings. William's view is a superb example of his considerable talent in making stereographs and the studio's growing reputation for this type of photograph. The contrasts that he was able to capture between the bright but filtered light pouring through the glass panes and the dark depths of the massed vegetation, the rigid structures of the greenhouse frame and the benches and shelves, and the feathery mass of the plants themselves, all enhance the impact of the photograph. In addition, William carefully manipulated the fab-

rication of the mounted stereo. The extraordinary size of the left half of figure 4.30b, 3⅝ inches, in contrast to the right, 2⅞ inches, was designed to focus the viewer's attention on the large-leafed plant in the aisle between the benches in the foreground. At the same time, the inherent structure of the photograph draws the viewer's attention to the more distant focal point, the end of the aisle at the rear of the greenhouse. The contest between the two focal points for the viewer's attention results in an especially effective stereo view.

It is interesting to note that the large plant in the foreground appears to be a *Zantedeschia aethiopica,* or calla lily, a most popular conservatory flower at the time and one often associated with cemeteries. This one may have been in the aisle and became very much a part of the photograph because it later went home with William. A brief notice in the October 3, 1879, *Saginaw Morning Herald* reported that the "Goodridge Bros. have a curiosity at their photograph rooms in the shape of a double calla lily of the pure white variety."[66]

A year or two later, William created a stereograph of a "Victorian Parlor," figure 4.30c, that remains one of his most extraordinary interior views. Once again he made use of only the available natural light. In this case, however, the success of the view is due not to his manipulation of the light or to the size ratio of the twin images, but instead to carefully chosen camera placement. By locating his camera in one parlor and directing his lense over tables, chairs, and footstool, and through the archway but under the chandeliers toward the seated woman reflected in the mirror, William achieves the illusion that one is looking through several rooms, not merely from one to the other. It was a photographic convention that had already become a cliché. William, however, was able to soften the effect of the cliché and reinforce the illusion of multiple spaces by creating "pictures within a picture." Notice that the woman seated on the sofa and reflected in the mirror is presented much like the framed portrait above her left shoulder or the several cabinet photographs artfully arranged on either side of the archway between the rooms. It has not been possible to identify the woman or to

Figure 4.31a. "Ruins, Thomas Saylor & Co. Mill Fire," 1874, stereograph. Albumen image, 6¹¹⁄₁₆ x 3⅝ inches, yellow bristol board mount, 6¹⁵⁄₁₆ x 3¹⁵⁄₁₆ inches. Goodridge Brothers Studio, East Saginaw, Mich. Collection of Dave Tinder.

Figure 4.31b. "Offices, Flint & Pere Marquette Railroad," 1874, stereograph. Albumen image, 6¹³⁄₁₆ x 3⅝ inches, yellow bristol board mount, 7 x 3¹⁵⁄₁₆ inches. Goodridge Brothers Studio, East Saginaw, Mich. Collection of Dave Tinder.

determine the location of the residence. She does not appear to be a Goodridge family member. Nonetheless, the impact of the stereo in the viewer is most dramatic.

The increasing number of "Michigan Views" series and their apparent popularity prompted Wallace and William to introduce yet another group of stereo series by 1874. Originally titled "The Saginaws and Tributaries—the Great Lumbering and Salt District of Michigan," but soon modified to "In and about the Saginaws—the Great Lumber and Salt District of Michigan," the new group of series may have been launched to take advantage of the studio's success with the "Michigan Views" or simply to utilize and promote as effectively as possible an expanding inventory of stereo views. Initially the subject matter of the various new series was

much like that of the "Michigan Views." In the summer of 1874, for example, an explosion and fire at the T. P. Saylor lumber mill resulted in a series of views that included figure 4.31a. The Saylor mill was located on the west bank of the river in Carrollton at the foot of Sherman Street. Although a boiler explosion and fire destroyed the mill on June 30, 1874, Saylor later rebuilt it at the same location. Only two views in the series are known to exist, but the numbering system used to identify specific views within the series—notice the "108" in the lower right corner of figure 4.31a—indicates that it contained at least four views.[67]

That same summer, William added a series of city views to "The Saginaws and Tributaries." Most interesting of the group is figure 4.31b, the new general offices of the Flint & Pere Marquette Railroad at the southeast corner of Washington and Tuscola in East Saginaw. Although the view is not an especially distinguished one, it suggests the existence of a formal commercial relationship between the railroad and the Goodridges that had become increasingly important to the studio by 1874. The railroad had been organized in 1857 to capitalize on government land grants that had begun with the subsidy to the Illinois Central Railroad in 1850. Designed to link Flint and East Saginaw with Detroit and Pere Marquette (Ludington) on Lake Michigan, the line eventually was completed in 1874, although track was opened to East Saginaw in 1862, Midland in 1867, Clare in 1870, and Reed City in 1871.[68] No record exists officially linking the Goodridge studio and the railroad, but it is clear that William used the railroad to reach locations along its route through Midland and Clare Counties and, at least once, to its western terminus at Ludington (see figure 4.38b). And an 1881 newspaper account detailing the Goodridges' success reported that the brothers were "special photographers" for the "G. R. & I. railroad and F. & P. U. [sic] R.R.," implying such a formal connection.[69]

No doubt William followed the route of the Flint & Pere Marquette, perhaps even riding "The Peggy" into Midland County during the winter of 1874–75 to create the most important of the "Lumber and Salt District" series. Titled "Scenes in the Pineries of Michigan," the series soon became the basis for much of the Goodridge studio's financial success and professional recognition through the 1880s. Made by William "At P. Glynn & Co.'s Camp, Midland County, Michigan" (see figure 4.32a), the series, as later included in "Picturesque Michigan" (see figure 4.37a), contained twelve views.

The choice of the "P. Glynn & Co.'s Camp" was an excellent one in that the camp was a fair representation of a Saginaw Valley pine lumber operation at the time. The owner, Patrick Glynn of East Saginaw, had come to the Saginaw Valley from Ireland in 1863. His early years working as a land-looker for various timber companies had taught him to recognize valuable pineland, and his experience as a "river rat" served Glynn well when he later became superintendent of the Tittabawassee

Boom Company from 1883 to 1885.[70] Only eight years after coming to Michigan, however, Glynn had jumped from employee to employer status when, in August 1871, in partnership with Charles W. Grant, Thomas Saylor, and James F. Brown, all well-established East Saginaw businessmen, he purchased approximately four thousand acres of pinelands in Warren and Edenville Townships in Midland County and Beaverton Township in Gladwin County for $29,700 from Horace Thurber of East Saginaw and Giles and Mary Williams of New York City. In 1874 and 1876, Glynn added small parcels of 40 and 240 acres, respectively, to the original purchase.[71] The operation was well situated in that the acres were a contiguous unit extending across more than ten sections in northeast Warren Township. The flat to gently rolling land was well drained by the Bliss and Howe Drains, which formed Bluff Creek in Section 25. The creek flowed southeast to North Bradley, where it joined the Salt River, which flowed into the Tittabawassee near Sanford. In addition, the camp itself was located only four miles due east of Coleman, a regular stop on the main line of the Flint & Pere Marquette, near the present junction of MacGruder and Shaffer Roads, where the Bliss and Howe Drains join Bluff Creek. Most important, however, as William's views clearly demonstrate, the land was covered by magnificent forest with many fine specimens of primal white pine.

By the time William visited the camp in the winter of 1874–75, Glynn and his partners already had fallen on hard times—suffering, according to one source,[72] the effects of the Panic of 1873. In November 1875, Glynn, Grant, Saylor, and Brown declared bankruptcy, and the following year, in October, William L. Webber acted as their agent in selling the entire operation to Newell Avery and Simon P. Murphy of Detroit for $51,000.[73]

As figures 4.32b–c and 4.33a–c show, however, William's views were considerably more successful than Glynn's lumbering operation. Figure 4.32b simply is titled "General View of the Camp," but with the large log in the left foreground, the nice curve to the muddy logging road, and sharp contrast between the smoothness of the snow and the rugged

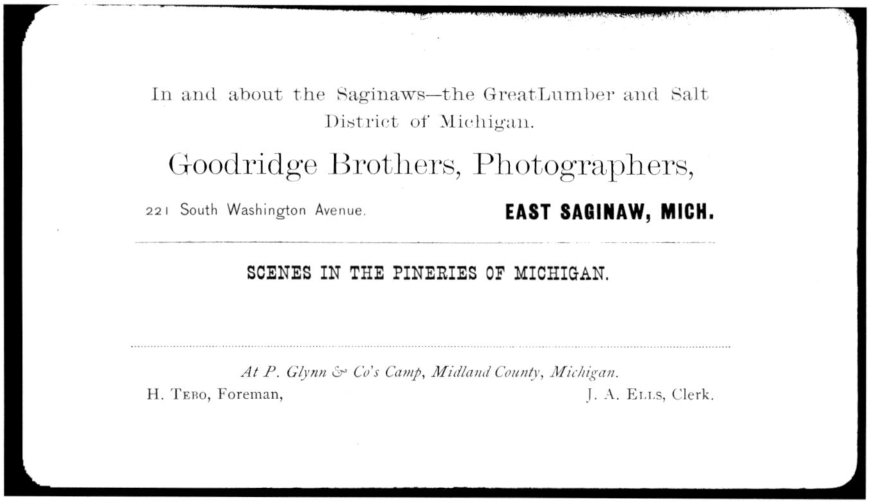

In and about the Saginaws—the Great Lumber and Salt
District of Michigan.

Goodridge Brothers, Photographers,

221 South Washington Avenue.   **EAST SAGINAW, MICH.**

SCENES IN THE PINERIES OF MICHIGAN.

At P. Glynn & Co's Camp, Midland County, Michigan.
H. TEBO, Foreman,   J. A. ELLS, Clerk.

Figure 4.32a. "Verso of Stereograph Mount," 1874–75, 7 x 3¹⁵⁄₁₆ inches. Goodridge Brothers Studio, East Saginaw, Mich. Collection of Dave Tinder.

Figure 4.32b. "General View of the Camp," 1874–75, stereograph. Albumen image, 6¹¹⁄₁₆ x 3⅜ inches, green bristol board mount, 7 x 3¹⁵⁄₁₆ inches. Goodridge Brothers Studio, East Saginaw, Mich. Collection of Dave Tinder.

Figure 4.32c. "Interior of Sleeping Camp," 1874–75, stereograph. Albumen image, 6⅝ x 3⅜ inches, orange bristol board mount, 7 x 3¹⁵⁄₁₆ inches. Goodridge Brothers Studio, East Saginaw, Mich. Clarke Historical Library, Central Michigan University.

Figure 4.33a. "Falling," 1874–75, stereograph. Albumen image, 6¼ x 3⅜ inches, yellow bristol board mount, 7 x 3¹⁵/₁₆ inches. Good-ridge Brothers Studio, East Saginaw, Mich. Collection of Dave Tinder.

Figure 4.33b. "Champion Log," 1874–75, stereograph. Albumen image, 6¼ x 3⅜ inches, yellow bristol board mount, 7 x 3¹⁵/₁₆ inches. Goodridge Brothers Studio, East Saginaw, Mich. Collection of Dave Tinder.

Figure 4.33c. "Banking Ground," 1874–75, stereograph. Albumen image, 6¼ x 3⅜ inches, yellow bristol board mount, 7 x 3¹⁵/₁₆ inches. Goodridge Brothers Studio, East Saginaw, Mich. Collection of Dave Tinder.

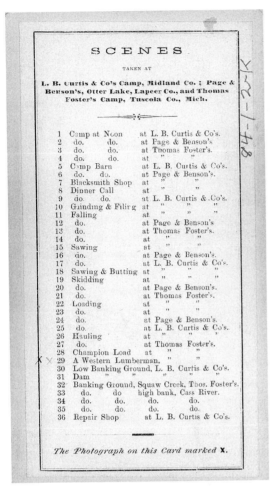

SCENES

TAKEN AT

L. B. Curtis & Co's Camp, Midland Co. ; Page &
Benson's, Otter Lake, Lapeer Co., and Thomas
Foster's Camp, Tuscola Co., Mich.

1	Camp at Noon	at L. B. Curtis & Co's.
2	do. do.	at Page & Benson's.
3	do. do.	at Thomas Foster's.
4	do. do.	at " "
5	Camp Barn	at L. B. Curtis & Co's.
6	do. do.	at Page & Benson's.
7	Blacksmith Shop	at " "
8	Dinner Call	at " "
9	do. do.	at L. B. Curtis & Co's.
10	Grinding & Filing	at " " "
11	Falling	at " " "
12	do.	at Page & Benson's
13	do.	at Thomas Foster's.
14	do.	at " "
15	Sawing	at " "
16	do.	at Page & Benson's.
17	do.	at L. B. Curtis & Co's.
18	Sawing & Butting	at " " "
19	Skidding	at " " "
20	do.	at Page & Benson's.
21	do.	at Thomas Foster's.
22	Loading	at " " "
23	do.	at " " "
24	do.	at Page & Benson's.
25	do.	at L. B. Curtis & Co's.
26	Hauling	at " " "
27	do.	at Thomas Foster's.
28	Champion Load	at " "
29	A Western Lumberman,	" "
30	Low Banking Ground,	L. B. Curtis & Co's.
31	Dam "	" " "
32	Banking Ground, Squaw Creek, Thos. Foster's.	
33	do. do	high bank, Cass River.
34	do. do.	do. do.
35	do. do.	do. do.
36	Repair Shop	at L. B. Curtis & Co's.

The Photograph on this Card marked X.

Figure 4.34. "Verso of Stereograph Mount," 1871–75, 3¹⁵⁄₁₆ x 7 inches, J. A. Jenney, Photographer, Flint, Mich. Historical Society of Saginaw County, Inc.

forest that surrounded the camp, the image is very much enlivened in the stereo viewer. "Interior of Sleeping Camp" (figure 4.32c) is not only one of William's best-known and most often reproduced views (Mills, *History of Saginaw County,* 1:406, for example, includes it without attribution) but also may be the most effective example of three-dimensional stereo effect achieved by William in any of his views. The remaining images in the series (see, for example, figures 4.33a–c) are devoted to documenting procedure and demonstrating the seemingly limitless abundance of the Saginaw Valley's timber resources. Notice that the four-foot-diameter log in figure 4.33b clearly shows the "GLYN" logmark and also records that the log contained 2,029 board feet of lumber, worth at least $20 on the wholesale market.

William was not the only Michigan photographer who toured the lumber camps during the boom years. The Goodridges' Flint competitor James A. Jenney visited at least three in the early 1870s (see figure 4.34). That Jenney was a formidable contender is clear from the fact that he invaded Goodridge territory in 1874 and showed a "large collection of stereoscopic views of Michigan scenery" at the Agricultural Society Fair that year. Only a month later, possibly the same set of "Stereoscopic views" won Jenney a "1st Premium" at the state fair that was held for the first time in East Saginaw in 1874.[74] Jenney's success and the quality of his work may have prompted William's initial attempts to create a lumber camp series of his own. The *Saginaw Daily Courier* reported in the spring of 1873 that it had received "some excellently executed views in the lumber camp of Henry Gamble, Esq., on Tittabawassa [*sic*], some three miles from Midland," made by the Goodridge studio. "The views taken in dead of winter," the newspaper declared, "are life like, and reflect credit on the workmanship of the house named."[75] Made in the winter of 1872–73 during the weeks following the October 1872 Crouse Block fire, the views may have been an attempt to revive the studio's diminished fortunes. However, no example from the "Gamble Camp" series is known to exist. If William had created such a series, it likely did not contain many views or circulate widely. Jenney's "Pineries" series, on the other hand, was quite large, with thirty-six views made at three different lumber camps in Midland, Lapeer, and Tuscola Counties. Between 1871 and 1875 the series evolved from the engaging "Gems in the Pineries of Michigan," with its scenes of camp life (as in figure 4.35a), to the more direct and dramatic "In the Pineries" of figure 4.35b. Darrah, in fact, singles out Jenney's "logging camps" views as classics of the genre.[76]

Ultimately, as we shall see, William's lumber camp series matched and even surpassed Jenney's success by serving as the basis for an extensive group of large-format lumber camp photographs that received both national and international attention. As early as the spring of 1875, *Anthony's Photographic Bulletin,* the leading professional journal

Figure 4.35a. "Dinner Call," 1871–75, stereograph. Albumen image, 6⅛ x 3¹³⁄₁₆ inches, green bristol board mount, 7 x 3¹⁵⁄₁₆ inches. J. A. Jenney, Photographer, Flint, Mich. Historical Society of Saginaw County, Inc.

Figure 4.35b. "Champion Load," 1871–75, stereograph. Albumen image, 6¹⁵⁄₁₆ x 3¹³⁄₁₆ inches, yellow bristol board mount, 7 x 3¹⁵⁄₁₆ inches. J. A. Jenney, Photographer, Flint, Mich. Historical Society of Saginaw County, Inc.

Figure 4.36. "The Letter or Poem," 1877–78, stereograph. Albumen image, 6¾ x 3⅜ inches, yellow bristol board mount, 7 x 3¹⁵⁄₁₆ inches. Goodridge Brothers Studio, East Saginaw, Mich. Collection of Lloyd C. Wright.

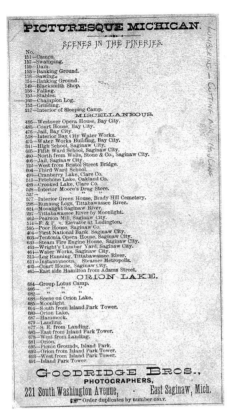

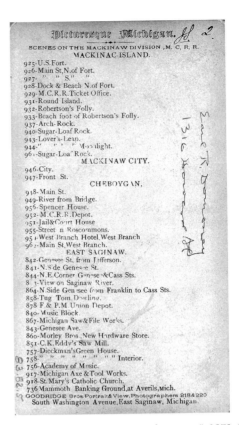

Figure 4.37a. "Verso of Stereograph Mount," 1873–90, 3¹⁵⁄₁₆ x 7 inches. Goodridge Brothers Studio, East Saginaw, Mich. Clarke Historical Library, Central Michigan University.

Figure 4.37b. "Verso of Stereograph Mount," 1873–90, 3¹⁵⁄₁₆ x 7 inches. Goodridge Brothers Studio, East Saginaw, Mich. Historical Society of Saginaw County, Inc.

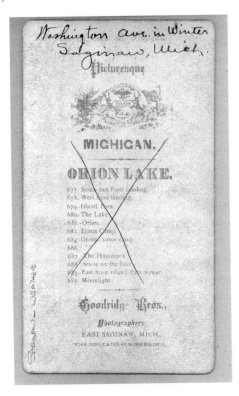

of its day, noted that it had received "From Goodridge Bros., East Saginaw, some very characteristic stereos of the great lumber business of that region," no doubt a reference to William's recently completed "P. Glynn & Co.'s Camp" series.[77]

In addition to William's noteworthy views of East Saginaw and the very successful "Scenes in the Pineries" singled out above by *Anthony's,* the "In and about the Saginaws" series included at least one view (figure 4.36) that is unusual if not unique. The view of the three well-dressed young ladies, which might appropriately be titled "The Letter" or "The Poem," was made during 1877 or 1878[78] and may have been an attempt to create what Darrah has characterized as the "Literary" view, where the photographer employed "verses of

Figure 4.37c. "Verso of Stereograph Mount," 1880, 3¹⁵⁄₁₆ x 7 inches. Goodridge Brothers Studio, East Saginaw, Mich. Clarke Historical Library, Central Michigan University.

poetry" as the focal point for his subjects.[79] Of even greater significance, however, is that fact that the view is the only extant example of a Goodridge stereo made in the studio and not in the field, and consequently, given the division of labor between Wallace and William, may be the only example of a stereo view made by Wallace Goodridge.

Success with the city view and lumber camp series led Wallace and William to launch their boldest venture to date. The March 7, 1880, edition of the *Saginaw Morning Herald* announced that the "Goodridge Bros. will publish a monthly journal, 'Goodridge's Picturesque Michigan.' The first number will appear next month. Each part will contain three photographs of various scenes in the lumber camps, saw mills, salt blocks, State public buildings, summer resorts, and many other views that will be interesting to the general public."[80] The proposal demonstrates clearly the extent to which the Goodridges were aware of and to some degree even anticipated the rapid development of their profession during the 1870s and 1880s. The mass production of stereo views for a national market was well established by 1865 under the leadership of publishers like E. & H. T. Anthony of New York, the Kilburn Brothers of Littleton, New Hampshire, and Charles Pollock in Boston, with each capable of printing more than a million stereo views annually. In 1879 B. W. Kilburn, who had assumed sole control of the family firm at his brother's retirement, introduced a most important marketing innovation by sending "canvassers . . . to several selected New England towns to demonstrate a variety of views, take orders, and a week later, deliver the stereo views and collect the money due." And, by the turn of the century, Underwood and Underwood of Ottawa, Kansas, introduced an innovation to the mass distribution of stereos that was soon taken up by the Keystone View Company, which was to become "the most important stereo publisher in the twentieth century." According to Darrah, "Underwood introduced the 'boxed set' and the 'stereographic library,'" which was "a selection of a series of cards, usually one hundred, arranged in a sequence that would simulate a tour to the country depicted. . . . A descriptive guide-book was prepared to accompany each card set," and "an ingenious copyrighted map system showed the exact position of the camera when each photograph was taken." Darrah acknowledged that "the basic idea of the travel set" was as old as photography itself but pointed out that the "idea of Underwood & Underwood went much further." It was "not merely a series of views of a particular region, it was a carefully integrated sequence of views that would show cities, governmental buildings, industry, topography, natural resources, agriculture and people." He concluded that "Nothing like it had appeared in stereo before."[81] The *Herald's* description of "Goodridge's Picturesque Michigan" reveals that their proposal included elements of both Kilburn's recently established serial publication system (the "monthly journal") and also anticipated Underwood's later "carefully integrated sequence of views" ("photographs of various scenes"). Goodridge relative Joseph H. Gray also was to be employed as the studio's "canvasser" in marketing the "Picturesque Michigan" series.

No complete inventory of "Picturesque Michigan" exists, but as figures 4.37a and b reveal, the venture, as it evolved, came to include a variety of elements. Existing series of views such as the "Scenes in the Pineries," made in 1874–75 at "P. Glynn & Co.'s Camp," were incorporated as a unit. Selections from the "Michigan Views" and "Lumber and Salt District" series, such as No. 297, "Tittabawassee River by Moonlight," No. 736, "Mammoth Banking Grounds at Averill," and No. 577, "Interior Green House, Brady Hill Cemetery," also were included to achieve the goals announced for the undertaking. By listing views from Mackinac Island, Mackinaw City, Cheboygan, Roscommon, West Branch, Ludington, Clare and Oakland Counties, and Bay City, in addition to the East Saginaw and lumber camp series, it also is clear that the emphasis was to be on picturesque "Michigan" and not merely on the Saginaw Valley, as in earlier series. Including the state seal and motto between "Picturesque" and "Michigan" on the verso of the card listing the "Orion Lake" series conspicuously reinforced Wallace and William's intention to focus

Figure 4.38a. "Group Lotus Camp, Orion Lake," 1880, stereograph. Albumen image, 6¹³⁄₁₆ x 3⁷⁄₁₆ inches, orange bristol board mount, 7 x 3¹⁵⁄₁₆ inches. Goodridge Brothers Studio, East Saginaw, Mich. Collection of Dave Tinder.

Figure 4.38b. "F. & P. M. Elevator at Ludington," 1880s, stereograph. Albumen image, 6⁶⁄₁₆ x 3⁶⁄₁₆ inches, orange bristol board mount, 7 x 3¹⁵⁄₁₆ inches. Goodridge Brothers Studio, East Saginaw, Mich. Historical Society of Saginaw County, Inc.

Figure 4.38c. "Cranberry Lake," 1880s, stereograph. Albumen image, 6⅞ x 3⁶⁄₁₆ inches, orange bristol board mount, 7 x 3¹⁵⁄₁₆ inches. Goodridge Brothers Studio, East Saginaw, Mich. Historical Society of Saginaw County, Inc.

on Michigan (see figure 4.37c). That the studio considered "Picturesque Michigan" especially important at this time is clear from an examination of figure 4.10 (the Goodridge brothers and their assistants, Morris and Brown), which features display boards of stereo views that were major components of the series.

A notice in the August 12, 1880, *Saginaw Morning Herald* suggests, however, that intention and its accomplishment did not always concur. The notice stated that the "Goodridge Bros. have a fine selection of Orion Lake views at their photograph gallery. Those wishing them *can obtain them by calling*."[82] Inviting their customers to purchase views "by calling" for them in person at the studio did not preclude continued publication of a serialized "monthly journal," the original description of "Goodridge's Picturesque Michigan." It does suggest, however, that the studio may have altered its intended system of distribution for the series or, at the very least, provided alternatives to it. Furthermore, while multiple copies of the lumber camp and city view stereos that were made before 1880 and the creation of "Picturesque Michigan" exist, only one probable view from the "Orion Lake" series is known (see figure 4.38a). It is most likely either No. 682, 684, or 686, all titled "Group Lotus Camp," although no specific evidence from the view itself other than a "Picturesque Michigan" label on the verso of the card (see figure 4.37a) so identifies it. And, indeed, if the intention of the "Orion Lake" series was to showcase a Michigan resort, the week the photograph was made must have been a rainy one from the expressions on the faces of the "Lotus Camp Group"! Notice, as well, in figure 4.37c, that the card stock with the "Picturesque Michigan"—"Orion Lake" series labels had become surplus and was being used to publish scenes of "Washington Ave. in Winter," although exactly which "winter" is impossible to determine.

A meticulous search also has yet to uncover a single example of a Goodridge stereo view in the Mackinac Island, Mackinaw City, Cheboygan, Roscommon, West Branch, or Bay City series listed under "Picturesque Michigan" in figures 4.37a and b. William may have planned and even advertised

these several series as part of the "Scenes on the Mackinaw Division, M. C. R. R." (figure 4.37b), but then was not able to create the photographs. If he did eventually make some or all of the views listed, it also is possible that the studio simply did not publish them as part of "Picturesque Michigan." Figure 5.23 does reveal, however, that in 1878 William had made a series of "Views in Bay City, Michigan" that were published by the *New York Daily Graphic* that year. Four of the views from the publication—No. 5, "Holly Water Works," No. 7, "Bay County Jail," No. 8, "Westover Opera House," and No. 9, "Bay County Court House"—correspond exactly to the "Miscellaneous" stereo views listed under "Picturesque Michigan" (see figure 4.37a) as No. 475, "Water Works Building," No. 476, "Jail, Bay City," No. 486, "Westover Opera House," and No. 485, "Court House, Bay City," although none of these four stereo views is known to exist at present.

As late as 1906, many years after William's death, the studio continued to advertise itself as "special photographers" to the Michigan Central Railroad, for which the Mackinac, Cheboygan, Roscommon, and West Branch series were to have been made. Also, a newspaper account published only two years before his death reported that William was then actively "taking landscape views for his 'Illustrated Michigan,'" most likely a later version of "Picturesque Michigan."[83]

The stereo views that are known to have been added to "Picturesque Michigan" after 1880 were included either in the "East Saginaw" or "Miscellaneous" series and represent some of William's best work at that time. For example, No. 514, "F. & P. M. Elevator at Ludington" (figure 4.38b), was made at the western terminus of that rail line. The view shows the steamer *Depere*, later renamed the *State of Michigan*,[84] powering up—smoke appears to be coming from the funnel—to depart the Flint & Pere Marquette Railroad dock at the elevator at Ludington on Lake Michigan. William used both the dull sky and the light reflecting off the water of Lake Michigan to create a series of silhouettes of the elevator and the pilings of the projecting docks to surround, almost to restrain, the steamer as it prepared to depart. The result is especially dramatic and energetic in the stereoscopic viewer.

Its companion, No. 490, "Cranberry Lake" (figure 4.38c), is an intriguing view. Like "Elevator at Ludington," it was made along the route of the Flint & Pere Marquette. Known today as Big Cranberry, the lake is located adjacent to the main line of the former Flint & Pere Marquette Railroad between Farwell and Evart and present highway U.S. 10 in Garfield Township in Clare County. According to Clare County historian Forrest B. Meek, Cranberry Lake was an important source of ice for the Flint & Pere Marquette Railroad, which by 1890 had built "over twelve ice houses . . . each holding approximately 30,000 tons" and "had a crew of men working full time either loading the ice houses or unloading them in the warm weather when the refrigerator cars required large quantities of ice." Earlier a local lumber mill had operated briefly on the lake, and in the twentieth century it became a popular recreation site.[85] William's view presents five men almost enveloped by trees and brush against the background of the lake and its distant shore. The heavy vegetation and thick forest suggest the view was made in summer, no later than the early 1880s, before serious logging had begun in the area. The second individual from the right may be William himself, and the homburg-topped figure at the far left is either brother Wallace or possibly William Q. Atwood, a wealthy lumberman, prominent leader of Saginaw's African American community, and a close family friend. The occasion may have been an Emancipation Day picnic similar to the one held at Oa-at-ka Beach in 1889, with the Goodridge brothers serving as official photographers for the day.[86]

The view also is a thought-provoking one in that in it William addresses, perhaps only unconsciously or inadvertently, the relationship between people and nature. The vast majority of Goodridge views, whatever the series, present a natural world that has been subdued if not completely vanquished by human activity—the lumber camp series is only the most obvious example. Certainly the tone of William's approach in the lumber series is to celebrate human accomplishments—champion logs, record loads, and mammoth banking

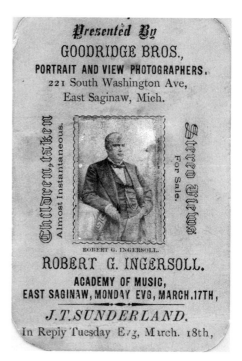

Figure 4.39. "Ingersoll-Sunderland Debate," March 1879, advertising card. Albumen image, ⅞ x 1⅛ inches, gray bristol board mount, 2½ x 3¾ inches. Goodridge Brothers Studio, East Saginaw, Mich. Collection of William Wegner.

grounds—as the measurement of success. At the same time, there is in the lumber camp stereo series (and in the larger-format lumber photographs that would soon follow) the implicit sense that the photographs were recording not just the pinnacle but also the finale of the process. Only rarely, however, does a Goodridge view clearly present nature as ascendant. By framing the human group with the lateral branch to the left and the large pine at the right, by enveloping the sightseers in the wild brush along the shore, and by metaphorically sinking them into the waters of Cranberry Lake, William presents a view of nature that departed directly and dramatically from that in the rest of his work. The missing views from the Mackinac Island and Orion Lake series, as well as No. 515, "Pete-bone Lake, Oakland County," and No. 489, "Crooked Lake, Clare County," become then an even greater loss in that they might have been the means to test the uniqueness of the "Cranberry Lake" view.

In the absence of those views, a clue to William's thinking about people and the natural world may lie in the fact that during the family's years in York father William C. Goodridge, and presumably his sons and daughters, were strongly influenced by the writings of the Swedish mystical philosopher Emanuel Swedenborg. According to his "doctrine of correspondance . . . all phenomena of the physical world have their spiritual correspondances. Consequently, the substitution of corresponding terms of a spiritual import for key words in sentences referring to nature *transforms a natural statement into a spiritual statement* or a theological dogma."[87] Swedenborg's doctrine was especially attractive to the American transcendentalists. Ralph Waldo Emerson, for example, included Swedenborg as one of his *Representative Men* (1850). Swedenborg's New Church continues worldwide to this day, with its most important center at the New Church Academy in Bryn Athyn in suburban Philadelphia. There is no record that William O. Goodridge was a member of any Saginaw Valley church, and Wallace only joined Zion Baptist Church after his marriage to Miss Margaret Jacques of Baltimore in 1889. Goodridge sponsorship of a debate at the Academy of Music on March 17 and 18, 1879 (see figure 4.39), between the celebrated American agnostic Robert Green Ingersoll and the equally prominent Unitarian Jabez Thomas Sunderland suggests, however, that Swedenborg's "anthropocentric theological system" remained attractive to the Goodridge family long after its move to East Saginaw.[88]

Not all of William's stereo views were destined for inclusion in one of the studio's many series. Regularly during the 1870s and 1880s the studio accepted private commissions for a single view or two to commemorate an event such as a wedding or to preserve the memory of the family homestead. Figure 4.40a was made for Miss Carrie R. Bliss and Mr. F. M. Luther, who were married at First Congregational Church in 1875. The view shows the garlands of flowers used to decorate the main aisle for the ceremony. The "tunnel of blooms" accentuates the Romanesque arches of the church, creating a dramatic stereo view and keepsake for the newlyweds. Unfortunately, the joy that the view celebrates was short-lived. Less than a year later, the February 20, 1876, *Saginaw Daily Courier* informed the community that Carrie Bliss-Luther had died after a prolonged illness only the day before in Saltville, Virginia.[89]

The May 23, 1880, edition of the *Saginaw Morning Herald* published a notice that during the previous week the "Goodridge Bros. made some fine views of the residences in the Washington avenue grove, and have orders to photograph a number of residences both in this and Saginaw City. Having just received a new camera they now have the largest collection of photographic instruments for portraits and views in the state."[90] Although it had been made the previous year, figure 4.40b certainly was the sort of view the Goodridges were promoting that following spring. A note on the verso of the mount describes the view as the "Cottage in which Alfred Owen Dunk & Mary Rust Dunk were born . . . three doors from Hoyt Street on West & South side of Washington Ave." Sadly, Alfred A. Dunk, Alfred O. and Mary Dunk's father, died in December, only months after this view of the family home was made. He was born thirty-three years earlier in Syracuse, New York, and had come to East Saginaw in 1864 when he was nineteen. He purchased the drugstore run by Leander Simoneau in the Crouse Block, where he was a Goodridge studio neighbor (see figure 3.3) until fire destroyed the block in October 1872. Dunk returned to the identical location when Hoyt's new block was completed. The "new and elegant fixtures" he installed in the store were "said to have been the finest ever placed in a store of the kind in this part of Michigan."[91] Following Dunk's untimely death in 1879, the drug store, including fixtures, was sold to William B. Moore, who poses next to the store's "elegant" soda fountain in figure 4.40c.

From their Crouse Block studio the Goodridge brothers had supplied Saginaw merchants with carte de visite views to advertise their various goods and services. At the new Washington Avenue facility the service continued, but the larger and more "lively" stereo views now replaced the smaller carte de visite ads. The Bullock music store, for example, was justly proud of "two pho-

Figure 4.40a. "Bliss-Luther Wedding, First Congregational Church," 1875, stereograph. Albumen image, 6¾ x 3⅝ inches, yellow bristol board mount, 7 x 3¹⁵⁄₁₆ inches. Goodridge Brothers Studio, East Saginaw, Mich. Collection of Val R. Berryman.

Figure 4.40b. "Dunk Cottage, Washington Avenue," 1879, stereograph. Albumen image, 6⁹⁄₁₆ x 3½, yellow bristol board mount, 7 x 3¹⁵⁄₁₆ inches. Goodridge Brothers Studio, East Saginaw, Mich. Eddy Local History and Genealogical Collection, Hoyt Public Library.

Figure 4.40.c "Fountain, Dunk's Drug Store," after 1879, stereograph. Albumen image, 7 x 3⁵⁄₁₆ inches, orange bristol board mount, 7 x 3¹⁵⁄₁₆ inches. Goodridge Brothers Studio, East Saginaw, Mich. Collection of Dave Tinder.

Figure 4.41a. "Little Jake's," 1874–76, stereograph. Albumen image, 7 x 3⅞ inches, green bristol board mount, 7 x 3¹⁵⁄₁₆ inches. Goodridge Brothers Studio, East Saginaw, Mich. Historical Society of Saginaw County, Inc.

TRADE WITH LITTLE JAKE
THE GREAT CLOTHIER OF THE WEST.

The largest stock of Ready-Made Clothing, Cloths, Cassimeres, Vestings, Gents' Furnishing Goods, Hats, Caps, and Lumbermen's Supplies ever on exhibition in Michigan.

Goods marked in plain figures and strictly one price, and the lowest in the market.

For custom work we cannot be surpassed. The best Cutters and Tailors employed.

Goods in this department are chiefly of my own importation.

Stores on Genesee Avenue and Franklin Street, East Saginaw, Michigan.

Call and see me.

Goodridge Bros., Photographers, 221 S. Wash. Ave.

LITTLE JAKE,
THE POPULAR CLOTHIER.

85.142

Figure 4.41b. "Verso of Stereograph Mount," 1874–76, 7 x 3¹⁵⁄₁₆ inches. Goodridge Brothers Studio, East Saginaw, Mich. Historical Society of Saginaw County, Inc.

tographs showing the exterior and interior of their . . . store. . . . They are the work of Goodridge Bros. and finished in their best style. The interior view shows distinctly the arrangement of the different pianos and organs on sale."[92]

By all accounts, however, the studio's best and most flamboyant commercial customer was Jacob "Little Jake" Seligman. Already something of a legend before his death in 1911, the young Seligman had come to the United States in 1859 from Darmstadt, Germany, where he was born in 1843. The basis for his future success was established, with the help of the Heavenrich brothers, in Pontiac, Michigan, in 1863 when Seligman opened his first clothing store there. By 1870 he had branched out to East Saginaw, where he then moved the headquarters of his expanding commercial empire in 1874. Much of his success came as a wholesale supplier to other

clothing retailers. According to his biographer, "As the Flint & Pere Marquette Railroad inched its way across the state in the 1870s, Little Jake picked up additional towns which were built along the line. From as far away as Hersey in Osceola County, Richard B. Sheridan, proprietor of the store there, came to Little Jake for his clothing stock."[93] Success came not only from Seligman's astute business acumen—at one time he owned the Union Street Railway, the Bank of Commerce, and several business blocks in East Saginaw—but also from his determination to keep "Little Jake" in the public eye. Figures 4.41a and b represent only one of the means he chose. The view was made sometime between 1874 and 1876 when his neighbor, Doughty's Jewelry Store, moved out and Little Jake took over the entire Wisner Block. Featured prominently is one of the horse-drawn wagons that Seligman often used to advertise his famous clothing auctions or to carry the brass band that he hired to attract customers. Not surprisingly, the stereo view is the largest, 7 x 3⅞ inches, that the Goodridge studio ever produced. Seligman obviously recognized quality and remained a Goodridge customer throughout the 1880s. In September 1884, for example, the *Saginaw Evening News* reported that the "Goodridge Bros. have commenced photographing our principal business blocks and took a fine picture of Little Jake's bank this morning. The Music block [which Seligman purchased in 1890] will be taken next."[94]

Among the many hundreds of stereo views the Goodridge brothers produced between 1860 and 1880, there are none that might be considered "personal" in the sense of portraits of either brother, although both Wallace and William do appear peripherally or inadvertently in some of their views (see, for example, figures 4.38c and 5.12b). There are a few stereo views extant, however, which do reveal something of the brothers' interests and possibly their thinking about issues of national concern. Figure 4.42a is a view of the grandstand and finish line at the East Saginaw Driving Park. The park was located on a large tract of land in the southeast corner of the city bounded by Jefferson, Webber, and Sheridan. The site originally was developed as the location for its annual fair by the Saginaw Valley Agricultural Society, which built a half-mile track there shortly after its organization in 1866. The society continued to use the park for its autumn festival until the land was sold to the Saginaw Improvement Company in 1890 and subdivided into residential lots.[95] When the driving park was created in 1872 by a group of twenty East Saginaw investors (including well-known business leaders such as C. K. Eddy, H. D. Wickes, and G. W. Morley), they added an excellent one-mile track and grandstand to the site. According to its "Articles of Association," the park was created "for riding, driving and walking of horses with and without carriages and other vehicles, . . . and such other purposes as Driving Parks are usually used for."[96] The latter, of course, referred to horse racing. One Saginaw historian has written that the park was built specifically to attract the "Grand Circuit."

When the event came to town, usually in July, "sportsmen from miles around attended and crowds up to 10,000 were common. The most famous race took place on July 18, 1874, when the legendary Goldsmith Maid ran Judge Fullerton into the ground, setting a new world record of two minutes and sixteen seconds in the third heat. It was considered such a feat the *Daily Republican* was on the street with an extra less then [*sic*] thirty minutes after the finish."[97] Another account of the race adds that the event was so important that "Currier and Ives memorialized it in colorful lithographs."[98]

The chances are quite good that the day Goldsmith Maid broke the record the Goodridge brothers and their friend the barber Abraham Reyno were in the grandstand. As early as 1866, Reyno won an "$8.00 Premium" at the Agricultural Society Fair for "Best mare or gelding." In September 1870 it was reported that Reyno had entered a bay gelding named John Stewart in an open trot during the first day of the annual fair. The results of the race were not recorded. And three years later Reyno not only entered a grey gelding named Storm in the first race at the 1873 fair but also drove his black stallion, General Sherman, in the third race.[99] Figure 4.42b may well be Reyno and the General. Several years later the *Cleveland Gazette* noted that "Wm. O. Goodridge and his trotter, Billy G. have gained quite a reputation." While Billy's time, 2:38, did not quite match Goldsmith Maid's record, the *Gazette* reported that Goodridge had "refused an offer of $1,100 for the horse."[100] In 1871 a "W. Goodridge" (likely William but possibly Wallace) had entered a "mare 3 years old" in the fair. Unlike family friend Reyno, however, there was no report of a premium for the entry. Then, in 1890, during the driving park's final season and shortly before William's own death, the *Detroit Plain Dealer* observed that "Mr. W. O. Goodridge talks of entering his fine pacer for a prize at the Driving Park the coming season."[101] Whether he raced before William's death in August that year is not known.

A much more intriguing and perhaps revealing view is figure 4.42c. James Webber had numbered it "146" in his collection of views and noted that its vintage was 1873. Unfortunately,

Figure 4.42a. "East Saginaw Driving Park," 1873–82, stereograph. Albumen image, 6³⁄₁₆ x 3⅜ inches, green bristol board mount, 7 x 3¹⁵⁄₁₆ inches. Goodridge Brothers Studio, East Saginaw, Mich. Collection of Dave Tinder.

Figure 4.42b. "Abraham Reyno and 'General Sherman,'" 1873, stereograph. Albumen image, 6⅜ x 3⅜, black bristol board mount, 6¹⁵⁄₁₆ x 3¹⁵⁄₁₆ inches. Goodridge Brothers Studio, East Saginaw, Mich. Historical Society of Saginaw County, Inc.

Figure 4.42c. "Charter Oak," 1873, stereograph. Albumen image, 7 x 3⅜ inches, green bristol board mount, 7 x 3¹⁵⁄₁₆ inches. Goodridge Brothers Studio, East Saginaw, Mich. Historical Society of Saginaw County, Inc.

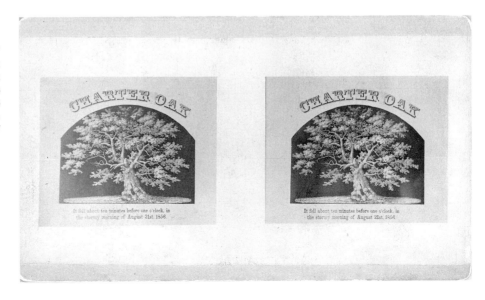

Webber gives us no information as to why he chose the view for his collection or why the Goodridge brothers had published it. The stereo is of a woodcut print of Connecticut's celebrated "Charter Oak." According to tradition, a hollow in the tree was used in 1687 to hide Connecticut's 1662 charter from Sir Edmund Andros, who had been sent to Hartford by King James II to seize the colony's liberal constitution. The tree, which stood on property owned by Samuel Wyllys, was reported to have been a thousand years old and thirty-three feet in circumference when "It fell about ten minutes before one o'-clock in the stormy morning of August 21, 1856." According to one source, "the wood of the Charter Oak has been made into chairs, gavels, and other odd articles" and "the name 'Charter Oak' has been freely used on all manner of places and articles." Mark Twain, a Hartford resident, wrote that "he had seen 'a walking-stick, dog collar, needle-case, three-legged stool, bootjack, dinner table, tenpin alley, toothpick, and enough Charter Oak to build a plank road from Hartford to Salt Lake City.'"[102] The tree had become an icon of freedom, even before it fell, because of its reputed role in protecting American constitutional rights against British tyranny. For a time, in fact, the name "Charter Oak" was taken by an abolitionist newspaper published in Hartford.[103] Given William C. Goodridge's earlier and costly commitment to the Underground Railroad and the abolition of slavery, as well as the family's later involvement in organizations established to protect and promote the progress of free African American citizens, which we will consider in chapter 6, the Goodridge studio's publication of the "Charter Oak" view, then, becomes most appropriate.

5

The Large-Format Photographs: National and International Acclaim, 1872–1890

In 1857 a bellows-style camera capable of making photographs as large as 18 x 22 inches was introduced in Paris. The same year, Professor David A. Woodward of the Maryland Institute in Baltimore patented the solar camera, which was an enlarging device that made use of natural sunlight. By 1864 improvements to Woodward's original design enabled the solar camera to print photographs 17¾ x 23¼ inches from a carte de visite–sized negative in less than seventy minutes.[1] Although by 1865 both devices (but especially the solar camera, according to John Towler in *Humphrey's Journal*) had become "the favorite mode" of making "enlarged photographs,"[2] before 1872 the Goodridge studio did not advertise that it possessed such equipment, nor did it actively promote large-format photography. Given the competition among Saginaw Valley photographers at the time, any opportunity to publicize a competitive advantage, whether a Sarony posing device or a wife to assist female customers with their toilette, was rarely ignored. In their initial 1865 newspaper advertisement the Goodridges did include "the life-size Photograph" which, depending on the process and the camera used, could have been anything from a 6½ x 8½ daguerreotype to a paper positive made from a collodian-coated glass negative usually no larger than 8 x 10. There was no mention of "enlargements."[3]

By 1872, however, even before the fire and move to the new studio, the Goodridges had begun to promote their "New American Portraits" (cabinets) and "copies small or enlarge [sic] in Ink, Oil or Pastell"[4] (see figure 3.6b). In fact, the portrait of the Goodridges' favorite actress, Effie Ellsler, which was featured in the brothers' 1879 New Years greeting (see figures 4.21a and b), was exactly this sort of enlargement made from an original cabinet-sized portrait. Enlarged portraits such as Ellsler's no doubt were made using a solar camera, but even after 1872 there is no record confirming that the studio had acquired one.

More than once after the 1872 move, the Goodridges also purchased new cameras that enabled them to make ever larger portraits and landscapes by using a direct printing process. In fact, an 1882 notice in the *Saginaw Evening Express* reported that the brothers had "completed arrangements to make some mammoth views, 20 x 25 inches, for some of the leading railroads of Michigan, when the season opens."[5] At the time, a camera with the capacity to use such large glass-plate negatives was at the limits of the available technology. By the end of the decade, introduction of the electric light enlarger made both the solar camera and the mammoth-plate camera obsolete.[6]

Attention to the latest developments in photo technology and a growing reputation for the quality of their portraits and stereo series enabled Wallace and William between 1872 and 1890 to make numerous large-format photographs and photo series that brought them not only national but also international attention by the time of William's death in 1890. One visitor to the studio in December 1889, for example, reported that he had "stepped into the photograph parlors of the Goodridge brothers and found them doing a thriving business, having more orders than they can

Figure 5.1a. "Members of the Tuesday Club at Mrs. Buckhout's Home," 1885, original size and format unknown. Goodridge Brothers Studio, East Saginaw, Mich. Mills, *History of Saginaw County,* 1:309.

fill."[7] Presumably the division of labor that the brothers had established earlier, with Wallace in the studio concentrating on individual and group portraits and William farther afield making landscapes and views, carried over into their large-format work as well.

Increasingly during the 1870s and 1880s, having a "Photograph by Goodridge" made to document an achievement, record a special event, or simply for the joy of it came to be of ever greater importance to Saginaw residents.[8] In the summer of 1885, for example, William was invited to celebrate in a group portrait the meeting of East Saginaw's most exclusive and influential women's organization (figure 5.1a). According to Mills, the Tuesday Club "was a small but very exclusive club of women, all very close friends, who were prominent in the social and religious life of the city. . . . The membership was limited to fifteen, and there was always a waiting list of leading women eager to enter the inner circle of their friends." Mills identifies the members present for the photograph as

"Mrs. Chauncey Wisner, Mrs. Farnum Lyon, Mrs. C. Stuart Draper, Mrs. Gurdon Corning, Mrs. Edward Mershon, Mrs. Henry D. Wickes, Mrs. William F. Potter, Miss Lizzie Thurber, Mrs. James F. Brown, Mrs. L. A. Clark, Mrs. Sanford Keeler, Mrs. Bryon B. Buckhout, and Mrs. John J. Wheeler. Mrs. Robert Boyd and another member of the club not now recalled, were not present at the time this picture was taken." The Buckhout residence at 226 North Washington Avenue, the setting for the portrait, was described as "in its day the most palatial mansion in Saginaw." It later became home to the Knights of Columbus.[9]

A much larger, certainly less influential, but no less solemn group (see figure 5.1b) invited the Goodridge studio to record its gathering on the banks of the Cass River near the Dixie Highway bridge one summer in the 1880s. Most likely this was a church group—notice the patriarchs among the children and seated on the stump in the foreground—or one of Saginaw's several fraternal organizations, although the latter rarely failed to feature an identifying banner for such a group portrait. The presence of the brass band, if not the occasional smile here and there among the group, suggests that this was a joyful occasion. Technically the portrait is weak, with individuals severed from the group at both margins and others in the background lost in the dappled forest sunshine. At the same time, use of the fallen log to define the foreground, the riverbank to bring some order to the multitude, and even the lack of definition as the most distant members blend into the surrounding forest present a pleasing result.

Increasingly, the Goodridges also were called upon by the community to record important events. Some were of lasting, others of more passing, consequence. For example, in August 1882 several performances of a light operatic version of *Cinderella*, with at least some of the music based on

Rossini's more formal work, were staged in both East Saginaw and Saginaw City as a "Grand testimonial benefit to Mrs. Agnes Benton." On Saturday the twenty-fifth the Goodridge brothers were engaged to photograph the young thespians who were honoring Mrs. Benton. Figure 5.2a is the result of both their and the Goodridges' effort.[10]

The East Saginaw performances of *Cinderella* were staged in the original Academy of Music a few doors from the Goodridge studio at the northeast corner of Washington and William (now Janes) Street. Little more than a year after the benefit, the academy, which lumberman Charles Lee had decorated lavishly, was destroyed by fire. Within the year an Academy of Music Company was formed by thirty investors with William C. McClure as secretary. By December 1884 the new and even more impressive Academy of Music opened at the same

Figure 5.1b. "Picnic on the Cass River," 1880s. Silver print, 8¹⁵⁄₁₆ x 7⁷⁄₁₆ inches, beige bristol board mount, 9⅞ x 8 inches. Goodridge Brothers Studio, East Saginaw, Mich. Collection of Frankenmuth Historical Association.

Figure 5.2a. "Cinderella," 1882. Silver print, 7¹⁄₁₆ x 5¹⁄₁₆ inches, dark gray bristol board mount, 9¹⁵⁄₁₆ x 7⁵⁄₁₆ inches. Goodridge Brothers Studio, East Saginaw, Mich. Historical Society of Saginaw County, Inc.

Figure 5.2b. "Academy of Music," 1885. Silver print, 9½ x 6⅞ inches, ivory bristol board mount with gold trim, 9⅞ x 6⅞ inches. Goodridge Brothers Studio, East Saginaw, Mich. Eddy Local History and Genealogical Collection, Hoyt Public Library.

Figure 5.3. "Hoyt Library," 1889–90. Silver print, 9 ¾ x 7¹³⁄₁₆ inches, beige bristol board mount, 12 x 9 ¹⁄₁₆ inches. Goodridge Brothers Studio, East Saginaw, Mich. Historical Society of Saginaw County, Inc.

location as the original. The new structure was of brick, could seat more than fifteen hundred patrons, and "was regarded as one of the finest theatres in Michigan, its furnishings and appointments being first-class in every respect."[11] Between 1884 and its destruction by fire the night of April 17, 1917, the new academy enjoyed the talent of local aspirants as well as the cream of the American stage, including "the youthful, 43-year-old Sarah Bernhardt who arrived on March 10, 1892, with six coaches and baggage cars and her pets: St. Bernard dog, 10 Paris snakes, and Australian kangaroo, Tilda."[12] Shortly after opening night, most likely in the spring of 1885, Wallace (notice William standing to the right of the main entrance in figure 5.2b) recorded the

impressive presence of the Goodridges' newest neighbor. Visible at the very edge of the lower left corner of the photograph are the chimneys and outline of the roof of the Goodridge studio. A note on the verso of the print states that the "House with cupola in the distance at the lower right was Dr. Stewart's home. Stood at corner of Janes & Jefferson across from Hoyt Library." The verso bears a stamp inscribed "W. L. Webber, May 28, 1886, East Saginaw, Mich.," indicating that this photograph was at one time part of the collection of Goodridge photographs begun earlier by James S. Webber and continued by his son William.

Some years later, most likely in 1889, one of the Goodridges recorded the remarkable achieve-

Figure 5.4a. "East Saginaw Fire Department, Chief George Wallis and Staff," 1887. Unmounted silver print, 9½ x 7½ inches. Goodridge Brothers Studio, East Saginaw, Mich. Historical Society of Saginaw County, Inc.

ment of the stonemasons and sculptors as the exterior of the new Hoyt Library neared its completion (figure 5.3). In 1882 the estate of lumber baron Jesse Hoyt, who had died that August, bequeathed four lots on William between Jefferson and Warren and a trust fund of $100,000 to the community for "the establishment of a library for the benefit and free use of all the people of Saginaw." In 1887, after an initial delay, the trustees chose the Boston architects Van Brunt and Howe, who designed "a building of dignified and artistic proportions" in what is usually described as the Richardsonian Romanesque style, with "walls of stone from the Bay Port quarries, [and] trimmed with Lake Superior red sandstone."[13] When the library opened to the public in October 1890 it was hailed as "the pride of all Saginawians."[14] The photograph effectively captures the massive grace that was the hallmark of the Richardsonian style, as well as the pride of the artist-craftsmen who, with their mallets under their arms, were responsible for the graceful de-

tailing that defined the massive arches of the library's main entrance.

After 1872 a variety of organizations, both from within the city itself as well as those that visited, if only for a short time, also chose the Goodridge studio to create their official portrait. In 1878, for example, it was reported that "The Goodridge Bros. photographed the Congregational association of the state, during the recent session here, the physiognomy of the delegation being readily recognized by all who are acquainted with them."[15] Although the portrait is no longer extant, the report reveals that it met the studio's well-known standards for quality.

In 1887, newly appointed fire chief George Wallis made a similar choice. He invited the Goodridges to commemorate his promotion in a portrait flanked by his staff at department headquarters (figure 5.4a). The former Valley City Engine House No. 3, at the northeast corner of Cass (now Baum) and Germania (now Federal) Streets, had served as the department's headquarters since

Figure 5.4b. "Saginaw Fire Department, Hose House No. 10," after 1890. Silver print, 9⁹∕₁₆ x 7⁷∕₁₆ inches, dark gray bristol board mount, 14 x 10 ¹⁵∕₁₆ inches. Goodridge Brothers Studio, Saginaw, Mich. Collection of Beth Cordes Thompson.

its initial formal organization in 1865. Wallis was chief of the department and, from 1890, of the consolidated departments of East Saginaw and Saginaw City until 1915. That year he was succeeded by assistant Robert Hudson, who is seated to Wallis's right, behind that very abundant mustache.[16]

Some years after 1890 (the exact date is not known), Wallace crossed the river to complete yet another commission for the fire department. Figure 5.4b shows Hose House No. 10, formerly located in the 1800 block of North Michigan Avenue. It was one of four companies of the consolidated fire department on the west side of the river. Its captain was George Fradd, the mustached individual seated next to the driver, and three fire-

men were under his command. Whether Wallace made portraits of the other west side hose houses (Nos. 13, 15, and 19) is not known. Although Mills includes a photograph similar to figure 5.4b of Hose House No. 13 at Harrison and Van Buren Streets, which served as the west side headquarters of Assistant Chief Robert Hudson at the time, the view is not attributed to a specific studio.[17]

Not to be outdone by their fellows in the fire department, the combined police force of the recently consolidated Saginaws gathered around Chief Patrick Kain for a Goodridge portrait in May 1890 (see figure 5.5). Kain, who had succeeded T. Daily Mower upon the latter's retirement in January 1890, had been chief in East Saginaw only

Figure 5.5. "Saginaw Police Force," May 1890. Unmounted silver print, 13⅜ x 12¾ inches. Goodridge Brothers Studio, Saginaw, Mich. Historical Society of Saginaw County, Inc.

three months when he was chosen to head the consolidated force on April 22, 1890. Kain had come to the valley from Canada to work as a blacksmith but joined the East Saginaw force in 1873 on the recommendation of Sanford Keeler, superintendent of the Flint & Pere Marquette Railroad. Kain was assigned the difficult Potter Street beat, home to the "red sash brigade" of lumberjacks who regularly visited the city and especially the attractions in the neighborhood of the railroad's Potter Street station. According to Mills, Kain "sized up the situation . . . and came to the conclusion that the first duty of an officer was to keep the peace." In a short time, by jumping "right in to the thick of

it" but getting "in the way of a good many blows," Kain had made the Potter Street beat "as orderly as any business street" in the city. "This condition of affairs soon came to the notice of the commissioners," and Kain rose steadily through the ranks. Under his direction the force grew from the forty members pictured with Kain to sixty-four in 1915. By that time, Mills tells us, Kain's "natural aptitude for the business of running down criminals" and "his record as a sharp tracer of thugs and confidence men" was so well known that "His name is such a terror to a long list of crooks that they give Saginaw a wide berth."[18] Sergeant Tim McCoy, seated second from the left, who succeeded Kain as

Figure 5.6. "Parade on Genesee Avenue," 1879–80. Unmounted silver print, 9 ½ x 7¹¹/₁₆ inches. Goodridge Brothers Studio, East Saginaw, Mich. Collection of William Oberschmidt.

chief in 1919, was the father of Tim McCoy, a star of many early Westerns, including *The Indians Are Coming* (1930).[19] Willie Goodridge, who slipped in between Chief Kain and Captain Baskins, was, of course, the son and nephew of the photographers William and Wallace Goodridge.

Young William Goodridge was not yet born when his father photographed the procession of wagons in figure 5.6 as it paused on its march along Genesee Avenue. The purpose of the parade and the nature of the organization responsible for it are lost to history, but internal evidence from the photograph reveals much about the time and the place. William Goodridge, the studio's outdoor specialist, made the photograph in the summer of 1879 or 1880. At the far left of the image, beyond the business blocks along Genesee and across the river, the trees are in the full leaf of summer. In addition, the city directories reveal that Billy Herb, at 411 Genesee, operated his jewelry store at that location only in 1879 and 1880 and not before or after. The band in the second wagon and the more

ample supply of lager in the kegs that filled the third and fourth wagons suggest that this was to be a very social occasion. There are no lodge banners or fraternal symbols to indicate the identity of the organization, but a large number of gentlemen in dark suits and white shirts are gathered on the sidewalk around the "Fresh Oysters & Choice Butter" sign at the right middleground of the photograph who appear ready and eager to board their rigs and join the parade. The fourth and fifth wagons reveal that they and possibly the lager were supplied by the Flint & Pere Marquette Railroad. The photograph also demonstrates the significant growth that East Saginaw had experienced during the 1870s in spite of a nationwide depression. Morley's and Boyd & Co. were well established in the 100 block at the river. Jessie Hoyt's impressive four-story replacement for the Crouse Block stands out at the corner of Washington and Genesee. Little Jake's complex occupied much of the 300 block. And the 400 block displays not only the grace and style of nineteenth-century commercial architecture but also the range of goods and services available to residents of a smallish Midwestern metropolis like East Saginaw. The photography studio advertising its presence on the first-story wall of the National Block at the northwest corner of Cass and Genesee was run by the Beals brothers, Ferris and Ferrin, who had only recently rented this location at 325 Genesee and would prove to be active competitors to the Goodridges until at least 1885.[20]

On May 23, 1880, it was reported that earlier in the month the "Goodridge Bros. made some fine views of the residences in the Washington avenue grove, and have orders to photograph a number of residences in both this and Saginaw City."[21] Among the architectural portraits that resulted is figure 5.7a, the Morley-Boyd residence at 1617 South Washington. George W. Morley was listed as living at that address as early as 1876 and continued to reside there until his death in 1914. There is no record indicating the year Morley built or purchased the structure, but its eclectic style with slate mansard roof and neogothic and Italianate elements suggests a date in the mid- to late 1870s. By that time Morley, who had been born in Brockport, New York, in 1831 and grown up in Painesville,

Ohio, would have experienced the goldfields of California and British Columbia and then settled comfortably as a partner into a series of successful hardware and banking ventures in East Saginaw. He married Miss Letitia Johnson of East Saginaw. She died following the birth of the couple's second child, Letitia May Morley. When Miss Morley married George H. Boyd in October 1895 the newlyweds joined the bride's father at 1617 South Washington and continued to occupy the residence after George Morley's death in 1914.[22] By effectively using the bright springtime sunshine and shooting from a low angle, William's photograph easily captures the busy angularity of the home's style as well as its impressive magnitude. The structure now exists only in the photograph the Goodridge brothers made of it that spring of 1880.

It may have been later in the summer of 1880 or, more likely, on one of their occasional visits to Saginaw City during the previous decade—the date cannot be determined precisely—that the Goodridge brothers made the photographs of the seat of county government and the first Roman Catholic parish in the Saginaw Valley (see figures 5.7b and c). Saginaw County had been created in January 1835, but it would not be until three years

Figure 5.7a. "Morley-Boyd Residence," 1880. Albumen image, 8 x 4¾ inches, beige bristol board mount with gold trim, 8⁹⁄₁₆ x 5⁷⁄₁₆ inches. Goodridge Brothers Studio, East Saginaw, Mich. Clarke Historical Library, Central Michigan University.

Figure 5.7b. "Saginaw County Court House Square," 1873–80. Original format unknown, 9½ x 6⁹⁄₁₆ inches. Goodridge Brothers Studio, East Saginaw, Mich. Bosch-Devers Collection.

Figure 5.7c. "St. Andrew's Roman Catholic Church," 1871–80. Albumen image, 9⅝ x 7¹³⁄₁₆ inches, beige bristol board mount, 12 x 10 inches. Goodridge Brothers Studio, East Saginaw, Mich. Clarke Historical Library, Central Michigan University.

later that the county board proposed construction of a courthouse. Bids were let and Asa Hill's for $9,925 was accepted after he had lowered his original proposal by nearly $1,600. The neoclassic plan with its double portico and Ionic columns was based on the Livingston County, New York, courthouse where county board member Jeremiah Riggs had served as an associate justice before coming to Saginaw City. Construction was delayed first by the death of Asa Hill from malaria in October 1838 and then by the failure of the Saginaw City Bank, which had agreed to loan the county $10,000 for the project. It was not until Eliel Barber was hired by the county building committee in 1841 that construction actually began. According to Mills, Barber "hired carpenters at one dollar and twenty-five cents a day, and laborers at a dollar a day, and went on with the building operations until the outside was finished and all the rooms on the lower floor were made ready for occupancy. A large room intended for the grand jury was used for a long time as a court room; and it was not until fifteen years after the contract had been let that the court room on the upper floor was finished. It was said that when first occupied the members of the Saginaw County bar were justly proud of the fine appearance of their court room."[23]

Figure 5.7b was made by William from the northeast corner of Adams and Washington (now Michigan Avenue) Streets looking west up Court Street. Washington had not yet been paved, and the young saplings lining that main thoroughfare had only just been planted. The squarish building to the south of the courthouse was the county office building. Leeson recalled that "The county offices comprise the Clerk's, Treasurer's, Registrar's rooms, and that of the Judge of Probate; all located in a low, French roofed building. There is nothing architecturally beautiful about it, yet the records which it contains are very complete, and the county officials genial, affable gentlemen. Such men and records lend to the county offices an importance which the building under any other circumstances never possesses."[24] The spire above the courthouse is that of the new Holy Cross Lutheran Church,

which had been dedicated in February 1869. The buildings across Court Street to the right of the large oak tree are the sheriff's residence and the jail. The courthouse was replaced by a new and much larger structure in a distinctly different architectural style in 1884. According to one source, "the graceful ionic pillars that graced the facade" of the original courthouse later were incorporated into a Saginaw residence.[25]

Members of St. Andrew's Roman Catholic parish had been gathering for services and instruction since May 1841, when the Reverend Martin Kundig first visited from Detroit that year. However, it was not until the appointment of Father Reinurus J. Van Der Heyden as pastor in 1862 that formal organization came. Three years later the growing congregation, which had been meeting in a renovated carpenter shop that it had moved to parish land at the northeast corner of Monroe and Washington Streets, built the simple but stately structure that appears in figure 5.7c. William's photograph was made sometime after 1871, when the original edifice was enlarged to accommodate additional parishioners, but before construction of a home for Father Van Der Heyden, when the schoolhouse that appears next to the church was moved to Monroe and Fayette Streets and became St. Andrew's Academy.[26] Close examination of the photograph reveals that there were few pupils at St. Andrew's that day who were not aware of William Goodridge's visit.

Later during the 1880s two other Saginaw City religious institutions followed St Andrew's lead and also chose the Goodridge studio to document memorable occasions. As the *Saginaw Evening News* reported in its Monday August 29, 1887, edition, "At 1:30 o'clock yesterday, after services at the Lutheran Church in Saginaw City, a long procession formed and proceeded, under the direction of Rev. [Christoph L.] Eberhardt, to the grounds . . . [of] the New Lutheran Seminary on Court Street."[27] On that day, or more likely a few weeks after, on September 20, when classes officially began, the directors of the seminary had contracted with William Goodridge to record the event. Figure 5.8a is the result. For the portrait

Figure 5.8a. "'Old Main,' Michigan Lutheran Seminary," September 1887. Silver print, 7⅜ x 9½ inches, beige bristol board mount, 9½₁₆ x 11½₁₆ inches. Goodridge Brothers Studio, East Saginaw, Mich. Collection of Dave Tinder.

Figure 5.8b. "St. John's Episcopal Church, Washington Centennial," April 1889. Silver print, 13⅜₆ x 10¼ inches, black bristol board mount with gold trim, 13¹³⁄₁₆ x 10⅞ inches. Goodridge Brothers Studio, East Saginaw, Mich. Collection of St. John's Episcopal Church.

William posed the seminary's four faculty members (Professor Alexander Lange, Pastors Eberhardt and Ferdinand Huber, and Ernst Sperling) and their fourteen students on the front steps of "Old Main" in a manner that mirrored the shape of the pediment and decorative arches of the front portico and bell tower but which also suggested the stability and substance to which the new institution aspired. William made the photograph from the sidewalk along the north side of the 1900 block of Court Street at an angle that captured both students and faculty but which also featured the city's newest and most impressive academic structure. A second portrait—a close-up of students and faculty in the same pose—made shortly after from the sidewalk leading directly to the front steps of "Old Main" also exists but does not bear the Goodridge studio imprint on its mount.

Construction of "Old Main" had begun in April 1887 on land donated for the purpose by Pas-

tor Eberhardt of Saginaw. The Evangelical Lutheran Synod of Michigan had decided to train its own clergy rather than continue to fill its pastoral needs with men sent over from Germany, as it had been doing for the previous twenty-five years. Initially the seminary had been established in 1885 in Manchester, Michigan, where it functioned for two years. Most likely as a result of Eberhardt's influence and the land he donated, the institution relocated to Saginaw, where "Old Main" was built and furnished at a total cost of $8,871.61. The seminary continued to train clergy only until 1907, when the Michigan Synod rejoined the Synodical Conference and simultaneously merged with the Minnesota and Wisconsin Synods. As a result, although Michigan Lutheran Seminary retained its name, it functioned thereafter as a preparatory and secondary school. "Old Main" stood until 1963, when it was demolished to make way for new construction.[28]

On April 30, 1889, East Saginaw and Saginaw

City, like most communities throughout the land, marked the centennial anniversary of the inauguration of George Washington as the first president of the United States. According to a report in the *Saginaw Courier-Herald,* the "occasion will be observed in East Saginaw, as it will in all parts of the Republic, by the closing of public offices, banks, courts, many of the stores and factories, and the holding of church services." In Saginaw City the "clergy, choirs and congregations of St. Paul's and All Saints' will join with St. John's . . . in an appropriate observance of the day." William Goodridge was commissioned to create figure 5.8b to commemorate the "Centennial Celebration," as the caption on the mounting board of the photograph indicates. The portrait is of the combined choirs of St. Paul's, All Saints', and St. John's Episcopal Churches, which had joined together at St. John's to celebrate the nation's first president.[29]

Although St. John's, the first of the Episcopal churches in the Saginaws, had been formally organized only in 1851, there were "communicants of the Episcopal Church . . . in [the] Saginaw Valley," according to Mills, "as far back as 1836 . . . [which] was the nucleus of the present St. John's." Both St. Paul's and All Saints' had been established in East Saginaw as a result of the mission efforts of St. John's shortly after its own formal organization, and as the portrait suggests, the relationship among the three remained close. During the rectorship of the Reverend Benjamin F. Matrua, from 1883 to 1890, St. John's established a men's and boys' choir that Mills described as "a leading feature of the church services, and [which] under the able direction of Henry B. Roney soon came to be regarded as one of the best in the diocese, winning fresh laurels of praise and appreciation whenever heard in neighboring cities." Not surprisingly, therefore, St. Paul's and All Saints' had followed St. John's leadership in establishing their own choirs, and their combined effort became one of the focal points of the centennial celebration.[30]

William made the photograph from the center of Hancock Street with Michigan Avenue just visible to the left. Notice Hancock's lack of pavement and the well-trod wooden sidewalk along which the choir members are aligned for the portrait. Although it is now impossible to identify the individual choirs or their members, it appears from the location of the three crossbearers that the St. Paul's and All Saints' choirs, composed exclusively of boys, are to the left and center and that the larger St. John's combined men's and boys' choir is to the right. The individual to the far left may well be Henry B. Roney, director of the St. John's choir and the most logical leader for the combined effort. Beneath the gothic arch of the side entrance to the nave of St. John's are five clergymen distinguished by their birettas. The bearded individual closest to the banner proclaiming "In Hoc Signo Vinces" is most likely Rector Matrua of St. John's. The most intriguing individual in the portrait, however, is the St. John's crossbearer, who, from her long curly locks, delicate features, and distinctive cassock appears to be the only female among the more than one hundred individuals in the portrait.

During August 1887 a reporter for the African American *Cleveland Gazette* visited East Saginaw to give readers of the *Gazette* "Something of the City and Those of the Race There." One of the businesses that he showcased in his report was, of course, the Goodridge brothers' studio. Among other things, he wrote that they were "special photographers for the New York *Daily Graphic, Harper's Weekly,* G. R. & I. [Grand Rapids & Indiana] railroad and F. & P. U. [sic] R.R."[31] While there were few photographers during the second half of the nineteenth century who did not claim a "special" or "official" appointment of one type or other, it is clear that the Goodridge brothers did have a "special" connection with the Flint & Pere Marquette and Michigan Central, if not other railroads in Michigan. Specific segments of the proposed "Picturesque Michigan" series were to be "Scenes on the Mackinaw Division, M. C. R. R." (see figure 4.37b) and several of Flint & Pere Marquette Railroad Company facilities (for example, figures 4.38b, "F. & P. M. Elevator at Ludington," and 4.31b, "Offices, Flint & Pere Marquette Railroad"), also were included in the stereo series.

A July 1882 notice in the *Saginaw Morning*

Figure 5.9. "Potter Street Depot, Flint & Pere Marquette Railroad," 1882. Tinted silver print, 9¹⁵⁄₁₆ x 8¹⁄₁₆ inches, ivory bristol board mount with gold trim, 10 x 8¹⁄₁₆ inches. Goodridge Brothers Studio, East Saginaw, Mich. Collection of John V. Jezierski.

Herald confirmed the connection when it reported that the "Goodridge Bros. were engaged yesterday afternoon in taking views of the new F. & P. M. depot."[32] It was to be the first of many visits to the new facility. The resulting photograph (figure 5.9) reveals a busy scene. The "Depot Car" from one of the Saginaws' street railways is prepared to deliver a group of recently arrived passengers. Others will soon be met by one of the line of carriages drawn up along the platform. And ghosts of a group already crossing Potter Street are visible as they move through the photograph and approach the street railway track and the two commercial travelers who had paused in the middle of the street for a brief discussion. Most impressive, however, is the new depot building itself.

The Flint & Pere Marquette had had a passenger and freight station of some sort on the east side of the Saginaw River near Potter Street and Washington Avenue as early as the summer of 1859, when the first rail was laid for the new road at that location on August 19.[33] By 1877 the county atlas reveals that the original facility had evolved into an impressive complex that included two engine- or roundhouses, a car house, a blacksmith shop, a machine shop, and a car manufactory. There also was a large freight house, but only a small passenger depot and a separate baggage room.[34] Completion of the road to Ludington in 1874 and its resulting success by 1881 convinced the directors to undertake construction of a new main depot in East Saginaw that more properly fit the Flint & Pere Marquette image. The railroad chose as its architect the young but promising Bradford Lee Gilbert. A graduate of Yale, where he had studied with Josiah Cleveland Cady, Gilbert ultimately would design depots for sixteen U.S. railroads, including the Illinois Central in Chicago in 1892–93 and a major renovation of Grand Central in New York City in 1898–99. In 1882, however,

Figure 5.10a. "Potter Street Depot, Looking East from Washington Street," 1890. Silver print, 13⅞ x 11 1/16 inches, gray bristol board mount, 13 15/16 x 11 1/16 inches. Goodridge Brothers Studio, Saginaw Mich. Collection of John V. Jezierski.

Figure 5.10b. "Looking Northwest from Roof of Potter Street Depot," 1892. Silver print, 14 1/16 x 11 inches, white bristol board mount with gold trim, 14 1/16 x 11 inches. Goodridge Brothers Studio, Saginaw, Mich. Collection of John V. Jezierski.

Gilbert was not yet thirty years old, and the new Potter Street depot was to be one of his most important early commissions. Figure 5.9 displays the practical elegance that became the basis for Gilbert's success. In addition, figures 5.10a and b demonstrate what a recent student of the depot's history has described as Gilbert's appreciation for locally derived materials—timber and brick—and a keen sense of the station's "fit" with its surroundings.[35] Notice in figure 5.10a that the depot and adjacent Potter Street business district complement each other both commercially and architecturally. A view from the depot tower down into the railroad's maintenance and manufactory complex (figure 5.10b) also makes clear that Gilbert's depot was not so dainty as to be apart from the smoke and grime that was a part of any railroad at the time. These two photos document the impressive growth of the Flint & Pere Marquette at its Potter Street location by 1890.[36] The photographs also confirm a continuing connection between the railroad and the Goodridge studio even after William's death in 1890. In fact, in one of the studio's last commercial notices, published in 1906, Wallace stated that the studio had remained "special photographers to the M. C. and the P. M. railroad companies."[37]

━━━◆━━━

It was from the new Potter Street depot that William Goodridge set off on a most important excursion in the spring of 1883. Although it was a trip that he had made regularly in the past, this time more than one East Saginaw newspaper reported his departure, noting that "Wm. Goodridge, of the firm of Goodridge Bros., left this morning for Averill to take photographic views of Wright & Ketcum's [sic] seven camps near that place, and also several views of the big rollway at Averill."[38] William's destination was not surprising. He had begun making stereo views at Averill as early as 1868 or 1869 (see figure 3.27a), and had made a photographic expedition to the giant banking ground on the bend of the Tittabawassee River there as recently as March 1881 (see figure 4.29b). Furthermore, as in the past, William was again rid-

ing the Flint & Pere Marquette and may even have hitched a ride on "The Peggy." The 1883 journey was different and important, however, because for the first time William would create a significant number of large-format photographs of Michigan's booming white pine lumber industry. He had been photographing the pine lumber industry for more than a decade by 1883. With only rare exceptions, the results had been presented as stereo series—for example, the views made at P. Glynn & Co.'s camp in Midland County in 1874 and 1875 (see figures 4.32a–c and 4.33a–c). William also may have created stereo views at Wright and Ketcham's camps in 1883, but none are presently known or listed among the various stereo series. Large-format Wright and Ketcham views are extant, however, and from 1883 to his death in 1890 William continued to make ever more important and often extraordinary large-format lumber photographs. Almost simultaneously, the lumber camp stereo series lost the place of preeminence they once had held.

Several factors, local and national as well as technical and conceptual, explain this important shift in William's work by and after 1883. Darrah has written that by 1881 many stereo markets had become saturated with views as a result of so many producers entering the profession during the 1870s. There followed a period of market adjustment that dramatically reduced the number of local studios creating stereo views but simultaneously witnessed the emergence of mass-production companies that dominated the field into the next century.[39] The Goodridges did not have any serious competitors making stereo views locally, and James A. Jenney had moved on from Flint after 1875. Views were readily available by mail order, however, from national suppliers like B. W. Kilburn and Underwood & Underwood during the late 1870s and throughout the 1880s.[40] The Saginaw stereo market may, therefore, have been at its capacity for a time, and Wallace and William responded by making this necessary adjustment. In addition, in 1880 the studio acquired a new camera that gave it "the largest collection of photographic instruments for portraits and views in the state."[41] The new camera may have been the one that enabled the Goodridge studio to create "mammoth views, 20 by 25 inches, for some of the leading railroads of Michigan," and also to market them to a public that had come to recognize the railroad as the primary engine of nineteenth-century material progress.[42] Close examination of figures 4.4 and 4.5 reveals that the walls of the Goodridge studio were hung with large-format photographic views presumably available for sale.

Two important and closely related developments in Michigan's forests and the Saginaw Valley's lumber mills also accelerated the Goodridges' shift to the larger view photographs. In 1876 Clare County lumberman Winfield Scott Gerrish and his partner E. H. Hazelton began operating Michigan's first logging railroad, the Lake George & Muskegon River Railroad. Gerrish was a native of Maine but raised in Michigan. By the time he was twenty-five, in 1874, he had settled in Clare County and began lumbering in Freeman and Lincoln Townships. The timber there remained pristine largely because its distance from navigable streams made the expense of moving it to the mills in Muskegon or Saginaw prohibitive. In addition, several dry and mild winters through the 1870s made the traditional skidding methods even more difficult. During a summer 1876 visit to the Centennial Exhibition in Philadelphia with his family, Gerrish viewed a small but powerful railroad steam engine that he reportedly described as "Just the kind of a horse to haul logs without snow." Gerrish ordered an engine named "Sampson" from the Porter, Bell & Company of Pittsburgh, along with thirty cars and enough rails for an initial five miles of track, all of which the Flint & Pere Marquette delivered to Evart in November 1876. The equipment was rafted up the Muskegon River near to the town of Temple, where the novel railroad was begun and extended southeast to Gerrish's operations at Lake George. The road opened on January 28, 1877, and by the spring of the same year had moved twenty-nine million feet of prime timber to the Muskegon River at a net profit of more than $25,000 to its investors on an initial investment of approximately $50,000. That same season, other lumber companies suffered through another dry and mild winter of little or no profit. The Lake George & Muskegon River Railroad continued to expand and enjoyed general profitability until Gerrish's untimely death in 1882, when part of the railroad was dissolved and the remainder eventually absorbed by other roads.[43]

Although Gerrish's success was short-lived, his idea helped to transform the timber industry in Michigan. By 1882 there were thirty-two logging railroads in the state, and in 1885 forty-nine were counted.[44] Specific research has yet to equate the success of logging railroads with the rapid depletion of Michigan's forests in the 1880s, but the connection appears reasonable and leads to the second development of local consequence that influenced the theme of William Goodridge's large-format lumber views in April 1883 and thereafter. According to one source, Saginaw River lumber mills began to produce more than 100 million feet of lumber by 1854. Their output expanded steadily through the 1860s and continued to grow, although not without the impact of the Panic of 1873 and the mild and dry winters of the 1870s, until the peak year of 1882, when Saginaw River mills cut more than 1 billion feet of lumber and almost 300 million shingles. Thereafter the total dropped annually until in 1896 the mills cut less lumber than they had in 1866.[45]

As important as were new cameras and glutted stereo markets or new logging railroads and record cuts of lumber by Saginaw Valley mills, it is only when these facts are understood in combination with other, more subtle changes at the time that their impact on William's work and his shift to the larger view photographs of Michigan's timber industry during his 1883 Wright and Ketcham expedition takes on its true significance. According to a recent analysis of nineteenth-century view photography, Americans who wished "to see their country" in the years after the Civil War turned increasingly to photography "to understand not just its topography but [also] its underlying values and beliefs."[46] Photography, in other words, had become a means to document and, in fact, to justify man's mastery of nature. Among the most successful but also most visually impressive of the instruments that Americans were now employing to dominate their natural world was the railroad. The recently completed transcontinentals had achieved, but only on a grander scale, the same sort of triumph that Gerrish's Lake George & Muskegon River Railroad was accomplishing almost simultaneously in the forests of Michigan by redefining space and affording access to heretofore inaccessible resources.[47] Among the consequences of this technological triumph over nature was, ironically, an increased willingness to value nature, but now as a commodity, where quantity, size, magnitude, or amount had become the measure of man's success.[48] By 1880 William Goodridge's work reflected and in fact may have helped to stimulate such a shift in photographic style and function, as his Wright and Ketcham photographs of ever more effective timber-related technology and the resulting, for a time at least, ever larger cut of pine clearly demonstrate.

The 1883 photographic expedition to Wright and Ketcham's seven camps at Ketchamville in Midland County was different from William's earlier photographic trips to the timber country. Not only did he create primarily large-format photographs, but the resulting subject and ultimate function of the photographs also shifted dramatically. In 1874–75, William's "Scenes in the Pineries of Michigan" stereo series, made at P. Glynn & Co.'s camp in Warren Township in Midland County, was concerned with camp life and the techniques of felling and moving timber to the banking ground. The impressive magnitude of individual logs and the size of the season's "cut" are apparent in the series but of less consequence than the series' primary and more informative function of documenting life and labor in the "pineries" of Michigan. By the 1883 Wright and Ketcham trip, however, William's attention—in fact the entire perspective of his fieldwork—had shifted from camp life and the techniques of felling and banking timber to a much more focused look at logging railroads and the resulting record amounts of timber being cut from Michigan forests. In other words, documentation had given way to evaluation, and simple observa-

tion had been replaced by an attempt to present "underlying values and beliefs."

According to the newspaper reports, William's destination in April 1883 was the Wright and Ketcham Lumber Company's camps north of Averill in Midland and Gladwin Counties. In addition, he also may have traveled farther afield to A. W. Wright & Company's operations along the Tobacco River in Clare County. By 1882 Ammi W. Wright had become one of the Saginaw Valley's and the state's leading lumber producers. His partnership with Philip H. Ketcham was only one of several ventures that ultimately extended from Michigan to Minnesota and south to Mississippi. Forrest Meek has described Wright as "one of the most constructive capitalists in the timber producing regions. Other business men took their profits and left counties like Clare holding nothing but pine stumps in great profusion. Wright invested his capital in agricultural equipment manufacturing and indirectly assisted the men who cut his timber many years previously."[49]

Like many of his contemporaries, Wright, who was born in Grafton, Vermont, in 1822, had come west to Michigan to take advantage of the opportunity there. He settled in Saginaw City in 1851 and the same year purchased his first pinelands on the Cass River. According to Mills, Wright "had the great good fortune of choosing some of the finest tracts of pine in this section."[50] Continued good fortune, combined with a keen business sense, brought Wright repeated and widespread success. By the time that he and Ketcham had formed their partnership in 1878, Wright, on his own and with other partners, already owned tens of thousands of acres of timberlands throughout Michigan and had interests in various mills, railroads, and plank roads, the Tittabawassee Boom Company, extensive farmlands, and several banks and manufacturing companies.[51]

The younger Ketcham was born at Staten Island, New York, in 1845 but moved to De Kalb County, Illinois, with his family soon after. He left the family farm in 1866 and settled in Saginaw. After ten years as a partner in the modestly successful lumber firm of Ketcham, Edsell & Dunning he joined Wright & Co. in an undefined capacity.[52] By 1878 he had attracted Wright's attention and the two formed the Wright and Ketcham Lumber Company. Between 1878 and 1883 the partnership spent more than $107,000 to purchase nearly ten thousand acres of timberland in Midland and Gladwin Counties. Most of the acreage was located north of Averill in Lincoln, Hope, and Mills Townships in Midland County.[53]

Wright and Ketcham based their operations at the small village of Ketcham (or Ketchamville) where the Hope Road crosses Sturgeon Creek. In 1881 they began building a narrow-gauge logging railroad that ran from "a high bluff of the Tittabawassee River . . . a trifle north and west of Averill" due north to Ketchamville and then northeast across Mills Township into Gladwin County. When it was completed in 1886, the Wright & Ketcham Logging Railroad—or Tittabawassee & Hope Railroad, as it also was known—was described as: "32 miles of roadbed; their average hauls are 18 miles; they dump into the Tittabawassee River, Midland County; 36" gauge; two Brooks & one Porter locomotives, 7.5, 15, and 21 tons; 96 Russell cars; 1.5 M ft/car; 45.0 MM ft/yr." The road was dismantled in 1888 when the timber was gone and the partnership dissolved. At its peak in the winter of 1883–84 Ketchamville boasted a "post office, a large general store, the boarding house for the trainmen, stables, a small mill, used chiefly to saw hardwood lumber, an engine house, a new structure for the latter purpose being about completed. The coal for the locomotives, hauled from Averill during the winter, is also stored at this point. The general store handled during 1883 some $100,000 worth of goods, $25,000 of which was sold to surrounding settlers and the balance consumed by the firm in their operations. Along the line are seven camps, all connected by telephone. During the last winter 500 men were employed at wages ranging from $18 to $30 a month and board." That year alone, forty million feet of timber were shipped along the railroad to the banking ground at Averill.[54]

If William created views of Ketchamville and its busy general store or any of the company's sev-en camps, they are no longer extant or presently are unknown. The views that have survived, however, focus on at least part of the forty million feet of timber that Wright and Ketcham shipped along their railroad to the banking ground at Averill in 1883. In fact, William not only followed the timber from Ketchamville to Averill but kept track of it as it moved along the Tittabawassee River to Bryant's Trip and then on to the booming grounds at the Merrill Bridge. The timber, and William, ended up at the A. W. Wright Lumber Co. along the west bank of the river in Saginaw City.

Figure 5.11a, "Log Train," reveals Wright and Ketcham's small but powerful N. D. Porter engine pulling at least nine cars heavily laden with six prime logs each. The engine is a near duplicate of Gerrish's "Sampson," except that the Wright and Ketcham version was configured for a narrow-gauge track and sports a pilot or "cow-catcher" fitted with a blade to move the winter's snows. The hose snaking along the log cars provided the water or air pressure to operate the braking system located on the final car, barely visible at the far right of the photograph. The Porters were "tank engines." The semicircular "tank" supporting the engine's bell was used to store water, which was converted into steam in the boiler that it enveloped.[55] William's choice of a horizontal perspective, with the looming presence of the engine to the left and the seemingly limitless line of cars with their load of logs, accentuated by a blank sky and appearing to vanish to the right, not only introduces but also affirms his concern with the record amounts of timber being cut from Saginaw Valley forests in 1883.

At the banking ground on the Tittabawassee River near Averill (figure 5.11b), William again used his camera to comment on the magnitude of the year's cut. In this view the subject and William's careful technique complement each other to produce the desired result. Obviously the banking ground held thousands of prime logs. Yet particular concern for the depth of field in this shot kept the logs in the immediate foreground as well as those on the distant bank in sharp focus and made each of the thousands of logs a recognizable

Figure 5.11a. "Log Train," 1883. Unmounted silver print, 9¹⁵⁄₁₆ x 8¹⁄₁₆ inches. Goodridge Brothers Studio, East Saginaw, Mich. Collection of Beffrey Family.

Figure 5.11b. "Banking Ground, Averill," 1883. Unmounted silver print, 10 x 7¹⁵⁄₁₆ inches. Goodridge Brothers Studio, East Saginaw, Mich. Collection of Beffrey Family.

Figure 5.12a. "No. 52, F. & P. M. Railroad, Banking Ground, Averill," 1883. Unmounted silver print, 10 x 8 inches. Goodridge Brothers Studio, East Saginaw, Mich. Collection of Beffrey Family.

Figure 5.12b. "Log Drive, Tittabawassee River," 1883. Unmounted silver print, 10 x 8 inches. Goodridge Brothers Studio, East Saginaw, Mich. Collection of Beffrey Family.

individual, further enhancing the impact of their number. In addition, the composition of the view is strongly three-dimensional and reveals William's longtime success with stereographs. Notice that there are three groups of logs, in the fore-, middle-, and background. Each is separated from the other by a band of icy-smooth water, and the division is reinforced by the vertical pilings. Placement of the men atop the logs across the middleground, however, enhances the dynamics of the view and unites the middle- with the fore- and backgrounds. The third individual from the left, with his hands in his pockets and the prominent watch chain, is most likely John Stratton, who managed the banking ground for Wright and Ketcham at the time.[56]

That same spring of 1883 William also was able to photograph the Flint & Pere Marquette Railroad's engine No. 52 pulling into the Averill banking ground with an extraordinary cargo of timber (figure 5.12a). Although the depth of field is not as sharp as in the previous illustration, it still is possible to count at least thirty log cars trailing around the bend behind No. 52, its tender, and a single boxcar. Each car held a minimum of twelve logs similar to those lying end-to-end across the foreground of the view. No. 52 was a powerful 2–6–0 engine that the Flint & Pere Marquette classified as one of its "Moguls." It was built by the Brooks Locomotive Works in September 1880, and with its six forty-nine-and-a-half-inch drive wheels and sixteen- by twenty-four-inch cylinders developed more than enough power to pull many carloads of logs. In later years it was reconfigured to 0–6–0 and renumbered 258 and then 440.[57]

As in figure 5.11b, William here also employs both subject and technique to gain his intended effect. Not only do the railcars with their burden of hundreds of logs follow the bend of the river as they appear to vanish into the distant forest of their origin, but the countless logs lying end-to-end along the banking ground between track and river reveal that No. 52 had made the same trip regularly in recent days. William's choice of perspective and camera angle also are essential to the result. By placing his tripod and camera immediately upon the logs themselves, only a few feet from the track,

and shooting from a rather low, eye-level angle, he is able to capture the immensity of the banked logs as they bend off into the distance between No. 52 and the Tittabawassee.

Some weeks after leaving Ketchamville and Averill—the lush foliage suggests late May or early June—William again caught up with some of Wright and Ketcham's forty million feet of timber. Here, in figure 5.12b, he was accompanied by two young friends and Wallace, whose characteristic profile and homburg are visible along the bank. Ralph Stroebel has identified the location as Bryant's Trip on the Tittabawassee River, with present-day Immerman Park located on the east bank of the river to the right. Bryant's Trip was a massive dam of logs chained end-to-end across the river and anchored to heavy pilings set deep into each bank. The "Trip" held back the thousands of logs that had made the journey down the Tittabawassee from Averill and other locations. Notice that the year's drive had been a very large one, with innumerable logs extending back from the "Trip" for more than a mile upriver and along the banks as the water level had dropped by late spring and into summer. Near the middle of the "Trip" was a log gate which was opened regularly but briefly so that a few logs could pass through or "be tripped" and sorted into booms according to their respective log marks for shipment to the mills.[58]

In this instance William has chosen a perspective and camera angle that magnify the size of the drive. The effect is similar to that which a contemporary photographer might achieve with a wide-angle lens. By placing his camera on the bank above the river just at the apex of its bend here, William is able to present both banks of the river upstream to its next bend and a horizon that extends beyond 135 degrees. The result is a sense that the banks of the river—perhaps even the extent of the valley itself—are unable to contain the year's harvest of timber. At the same time that William's camera looks upriver for the source of this cornucopia of timber, it looks down the bank to Wallace and his companions. The angle not only diminishes Wallace's size but simultaneously enlarges the expanse of this river of logs. The fence rails that run just across the lower right of the view further reduce Wallace's size in spite of his proximity to the camera, but at the same time serve to amplify the vista that William presents.

A bit more than seven miles from Bryant's Trip, Wright and Ketcham's logs found their way to the booming or sorting pens operated by the Tittabawassee Boom Company (figure 5.13a). The company was organized in 1864 by a group of twenty-two investors who took over and expanded existing "booming" operations on the Tittabawassee River. In 1867 Joseph E. Shaw served as president; Ammi W. Wright was treasurer, although he had not been one of the original investors. That same year the company was operating twelve miles of booms and employed nearly 250 men. Its peak year of activity was 1882, when 611,863,000 feet of pine logs were sorted and transported to Saginaw River lumber mills.[59]

The company's largest and most important of several booming or sorting facilities was located on the Tittabawassee River at the Merrill Bridge, which William visited to make this view in early summer 1883. The bridge crossed the river little more than two miles from Greenpoint, where the Tittabawassee joined the Shiawassee and the Cass to form the Saginaw itself. The location, near present-day St. Peter and Paul Church on West Michigan, was an excellent one. It enabled the company's boom operators to sort individual logs on the basis of their log marks as they came down the river from Bryant's Trip into rafts of timber in the sorting pens. The rafts were formed by aligning the timber and hammering hardwood rafting pins over the rope into the softer pine. Individual "strings" or "rafts" contained up to one hundred logs. Larger rafts or "tows," up to a half mile in length, were made up of several "strings" or "rafts" and delivered by company tugs or independent operators to the mills along the river. Men known as "runners" rode the large rafts behind the tugs and were responsible for cutting free and delivering smaller "strings" or "rafts" of logs from the larger "tows" to the appropriate mill. The company annually purchased $30,000 to $50,000 worth of rope and in 1879 ordered fifty tons with a special

color strand in an attempt to cut back on its losses. Rafting pins must have been counted in the millions over the years.[60]

William's view (figure 5.13a) was made from the south bank of the Tittabawassee looking upstream beyond the bridge toward Bryant's Trip. For the shot, company employees momentarily suspended their labors to face the camera, and a local resident headed into town with a wagonload of what appears to be fenceposts has decided to join them. Although William's focus is a bit fuzzy at the perimeter, it is sharp across the center of the view, capturing the thousands of feet of barely visible rope and the multitude of individual rafting pins used to create the rafts of logs that blanketed the river from bank to bank.

The timber which William had been following now by rail and river from the forest near Ketchamville ultimately arrived at its final destination, the A. W. Wright Lumber Company mill at the foot of Throop Street in Saginaw City (figure 5.13b). Here it was sawed into lumber for shipment throughout the East and Midwest. A lumber mill had operated at the location since at least 1853, but only in 1865 did it become part of the Pearson & Wright Company. The original mill was destroyed by fire the same year but replaced almost immediately by a larger one that came to be known as the "Big Mill." Wright's partner in the venture, James H. Pearson, retired from the firm in 1871 but maintained an interest until 1880, when the business was reorganized and the mill brought under the sole control of the A. W. Wright Lumber Company.[61] In 1882 the "Big Mill" cut twenty-six million feet of lumber, which was surpassed only by the larger H. W. Sage & Company mill of Bay City, which cut thirty-one million feet, and Birdsall and Barker's two mills, also in Bay City, which combined for a total cut of forty million feet that year.[62]

For the shot William had located his camera on the Bristol Street Bridge (later the Remington-Holland Bridge) only a few hundred yards downstream from the mill. The placement allowed him to create a large but well-balanced view of Wright's operation. The extant print is 14 x 10 inches, one

Figure 5.13a. "Tittabawassee Boom Company," 1883. Unmounted silver print, 10 x 7¹⁵⁄₁₆ inches. Goodridge Brothers Studio, East Saginaw, Mich. Collection of Beffrey Family.

Figure 5.13b. "Mill, A. W. Wright Lumber Company," 1883. Unmounted silver print, 14 x 10 inches. Goodridge Brothers Studio, East Saginaw, Mich. Collection of Beffrey Family.

Figure 5.14a. "Saginaw Fire Tug," 1883. Silver print, 9½ x 7⅝ inches, beige bristol board mount, 9¹⁵/₁₆ x 7¹⁵/₁₆ inches. Goodridge Brothers Studio, East Saginaw, Mich. Clarke Historical Library, Central Michigan University.

Figure 5.14b. "Edgers, Sears and Holland Lumber Mill," 1879–1883. Unmounted silver print, 9¹¹/₁₆ x 6⅛ inches. Goodridge Brothers Studio, East Saginaw, Mich. Originally published July 29, 1951. ©1999 *The Saginaw News*. All rights reserved. Reprinted with permission.

of the largest from that period in William's career. While few employees are visible, the log rafts moving in the river before the mill and the smoke pouring from the tall stack present a scene of businesslike activity. In addition, the camera placement allows the "Big Mill" to be shrunk a bit by the large piles of drying lumber that cover the riverbank. Notice how the mass of the mill at the left is balanced by an equally large volume of drying lumber to the right. The balance is strengthened by the fortuitous location of the brine well towers at the immediate left and right of the horizon.

At or near the same location, but from the deck of a vessel in the river and not the Bristol Street Bridge, William captured a "Saginaw Fire Tug" (figure 5.14a) protecting the drying lumber that had been cut by Wright's and other mills on the river. The unidentified and unmarked tug was operated by the Shaw Transfer Company. There are no documents detailing the activities of the Shaw Transfer Company on the Saginaw River. It may have been a subsidiary of the Tittabawassee Boom Company or, more likely, an independent but related operation controlled by Joseph E. Shaw, president of the boom company. While the tug is demonstrating its fire-fighting capability for the camera, it also is clear from the flag, the decorative canopy, and the relaxed attitude of the three passengers on the foredeck and engineer in the window that the tug was on an excursion and not headed for an emergency.

With only one exception, all of the surviving large-format lumber views that William made during the 1883 Wright and Ketcham expedition (and thereafter for that matter) are outdoor shots of the forest, railroad, or river. The sole large-format interior lumber view from the period is figure 5.14b. Many years after the view was created, a caption was added to the verso that identifies it as "edgers at Sears and Holland mill on South Tildon (Water) street. 1879." The caption is typewritten, not in the usual Goodridge hand identifying vintage prints, and was appended to this copy of the now lost original print in the 1950s or 1960s. Its accuracy, therefore, is questionable. Sears & Holland did have a mill on South Tildon Street into the 1880s.

It was a modest operation, however, and most likely did not include the extensive finishing facility pictured. A. W. Wright Lumber Company, on the other hand, did have a separate, specialized finishing mill located just to the south of the western terminus of the Bristol Street Bridge, and William may have chosen to include it in his Wright and Ketcham portfolio.[63]

The view is intriguing not only because it is an uncommon interior shot but also because William has made excellent use of the light to transform the grimy factory setting into an essay on line and form. The light accentuates the various series of parallel lines created by the roof studs and rafters, the chains and tie rods used to anchor the edgers, the ribs of the edging tables themselves, and the floorboards and tracks of the lumber carts. All are nicely contrasted with the roundness of the tables' drive and control wheels with their serpentine spokes. While the natural lighting was sufficient to create this view, the shot may be a rare example of William's use of artificial lighting at this time. The circular intensity of the lighting and the direction of the shadows cast by the table legs suggest a powerful and probably artificial source of light near the camera. Chapter 7 will consider this subject in greater detail.

William O. Goodridge's April 1883 Wright and Ketcham expedition was a significant turning point in his career. He did not abandon the stereo views that had served the studio so well for almost two decades, but more and more he came to prefer the large-format views that he created while following Wright and Ketcham's timber from its origin in the forests of Midland County to Averill and then along the Tittabawassee to Wright's mill in Saginaw City. William's success with Wright and Ketcham in 1883 may explain why the "Picturesque Michigan" stereo series which the studio had launched in 1880 and had planned to issue on a monthly basis did not develop as anticipated. Of even greater consequence, however, was William's shift from a straightforward, descriptive documentation of process and technique in the stereo views to a more discerning assessment of the impact of the logging railroads (technology) and magnitude of the season's cut of timber (commodity) during the peak years of production in the early 1880s that is the essence of these larger views.

The new perspective and the momentum that William had generated in 1883 continued to the end of the decade. In fact, during the winter of 1884 or 1885 William made the first of a series of trips along the Mackinaw Division of the Michigan Central Railroad into northern Michigan. Earlier William had planned an identical journey to make stereo views of Cheboygan, Mackinaw City, and Mackinac Island for the "Picturesque Michigan" series (see figure 4.37b), but the views do not exist and it is impossible to determine if William had, indeed, made the trip. In 1884 or 1885, however, he traveled to Mackinaw City on the Michigan Central, crossed the Straits of Mackinac to St. Ignace, and from there made connections that took him to Manistique and a bit farther west to Thompson on Lake Michigan in Schoolcraft County, the headquarters of the Delta Lumber Company. During 1884 the company began operating a camp at Walsh's Siding in a rugged but pine-rich area twelve miles west of the town of Seney.[64]

At least six large views survive from William's trip to Schoolcraft County, but two examples represent well his goals for the expedition. The Delta Lumber Company was an extensive operation that was begun in 1881 by E. L. Thompson of Lapeer and his partner R. B. Warrior. By 1883 the two controlled more than seven thousand acres of timber in the Seney area, and as late as 1888 they sent six million feet of logs down the Driggs River.[65] Figure 5.15a, "The Start (Morning)," momentarily stops several crews and their teams and sleds as they leave camp at Walsh's Siding for the day's labor. The individual in the greatcoat and fur hat facing the camera from the center of the view was probably foreman Walsh in the midst of directing the departing traffic. Somewhat later in the day William captured one of the crews returning with a considerable load of timber. The most interesting aspect of figure 5.15b, "Select Logs," is not the size of the load or the crew who posed for the view (William created several that are nearly identical); but notice that when he later printed the photo-

graph, William had retouched the negative to highlight the numerals indicating the board feet in each piece of timber—810, 836, 884, and so forth. Clearly he wished to be certain that his audience appreciated the magnitude of the crew's accomplishment.

The following year, most likely in late winter or early spring 1886, William again traveled north, but not so far as the Straits of Mackinac or Schoolcraft County. His destination on this trip was the camps of the Gratwick, Smith & Fryer Lumber Company in southeastern Otsego County. The company had begun operations in 1882 with construction of a railroad from Crapo Lake to its main camp eight miles distant in Charlton Township near Johannesburg. In only a few years the operation had grown to include the substantial complex shown in figure 5.16a. And by 1886 the company's railroad, the Crapo Lake & Northwestern, was operating two Baldwin locomotives and twenty-six log cars with an annual capacity of twenty million feet of timber.[66] In figure 5.16a, one of the Baldwins, a 0–6–0, had paused briefly so that William could record the carloads of timber that were more than sufficient to rebuild the dining hall, bunkhouses, and work sheds across the track. William's decision to create a semipanoramic view—the original print is an unusual 14 x 8 inches—not only emphasizes the line of log cars and camp structures but also demonstrates very dramatically the end result of an effective lumber operation. By 1886 much of Michigan resembled the stumpland and slash that fills the foreground of William's view. The contrast between the methodical organization represented by the railroad and the camp and the ravaged disorder between the camera and the track is especially telling.

Who among the individuals posed on the length of timber at the left in figure 5.16a may have been Gratwick, Smith, or Fryer? Although we do not know, one of the three at least also was present when William celebrated the "Champion Load" created for figure 5.16b. Notice that the individual with the high-button jacket, heavy mustache, and little hat with the turned-up brim appears in both shots. In figure 5.16a he is second from the left; in

Figure 5.15a. "'The Start, Morning,' Delta Lumber Co.," 1884–85. Unmounted silver print, 8⁹⁄₁₆ x 6⁷⁄₁₆ inches. Goodridge Brothers Studio, East Saginaw, Mich. Collection of Beffrey Family.

Figure 5.15b. "Select Logs," 1884–85. Unmounted silver print, 8⁹⁄₁₆ x 6⁷⁄₁₆ inches. Goodridge Brothers Studio, East Saginaw, Mich. Collection of Beffrey Family.

Figure 5.16a."Lumber Camp and Railroad of Gratwick, Smith & Fryer," 1886. Unmounted silver print, 14 x 8 inches. Goodridge Brothers Studio, East Saginaw, Mich. Collection of Beffrey Family.

Figure 5.16b. "'Champion Load,' Gratwick, Smith & Fryer," 1886. Unmounted silver print, 14 x 10 inches. Goodridge Brothers Studio, East Saginaw, Mich. Collection of Beffrey Family.

5.16b he stands to the right of the cutter with its frisky team and trio of generations, each bedecked in her Sunday-best bonnet. All, however, are overshadowed by the focal point of the view, the "Champion Load." Such views were not uncommon during the boom years of the early 1880s, but this one is exceptional for several reasons. At 14 x 10 inches, the print is one of William's largest extant lumber views. Notice that here, as in figure 5.15b, William has retouched the negative to highlight the numerals indicating the size of each log and the total of 20,270 board feet in the load. In addition, the caption stamped across the lower front of the print stipulates that a copyright had been "secured," a clear indication that the studio considered this a view worthy of special attention. Beyond all of that is the sheer magnificence of the timber itself, which indicates the quality of the pine still available in Michigan forests even at this late date. Eight of the twenty-one prime twelve-foot logs that comprise this champion load scaled out at more than a thousand board feet each. The largest, containing 1,225 board feet, is at the far right of the second tier. Several are more than thirty inches in diameter. And together the twenty-one constitute a load that certainly weighed at the very least twenty-five tons, if not twice that amount. Furthermore, the photograph is a telling example of the extent to which nature, in this case Michigan's forests, had been "commodified" by the 1880s. Beyond the focus on this extraordinary load of pine timber with its prominently highlighted board footage is the fact that the individual—Gratwick, Smith, or Fryer—standing authoritatively before "his" pine logs is holding, and flexing a bit so it is impossible to identify it conclusively, what may well be a log scale. The scale was a measuring tool that was used to determine the board footage of individual logs and as such therefore becomes the ideal symbol of the process by which nature was converted into commodity, trees into board feet.[67]

Not long after William's visit to Otsego County, two men were killed and three badly injured when one of Gratwick, Smith & Fryer's locomotives hit a broken rail and jumped the track. According to the newspaper account: "While nearing the camp of Thomas Judge a log train on the Gratwick, Smith & Fryer Lumber Company's road jumped the track and the engine rolled into the ditch killing John Reardon and James Morrissey. Three others were badly injured, and of these Charles Boney and James Stinson were yesterday brought to this city [East Saginaw] and taken to St. Mary's Hospital for surgical attention. The engineer and fireman escaped with slight bruises. A broken rail caused the accident."[68] Which of the men pictured in William's Gratwick, Smith & Fryer views were dead or badly injured in 1888 as a result of the reported or a similar accident in Michigan's forests is not known at this time.[69]

The same winter as the Gratwick, Smith & Fryer tragedy but in March, William made yet another trip north to the lumber camps. This time his destination was the A. J. Scott camp on Hope Creek in Iosco County. Hope Creek flows into Londo Lake near the west-central boundary of the county. Little is known of the Scott operation except that it was a large one in 1888. In one of the views William made of Scott's camp, more than eighty men, representing all possible lumber camp occupations, posed for his camera. The most impressive result of William's visit, however, is figure 5.17. This "Champion Load" topped the one created by Gratwick, Smith & Fryer's crew two years earlier by almost three thousand board feet, contained twenty-five logs, and weighed in at a hefty seventy tons. A Goodridge label on the verso identifies the men who were responsible for the feat and perched atop their accomplishment as Robert E. Law, Ralph A. Ballagh, Frank Bolton, John Donnelly, George Hess, Dave Bolton, and Charles Hess. The fifth individual from the left, with his left foot forward a bit and the middle buttons of his vest open, is probably A. J. Scott, as he appears in a position of authority in this and the other Goodridge views of the camp.

William composed the view as carefully as the men pictured had created this champion load. His camera angle, shooting from below, and use of the large tree to the right to frame the shot magnify the size of the timber mountain. The three groups of

Figure 5.17. "'Champion Load,' A. J. Scott Lumber Camp," 1888. Unmounted silver print, 14⅛ x 10 inches. Goodridge Brothers Studio, East Saginaw, Mich. Collection of Beffrey Family.

men, one on each side and atop the pyramid of logs, define its shape and also separate these cut timbers from the forest that had for so long been their home. All of them—from the men at the top holding reins and resting the tools that represent their accomplishment, to the two men clinging to the left side of the load, to the groups at its base, even the team of horses—seem to be telling William's camera, "See what we have done!" "Celebrate our conquest of this magnificent timber!"

William apparently agreed. Not only did he make the view one of his largest, 14 x 10 inches, but he titled it "Champion Load of the World, 23,210 ft.," secured a copyright, and printed a special label for the verso, most of which is now lost, that recorded all of the necessary vital statistics including location, size, and the names of those present. In addition, William and Wallace had special plans for the view. Only a week after William's visit, under the headline "The Champion, One Team Log Load," the *Saginaw Courier* reported that "At A.

J. Scott's camp on Hope Creek, Iosco County, with one team there was hauled March 14 at one load, 25 pine saw logs scaling 23,210 feet. The haul was about one mile, Goodridge Bros., of this city, neatly photographed the load, and copies of the same will be placed on exhibition here and engraved for Frank Leslie's."[70] Unfortunately, a close reading of *Leslie's Illustrated,* one of the popular news magazines at the time, reveals that the Scott "Champion Load of the World" was not reproduced as announced during 1888 or 1889. Exactly why is not known.

In January 1889 William made his last trip to the north. Appropriately, he visited, once again, the giant banking ground on the Tittabawassee River at Averill. The occasion was a special excursion to Averill by members of the United Association of Lumber Dealers, all of whom were lumber retailers from Ohio, Pennsylvania, Indiana, Kentucky, or Michigan. The group had been holding its annual convention in Columbus, Ohio, since

Figure 5.18. "'Banking Ground,' Tittabawassee River, Averill," 1889. Silver print, 14 x 10 inches. Goodridge Brothers Studio, East Saginaw, Mich. Collection of Beffrey Family.

January 21. Approximately one-half of the three hundred conventioneers made their way north from Columbus to the Saginaws to continue the meeting. The *Saginaw Courier* minutely traced their route along several rail lines from Columbus to Springfield and Toledo and then on the Flint & Pere Marquette to East Saginaw, noting that at Toledo, even though it was long after midnight, "a large number had remained out of bed, and to these the Saginawians gave cordial greeting and a hearty welcome to Michigan." For four days after their arrival on Thursday, January 24, the visitors were feasted and feted, toasted by the present and ex-mayors of both cities, and serenaded by Miss Minnie Madders at the Academy of Music. As was the custom at the time, the *Courier* listed each guest by name and city of origin and even printed the banquet menu, which included everything from oyster patties to hickory nut cake. Among the highlights of the weekend was the Friday afternoon trip to Averill. The "Programme" printed by the *Courier* listed a "2 P.M. excursion to Averill to

visit the great log roll-way, 20,000,000 feet of logs, the largest roll-way in the world, returning at 5 P.M." The Goodridge studio was engaged by the city fathers to commemorate the event.[71]

William traveled with the visitors on the Flint & Pere Marquette to Averill, and his contribution to the excursion appears as figure 5.18. The peak of the true boom years for Averill had already passed. The town's historian has written that "In 1889, the business directory of Averill consisted of only the following businesses: East Saginaw Lumber Company, general store; F. A. Girswold, railroad express agent; Charles Inman, dog breeder; Alexander McMullen, general store and postmaster; and Wright and Ketcham, general store. The population meanwhile had dropped to a low of 50, with most of the men pulling up stakes and going to Edenville, or Camp 16, where the boom was still in progress."[72] Nonetheless, twenty million feet of saw logs was an impressive accumulation, and all but one of the visitors—the fellow presenting the five-finger salute to the left of center—appears to be considering its retail possibilities. Notice that the visitors and camera, as always, have attracted the attention of a group of young Averill residents whom William has included in the view.

For the occasion, and presumably for the conventioneers as well, William made several copies of the view. At least three vintage 14 x 10 prints are extant. One of the three is mounted on a dark green, bevel-edged, gilded board that is 14⅞ x 10⅞ inches. Across the lower front is stamped "UNION ASSOCIATION OF LUMBER DEALERS, At Averill Banking-Ground Tittabawassee River, Midland County, Michigan. January 25th, 1889. Goodridge Bros., East Saginaw, Mich." It appears to be an example of the view presented to or available as a souvenir to the visiting lumber dealers.

The large-format views that William had been making since his April 1883 Wright and Ketcham expedition were consistent in their point of view. Each is concerned, in one way or another, with the impact of the railroad on the timber industry and the resulting record levels of production that were achieved during the 1880s. It would be presumptuous, however, to assume that William created these views in direct response to the decline of the industry and the disappearance of Michigan's once seemingly limitless forest resources during the same decade. Yet it also is clear that his purpose and his perspective had evolved in the quarter century since 1865. The stereo views' simple and straightforward attempts to describe camp life and to document forest technique had been responsible for the studio's initial success. After 1883 that directness was supplanted by William's more subtle but no less successful evaluation of the results of the pine lumber boom. It is ironic but fitting that the last of William's large-format lumber views is of the men responsible for the final phase of the process that he had been photographing now for so many years.

⬥≡⬥

This most active and successful period in the long history of the Goodridge studio's development ended abruptly on Sunday evening, August 17, 1890. The following day the *Saginaw Evening*

News reported that "Wm. Goodridge, of the firm of Goodridge Bros., the veteran photographer, and a prominent and respected colored citizen, died last evening, of an affection [*sic*] of the kidneys after an illness of about two weeks." (Figure 5.19 is a vignetted portrait of a mature William made by Wallace shortly before August 1890.) A subsequent report in the *Saginaw Courier-Herald* revealed that William had "received careful nursing, and physicians did all in their power to repel the advance of the disease, but in vain, and at the close of last week it was evident the end of life was near." The funeral service was held at the studio and family residence, 220 South Washington, on Tuesday, August 20, and William became the first of several family members to be interred in the Goodridge plot in Forest Lawn Cemetery.[73]

The exact cause of William's sudden and untimely death—he was only forty-four years old—is not clear. The newspaper accounts report it as a "disease of the kidneys," but William's death certificate attributes it to "blood poisoning."[74] The two certainly are not incompatible. It may be, in fact, that the source of William's success also became the occasion for his death. A studio or darkroom accident involving the sharp metal or glass edges and variety of chemical agents common there easily could have caused the blood poisoning that was responsible for William's kidney failure.

William's death not only left Wallace as the last of the three original "Goodridge Bros., Photographers," but William also was survived by a young widow and three small children. On October 1, 1867, William O. Goodridge had married Alice Guin Hayner, who died in January 1874. There were no children.[75] The 1880 census reveals, however, that William had remarried by that time. He and the new Mrs. Goodridge (see figure 5.20 for a portrait made some years after the marriage), who was born Gertrude Watson in December 1861 in Michigan, had three children before William's death. A son, William O., Jr., was born in 1883. Young "Willie," as he was known, appears in the studio's May 1890 portrait of the recently united Saginaw Police Force (see figure 5.5). By 1900 William, Jr., was working as a photographer with

Figure 5.19. "William O. Goodridge," 1889–90. Albumen image, 3¹⁵/₁₆ x 6¹¹/₁₆ inches, beige bristol board mount with gold trim, 4 x 8 inches. Goodridge Brothers Studio, East Saginaw, Mich. Collection of Beverly S. Osborne Pearson.

Figure 5.20. "Gertrude Watson Goodridge," 1885–90, cabinet card. Albumen image, 4 x 5⅞ inches, beige bristol board mount, 4 x 6 inches. Goodridge Brothers Studio, East Saginaw, Mich. Collection of Beverly S. Osborne Pearson.

his uncle Wallace, but he died in November 1904 of unknown causes shortly after his twenty-first birthday. A second son, John F., was born in 1885. As a teenager John worked for the Flint & Pere Marquette Railroad, but he joined uncle Wallace in the studio in 1903 shortly before the death of William, Jr. In 1908 John left the studio to work as an electrician and film projectionist at a succession of Saginaw theaters, including the Jeffers and the Franklin, until his death in 1947. William's only daughter, Alta (or Altena), was born in February 1891, nearly six months after her father's death.[76] Although she never knew him, Alta later helped to preserve the community's awareness of her father's accomplishments as a photographer. In 1926 she married Oliver J. Murchison of Muncie, Indiana, who settled in Saginaw. He died in 1956. As a widow, Alta Goodridge Murchison was active in sever-

al religious and fraternal organizations until her own death in 1966. She was the last of the family living in Saginaw, and her death became an occasion for the city to recall the Goodridge studio's importance to it. She was survived by a stepson, Jewett Murchison of Battle Creek, Michigan. Gertrude Watson Goodridge, who was only twenty-eight when she was widowed, worked as a hairdresser with her sister-in-law Mary Nicholas until 1899, when she married Fred Jackson and moved to Geneva, Ohio. He died in 1926, and Gertrude returned to Saginaw, where she lived until her own death in 1948. There were no known children from the Jackson marriage. Both Fred and Gertrude were buried with William in the Forest Lawn plot.[77]

During the decade or so between William's second marriage and his untimely death, he and Gertrude assembled an album of family portraits that is a rare glimpse into the private lives of the Goodridges. Some of the portraits may have been

Figure 5.21a. "Gertrude Watson Goodridge and William O. Goodridge, Jr.," 1883, tintype, 2½ x 3⁷⁄₁₆ inches. Goodridge Brothers Studio, East Saginaw, Mich. Collection of Beverly S. Osborne Pearson.

Figure 5.21b. "William O. Goodridge and William O. Goodridge, Jr.," 1883, carte de visite. Albumen image, 2⁵⁄₁₆ x 3¹¹⁄₁₆ inches, beige bristol board mount 2½ x 4³⁄₁₆ inches. Goodridge Brothers Studio, East Saginaw, Mich. Collection of Beverly S. Osborne Pearson.

made by William, but it is likely that most were created by Wallace in the studio's portrait rooms adjoining the family residence. The album is an extraordinary one in that it reveals that although the Goodridges then were at the pinnacle of professional achievement, they also could use their cameras to create a series of family "snaps" not unlike those that countless parents would and still create many decades later. Figures 5.21a and b are first Gertrude and then William in June 1883, each posing with the three-month-old William O., Jr. The following year, perhaps it was a birthday or Christmas 1884 (figure 5.21c), young William appears with his mother and maternal grandmother, Mrs. Watson, and a new hobbyhorse. At about the same time, Christmas 1884, when young William, Jr., was twenty-one months (figure 5.21d), either his father or his uncle captured his thoughtful mood as he rested on the arm of one of the studio's plush chairs. The following September, in poses which were a bit more contrived, William, Jr., is accompanied first, in figure 5.21e, by his favorite toy—notice the

hobbyhorse to the left—and then, in 5.21f, by the studio dalmatian. About a year after John was born, William and Gertrude (see figure 5.21g) posed with their two sons on the studio's hallmark rustic steps. During 1888 and 1889 William created a series of family portraits that were sometimes fantastic, as in figure 5.21h, with William, Jr., and John in outlandish costume, or in more formal poses, as in figure 5.21i, with their mother and maternal grandparents. Following William's death, Wallace would continue the tradition and add several photographs to the family album (see figures 7.9a–b and 7.10a–b).

Within days of his death, personal and professional tributes recognizing William O. Goodridge's achievement appeared in local, state, and national publications. The *Saginaw Evening News* characterized him as "an industrious man, a good citizen, a kind husband and father, and . . . respected by all who knew him." The *Courier-Herald* described him as "a man of intelligence and discernment, thoroughly posted on important questions of the day, and . . . a student of nature

Figure 5.21c. "Gertrude Waston Goodridge, Mrs. Watson, and William O. Goodridge, Jr.," 1884, tintype, 2⅞₆ x 3½ inches. Goodridge Brothers Studio, East Saginaw, Mich. Collection of Beverly S. Osborne Pearson.

Figure 5.21d. "William O. Goodridge, Jr.," 1884, cabinet card. Albumen image, 4⅛ x 5⅞ inches, beige bristol board mount, 4⁵⁄₁₆ x 6⁹⁄₁₆ inches. Goodridge Brothers Studio, East Saginaw, Mich. Collection of Beverly S. Osborne Pearson. of Beverly S. Osborne Pearson.

Figure 5.21e. "William O. Goodridge, Jr.," 1885, cabinet card. Albumen image, 4¹⁄₁₆ x 5¼ inches, beige bristol board mount with gold trim, 4¼ x 6½ inches. Goodridge Brothers Studio, East Saginaw, Mich. Collection of Beverly S. Osborne Pearson.

Figure 5.21f. "William O. Goodridge, Jr., and Dalmatian," 1885, tintype, 2⅞ x 3⁹⁄₁₆ inches. Goodridge Brothers Studio, East Saginaw, Mich. Collection of Beverly S. Osborne Pearson.

Figure 5.21g. "William O., Gertrude W., William O. Jr., and John Goodridge," 1887, tintype, 2⁹⁄₁₆ x 3⁹⁄₁₆ inches. Goodridge Brothers Studio, East Saginaw, Mich. Collection of Beverly S. Osborne Pearson.

Figure 5.21h. "William O. Jr. and John Goodridge," 1888, cabinet card. Image, 4 x 5½ inches, beige bristol board mount with gold trim, 4³⁄₁₆ x 6½ inches. Goodridge Brothers Studio, East Saginaw, Mich. Collection of Beverly S. Osborne Pearson.

Figure 5.21i. "Gertrude W., William O. Jr., and John Goodridge with Mrs. and Mrs. Watson," 1889, cabinet card. Albumen image, 3¹³⁄₁₆ x 5⁵⁄₁₆ inches, black bristol board mount, 4¼ x 6½ inches. Goodridge Brothers Studio, East Saginaw, Mich. Collection of Beverly S. Osborne Pearson.

and art." Both papers noted that major contemporary publications such as "*Harper's, Frank Leslie's,* the *New York Graphic* and other illustrated papers have frequently born[e] traces of his handiwork." The *Detroit Plain Dealer* labeled the death "Saginaw's Loss" and memorialized William as "a man of more than average intelligence, . . . [who] took an active part in politics, . . . whose upright character had gained the respect of all classes," and whose "death is sincerely lamented." The profession's national journal, *Anthony's Photographic Bulletin,* in its "Views Caught with the Drop Shutter" section, published the following: "We regret to note the death, on August 17th, of W. O. GOODRIDGE, of the firm of Goodridge Bros., Saginaw Mich. he was forty-four years of age, and leaves a widow and two children to mourn his loss. Those who knew him best found him a good citizen and respected by all classes."[78]

The two decades of collaboration between William and Wallace following the death of their brother Glenalvin and subsequent move to the 200 block of South Washington after the 1872 Crouse Block fire were the most successful in the Goodridge studio's long history. The brothers continued to expand and improve the studio building they had begun in 1872, with major renovations of and additions to the original structure in 1881 and again in 1890 (see figures 4.4, 4.5, and 4.6).[79] The result was a facility that was variously described as surpassing "any other gallery in the state of Michigan" and "the largest concern of its kind in the United States."[80] While the latter description certainly was overly enthusiastic in its estimate of the studio's growth, the same correspondent also noted that "Among the *well-to-do* people of this city are the Goodridge Bros., composed of Wallace L. and William O., who are in the photographing business."[81] No account books or other financial records from the studio are extant to corroborate the above characterization, but a reporter for the *Detroit Plain Dealer* who visited East Saginaw in December 1889 wrote that he had "stepped into the photograph parlors of the Goodridge brothers and found them doing a thriving business, having more orders than they can fill."[82] The tax history of the Goodridge property at 200 South Washington also reveals that with only two exceptions, between 1872 and 1890 the brothers regularly paid their local and state taxes on time. The exceptions were 1877 and then 1883–84, when the property was sold for nonpayment of taxes in 1883 but then redeemed the following year.[83] The 1883–84 tax delinquency was most likely due to a loss of studio revenue when a price war broke out among Saginaw photographers in the spring of 1883. Beals and then Angell began advertising cabinet-sized portraits for $2.50 per dozen and other photographers, including the Goodridges, were compelled to follow.[84] The war lasted until the end of the following year and also affected the pricing of all photographs. For example, as late as November 1884 the Goodridge studio continued to advertise "Four cabinets or two panel photographs . . . for $1."[85] Interestingly, the price war advertisements were

the only ones run by the Goodridge brothers in the local newspapers or directories after 1872. The Goodridge reputation was so strong by that time and the volume of reports of their work so great that the brothers purchased advertising only in very special circumstances.

While the studio's financial success enabled Wallace and William and their families to live more comfortably than most other Saginaw Valley residents at the time,[86] the brothers' reputation as photographers placed them at the very pinnacle of their profession by the time of William's death. This success is confirmed by a variety of sources. Through the 1870s and into the 1880s, although local newspapers ceased printing lists of individual prizewinners after 1879, the Goodridge studio continued to amass "First" and "Second" premiums in the "Fine Arts" division at the annual East Saginaw Agricultural Society Fair. One reporter, in fact, was so impressed by the brothers' presentation at the 1878 fair that he devoted a major portion of his report to their work. The "Goodridge Bros., the photographers," he wrote, "make a very fine exhibit of 'Old Sol's' work in photography. They occupy one corner of the north wing. Thirty frames are exhibited by them—one containing 15 pictures of infants, and a moonlight photo—a double print." They had, he continued, "enlarged their exhibit of what may be done in the photographic line to a great extent. Although performing all work very excellently, they make a specialty of views, of which they exhibit some very fine specimens. They show views of the city which are superb, and also some railroad views, and one photo with porcelain finish. The tone and richness of their pictures throughout are very fine."[87] When the State Agricultural Society chose East Saginaw as the location for its annual fair in September 1874 and again in 1875, Wallace and William were even more impressive in competition with photographers from throughout Michigan, including Milo Hiler of Lowell, J. A. Jenney of Flint, and C. C. Randall of Detroit. At the 1874 fair the brothers won two "Firsts" for "Pastel painting of a face" and "Three cabinet photographs" and two "Seconds" for "Landscape photograph" and "Half dozen miniature photographs" among the eleven categories judged.[88] In 1875, however, they were dominant. Thirteen categories of photographs were judged at the 1875 fair. William was awarded two "Firsts" for "Pastel painting of [a] face" and "Collection of photographs by any person," a "Second" for "Three cabinet photographs," and a "Recommendation" for a "Landscape photograph." Wallace did not gain a "First," but was awarded a "Second" for a "Set [of] stereoscopic views" and two "Recommendations" for "Specimen photographs on Linen" and "Specimen photographs on Porcelain."[89]

The purpose of such competitions at local and state fairs was to showcase the work of the various competitors, which would increase sales or make it possible to obtain special photographic commissions. For the Goodridge studio the fairs produced the anticipated result. Beginning in 1878 and continuing to the year of William's death, popular national journals like the *New York Daily Graphic, Harper's,* and *Leslie's Illustrated,*[90] as well as various government agencies and privately funded publications, turned to the Goodridge brothers for visual documentation to illustrate both Saginaw's and the entire valley's rapid development during the heyday of the pine lumber boom.

The first of several important commissions came in 1878 when the *New York Daily Graphic* printed "Views in East Saginaw, Mich." (see figure 5.22). The photocollage was part of a series that the *Graphic* ran once or twice a month to promote the rapidly growing cities of the West and Midwest, including Salt Lake City, with photographs by C. R. Savage; Rochester, New York, by George E. Munroe; and Cleveland, by "Sweeny"—indeed fine company for both East Saginaw and the Goodridge brothers.[91]

The *Saginaw Daily Courier* noted during July that year that "Mr. L. H. Hopkins of the New York *Graphic* is in the city for the purpose of writing up some of our more prominent points, which will be illustrated in the *Graphic*." In December both the *Courier* and the *Saginaw Morning Herald* reported that "East Saginaw [had been] Graphicized," and described in detail the illustrations and accompanying description of East Saginaw that the *Daily*

Graphic had printed on December 3. The reports indicated that the "illustrations were furnished by Goodridge Bros., and are excellent," and that "orders for extra copies [of "Views in East Saginaw"] can be left with Gibbs at the postoffice news rooms, which will be filled at the usual rates."[92]

During the previous two decades of rapid growth East Saginaw had flourished, and the Goodridge views, both cartes de visite and stereographs, were exactly what the *Graphic* required to substantiate the following characterization of the city: "The growth of East Saginaw has not been of an ephemeral nature, but has been honest and its future is assured, situated as it is in the heart of the great pine district of Michigan with good railroad facilities and a river running by it navigable for vessels drawing 11 feet of water and whose banks are lined with sawmills and salt works."[93] Each of the collages included views of banks, hotels, schools, hospitals, and churches, as well as major commercial structures. The goal was to demonstrate the rapid progress but also the institutional stability that had been achieved. Each usually contained a vista of the main street from a vantage point that presented the city in its most positive light. Goodridges' East Saginaw was no exception. "Genesee Street from the Bridge" is framed by views of the Congregational Church, Central High School, Germania, the public library, the Bancroft Hotel, Merchants' National Bank, the Flint & Pere Marquette Railroad Building, St. Mary's Hospital, and the Jefferson Avenue Methodist Church. However, the foundation for the entire presentation—emphasized by its dark border—is a magnificent panorama titled "Looking Down [North] the Saginaw River from the Middle [Bristol] Bridge." The original print of the photograph is not known to be extant, but there is no doubt that this large panorama—one of the studio's first—was created two years earlier and described by the *Saginaw Daily Courier* as a "Fine Photographic View." According to the newspaper report, the "Goodridge Bros., the enterprising photographers on Washington avenue, have taken photographic views showing the entire river front of East Saginaw at highwater. Carrollton and Saginaw City also appear in the dis-

Figure 5.22. "Views in East Saginaw, Mich.," December 3, 1878, *New York Daily Graphic*. Clarke Historical Library, Central Michigan University.

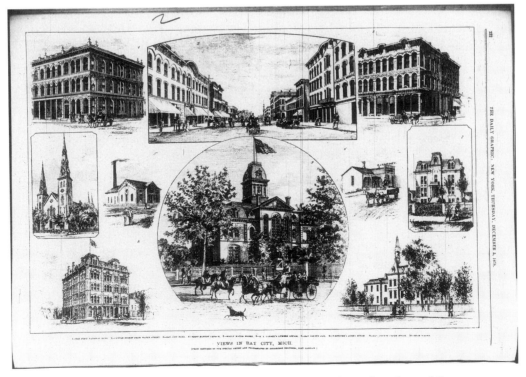

Figure 5.23. "Views in Bay City, Mich.," December 5, 1878, *New York Daily Graphic*. Library of Congress.

tance. The picture is forty-three inches long, and every family in the city should have one."[94]

Certainly the view was a much more ambitious one than the two-part carte de visite panoramas (see figures 3.15a–c) that the studio had created in 1870. Without the original print, however, it is impossible to determine if the forty-three-inch panorama was constructed from only two or more probably three separate views. A camera capable of making a true single-piece panorama would not be commonly available until after 1880.[95] Nonetheless, the result, even in its reduced and reproduced state, is impressive. The Middle Bridge crossed the Saginaw River at Bristol Street and was an excellent vantage point from which to capture the river's expanse. William later used the same location to photograph the A. W. Wright Lumber Company mill at the foot of Throop Street up the river in Saginaw City (see figure 5.13b). This view is exceptional, however, in that it is the only one in any format William is known to have made downriver, to the north, from this perspective. Shooting north and east, the direction of the river's flow here, into the bright morning light, was difficult at best, and afternoon moved the shadows around to the wrong direction. Given the result, it is a wonder that he did not attempt the location more often. The composition of the view shows William at his best. The sky and broad plain of the river divide the view into nearly equal horizontal halves. The lower or river half is framed on the east bank, right side, by the booms and buildings and especially the smokestack of Sears & Holland Company's sawmill, with the impressive expanse of East Saginaw filling the middleground in the distance. On the west, left side, along the northern perimeter of Saginaw City is another of A. W. Wright and Company's sawmills with smoke also coming from its stack. And, in the distance, beyond the Genesee Street Bridge, other smokestacks of various Carrollton sawmills also are visible. Joining river to sky, east to west, and mill to mill, is the reason for it all, the rafts of white pine logs waiting to play their part in the valley's lumber boom. In the immediate foreground, between the rafts of timber and the Sears & Holland mill,

William has introduced a softer, more human element into the midst of all the industry and progress. Although an obvious convention, it is an effective one and characteristic of William's work.

On December 5, two days after publishing "Views in East Saginaw," the *Daily Graphic* featured a second "Thriving Michigan City" in "Views in Bay City" (see figure 5.23), which it characterized as "One of the Most Important Shipping Points on the Great Lakes."[96] The collage is interesting for a number of reasons. It is faithful to the formula that the *Graphic* had earlier established for the series. Ten illustrations based on photographs present the most important and impressive structures in Bay City, including the courthouse and jail, Holly Water Works, Westover's Opera House, and a semipanoramic view looking up "Center Street from Water Street." For the series the *Graphic* also chose to use "Photographs by Goodridge." At the time, 1878, Bay City was well served by several photographers, including Charles B. and Elizur J. Colburn, J. J. Gibson, and George A. Harman and J. C. Verner, all of whom were more than capable of producing the necessary views.[97] Nonetheless, as the description accompanying the collage noted in its concluding remarks, "For our excellent views of Bay City we are indebted to the Goodridge Bros., the colored photographers of East Saginaw, who make a specialty of out-door work."[98] Probably because of the Goodridges' reputation, possibly because of their near unique status as "colored photographers," but likely because they had almost simultaneously supplied the views for East Saginaw, the editors of the *Graphic* had chosen them rather than any of their Bay City competitors to make the Bay City views. Subsequently, four of the ten Bay City photographs upon which the collage was based (the Holly Water Works, Westover's Opera House, and the courthouse and jail) were included as part of the "Picturesque Michigan" stereo series (see figure 4.37a) introduced in 1880. The ten images, including the four later reproduced as stereo views, are the only photographs of Bay City that presently are known to have been made by the Goodridges.

In January 1882, four years after the first commission, the *New York Daily Graphic* turned once again to the Goodridge studio when it wished to publish yet a second collage of "Views in East Saginaw, Michigan" (see figure 5.24). During the previous December the *Saginaw Evening Express* had reported that "Goodridge Bros. have been appointed photographers for the New York Graphic, and will furnish that paper with views for publication, including the principal buildings in the valley, lumber scenes, railroad bridges and summer resorts. The Graphic will make a specialty of the scenery of Northern Michigan during the coming year."[99] Obviously the *Graphic* had been impressed with the studio's earlier work and may have hoped to use the Goodridges as a source of illustrations for locations in Michigan beyond the Saginaw Valley. It has not been possible, however, to identify conclusively illustrations of Michigan published in the *Graphic* during 1882 or later other than the "Views in East Saginaw" based on Goodridge photographs. Nonetheless, the 1882 "Views in East Saginaw," which was published from Goodridge photographs, was part of a larger series focusing on the rapidly growing cities of the West and Midwest, and East Saginaw and the Goodridges were in even more impressive company than they had been in 1878. The series featured Toledo with photographs by Alley, North, and Oswald, Council Bluffs by "Barker," Little Rock by "Dawson," and Denver with the photographs of William Henry Jackson.[100]

The *Graphic's* decision to run a second collage so soon was based on the fact that 1881 and 1882 were the peak years of lumber production in Saginaw Valley mills—more than nine hundred million board feet in 1881 and over one billion board feet of lumber cut in 1882[101]—and East Saginaw had come to stand as the symbol of that achievement. As a result, the *Graphic's* presentation and choice of Goodridge views had a somewhat different emphasis than in 1878. Rather than providing a cross section of institutions that included churches, schools, hospitals, libraries, and social clubs, the 1882 photocollage focused almost exclusively on business, especially lumber and the various enterprises related to it. As if to emphasize this theme, the presentation is capped, in the upper left corner, by a symbolic pine log, crosscut saw, and ax. At its heart, however, taking up most of the upper half of the page, are three large views, including two panoramas, of the pine lumber industry. Each, in its own way, represents the abundance of timber coming from the valley's seemingly inexhaustible forests down the river to Saginaw's mills and serves as a prelude to the perspective on timber as "commodity" that was soon to appear so strongly in William's series of large-format photographs made for Wright and Ketcham beginning in 1883.

The first of the panoramas (top of figure 5.24) is a sweeping view of East Saginaw between Potter Street and Genesee made from the west bank of the river near the Whittier & Co. sawmill and saltworks located at the western terminus of the Flint & Pere Marquette Railroad bridge. The structures visible immediately across the river are the machine shops of the Wickes Bros. Co., where the gang saws that made it possible to saw millions of board feet of lumber each year were manufactured, and the Mayflower Mills, which supplied flour and other staples to lumber camps throughout the valley.[102] In the distance, a bit upriver, is the Genesee Bridge and the skyline of East Saginaw proper. Most important, however, are the rafts of logs tied up near the sorting pens of the various lumber mills, literally making the Saginaw a river of wood from bank to bank. Notice that William again has included the convention of the boatmen, although certainly not the same individuals who appeared in the 1878 panorama. The second of the lumber views, titled "Rafting Logs," is a copy of figure 5.13a, which William had made for the Tittabawassee Boom Company's "booming" facilities near the Merrill Bridge as part of the Wright and Ketcham series of large-format views. Again the emphasis is on "commodity," the abundance of pine saw logs peacefully awaiting their fate and the journey downriver to the mills. The last of the three lumber views and the second of the panoramas is described as "The Largest Banking Ground in the World, Containing 40,000,000 Feet of Lumber." It is, of course, the banking ground at Averill

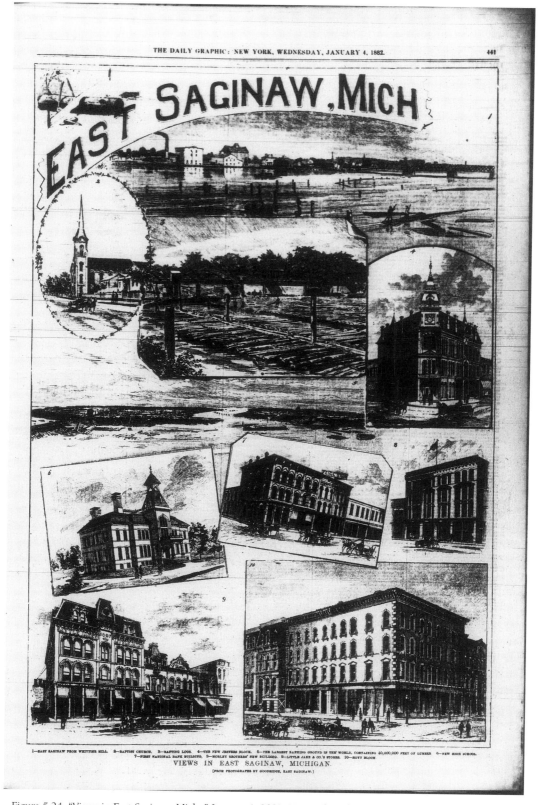

Figure 5.24. "Views in East Saginaw, Mich.," January 4, 1882, *New York Daily Graphic.* Library of Congress.

in Midland County which William had been photographing regularly during the 1870s and 1880s, and which, better than any other place in the valley, represented "commoditization" of the extraordinary abundance of timber that was the basis for the pine lumber boom. Although the *Graphic*'s editors chose to include views of the First Baptist Church, which had been located at the northeast corner of Jefferson and German Streets since 1868, and the "New High School," which was built at the northwest corner of Warren Avenue and Millard Street in 1880, the remaining five views in the collage all are business blocks or organizations with close ties to the timber trade. As if to emphasize the support they derived from but also provided to the industry, they are grouped together across the bottom half of the page, serving as a "foundation" for the three lumber views. Each of the five was a new or at least recently renovated structure. Included are "The New Jeffers (Tower) Block" at the corner of Genesee and Warren, which Michael Jeffers had earlier purchased from Jesse Hoyt and only recently refurbished; the "First National Bank Building" located at the southwest corner of Genesee and Cass in 1876; the "Morley Brothers' New Building" on Washington, which was to open on April 1, 1882; "Little Jake & Co.'s Stores" at Genesee and Franklin; and the new Hoyt Block, which had replaced the Crouse Block at the northeast corner of Washington and Genesee in 1873.

The *Graphic*'s "Views in East Saginaw, Michigan" presented a most positive image of the city and also provided a national audience for the Goodridge brother's photographs. In fact, the *Graphic*'s editors concluded the text which accompanied the collage by stating that "We are indebted to the Messrs. Goodridge Brothers of East Saginaw, for the *very excellent photographs* we present today. The Messrs. Goodridge are *photographers of no little reputation,* and the character of their work has *justly won the high estimation in which it is held.*"[103] Whether the *Graphic* thought so highly of the Goodridges' work that it actually continued to use the studio's photographs of Michigan as a basis for its illustrations has been impossible to determine. No illustrations based on photographs are specifi-

cally attributed by the *Graphic* to the Goodridges after January 1882. However, on September 5, 1882, the *Graphic* did publish a very elaborate two-page spread of "Some of the Prominent Scenes in the Lumber Camp of Alger, Smith & Co., at Black River, Michigan" that included twelve illustrations "From Photographs and Sketches by Our Special Artist." The accompanying description does not identify the "Special Artist," nor did a lengthy notice describing the presentation that was published two weeks later in the *Lumberman's Gazette*. And while the "Black River" illustrations do not correspond to any Goodridge lumber photographs presently known, their style is similar to William's work and he did make several photographing expeditions to that part of the state during the early 1880s.[104]

Shortly after the publication of the *Graphic*'s second presentation featuring East Saginaw based on Goodridge photographs, the *Saginaw Evening Express* reported that the "Goodridge Bros., the leading portrait and [*sic*] photographers and special artists for the New York Daily Graphic, of this city, have now pending negotiations to make a number of stereoscopic and large views of Colorado, and have also completed arrangements to make some mammoth views, 20 by 25 inches, for some of the leading railroads of Michigan, when the season opens."[105] Unfortunately, it is not known if negotiations for the Colorado commission ever were concluded successfully. The presumption must be that they were not. No subsequent notice appears in the local newssheets reporting a trip to Colorado by Wallace or William—such a venture would have been reported—and no stereoscopic or large views of Colorado by the Goodridge studio presently are known. Nevertheless, it is clear that the negotiations were prompted by their work for the *Graphic,* and Goodridge views of Colorado may yet appear. It is more likely that Wallace and William did, indeed, complete a variety of commissions for Michigan railroads, as was regularly reported,[106] and, in fact, figures 5.9 and 5.10a and b of the Potter Street complex of the Flint & Pere Marquette Railroad Company are examples of just this sort of commission.

Locally, both the actual and the reported commissions also enhanced the Goodridges' already considerable reputation as "leading photographers" and "special artists." In January 1888, for example, the *Saginaw Evening News* announced that the International Publishing Company, in association with H. R. Page & Co. of Chicago, was studying the feasibility of publishing a *Saginaw Illustrated.* The volume would "contain views taken from the most romantic, artistic and picturesque points" of both East Saginaw and Saginaw City, with "Due prominence . . . given to churches, public buildings, businesses and manufacturing interests." The illustrations were to be accompanied by a text of "a historical and descriptive nature."[107] International Publishing and H. R. Page were well known as producers of such "illustrateds." The idea, however, was based on the earlier popularity and success of the hundreds of county histories created for the 1876 Centennial celebration and, more recently, the fascinating "Bird's Eye Views" produced by publishers such as A. W. Morse and Co.[108] The key to success in each instance was to

obtain as many subscribers as possible before publication and then to produce the "view," history, or "illustrated" as quickly as possible. Both the centennial histories and bird's-eye views obtained subscribers by including brief biographical sketches or views of homes and businesses around the perimeter of the bird's eye in exchange for the subscription. The "illustrateds" do not appear to have followed this practice. According to subsequent reports in the *Evening News,* International Publishing and H. R. Page's success in the Saginaws was due to signing up at least three hundred subscribers to the *Illustrated* before going to press and then producing and delivering the nine parts of the *Illustrated* before the end of the year. Most of this success resulted from the efforts of R. H. Morrish, who was the "active man in the field" for H. R. Page & Co. It was Morrish who signed up the three hundred subscribers, contracted William F. Goldie, assistant editor of the *Evening News,* to write the accompanying text, and both created and collected the photographic views that were the essence of the *Illustrated.* As was Page & Co.'s practice, Mor-

Figure 5.25a. "View of East Saginaw to Southeast," 1888. Copy of original image, 10 x 8 ⅛ inches. Goodridge Brothers Studio, East Saginaw, Mich. Bosch-Devers Collection and published in *Saginaw Illustrated.*

Figure 5.25b. "William L. Webber Residence," 1888. Copy of original image, 10 x 8⅛ inches. Goodridge Brothers Studio, East Saginaw, Mich. Bosch-Devers Collection and published in *Saginaw Illustrated.*

Figure 5.25c. "Wickes Bros. Iron Works," 1888. Copy of original image, 10 x 8⅛ inches. Goodridge Brothers Studio, East Saginaw, Mich. Bosch-Devers Collection and published in *Saginaw Illustrated.*

rish or one of their other field men created the majority of the views that went into any of the "illustrateds." But Morrish also purchased existing views and commissioned new ones from local photography studios. In the case of *Saginaw Illustrated,* approximately twenty-seven of the ninety-four views included were commissioned and/or purchased from the Goodridge studio during the summer of 1888.[109]

Among the Goodridge views included in the *Illustrated* are figures 5.25a–c. The first is a view looking southeast taken from the roof of the Academy of Music near the Goodridge studio on South Washington. Jefferson Avenue Methodist and First Congregational Churches are clearly visible to the left and right, and the new high school and Presbyterian Church at Warren and Millard also can be seen in the center and a bit more distant. In the immediate foreground is William (later Janes) Street and the houses and lumber mill (Cooper & Avery) that have replaced those damaged or destroyed by the June 1873 fire that the Goodridges had recorded in one of their earlier stereo series (see figures 4.27b and c). The Goodridge selection also included several examples of East Saginaw's finest domestic architecture. Among them is the William L. Webber residence (figure 5.25b). It was located on Millard between Warren and Sheridan Avenues (just visible to the left of the steeple of First Congregational Church in figure 5.25a). An extraordinary example of Victorian eclectic, with elements of both Italianate and mansard styles, the Webber home was constructed in 1883–84. Unfortunately, it no longer stands. Both William L. and his father, James S. Webber, were regular Goodridge customers and are known to have been avid collectors of the Goodridge stereo series. A more immediate view of the Wickes Brothers Iron Works than in the 1876 panorama printed by the *New York Graphic* appears as figure 5.25c. After an earlier beginning in Flint, Michigan, as the Genesee Iron Works, in partnership with H. N. Wood of that community, Henry D. and Edward N. Wickes moved the business to East Saginaw in 1860, purchased Wood's interest four years later, and renamed it Wickes Brothers. From this site bounded by Washington,

Miller, Water, and Carroll the firm grew in twenty years to become the most important manufactory in the Saginaw Valley. The basis for much of its success was the production of a gang saw that both speeded the sawing of timber and dramatically reduced wastage, making it the "standard sawing machine wherever timber and logs were made into lumber."[110]

The Saginaws' response to the combined efforts of the Goodridge brothers, William F. Goldie, R. H. Morrish, H. R. Page & Co., and International Publishing was even better than any of them had anticipated. According to a report in the *Saginaw Evening News* upon completion and delivery of *Saginaw Illustrated* to the more than three hundred subscribers: "The firm have more than lived up to their agreement, each number being larger than was originally intended, with also more reading matter and illustrations than the contract called for. Taking the elegant views and prose sketches together, the work jointly makes one of the most pleasing souvenirs of the Saginaws that has ever been brought forth."[111]

The same spring that the Goodridge studio had contracted with Morrish to supply views for *Saginaw Illustrated,* the *Saginaw Courier* reported that the Goodridge brothers had photographed a "Champion Load" of "25 pine saw logs scaling 23,210 feet" at A. J. Scott's camp on Hope Creek in Iosco County (see figure 5.17). The view was placed on exhibition at the studio and was to be published in *Leslie's Illustrated.*[112] However, it was not published in 1888 or later in 1889. The decision to withhold it from publication in *Leslie's* was motivated by a singular opportunity presented to Wallace and William Goodridge at the end of 1888.

On November 28, 1888, Bernhard E. Fernow, chief of the Forestry Division in the Department of Agriculture from 1886 to 1898, wrote to the Goodridges with the following request: "I have your list of photographs of Lumbering Scenes from Mr. Kern. I should like to have a full set of them, leaving out the River view, which will make 12 altogether. As I wish to bring this exhibit under one frame, I should like to know beforehand, how

Figure 5.26. "Scenes in Camp," 1880s. Copy of original image, 5 x 4⅟₁₆ inches. Goodridge Brothers Studio, East Saginaw, Mich. Collection of Beffrey Family.

many are high and how many wide views. The desirable size would be 8 by 10, or if you can make them as well larger, please let me know."[113] What Fernow did not explain in this initial request was that he was in charge of organizing the Forestry Division's component of the Department of Agriculture's enormous display that would be sent to Paris for the 1889 Universal Exposition celebrating the centennial of the French Revolution. The exposition was the most ambitious since the English had set the standard with the "Crystal Palace Exhibition" in 1851, and Paris also would serve as the model for Chicago's Columbian Exposition, already being planned for 1893. The 1889 Universal Exposition was an immense success, with more than twenty-eight million visitors between May and November—more than twice the twelve million who had attended the earlier 1878 Paris exposition.[114] Most of the 1889 visitors, no doubt, came intending to ride to the top of Gustave Eiffel's three-hundred-meter tower, which became the

icon of the exposition, and to marvel at the dazzling brilliance of electric light—the exposition was the first to be lit by electricity.[115]

After the French, the United States had created the largest and most elaborate series of exhibits for the exposition. U.S. motivation was varied but broadly based. The American and French people had shared a commitment to liberty since their mutual revolutions in 1776 and 1789. In 1886 the French gift of a "Statue of Liberty" was intended to demonstrate that mutuality. The first opportunity for a positive and substantive U.S. response came in 1889. Paris also would provide the American people with the occasion to recall with pride the earlier success of the Centennial Exhibition at Philadelphia in 1876 and to refine their plans for Chicago in 1893. But most of all it was an opportunity to demonstrate to the world America's growing power, the genius of her people, and the extraordinary abundance produced by her factories, farms, and forests. The Goodridge studio would play a small but important role in that demonstration.[116]

According to the records of Forestry Division correspondence, Chief Fernow had learned of the Goodridge lumber photographs from William M. Kern of Detroit. During the 1880s Kern owned a large cooperage works on River Rouge, with offices at 44 Buhl Block in Detroit. He regularly ordered publications from the Forestry Division, such as the 1884 "Report of Forests of North America," and may also have acquired the various series of Goodridge stereographs and lumber views that the studio was then marketing throughout the state.[117] Kern apparently had been able to acquire his Goodridge lumber views with much less difficulty than Fernow.

On December 28, "fearing that [his] letter or your answer must have been lost," Fernow sent a second request to the Goodridge studio "for a set of photographs of Lumbering Scenes, 12 altogether of your list, leaving out the River view." He also hoped that "If you can make bromide enlargements, I should prefer them to the 8 by 10 photographs" he had requested in his first letter. In the interim Wallace or William had responded to Fernow's first request with a proposal that included "12 small . . . and 2 larger-sized" views and a diagram of the display which Fernow approved. By January 31, however, the views had not arrived in Washington, and a frustrated Fernow wrote the Goodridges that "If you wish to sell me the Photographs of Lumbering Scenes, which I ordered, please send them at once, as I cannot wait any longer, and oblige." Within the following week the views finally arrived, and Fernow sent the Goodridge brothers a check for an unknown amount "in payment for material furnished for the Paris Exposition."[118]

Precisely which of the Goodridge lumber views Fernow ordered and the studio sent to the Paris Exposition is, unfortunately, impossible to determine. A notice published in the *Saginaw Morning Herald* offers only some hints:

> Goodridge Bros., the photographers, of this city, have attained a national reputation for their views in the Michigan lumber woods, which cover all

the chief features of the lumber business from the tree to the mill. The firm recently received an order for 14 of these views from the Agricultural Department at Washington, the order coming from the Chief of the Forestry Division, which will be placed on exhibition at the Paris Exposition this year. The views will be shipped by express to-day, and they are certainly fine *and cover all the varied operations in lumbering, including the famous big load of logs, which was heretofore referred to in these columns.* The views, interesting and beautiful as they are, will undoubtedly be given a prominent place in the Paris Exposition.[119]

The "famous big load of logs" refers, of course, to the "Champion Load" view from the A. J. Scott camp (see figure 5.17) that was to have been published in *Leslie's Illustrated* the previous summer but which the Goodridges decided to include in the Paris display instead. The other views certainly drew upon the Goodridge inventory that William had created on his various photographing expeditions to the Wright and Ketcham camp in Midland County, the Delta Lumber Company in Schoolcraft County, and Gratwick, Smith & Fryer in Otsego County during the 1880s. It also is possible that the display included enlargements of the earlier stereo series which William had made at P. Glynn & Co.'s Camp (see figures 4.32a–c and 4.33.a–c) and included in the "Picturesque Michigan" series. Figure 5.26, although not part of the display ordered by Fernow for the Paris Exposition, is certainly similar to what he did purchase and contained views from the various Goodridge series created during the 1870s and 1880s.

Whatever may have been its exact content, the display of lumber views that made its way from the South Washington studio in East Saginaw to Washington, D.C., and then to Paris, where it spent the summer in the shadow of the Eiffel Tower, was a modest but essential element in the success of the Department of Agriculture's exhibit and the general acclaim bestowed on U.S. participation in the 1889 Universal Exposition. One especially enthusiastic special correspondent to the *Saginaw Evening News*, who identified himself as "J.S.," concluded that "The greatest and best republic in the world, the United States, can congratulate its young sister republic on the success of its exposition, for to make a success in Europe of an undertaking on so grand a scale as this, independent of the crowned heads of the balance of the country, is very significant indeed, and shows intelligent people that imperial governments are not necessary to the success of undertakings or the happiness of any people. That is American and the writer likes it."[120] Through the summer of 1889 Miss E. A. Wright of East Saginaw, who was living in Paris at the time, also served as a "special correspondent" to the *Evening News,* which published a series of four of her letters describing in great detail her visits to the exposition. Miss Wright was most taken by the Eiffel Tower, the Egyptian dancing women, the magnificent floral displays, and an enormous "tun of campagne" which "When filled . . . contains wine enough to fill 200,000 bottles." "In coming from Epernay to Paris," she wrote, "drawn by a dozen pair of oxen, it overturned a house, broke down trees, and, as the guides humorously tell you, 'did almost a hundredth part of the mischief which its contents will do hereafter.'"[121] Apparently she managed to avoid the Quai d'Orsay where the agricultural and mechanical exhibits were located, including those from her own city and state.[122]

The Paris newspapers noted, however, that "the exhibit from the United States Department of Agriculture has received the highest degree of attention from economists and agronomists."[123] And the *Michigan Farmer* was justly proud when it reported later that year the "awards conferred upon American exhibitors . . . including several grand prizes and gold medals awarded to the Exhibit prepared under the direction of the U.S. Department of Agriculture, . . . [which] testified in a measure to the favorable recognition accorded to that exhibit by the several juries who sat upon it." The same report included a lengthy excerpt from the *London Morning Post* to the effect that

> There is probably no section of the Paris Exhibition which possesses greater interest to British farmers than that devoted to the agriculture of the United States. So large a portion of our food supply, particularly flour and beef, is derived from the United States, that it becomes instructive to inquire what account the American agriculturists render of themselves in the great Industrial Exposition which is now in progress. It may at once be said that the grouping together of the many and varied objects of interest and study in the American Agriculture Department, is a work that must have involved much patience, care and discrimination on the parts of the collectors. . . . The opportunity afforded by the Paris Exposition of displaying in Europe the remarkable agricultural resources of the United States had been utilized to the full by the government of that country. For no European country does the agriculture development of the American Republic possess greater significance than for Great Britain, and now that the United States Agricultural Exhibit at Paris is complete, attention may profitably be directed to its salient features. The whole display is based upon a scientific plan and is intended by means of illustrations, charts, models, and specimens of produce, to instruct as to the methods and processes of cultivating, harvesting and preparing each particular product for market.[124]

Since the early 1870s the momentum and the level of the Goodridge brothers' professional achievement had increased continuously and consistently. Had William's death not interrupted and, in effect, ended the progress, one wonders what the ultimate level of achievement might have been.

6

Political Activism and Social Responsibility:
The Saginaws, 1863–1922

ALLACE AND WILLIAM GOODRIDGE'S professional success thrust the brothers inevitably into positions as leaders of the Saginaws' small but spirited African American community. In 1870 the population of Saginaw County was slightly more than 39,000, of whom 19,000 lived in either East Saginaw or Saginaw City. Of those, 288—approximately 1.5 percent of the cities' residents—were African Americans. By 1900 the population of the consolidated Saginaws exceeded 42,000, and the African American population had grown to 364. As a percentage of the city's total population, however, the 364 had shrunk to less than 1 percent.[1] Furthermore, since 1870 the status of the city's African Americans had eroded in a variety of ways that called for action. During the 1870s and 1880s, therefore, Saginaw's African American community turned to its small group of elite for leadership. Wallace and William Goodridge were among those leaders.

The most obvious symptoms of the crisis were economic, and the primary response was political. But it also was clear that continued erosion of economic standing and the failure of a political solution were more than an immediate concern and threatened the long-term status of African Americans within the society as a whole. The abolition of slavery in 1865, enfranchisement in 1870, and the guarantee of civil rights at the federal level in 1875 and in Michigan in 1885 had promised much but had failed to eliminate proscription and prejudice based on race. For a time the Republican Party, nationally and locally, appeared to offer the prospect of success, but as the end of the century approached the reality became even more remote. By the 1890s, in fact, many African Americans—in Saginaw, in Michigan, and nationally—found their status with respect to society as a whole to be more precarious than it had been only a generation before.[2]

The nature of the economic threat becomes clear from an analysis of African American occupational patterns in Saginaw between 1870 and 1900. As Table 6.1 reveals, the percentage of African American males employed as barbers or in other service areas between 1870 and 1900 had fallen from 50 percent to 24 percent. At the same time, the percentage of those working as laborers had nearly doubled, from 38 to 68 percent. In addition, the percentage of those at the top end of the scale, craftsmen and professionals, had been reduced by a third. A large majority of laborers in 1900—90 of 107—were coal miners. Mining was always difficult and dangerous work, and most of the miners were young, single men from Virginia and Kentucky who had been brought to Saginaw by the coal companies to work in the valley's mines. In other words, nearly 60 percent of all employed African American males living in Saginaw by 1900 were young, single recent arrivals, engaged in a most dangerous occupation, with as yet little connection to the community or prospects for the future.

In addition, if the 90 miners—most of the recent arrivals—are subtracted from the 364 African American residents of Saginaw in 1900, the resulting figure, 274 African American residents who were not miners in 1900, reveals that the African

Table 6.1 Occupations, African Americans, East Saginaw
and Saginaw City, 1870–1900

	1879		1900	
	No.	%	No.	%
Barbers	19	22	5	3
Service	24	28	34	21
Laborers	33	38	107	68
Craftsmen	8	9	7	4
Professionals	5	3	6	4
Total	87	100	159	100

Source: Ruffin, *Black Presence in Saginaw*, 46–56; and Ruffin in *Saginaw Valley Documents II*, ed. Jezierski and Ross, 261–84

American population of Saginaw who were not primarily young, single, recently arrived male miners was actually smaller than the comparable African American population of the Saginaws, 288 individuals, in 1870. As a percentage of the total population of Saginaw in 1900, the 274 were only seven-tenths of one percent, less than one-half of what the comparable African American population had been as a percentage of the total population in 1870. Not only had the African American population experienced negative growth, but its composition had changed dramatically in a single generation.

The most telling statistic, however, is the significant reduction in the number of African Americans who were barbers. Since at least the 1840s—the 1820s in the case of William C. Goodridge in York—barbering, with the possibility of shop ownership, had provided one of the few routes of upward mobility to young African American males. Long hours, seven-day workweeks, and its early identification as personal service work open to African Americans enabled them to dominate the occupation for most of the century.[3] In East Saginaw and Saginaw City in 1870, for example, 19 of 26 barbers, or 73 percent, were African Americans. At least 6 of the 19, including Abraham Reyno, Lewis Reno, George Palmer, Johnson Bradley, Walter Walker, and Joseph Mayberry, either owned or at least controlled their own shop. By 1900 the number of barbers in Saginaw had

more than doubled, to 61. However, only 5 of these, 8 percent, can be identified as African American, and 3 of the 5 appear to have been shop owners. The surnames of Saginaw's other 55 barbers, 92 percent, suggest that the vast majority were of German or Irish ancestry and, if not recent immigrants, were recent arrivals in Saginaw.[4]

Tracking the occupational status of several of Saginaw's young, male African Americans between 1880 and 1900 also reveals that most were not able to duplicate the status achieved earlier by their fathers. For example, the Washington Foot family was living in East Saginaw by 1870. Foot was a self-employed mason who at thirty years of age had three children and owned real and personal estate valued at $2,000 and $300, respectively. Ten years later he continued to operate his own masonry business, and the family had increased to include a fourth child, four-year-old Elmor. The three eldest children, even including nineteen-year-old Albert, were attending school. By 1900 Washington Foot had died and the family's future was the responsibility of son Albert. In 1900 Albert Foot was thirty-nine years old, single, and living with his sister. In spite of an education that had continued until he was at least nineteen, Albert Foot had no profession—he was listed as a "common laborer"—and owned no real property.

Reuben Walker is a similar example. The Walkers were the first African American family listed as residents of Saginaw City, where Frederick (sometimes Theodorick) Walker owned his own barbershop on Water Street near Adams. By 1870 Walker's real and personal estate were valued at more than $6,600, and five of his seven children were attending school. Reuben was only five years old. By 1880 the family had increased to nine children, with Reuben in school and the eldest son, Theodore, established as a painter. Twenty years later, however, Frederick Walker was dead, the barbershop was gone, his widow, Mary, lived in a mortgaged house, and the family had scattered. Only three of the Walkers' eleven children, including thirty-four-year-old Reuben, remained at home. Reuben had married within the year, owned no property, and, like many other young, male African Americans in Saginaw, had only been able to find work in the valley's coal mines.[5]

Some, but very few, of Saginaw's African Americans were more fortunate, or perhaps more able. For reasons which are now impossible to determine, they had achieved professional success, were economically secure, and in one case acknowledged to be among the valley's wealthiest citizens. This small group of elite African American families had begun to emerge between 1860 and 1870, was in place by 1880, and exercised its leadership for the rest of the century.

When William Quincy Atwood died in 1910, the *Saginaw Daily News* eulogized him as a "Remarkable Colored Man and Pioneer, . . . a Self-Made Citizen."[6] For nearly half a century Atwood had been the most prominent and effective leader of Saginaw's African American community. His presence in East Saginaw was first noted in 1866 when he was reported to be the treasurer of the recently organized Colored Debating Society. At that time Atwood was twenty-seven—he had been born in 1839 in Wilcox County, Alabama—and had lived in Michigan since 1856 and East Saginaw since 1862. Atwood had left Alabama a young freedman, settled in Ripley, Ohio, across the river from Maysville, Kentucky, where he reportedly worked as an agent for the Underground Railroad, and later attended Berea College near Cleveland. The lure of California gold, however, cut short his academic career and for a time young Atwood and

a brother ran a restaurant, bought and sold horses, and prospected for gold. Atwood never said, but he must have had some success in California because he then came to Michigan to speculate in pinelands and by 1870 reported real and personal property worth more than $100,000. Between 1874 and 1888 Atwood also owned and operated a successful lumber mill on the west bank of the Saginaw River between Johnson Street and the Genesee Street Bridge. Before the end of the decade he had sensed the passing of the lumber boom and converted his timber interests into extensive real estate holdings that remained the basis for his wealth until his death.[7]

Atwood's wealth and presumably his considerable ability gained him recognition from a community that did not accept him as an equal but which was forced to acknowledge his presence. It was, nonetheless, a position that few African American males would attain in the Saginaw Valley before the end of the century. An indication of his status is the fact that between 1870 and 1890 Atwood was the only African American regularly included as a "contributor," "petitioner," or "participant" in the lists of civic or business leaders published in the local newspapers. For example, as early as May 1871 Atwood was listed as one of one hundred subscribers, each of whom had pledged ten dollars to support the library of the Young Men's Association of the City of East Saginaw. In September 1886 he was among a small group of Saginaw Valley residents who organized and conducted a railroad excursion to Grand Rapids for eight hundred of the area's most "Prominent Citizens" to "increase the bond of commercial and social interests" with "our sister city." And, by June 1890, Atwood's status was such that Mayor George W. Weadock had appointed him to serve as a member of the committee to entertain members of the Michigan Press Association who were holding their annual convention in Saginaw that year.[8] Atwood also consistently served as chairman or treasurer of various African American religious and social organizations in Saginaw. And his reputation as an intellectual and orator made him the popular and regular choice to address Emancipation Day or other special celebrations organized by African Americans in the Saginaw Valley and throughout the state.[9] A lifelong Republican, Atwood not only was one of the party's most visible African American leaders in Michigan but served as a state delegate-at-large to the 1888 national convention in Chicago.[10]

In 1872 Atwood married Charlotte M. Eckles of Cleveland. The couple had four children, William Q., Jr., Frederick S., Oliver K., and Alberta L. Atwood. Charlotte Atwood died in 1895. By the time of her death, however, the family was comfortably settled into a large house at 633 South Jefferson Avenue, where their needs were seen to by a Norwegian housekeeper, Laina Gilson. At the time of his own death in 1910, William Quincy Atwood's substantial fortune had diminished somewhat as a result of the reduced activity his long-term illness had imposed. Still, his estate listed thirteen properties throughout the city and four parcels of farmland (all that remained of more extensive timberlands) in Saginaw and Crawford Counties. The heirs, his children, shared equally in an estate valued at nearly $50,000.[11]

Charles W. Ellis was born a free man in Canada in approximately 1828, but during the Civil War he and his wife, Mary, crossed the border into Michigan and lived for a time at Adrian. By 1868, however, Ellis was working as the headwaiter in Saginaw City's Taylor House hotel and in 1870 reported owning personal property worth $1,000. During the decade he invested in his own restaurant, with some success, for by 1880 the Ellises lived in their own home on Granger Street in Saginaw City, employed a cook, had room for a boarder, and had taken responsibility for an orphaned niece in addition to their own children, Mary and Charles, Jr. The Ellises' sense of responsibility extended beyond the family into East Saginaw, where in 1876 Charles began serving as the superintendent of the Zion Baptist Church Sunday School. Some years later the Ellises moved to East Saginaw after having opened a Turkish bathhouse there in 1888 and a new restaurant in 1891. The East Saginaw correspondent for the *Detroit Plain Dealer* described the restaurant as "fitted up in first-class

style" with "a neat building, first-class waiters and meals served promptly." Apparently the move was not a financial success, for when Ellis died in 1897 his only asset was a $1,000 life insurance policy.[12]

Although Charles W. Ellis died leaving little material wealth, his legacy to his family and community was considerable. The Saginaw city directory for 1884 indicates that in addition to his restaurant Ellis worked, from the same location, as a "Professional Nurse" and employed his son as his assistant. Young Charles, who was twenty-two in 1884, had been born when the family lived in Adrian. He graduated from Saginaw City's high school and then attended Olivet College from 1881 to 1883. For a time he worked as a clerk in a local dry goods store, but by 1884 apparently had discovered his vocation while also serving as his father's nursing assistant.[13] A brief notice in the *Saginaw Morning Herald* for March 30, 1889, reported that "Charles W. Ellis, Jr., who has been a student in the office of Dr. Ross for the past four years, graduated at the Detroit college of medicine last Monday evening with honors. Dr. Ellis will continue with Dr. Ross during the coming year."[14]

Dr. Benjamin B. Ross was East Saginaw's best-known, but also one of the city's most independent-minded, physicians. He opened his practice in the city in 1864 upon graduation from medical school in the University of Buffalo. He quickly became chief surgeon to most of the lumber mills in the area and was instrumental in the establishment of St. Mary's Hospital, serving as a member of its first medical staff. His obituary remembered Dr. Ross, who was born in Ireland, as "Somewhat brusque in manner, outspoken, blunt, but true and steady in his friendships, [and] possessed of rare intelligence and a large and varied stock of information." His openness to all ideas no doubt led to a long-standing feud with Dr. Lyman W. Bliss of Saginaw City. The source of the disagreement was most probably a pronounced difference in personalities, but the crisis came when Dr. Bliss, who was president of the Michigan Medical Society in 1890, arranged to have Dr. Ross expelled from the society for having consulted with a homeopathic physician.[15]

Dr. Ross's same openness and independence may explain his decision to serve as mentor, friend, and eventually colleague to young Charles W. Ellis, Jr., the Saginaw Valley's first African American physician. Dr. Ross was instrumental in helping Ellis gain admission to the Detroit College of Medicine, and when Dr. Ellis graduated in 1889 he worked as an associate in Dr. Ross's East Saginaw office. During 1890 and 1891 Dr. Ellis, with Dr. Ross's assistance, toured Europe, where he continued his medical studies for six months in London, Paris, and Berlin. Two years later Dr. Ross died of acute suppurative nephritis—Dr. Ellis performed the autopsy—and Dr. Ellis inherited both Dr. Ross's practice and his home at 522 South Jefferson.[16]

In January 1892, shortly after his return from Europe, Dr. Ellis married Amy Watson of Detroit, whom he had met while a medical student there. For a time the newlyweds lived with the groom's parents, and it was not until 1896 that they occupied the former Ross home. There were no children from the marriage. Dr. Ellis, however, did continue to expand upon Dr. Ross's successful practice. During an unfortunately brief medical career, Dr. Ellis also served as the physician for St. Vincent's Orphans' Home, as health officer for the Saginaw Traction (Transit) Company, and was on the medical staff of St. Mary's Hospital. In April 1892 he was nominated to serve as city physician, but the Common Council chose not to make the appointment. Instead Dr. Ellis was chosen by the city to serve as health officer (one of two in the city) for the east side from 1892 until 1896. When he died of pneumonia in 1908 at age forty-five, Ellis was at the peak of his profession and one of the city's most respected physicians. The list of his patients included not only Atwoods, but Heavenriches, Seitners, Webbers, and Wickeses. The Saginaw County Medical Society, of which Dr. Ellis was a member, held a special Sunday afternoon memorial meeting at the Bancroft Hotel in his honor, attended the funeral as a group, and chose six of its members (Drs. H. M. Leach, C. H. Sample, T. M. Williamson, J. H. Crowell, W. L. Slach, and W. J. O'Reilly) to serve as pallbearers.[17]

The relative economic security and personal and professional success that the Ellises, the Atwoods, and the Goodridges had achieved during the second half of the nineteenth century naturally had made them the leaders of Saginaw's African American community and simultaneously the most obvious symbols of its potential for success. By the end of the 1880s, however, the actual success of a few individuals and the potential for success for all African Americans in Saginaw had become a problem for the community.[18]

From their beginning the Saginaws were a community that found consensus difficult to achieve. Geography was a factor, for even though the Saginaw River was the lifeblood of the community it also served as the boundary dividing Saginaw City from East Saginaw, and remained so after the state legislature had mandated consolidation of the two cities in 1889. Similarly, although the newly organized Republican Party dominated state politics after 1854, Saginaw County voters continued to oscillate between Republicans and Democrats through the nineteenth century. For example, between 1854 and 1880 a majority of county voters chose nine Democrats and five Republicans for governor. During the same period four Democrats and three Republicans were the county's choice for president.[19]

Attitudes toward race in the Saginaws also were inconsistent, although a discernible pattern did begin to emerge between 1870 and 1890. Like many northern communities at midcentury, the Saginaws were opposed to slavery and its extension as an institution, although local issues regularly took precedence.[20] James G. Birney, a founder of the Liberty Party, settled with his family at Lower Saginaw (later Bay City) in 1841. During his campaigns for national and state office, however, Saginaw County voters never gave Birney more than 38 votes. That was in 1844, when Birney was third in a three-man race for state representative. The Whig, Charles L. Richman, won with 105 votes, and Democrat Alfred Holmes was second with 71. There is no record that any Saginaw resident cast his vote for Birney as president in either 1840 or 1844.[21]

An analysis of attitudes toward race in Saginaw newspapers between 1870 and 1890 confirms this initial inconsistency and the emergence of a more negative attitude toward race by 1890. Newspaper references to African Americans in Saginaw by 1870 were clearly racial. The term "colored" appeared almost without exception. "Black" or "African American" was used only rarely. During the 1870s a majority of the references were, nonetheless, positive. The notices emphasized accomplishments and potential. For example, terms such as "colored citizen," "American Citizens of African Descent," and "Colored Masons" were regularly used. Reference to "merit" and "worthy motives" and "promoting the moral and educational improvements of the colored race" appeared often. African American religious and social organizations were lauded for their fund-raising and community consciousness, as when "the colored citizens [of East Saginaw] have sent $40 and 300 lbs. of clothing to the Southern refugees" in 1879. And when Sojourner Truth visited East Saginaw to speak at the Jefferson Avenue Methodist Episcopal Church in October 1877, she was described as a "colored centenarian" and "lady" whose "experience will undoubtedly be well worth listening to."[22] Negative references that often used dialect and focused particularly on race also appeared, though much less frequently during the 1870s. Throughout 1876, for example, the druggist Alfred A. Dunk, who had shared the Crouse Block with the Goodridge studio until 1872 (see figure 3.3), ran the advertisement that appears as figure 6.1 in the *Saginaw Daily Courier*.[23] That same year, a notice published in the same newspaper indicated that while African American children attended the city's public schools, it was not without penalty. The paper reported that "a colored pupil attends one of the schools in this city, and that when the teacher desires to punish the other scholars she makes them sit beside the little African. Grant should be advised at once, and no doubt he would send up a detachment of regulars . . . and declare martial law."[24]

Through the 1880s positive racial references continued to appear in Saginaw newssheets, but at

Figure 6.1. "Newspaper Advertisement," *Saginaw Daily Courier,* October 27, 1876.

a clearly reduced rate. At the same time, negative references to race, especially those that emphasized violence or caricatured racial characteristics, began to appear with increasing frequency. In 1881, for example, "a colored debating society" in the city was described as one in which "one of the contestants attempted to beat his side of the questions into his opponent's head with a club."[25] A boxing match in South Saginaw between C. A. C. Smith, "champion colored pugilist of America," and "Prof. Charles Hadley, winner of the Police Gazette colored championship," was described as a particularly "grand display of 'colored science'" in a November 1883 report.[26] In 1885, with "humor" no doubt in mind, the *Saginaw Evening News* even published a pseudo-report of "A colored fisherman of this city" who "was telling a funny story the other day with his mouth full of fish hooks. In the center of the funniest part of a guffaw," the fisherman "bunched the fish destroyers and forced the barbs of two of them through his lips which quickly changed his tune. A bystander remarked he had hooked a black bass."[27] Rather than "colored centenarians," elderly African Americans were parodied as "Uncle Ike Williams" and "Aunty Kate Brooks."[28] By 1890 the community's attitude toward race probably was best summarized in a report by the *Saginaw Courier-Herald* describing city schools superintendent E. C. Thompson's reaction to a recent tour of the South. Thompson found that "The negro of the South is much more immoral and ignorant" than in the North. "He is coarser in his make-up and more ferocious in temperament. He is bold and vindicative [sic] and seems to think the white man has no rights which he is bound to respect." The *Courier-Herald* suggested that the only way to solve "the race question" north or south was to "let *the superior white race show their superiority* by their magnanimity and justice, and if these influences do not solve the race question nothing will."[29] Whether Superintendent Thompson agreed with the recommendation is not known. The leadership of Saginaw's African American community certainly did not.

The development of an increasingly negative attitude toward race in Saginaw during the 1880s mirrors a similar growth nationally and in Michigan as well. In Saginaw this shift parallels and, to some extent, is magnified by a variety of causes. Between 1870 and 1900 the distribution of identifiable African American residences in East Saginaw and Saginaw City changed dramatically. In 1870 African Americans lived in specific areas of only four of East Saginaw's eight wards (the Second, Third, Fourth, and Fifth) and in five of Saginaw City's six (the Third was the exception). By 1900 African Americans resided in each of the consolidated city's fifteen wards, east and west. And, by 1900, African American residences were much more evenly distributed throughout the city rather than concentrated on a single street or two in a

particular ward.[30] Simultaneously, competition from new immigrants for control of service occupations, such as barbering, that had traditionally offered African Americans at least the possibility of some success made it quite evident that while a few African Americans might succeed, most would not. In other words, residential diversity was increasing at the same time that occupational opportunity was decreasing. As a result, the shrinking rate of success for Saginaw's African Americans coincidentally was becoming more apparent to all. Many in the community, unfortunately, equated the failure with race. But even for the few African Americans who achieved it, success was not without its problems. By 1880 the Atwoods, the Ellises, and the Goodridges, among others, were being pressed both by their fellow African Americans to solve these problems and, at the same time, by the larger community to justify the success that each had achieved. The solution, they hoped, lay in intensified political activity.

———— ❧ ————

Before 1880 there is little evidence that Saginaw's African American leadership, unlike its Detroit counterpart,[31] was openly or directly involved in local, state, or national politics. Nonetheless, there had been ample opportunity for political discussion and expression within the African American community during the preceding decades. For example, the Colored Debating Society, which was organized in East Saginaw in February 1866 and which elected Lewis Reno, Glenalvin and William Goodridge, and William Atwood as its officers, certainly considered the momentous political changes occurring at that time in its debates. In April 1870 Atwood also led a team from the society, comprised of H. R. Harris, P. P. Field, and a Mr. Sweeney and a Mr. Delano, in a Lyceum debate at Parsons College in East Saginaw against E. W. Haskins, Jacob Klein, and A. C. Parsons which considered the question: "That the Freedmen should be educated at the public expense." According to the report, "the question was first decided in the negative, but afterwards in the affirmative, by a vote of the audience, on the argument." Two years later the Colored Amateur Dramatic Association made a political statement with its successful presentation of *Uncle Tom's Cabin,* first at Eolah Hall and then at Jackson Hall in East Saginaw, to a "big card" with Miss Victoria Bings as "Topsey."[32] And there can be little doubt that politics was a perennial subject for discussion at the Emancipation Day celebrations organized by Saginaw's African American community each January and August.[33]

The first indication that Saginaw's African American leadership was at last being considered for an active and public role in local Republican affairs came only in August 1880, when the *Saginaw Morning Herald* announced the formation of a Garfield and Arthur Club and called upon "All voters who are in favor of free speech and a free ballot, of the maintenance of our unrivaled public credit and business prosperity, and of having the national government administered by the party who have been its constant and undoubted supporters" to join. Included on the list of the more than 250 of Saginaw's Republican political and economic elite who endorsed the call were William O. Goodridge and William Quincy Atwood, although neither was listed as a member of the Garfield and Arthur Club when its membership was published by the same newspaper six weeks later. In the days before the election, however, Atwood reportedly did make a "political speech," presumably in support of Garfield and Arthur, although its exact content is unknown. In spite of this effort, James A. Garfield failed to carry Saginaw County, losing to the Democrat Winfield Scott Hancock 5,234 to 5,208.[34]

During the 1880s and through the 1890s it also is clear that racial harmony within the Republican Party, both at the state level and in Saginaw County, was more superficial than substantive. In 1879 Zachariah Chandler, Michigan's longtime U.S. senator and leader of the Radical Republicans who had supported abolition, civil rights for African Americans, radical reconstruction of the South, and impeachment of President Andrew Johnson, died. As a result, earlier divisions within

the party were solidified and for the first time since 1854 a non-Republican, the Fusion Party candidate Josiah Begole, was elected governor in 1882. Continued Republican infighting led to further defeat. In 1890 Edward Winans became the first Democrat elected governor since before the Civil War, and his party also gained control of the Senate. At the state level the Republicans' problems were caused partly by a division in the leadership between party stalwart James McMillan and the newcomer Hazen S. Pingree, both of whom aspired to succeed Chandler as Michigan's "Mr. Republican." McMillan was a wealthy Detroit businessman with close ties to the railroads and utility companies and strong support among the conservative members of the state's racially integrated unit of the Grand Army of the Republic. McMillan sensed the Democrats' threat and believed that the loyalty of the state's seven thousand African American voters to the party was a key to maintaining Republican dominance in Michigan. As a result he continued Chandler's traditional commitment to African American rights. Under McMillan's leadership the party actively courted its African American members to the point of sending two African Americans, Dr. Samuel C. Watson of Detroit and William Quincy Atwood of East Saginaw, as delegates-at-large to represent the state party at the national nominating conventions at Chicago in 1884 and 1888. Pingree also was a wealthy businessman, but as mayor of Detroit he battled the same railroad and utility companies that supported McMillan in an effort to achieve progressive reform in the city and throughout the state. Initially Pingree ignored African American Republicans. And although he later sought their support even more actively than McMillan had, the reforms that followed from his leadership as governor after 1896 had the effect of reducing, not increasing, African American power within the party and making it vulnerable to Democratic inroads during the next century.[35]

During the 1880s and 1890s it also was evident to Michigan's African American leadership that its position was not a strong one. Race was an apparently unavoidable issue. During the 1884 state Republican Convention at Grand Rapids that ultimately chose Dr. Watson as a national delegate-at-large, for example, the *Detroit Post and Tribune*, the party's state organ, published the following sarcastic account of the debate over Watson's nomination: "A colored delegate caused considerable hilarity at this stage of the proceedings by announcing that Atwood's strength was not to be compared with that of Watson. In his judgment the latter could poll anywhere from 10 to 20 votes to every one Atwood would secure. He warmed up rapidly and wound up with a vigorous request that 'If a colored delegate must go to Chicago, for God's sake send the one who has got the most votes.'"[36] In an effort to counter the effect of such sentiments, Michigan's African American leaders subsequently organized the Michigan Protective League, the Afro-American League, and the Michigan Equal Rights League, and helped to create the National Federation of Colored Men in December 1895. Together the organizations sought to maintain and even enhance the African American position within the Republican Party for a time, but their influence did not extend much beyond the end of the century.[37]

At the local level—in Saginaw County, for example—African Americans found their status within the party to be even more precarious. The attempt to incorporate Saginaw's African American leadership into the local Garfield and Arthur Club in 1880 did not last beyond the election. As a result, it is clear that by 1884 they had begun to explore more independent options. In March "colored voters" in both Saginaw and Bay City chose delegates to represent them at the "Colored Citizens' State Convention" in Battle Creek. Saginaw sent William Quincy Atwood and Charles Ellis. William A. Susand and James H. Barker represented Bay City. In the keynote address to the convention, T. J. Martin of Cass County denounced the U.S. Supreme Court's decision in the 1883 Civil Rights Cases and warned the delegates against "half-breed" and "feather-head" Republicans who supported such a position. Martin and Atwood also were chosen to represent the state at the "National Colored Men's Convention" to be held in Richmond, Virginia, later that year.[38]

In September 1884, encouraged by the example of both state and national organizations, Saginaw's African Americans undertook their first independent political action. Wallace Goodridge invited all of Saginaw's "colored citizens to meet and form a Blaine and Logan club." According to a report of the meeting, it "was held at the rooms of [the] Goodridge Bros. The meeting was well attended and very enthusiastic, and speeches were made by W. Q. Atwood, W. L. Goodridge and other prominent colored citizens." The same report noted that "An invitation was extended to them by the Blaine and Logan clubs already organized to join them, and that was considered the best course and finally adopted."[39] Nonetheless, in spite of the fact that Atwood had attended the Republicans' state convention at Grand Rapids in April 1884 (not as an official Saginaw County delegate but as a "special colored delegate") and was considered by the convention as its "colored delegate-at-large" to the national convention at Chicago in June, neither he nor any other Saginaw African American was invited to participate actively or publicly in the political activities designed to support the Blaine and Logan campaign in the Saginaw Valley. Detailed newspaper accounts of both the Saginaw County Republicans' convention in August 1884 and Blaine's visit to East Saginaw on October 16, 1884, reveal that there was no role for Saginaw's African American Republicans at either event, even as "special colored delegates-at-large."[40]

Although Blaine carried the state in 1884, Grover Cleveland and the Democrats won in Saginaw County by more than one thousand votes out of a total of fifteen thousand cast. This pattern persisted through the 1890s with the Republican candidate winning the state's electoral vote but without help from Saginaw County Republicans. In fact, Saginaw County voters regularly during the 1880s and 1890s also chose the non-Republican candidate for governor. Because the margin of victory in both the presidential and gubernatorial elections in Saginaw County at the time was never less than five hundred votes, the county's Republican Party may have felt little need to actively court Saginaw's approximately 150 African American voters, who could not have given it the victory it sought in the county in any case.[41]

The failure to gain full admission to the local Republican circle caused Saginaw's African American leadership to seek political leverage elsewhere. While William Atwood represented African American interests at the 1884 state convention in Grand Rapids, Wallace Goodridge explored other possibilities at both the national and state levels. In 1884 Wallace accepted an appointment as a member of a committee of Michigan African Americans charged with the design and creation of an exhibit to demonstrate "the progress morally and intellectually of the colored people . . . in the arts, sciences and industries" for the World's Industrial and Cotton Centennial Exposition at New Orleans in 1885.[42] The exposition was one of a series held throughout the South between 1881 and 1907 that was designed to present "an image of a New South imbued with the spirit of progress and patriotism."[43] According to C. Vann Woodward, the "huge . . . structures of plaster and iron" created for the expositions "were temples erected to the alien gods of Mass and Speed. In their halls Southerners joined with millions of Yankee guests to invoke the spirit of Progress and worship the machine. Here they performed rituals of 'reconciliation' and nationalism, and held reunions of Blue and Gray—without which none of these affairs were complete. More prosaically, the expositions were modern engines of propaganda, advertising, and salesmanship geared primarily to the aims of attracting capital and immigration and selling the goods."[44]

According to the official report of the exposition, the "Colored Peoples' Exhibit," which was organized as a "separate department," occupied the entire north gallery of the Government Building. Thousands of artifacts contributed by African Americans from forty states and the District of Columbia were displayed in sixteen "state sections." Michigan was located in "Section O" with Missouri, Iowa, Illinois, Wisconsin, and Nebraska. Exactly what the state's African Americans contributed to their section is not known. According to the official report of the exposition, however, "the display of inventions" and "displays of art work" were "one remarkable feature" where "the visitors tarried the longest" in this department. An extant photograph of "Ohio's Afro-American exhibit" at New Orleans also reveals that it included many photographs. A selection of Goodridge views, therefore, may well have been a significant element of the Michigan display in the "Colored Department." In addition, the exposition report reveals that the state of Michigan's official exhibit occupied 6,740 square feet, that none "gave a finer idea of all of a State's resources," and that "Among the special features of the display were the mineral collection, forestry specimens, cereals and educational work." As the Forestry Division of the Department of Agriculture in Washington, D.C., would later invite the Goodridge studio to supply views of Michigan's pine lumber industry for the 1889 Paris Exposition, so the state may have obtained similar views from the Goodridges for its own extensive forestry exhibit at New Orleans.[45]

One account of the exposition's success concluded that "The number of articles exhibited in the colored department ranged in the thousands, and the attractiveness and beauty of the display *showed the wisdom of Director General [E. A.] Burke* in forming this department, and illustrated fully that the colored people are making great progress in all the various branches of industry."[46] Many African Americans, led by Bishop Henry A. Turner, agreed with Burke. Given the 1883 Supreme Court decision in the Civil Rights Cases, which sanctioned discrimination by individuals against any African American, they were surprised to have been invited to the exposition at all. Turner summed it up best in his opening ceremonies address when he concluded that "I cannot believe that I am in New Orleans. I am inclined to think it must be all a dream. All honor, I say, to Director General Burke. All honor to the managers of this Exposition. All honor to New Orleans."[47] Many others, instead, applauded a speech by African American attorney David A. Straker from South Carolina, who argued for more than simple acceptance. Straker and many other African Americans demanded political, social, and economic justice and argued that the exhibits at expositions like

New Orleans should bring all people together "in love, peace and unity, under equal laws, exact justice and common privileges, so that the antagonisms of race, the hatred of creeds and parties, the prejudice of caste and the denial of equal rights may disappear from among us forever."[48] Given Wallace Goodridge's political activities at the time, there can be little doubt that he would have agreed with Straker.

The spring and summer of 1885 also were especially busy in the Saginaws. Two events captured and held the public's attention for much of the year. On July 10 a sawmill hands' strike for "Ten Hours or No Sawdust" that had begun on July 6 in Bay City spread to the Saginaws. A month later, on August 4, shortly after the tension over the strike had peaked, Frederick Douglass visited East Saginaw to help celebrate Great Britain's abolition of West Indian slavery a half century earlier. Saginaw's African American leadership used both events to explore and to enhance their political options.

The mill hands' strike began when owners called for up to a 25 percent reduction in wages over the previous year for the same eleven-hour workday. Workers responded by demanding a reduction to ten-hour workdays to compensate for the lost wages, but with little success. As the most recent account of the strike concludes: "By the end of August the strike was broken. In general the mills reopened at either the old eleven-hour day or at ten hours with a corresponding pay reduction. . . . Mill hands gained little from their summer's effort. Although the ten-hour day was widespread, reduced wages undercut the original goal of recovering the spring pay reduction through fewer working hours."[49]

Although they had not initiated the strike, local assemblies of the Noble and Holy Order of the Knights of Labor quickly became involved in its direction. This was especially true in the Saginaws, where more than 40 percent of all mill hands, the county sheriff, and the Saginaw police chief were said to be Knights. In addition, Thomas B. Barry, who was elected to the state legislature in 1885 from East Saginaw as the Fusion Party candidate, was a Knight and quickly emerged as spokesper-

son for the striking Saginaw mill hands. At the beginning of August 1885, as enthusiasm for the strike began to wane and some mill hands began to drift back to work under pre-strike conditions, Barry delivered an impassioned speech to an assembly of several hundred Knights that certainly captured the attention of some in the audience. Barry denounced the hands who had returned to the mills as "scabs" who "would steal Christ's remains and sell them for ten cents." He warned the assembled strikers that "If the working men of the Saginaw valley go back today they will go back to a worse slavery than before and they will meet a worse fate than did the slaves of old."[50]

Precisely how many African Americans worked in the valley's sawmills during the 1880s and whether or not they were Knights is difficult to determine. According to Ruffin's analysis of the 1880 census of 91 employed African American males, 11 (12 percent) worked in the Saginaws' sawmills and 6 (7 percent) worked at the salt blocks, a closely related industry, although it is not clear whether salt-block workers were involved in the strike. In addition, 24 (26 percent) of the 91 employed males were classified as "laborers" and may have worked at the mills in some fashion or other.[51] Almost 20 percent were, but as many as 45 percent of all working African American males may have been, employed, therefore, in the Saginaws' mills.

Traditionally, during the nineteenth century Michigan's African American working people had remained outside the labor movement. Most were employed in service occupations ignored by the unions, and when they did express an interest they had been rebuffed. The Knights of Labor did attempt to organize a segregated assembly in Detroit for African Americans in 1886, but there was little interest and no evidence that it was established. In fact, David A. Straker, a nationally known African American lawyer then living in Detroit, denounced a labor movement whose "hidden purpose is to shut out and keep shut the doors of industry against a class of people on account of their race, color and past condition."[52]

For a time at least, likely because of the crisis

precipitated by the 1885 strike, the Knights of Labor did successfully incorporate African American
workers into its ranks in the Saginaw Valley.
Whether the initiative came from the union or
African Americans is impossible to determine. In
either case, Wallace Goodridge is listed as the delegate from Labor Assembly 2856, South Saginaw,
to the January 1884 State Assembly of the Knights
of Labor in Detroit. Wallace served, with six other
Knights, on the Committee on Organization that
was charged by the convention with drafting a
constitution for the state assembly. The convention
adopted the committee's recommended constitution with only a few minor changes. It also passed
resolutions calling on Congress "to prevent the importation of all foreign labor under contract," recommending that the "Convention take action to
extend co-operation with the trades unions in this
State," and calling for a boycott of "the Detroit Free
Press and Detroit Post and Tribune until they shall
employ union men or Knights of Labor." The convention also agreed to hold its next state assembly
in East Saginaw.[53]

By the time the delegates gathered in East Saginaw in June 1885, some progress had been made
in recruiting African American Knights. A local
"Black" assembly, for example, had been organized
in Bay City. Yet Wallace Goodridge is not listed as
a delegate to the convention he likely helped bring
to East Saginaw. The exact reason is impossible to
determine, but it may be that the Knights and Saginaw's African Americans had had an uneven relationship during the intervening year. In February
1884, shortly after Wallace had returned from the
Detroit convention, the local press announced that
"Our colored citizens indulged in a grand ball at
Knights of Labor hall last evening, which was
largely attended and highly enjoyed by all atten-
dants."[54] Less than two months later the same
newspaper reviewed a performance of the "Knights
of Labor Minstrels at the Academy [of Music]" and
concluded that "the boys" gave "a performance
equal to those of the best burnt cork troupes on
the road." The highlight of the evening was a most
interesting choice given the labor troubles the valley soon would be experiencing. According to the

reporter, a short piece titled "'Brown's Intelligence
[employment] Office, or the Demon of Cass Street,'
. . . showed Brown as engaging a number of [black]
men to work in places where situations were not to
be had, and wound up by the whole force pounc-
ing in upon the intelligence office for satisfaction in
various and diverse ways."[55] If any Saginaw African
American had joined the Knights, it is unlikely that
he or she attended their performance that evening.
It also is interesting to consider the degree to
which William Quincy Atwood may have influenced African American attitudes toward the
Knights of Labor in Saginaw.

This is especially important because in the
spring of 1885, as the valley's labor unrest had begun to escalate toward a strike, Atwood and the
Goodridges invited Frederick Douglass to East
Saginaw to head the state's Emancipation Day celebration that August. Atwood had been introduced
to Douglass by the Goodridge family. Family patri-
arch William C. Goodridge had been associated
with Douglass during the struggle against slavery;
Douglass had entertained the elder Goodridge in
Rochester during the latter's 1853 trip to Canada;
and Douglass had visited East Saginaw earlier, in
1868, again as a result of an invitation from the
Goodridge family. The 1885 visit, however, was
quite different from Douglass's earlier trip to the
Saginaw Valley. Although Douglass stayed with the
Atwood family and the occasion and address were
advertised as an "Emancipation Day Celebration,"
it is clear that the valley's African Americans were
able to spend little time with Douglass and quickly lost control of their own celebration to several
planning committees and an ever-larger number of
invited dignitaries.[56]

Douglass's speech, nevertheless, delivered a
message that Atwood, the Goodridges, and certainly other members of the audience applauded.
He recalled the struggle for emancipation, both in
Britain and the United States, commemorated the
efforts of abolitionists Garrison, Phillips, Sumner,
and Stevens, and with reference to the direction
lately taken by the Republican leadership in Michigan and nationally, eulogized the memory of
Ulysses S. Grant, who had died only days before,

as the one "to whom more than any other man the negro owes his enfranchisement," whose "moral courage surpassed that of his party; hence his place at its head was given to timid men, and the country was allowed to drift instead of stemming the current with stalwart arms." Douglass also called upon African Americans in the audience "to consider your opportunities and the immense distance you are in the rear of your white fellow citizens, and strive to decrease that distance and to diminish that disparity so terribly unfavorable to you. You have done well, but you can do better." And, he finished with a challenge that no doubt rang in the ears of the Atwoods, Goodridges, and Ellises present. "Until colored people can point to successful and prosperous men among them, and a good many of them," he declared, "it will be idle to talk much of their equality with the white race. While all other varieties of the human family, whether Caucasian, Mongolian, East Indian, or Malay can come here and make themselves good citizens, and acquire comfortable homes and even make themselves rich, if we move on from year to year without improving our physical condition," he concluded, "we shall dwindle and go down under the weight of the popular judgment concerning us."[57]

Two days after Douglass's address, a reporter for the *Saginaw Evening News* editorialized a bit by recommending that "Every colored man in the United States, and a good many white men, ought to read the advice Hon. Frederick Douglass gave to his race in the lecture delivered recently at Arbeiter hall. It is sound in every particular, and if heeded would be of more benefit to that race than all the colored pulpit oratory since the war."[58] Given the recent deterioration of their standing within the Republican Party, the continued erosion of their hard-earned economic achievements, the failure to benefit from even modest participation in the organized labor movement, and especially the rhetoric provided by Turner and Straker at New Orleans and Douglass in East Saginaw, all within the crisis atmosphere created by the mill hands' strike in 1885, it is clear that the valley's African American leadership intensified its efforts to estab-

lish and to protect a more independent political standing, for the time being at least, within the existing structure of the Republican Party.

The evidence indicates that Atwood, the Goodridge brothers, and Charles Ellis, Sr., initiated a movement that determined the direction of African American political activity in Michigan after 1885. The effort began in 1886 with the organization of a Saginaw County "colored voters political club" that met regularly through the year. In January 1887 the new organization, at a caucus held "at Goodridge Bros.' gallery on South Washington," chose Ellis to represent it at a meeting of the Central Committee of the Michigan Colored Men's Association at Jackson the following week. Ellis was already chairman of the association, which had been created to promote "the interests of the colored voters of this State." At the Jackson meeting the Central Committee chose Atwood as its new chair, and he led the association during the year in "considering the political situation and making arrangements for the best disposition of the colored vote in the State."[59]

Atwood's judgment was that continued loyalty to the Republican Party, but on a more independent, self-help basis, was in the best interest of Michigan African Americans. His position was endorsed by his Saginaw County fellows in November 1887, when after a heated debate they voted to disband the county Colored Men's Association in favor of a new Saginaw Colored Men's Protective League with Charles Ellis, Sr., as its president. The decision was made because "though the colored men are naturally Republicans they have a considerable number who are in sympathy with other political parties, and that is the main cause of the present trouble."[60] That winter, Saginaw African Americans, led by William and Wallace Goodridge, also organized a Colored National Monument Association. The specific purpose of the organization was never spelled out, but it appears that the Goodridges, especially the artist William, proposed creating a monumental sculpture honoring the nation's African American veterans, living and deceased. Together with the Protective League, the Monument Association called on the Central Committee of the Michigan Colored Men's Association to hold a convention at East Saginaw no later than March 20, 1888, for "the enlargement and [making] more perfect [the] organization of the State Central Committee" and for "the organization of a Colored Soldiers National Monument Association."[61]

The Central Committee responded by voting to hold the association's annual convention in Jackson that April. Atwood, Wallace Goodridge, and Charles Ellis, Sr. and Jr., represented Saginaw County. The gathering decided the direction of African American political activity in the state for the remainder of the century. According to a report of the convention's proceedings, Atwood and his Saginaw cohorts carried the day. The convention endorsed "the Republican party and its principles as opposed to the Democracy," called on "Afro-American delegates from the South" to support the presidential candidacy of Russell Alger, "our distinguished and philanthropic fellow citizen," and heartily supported "the Blair educational bill" and other self-help "movements that lead to industrial education." And, in a move that signaled Atwood's ascendancy at the state level, the convention voted to change the name of the association to the Michigan Protective League and chose Atwood as its first president.[62]

Less than a week after the convention, the *Detroit Tribune* printed a report of an interview that the *Lansing Journal* had conducted with H. L. Lewis of East Saginaw. Lewis was the spokesperson for a small group of Saginaw African Americans who apparently were dissatisfied with the Republican Party and especially with Atwood-Goodridge-Ellis leadership. Lewis claimed that the Jackson convention had "only two objects in view." "One," he said, "was to put W. Q. Atwood forward as a delegate to the National Republican convention, and the other to fully endorse the Republican party." According to Lewis, the results of the convention were "not in accord with the general will of the colored people, and was the work of a few scheming politicians." The same reporter also interviewed Atwood (whom he characterized as "a respected citizen of East Saginaw" who "has secured a com-

fortable income and home") with regard to Lewis's claims. Atwood conceded that there were a few dissenters in Saginaw County but noted that "nearly all of the colored voters were staunch Republicans, with a few Prohibitionists." They had come to Jackson for the purpose of "centralizing and infusing life" into a politically moribund organization. The new Michigan Protective League would seek affiliation with a national organization and oppose "discrimination and disfranchisement on account of race" in Michigan and throughout the United States, especially in the South. The reporter concluded that "Mr. Atwood is very earnest in his endeavors to better the condition of his race."[63]

There was, nonetheless, substance to Lewis's claim. In May Atwood was chosen as one of four delegates-at-large by the state Republican Party to represent it at the national convention in Chicago in June.[64] Although there is no record of Atwood's activity in Chicago that summer, it is clear that he found the appointment energizing. From May through September 1888 he crisscrossed the state from Lansing to Mecosta addressing meetings of both African American and white Republicans.[65] In September sixty-five Saginaw County African Americans organized a Harrison and Morton Club to support the Republican presidential candidate. That October state Republicans invited James G. Blaine to visit East Saginaw to campaign for Benjamin Harrison. Extensive preparations were for naught, however, when Blaine became ill during a similar stop in Detroit. Unlike the preparations for Blaine's 1884 visit to East Saginaw, in 1888 the "Colored Harrison and Morton Club" was at least invited to march in the torchlight parade planned for the evening of Blaine's visit with the other Republican clubs from across the valley. But once again the Republicans failed to deliver, and Grover Cleveland and the Fusion Party candidate for governor carried the county by margins that exceeded 25 percent.[66]

Harrison's narrow electoral victory did provide Atwood and Michigan's African Americans one last opportunity to advance their standing within the party. In February 1889 the *Saginaw Evening News* reported that the Michigan Protective

League had recommended Atwood to president-elect Harrison for appointment as recorder of deeds in the District of Columbia as "fitting tribute . . . and reward [to] a faithful worker in the ranks of his political party." The position was largely a symbolic but visible one, and had been held by an African American Democrat during the previous Cleveland administration. Atwood traveled to Washington at the end of the month to attend the inauguration and to lobby for his appointment.[67] For whatever reason, he returned to East Saginaw without it. Perhaps Harrison was aware of the county's electoral record and chose not to reward failure. In any case, the 1889 Washington visit proved to be the pinnacle of Atwood's and the Protective League's attempt to rise within and to enhance the position of Michigan African Americans within the Republican Party.

When delegates from across the state gathered in Detroit on May 13, 1890, for the annual convention of the Michigan Protective League, it became clear that a division had developed within the ranks of the league since, and perhaps because of, Atwood's failure to obtain the District of Columbia appointment from the Harrison administration.[68] The Saginaw league was represented by a large delegation that, in addition to Atwood, Charles Ellis, Sr., and Wallace Goodridge, included George Washington, George L. Henry, Arthur Hammond, Sterling Brown, James H. Gray, Robert Robinson, Richard Combine, Richard Brown, Thomas Cotillier, Henry Smith, and the Reverend George Cotman.[69] Atwood, as president of the state league, opened the convention with an address to the assembled delegates. He asked the convention to continue "that patience that is characteristic of us . . . until that great majority that was once against us has become a solemn help in the interests of justice and right" and, in effect, apologized to the delegates that his "administration perhaps has not been unanimously satisfactory." That same afternoon, the convention proceedings reported that "a controversy in which some warmth was displayed by delegates from Saginaw, Wayne and Kent . . . was satisfactorily adjusted," but only with effort. The exact nature of the disagreement is un-

known, but the result was the near-total exclusion of members of the Saginaw delegation from responsible positions within the league, which was then reorganized as the Afro-American League of the State of Michigan. All new league officers and members of the executive committee were chosen from delegates who represented downstate constituencies. The single exception was Wallace Goodridge, who was elected a member of the executive committee.[70]

Unlike the earlier Protective League, which some Michigan African Americans believed had as its primary objective the enhancement of their and especially William Quincy Atwood's position within the state Republican Party, the new Afro-American League made no mention of the Republicans at all. Instead, it sought to base Atwood's concept of "self-help" for African Americans within the Republican Party not exclusively on the continued tradition of membership in the party but more so on the joint efforts of African Americans organized at the state and national levels. The newly reorganized league, therefore, sought immediate affiliation with the national Afro-American League, formed only the previous January in Chicago, and endorsed its goals "to assist . . . all local leagues in their efforts to break down all color bars which prevent the Afro-American from securing equal opportunities in the avocation of life, or enjoying the rights and privileges of citizenship, to help upbuild the material interests of the Afro-American in the State, by encouraging local leagues to undertake cooperative enterprises, and by suggesting to them such policies as will best enhance that interest." The convention endorsed no political candidate and did not commit Michigan African Americans to continued support of the Republican Party.[71]

The convention, however, ended amicably, with the proceedings noting that "Mr. Goodridge submitted himself to the eloquence of the ladies" who had provided the entertainment at the convention, by his declaring that "as one of old, 'Almost thou persuadest me,'" and that the "two or three members of the Saginaw delegation who put their prejudice in their pockets and came up smiling at the finish won hearty approval from all present."[72] Still, the parting amity was superficial and short- lived. By late June the *Detroit Plain Dealer*, in an especially pointed editorial, took note of the Saginaw delegates' continued discontent:

FOUR or five disgruntled members of the Saginaw delegation to the recent State convention in Detroit, after nursing their ignorant malice for over a month, are out in a set of circulars scrurlously [*sic*] abusing their betters. The maliciousness of the attack and the sneaking manner in which it is placed before the public puts this cats paw committee beneath the notice of honorable mention. Who are they? What are they? They are not known outside of Saginaw, and if they can get some reputable citizens to vouch for their standing, THE PLAINDEALER will deign to notice them.[73]

No account of the "malicious attack" by the Saginaw delegation on its "betters" exists, so it is impossible to determine precisely the contents or the authors' identity. Nonetheless, relations between Saginaw's African American leadership and its counterparts across the state, especially those from Wayne and Kent Counties who continued to support the new Afro-American League, remained cool for some time. In fact, it was nearly six months before the *Detroit Plain Dealer* again printed any news from Saginaw, and then only when its Saginaw correspondent humbly noted that "It has been some time since we have seen any Saginaw items in THE PLAINDEALER and feeling confident that we have as much intelligence and intellect here as any place we do not want to be behind or forgotten, therefore we once more ask a small space in your most highly esteemed paper."[74]

Political discontent among Saginaw's African American leadership, including Atwood, Ellis, and the Goodridges, continued until at least 1892. That March the *Plain Dealer* reported a call issued by the Saginaw Protective League for a convention to meet at Lansing in April "to better organize for political purposes and otherwise for the general good." According to the report, "about twenty letters thus far have been received from leading citizens, in as many localities throughout this state, all favoring a state convention." Two weeks later, how-

ever, the same newspaper printed a series of letters from Michigan African Americans who described themselves as "within the bounds of the Republican party" and who "cannot see how a convention at this time will benefit us as a race." The paper concluded that "the promoters [of the convention] have utterly ignored the Afro-American League" and aroused "useless antagonism."[75]

Nonetheless, eighty delegates—almost exclusively from Jackson, Calhoun, Saginaw, and Ingham Counties—gathered in Lansing on April 6, 1892, in response to the call. Wallace Goodridge brought the convention to order, and Saginaw delegates including Charles Ellis, Jr. and Sr., J. H. Gray, and William Quincy Atwood assumed major roles throughout the meeting. Still, the results were not completely as the Saginaw delegation might have expected. At least twice the convention turned to "a [more] representative young man" as opposed to a delegate with more long-term experience. For example, it chose Walter L. Burton of Lenawee to serve as temporary chairman of the convention instead of Charles Ellis, Sr., who had been Wallace Goodridge's choice. And the assembly also chose to reestablish a closer, although not formal, relationship with the state Republican Party. It endorsed the Harrison administration. It voted its thanks to the state Republicans for "recognizing the Afro-American," but also "recommended that the list of [African American officeholders] be increased by the coming republican administration." It called upon Michigan Republicans at their upcoming Detroit convention to choose as a delegate-at-large to the national party convention John J. Evans, whom it had unanimously recommended. And finally, as if to signal both state and Saginaw Republicans of this subtle but significant shift, the convention voted with "no little feeling exhibited" to change the name of the former Michigan Protective League to "The Michigan Equal Rights Association."[76]

Less than a week after the convention closed, a brief notice appeared in the *Plain Dealer* stating that the Saginaw "protective league has reorganized, and now bears the name of the Michigan

Suffrage League."[77] The change signified Saginaw's acquiescence to the will of the majority, both in the Afro-American and the Equal Rights Leagues across the state. Although Goodridges, Atwoods, and Ellises continued to participate in local and state politics as Republicans through the end of the century, it was with much less enthusiasm and much less effect than had been the case during the preceding decade. The attempt that Saginaw's African American leadership, with Atwood at the head, had made to establish a more independent, self-help position within the Republican Party had been only modestly successful. The result was an invitation here and an appointment there, but little of lasting consequence. As the century ended, the very political reforms that were the essence of state and national Republican platforms had the effect of denying to African Americans access to the positions of real power within the party that they so long had been seeking.[78] Independence and self-help ultimately had come to mean functioning apart from, not as a part of, the Republican Party. Whether African Americans would be able to protect what a few had achieved but also generate continued progress for as many as possible as members of the Democratic Party would remain for the next century to determine.

——◆——

The political activism of Saginaw's African American leadership during the 1880s and into the 1890s also provided ample opportunity for family members to combine business with a full schedule of social activities. For example, the *Detroit Plain Dealer* reported in April 1890 that "There will be quite a large delegation of ladies from this city [Saginaw], Midland and other surrounding cities" traveling to Detroit for the state Protective League convention. "Among those who will attend from this city are: Mrs. W. Q. Atwood, Mrs. Geo. L. Henry, Mrs. R. Combine, [Mrs.] Wm. F. Countee, Mrs. W. L. and W. O. Goodridge, Mr. & Mrs. Peter Thurman and a host of others."[79]

William Goodridge, a widower by 1874, had

remarried and was the father of two sons and a daughter by the time of his own death in August 1890. Wallace, however, for reasons he never revealed, had chosen not to marry until the winter of 1889–90, shortly before his brother's death. After nearly a half century as a bachelor, Wallace married Miss Margaret Jacques of Baltimore, Maryland, in that city in the autumn of 1889 or early winter 1890. Miss Jacques, who was approximately thirty-five at the time of her marriage, was the daughter of Henry and Mary Brooks Jacques. Exactly how the two met is not known, but the Goodridges had maintained family connections in Pennsylvania and Maryland, and Wallace and Maggie, as she was known, may have first met during a trip east that Wallace made in 1887. On their return to Saginaw the newlyweds occupied "a nice little residence on Phelon street" that Wallace had built in the fall of 1889.[80]

Maggie Goodridge not only accompanied Wallace on his various political excursions in Michigan but also dramatically expanded the sphere of his social activity beyond business and politics both in Saginaw and "back home" in Maryland and Pennsylvania. She regularly spent summers with her family in Baltimore and was an active member of Saginaw's Zion Baptist Church, which often called upon her talent as a pianist. During the early 1890s the "Saginaw Valley" report in the *Detroit Plain Dealer* followed the couple's active social life on an almost month-to-month basis and noted that as a result of the new Mrs. Goodridge's enlisting his assistance in a variety of church-related social events, Wallace came to be known as "Saginaw's silver-tongued orator."[81]

Margaret Goodridge was not only a wife but in effect also became Wallace's partner when he was left the last of the Goodridge brothers following William's death. Margaret and Wallace's "partnership" continued for nearly a quarter century until her own death from a cerebral hemorrhage in May 1914.[82] Wallace's decision to marry shortly before his brother's death, which had ended a most successful half century of professional partnership, was also the beginning of a successful but more personal partnership that lasted nearly a quarter of a century.

———◆———

The remarkable growth and success of the Goodridge studio between the 1872 Crouse Block fire and William's death in 1890 reflected, to a considerable extent, a similar pattern of development by the family's adopted home, East Saginaw. From a small and struggling frontier community on the banks of the Saginaw River at midcentury, the town had expanded rapidly to become the focal point of Michigan's pine lumber boom during the second half of the century. The dramatic population increase and considerable revenue that resulted from the boom not only provided the studio with eager customers, but the timber industry and its impact on the valley and state also became the basis for the Goodridge brothers' regional, national, and international reputation. Their professional success enabled Wallace, William, and their families to maintain, and at times even to exceed, the living standard established by their father in York a

half century earlier. As William C. Goodridge's wealth had begotten a strong sense of responsibility and political activism in antebellum York, his sons' achievements also thrust them into the forefront of an attempt by Michigan's African American community to protect and promote its accomplishments at the end of the century.

For the Goodridge family, most of its political activism and much of its professional achievement would have peaked with William O. Goodridge's death in 1890. The boom years of the timber industry by then were gone, and for a time at least so too were the customers, the revenue, and the drama that had come from more than two decades of documenting the process. Coincidentally with the end of the timber boom and William's death there occurred a series of profound changes in photography both technically and commercially. For more than three decades following William's death it was Wallace, the last of the three Goodridge brothers, therefore, who guided the development of the studio into this new era in the history of the family and the profession which it had helped to create.

7

The Final Years:
Change with Continuity, 1890–1922

I N JUNE 1889 the state legislature mandated action which a majority of the populace in both East Saginaw and Saginaw City had debated for years but certainly did not support with any enthusiasm. The consolidation of the two cities as one "united" Saginaw became official in March 1890 with the election of Mayor George W. Weadock and a council composed of thirty aldermen from both sides of the river. While more than a symbolic union would be achieved only in the next century, the action was typical of that taken by a number of "twin" cities across the United States at the end of the century. Economic efficiency and political expediency transcended geographic and psychological divisions that had existed for decades and even longer. In the case of the Saginaws, it was the possibility of economic stagnation or even extinction that had forced the political union.

By the end of the 1880s, what some in the Saginaw Valley may long have suspected but few had articulated publicly had occurred. The seemingly inexhaustible pine forests, at least those reasonably close to the valley's mills, were gone. Lumber camps and sawmills remained an essential part of Michigan's economy into the next century, but only so long as the forests to the north and in the Upper Peninsula lasted. Throughout the Saginaw Valley, however, the saws were still and the mills began to close. The amount of lumber cut by the mills that lined the Saginaw River had peaked in 1882 when over one billion board feet was produced. By 1892 the amount had dropped to little more than 700 million board feet, and by 1897 the

total was less than 340 million board feet.[1] The impact of the depletion of the pine forests was pervasive and extensive. For example, the combined population of the Saginaws had grown with the timber industry by more than 50 percent between 1880 and 1890, from 29,500 to 46,000. Yet by 1900 the population of Saginaw, reflecting the hard times of the 1890s, had dropped by almost 10 percent, to 42,300. Not until 1910 did the population again reach its 1890 level and then begin a period of rapid growth, reaching nearly 62,000 by 1920.[2] In spite of the fact that business and community leaders on both sides of the river had thought about and even initiated some economic diversification before 1890, it would be only after 1920 that the prosperity of the lumber boom years would be replaced by and then surpassed with the establishment of the mass-production automobile industry.[3] By 1890, therefore, many in Saginaw feared for the future, and only a few were optimistic. It was the optimists who pushed for consolidation.

The union of the Saginaws had little direct impact on the Goodridge studio. The end of the pine lumber boom, however, did present Wallace with enormous challenges. Given the division of labor in the studio, with William having been responsible for the stereo series and larger views of forest, lumber camp, river drives, and mills and Wallace doing the portraits and overseeing studio operations, it is likely that William's death would have cut short this most significant portion of the studio's annual production even had the timber boom not peaked and passed from the Saginaw

Valley almost simultaneously. For a time after 1890 Wallace did continue to print and market William's stereo series and views from the original negatives, and he also recycled the negatives and prints in various forms. But he created no new stereo series subsequent to William's death. Furthermore, as the camps were abandoned and the mills closed, not only did subject matter disappear but so too did much of the market for stereos, views, and even the inexpensive studio portraits popular with shanty boys and mill hands that had been the mainstay of Wallace's work.

Almost simultaneously with William's death and the end of the pine lumber boom, significant technical changes also would transform photography as a profession. Since the work of Niepce, Talbot, and Daguerre in the 1830s, photographic technology had continued to evolve regularly through the second half of the nineteenth century. The changes, however, whether to film or camera, had been such that control of the technology had remained largely in the hands of the studio-based professional. Then, during the 1880s, two dramatic technical changes permanently altered the direction of the profession's evolution. The first was the introduction in the early 1880s of the gelatin dry plate and shortly thereafter of celluloid roll film, both of which removed "the delicate and very technical operation of producing the photosensitive material [film] . . . from the hands of the photographer and placed [it] in the hands of production experts in factories," where it remains to this day.[4] And then in 1887 George Eastman introduced the Kodak camera system. The Kodak was loaded with a one-hundred-exposure roll of film and initially sold for twenty-five dollars. Anyone could now become a photographer simply by turning the key (to position the film), pulling the cord (to cock the self-capping shutter), and then pressing the button (to release the shutter and expose the film). When the roll was completed the entire Kodak system was sent to the Eastman factory, where the exposed film was unloaded, developed, and printed. The negatives, prints (photographs), and the Kodak reloaded with a new roll of film were then returned by the factory to the customer, and the process be-

gan once again. The momentous impact of the Kodak was such that

> The basic elements of the photographic process had been isolated and technical specialists trained to perform all the functions except aiming the camera and pressing the button. That separation of functions, fully realized by the Kodak camera system, revolutionized photography, for how the novices liked to press the button! The Kodak camera system also solved the basic problem with American Film [strip film]. Too complicated for professional photographers to operate conveniently, the film could now be fully processed by the Eastman Company, and the novices were quite willing to pay for that service.[5]

Saginaw photographers reacted to these changes in various ways. Many were forced to abandon the profession. Between 1885 and 1895 twenty-one of the thirty-three studios operating in Saginaw closed. Some, like Daniel Angell, the Beals brothers, and John T. Butterworth, had been in Saginaw for more than a decade. Most had lasted only a year or two. Of the twelve studios that did survive, only two, Duncan J. McIntyre and William L. Smith, had opened before 1885, and six had begun operations in 1890 or later.[6] Some of those who struggled to survive, like Powe & Howell at 305 East Genesee, sought a share of the shrinking market by cutting prices. Their ad in the *Courier* hoped to lure customers by informing Saginaw that "the reduction on cabinet photographs [$2 per dozen] will continue until the 20th inst. as an accommodation to the hundreds of people who came to the gallery during the past month and were unable to secure a sitting, owing to the rush of business then on hand from early morn until late at night!"[7] Studio professionals also were forced to compete with and, increasingly, to accommodate the amateur photographer. For example, as early as the summer of 1887 Frey & Wicklein, who sold a variety of "notions," began to advertise "Horsman's 'Eclipse' Outfit, The Neatest and Most Complete Photographing Outfit ever offered to the public."[8] And, as if to enforce an already growing trend, the *Saginaw Courier* in the spring of 1888 reprinted the following vision of the near future, titled "The

Camera at Home," that it had picked up from the *New Orleans Times-Democrat*:

> It is believed that in time a photographic apparatus will become part of the general household furniture. Its use will be as distinct a source of pleasure and profit as a telescope or a tennis set. Besides the fun to be derived from taking portraits of one's friends, it would be the dearest comfort to those at a distance to have illustrated letters from home. It is the easiest thing imaginable to buy the dry plates by the dozen, and when the arrangement of an apartment is changed, an entertainment in process, additions made to the house or grounds or any of the numberless little variations going on that make up the interest of private life, it could all be charmingly presented to the absent ones by means of the camera.[9]

Sensing the deluge to come, some professionals decided to join what they could not fight. William Von Glazer, whose studio did not last the year in 1888, sought to establish himself in Saginaw City by advertising that as "a first-class Scientific Photographer, [he] will give instructions to amateurs in all branches of this art from plain to the Most Artistic Photography."[10] And somewhat later, in a rare 1906 advertisement, Wallace Goodridge made it very clear that although he had been in Saginaw for more than half a century, his studio continued to lead the competition. He was ready, he declared, to "teach photography in all its branches, or in any special department, instruments and accessories being furnished direct from [the] factory." In addition, he had "kodaks and cameras for sale or rent, and [carried] a full line of photo buttons and jewelry, films and dry plates."[11]

Decades of experience had attuned Wallace and William Goodridge to changes in their profession. Their long-term success also made them optimistic about the future. Rather than cutting back, therefore, they decided to meet the future with a major expansion of the studio. And even though William's death occurred in the midst of the expansion, Wallace decided that the best course of action was to complete it. The newspaper notice that announced the expansion also made it clear that the studio was not only expanding physically

Figure 7.1. "Goodridge Brothers Studio, 220 South Washington," 1910, enlarged from original postcard. Goodridge Brothers Studio, Saginaw, Mich. Hurley Family Collection.

but also evolving functionally along with the profession. The announcement stated that the "Goodridge Bro's will break ground for their new store building next week."[12] No longer was the studio at 220 South Washington (see figure 7.1) to be a facility simply for creating and selling photographs. Henceforth, as Wallace later advertised, it would be a modern and complete photography center where customers also could learn "photography in all its branches," purchase or rent "kodaks and cameras," and obtain all necessary supplies. The same advertisement also reminded Saginaw that "portraiture" continued to be "the speciality" and that the studio also would continue to do "a large amount of commercial and landscape" photography.[13] Obviously, Wallace had decided to meet

Figure 7.2. "William O., Jr., Glen J., and John F. Goodridge," 1887, tintype, 2½ x 3⅜ inches. Goodridge Brothers Studio, East Saginaw, Mich. Collection of Beverly S. Osborne Pearson.

the challenges presented by the changes that surrounded and threatened to envelop him by maintaining a certain continuity with his brothers and the past, but also by striking out in some new directions now that he was alone.

＊

Although he was the last of the Goodridge brothers, Wallace was not completely on his own at the studio. Even before William's death and until shortly before his own, Wallace continued to employ family members as his assistants and also hired an occasional technician to provide specialized services at the studio. By the end of the 1880s the Goodridges' longtime assistants—John Freeney, James H. Morris, Arthur W. Brown, and William Edwards—all had moved on or established studios of their own. In May 1890 a George W. Watson of Clio, who may have been a relative of William O. Goodridge's second wife (born Gertrude Watson), was taken on as an apprentice, but there is no record of a continuing association with the studio after that year. It was to his nephews, therefore, that Wallace turned most often for assistance after 1890.

Figure 7.3. "Gertrude Nichols, William O. Jr. and John F. Goodridge," 1888–89, cabinet card. Albumen image, 4 ⅜ x 3 7/16 inches, beige bristol board mount with gold trim, 4 9/16 x 6 7/16 inches. Goodridge Brothers Studio, East Saginaw, Mich. Collection of Beverly S. Osborne Pearson.

Glenalvin's eldest son, Glen J. Goodridge, Jr., worked with his uncles from 1884 until approximately 1891, when he returned to York to reestablish the family barbershop there. The young man in figure 7.2, with his cousins William O. Goodridge, Jr., and John F. Goodridge in July 1887, is Glen J. Goodridge. In York he lived for a time with his mother, Rhoda Goodridge, who had moved back east after her husband's death. But by 1898 he had married and had purchased his shop and home at 104 N. Duke Street just around the corner from the original Goodridge home on East Philadelphia. There is no evidence that he worked as a photographer in York. Glen J. Goodridge died in 1928.[14]

As figure 7.3 indicates, the Goodridge children, William, Jr., and John F.—the young girl is most likely Gertrude Nichols, daughter of Mary Goodridge Nichols, as William's daughter Alta Goodridge had not been born when this photograph was made—were at ease in the family studio and from an early age even encouraged to emulate their father and uncle. It was to be expected, therefore, that William's sons would follow his example and begin to work with their uncle Wallace as soon as possible after their father's death. The Goodridge children attended Saginaw public schools, although by 1900 William O. Goodridge, Jr., had completed his formal education and was listed by the census that year as a full-time photographer in the family studio. Figure 7.4 is an extraordinary example of a photo-charcoal portrait of the young man a few years before his untimely death at age twenty-one in 1904. It was made by Wallace and colored by Goodridge studio artist Otto A. Shulz in the style made famous locally by William O. Goodridge at least three decades earlier. Had young William, Jr., not followed his father in death, it is certain he would as well have followed him as Wallace's partner in the studio.[15]

When not at school, Alta Goodridge (see figure 7.5a) worked with her mother, Gertrude Watson Goodridge, who was a partner for a time with Goodridge sister Madame Mary Nichols and her daughter Gertrude Nichols in one of Saginaw's most celebrated hairstyling salons. Subsequently

Alta may have attended St. Frances Academy in Baltimore, as her father's sisters had before her.[16] Figure 7.5b is a photograph of a wig shop and styling salon in Saginaw made by Wallace between 1915 and 1920. At that time Madame Nichols's shop operated separately from the photo studio and was located at 121 N. Franklin Street. The extensive collection of prints and photographs lining the walls and aisles of the shop reveals Madame Nichols's affinity for her brothers' work. The shop also served to train young African American women from the area as stylists and wigmakers. For example, figure 7.5b belonged to Mrs. John Johnson of Midland, Michigan, who was born Violet Victoria Edmonds of Detroit and Bay City, Michigan. Miss Edmonds had earlier trained as a hairdresser and wigmaker at the Nichols's shop in East Saginaw before marrying the barber John Johnson of Midland in 1872.[17]

It was William's youngest son, John F. Goodridge (see figure 7.6), who took his father's place in the studio next to Wallace as the new century began. John apparently was mechanically inclined. As a teen he used family connections with the Flint & Pere Marquette Railroad to begin training for a career as a brakeman and conductor. By 1903, however, the year before his brother's death, John had left the railroad and replaced his brother at Wallace's side. In 1907, when John was twenty-three, Wallace made him a partner in the studio. Both were listed as proprietors of the Goodridge studio in the directory that year, a position that no other assistant or family member with the exception of William O. Goodridge had or would attain. The following year, for reasons which are not known, John left the studio and was not again listed as partner or assistant. Until his death in 1947 John Goodridge worked as an electrician and projectionist at a succession of Saginaw theaters, in particular the Jeffers and the Franklin. Although his formal connection to the studio had ended in 1908, it is very likely, as we will discuss later in this chapter, that John's talent and technical ability as an electrician and film projectionist had a significant impact upon and were employed regularly by Wallace on at least a part-time basis until the studio closed in 1922.[18]

Figure 7.4. "William O. Goodridge, Jr.," ca. 1900, photo-charcoal, 16 x 20 inches. Goodridge Brothers Studio, Saginaw, Mich. Collection of Beverly S. Osborne Pearson.

Figure 7.6. "John F. Goodridge," ca. 1907. Silver print, 4 x 5¹⁵/₁₆ inches, on trimmed mount, 5¹/₁₆ x 7 inches. Goodridge Brothers Studio, Saginaw, Mich. Collection of Beverly S. Osborne Pearson.

Figure 7.5a. "Alta Goodridge," ca. 1900. Silver print, 3⁷/₁₆ x 5 inches, dark gray bristol board mount, trimmed to 4 x 6 inches. Goodridge Brothers Studio, Saginaw, Mich. Collection of Beverly S. Osborne Pearson.

Figure 7.5b. "Nichols Wig and Style Shop," 1915–20. Copy of original image, 7 x 5 inches. Goodridge Brothers Studio, Saginaw, Mich. Midland County Historical Society.

Figure 7.7a. "Goodridge Brothers Studio, 220 South Washington," 1915. Copy of original image, 3¹⁵⁄₁₆ x 3¹⁵⁄₁₆ inches. Goodridge Brothers Studio, Saginaw, Mich. *Michigan Manual of Freedmen's Progress*, p. 209.

For a time in 1894–95, a few years after they had married, Margaret Goodridge also served as Wallace's studio assistant.[19] While the marriage was successful, Margaret's work in the studio did not survive the year. In 1900 a notice in the *Saginaw Evening News,* describing an addition to the studio, referred to a different sort of partnership. According to the notice, the "Goodridge Bros. & Schulz . . . are fitting up a fine photograph enlarging room that will have a capacity of 200 enlargements a day." "Prof. Otto Schulz" was described as "an accomplished artist in crayon, ink and water colors, [who] is turning out some fine work." Schulz's talent as an artist is apparent in figure 7.4, but it is unlikely that Wallace went so far as to share the studio's long-established name with him in 1900. The census for that year lists the "professor" as a twenty-year-old "artist" who had immigrated to the United States from Germany in 1889. There is no record of Schulz in Saginaw after 1900.[20]

William O. Goodridge died before the major renovation of the studio that he and Wallace had planned was completed. A comparison of a 1910 photograph of the exterior of the studio (see figure 7.1) with photographs made in 1915 (figure 7.7a) and 1916 (figure 7.7b) reveals little change in the exterior of the structure. Even the canvas awning

Figure 7.7b. "Goodridge Brothers Studio, 220 South Washington," 1916. Close-up from "Schust's Third Auto Fleet," panorama. Goodridge Brothers Studio, Saginaw, Mich. Originally published August 8, 1948. ©1999 *The Saginaw News.* All rights reserved. Reprinted with permission.

Figure 7.7c. "Office, Goodridge Brothers Studio," before 1902, original format and size unknown, *Goodridges' Art Souvenir of Saginaw, Michigan, U.S.A.,* p. 21. Collection of John V. Jezierski.

Figure 7.8a. "Erna Schreyer," 1910. Silver print, 3 x 5½ inches, gray bristol board mount, 5⅞ x 8⅞ inches. Goodridge Brothers Studio, Saginaw, Mich. Collection of Eugene Schreyer Family.

Figure 7.8b. "Eugene Schreyer," 1910. Silver print, 3¹¹⁄₁₆ x 6 inches. Goodridge Brothers Studio, Saginaw, Mich. Collection of Eugene Schreyer Family.

remained the same. The studio's window displays, however, did change regularly, reflecting the ebb and flow of photographic fashions. Increasingly, the displays also included the cameras and supplies that had become an essential part of the inventory of any successful studio.

For most of the period after 1890, with only brief interruptions, the city directories reveal that Wallace and his family, as well as an ever-changing group of other Goodridges, continued to make the rooms behind the studio their private residence. For example, John Goodridge lived there in 1906 and may have saved the studio from considerable loss. A report in the *Saginaw Courier Herald* for August 30, 1906, noted that "John F. Goodridge has been sitting up nights since about 1 o'clock Monday morning watching for a man about 30 years old who threw a bright light from a huge bull's eye lantern into his eyes through a screen door. Goodridge was sleeping in the rear of the photograph gallery of his uncle Wallace L. Goodridge,

South Washington avenue, when he was awakened by these bright rays. Grasping a big revolver he prepared to do battle but the would-be burglar calmly walked away. The young man expects him back and has a big charge of bird shot in his gun."[21]

Figure 7.7c, an undated photograph simply titled "Office, Goodridge Bros. Studio," is of a comfortable room that obviously served a variety of functions. It was Wallace's office and the family parlor. The upright piano visible to the right was a replacement for the infamous "Emerson's Piano with legs and cover" that had been the subject of a lawsuit brought against the family in 1870 and which was destroyed in the 1872 Crouse Block fire. In an interview the author conducted with Mr. Eugene Schreyer in 1991, Mr. Schreyer recalled visiting the Goodridge studio with his sister Erna in June 1910 for confirmation portraits. Figures 7.8a and b are the result of the visit. Mr. Schreyer remembered the piano. He also described the studio and its various rooms as small but neat and filled with photographs and many different cameras. He characterized Wallace Goodridge as a quiet and dignified man with dark hair who used a large view camera with a cloth cover over his head to make the portraits. There also was an elderly African American woman present whom Mr. Schreyer remembered as being partially blind. This most likely was Wallace's sister Mary Goodridge Nichols, who is listed as blind in the 1910 census.[22]

Unlike the exterior, the interior of the studio underwent regular renovation. At times it was the result of purposeful change meant to keep pace with professional development. For example, in 1900 the Goodridge studio was "fitting up a fine photograph enlarging room that will have a capacity of 200 enlargements a day." This was most likely the result of Wallace's having hired "Professor" Otto Schulz that same year to create large numbers of oversized "hand-colored" portraits similar to that of William O. Goodridge, Jr., in figure 7.4. In 1908 more extensive interior renovation was necessary as a result of a fire that nearly destroyed the entire studio. According to an article in the *Evening News,* on Sunday afternoon, May 3, "Wallace L. Goodridge had [a] narrow escape from being cremated!" Wallace had been working in the darkroom at the time and accidently overturned an oil lamp used for drying prints. "Instantly the small room . . . was a mass of flames." The intensity of the fire and the size of the room made it difficult for Wallace to escape, but "he managed to open the door, which he had locked, and push his way through the flames into the other room, from whence he gave the alarm." By the time the fire department arrived "the entire outside rooms were on fire and 15 picture backgrounds . . . were destroyed." The fire department did manage to "prevent the spread of the flames to the front of the building," but the "entire photo rooms were gutted and Mr. Goodridge was quite badly burned about the head." In an interview the next day, Wallace stated that he "was unable to say definitely as yet what his damages would amount to, but they would aggregate in the neighborhood of $400, which in the main was covered by insurance." In addition, the fire destroyed the "numerous new photos which Mr. Goodridge had just fin-

ished" and there also was "some damage to the machines [cameras and equipment]."[23] Apparently there was more extensive damage to the studio and its equipment than Wallace originally had estimated or which was covered by insurance. In November, six months after the fire, Wallace and Margaret Goodridge obtained a mortgage on the studio in the amount of $550 from Peoples Savings Bank to complete the restoration. The amount was not completely repaid until 1922, shortly before Wallace's death.[24] The records reveal no major alterations to the studio interior or exterior after 1908.

—◆—

Eastman's Kodak ushered in the era of the "snap-shot," making it simple and convenient for most anyone who chose to create his or her own portraits. The Kodak system ensured the demise of the tintype, carte de visite, and cabinet, the inexpensive portraits that had been the mainstay of studio photographers for nearly half a century. Its introduction did not mean, however, that professional photographers, including Wallace Goodridge, altogether abandoned portrait photography. On the contrary, the stimulus to the profession from the Kodak revolution provided some photographers, especially those with the confidence that came from solid ties to the past but also an eye to future innovation, with even greater opportunities. Wallace Goodridge was among them.

Wallace's commitment to portrait photography continued through the end of his career. For a time, in fact, because he appreciated their quality and long ago had mastered the technique of the processes, Wallace continued to make old-style tintype and cabinet portraits. Most that have survived from after 1890 are of Goodridge nieces and nephews. For example, figures 7.9a and b are tintype portraits of William and Gertrude Goodridge's daughter Alta with her brother William, Jr. (a), made by Wallace shortly after her birth in 1891, and of Alta (b) perhaps eighteen months later as a toddler just beginning to walk. At about the same time, Wallace also made an excellent portrait (figure 7.10a) of his nephews William, Jr., and John in matching knickered suits and flamboyant "bow" ties. In 1898 he

Figure 7.9a. "William O., Jr. and Alta Goodridge," 1891, tintype, 2¹⁄₁₆ x 3⁵⁄₁₆ inches. Goodridge Brothers Studio, Saginaw, Mich. Collection of Beverly S. Osborne Pearson.

Figure 7.9b. "Alta Goodridge," 1892, tintype, 2½ x 3⅜ inches. Goodridge Brothers Studio, Saginaw, Mich. Collection of Beverly S. Osborne Pearson.

Figure 7.10a. "William O., Jr. and John F. Goodridge," 1891, cabinet card. Silver print, 3⅞ x 5½ inches, ivory bristol board mount, 4¼ x 6½ inches. Goodridge Brothers Studio, Saginaw, Mich. Collection of Beverly S. Osborne Pearson.

Figure 7.10b. "William O., Jr., Alta, and John F. Goodridge," 1898, cabinet card. Silver print, 3⅞ x 5⁷⁄₁₆ inches, gray bristol board mount, 4⁷⁄₁₆ x 6¹¹⁄₁₆ inches. Goodridge Brothers Studio, Saginaw, Mich. Collection of Beverly S. Osborne Pearson.

Figure 7.11. "Unidentified Woman," after 1890, cabinet card. Albumen image, 4 x 5⁵⁄₁₆ inches, beige bristol board mount with gold trim, 4¼ x 6½ inches. Goodridge Brothers Studio, Saginaw, Mich. Historical Society of Saginaw County, Inc .

disguised by the rug—are duplicates of or similar to props found in Goodridge portraits made a half century earlier. Even the pose, with the brothers flanking their sister and the three directly confronting the camera, is typical of a much earlier style. At the same time, the whole tone of the photograph is one of a relaxed comfort with the camera and the whole process that only became possible as split-second shutter speeds eliminated posing apparatuses and the other rigors of earlier portraiture.

Wallace also employed a similar blend of format and technique, pose and tone, in the portraits that the studio continued to make for Saginaw Valley residents. Figure 7.11, a cabinet portrait in the "Rembrandt" style that Wallace had popularized locally a generation earlier, could easily have been made in 1875 rather than in 1895. The traditional lighting style obviously was chosen to highlight bow, buttons, kerchief, and pearls as well as the most up-to-date "gay '90s" bouffant hairstyle. Twenty years later, in 1915 (see figure 7.12), for Erna Schreyer (who had visited the studio for a confirmation portrait in 1910—see figure 7.8a), Wallace chose similar lighting—highlighted subject against dark background—but in a full-length pose to help Miss Schreyer remember a "new party dress" and an especially enjoyable evening.[25] The contrast and counterpoint that Wallace was able to create in this very traditional portrait give it considerable "life." For example, the brilliant white fluffy puff of the fan contrasts very nicely with the smooth and subtle highlights of the satiny smoothness of the dress. Miss Schreyer's long, bare arm with its four folded fingers also mirrors the one long and four shorter white lines of lace that define the collar and bodice of her dress. And the peak formed by the parting of her hair is emphasized by the downward-pointed white fan, which together help to define the length of the portrait. For the mount, subject and photographer chose the then very popular oval vignette that complements Miss Schreyer's full features, slightly bending left arm, and the fluffy white oval of her ostrich feather fan. The mounting board is a most contemporary mottled brown that enhances the rich tones of the portrait itself.

again chronicled the family's continued growth with the elegant but relaxed portrait of William, Jr., Alta, and John in figure 7.10b. The photograph demonstrates not only Wallace's continued mastery of portraiture but also his ability to synthesize the traditional and modern elements of his craft. The portrait is a cabinet, a most traditional format. The size of the image is a standard 3⁷⁄₈ x 5⁵⁄₁₆ inches, but Wallace has mounted it on a board of 4⁷⁄₁₆ x 6¹¹⁄₁₆ inches, a bit larger than in the past. And for the board he has chosen a new pearl gray stock with a smoothly dimpled surface that the studio used regularly to mount a majority of its work after 1890.

The props that Wallace used to pose his subjects—the ornate pillar and rail, the chair and table

Figure 7.12. "Erna Schreyer," 1915. Silver print, 4 x 6⅟₁₆ inches, mottled brown paper mount, 6⅝ x 11⅜ inches. Goodridge Brothers Studio, Saginaw, Mich. Collection of Eugene Schreyer Family.

During this period Saginaw residents also continued to choose the Goodridge studio to make their wedding portraits. In approximately 1895 the unidentified newlyweds in figures 7.13a and b visited the Washington Avenue studio. Wallace created for them two wonderfully contrasting portraits. In the first he chose a very typically formal pose reminiscent of the tintype, cartes, and cabinet portraits of the previous half century. Contact between bride and groom is minimal, and their attention is focused

Figure 7.13a. "Unidentified Wedding Portrait," ca. 1895. Silver print, 3¹⁵⁄₁₆ x 5⁵⁄₁₆ inches, black bristol board mount, 6 x 8¹⁵⁄₁₆ inches. Goodridge Brothers Studio, Saginaw, Mich. Historical Society of Saginaw County, Inc.

Figure 7.13b. "Unidentified Wedding Portrait," ca. 1895. Silver print, 5¹/₁₆ x 3⁷/₁₆ inches, gray bristol board mount, 8 x 6 inches. Goodridge Brothers Studio, Saginaw, Mich. Historical Society of Saginaw County, Inc.

on the camera and not each other. The emphasis of the photograph is the event—the marriage—and not necessarily the human participants. The lighting from the upper left helps to soften the portrait somewhat by highlighting curly hair, bent elbows, and flowers, ruffles, and ties. The few blossoms scattered on the floor at the lower right not only achieve the same effect but effectively camouflage the carpet seams as well. The effect of 7.13b, however, is dramatically different. While a formal studio portrait, it is a much more personal and relaxed one. Husband and wife are presented as close both physically and emotionally. In fact, the effect of the oval vignette of the mount is almost embarrassing in that it serves as

a window that allows the observer to view the couple's obvious intimacy. The intensity of the portrait is lightened somewhat by backlighting and especially the structure of multiple triangles within the oval window of the mount resulting from the couple's selection of costume and Wallace's choice of pose. All in all, the result is one of Wallace's most striking and memorable portraits.

In addition to continuity seasoned with a bit of innovation in his portrait work, Wallace maintained his own and the studio's interest in a variety of subject areas. Since the early days of Glenalvin's

Figure 7.14. "Sid Thorne," 1907. Silver print, 10 x 8³⁄₁₆ inches, gray bristol board mount, 11¹¹⁄₁₆ x 10¹⁄₁₆ inches. Goodridge Brothers Studio, Saginaw, Mich. Collection of Dave Tinder.

work in York (see figure 2.7), the Goodridge family had maintained a strong interest in horses and racing. During the fall of 1907, probably in Saginaw but possibly in Pontiac, Michigan, or Ft. Wayne, Indiana, Wallace made the portrait of Sid Thorne (figure 7.14), a nine-year-old bay born in 1898 of Sidney (sire) and Hawthorne Belle (dame). He was owned by the Westwind Stock Farm of Pontiac, which ran him as a "short-track" racer. On September 19, 1907, he set a track record of 2:16 1/4 for the mile at a racing park in Ft. Wayne.[26] There is no known direct connection between the Goodridge family and the horse or Westwind Farm.

Alta Goodridge later married Ollie J. Murchison of nearby Muncie, but there is also no apparent link tying the Goodridge family to Ft. Wayne or Indiana in 1907. It may be that Sid Thorne simply was in Saginaw to race at the fairgrounds and Wallace used the occasion to recognize his achievement. In any case, the young observer leaning against the sapling along the right edge of the portrait found the whole process a most interesting one.

Although the drama and excitement of the pine lumber boom would have peaked by the 1890s, Wallace also continued to market the stereo series and large-format views of forest, river drive,

GOODRIDGE BROS., PHOTOGRAPHERS E.Saginaw,Mich.

R.H. NASON'S MILL.

Figure 7.15a. "R.H. Nason's Mill," 1885–95. Albumen image, 9⅛ x 7¼ inches, beige bristol board mount, 14 x 10¹⁄₁₆ inches. Goodridge Brothers Studio, East Saginaw, Mich. Historical Society of Saginaw Country, Inc.

GOODRIDGE BROS., PHOTOGRAPHERS E.Saginaw,Mich.

VIEW OF MARSH CREEK.

J.L. & S.R.W Saginaw County, Michigan.

Figure 7.15b. "View of Marsh Creek," 1885–95. Albumen image, 9¹⁄₁₆ x 7³⁄₁₆ inches, beige bristol board mount, 14 x 10¹⁄₁₆ inches. Goodridge Brothers Studio, East Saginaw, Mich. Historical Society of Saginaw County, Inc.

Figure 7.16. "Maple Lawn Farm," after 1889. Silver print, 9⅝ x 7¾ inches, ivory bristol board mount, 13¹⁵⁄₁₆ x 10 inches. Goodridge Brothers Studio, Saginaw Mich. Historical Society of Saginaw County, Inc.

and mills that William had created previously. For example, William's view of the Tittabawassee River log drive at Bryant's Trip (figure 5.12b) is included in the 1904 *Views of Saginaw and Vicinity* published for the S. H. Knox & Co. variety store. And more than thirty Goodridge photographs, including William's earlier stereo views and Wallace's more recent portraits and panoramas, are used as illustrations in Mills's 1918 *History of Saginaw County*.[27] In addition, Wallace accepted an occasional special commission to photograph one or other of the timber operations that continued to function throughout the valley. Among them was a series of large views that he made for the Nason family of Chesaning, Michigan, shortly after William's death. Charles and Harriet Nason had immigrated to the United States from Northampton, England, in 1834 and settled on a farm near Buffalo, New York.

Two sons, Charles F. and Robert H., were born in Northampton, and three additional sons, George N., John C., and William, and two daughters, Harriet and Jane, were born in New York. Robert H. Nason, who married Susan Odell in 1851 and moved to Michigan the same year, was the first of the brothers to settle in Chesaning. The couple owned and operated the "Hotel Central" for a time, speculated in the timber market, and Robert even left Chesaning and his family for a time to prospect for gold during the Pikes Peak rush, but with little to show for it "except the journey and experience." Nonetheless, upon his return Robert Nason prospered from a variety of enterprises, including the mill in figure 7.15a. It was one of several mills and salt blocks that Nason owned throughout Saginaw County which served as the basis for even more extensive investments made later in Calcasieu

Parish, Louisiana.[28] Figures 7.15a and b are among a series of photographs that the Goodridges made for Nason. The mill was located at Garfield on the route of the Jackson, Lansing & Saginaw Railroad (after 1871 the Saginaw Division of the Michigan Central), about a mile north of St. Charles and eight miles west and south of Saginaw. As late as 1896 Nason owned more than three hundred acres of prime timberland on Marsh Creek, a tributary of Swan Creek, that flowed through Garfield.[29]

Sometime after 1889 (note the date on the barn in figure 7.16), Wallace also traveled to Chesaning to make a family portrait for the Nasons at Maple Lawn Farm. The farm was located on forty acres at the junction of Main and Peet Streets on the east side of the Shiawassee River south of town. The land was among Robert Nason's earliest investments in the area and by 1889 had been deeded to his son Charles. Robert is seated to the left and Charles to the right in the photograph. Father and son are surrounded by family members and farmhands.[30]

A major element of the studio's activity during the peak years of the pine lumber boom had been its contract work for the railroads that owned the timberlands and transported the logs. After 1890 the Goodridge connection with the railroads continued, but like the railroads themselves, it also was transformed somewhat as the forests disappeared. Rather than narrow-gauge locomotives, trestles, and cars piled with pyramids of timber, the studio's focus shifted to the men who worked for the railroads that continued to operate throughout the valley. For example, figure 7.17 is a portrait that Wallace made at Saginaw of the famous baseball team sponsored by the Flint & Pere Marquette Railroad.

The team was organized for the railroad during the early 1890s as a shop team by Herman Grobe, its first manager. According to the sport's best-known historian, such teams were originally a major element of a "paternalistic and manipulative system of recreation set up as a method of social control by businesses for motives of enlightened self-interest, such as increased production, less employee turnover, and, above all, prevention of

unionism and strikes." In addition, baseball, for players and fans, would positively occupy increasing leisure hours as average workweeks dropped to sixty hours by 1900.[31] If such motives were, indeed, behind the railroad's sponsorship, they were effective. By 1895 the Flint & Pere Marquette team had become "one of the greatest teams in the middle west . . . [taking] on all comers, including the Detroit team [professionals] of the Western League, and it whipped them regularly." In fact, at the height of its popularity in 1895 the team drew 3,939 paid admissions—the most to view a game in Saginaw for many years to come—at its home field located near the old car repair barns for a game at which it defeated the Saginaw Interstate League team 2–0 in eleven innings.[32]

Some years later Wallace also made a portrait of the office staff and yard crew of the Saginaw Division (the former Jackson, Lansing & Saginaw Railroad) of the Michigan Central (figure 7.18). The freight office was located on Niagara Street between Van Buren and Cass on the west bank of the river. A portion of the structure stands there today. In 1884, in order to improve its poor position in competition for freight with the Flint & Pere Marquette, the Michigan Central brought Spencer Goseline to Saginaw as its freight agent. Goseline, the tall man in the white shirt at the center of the photograph, is described by Mills as "a man of vital force, . . . genial nature, [and with] a firm grasp of the whole situation." By "improving freight schedules, speeding up freight deliveries, and by extending track connections," he gradually gained for the Michigan Central its "rightful share of the freight business" and became "highly regarded by our substantial citizens." Goseline died of pneumonia in Saginaw on October 12, 1905. His obituary described him as "One of Saginaw's best known citizens," who was "welcome company wherever he appeared."[33]

In addition to continuing his work for the long-established railroads, Wallace also regularly photographed Saginaw's new electric interurban and expanded street railway systems. The Saginaws had been served by a trolley system since the organization of the Saginaw City Street Railway Compa-

Figure 7.17. "Baseball Team, Flint and Pere Marquette Railroad," after 1890. Copy of original image, 10 x 8⅛ inches. Goodridge Brothers Studio, Saginaw, Mich. Collection of John V. Jezierski.

Figure 7.18. "Freight Office Staff, Michigan Central Railroad," after 1890. Silver print, 8¹¹⁄₁₆ x 6⁹⁄₁₆ inches. Goodridge Brothers Studio, Saginaw, Mich. Collection of William Oberschmidt.

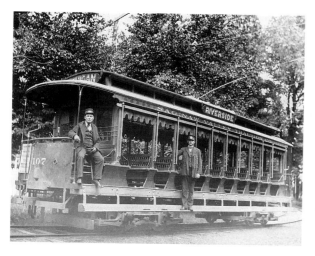

Figure 7.19a. "Trolley No. 107, Union Street Railway Company," after 1894. Copy of original image, 10 x 8⅛ inches. Goodridge Brothers Studio, Saginaw, Mich. Bosch-Devers Collection.

Figure 7.19b. "Picnic Grounds, Riverside Park," after 1894. Copy of original image, 10 x 8⅛ inches. Goodridge Brothers Studio, Saginaw, Mich. Bosch-Devers Collection.

Figure 7.20. "Electric Interurban, Saginaw-Bay City," after 1894. Copy of original image, 10 x 8⅛ inches. Goodridge Brothers, Saginaw, Mich. Bosch-Devers Collection.

ny in 1863 and the East Saginaw City Street Railway two years later. In 1888 "Little Jake" Seligman gained control of the East Saginaw line, which had been reorganized as the Union Street Railway Company. During 1889 Seligman converted the Union line to an overhead electric trolley system and extended it to Saginaw City. So successful was this innovation that by 1895 the Union line was able to absorb the nearly defunct Saginaw City line.[34]

In 1894 the Union line, like many other street

railway companies throughout the United States, opened Riverside Park at the end of the line where the Tittabawassee joins the Saginaw River. Figure 7.19a is a shot of trolley No. 107, which carried many Saginaw families to the fun at the river's edge. Riverside Park's seventy-two acres ultimately included a variety of rides, a large dance pavilion, and an extensive picnic area (see figure 7.19b) along the river. The park operated for more than forty years, until 1937, and served as Saginaw's most popular "breathing place."[35]

The same year that the Union line opened Riverside Park, Saginaw lumberman Isaac Bearinger invested nearly $500,000 of his own capital in an electric traction interurban system that joined Saginaw to Bay City (figure 7.20). The line, which was "well built and equipped with the best type of electric cars then used," traveled the fifteen miles between the two cities at thirty-minute intervals. The interurban proved "to be very successful," and Bearinger sold it to the Saginaw Traction Company in 1898.[36]

As it had since the Goodridges' arrival in East Saginaw almost half a century earlier, the Saginaw River continued to attract the studio's attention. For most of the period William and Wallace's photographs had focused on the river as the key to the region's economic and industrial development (see,

Figure 7.21a. "Saginaw River from Southwest to Northeast," after 1913. Silver print, 7 x 5⅟₁₆ inches, dark gray bristol board mount, 9¹⁵⁄₁₆ x 7⅞ inches. Goodridge Brothers Studio, Saginaw, Mich. Historical Society of Saginaw County, Inc.

Figure 7.21b. "Saginaw River from Southeast to Northwest," after 1913. Silver print, 7 x 5⅟₁₆ inches, dark gray bristol board mount, 9¹⁵⁄₁₆ x 7⅞ inches. Goodridge Brothers Studio. Saginaw, Mich. Historical Society of Saginaw County, Inc .

for example, figures 4.28a–c and 4.29a–c). During the final decade of Wallace's career, however, he began to view the river with a bit more nostalgia. Figure 7.21a was made looking from west to east sometime after 1913, when the new Genesee Avenue Scherzer Lift bridge had been completed.[37] Although the bridge was new, the whole tone of the photograph tends to emphasize what had been rather than what could be. There is no human presence, and even the roofline of Saginaw's east side is blurred and without definition. The very prominent piles of scrap lumber that occupy the lower left third of the image sadly recall busy mills and riverbanks lined with rafts of logs. The mood is strongly reinforced by figure 7.21b, made at about the same time. Shot from Ojibway Island, the site of numerous mills and a variety of industries since midcentury, the vacant banks, empty river, and trafficless bridges seem to cry out for activity.

A decade earlier, in 1904, Wallace also had joined with other Saginaw photographers to create a more traditional but also tragic view of the river's impact on the valley. Headlines in the Saturday, March 26, edition of the *Saginaw Evening News* proclaimed "WORST FLOOD IN MANY YEARS" An unusually long cold spell had held the ice in much of the Saginaw River system. Several inches of rain in late March therefore had no place to go but over the riverbanks. By March 29 the river at Saginaw had risen to 12.46 feet above its low-water mark, more than a foot above the previous flood record set in 1884. Most of East Saginaw and parts of Saginaw City within four blocks of the river were under as much as four feet of water as a result, and thousands of rural residents throughout the valley were completely cut off for more than a week. Losses were estimated at more than one million dollars, with businesses along Genesee Avenue losing more than $100,000 in inventory. The previous week the Grand River had similarly visited Grand Rapids, with a "$1,000,000 LOSS, . . . 8,000 Men Out of Work and 2,500 Houses . . . in [a] Sea of Water."[38] On April 1 and 2 the *Evening News* published a series of photographs of the high water which proved to be so popular that later the same month Appleby Brothers, an East Saginaw job printer, published

a commemorative booklet of flood photographs titled *Souvenir Views of Saginaw's Greatest Flood*. The introduction noted that "Lives were lost; millions of dollars worth of property destroyed; factories shut down; railway and street car service suspended; and business throughout the Valley being practically at a standstill." The photographs were designed to "give one an excellent idea of this great flood, the water having attained a height of nineteen inches over the memorable flood of 1884."[39] Appleby Brothers solicited photographs from six of the Saginaws' studios (Beckmann Bros., M. L. Hendricks, J. R. Nichols, C. J. L. Bush, Michigan View Company, and Goodridge Bros.) and an unidentified source or two. The booklet contained thirty-two photographs, with the Goodridge, Beckmann, and Nichols studios providing more than half.

Figure 7.22a was made by Wallace from the roof of city hall looking west across the river over the Bristol Street Bridge as the water began to rise. The submerged tip of Ojibway Island and a siding of the Saginaw Branch of the Michigan Central Railroad are visible to the left. Across the river floodwaters have begun to inundate both the A. W. Wright Planing Mill and the Wylie Bros. Shingle Mill as well as low-lying residences along the riverbank. The ice beginning to build up against the eastern terminus of the Bristol Street Bridge would threaten but not destroy it as ice floes did most of the other bridges across the river. At the corner of Baum and Germania, more than four blocks from the river, the crew from Valley City Fire Station No. 3 (see figure 7.22b) did "a Wading Stunt" for Wallace in more than a foot of water. If the number of times that the photographs from Appleby's *Souvenir Views* have been reproduced over the years is an indication of its popularity, the publication was a resounding success.

The continued success of Wallace's portrait work, resulting from his ability to blend traditional style with innovative technique, led, after 1900, to a series of important photographic commissions for the studio from Saginaw's increasingly varied corporate community and from the city fathers as

Figure 7.22a. "Looking across the River from City Hall," 1904, *Souvenir Views of Saginaw's Greatest Flood,* p. 19. Collection of William Oberschmidt.

Figure 7.22b. "Corner Baum and Germania Avenue—Fire Laddies during a Wading Stunt," 1904, *Souvenir Views of Saginaw's Greatest Flood,* p. 21. Collection of William Oberschmidt.

well. Given the fact that the studio was approaching its golden anniversary in Saginaw and that Wallace, at fifty-nine years of age in 1900, had entered the final phase of his career in photography, the decision by the valley's business and political leadership to entrust the Goodridge studio with such noteworthy commissions is testimony to the position that Wallace and the Goodridge family had earned in Saginaw during the previous half century. By 1900 the revolutionary changes that also had been transforming photography as a profession since before the introduction of the Kodak would have weeded out the weakest and least adaptable of Saginaw's photography studios. At the turn of the century there were sixteen studios besides the Goodridges' active in Saginaw. Five closed within five years. The remaining eleven, however, demonstrated remarkable stability and continued in business for an average of nineteen years. Although none equaled the fifty-nine-year record of the Goodridge studio, some, like Charles Busch, Alfred Glover, Benjamin Krupp, A. E. Lyon, and Duncan McIntyre, were open for more than a quarter century, with Busch, at forty years, second only to the Goodridges.[40] The business community and city fathers, therefore, had several well-established and successful studios from which to choose when they decided to award photography

Figure 7.23. "Reider Family, Tollhouse, Saginaw and Genesee Plank Road Company," 1907. Silver print, 10 x 8 inches, gray bristol board mount, 14 x 12 inches. Goodridge Brothers Studio, Saginaw, Mich. Citizens Bank - Saginaw.

commissions. More often than not, Wallace Goodridge continued to be their choice.

For example, in 1907, shortly before the Saginaw and Genesee Plank Road Company terminated its franchise and turned control of the road over to Bridgeport and Buena Vista Townships, the company hired the Goodridge studio to photograph the last family to maintain the tollhouse near the present intersection of East Genesee and Hess. Figure 7.23 is the resulting portrait. Seated at the center of the photograph are Jacob and Marie Reider, surrounded by their six children, Charles, Clara, Fred, Jacob, Florence, and Barbara, and their spouses and children. In February 1976 the *Saginaw News* interviewed Florence Reider Dulmage (standing at the right in the back row), who remembered "the tollhouse as being an exciting place for children to grow up." "It had," she re-

called, "a front parlor, a living room, dining room, kitchen and upstairs . . . bedrooms." In the family parlor was the wheel that was used to open and close the gate to the toll road. At that time the Reiders collected two cents per mile per horse from each traveler using the road.[41]

The Reider family had come to work for the company in 1899 when the plank road, visible through the toll gate as it headed north into Saginaw, was already half a century old. The road was the creation of Norman Little, the driving force behind the establishment of East Saginaw in 1850. Little realized from the beginning that the success of his East Saginaw venture depended upon transportation links with the rest of the state, especially to the south and east toward Detroit. As a result, he elicited a charter from the state legislature, organized the road corporation, and undertook con-

Figure 7.24a. "Hoyt Park, Semi-Centennial Celebration," 1907. Copy of original image, 10 x 8 inches. Goodridge Brothers Studio, Saginaw, Mich. Collection of John V. Jezierski.

Figure 7.24b. "Hoyt Park, Semi-Centennial Celebration," 1907. Copy of original image., 10 x 8 inches. Goodridge Brothers Studio, Saginaw, Mich. Collection of John V. Jezierski .

struction. The road, which ran thirty-two miles along the Cass River and Pine Run, was completed from East Saginaw to Flint in 1851. Its almost immediate success led to the establishment of the first post office at East Saginaw and daily stage service to Flint and beyond. Within twenty years, similar plank roads connected Saginaw with Vassar and Watrousville in Tuscola County and St. Louis in Gratiot County.[42]

That same summer of 1907 was an especially busy one for Wallace when several civic organizations asked the studio to photograph the city's semi-centennial celebration. During the week of August 17–24 the city celebrated the fiftieth anniversary of its incorporation with a series of events that began with an illumination of the city by more than three thousand electric lights during the evening of Saturday the seventeenth and concluded with several bands throughout the city simultaneously playing "Auld Lang Syne" at 10 P.M.a week later. Between the two Saturdays city residents and visitors enjoyed a multitude of parades, proclamations, dinners, and pageants. Wallace was called upon to record several of the most important. For example, during the afternoon of Sunday, August 18, Wallace was among the more than thirty thousand Saginaw residents and visitors who gathered in Hoyt Park to kick off the festivities with a series of speeches and songs, including "Saginaw, My Saginaw," "Queen of the Saginaw Valley," "Home Again," "Dixie," the "Star-Spangled Banner," "La Marseillaise," and the Polish national hymn, among others.[43] Wallace made several series of photographs of the various celebrations, including the throngs of celebrants (figures 7.24a and b) who gathered in the park in their Sunday best with bicycles and carriages and perhaps even cameras of their own. Notice the young man in the left foreground of figure 7.24a.

Throughout the week, Saginaw's newspapers published a series of reminiscences covering the half century, including a selection of photographs in the *Evening News* titled "Scenes in Saginaw Long Ago," a collage of Goodridge photographs of East Saginaw buildings and street scenes from the late 1860s and early 1870s.[44] On Wednesday afternoon, August 21, Wallace also was called to the

Saginaw Club on North Washington to photograph (figure 7.25a) the reunion of residents and visitors organized by Mrs. W. S. Linton and Mrs. Max Heavenrich and the Ladies Auxiliary of the Semi-Centennial Committee. A variety of refreshments and music provided by the Boos and Hinte bands had attracted most of Saginaw's "most prominent citizens," including seventy-one-year-old Mrs. T. S. Kennedy, Saginaw's oldest continuous resident, who had come to the valley with her father, John Sitterling, in 1836. The newspaper account reporting the event noted that the "historical photograph was taken by Photographer Goodrich."[45] Perhaps that same evening, at either the Saginaw Club or the Bancroft Hotel, Wallace again was called upon to record a festive dinner gathering of some of the city's most powerful leaders. Included in figure 7.25b are, standing from left to right, Paul F. H. Morley, Charles H. Peters II, Frederick Stevens, Herbet Cross, Lewis Slade, James Malcolm, George Potter, Robert H. Cook, Archie Patrick Milne, and Wallis Craig Smith. Seated, from left to right, are Frederick Carlisle, George W. Weadock, Frederick Potter, Ernest Goff, Bert Saylor, Ezra Rust, Frederick Jerome, Benton Hanchett, W. S. Linton, and Edward W. Morley.

Several of Wallace's semi-centennial photographs were printed as postcards and sold as souvenirs to city residents and visitors who wished to remember Saginaw's grandest celebration. For a detailed discussion of Goodridge postcard production, see figures 7.35a–e and the accompanying text.

Six years after the semi-centennial celebration, in 1913, Edward W. Morley and his brother George hired Wallace to create a series of photographs of their remarkably successful hardware and supply business. The Goodridge studio had worked for the Morley family regularly over the years. In fact, more than thirty years earlier, in 1880, William had photographed the Morley residence at 1617 South Washington, which George W. Morley continued to occupy with his daughter Letitia and her husband, George H. Boyd (see figure 5.6b). In 1913 Wallace's series for the Morleys began with a portrait of the brothers in their private office (figure 7.26a). The photograph is a remarkable one for several reasons.

Figure 7.25a. "Saginaw Club, Semi-Centennial Reunion," 1907. Silver print, 10 x 8 inches. Goodridge Brothers Studio, Saginaw, Mich. Historical Society of Saginaw County, Inc.

Figure 7.25b. "Semi-Centennial Banquet," 1907. Silver print, 10 x 8 inches. Goodridge Brothers Studio, Saginaw. Mich. Historical Society of Saginaw County, Inc.

Figure 7.26a. "Edward W. and George W. Morley," 1913. Silver print, 7³⁄₁₆ x 5 inches, dark gray bristol board mount, 9¹⁵⁄₁₆ x 7¹⁵⁄₁₆ inches. Goodridge Brothers Studio, Saginaw, Mich. Historical Society of Saginaw County, Inc.

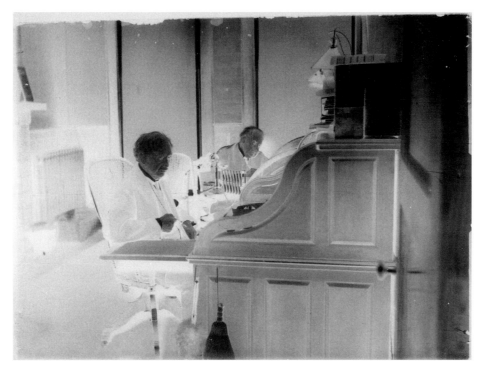

Figure 7.26b. "Edward W. and George W. Morley," 1913. Dry plate negative, 6⅞ x 4¾ inches. Goodridge Brothers Studio, Saginaw, Mich. Historical Society of Saginaw County, Inc.

Figure 7.27. "The Hunters," ca. 1913. Silver print, 6¼ x 4¾ inches, dark gray bristol board mount, 10 x 7¹⁵⁄₁₆ inches. Goodridge Brothers Studio, Saginaw, Mich. Collection of Dave Tinder.

Less than a year after the portrait of the brothers was made, George W. Morley died on April 10, 1914. The photograph also is signed by Edward W. Morley and was given to his son Albert J. Morley. Mr. Morley wrote on the back of the portrait: "For A. J. Morley. Edward Morley and George W. Morley. In their Private Office, November 13, 1913. Edward W. Morley has a newspaper in his hand. The above writing was done by me. Saginaw, Michigan Dec 27th 1913. Edward Morley." And of most significance is the fact that although several hundred Goodridge photographs are presently known, few negatives are extant, among them figure 7.26b, that of Edward and George Morley at their desks in their private office, also made on November 13.

For the same series, Wallace also made several photographs of the Morley Brothers store win-

dows along the west side of North Washington. Perhaps because it was November, one of the window displays featured a variety of pheasant-, duck-, and deer-hunting supplies for immediate use or to be purchased as Christmas presents. The selection of shotguns and rifles, priced from less than $20 to more than $100, reveals that Morleys had something for just about every hunter. A prominently featured painting of a brace of pheasants in one of the displays may well have caught the attention of the two hunters in figure 7.27 who stopped at Morleys before heading out and at the Goodridge studio upon their return.

As it became increasingly successful, the Herzog Art Furniture Company, which had been founded by John L. Herzog, Sr., in 1899, also regularly turned to the Goodridge studio to document

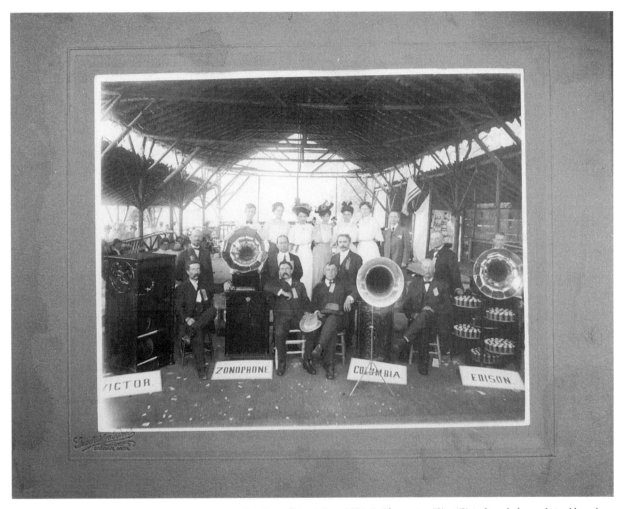

Figure 7.28a. "Herzog Art Furniture Company, Display, Annual Picnic," ca. 1906–7. Silver print, 9¾ x 7⅞ inches, dark gray bristol board mount, 13⅞ x 10⅞ inches. Goodridge Brothers Studio, Saginaw, Mich. Collection of Frankenmuth Historical Association.

its success. Herzog was born in Frankenmuth in 1867 and studied furniture design and construction in Saginaw and Grand Rapids and throughout Europe for more than a decade after 1885. In the spring of 1899, shortly after his return from Europe, Herzog and two friends, Joseph Grohman and August Miessler, organized a small cabinet-making business on Saginaw's west side at the corner of Cass and Niagara Streets. Within months of its organization the business ran short of capital, and Herzog turned for assistance to John L. Jackson.[46]

By 1899 Jackson, a forty-five-year-old Saginaw County native, had organized three successful businesses—the McGregor & Jackson Boiler Works, the Saginaw Plate Glass Factory, and the Saginaw Brick Company—and kept a sharp eye out for other potentially successful investment opportunities. He judged John Herzog to be one and provided the capital that allowed the fledgling furniture business to establish itself and quickly prosper. Within the year Jackson became president and Herzog general manager of the rejuvenated company.[47] Jackson's judgment was excellent. In 1910 or possibly 1912, when Herzog introduced his "bulge arch" design, especially well suited to wooden phonograph cabinets, the company received its first order from the Sonora Phonograph Company. By 1916 Herzog and Jackson were producing more than sixty thousand phonograph cabinets for Sonora alone and continuing to supply

Figure 7.28b. "Herzog Art Furniture Company, Sales Staff, Annual Picnic," ca. 1906–7. Silver print, 9¾ x 7⅞ inches, dark gray bristol board mount, 13⅞ x 10⅞ inches. Goodridge Brothers Studio, Saginaw, Mich. Collection of Frankenmuth Historical Association.

other phonograph producers as well. Figure 7.28a, made by Wallace in 1906 or 1907, has Herzog seated to the left and Jackson to the right in the center of the photograph. Seated to the left of Herzog is Joseph Grohman, his original partner, who had become personnel manager. They are flanked by company staff, family members, and examples of the cabinets produced in Saginaw for the phonograph companies represented.[48] According to Herzog's obituary, it was shortly before this photograph was made that he had met Thomas A. Edison and had won a contract to produce cabinets for the Edison phonograph in the photograph. Herzog became "a close friend of the inventor and . . . was given a portrait of Edison by the inventor"

himself.[49] A photograph of Edison presenting his portrait to Herzog remains among the family photographs.

Herzog and Jackson were known as progressive employers. Herzog in particular organized a night school at the factory where "young men and [apprentice] boys are afforded practical instruction in drawing, designing and woodworking—advantages equal to what a student gets in a technical school." In addition, Herzog's policy of generous incentive bonuses and promotion from within the ranks of the company served as the basis for positive relations with the company's more than one thousand employees. Each summer the company also celebrated the year's success with "a huge excursion and picnic at some lake or city, which is financed by the company, though earned by the workers."[50] Figure 7.28b, made by Wallace at the same time as 7.28a, is a photograph of Herzog and company salesmen, including John Gottschalk and Otto Carpell, both to Herzog's right, at the annual celebration. Notice the rustic pavilion to the left rear (the location for figure 7.28a), the ladies in their summer dresses, and the picnic tables scattered throughout the grove.

In 1917 the Herzog Art Furniture Company contracted with the Sonora Phonograph Company to furnish $25 million worth of phonograph cabinets for Sonora within the next ten years. As a result, Sonora moved much of its assembly operations to Saginaw the same year and the companies, for all practical purposes, merged into a single production facility ultimately controlled by Sonora. In 1927, for reasons which remain unclear, Herzog resigned from Sonora, and two years later he once again started his own furniture company, which he directed until his death in 1955. Jackson stayed on at Sonora until 1934, when he retired.[51]

During the same period, Wallace returned to Hoyt Park at the request of Saginaw's Thirty-third Infantry Regiment of the Michigan National Guard to photograph its preparations for service. The regiment originally was organized as two independent volunteer militia companies, the East Saginaw Guards and the Flint Union Greys, in December 1857 and January 1858, respectively. The units were consolidated as the Second Michigan Volunteer Infantry Regiment in April 1861 just in time for a variety of campaigns from Bull Run to Appomattox. Several subsequent reorganizations designated it as the Second and then Third Infantry Regiment of the Michigan National Guard and took the unit to Michigan's Upper Peninsula during the copper miners' strike there in 1913. Figures 7.29a and b were made either in June 1916, when the unit was mustered into federal service along the Mexican border in support of General John J. Pershing and the eleven thousand U.S. troops chasing Pancho Villa, or in August 1917, just before leaving for the French-German line and

heavy fighting in Alsace, the Marne, and Meuse-Argonne during World War I.[52]

In figure 7.29a the Supply Company and Sanitary Detachment of the regiment, which were headquartered in Saginaw, pass in review before several hundred family, friends, and neighbors scattered across the shaded ridge overlooking the playing fields in the park. The mounted officers leading the column are most likely Colonel John B. Boucher, Lieutenant Colonel Edward G. Heckel, and Majors Augustus H. Gansser, Guy M. Wilson, and Charles D. Mathews. Figure 7.29b presents several companies of the regiment as they pass before the close scrutiny of the four observers aligned to the left of the photographer. In September 1917 the regiment, shortly before it left for Europe, was redesignated as the 125th Infantry (Third Michigan), which it remains today.[53]

✦

Wallace Goodridge's ability to maintain the studio's long-standing reputation for outstanding photography for more than a quarter century following William's death was based on continuity with the past and a simultaneous but selective acceptance of change and innovation. Continuity meant that he maintained the studio's traditional commitment to the highest-quality portrait and landscape photography, as it had under Glenalvin's original leadership in York and then during William's partnership with Wallace in East Saginaw. The community's recognition of Wallace's success in continuing that tradition was demonstrated by its regularly identifying "Goodridge" as Saginaw's "official" photographer. Selective innovation meant that Wallace anticipated and incorporated the most up-to-date technical, artistic, and market-oriented changes into the studio's already well-established traditions. Much of his effort after 1890 was devoted to that goal.

As early as 1851, European photographers, including Talbot and Nadar, began experimenting with artificial lighting to create interior photographs. Although both achieved some success,

Figure 7.29a. "Parade, Hoyt Park, Third Infantry Regiment, Michigan National Guard," 1916–17. Copy of original image, 7 x 5 inches. Goodridge Brothers Studio, Saginaw, Mich. Collection of John V. Jezierski.

Figure 7.29b. "Parade, Hoyt Park, Third Infantry Regiment, Michigan National Guard," 1916–17. Copy of original image, 7 x 5 inches. Goodridge Brothers Studio, Saginaw, Mich. Collection of John V. Jezierski.

the cumbersome batteries, cables, and equipment that made the lighting and photographs possible were impractical. A decade later photographs were made in England using the intense light produced by burning magnesium wire. In October 1865 the method was first used in the United States to make a series of photographs at the home of John C. Browne in Philadelphia. Included in the portraits was Edward Wilson, editor of the influential *Philadelphia Photographer,* where the experiment was given extensive coverage. About the same time, the method of using powdered magnesium to produce an intense flash of light was proposed, but it did not become practical until two decades later.[54] There can be little doubt that the Goodridge studio experimented with magnesium wire as a light source during the 1880s (figure 5.14b is the best example extant), although it is unlikely that William or Wallace used this technique very often. In February 1888, however, the *Cleveland Gazette* reported that the "Goodridge Bros. are successfully taking pictures at midnight by the flash process."[55] Because the flash process resulted in a cloud of acrid white smoke that dispersed only very slowly, and because the flash process could be dangerous (there were five deaths attributed to it in Philadelphia alone the first years after its introduction), Wallace and William used it more often than magnesium wire, but very carefully. Few Goodridge photographs from the period before 1900, therefore, can be attributed to the magnesium flash process. After the introduction in June 1897 of A. E. Johnstone's "Safe, Clean, and Rapid Flash Machine," which made the powdered magnesium flash process efficient and practical until it was supplanted by the electric flashbulb after 1925, Wallace used Johnstone's new technology regularly to create studio and "at home" portraits.[56]

By far the most intriguing photographs created by Wallace using the new magnesium flash process after 1900 can be described, for lack of a better term, as the "Women's Night Out" series. This group of photographs, represented by figures 7.30a–d, presents an interesting case study in photo interpretation. The first image was identified more than a decade ago, and additions to the series are discov-

ered almost annually. At the present time thirteen are known. Each photograph is of a group of women in a caricature of male dress or in rather outlandish female costume. The groups range in size from nine to twenty-four individuals. Only one group (7.30b and c) appears twice. Most are mature individuals in their thirties, forties, or fifties, although one young girl and two or three teens (see, for example, the person third from the left in 7.30a) are present. Some familial connection is apparent in the faces of the subjects (see 7.30a), but most of the other individuals in the series appear to be more friends than family. All are white and, judging from the quality of dress and furnishings, at least middle class. With the exception of 7.30b and c, where the same group of women is photographed in different costume in the same room, each of the photographs was made at a different location. Nonetheless, the settings are all similar in that each is a parlor or sitting room with furnishings typical for the time, including lace curtains, brocaded wallpaper, a "Turkey" carpet, heavy wooden furniture, gas lighting, parlor stoves, elaborately framed prints, paintings, and photographs, and (in 7.30a and c) a piano. Each photograph in the series was made by Wallace on location rather than in the studio, between approximately 1905 and 1915, using the new magnesium flash process. Notice the harsh quality of the light, especially as it is reflected back from the lightest elements of each photograph (using reflectors to soften and direct the light from the flashing magnesium powder was not a practical option outside of the studio as yet) as in figure 7.30d, and the very dark, contrasting shadows directly behind each subject resulting from the brilliance of the flash.

The first photograph to be discovered in the series certainly appeared to be interesting, even unusual, in comparison to the sort of landscape and portrait work done by the studio previously. As regular additions to the series were made, however, it became more of a challenge to interpret its meaning. One collector believed that the women might be prostitutes. There are 148 different individuals in the twelve (two of the same subject) photographs. Although Saginaw was well served by brothels at the time, it is does not seem possible

272   The Final Years

Figure 7.30a. "Women's 'Night Out,'" after 1900. Silver print, 7¹⁄₁₆ x 5⅛ inches, gray bristol board mount, 9¹⁵⁄₁₆ x 7¹⁵⁄₁₆ inches. Goodridge Brothers Studio, Saginaw, Mich. Collection of John V. Jezierski.

Figure 7.30b. "Women's 'Night Out,'" after 1900. Silver print, 7⅛ x 5 inches, gray bristol board mount, 10 x 8 inches. Goodridge Brothers Studio, Saginaw, Mich. Historical Society of Saginaw County, Inc.

Figure 7.30c. "Women's 'Night Out,'" after 1900. Silver print, 7³⁄₁₆ x 5 inches, gray bristol board mount, 10 x 8 inches. Goodridge Brothers Studio, Saginaw, Mich. Historical Society of Saginaw County, Inc.

Figure 7.30d. "Women's 'Night Out,'" after 1900. Silver print, 7³⁄₁₆ x 5 inches, dark gray bristol board mount, 9¹³⁄₁₆ x 8 inches. Goodridge Brothers Studio, Saginaw, Mich. Collection of Barbara and Michael Slasinski.

that Wallace would have been able to gather and photograph such a significant portion of the profession unless as a result of some now unknown special commission. Another thought that the women were lesbians who gathered for each other's company in these private settings to which Wallace was called to make the photograph. Certainly this is a possibility, but the nature and variety of the theatrical costumes in 7.30a and d, for example, argues against such an interpretation. Both of the above perspectives, in fact, reflect more of a late-twentieth-century view of same-sex gender relations rather than the actual circumstances in the photographs. The groups actually were women who gathered regularly to enjoy each other's company and to perform, for their own pleasure, a variety of amateur theatricals. According to Carroll Smith-Rosenberg, the "twentieth-century tendency to view human love and sexuality within a dichotomized universe of deviance and normality, genitality and platonic love, is alien to the emotions and attitudes of the nineteenth century and fundamentally distorts the nature of women's emotional interaction." "Women," Smith-Rosenberg concludes, "did not form isolated dyads but were normally part of highly integrated networks. Knowing one another, perhaps related to one another, they played a central role in holding communities and kin systems together." The resulting relationships "were close, often frolicsome, and surprisingly long-lasting and devoted."[57] The costumes in 7.30a and d, the enthusiasm apparent in 7.30b and d, and the piano to the right in 7.30b and c all testify to the validity of Smith-Rosenberg's conclusions. In fact, in the summer of 1985 the author was able to interview a person who as a young girl had regularly accompanied her mother to meetings of the mother's amateur theatrical group and was included in the photograph of the group that Wallace made one evening. The interviewee, who wished to remain anonymous and who has since died, recalled Wallace as an elderly man with curly gray hair who was very businesslike in organizing the group for the pose. She remembered the large camera with the focusing cloth that the photographer used to cover his head, as well as the very bright flash and resulting smoke from the magnesium powder. She noted that her mother's club was one of several such organizations common throughout the city at the time and that they served as an effective communications network and as an informal means of integrating girls and young women into Saginaw society.[58] Obviously, the Goodridge studio's long-standing reputation for quality portraiture, but even more Wallace's use of this latest technical innovation, had made him their "official" photographer as commissions came from one Saginaw women's group after another.

At about the same time that Wallace regularly began to use the magnesium flash process as a means of making "at home" portraits for a variety of organizations and individuals, he also had contracted with the Albertype Company of Brooklyn, New York, to mass-produce prints derived from Goodridge studio photographs for a larger audience than had ever been possible before. The Albertype was a photomechanical gelatin-based printing process perfected in 1868 by Bavarian court photographer Josef Albert. The technique was patented in the United States the following year, and the rights were sold to Edward Bierstadt, brother of the painter Albert Bierstadt, who became a well-known champion of the process.[59] In 1867 Hermann Wittemann founded a printing company in Brooklyn that later obtained the rights to the Albertype from Bierstadt and, as the Albertype Company, used the process well into the next century to produce gravure-style booklets of photographic prints and postcards for customers throughout the United States, including the Goodridge studio.[60]

The most immediate result of the Goodridge-Albertype contract was the publication in July 1902 of *Goodridge's Art Souvenir of Saginaw, Michigan, U.S.A.* The *Souvenir* was a twenty- seven-page 7 ⅛ x 5 ¼ inch booklet (figure 7.31a) that was designed to celebrate both the city and the studio. A notice in the July 17, 1902, edition of the *Saginaw Evening News* reported that "Last Monday's patrons of Goodridge Brothers' photograph studio . . . were somewhat surprised at having their money refused and the work presented as a free gift instead. Mr. Goodridge . . . [explained] that he was celebrating

Figure 7.31a. "Cover, *Goodridges' Art Souvenir of Saginaw, Michigan, U.S.A.*," 1902, 7⅛ x 5¼ inches. Goodridge Brothers Studio, Saginaw, Mich., and The Albertype Co., Brooklyn, N.Y. Collection of John V. Jezierski.

Figure 7.31b. "'Residences,' *Goodridges' Art Souvenir of Saginaw, Michigan, U.S.A.*," 1902, p. 4, 7 x 5 inches. Goodridge Brothers Studio, Saginaw, Mich., and The Albertype Co., Brooklyn, N.Y. Collection of John V. Jezierski

Figure 7.31c. "'Saginaw Views,' *Goodridges' Art Souvenir of Saginaw, Michigan, U.S.A.*," 1902, p. 22, 7 x 5 inches. Goodridge Brothers Studio, Saginaw, Mich., and The Albertype Co., Brooklyn, N.Y. Collection of John V. Jezierski.

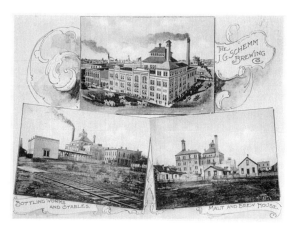

Figure 7.31d. "'The J.G. Schemm Brewing Co.,' *Goodridges' Art Souvenir of Saginaw, Michigan, U.S.A.*," 1902, p. 23, 7 x 5 inches. Goodridge Brothers Studio, Saginaw, Mich. Collection of John V. Jezierski.

Figure 7.31e. "'City of Saginaw,' *Goodridges' Art Souvenir of Saginaw, Michigan, U.S.A.*," 1902, p. 25, 7 x 5 inches. Goodridge Brothers Studio, Saginaw, Mich. Collection of John V. Jezierski.

the thirty-ninth anniversary of his business career in Saginaw. . . . Each customer also received a pictorial souvenir of Saginaw."[61]

The brief introductory text of the anniversary *Souvenir* presented to Goodridge patrons that day described Saginaw as "a city of beautiful homes, broad streets and avenues lined with shade trees, . . . unsurpassed rail and water facilities, . . . inexhaustible mineral resources, . . . [and situated in] the center of the richest agricultural district in the United States."[62] There then followed a photographic collage of private residences (7.31b), civic structures and landmarks (7.31c), commercial and industrial establishments (7.31d), and a concluding bird's-eye-view panorama of the city of Saginaw and the valley north to Saginaw Bay (7.31e).

Unlike the 1878 and 1882 photographic collages that the studio created for the *New York Daily Graphic* (see figures 5.22 and 5.24), which emphasized the commercial development and economic potential of a youthful East Saginaw in the midst of the peak years of the pine lumber boom, the 1902 *Souvenir* took the measure of a much more mature metropolitan area. The montage of private homes that Wallace presented (it is not clear whether the *Souvenir* was financially subsidized by subscribers) included not only the mansions of the few lumber barons or industrial magnates who had dominated the city's early development but now also the more modest dwellings of a comfortable middle class who had become the basis for the city's future. Notice that figure 7.31b features the substantial but not opulent residences of seven of Saginaw's physicians, with the home of close Goodridge friend and political compatriot Dr. Charles W. Ellis, Jr., given a most prominent position in the upper left. Also included were the homes of Saginaw haberdashers Max and Carl Heavenrich and merchants R. H. Roys, Corning Gurdon, and J. C. Mercer. Views of the city (figure 7.31c), which included both east and west banks of a now consolidated Saginaw, emphasized the growth that already had taken place and the structures (courthouse, post office, and city hall) that would provide a solid foundation for the future. A broadly based cultural life, fostered by institutions like the Academy of Music and Hoyt Library, even extended to the river, which had come to be viewed as a place for leisure and recreation and not merely as a commercial artery. Where commerce and industry were included (figure 6.31d), the emphasis was on the necessary diversification that had taken place as the pine lumber boom had passed. Saginaw Plate Glass and J. G. Schemm Brewing Company, for example, were industries that had begun during or as a consequence of the lumber boom but which

now would survive on their own. More than any of the others, however, figure 7.31e best summed up the *Souvenir's* sense of the past and vision for the future. In it Wallace placed the city of Saginaw at the very center of a vast industrial, agricultural, and commercial region. More than any other of the *Souvenir's* illustrations, the bird's-eye view also served as a symbol of the technological innovation and bold enterprise that Wallace had identified as the themes for the studio's final decades as it entered the twentieth century.

Since its establishment in East Saginaw, the Goodridge studio regularly had provided photographs to national publications like *Leslie's Illustrated* and the *New York Daily Graphic,* and to the H. R. Page & Co. for inclusion in its *Saginaw Illustrated.* The studio also would continue to collaborate with other Saginaw photographers in joint ventures such as the *Souvenir Views of Saginaw's Greatest Flood* of 1904 (see figures 7.22a and b). And to this day Goodridge photographs continue to serve as the most important visual documents and most often used illustrations for the period. Yet the 1902 *Souvenir* differs from these other ventures on two accounts. First, it was an attempt by Wallace to revive the studio as a major local *publisher* of photographs on a basis not unlike that which he and William had envisioned with the 1880s "Picturesque Michigan" series of stereo views that the studio had continued to advertise even after William's death. The Albertype Company was credited as the producer and printer of the *Souvenir,* but it was "Copyrighted 1902 by Goodridge Bros., photographers *and* publishers of Photo Art Souvenirs, Saginaw, Michigan, U.S.A.," clearly suggesting Wallace's intention not to limit the studio to this lone 1902 publication.[63]

The same *Saginaw Evening News* article, in fact, which reported publication of the *Souvenir* also stated that "Mr. Goodridge has an unusually fine collection of lumbering views, most of which were taken in the height of the lumbering industry of the Saginaw Valley," and apparently Wallace saw no reason not to make profitable use of them.[64] It also is clear that in serving as the publisher of the Photo Art Souvenirs the studio intended to integrate the work of other Saginaw Valley photographers into its own large inventory of photographs. The 1902 *Souvenir* contains 147 individual images organized as seventeen photocollages. Some of the views—"Saginaw River from R.R. Bridge" in figure 7.31c, for example—obviously were selected from the Goodridge photo archives, but the great majority were of more recent vintage, such as the view of the new city hall, the recently completed federal building and post office in the same illustration, and the bird's-eye view of the city which Wallace most likely had purchased from a now unidentifiable source. Few of the contemporary residential, civic, or commercial and industrial views in the *Souvenir* correspond to Goodridge photographs made before 1902. No doubt Wallace or a studio staff photographer made most of the new views for the *Souvenir*, but as *publisher* Wallace also purchased the rights to photographs from other Saginaw sources. Which photographs fall into either category is now impossible to determine.

The 1902 *Souvenir* also is significant because the contract with the Albertype Company, a major publisher of photo-derived postcards, opened to Wallace a whole new medium and market for Goodridge photographs, especially the multitude of images that had been created for the *Souvenir*. And it may have been this opportunity to sell photographs to postcard publishers after 1902 that caused Wallace not to issue the additional "Photo Art Souvenirs" that he had earlier planned. Postcards, both printed by individuals and issued by government postal systems, were introduced in Europe and the United States between 1861 and 1870. These early postcards were designed to be an inexpensive and practical means of communication and often did not bear illustrations. The Chicago Columbian Exposition of 1893 popularized the illustrated postcard as a "souvenir," but because no writing was permitted on the back of the card they were not especially successful, usually resulting in brief "Greetings From" messages or disfigured illustrations. In addition, privately printed postcards were subject to the two-cent first-class letter rate, while government-issued cards were mailed for one cent. On May

19, 1898, however, Congress passed an act that standardized the format of the cards and allowed private printers to publish and sell postcards that could be mailed at the one-cent rate. Subsequently, in 1907, the law provided for illustrated cards with divided backs that allowed for both an address and a written message.[65] As a result, untold millions of postcards have flowed from every corner of the world since and have become an accepted and expected means of documenting "I was here!"

Congressional action had been prompted by the large publishing companies like Albertype, the American Souvenir-Card Company, and especially the Detroit Publishing Company, which issued its first set of the new one-cent private mailing cards on July 1, 1898, the very day the new law went into effect. The large publishers dominated the national and international markets, but room remained for the regional and local publisher who often had a specialized market in view. Quite often the large national or even smaller regional publishers also purchased views from or printed postcards for local news agents, tobacconists, druggists, dry goods shops, and photography studios.[66] It was here, in particular, as a source of photographic views for the major postcard publishers but also as one of the multitude of clients for whom they printed local issues, that Wallace Goodridge sought his niche in the rapidly expanding postcard industry.

Between 1902 and 1910 most of the photographs of the commercial, industrial, cultural, and civic institutions included in the 1902 *Souvenir* published by the Goodridge studio also were issued as postcards. For reasons of privacy or market size, however, none of the residences included in the *Souvenir* are known to have been published as postcards. During the decade Wallace also sold existing photographs to and created new images for national, regional, and local postcard publishers. Because catalogues and checklists for most publishers, large and small, do not exist, it is impossible to determine with any certainty the exact number of Goodridge photographs published as postcards or which publishers purchased more or less of the studio's photographs. An analysis of both private and public holdings of

Figure 7.32a. "City Hall, Saginaw, Mich.," 1902–10, postcard, 5½ x 3½ inches. Goodridge Brothers Studio, Saginaw, Mich., and Tom Jones, Publisher, Cincinnati, Ohio. Collection of William Oberschmidt.

Figure 7.32b. "U.S. Post Office, Saginaw, Mich.," 1902–10, postcard, 5½ x 3½ inches. Goodridge Brothers Studio, Saginaw, Mich., and Illustrated Post Card Company of New York City. Collection of Frank M. Polasky.

Figure 7.32c. "Masonic Temple, Saginaw, Mich.," 1902–10, postcard, 5½ x 3½ inches. Goodridge Brothers Studio, Saginaw, Mich., and Western Post Card Co., Detroit, Mich. Collection of Frank M. Polasky.

Figure 7.32d. "Saginaw River Scene, Saginaw, Mich.," 1902–10, postcard, 5½ x 3½ inches. Goodridge Brothers Studio, Saginaw, Mich., and Tom Jones, Publisher, Cincinnati, Ohio. Collection of Frank M. Polasky.

Figure 7.32e. "Saginaw River, South from Pere Marquette Railroad Bridge—Saginaw, Mich.," 1902–10, postcard, 5½ x 3½ inches. Goodridge Brothers Studio, Saginaw, Mich., and J. Murray Jordan, Publisher, Philadelphia, Pa. Collection of Frank M. Polasky.

Figure 7.32f. "Saginaw River and East Side, Saginaw, Mich.," 1902–10, postcard, 5½ x 3½ inches. Goodridge Brothers Studio, Saginaw, Mich., and Illustrated Post Card Company of New York City. Collection of William Oberschmidt.

Figure 7.33a. "Court St., Saginaw W., Mich." 1902–10, postcard, 5½ x 3½ inches. Goodridge Brothers Studio, Saginaw, Mich., and Western Post Card Co., Detroit, Mich. Collection of William Oberschmidt.

Figure 7.33b. "Coal Mine, Saginaw, Mich.," 1902–10, postcard, 5½ x 3½ inches. Goodridge Brothers Studio, Saginaw, Mich., and Western Post Card Co., Detroit, Mich. Collection of William Oberschmidt.

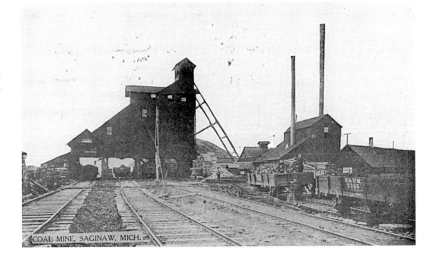

Figure 7.33c. "Women's Hospital, Saginaw, Mich.," 1902–10, postcard, 5½ x 3½ inches. Goodridge Brothers Studio, Saginaw, Mich., and Western Post Card Co., Detroit, Mich. Collection of Frank M. Polasky.

Figure 7.33d. "Genesee Ave., Saginaw, Mich.," 1902–10, postcard, 5½ x 3½ inches. Goodridge Brothers Studio, Saginaw, Mich., and Western Post Card Co., Detroit, Mich. Collection of William Oberschmidt.

Figure 7.33e. "Pere Marquette R.R. Station, E. Side, Saginaw, Mich." 1902–10, postcard, 5½ x 3½ inches. Goodridge Brothers Studio, Saginaw, Mich., and Western Post Card Co., Detroit, Mich. Collection of Barbara and Michael Slasinski.

Figure 7.33f. "Central School, Saginaw, Mich.," 1902–10, postcard, 5½ x 3½ inches, Goodridge Brothers Studio, Saginaw, Mich., and Western Post Card Co., Detroit, Mich. Collection of William Oberschmidt.

Figure 7.34a. "Riverside Park, Saginaw, Mich.," 1902–10, postcard, 5½ x 3½ inches. Goodridge Brothers Studio, Saginaw, Mich., and C. H. Stephens, Saginaw, Mich. Collection of William Oberschmidt.

Figure 7.34b. "Eddy Building, Saginaw, Mich.," 1902–10, postcard, 5½ x 3½ inches. Goodridge Brothers Studio, Saginaw, Mich., and F. J. Kelsey & Son, Saginaw, Mich. Collection of William Oberschmidt.

Figure 7.34c. "Genesee Avenue, Saginaw, Mich.," 1902–10, postcard, 5½ x 3½ inches. Goodridge Brothers Studio, Saginaw, Mich., and F. J. Kelsey & Son, Saginaw, Mich. Collection of William Oberschmidt.

Figure 7.34d. "Moonlight Scene on the Saginaw River, Saginaw, Mich.," 1902–10, postcard, 5½ x 3½ inches. Goodridge Brothers Studio, Saginaw, Mich., and John E. Ferris Color Press, Saginaw, Mich. Collection of William Oberschmidt.

Figure 7.34e. "Arbeiter Hall," 1902–10, postcard, 5½ x 3½ inches. Goodridge Brothers Studio, Saginaw, Mich., and H. Watson & Co., Saginaw, Mich. Collection of Frank M. Polasky.

Saginaw postcards reveals that more than fifty Goodridge photographs were issued as postcards between 1902 and 1910. At the present time, for reasons which remain unclear, only two photographs among the fifty (figures 7.35a and b) are known to have been created, printed as postcards, and distributed directly by the Goodridge studio.

Three of the large, national postcard publishers purchased Goodridge photographs. The Rotograph Company of New York City issued at least two, but the numbering system suggests it may have printed ten or more Saginaw postcards. The Detroit Publishing Company, which typically used its own staff photographers, published eighteen Saginaw postcards, only two of which it purchased

from the Goodridge studio (see figure 4.1b for the company's No. 11914, "Washington Avenue, Saginaw, Mich."). The Illustrated Postcard Card Company of New York City appears to have been Wallace's best national customer, publishing seven of his photographs, including figures 7.32b and f.[67]

Goodridge photographs were most popular with regionally based postcard publishers. Tom Jones, located in Cincinnati, issued at least four Saginaw postcards from Goodridge photographs, among them figures 7.32a and d. A postcard publisher based in Philadelphia, J. Murray Jordan, purchased nine Goodridge images and issued them as postcards. Figure 7.32 is representative of his work. Goodridge photographs were, however, most appreciated a bit closer to home. Between 1902 and 1910 the Western Post Card Company of Detroit produced more than twenty Saginaw postcards from Goodridge photographs. Figures 7.32c and 7.33a–f, demonstrate the extent of the company's interest.

Local postcard publishers produced the greatest variety of cards from Goodridge photographs. Of the five known local publishers only one, the John E. Ferris Color Press, however, actually printed and published as postcards the photographs it had purchased from Wallace. See figure 7.34d, "Moonlight Scene on the Saginaw River," for an example of one of at least six known Goodridge photographs printed by Ferris. Since the studio's earlier stereo view "Moonlight—Tittabawassee River" (figure 4.29c), which was actually sunlight manipulated to represent moonlight, technical advances in both cameras and film now allowed Wallace to create true moonlight views.

The Ferris Press also printed postcards from the photographs made by the Goodridge and other Saginaw studios that had been published as the 1904 *Souvenir of Saginaw's Greatest Flood* (see, for example, figure 7.22b). The other local "publishers," unlike Ferris, did not actually print the postcards they published. They were either news agents, tobacconists, stationers, or dry goods merchants and simply did not have the equipment or capital needed for such a production. Furthermore, it was not necessary. Dorothy Ryan describes the procedure:

> In the smaller towns . . . the druggist, department, or novelty store would send photographs or negatives to Germany to be printed as postcards. Hence the name of an obscure druggist appears frequently as the "publisher." . . . A New York City firm advertised to "make Post Cards exclusively for you from any size Photo or Print you send us, deliver them in 10 days' time, guarantee not to use your subjects for any one else and put you name on each one of them as the Publisher." Prices were quoted as five hundred cards for $4.00, one thousand for $6.00.[68]

There is no evidence that Wallace used a German printer, although that was entirely possible. A number of Saginaw postcards made from Goodridge photographs bear no publisher's name, and the studio may have had them printed locally or in Germany. In any case, Wallace was busy supplying photographs to a variety of national, regional, and local postcard publishers, wherever they may have been printed.

The end result not only was inexpensive to produce but often could be quite beautiful. Figures 7.34a, b, c, and e were each printed in Germany. "Riverside Park" (7.34a), published by Charles H. Stephens, who sold newspapers, tobacco, and office supplies from two locations in Saginaw between 1905 and 1911, is an excellent example of an Albertype. Printed in Germany in various tones of greenish black, it was well suited to the massed foliage and contrasting light and shadow of the trees lining the riverbank at the park. The depth of field of the original photograph was very sharp, and Wallace had chosen the same photograph, in fact, to grace the front cover of the 1902 *Souvenir* (see figure 7.31a). "Genesee Avenue" (7.34c) and "Eddy Building" (7.34b) were published by Frank J. Kelsey and his son Charles, whose shops on Genesee and Jefferson Avenues sold everything from books and china to jewelry and cameras between 1897 and 1914. Both postcards are fine examples of the often hand-colored lithographs that were mass-produced in Germany at the time for local markets like Saginaw. In each case the printing and the tinting have enhanced somewhat the original photographs. "Eddy Building" (7.34b) and "Arbeiter Hall" (7.34e), the latter published by H. Watson and Company, the wholesale and retail china and glassware dealer at 420 Genesee, also demonstrate how the printer could manipulate and often improve the original photograph when printing it as a postcard. In the original of the "Eddy Building" four large telephone poles and their wires cut the building into a maze of windows and floors. The postcard simply eliminates them. Similarly, in the photograph of Arbeiter Hall the young man is leaning against a telephone pole identical to those along the tree line to the left of the building and towering over its roof. In the postcard the pole has been cut down to a post so that the young man has something to lean on, but it does not obscure the view of the hall.[69]

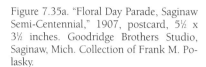
Figure 7.35a. "Floral Day Parade, Saginaw Semi-Centennial," 1907, postcard, 5½ x 3½ inches. Goodridge Brothers Studio, Saginaw, Mich. Collection of Frank M. Polasky.

Figure 7.35b. "Fraternal Day Parade, Saginaw Semi-Centennial," 1907, postcard, 5½ x 3½ inches. Goodridge Brothers Studio, Saginaw, Mich. Collection of Dave Tinder.

During summer 1907 Wallace used the week-long Saginaw semi-centennial celebration to issue the studio's own series of postcards. Figures 7.35a and b, "Floral Day" and "Fraternal Day," are the only known examples of a series which may have included seven to ten postcards. In fact, at about the same time, the Goodridge studio also had teamed up with a manufacturer on the west bank of the Saginaw River, the Hatfield Card Company, to produce figures 7.35c–e, "Eleven Photo Views of Saginaw, Mich., Semi-Centennial Week, August 18 to 24, 1907." The eleven views, in both perspective and process, are identical to figures 7.35a and b, which the studio published and printed on its own, and may even duplicate as yet unidentified post-

cards from the Goodridge series. The Goodridge-Hatfield collaboration is a superb example of the technical and artistic quality possible at the local level in photography and printing at that time. Unfortunately, little is known of the Hatfield Card Company beyond its west Saginaw location, and no individual postcards of the eleven views are extant.

Analysis of the postcards published from Goodridge photographs also reveals that the same photograph often was used by several different publishers. Whether Wallace sold the rights to each of them or the photograph circulated from company to company is not clear. According to Ryan, postcard printers, both in Europe and in North America, offered a "guarantee not to use

Figure 7.35c. "Cover, Eleven Photo Views . . . Semi-Centennial Week," 1907, postcard folder, 5½ x 3½ inches. Goodridge Brothers Studio, Saginaw, Mich., and Hatfield Card Company, Saginaw, Mich. Collection of William Oberschmidt.

are all made from the same Goodridge photograph, but publisher Tom Jones has cropped "d" to reduce the foreground, while publisher J. Murray Jordan has retained the entire photograph in "e" but reduced its size to fit the format of his postcard series. Illustrated Post Card Company in "f" went even further and added light blue hand-tinting to sky and river and silver glitter to enhance all horizontal lines ashore, on the bridge, and along the rafts of logs. We can only guess which of the versions sold the best.

Western Post Card Company of Detroit, which was operated by Alex I. Kaufman at 275 Gratiot Avenue until 1911, also printed Goodridge photographs as postcards.[71] For example, it issued versions of figures 7.32a, "City Hall," and 7.32c, "Masonic Temple," and also published a black-and-white copy of figure 4.1b, "Washington Avenue," which the Detroit Publishing Company had printed in color in 1907. Most often Western Post Card, which published more postcards based on Goodridge photographs than any other national, regional, or local company, chose its postcards from a distinctive but very typical group of Goodridge photographs. Figures 7.33a–f include many of the Goodridges' favorite photo subjects—schools, stations, and street scenes—but also more recent additions to the Saginaw scene like the Flint & Pere Marquette's "Coal Mine" and the recently organized "Women's Hospital."

Goodridge photographs from the 1902 *Souvenir* not only were the source for a multitude of postcards published during the first decade of the century but also served as the illustrations for *Views of Saginaw and Vicinity* published for the S. H. Knox & Company, a Saginaw variety store, by the L. H. Nelson Co. of Portland, Maine, in 1904. The 1904 *Views of Saginaw* was larger, 8 x 10 inches, and a bit longer, thirty-two pages, than the *Souvenir*. And rather than print several pages of photocollages of private residences, as Wallace had in 1902, the 1904 *Views* concentrated instead on larger photographs of streetscapes and commercial and civic structures. The difference was dictated largely by the purpose of the publication. Unlike the 1902 *Souvenir*, which was a celebration of indi-

your subjects for any one else," but with the exception of the Detroit Publishing Company, postcards rarely were copyrighted and the same image often served several masters.[70] For example, figure 7.32a, "City Hall," was published by at least five postcard companies (Tom Jones, Western Post Card, J. Murray Jordan, Illustrated Post Card, and F. J. Kelsey) between 1900 and 1910, all using exactly the same Goodridge photograph in exactly the same form. Four companies similarly printed postcards of the 1898 chateau-style post office (figure 7.32b), and three of the Masonic Temple (7.32c). On occasion printers and publishers might also employ the same photograph to create a postcard but alter it in a variety of ways to suit their needs. For example, figures 7.32d, e, and f

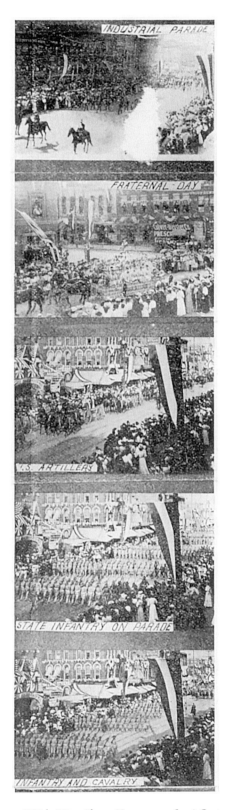

Figure 7.35d. "Five Photo Views . . . Semi-Centennial Week," 1907, postcard folder, 1¼ x 5¼ inches. Goodridge Brothers Studio, Saginaw, Mich., and Hatfield Card Company, Saginaw, Mich. Collection of William Oberschmidt.

Figure 7.35e. "Five Photo Views . . . Semi-Centennial Week," 1907, postcard folder, 1¼ x 5¼ inches. Goodridge Brothers Studio, Saginaw, Mich., and Hatfield Card Company, Saginaw, Mich. Collection of William Oberschmidt.

Figure 7.36a. "Lumber Yard of Booth & Boyd," 1904. Silver print, 7 x 5 inches. Goodridge Brothers Studio, Saginaw, Mich. Published in S. H. Knox & Co., *Views of Saginaw and Vicinity*, p. 10. Collection of William Oberschmidt.

Figure 7.36b. "Scene in Sugar Beet Field," 1904. Silver print, 7 x 5 inches. Goodridge Brothers Studio, Saginaw, Mich. Published in S. H. Knox & Co., *Views of Saginaw and Vicinity*, p. 30. Collection of William Oberschmidt.

Figure 7.36c. "At Federal Park, Gov. A. T. Bliss Presenting the Soldiers' Fountain to the City of Saginaw," 1904. Silver print, 7 x 5 inches. Goodridge Brothers Studio, Saginaw, Mich. Published in S. H. Knox & Co., *Views of Saginaw and Vicinity*, p. 32. Collection of William Oberschmidt.

vidual accomplishment, the Goodridge studio, the S. H. Knox & Company, and L. H. Nelson had designed the 1904 *Views of Saginaw* to explain, facilitate, and publicize Saginaw's transition from the lumber-based economy of the previous decades to the industrial and agricultural diversification that was only beginning to take hold after 1900. The introductory page set the theme for the publication by observing that while "the disappearance of the pine forests before the axe of the woodsmen led to

a great change in the character of the industries of Saginaw, . . . [and] while it is true that many wealthy and prosperous firms yet engage in the lumber trade and allied lines of business, it is of especial note that no city in Michigan has a more varied total of manufactured products, . . . [that] the adjacent land has been found admirably adapted to the raising of beet sugar and nine thousand eight hundred acres are under cultivation for that purpose, . . . [and that] this busy community . . . will compare favorably with any city in the country."[72] Consequently, the *Views of Saginaw* not only duplicated most of the images contained in the 1902 *Souvenir*, including figures 7.32a–d, 7.33d, and 7.34a–c, but added a significant selection from the Goodridge photo archives to celebrate Saginaw's glory during the heyday of the timber boom, such as copies of figures 5.12b, "Log Drive, Tittabawassee River," 3.14c, Curt Emerson's "Halls of Montezumez" (sic) and 7.36a, "Lumber Yard of Booth & Boyd," which continued to operate a planing and finishing mill at the corner of Holden and Baum Streets under the direction of George H. Boyd, although James L. Booth had died the previous year.[73]

Rather than focusing on the past, the *Views of Saginaw* concentrated on the city's potential for the future. Coal mining, manufacturing, and especially agriculture were singled out for particular attention. Figure 7.36b, "Scene in Sugar Beet Field," for example, with father and young son obviously photographically spliced into the midst of a sea of sugar beets, blatantly promotes the crop as the valley's agricultural salvation in the new century.[74] And as if to signal its respect for the past but optimism for the future, the *Views of Saginaw* concluded with figure 7.36c, a Goodridge photograph of Governor Aaron T. Bliss presenting his "Soldiers' Fountain" to the citizens of Saginaw at Federal Park. The park was located on land between the new post office and Hoyt Library bounded by Jefferson, Warren, Janes, and Germania (now Federal) Streets. The "Soldiers Fountain," with its six-foot, three-inch bronze statue of a Union infantryman in full uniform, was later moved to Bliss Park with the expansion of the post office.[75]

———◆◆◆———

At the same time that Wallace was able to continue the Goodridge studio's long tradition of quality portraiture and explore new media for land and urban scapes, he also actively directed the studio in its experiments with a variety of new film and photographic technologies. In these ventures Wallace was ably assisted by nephew John F. Goodridge, William's youngest son. Only six years old when his father died in 1890, John naturally turned to his uncle for support and direction. Wallace saw to his education and by 1903 had brought John into the family business, making him a partner in 1907. Unlike his father, however, John Goodridge was attracted more by the technical than the artistic aspects of photography. He had worked for a short time as a teenager for the Flint & Pere Marquette Railroad, where he discovered an interest in mechanics and electricity. Even after he had joined Wallace at the family studio he also continued to work as an electrician and projectionist at several local vaudeville and movie theaters.[76] John became, therefore, the logical person to implement Wallace's ideas about the possibilities of the new technologies. Together uncle and nephew explored the potential of three new and exciting techniques.

At just about the time that John joined the studio on a full-time basis, Wallace placed an advertisement in the 1906 *Illustrated and Commercial Review of Saginaw, Michigan,* which stated that "while portraiture is the specialty [of this studio and] a large amount of commercial and landscape work is done," the Goodridges also were "experts in X-ray and surgical operative cases."[77] The ad is an interesting one for several reasons. It had been little more than a decade since the discovery of X-rays by Wilhelm Konrad Röntgen at Würzberg in 1895. Yet within a year of the discovery, according to one scholar, "more than a thousand publications about X-rays appeared" and stimulated "their immediate use in camera images for medical diagnoses."[78]

Initially, studio photographers, in association with the medical profession, led the way in the development of the technology until radiology attained a more formal organization during the following decade. For example, John Carbutt, the highly regarded English-born photographer who had settled in Philadelphia, where he pioneered the mass production of gelatin dry plates, lantern slides, and magnesium flash powder, also began the production of X-ray film there before 1900.[79] As a result, scores of photographers across the United States advertised, like the Goodridges, X-ray photography in their studios. By 1905, however, most had abandoned the technology to their medical brethren in the face of an increasing awareness of its hazards.[80] The Goodridge studio advertisement is significant in that it first appeared only at the very end of this "X-ray in the photography studio" period. By 1905 most X rays were being made in a medical setting by trained technicians. In the past the Goodridge studio had often been the first, in either York or East Saginaw, to experiment with the latest innovations. Perhaps the studio had been making X rays for years before including the information in the 1906 advertisement. Furthermore, the ad does not tell us whether Wallace and John were aware of the dangers X-ray photography posed, whether the studio made more than a few experimental X-ray photographs, or whether it was simply a well-designed ploy to attract customers, much like the company that used a similar technology during the 1950s to test the fit of children's shoes. Figure 7.1 shows a photograph of the silhouette of a hand that is a positive print made by using an X ray as the negative. This had been a very popular form of commercialized X-ray photography for a short time at the turn of the century.[81] No other examples of Goodridge X-ray photography are known to exist, and the technology likely never became more than a curiosity for the studio. Soon thereafter Wallace and John Goodridge turned their attention to another technology which, unlike the occasional X ray, provided the studio with a regular clientele through at least 1920.

Soon after the introduction of the daguerreotype, photographers began searching for a camera technology that would enable them to duplicate the wide-angle vision of the human eye. Friedrich von Martens, an engraver-photographer living in Paris in 1844, is credited with development of the Megaskop, a camera with a movable lens that panned across a 150-degree field resulting in a 4½ x 15 panoramic view on a curved daguerreotype plate. Other systems followed. For example, in 1862 two Englishmen, John R. Johnson and John A. Harrison, patented a camera, the Pantascope, that rotated on a circular base while a string-pulley arrangement exposed a wet collodian plate as it moved past the exposing slot. Neither the von Martens nor subsequent improvements like the Johnson-Harrison system proved to be practical. Most studios that created panoramic photographs before 1900 did so by making a sequence of overlapping photographs and then piecing them together to form a single panoramic image. The Goodridge brothers apparently did not employ either the von Martens or Johnson-Harrison cameras, but as early as 1870 they had begun to construct a variety of panoramic views. Figures 3.15a–c, for example, were made by printing portions of a larger wet-plate collodian negative on two cartes de visite and then joining the two-part image with linen tape to create a panoramic view of the river and/or city. In 1876 the studio also created and displayed a multi-part

panorama described as "photographic views showing the entire river front of East Saginaw at highwater . . . [with] Carrollton and Saginaw City . . . in the distance. The picture is forty-three inches long, and every family in the city should have one." A portion of it was published two years later in the *New York Daily Graphic* as the centerpiece of "Views in East Saginaw, Mich." (see figure 5.22).[82]

It was only after the introduction of celluloid roll film by George Eastman in 1888, however, that the creation of single-negative panoramic photographs became a practical possibility. By 1899 Eastman Kodak Co. was marketing its No. 4 Panoram Kodak, which enabled amateur photographers to create panoramic prints as large as 3½ x 12 inches. Professional photographers required something more substantial to produce larger and sharper commercial views. The solution came in 1905 in the form of the Cirkut camera developed and introduced by the Rochester Panoramic Camera Co., which soon merged with Century Camera Co., a subsidiary of Eastman Kodak. The Cirkut resembled the typical view camera but was designed to make panoramas, which it did "by revolving on a geared tripod head while the film moves in the opposite direction past a narrow slit at the focal plane." The cameras were numbered according to the width of the film, for example, the No. 5 or No. 10 Cirkut. The latter was the most versatile available in that it could be loaded with 6-, 8-, or 10-inch film and expose a negative up to 12 feet long. Panoramas of 2 to 4 feet were typical. The Cirkut's primary limitation was its inability to freeze action, and panoramas from the period sometimes include blurred faces or "ghost" images as persons and vehicles moved through the field of the camera's vision. The camera's slow but steady panning action also allowed Cirkut photographers to employ "a popular trick . . . [by having] a person at one end of a group run behind the camera and pose at the other end as the camera panned across the scene. By doing this the same person could appear on both sides of the photograph."[83] As a result there were few communities, either small towns or large cities, across the United States which during the first decades of the new century did not have their own or were visited for a time by a Cirkut photographer. The Goodridges, of course, served the Saginaw area.

Between 1910 and 1920 Wallace, but more likely John Goodridge, used a No. 10 Cirkut to create a wonderful series of panoramic photographs for Saginaw Valley clients. Some of the photographs were quite small by the standards of the day, only 6 x 24 inches, but others would be mammoth 8 x 42 panoramic views of most of the residents of an entire community. In 1913 the studio made several panoramas. Among them is figure 7.37, which was commissioned to commemorate the May 10 laying of the cornerstone for a substantial addition to the Herzog Art Furniture Company manufacturing complex on the east side of South Michigan Avenue between Stewart and Florence Streets. John Herzog only recently had introduced his "bulge arch design" cabinet, and the company had begun to receive regular orders from Sonora and other phonograph manufacturers. Hence the need for the additional manufacturing, display, and office space. And in the tradition of positive Herzog management-employee relations, the lower level of the addition was to include a "modern lunch room . . . for the use of the employees."[84]

The ceremony and, of course, the photographer attracted a diverse group of company officers and employees (John Herzog and John Jackson are standing side-by-side immediately to the left of the cornerstone); city officials, including Mayor Albert W. Tausend, Postmaster W. S. Linton, and the newly elected president of the Saginaw Board of Trade; and the interested public, especially several local children who under the watchful eye of at least two of Saginaw's "finest" were successful in their quest to become part of the photograph. Benton Hanchett, one of the community's most important business leaders and president of the Bank of Saginaw, delivered the principal speech of the day, which traced the origins and growth of the Herzog Art Furniture Company. John Herzog himself addressed the company's future and stated that "I will not be satisfied until Herzog furniture is in every home in the Saginaw Valley." The *Couri-*

er Herald's account of the event concluded by stating that "following the lowering of the [corner]stone, a large picture of the grounds will be taken."[85]

The resulting photograph is one of the Goodridge studio's most ingenious yet effective early panoramic views. Camera placement—in the middle of South Michigan Avenue—although awkward, is the key to the success of the photograph. The effect is the illusion of the division of South Michigan into the two parts, one on either side of the photograph. Yet at the same time, the placement enhances the impact of the photograph by using the bisected street to create a V-shaped structure within the photograph with the dark mass of the factory on the left balanced by the smaller group of houses and trees on the right and with the assembled guests and open sky between. The impact is almost three-dimensional, drawing the viewer immediately into the photograph itself.

Several personal touches also add poignancy to the photograph. The only individual in the panorama who appears to be uninterested in the camera and the ceremony is the young fellow playing on the plank at the very base of the factory foundation to the far left. Ironically, only a few years later, in 1915, the same young John L. Herzog would discover a lifelong fascination with photography that gained him a national reputation as a master of the dye transfer printing process. In addition, the modest house with carriage barn immediately to the right of the construction site had been the Herzog family home since 1903. As a result of the company's expansion, which the photograph records, John Herzog became increasingly prosperous and moved his family to a larger home at 1025 Gratiot in 1922. The day following the ceremony, company officials also sealed a copper time capsule measuring 12 x 12 x 21 inches within the cornerstone. When the building was razed and the capsule opened years later, it was found to contain an extraordinary array of company memorabilia and souvenirs from the ceremony. The inventory lists copies of several local newspapers, company catalogues and stationery, the business cards of many of the dignitaries present at the ceremony, congratula-

tory letters from customers and competitors, photographs of Herzog products, a can of Automobile Pale English Varnish, and a copy of figure 7.37, the Goodridge panorama created for the event and mentioned in the newspaper report.[86]

The Herzog panorama also is interesting from an entirely different perspective. The decade following 1910 was a most important time of transition in the Saginaw Valley. By then there were few who did not realize that more than two generations of seemingly limitless growth fueled by the pine lumber boom had ended. At the same time, a more diversified economic base founded on agriculture, mining, and the manufacture of everything from phonographs to automobile components had only recently replaced the timber boom, and its future could be anticipated but not predicted with any accuracy. This sense of anticipation certainly is evident in the subject matter of the panorama. But the photograph also discloses, in a very direct way, much about the nature and magnitude of the transition Saginaw's citizens faced at the time. Even a cursory examination of its content reveals that the photograph is literally a catalogue of the longtime but also most up-to-date modes of transportation then available and suggests the already keen competition among

Figure 7.38. "First Saginaw Horse Show," 1914. Cirkut panorama, silver print, 8 x 36 inches. Goodridge Brothers Studio, Saginaw, Mich. Historical Society of Saginaw County, Inc.

Figure 7.37. "Laying the Cornerstone, Addition to Herzog Art Furniture Company," 1913. Cirkut panorama, silver print, 8 x 42 inches. Goodridge Brothers Studio, Saginaw, Mich. Historical Society of Saginaw County, Inc.

them. Many of the onlookers obviously had walked to the ceremony, but others had ridden in horse-drawn carriages or had driven in the several new automobiles parked along South Michigan. Two or three had come on their bicycles. Several, no doubt, had taken the trolley from the center of town, and at least one had arrived on a motorcycle. In addition, construction supplies already had been delivered to the site by horse-drawn wagon, on the trains that used the Michigan Central track running between the Herzog home and the factory, and likely had been brought to town aboard the vessels on the Saginaw River that flowed to the north just beyond

the factory itself. In little more than a generation, however, the horses would have disappeared, the trolleys become a novelty, and the cycles toys. But the automobile would have become the necessity that drove the valley's economy.

The transition also is apparent in a comparison of two Goodridge panoramas made shortly after the Herzog Art Furniture cornerstone ceremony. On April 9, 1914, the Goodridge studio was called on to photograph the city's first annual horse show, parade, exhibition, and sale that had been organized to celebrate the opening of the new city market in the block bordered by Franklin,

Figure 7.39. "Schust Baking Company Traveling Salesmen," 1916. Cirkut panorama, copy of original silver print, [8 x 42 inches]. Goodridge Brothers Studio, Saginaw, Mich. Originally published August 8, 1948. © 1999 *The Saginaw News.* All rights reserved. Reprinted with permission.

Baum, Janes, and Germania (Federal) just around the corner from the Goodridge studio. A notice in the *Courier-Herald* stated that "a large number of very valuable animals will be exhibited . . . from the small driving horses to heavy farm and draft stallions." The parade would form at the courthouse and proceed north on Michigan Avenue to Genesee and thence across the Genesee Bridge to the market. The paper noted that "both on the west and east sides photographs will be taken of this great exhibition of horse flesh."[87] Given the family's longtime interest in horses, there was little chance that Wallace and John Goodridge would have missed the festival even if the studio had not been invited to photograph it. The result is figure 7.38. In spite of the obviously chilly early spring day, the parade and sale attracted quite a crowd of horses and spectators. The pagoda-roofed market pavilions that opened that day continued to serve city residents for nearly a quarter century until they were dismantled in the 1930s. Later in the day the *Daily News* reported that the "First Horse Show Is Great Success."[88] Unfortunately, a "second annual" horse fair failed to follow the "first."

As if to emphasize the by then rapidly progressing transformation from horseflesh to horsepower, only two years later, in 1916, John or Wallace positioned their Cirkut almost directly across South Washington from the studio and created figure 7.39. The photograph was made to mark the deployment of the Schust Baking Company's third fleet of automobile-propelled traveling salesmen. The company was Saginaw's premier manufacturer of crackers, cookies, biscuits, and candy. According to Gustave A. Schust, the last of the family to be associated with the company after it became a division of Sunshine Biscuits, the company had first equipped its sales force with Maxwells in 1912, Fords in 1914, and then, to be fair, switched to the Chevrolets pictured here in 1916. According to the caption accompanying a later reprint of the photograph in the *Saginaw News:* "Standing proudly beside their new cars are (left to right): Adam Hilles, Pearl Pidd, Frank Pinkey, Albert Baum, Eugene Brouillette, an unidentified spectator, Albert Lunger, Harry Barin, Clyde Jennings, Eugene Schust, then vice-president and sales manager; Loren Colton, James McKay, Martin A. Salvner, William Stout, [and] John Lowe."[89]

Of even more interest than the new Chevys, however, is the 200 block of South Washington. The block was anchored on the north by the Hotel Vincent and on the south by the Academy of Music. Notice how the wide angle of vision of the Cirkut camera bends the trolley tracks running down the middle of South Washington and en-

ables them to pull both ends of the image toward the middle. Unfortunately, before the decade ended both "anchors" had been destroyed by fire and were then razed. Nonetheless, the focal point of the block, the "Goodridge Bros." studio, with its ornate facade and entablature, still stands, although all of the ornamentation has long since been removed. Close examination of the studio window display (see figure 7.7b) reveals two unidentifiable panoramas, a large photo-pastel portrait of a young woman, and at least one example of a piece of John Rogers sculpture.

Rogers, who was born in the Boston area in 1829 and worked for most of his three-decades-long career in New York City, has been characterized as "something of a one-man phenomenon in American sculpture" between 1860 and 1890. His work has been described as "the sculpture counterpart of Currier and Ives prints—an answer to the demand of an art-conscious middle class for works of art at modest prices." Consequently, Rogers's sculptures were very popular in a rapidly developing community like Saginaw that was only beginning to make the transition to middle-class gentility in the decades after 1870—the local art museum, in fact, owns a large collection handed down from the turn of the century. Rogers's works were typically "genre pieces" that "may be either sly and amusing or gentle and warm," like his first success, *Checker Players,* or "an illustration of a scene from literature," such as the well-known *Is It So Nominated in the Bond?* from *The Merchant of Venice.* Yet it was his works of "piercing social comment," including *The Slave Auction, The Fugitive's Story,* and *Wounded Scout,* for which he was best-known. Although it is impossible to identify the Rogers sculpture in the Goodridge studio window with any certainty, it was most likely one from the latter group which would have touched Goodridge's political sensibilities most poignantly and, in fact, may even have been in the family's possession for several years by 1916. *The Fugitive's Story* is part of the local art museum's Rogers collection.[90]

Further comparison of the content of figures 7.38 and 7.39, however, also reveals much about the rapid rate of change that Saginawians were experiencing at the time. The horses in figure 7.38 and the Chevrolets in figure 7.39 represent two dramatically different and ultimately incompatible worlds. As recently as 1897 the Saginaw city directory listed 37 blacksmiths, 16 horseshoers, 17 wagon and carriage makers, and 16 livery stables, but no automobile dealers or automobile-related services. Less than twenty years later, in 1914, the year of the first and last horse fair, there were still 24 blacksmiths, but only 9 horseshoers and 6 car-

Figure 7.40. "'Community Day,' Breckenridge 'Tabernacle Meeting,'" 1918. Cirkut panorama, silver print, 8 x 42 inches. Goodridge Brothers Studio, Saginaw, Mich. Breckenridge United Methodist Church.

riage makers left. In their place had come 13 automobile dealers, including Argo Electric, Duryea Motor Company, Garber Buick, Saginaw Hudson, and Sutton Reo, as well as 18 auto repair garages and 14 other categories of automobile-related services from storage facilities to tire dealers. By 1916 there were even more.[91]

Nineteen hundred eighteen was the final year that the studio is known to have made panoramas, and Wallace and John may have saved one of the largest and best of them for last (see figure 7.40). During June that year the Goodridges rode the branch of the Flint & Pere Marquette Railroad that crossed the Saginaw River south of the Centre Street bridge and headed west to Hemlock, thence through Merrill and Wheeler, and finally to their destination in Gratiot County, the town of Breckenridge. The studio had been engaged to record Breckenridge's "Community Day," the highlight of the town's spring "Tabernacle Meeting" conducted by the Zoller Evangelistic Party for the United Methodist Church that June.

According to notices published in the *Gratiot County Herald,* "A series of Revival Meetings will be held in Breckenridge, commencing June 2nd and continue all thru the month." The "Rev. Zoller, a noted evangelist will conduct the meet-

ings with the assistance of Mr. Sutherland who will have charge of the singing. Mr. Holmes, a conservatory graduate will preside at the piano." Local arrangements were "in charge of Rev. Geo. Osborne of the M. E. Church," and "other churches in the village have been invited to unite . . . and help in these meetings." Reverend Zoller, a member of the Interdenominational Association of Evangelists, was described in a letter to the *Herald* from Reverend Robinson of nearby Middleton as a "real Christian gentlemen" who was "a good preacher" and whose "work is thorough in every sense." The Zoller organization lived up to its advanced billing and served as the catalyst for a series of community activities throughout June, even attracting visitors from other towns in the area.[92]

The "Community Day" celebration was designed to be the culmination of the month-long series of revival meetings, and the panoramic photograph was commissioned to record their success. At 8 x 42 inches the panorama is not only one of the largest Cirkut photographs the studio is known to have made but also demonstrates most effectively the indispensable position the professional photographer continued to occupy in all communities, large and small, even a generation

after the introduction of the Kodak. Consider the fact that the organizers of the revival had chosen to send all the way to Saginaw in the next county for this particular photographer and likely had to pay a premium fee for the service as well. And further-more, consider that 243 men, women, and chil-dren—nearly half of the town's residents at the time—chose to join together for the photograph. And yet while the photograph certainly was not the only or even the essential result of Brecken-ridge's "Community Day" or month-long "Taberna-cle Meeting," it did serve then and has become since the symbol of what the gathering did accom-plish for the town. Is it possible to view the image without appreciating the positive sense of fellow-ship and neighborliness that the photographer has managed to record? Perhaps it is the sea of sum-mery white dresses, or the smiling faces that all seem to be related to each other, or the fact that the congregation gravitates toward the Reverend Os-borne and his wife and daughter at the very center of the photograph. Each and all of the possibilities argue for a strongly unified community—people who chose to stand with each other—even had a photographer not been there to document it.

This last of the Goodridge panoramas also of-fers some clues as to relationships within the

Goodridge studio and family at this time. In Sep-tember 1918 Wallace would celebrate his seventy-eighth birthday. Although he had been healthy and active for more than three-quarters of a century it is clear that he continued to work, especially in the field, only with the assistance of his nephew. Fig-ure 7.40 testifies to the nature of their partnership. Close analysis of the panorama reveals the pres-ence of a youngish African American male (John Goodridge) standing in three-quarter profile be-hind the last row of Breckenridge residents. His position also marks the very center of the photo-graph, with John stationed directly behind but also directly between the Reverend Osborne and his wife and daughter, who are the focal point of the panorama. It appears that John arranged the shot and then remained within it to allow Wallace, who operated the Cirkut, to position and aim the cam-era precisely in order to make this very large panoramic view.

The woman standing fifth from the right side of the photograph is most likely a member of the Goodridge family who had accompanied Wallace and John on their day-long expedition to Brecken-ridge. The woman, who appears to be an African American, was not Margaret Goodridge, Wallace's wife, who had died some years before. She is too old to be Ethel Goodridge, John's wife, and too young to be Mary Goodridge Nichols, Wallace's sister, who continued to live and work in Saginaw at the time. She does, however, bear a remarkably strong resemblance to Gertrude Goodridge (see figure 5.20), John's mother and Wallace's sister-in-law, who had earlier moved to Geneva, Ohio, after William O. Goodridge's death but who continued to make regular visits to family in Saginaw thereafter. Apparently she chose to travel with her son and brother-in-law on this fine day in June and as a result was invited to join in the photograph. Gertrude Goodridge had worked as a hairdresser with her sister-in-law Madame Nichols in Saginaw and continued her craft after moving to Ohio. The meticulous hairdo of the woman in the photograph suggests a person who best represented the results of her own skill. Goodridge family members often had accompanied William and Wallace to photo locations throughout the state, and this was simply another and ultimately final example of that long-time tradition.

At the same time that John Goodridge collaborated with his uncle Wallace in maintaining the family's reputation for the highest-quality photography, he also continued his own career as an electrician and projectionist at Saginaw's Jeffers Theatre. As a result he may have been responsible for introducing the Goodridge studio to one last innovation during its final decade. The week of June 8, 1913, the second annual convention of the Michigan Motion Picture Exhibitors met in Saginaw. The organization had been created the previous year to foster positive development of the industry statewide. During the two-day meeting in Saginaw the delegates endorsed the state legislature's recently passed law requiring annual inspection of theaters by the state fire marshal and committed themselves to work for "cleaner pictures" and "the uplifting of this important amusement." The convention also warmly applauded Miss Kate Carlisle, president of the Saginaw Federation of Women's Clubs, who called on the industry "to use their influence for the betterment of moving pictures, and particularly to join in presenting educational pictures on Saturdays for the benefit of the school children."[93]

The business sessions were tempered with the usual series of concerts and banquets, an automobile parade around the city, and special screenings of Kinemacolor[94] films at the Jeffers Theatre. The feature was *Romance of the Princess of Romania* in two reels, accompanied by a "scientific" short titled *The Moth of Asia Minor.* In addition, the delegates were treated to a film that had been made in Saginaw only shortly before the convention opened. According to the local newssheets, during April 1913 Mr. I. G. Ries of the Industrial Moving Picture Company of Chicago had visited Saginaw to create a series of films for W. S. Butterfield's Bijou Amusement Company, which operated the Jeffers Theatre (where John Goodridge was employed as a projectionist and electrician) among several others in the state at that time. The films were to be shown as short subjects in Butterfield's chain of theaters. Ries shot more than a thousand feet of film that was edited into vignettes of approximately two hundred feet each that included "the Wickes Brothers plant, the Grove and other residential scenes." In its initial form, as created by Ries, the film was titled *Saginaw in Motion* and shown first to local audiences at the Academy of Music for a run of five days starting May 7. Then it was added to the program screened for the Motion Picture Exhibitors later in June.[95]

In its much edited and spliced present form— a collage of eleven segments each a bit more than a minute in length—*Saginaw in Motion* has been retitled *Saginaw in Action,* described as being "Taken in 1913," and now sponsored by the Saginaw Firemen's Relief Association, "Whose hope it is to preserve this film so that the Saginaw of tomorrow can see the action of the Saginaw of yesteryear" (see figure 7.41).[96] There are no credits assigning the retitled and expanded film to a specific studio or source. Local tradition, however, supported by considerable internal and circumstantial evidence, attributes *Saginaw in Action,* at least in part, to the Goodridge studio. Five of the eleven segments of *Saginaw in Action,* including "City Officials," "Typical Saginaw Scenes," "John Moore School," "Herzog Art Furniture Co.," and "Saginaw Police," were

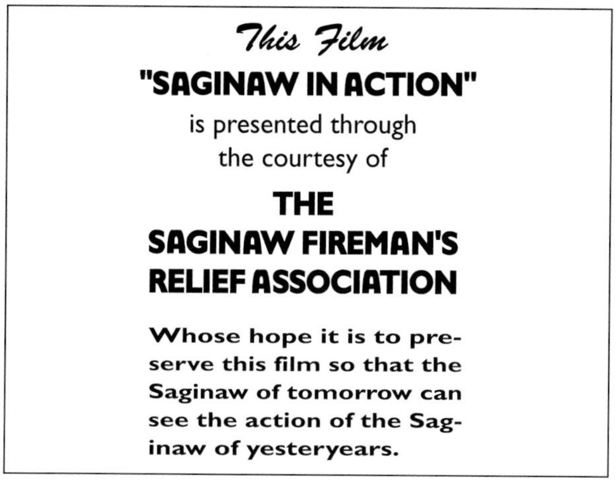

This Film

"SAGINAW IN ACTION"

is presented through
the courtesy of

THE
SAGINAW FIREMAN'S
RELIEF ASSOCIATION

**Whose hope it is to pre-
serve this film so that the
Saginaw of tomorrow can
see the action of the Saginaw of yesteryears.**

Figure 7.41. "Saginaw in Action," 1913. Film frame from contemporary video copy. Goodridge Brothers Studio, Saginaw, Mich., and Industrial Moving Picture Company, Chicago, Ill. Collection of John V. Jezierski.

originally shot by Ries in April 1913 and constituted the majority of the one thousand feet of film that became *Saginaw in Motion.* Subsequently, film segments made by the Goodridge studio titled "Houghton Normal School," "Normal Training School," "Matinee at the Bijou," and especially a long sequence devoted to the "Saginaw Fire Department" were added and the expanded version of the film was retitled *Saginaw in Action,* with the Saginaw Firemen's Relief Association as its sponsor. Whether the Goodridge studio, specifically John Goodridge, cooperated with Ries or worked independently in revising and expanding the film cannot be determined conclusively, although the former seems likely. As reported in the *Courier Herald* at the time, Ries was "enthusiastic about a picture at the Houghton School," but his "reaction to footage of the Saginaw Fire Department in action was not noted." Both segments were among the Goodridge additions to Ries's original footage.[97] Goodridge participation in the film, whether in cooperation with Ries or later on a more independent basis, clearly fits the pattern of innovation and experimentation that had become and remained one of the guiding themes of the studio's development during its final years under Wallace's direction.

The decades following William O. Goodridge's death in 1890 were a period of remarkable and continued technical innovation for the studio. Perhaps, as a result, the very same years also were a time of increasingly reduced professional, political, and personal activity for Wallace. That he continued to command the respect of his colleagues and competitors, however, is clear from the fact that in December 1906 Wallace was elected vice president of the Professional Photographers Association of Saginaw.[98]

The association has left no records, and it is not clear whether it had descended from a similar attempt to organize Saginaw Valley photographers in 1874, the union activism of the Knights of Labor during the 1880s, or as an effort on the part of the profession locally to cope with the significant changes photography continued to experience more than a decade after the "Kodak" revolution. In 1906 Saginaw's professional photographers were a small but select group. At the time the profession had achieved a remarkable degree of stability, and the association, no doubt, was created to maintain it. Of the fourteen studios operating in Saginaw at the time, two—Gem Photo and W. W. Hunt—had opened only that year but would be gone by 1908. The others had been in business an average of fifteen years by 1906, and most would continue for at least another decade. Second only to the Goodridge studio's singular six decades would be the forty-eight years of the Beckmann Brothers studio, which had begun in 1890, and the forty-year career of Charles J. Busch, which had started more recently, in 1903.[99] It was, of course, from this elite that the association chose its leadership. Benjamin S. Krupp, a Saginaw photographer from 1889 to 1913, was selected president, Wallace became vice president, and C. J. Busch and Hugo Beckmann were made secretary and treasurer, respectively.

Whether the association was as persistent as its membership is not known. If it was in existence in 1920, it may have been as a representative of this group that Wallace attended his last Photographers' Association of America convention in Chicago that August. Unfortunately, this last was not a pleasant experience for Wallace. A notice in the August 27 issue of the *Saginaw News Courier* reported that while attending the convention, "Wallace Goodridge, local photographer, . . . was the victim of pickpockets Thursday in Chicago. He lost a pocketbook containing $110."[100]

The political activism that had resulted in some degree of influence for Saginaw's African American leadership within the Michigan Republican Party during the 1870s and 1880s also gradually dissipated during the 1890s. The causes were political and personal and derived from changes at both the state and local levels which mirrored a nationwide movement away from the "Grand Old Party" on the part of many African Americans at that time.[101] Ironically, in Michigan the reforms proposed by the Pingree anti-MacMillan wing of the party during the 1890s that resulted in the establishment of a more open primary rather than managed convention system for nominating Republican candidates also had the effect of accelerating the process by blocking African American Republicans from elective office. According to David Katzman:

> The conventions had not been deliberative bodies, and they tended to approve the party committees' choices. With blacks represented at every level, and logrolling and a balanced ticket important means and ends, blacks were ensured representation on the ticket. With the primary system, however, the horse-trading and slate balancing of conventions were eliminated and majority rule prevailed. Voters who might cast their vote for any Republican, even a black one, against a Democrat in the general election were not obligated to support black candidates in the primaries.[102]

As a result, no Saginaw African American leader after 1892 attained the level of substantive or even symbolic influence within the party that William Quincy Atwood had before.

At the local level, Saginaw's African American elite—the Atwoods, the Goodridges, and the Ellises, among others—also failed to transfer its political activism and resulting power to a next generation of leaders. For example, there is no record of any po-

Figure 7.42. "The M'Kinley Minstrels," F. Opper. Cartoon, September 17, 1900, *Saginaw Evening News.*

litical activity at all on the part of Wallace L. Goodridge, Jr., or John Goodridge, and while William Atwood's sons William, Jr., Frederick, and Oliver achieved some modest success in business, largely on the foundation of their father's estate, none sought or gained any position of political consequence. In addition to the political reforms in state party organization noted above, locally the passing of the pine lumber boom, which had resulted in several decades of significant economic opportunity even for some in Saginaw's African American community, and the arrival of a new wave of black migrants who came seeking employment on production and assembly lines and who consequently found security in union activism and ultimately within the Democratic Party, combined to inhibit and to redirect the political activism of the previous two decades. Furthermore, by the mid-1890s an overt racism, perhaps stimulated by the Supreme Court's 1896 decision in *Plessy v. Ferguson,* had once again become evident. The cartoon by "F. Opper" published in the September 17, 1890, issue of the *Saginaw Evening News* (see figure 7.42) depicting McKinley, Roosevelt, and Hanna dancing as black-faced minstrels before an audience of black-faced "trusts" with Roosevelt answering Hanna's question in "black dialect" is a clear example of the prevailing attitude toward race held by some members of the community at the time.[103]

By 1900, while Saginaw's African American community continued to celebrate its race and achievements, it now did so in a manner that was less openly political and which served more often as an opportunity for socialization. In addition, there was a subtle but evident shift in the purpose and tone of the activity. It was as if Saginaw's African Americans had accepted the premise of "separate but equal" and then set out to demonstrate it to themselves and to the community at large. For example, after a lapse of more than a decade the August 1 celebration of West Indian Emancipation Day again became a significant summer holiday. In fact, in 1901 a committee headed by Wallace Goodridge that included Frederick Atwood, Emmanuel Van Dyke, and Joseph Goat of Saginaw and C. T. White and Daniel Fairfax of Bay City had planned "to make [it] a grand demonstration and secure the presence of Booker T. Washington." But Washington was unable to attend and, as a result, the *Evening News* carefully pointed out that the "demonstration" became "simply an old fashioned basket picnic and all . . . of the colored people . . . went out to have a good time."[104] During the 1860s and 1870s such Emancipation Day celebrations had been as much political as social events, with numerous speeches, bands playing patriotic marches, and often a parade through town to the picnic ground. In addition, city officials and all residents were invited to participate, and many did.[105]

This renewed emphasis on African American holidays likely had resulted from the organization in September 1900 of a committee "to work for the betterment of the black race," with Wallace Goodridge as its president, that had begun to meet regularly that year at Pastor T. W. Beck's African Methodist Church on Janes. By 1903 the commit-

tee also may have been responsible for the formation of East Star Lodge No. 6, an affiliate of the Grand Lodge of Prince Hall Masons chartered in Boston in 1787. By 1913 there were thirteen Prince Hall lodges in Michigan, with a membership of more than five hundred Masons.[106] East Star No. 6 was well established in the Saginaw Valley by 1903, and although its original membership roster remains confidential, a list of officers was published in the Saginaw city directories for the years 1903 to 1912.[107] The directory lists provide an opportunity to analyze the leadership of a fraternal organization that doubtless enjoyed considerable economic, social, and political influence within the Saginaw Valley's African American community at this time in the same manner that African American members of the Republican Party had a generation earlier.

Between 1903 and 1912 thirteen individuals held the eight lodge offices recorded by the directories. In 1905 Wallace Goodridge was listed as senior grand warden and in 1907 became secretary, a position he retained until his death. For the period the other senior offices of master, warden, and treasurer were shared among several members, including Joseph Hatfield, Arthur Hammond, Daniel Fairfax, Louis L. Stafford, George Henry, William Clark, J. B. Jackson, and Richard Combine, who together constituted, in a sense, the valley's new African American "elite." Although he was not listed as an officer, prominent Bay City attorney Oscar W. Baker is known to have been a member and likely exercised considerable influence within the lodge.[108]

The average age of the officer group was fifty in 1903, with Wallace the eldest at sixty-three and Jackson the youngest at thirty-two. Only two, Combine and Henry, were born in Michigan, and all but Stafford and Goodridge, who had made Saginaw their home since before 1880, were recent arrivals to the Saginaw Valley. Of more interest than age or place of origin, however, is status within the community. Eight were married but among them counted only three children still living at home. Five of those eight owned homes that were mortgaged, and the others either rented or, if single, were boarders. Only two, Goodridge and

Combine, a barber (three if Baker the lawyer is included), owned their own businesses and might be considered professionals. The others, while employed, worked as janitors, miners, drivers, laborers, messengers, or for the railroad—occupations demanding muscle or service to others. The members of this new elite had inherited neither their position nor any significant wealth and, in fact, were all of modest means. Most were recent residents who had doubtless come to the valley seeking opportunity. The East Star Lodge offered one occasion to pursue it.[109] Among them, however, only Wallace and Baker had been active in Republican politics prior to 1890 and, in a sense, served as the link between the old Republican elite and the new Masonic leadership.

The connection becomes clear from an analysis of the goals and membership of the 1915 Freedmen's Progress Commission, which published the *Michigan Manual of Freedmen's Progress* that same year. In January 1915 Governor Woodbridge N. Ferris chose fifty-seven African American citizens of Michigan as the state's delegation to the "Lincoln Jubilee and Celebration of the Half-Century Anniversary of Negro Freedom" to be held in Chicago between August 22 and September 16. The duties of the delegation included meeting "with the Governor to discuss ways to gain legislative support and an adequate appropriation to plan, collect, prepare, install and care for an exhibit at the Lincoln Jubilee, and to prepare a manual showing the professional, political, religious and educational achievements of citizens of this State of Negro ancestry." In April the Republican legislature endorsed the plan with a $5,000 appropriation and appointed a nine-person commission to implement it. Attorney Oscar W. Baker of Bay City was chosen president of the commission, and, perhaps as a result, seventeen of the ninety-four "Honorary Vice-Presidents" appointed by the commission were from Saginaw or Bay City. Only Detroit enjoyed greater representation. Among the seventeen were Daniel Fairfax, Wallace L. Goodridge, George Henry, John B. Jackson, William E. Cole, and Charles White, all of whom were past or current officers of East Star Lodge No. 6. In addition, the

commission's report noted that "Many of the prominent Afro-Americans of the state, most of whom are mentioned in this manual, are members of the [Prince Hall] Masonic order."[110]

The commission, with the able assistance of its honorary vice presidents, designed an exhibit that celebrated the achievements of Michigan's African American citizens and installed it in the Chicago Coliseum in time for the August 22 opening of the Jubilee Exposition, where it was applauded as "one of the finest of the displays." Photographs of the display included in the *Manual* reveal an extensive array of photographs featuring Frederick Douglass and Booker T. Washington and a painting of Lincoln and Sojourner Truth. Special sections were devoted to the more than fifty inventions patented by Elijah McCoy of Detroit and to Robert A. Pelham, founder and editor of the *Detroit Plaindealer* from 1883 to 1895 and subsequently appointed to the staff of the Director of the Census. Pelham had traveled from Washington specifically to create the political component of the display, distinguished by a banner calling for "Equal Suffrage" and a flag-draped portrait of "Our Governor" Ferris.[111]

A more daunting task was preparation of the *Manual* in time for distribution before the exposition. In less than four months the commission was able to gather an extensive range of data and to organize it somewhat less successfully into sections devoted to "brief biographical sketches of prominent Negroes in the professions, business and industry, and education," a listing of "Negro Home and Property owners" in the state, a "brief history of the Negro in Michigan," a section devoted to "Negro organizations," chapters on "Occupations" and "Mortality," and a list of "Negro soldiers serving in the Civil War." Each section is enriched with an extensive selection of photographs. A subsequent edition added an index.[112]

Featured prominently throughout the *Manual* are commission president Baker and his Saginaw Valley masonic colleagues. Baker understandably received the most attention, with two biographical sketches, a formal portrait, and photographs of his Bay City properties and law office. In addition to listing them as "Honorary Vice Presidents" and including them among the listing of "Home and Property Owners," the *Manual* also published photographs of the homes of Daniel Fairfax, George Henry, John Jackson, and Charles White. The section of the *Manual* devoted to "Michigan's Volunteer Negro Soldiers" concluded with a photograph of Civil War veterans James McConnell of Detroit and Arthur L. Hammond of Saginaw. Hammond, though not an "Honorary Vice President" of the commission, had served the East Star Lodge since its organization in each of its major offices. Perhaps because Wallace Goodridge, a widower since May 1914, had sold his home and lived once again at the studio on South Washington, the *Manual* printed a photograph of Wallace in the doorway of the studio (see figure 7.7a) and included a paragraph describing the Goodridges as "the leading photographers of Northern Michigan . . . [whose] work was not excelled in the state. One specialty was the taking of noted views all over the country."[113] No doubt the Goodridge studio had supplied the commission with the Saginaw Valley photographs.

———◆◆———

Until her death in May 1914, Margaret Goodridge, who was twenty years younger than her husband, Wallace, provided much of the social vitality in the family. From the time of her arrival in East Saginaw, Margaret was a member of Zion Baptist Church, where she often served as both pianist and organist. During most of the twenty-five years of their marriage, Zion also served as a focal point of the Goodridges' social life, with Wallace, as a result of Margaret's influence, acting as one of the congregation's lay leaders. For a time each summer Mrs. Goodridge also traveled east to visit her parents in Baltimore and on her return usually stopped in York and Philadelphia to visit Goodridge family members living there. In Saginaw she gave piano lessons, worked as her husband's assistant in the family studio, and for a time, between 1897 and 1902, was in partnership with her sister-in-laws Gertrude Goodridge, William's

widow, and then Madame Mary Nichols, Wallace's sister, in the hairdressing business.[114]

In anticipation of his marriage, Wallace had built a new house for his bride at 1821 Phelon Street. The newlyweds lived there only a few years before moving to residences in the 600 block of South Washington and then 115 Bagley Street. In 1896, however, they settled into 220 South Washington (the Goodridge studio building), where Wallace continued to live until shortly before his own death in 1922. The moves likely were tied to an initial $1,300 mortgage against the studio, which Wallace signed in 1889 for five years at 8 percent interest. The mortgage was intended to pay for the new home on Phelon Street and renovations to the studio. The note was not repaid in full, however, until 1907, when a second mortgage, for $550, was signed with People's Savings Bank. In 1916 an additional $200 was added to the $550, with both discharged only in 1922.[115] During the first decades of the new century Wallace remained technically innovative and continued to be recognized as the Saginaw Valley's preeminent photographer, but the prosperity that the studio had enjoyed earlier obviously had begun to fade away.

According to both the 1900 and 1910 manuscript censuses for Saginaw, Margaret Goodridge was childless. Given that Wallace was nearly fifty when he and Margaret married, the absence of children may not have been unusual. However, at Wallace's death in 1922 both the tribute to him published in the *Saginaw News* and his last will and testament stated that Wallace was survived by a son, Wallace L. Goodridge, Jr., of Philadelphia. The manuscript censuses for Philadelphia which confirm the younger Wallace's residence there between 1900 and 1920 provide conflicting data regarding his place and date of birth. According to the 1900 record, Wallace, Jr., was born in 1862 in Pennsylvania (both his parents were born there also) and was a thirty-eight-year-old single, educated African American male who worked as a waiter and lodged at 1624 Waverly Street. By 1910 he had become a widower who lived with his brother-in-law Charles Sweeny and family, first at South Smedley (1910) and then (1920) at South Ruby Streets. In 1910 he was described as a forty-two-year-old educated mulatto who worked as a public school teacher and was born in Pennsylvania in 1867 or 1868. The 1920 census once again listed Wallace, Jr., as single, but now an African American school-teacher, and recorded his place and date of birth as Michigan in 1867. Apparently he also had left Philadelphia and headed west shortly after the 1920 census, for a deed dated August 24, 1923, recording the sale of the Goodridge studio in Saginaw by Wallace's heirs lists "Wallace L. Goodridge, Jr. [as] a single man of Chicago, Illinois." The Chicago city directory for 1923 lists a Wallace J. Goodrich who lived at 1426 Elmdale and was employed as a salesman.[116] These inconsistencies with respect to place and date of birth certainly may be due to the vagaries of the census-taking process or even the subject's own confusion as to his exact origin, but other explanations also may account for his circumstances.

It is possible that Wallace did marry before he left York for East Saginaw in 1862 or 1863, or even during his first years in Michigan, and that although a son was born to the couple the marriage was not a successful one and mother and son returned to Pennsylvania shortly after the birth and the failure of the marriage. However, vital records in York and Saginaw Counties fail to document the marriage of a Wallace Goodridge or the birth of a son, Wallace, Jr., during the 1860s. In fact, the East Saginaw manuscript census which enumerated the Goodridge household in 1870, 1880, and 1900, and which even included studio staff who resided with the family, did not list Wallace, Jr., as a member of the family. Nor did the Saginaw city directories for the same decades—which normally recorded the presence of older children, especially if they were students or worked in the family business—list a Wallace, Jr.[117] It also is possible that although a child was born, there was no marriage and that even though Wallace acknowledged his son with his name, that was the extent of the formal relationship between father and son. Either possibility is supported by the fact that in Wallace's will the son, who lived in Philadelphia, was left a "dia-

mond ring and watch" but only "one-quarter" of the remainder of the estate, the same as nephew Glen Goodridge (Glenalvin's son) in York, but that John Goodridge (William's son), the nephew who lived and worked in the studio with Wallace in Saginaw, received not only the family's "Marble clock" but also "one-half" of the remainder of Wallace's estate.[118]

An additional possibility also may account for the birth of Wallace, Jr. The records of the 1862 trial in York (see chapter 2) that resulted in Glenalvin Goodridge's conviction and imprisonment for the rape of Mary E. Smith indicate that a sexual relationship had existed at that time between Smith and twenty-two-year-old Wallace L. Goodridge. In fact, it appears from the transcript of the trial that as a result of that relationship Smith had become pregnant, that Wallace already had left York for East Saginaw, and that Smith, in a desperate situation, had accused Glenalvin of rape in the hope of obtaining a financial settlement from the Goodridge family to ease her situation. For unknown reasons, the plan did not work and ultimately Wallace, Jr., was the result. Wallace's sense of guilt in the whole affair may explain the strong support he later provided for his brother in East Saginaw and to Glenalvin's wife, Rhoda, and son Glen until his own death in 1922. Unfortunately, there are no details of Wallace, Jr.'s, life or death once he moved to Chicago, and other than in his last will and testament Wallace, Sr., never publicly acknowledged his son or discussed the circumstances of his birth.

Margaret Goodridge's death on May 31, 1914, occurred only weeks before she and Wallace were to have celebrated their silver wedding anniversary. Although her death denied him both spouse and partner, Wallace's final few years in Saginaw were eased by the able assistance of his nephew John Goodridge in the studio and the companionship of sister Mary Nichols, who continued to operate her beauty parlor in the small shop at 218 South Washington adjoining the studio, although her failing eyesight had caused her to move into the family rooms in the studio building next door with brother Wallace. In addition, Gertrude A. Goodridge, widow of brother William, had moved to Geneva, Ohio, in 1899, had remarried, and returned to Saginaw as Mrs. Frederick B. Jackson. The Jackson home at 2026 Tuscola Street became the family gathering place for Gertrude's daughter Alta and son John as well as sister Mary and brother Wallace. It was here, in fact, that Wallace spent his final weeks when a failing heart forced him to abandon his residence in the Goodridge studio. Wallace died in the Jackson home on March 3, 1922.[119]

Wallace's death certificate listed the cause of death as a "disease of the heart." Whether he suffered a heart attack or the disease was a progressive one is not known. He was not hospitalized, had continued to work and live at the studio until a month before his death, and apparently died suddenly at 1:30 the afternoon of Friday, March 3. Other Goodridge family members, including Wallace's mother, Evalina, and sister Susan and brother Albertus, also had died of heart disease earlier in York, so it may be that heart problems were hereditary in the family although not affecting Wallace until late in his life. Final arrangements were handled by funeral directors W. Frazee and Sons, a Goodridge neighbor at 209 N. Washington, and conducted under the auspices of East Star Lodge No. 6 on Tuesday afternoon, March 7. Burial was in the family plot at Forest Lawn Cemetery where wife, Margaret, brother William, and nephew William, Jr., had preceded him.[120]

Only hours after Wallace's death, the *Saginaw News Courier* published a brief front-page notice of the event stating simply that "WALLACE GOODRICH [*sic*], PHOTOGRAPHER, DIES." It appeared directly above a report that the well-known merchant and entrepreneur Julius W. Ipple had suffered a stroke and that his condition appeared serious. From the location, brevity, and straightforwardness of the announcement, it is obvious that the *Courier* could assume that Wallace L. Goodridge, Saginaw's preeminent photographer, was well known to everyone in the community.[121] The following day the *Courier* expanded on its initial notice with a three-column obituary-tribute that included an excellent photographic portrait of Wallace made several years earlier

when he had been at the pinnacle of his profession (see figure 7.43). The headline proclaimed that "Goodridge, First Saginaw Photographer," had "Ranked as Oldest in His Profession in Michigan," and the article then reviewed the highlights of both the family's and Wallace's personal and professional history. The *Courier* chose to focus its report on Wallace as a professional photographer and as a person. And although the obituary-tribute did state that Wallace's father was "Born in Slavery" and that Wallace "was reputed the oldest photographer of colored blood in America," both references to race, in this final instance, were positive, part of the tribute, and not an attempt to set Wallace or other members of the Goodridge family apart as "colored" or "black," as had so often been the case with published reports in the past. In fact, although the *Courier*'s account appeared on page seven of the paper, its placement was not unusual. That it devoted three columns to the report and included a photograph of Wallace—ironically, the only time that a photograph of this photographer had appeared in the local newspapers—certainly was. Such a tribute typically was reserved only for the community's most illustrious individuals.[122]

As the executor of his estate Wallace had chosen fellow East Star Lodge member George L. Henry "on account of a friendship of many years." Wallace apparently had sensed the gravity of his condition, as his will is dated January 28, 1922, less than six weeks before his death. The will was drawn up by attorney John Hopkins at his offices in the Bearinger Building and witnessed by Thomas F. McComas, a former Goodridge neighbor at 1117 Phelon Street and likely a fellow East Star Lodge member. The document does not indicate the total value of the estate but suggests that Wallace was not particularly "well-off." Although specific bequests to relatives and friends included "the Falma & Zena statuary in my home" to George L. Henry, "the family dishes and silverware" to sister-in-law Rose in Baltimore, "my diamond ring and watch" to son Wallace, Jr., "one marble clock" to nephew John, and "my gold clock" to nephew Glen, Henry as executor was forced in November

Figure 7.43. "Wallace L. Goodridge," March 4, 1922, *Saginaw News Courier.*

1922 to seek permission from the probate court to obtain a mortgage against the studio building in the amount of $900 for one year at 7 percent interest in order to carry out Wallace's final wishes.

The mortgage was discharged the following October when the studio building was sold for $6,500 to Frederick R. Strutz and the proceeds distributed among Wallace's heirs according to his instructions.[123]

The structure has changed ownership several times since Wallace's death and in 1974 was remodeled and incorporated into its larger neighbor next door. As recently as 1952, however, the Goodridge building continued to function as a photography studio. In March that year the *Saginaw News* published a tribute to the Goodridge brothers in commemoration of the thirtieth anniversary of Wallace's death. The article included an interview with Charles E. White, "one of the real veterans of the Saginaw commercial photography field," who was then in the studio space. White remembered Wallace, "whom he counted among his friends, as 'a very fine man, a gentleman and a very fine photographer of noticeable refinement.'" White recalled that "the Goodridge brothers were much in demand in the early days here as both commercial and portrait photographers . . . [and] that they stood practically unchallenged here for commercial photography." He concluded that they "were keen businessmen and excellent photographers who really knew their trade."[124] White's 1952 assessment of the work begun by Glenalvin in York more than a century ago and continued by William and Wallace until only a few decades before remains the most fitting tribute to the Goodridges and their work.

Afterword

The Goodridge studio opened its doors in York in 1847 during photography's first decade, when the technology was still a mystery to most people and the resulting images near magical. The studio closed in Saginaw in 1922, exactly seventy-five years later, when almost anyone could own a camera and the photos it would churn out had become commonplace. In that three-quarters of a century Glenalvin, Wallace, and William Goodridge, like many photographers at the time, had made thousands of photographs in every format the profession afforded, from daguerreotypes to motion pictures. Unlike the vast majority of their colleagues, however, the Goodridges were African Americans, and the opportunity to work as photographers was available to them largely because of the enterprise and example of their parents, Evalina and William. Although a third generation of Goodridges—Glenalvin's, Wallace's, and William's children—choose not to maintain the studio after 1922, the several hundred photographs that are extant at present serve as its persistent heritage and our link to the studio and to the three men who had created it.

Wherein then lies the importance of these men and their work? In assessing their significance as persons and as professionals, it would be most easy to conclude that the Goodridge brothers deserve our attention primarily because they were African Americans. In fact, the Goodridge mystique that has evolved locally both in York and in Saginaw is based largely on that fact. Ancestry is certainly crucial to an understanding of the bases for their success, since both their parents and likely their grandparents before them had provided the Goodridge children with the material resources and the requisite example and guidance that enabled them to attain professional success and also to continue the family's tradition of political and social activism to the end of their lives. At the same time, the extant Goodridge photographic oeuvre reveals no clear or consciously articulated African American perspective. Among the images presently known, less than fifty are of African American persons, and most of those are family members and a few friends. In addition, the photographs reveal no obvious social or political message—only one or two (for example, the Lincoln portrait or the Charter Oak) might be interpreted in this fashion. Given the Goodridge family's opposition to slavery in antebellum Pennsylvania and its active role in Republican politics in Saginaw and in Michigan thereafter as well as its consistent social leadership in education and religion or lodge and lyceum, the fact that the photographs the Goodridge studio created over three-quarters of a century were almost without exception exactly like those made by most of the other studios who were their contemporaries may be surprising. But therein lies their significance.

The Goodridge studio deserves our attention because the Goodridges were African Americans, but even more so because the studio opened during the profession's first decade and remained, unlike the majority of its early and even later contemporaries, successful into the next century. The Goodridges' photographic heritage yields relatively little specific data about nineteenth- and early-twentieth-century African Americans in the United States. However, the hundreds of photographs that Glenalvin, Wallace, William, and their assistants made in every conceivable format reveal much about the Goodridges both personally and professionally. Like their parents, the sons believed that their effectiveness as individuals and as political leaders and social activists would derive from the degree of their success as enterprising businessmen and professionals. Consequently, their work, whether the earliest daguerreotype portraits, nineteenth-century lumber-era stereo series, or later the technically innovative flash, panoramic, or motion pictures, was shaped by the prerequisites of their profession. Success there easily could be transformed into effectiveness elsewhere.

That Glenalvin, Wallace, and William Goodridge had achieved both, the personal and the professional success which they sought, and that the two were essentially part of their singular talent is evident from their enterprise as individuals and the photographic images which will remain their heritage.

Notes

Preface

1. Michael Lesy, *Wisconsin Death Trip* (New York: Pantheon, 1973), xv.
2. Linda A. Ries, "Images of Common Wealth," *Pennsylvania History* 64 (1997): 169.

Chapter 1

1. *[Baltimore] American and Commercial Daily Advertiser,* 23 December 1806; and "Notebook of Daniel Lehman (1798–?)," MS A-778, The Historical Society of York County, York, Pennsylvania. William C. Goodridge may have been born in 1805 or as early as 1803. A birth certificate is not extant. His death certificate lists his age as "70 Yrs." on 15 January 1873, the recorded date of his death. Vital Records Division, Hennepin County, Minneapolis, Minnesota. Lehman's date is consistent, however, with census data for the Goodridge family and the datable events of William's life.
2. In 1912 Dr. I. H. Betz of York published an article on the Goodridge family based upon interviews with family members then living in York—in particular, Glen Goodridge, William C. Goodridge's grandson—that is the most accurate of the early accounts of the family's history. See *York Gazette,* 5 October 1912. An earlier, although less detailed, account of William's origin is contained in George R. Prowell, *History of York County, Pennsylvania,* 2 vols. (Chicago: J. H. Beers & Co., 1907), 1:595. An exchange of letters in 1953 between Mr. George Hay Kain of York and Mrs. Edna G. Bennett of Lawnside, New Jersey, who was William C. Goodridge's great-granddaughter (letters in possession of Mr. William H. Kain of York), and interviews conducted by the author and Mr. Georg R. Sheets of York in 1984 with Mrs. Catherine Grey Hurley of Washington, D.C., another Goodridge great-granddaughter, tend to corroborate Betz's account of the family's origins.
3. Eleanor S. Darcy, Assistant Editor, Papers of Charles Carroll of Carrollton, letter to author, 15 May 1996; and Allan Kulikoff, "The Origins of Afro-American Society in Tidewater Maryland and Virginia, 1700–1790," *William and Mary Quarterly* 35 (1978): 226–59. Doughoregan Manor is now located in Howard County, which was separated from Anne Arundel County.
4. *York Gazette,* 5 October 1912; Prowell, *History of York County,* 1:595; and Catherine Grey Hurley interviews, 1984. Mrs. Hurley noted that her grandmother, Emily O. Goodridge Grey, William's daughter, originally had been named Emily Carrollton Grey but dropped the Carrollton in favor of the middle initial "O." because Carrollton represented her family's connection to the Carrolls and slavery.
5. *York Gazette,* 12 October 1824. The ad, which ran until 25 January 1825, announced that "Wm. Goodridge, Hair-Dresser, had taken the shop in centre square, adjoining the store of William Jones, and lately occupied by Israel Williams, where he intends carrying on the Barbering Business in all its various branches."
6. See "A List of the Physicians and Surgeons of the Revolutionary Period, 1775–1783 in Maryland," *Maryland Historical Magazine* 24 (March 1929): 1–17.
7. Carl Douglass Oblinger, "New Freedoms, Old Miseries: The Emergence and Disruption of Black Communities in Southeastern Pennsylvania" (Ph.D. diss., Lehigh University, 1988), 59–61.
8. Ibid., 61.
9. A copy of the indenture is not extant. Details are from Betz, *York Gazette,* 5 October 1912.
10. Ruth Ellen Johnson, "The Development of a Unit of the Afro-American Entrepreneur in the United States before 1866: A Preliminary Field Test in Distributive Education Classes for Afro-American High School Students," 2 vols. (Ph.D. diss., Temple University, 1979), 1:235.
11. *York Democratic Press,* 6 April 1852.
12. "Deposition of Margaret Dunn, June 29, 1836," *Maryland Chancery Court Records,* 1836, vol. 157, p. 562. Archives of Maryland, Annapolis, Maryland.
13. Betz, *York Gazette,* 5 October 1912.
14. Ibid.; and *York Recorder,* 27 June 1826.
15. *York Democratic Press,* 13 July 1840; and Maryland, Manuscript Census Schedules, 1820, Baltimore County, Eleventh Ward, Baltimore City.
16. *York Democratic Press,* 9 November 1852; Pennsylvania, Manuscript Census Schedules, 1850, York County,

North Ward, York Borough; and Betz, *York Gazette,* 5 October 1912. When William and Evalina's son William O. Goodridge died in East Saginaw, Michigan, in 1890 his obituary stated that he was one of "eleven children, only three of whom are now living [Emily, Wallace, and Mary]." *Saginaw Evening News,* 18 August 1890. The Goodridges may have been the parents of eleven children, but the names of only seven of those children are known: Glenalvin, Emily, Albertus, Wallace, Susan, Mary, and William.

17. Georg R. Sheets, *To the Setting of the Sun: The Story of York* (Woodland Hills, Calif.: Windsor Publications, 1981), 72–73.

18. Oblinger, "New Freedoms, Old Miseries," 9–11. See also Julie Winch, *Philadelphia's Black Elite: Activism, Accommodation, and the Struggle for Autonomy, 1787–1848* (Philadelphia: Temple University Press, 1988), for a similar analysis.

19. *York Gazette,* 11 May 1830 and 1 November 1836.

20. *The New Grolier Multimedia Encyclopedia, Release 6* (1993).

21. *York Gazette,* 1 November 1836; and *Gopsill's York Directory, 1863–4* (York, 1863).

22. *York Gazette,* 25 September and 23 October 1832.

23. *York Democratic Press,* 24 February 1840. Goodridge last advertised the Philadelphia shop on 22 February 1841, ibid. The shop is listed in *M'Elroy's Philadelphia Directory for 1840* (Philadelphia, 1840).

24. *York Gazette,* 16, 30 June, and 11 August 1840; and *York Democratic Press,* 22 June, 27 July, and 14 September 1840.

25. *Democratic Press,* 21 December 1840.

26. See, for example, the lists published in the *York Gazette* for 6 June 1837 and 16 June and 8 December 1840.

27. Ira Berlin, *Slaves without Masters: The Free Negro in the Antebellum South* (New York: New Press, 1974), 236; and Johnson, "Afro-American Entrepreneur," 1:280.

28. Pennsylvania, Manuscript Census Schedules, 1830, York County, North Ward, York Borough; and Linda A. Ries and Ruth Hodge, letter to author, 16 August 1997.

29. Carter G. Woodson, comp. and ed., *Free Negro Owners of Slaves in the United States in 1830 Together with Absentee Ownership of Slaves in the United States in 1830* (New York: Negro Universities Press, 1924), v, vi, 26–27. Woodson identifies the Goodridge slave as aged "10–24," but the manuscript census lists his age as "twenty-four years of age and under thirty-six."

30. Pennsylvania, Manuscript Census Schedules, 1840 and 1850, York County, North Ward, York Borough.

31. A listing of "Retailers of Foreign Merchandise" who were required to purchase a license from the county was published annually in both York newspapers. The 5 December 1826 list in the *York Gazette* has Goodridge thirty-third of thirty-three on the list for "York Borough." By 1837 Goodridge was listed as fifth of fifteen "Retailers," and he retained his position thereafter. Ibid., 16 May 1837.

32. York County Tax Records, 1837–1843, North Ward, York Borough, The Historical Society of York County.

33. For the Goodridges' property holdings in York before 1840, see Register of Deeds, York County, 3K, 325–26; 3U, 594–95; 3V, 205, 486–87, and 487–88; 3W, 188–89, 195–96, and 196–97; and 3X, 217–18, 218–19, and 219–20. See, as well, the York County Tax Records, 1837–1838, The Historical Society of York County.

34. *York Democratic Press,* 26 February 1842.

35. William H. Shank, *Three Hundred Years with the Pennsylvania Traveler* (York: American Canal and Transportation Center, 1976), 123–26, includes an excellent discussion of early York railroads. For Borbridge and Lewis see *York Democratic Press,* 26 February and 12 April 1842. *M'Elroy's Philadelphia Directory for 1840,* 23, 95, and 145 lists Borbridge, Goodridge, and Lewis. *M'Elroy's Philadelphia Directory for 1839* (Philadelphia, 1839) includes an advertisement for the "Reliance Transportation Company's Line of Portable Iron Boats."

36. *York Gazette,* 27 June 1842, 31 October 1843, and 1 April 1845. The quotation is from Betz, ibid., 5 October 1912.

37. *York Democratic Press,* 17 March 1843.

38. "Col. John Hough and Wife Matilda to Wm. Goodridge (Barber)," 1 April 1843. Register of Deeds, York County, 3V, 487–88.

39. According to the 1 April 1843 deed, "the sd. Col. John Hough . . . assigns the privilege and the right of using the brick wall adjoining the above property whenever he the sd. Wm. Goodridge wishes to build against it agreeable to the agreement between sd. Hough and Goodridge on the 16th August 1842." Ibid.

40. "Wm. and E. Goodridge to David and Daniel A. Rupp," 21 February 1848, Register of Deeds, York County, 3U, 260–61, also records the 1844 and 1845 McGrath to Hartmann to Goodridge transactions. Property tax records for 1846–49 list the Goodridges as owning a "Barber shop and 1/8 lot" valued at $1,500 ($1,600 beginning in 1847) but do not specify its location. See York County Tax Records, 1846–1849, North Ward, York Borough, The Historical Society of York County.

41. See the *York Democratic Press,* 27 October 1846 and 6 April, 29 June, 27 July, and 28 September 1847; and "Goodridge to Rupp," 21 February 1848, Register of Deeds, York County, 3U, 260–61, for the rentals and sale of China Hall.

42. Betz, *York Gazette,* 5 October 1912; and George R. Prowell in the *York Dispatch,* 27 December 1897.

43. See Prowell in the *York Dispatch,* 27 December 1897, for an account of the Worth Infantry Band. For advertisements describing Goodridge's Centre Hall tenants see *York City Directory for 1856* (York, 1856), 70, 72, 73, 85; *York Gazette,* 21 April and 29 September 1857 and 5 and 19 January 1858; and the *Democratic Press,* 29 November 1849, 8 November 1853, 21 November 1854, 11 November 1856, 7 April 1857, 19 and 26 January 1858, and 25 January 1859.

44. "Peter McIntyre to Wm. Goodridge," 27 April 1849, 3U, 594–95; "William Matson and Wife Susanna to Wm. Goodridge," 2 August 1850, 3W, 188–89; "Wm. Goodridge and Wife Emily to York and Cumberland R.R.," 6 August 1850, 3V, 502–3; "William Goodridge, Barber and Wife Emily to Henry Small, Lumber Merchant," 28 May 1852, 3W, 673–74; "William Goodridge to John Pfleiger, Wm. Hess and John A. Nevin," 26 April 1854, 3X, 806–7; "Langley Meads Heirs to William Goodridge," 30 March 1848, 3W, 195–96; "Amelia Meads to William Goodridge," 30 March 1848, 3W, 196–97; "Jacob Stair and Wife Ann A. to William C. Goodridge," 30 March 1853, 3X, 217–18; and "John Stahle, esq. to William Goodridge," 31 March 1853, 3X, 219–20, document these real estate transactions by Goodridge between 1848 and 1854. All are Register of Deeds, York County.

45. Without family or business records, it is impossible to determine the extent of the Goodridges' wealth with any accuracy. My analysis of the real estate transactions yields a minimum figure of $25,000. The 1850 census lists the value of the family's "Real Estate" as $15,000. Pennsylvania, Manuscript Census Schedules, 1850, York County, North Ward, York Borough. In 1859, "Mifflin" in the New York *Weekly Anglo-African* for August 20 reported after a visit to York that "Mr. Goodridge was at one time worth one hundred thousand dollars, but, like many others, the money pressure did him no good." An 1890 obituary of son William O. Goodridge, printed when son Wallace L. Goodridge was available to provide the details of his father's circumstances, stated that Goodridge "was worth about $200,000. . . ." *Saginaw Evening News,* 18 August 1890.

46. Georg R. Sheets, *Children of the Circuit Riders: The History of Asbury United Methodist Church, York, Pennsylvania, 1781–1985* (York: Maple-Vail Press, 1985), 82. See also "Langley Meads Heirs to William Goodridge," 30 March 1848, 3W, 195–96, Register of Deeds, York County.

47. *Rochester (New York) North Star,* 26 August 1853.

48. Ibid., 15 December 1848.

49. Dorothy Burnett Porter, "The Redmonds of Salem, Massachusetts: A Nineteenth-Century Family Revisited," *Proceedings of the American Antiquarian Society* 95, no. 2 (1985): 275.

50. According to York historian Georg R. Sheets, "Goodridge's success inspired considerable envy among York's other businessmen, and one merchant [John Hartmann] began construction of a larger building that he hoped would literally 'overshadow' Goodridge's business complex." *To the Setting of the Sun,* 84–85. An 18 September 1948 account of Goodridge's success in the *York Dispatch* noted that "Goodridge's building was five stories high and the tallest in town. The older residents rather delighted in telling how this tall building aroused the envy of some of his white neighbors. One of them, not to be outdone, determined to surpass it and built on another corner of the square a seven-story building." The

earliest account in print that suggests such is Prowell's article on Goodridge in the 27 December 1897 issue of the *York Dispatch,* where he wrote that "In 1847 he [Goodridge] erected on the site of the Bernise home a building four and one-half stories high. John Louis Kuehn was the master carpenter of the new Goodridge building, which cost $6,000. It was the first four-story building in York and attracted wide attention, because it was built by a mulatto."

51. Board and Tuition Record for 1852–1875, Archives, Oblate Sisters of Providence, Our Lady of Mount Providence Convent, Baltimore, Maryland. See also Betz, *York Gazette,* 5 October 1912; and *The Colored Harvest* 24 (October–November 1936): 5.

52. Betz, *York Gazette,* 5 October 1912.

53. Ibid.

54. *York Democratic Press,* 22 December 1846 and 9 November 1852.

55. "Cathcart's Private Register, First Presbyterian Church, York, Pa. 1793–1837 & First Presbyterian Records," File No. 241, The Historical Society of York County; *York Democratic Press,* 29 January 1861; *York Gazette,* 29 January 1861; and Patricia C. Harpole, ed., "The Black Community in Territorial St. Anthony: A Memoir by Emily O. Goodridge Grey," *Minnesota History* 49 (Summer 1984): 43–45.

56. *York Gazette,* 28 December 1858. For the records of the sale see "Execution Docket, Court of Common Pleas, January 1859–August 1862," 14, County of York, Commonwealth of Pennsylvania; and "Grantor Index to Sheriff's and Treasurer's Deeds," County of York, Commonwealth of Pennsylvania. For reasons which are not clear, the *York Gazette* of 4 January 1859 reported the sale of only eleven Goodridge properties.

57. Sheets, *To the Setting of the Sun,* 88, 89.

58. *York Democratic Press,* 25 January and 9 December 1859, 20 March 1860, and 15 January and 26 March 1861; and *York Gazette,* 27 March 1860 and 5 October 1912.

59. *York Democratic Press,* 26 March 1861; and *Gopsill's York Directory, 1863–4,* 282.

60. *York Democratic Press,* 27 June 1862.

61. Ibid., 15 January 1864; and *York "Cartridge Box"* [Civil War hospital newspaper], 7 May 1865.

62. Johnson, "Afro-American Entrepreneur," 1:245–46.

63. *York Gazette,* 5 October 1912. For examples of Evalina (Emily) Goodridge's joint ownership of their property with William C. Goodridge, see 3V, 502–3; 3W, 673–74; and 3U, 260–61, Register of Deeds, York County.

64. *Saginaw Evening News,* 18 August 1890.

65. "Appearance and/or Common Pleas Dockets," No. 6, p. 40, Records of York County Prothonotary Office, York County Archives, York County, Pennsylvania.

66. "Appearance and/or Common Pleas Dockets," Docket No. 10, pp. 518, 535, 585; Docket No. 11, pp. 279, 289, 309, 310, 317, 341; and Docket No. 12, p. 106, Records of York County Prothonotary Office.

67. *York Gazette,* 1 December 1840.

68. *York Democratic Press,* 22 December 1846.

69. Bennett to Kain, 2 November 1953; *York Gazette,* 5 October 1912 and 10 June 1916; and Prowell, *History of York County,* 1:595.

70. Charles L. Blockson, *The Underground Railroad in Pennsylvania* (Jacksonville, N.C.: Flame International, 1981), 83; Charles L. Blockson, *The Underground Railroad* (New York: n.p., 1987); Charles L. Blockson, "Escape from Slavery: The Underground Railroad," *National Geographic Magazine* 166 (July 1984): 3–39; and William Still, *Still's Underground Railroad Records, With a Life of the Author,* rev. ed. (Philadelphia: W. Still, 1883).

71. Robert C. Smedley, *History of the Underground Railroad in Chester and the Neighboring Counties of Pennsylvania* (Lancaster: Office of the Journal, 1883; reprint, New York: Negro Universities Press, 1968), 45–46.

72. The best recent accounts of the "Christiana Riot" are Thomas P. Slaughter, *Bloody Dawn: The Christiana Riot and Racial Violence in the Antebellum North* (New York: Oxford University Press, 1991); and Jonathan Katz, *Resistance at Christiana: The Fugitive Slave Rebellion, Christiana, Pennsylvania, September 11, 1851: A Documentary Account* (New York: Crowell, 1974). For earlier accounts see also Smedley, *Underground Railroad in Pennsylvania,* 107–30; Wilbur H. Siebert, *The Underground Railroad: From Slavery to Freedom* (1898; reprint, New York: Arno, 1968), 280–83; and Larry Gara, *The Liberty Line: The Legend of the Liberty Line* (Lexington: University Press of Kentucky, 1961), 134–35.

73. *York Gazette,* 5 October 1912 and 10 June 1916; Katz, *Resistance at Christiana,* 247–61; and Slaughter, *Bloody Dawn,* 70–80.

74. William Parker, "The Freedman's Story," *Atlantic Monthly,* February 1866, p. 159; and Roderick W. Nash, "William Parker and the Christiana Riot," *Journal of Negro History* 46 (1961): 24.

75. Betz, *York Gazette,* 5 October 1912. When the Goodridge home was declared a historic site in 1987, the "cavern" beneath the kitchen floor was found to be in place. *York Daily Record,* 26 June 1995.

76. Katz, *Resistance at Christiana,* 28, 27.

77. *York Democratic Press,* 25 October 1859.

78. Osborne P. Anderson, *A Voice from Harper's Ferry: A Narrative of Events at Harper's Ferry; With Incidents Prior and Subsequent to Its Capture by Captain Brown and His Men* (Boston: Anderson, 1861), 55; and Jean Libby, *Black Voices from Harper's Ferry: Osborn Anderson and the John Brown Raid* (Palo Alto: Libby, 1979), 169.

79. *York Gazette,* 5 October 1912.

80. *Saginaw Evening News,* 18 August 1890; Bennett to Kain, 2 November 1953; Prowell, *History of York County,* 1:595; and *York Gazette,* 5 October 1912.

81. Stuart D. Gross, *Saginaw: A History of the Land and the City* (Woodland Hills, Calif.: Windsor, 1980), 129–30; Ed Miller and Jean R. Beach, *The Saginaw Hall of Fame: Biographical Sketches,* 2nd ed. (Saginaw: n.p., 1989), 127; Sheets, *To the Setting of the Sun,* 84; and Georg R.

Sheets, *Facts and Folklore of York, P.A.* (York: Sheets Books, 1993), 84.

82. Sheets, *To the Setting of the Sun,* 90; and *York Gazette,* 30 June 1863.

83. "Pardon, Glenalvin J. Goodridge," 13 December 1864, Record Group 26, Records of the Department of State, Clemency File, December 1864, Pennsylvania State Archives, Harrisburg.

84. Harpole, ed., "Black Community in St. Anthony," 42–53; *York "Cartridge Box,"* 7 May 1865; and "Wm. Goodrich," Certificate of Death Record, City of Minneapolis, County of Hennepin, State of Minnesota.

Chapter 2

1. The spelling of Goodridge's given name appears variously as Glenavlon, Glenalvan, and Glenalvin. See Linda A. Ries, "Glenalvon J. Goodridge: Black Daguerreian," in Peter E. Palmquist, ed., *The Daguerreian Annual 1991: Official Yearbook of The Daguerreian Society* (Eureka, Calif.: The Daguerreian Society, 1991), 38–41, for the "o" variant. See Harpole, ed., "Black Community in St. Anthony," 44–45, for the "a" variant. The "i" version, however, appears most regularly in both contemporary documents and family recollections, and I have adopted it for the sake of consistency.

2. Pennsylvania, Manuscript Census Schedules, 1830, 1840, and 1850, York County, North Ward, York Borough. The 1850 census was the first to list individual family members in addition to heads of households.

3. "M.R.D." in *Rochester North Star,* 15 December 1848. The fact that "M.R.D." had written from "Wilmington, Del." on 30 November 1848 has caused the assumption that Goodridge also taught school and may have worked as a daguerreotypist in Wilmington. See Ries, "Goodridge," 39; and Floyd Rinhart and Marian Rinhart, *The American Daguerreotype* (Athens: University of Georgia Press, 1981), 392. "M.R.D." was in Wilmington on 30 November and wrote his report there of a visit to York earlier that month.

4. For the historical development of the daguerreotype in the United States generally, see Rinhart and Rinhart, *American Daguerreotype,* 22–89. For early black photographers, see Deborah Willis-Thomas, *Black Photographers, 1840–1940: An Illustrated Bio-Bibliography* (New York: Garland, 1985), 3–7; Valencia Hollins Coar, ed., *A Century of Black Photographers: 1840–1960* (Providence: Museum of Art, Rhode Island School of Design, 1983), 9–10; and Deborah Willis, ed., *J. P. Ball: Daguerrean and Studio Photographer* (New York: Garland, 1993).

5. June Lloyd, Librarian/Archivist, The Historical Society of York County, letters to author, 26 September, 21 October, and 1 November 1997.

6. *Democratic Press,* 19 March 1842. It is possible that photographs were made in York before 1842. Given York's proximity to Philadelphia, where daguerreotypes were made as early as October 1839 by Joseph Saxton, cura-

tor of the United States Mint there, it is likely that they were. Rinhart and Rinhart, *American Daguerreotype,* 28. For a sampling of the itinerant photographers who visited York, see *York Gazette,* 29 March and 12 April 1842, 22 April 1845, 5 December 1848, and 16 January 1849, as well as *York Democratic Press,* 9 April 1842, 27 July 1843, and 21 February 1845. For advertisements from Philadelphia and Baltimore photographers, see *York Gazette,* 28 September 1847 and 4 July 1848; and *York Democratic Press,* 14 April and 13 October 1846 and 12 November 1850.

7. *York Democratic Press,* 6 and 13 April, 4 and 25 May, and 29 June 1847. Montgomery P. Simons (1817–77) was a well-known Philadelphia daguerreotypist, miniature casemaker, and author. Rinhart and Rinhart describe him as "a master of ivorytyping—an artistic treatment which brought out flesh tints in his portraits." In 1843 Simons patented a process for coloring daguerreotypes using a galvanic battery. Rinhart and Rinhart, *American Daguerreotype,* 105, 106, 195, 210–11, 409, 435–36.

8. *York Democratic Press,* 31 August 1847.

9. Ibid., 27 July 1847 and 11 July 1848.

10. See Patricia Poist-Reilly, "At First, It's an Empty Canvas: Goodridge Teaches Art of Business," *York Sunday News,* 11 August 1996; and Sheets, *Facts and Folklore,* 80.

11. *Rochester North Star,* 15 December 1848.

12. *York Democratic Press,* 27 July 1848; and Barbara McCandless, "The Portrait Studio and the Celebrity: Promoting the Art," in *Photography in Nineteenth-Century America,* ed. Martha A. Sandweiss (Fort Worth and New York: Amon Carter Museum and Harry N. Abrams, 1991), 52.

13. Alan Trachtenberg, *Reading American Photographs: Images as History, Mathew Brady to Walker Evans* (New York: Noonday Press, 1990), 25–26.

14. Rinhart and Rinhart, *American Daguerreotype,* 66. For the Simons daguerreotypes see pp. 105, 113.

15. Stanley B. Burns, M.D., *Sleeping Beauty: Memorial Photography in America* (Altadena, Calif.: Twelvetrees Press, 1990), [ii]. See also John Updike, "Facing Death," *American Heritage,* May–June 1992, pp. 98–105.

16. The spelling of the name appears as both Grey and Gray. For the sake of consistency I have chosen the former.

17. Pennsylvania, Manuscript Census Schedules, 1850, York County, North Ward, York Borough; *York Gazette,* 2 April 1850; and Oblinger, "New Freedoms, Old Miseries," 148.

18. Rinhart and Rinhart, *American Daguerreotype,* 113–15; Alan Trachtenberg, "Photography: The Emergence of a Keyword," in *Photography in Nineteenth-Century America,* ed. Sandweiss, 23; and Trachtenberg, *Reading American Photographs,* 22–23.

19. *York Democratic Press,* 28 January 1851 and 4 April 1861; *York Gazette,* 1 April 1862; and Rinhart and Rinhart, *American Daguerreotype,* 136–37.

20. Prowell, *History of York County,* 1:488–90. The caption that accompanies the photograph in the Latimer Family Collection in the Historical Society of York County misidentifies the subjects as, from left to right, Robert Jones, Anne Helen, and Emilie Shevall Fisher.

21. *Humphrey's Journal,* 1 January 1853, p. 287, and 1 October 1853, p. 191. Rinhart and Rinhart, *American Daguerreotype,* 98, describe the *Journal* as "the first periodical devoted to photography.... The new journal, its first issue being published in November 1850, explored both foreign and domestic improvements in the art and, of great interest to daguerreotypists, newsy items about fellow practitioners were recounted."

22. *York Gazette,* 18 October 1853; and Linda A. Ries, letter to author, 9 September 1993. Rinhart and Rinhart, *American Daguerreotype,* 108, note that for the regional daguerreotypist "a display at the county fair provided a chance to solicit patronage" as well as a contest among photographers.

23. *York Gazette,* 18 October 1853. Goodridge manufactured and distributed the coffee extract on both a wholesale and retail basis. His ads claimed that "a single pack of this Extract will save five pounds of Coffee, and it has a finer flavor and taste than any other article that is manufactured." *York Democratic Press,* 5 September 1854.

24. Pennsylvania, Manuscript Census Schedules, 1860, York County, First Division, York Borough; and Hamilton and Jane Grey to Glenalvin J. Goodridge, 1 April 1853, Register of Deeds, York County, 3X, 305–6. The price was $680 for "one-half part of . . ... [a] dwelling House and piece of ground 14′ 4½″."

25. *Thompson's Mercantile & Professional Directory, for the States of Delaware, Maryland, Virginia, North Carolina, & the District of Columbia . . . 1851–52* (Baltimore, 1851); and Ross J. Kelbaugh, Baltimore, Maryland, letter to author, 19 October 1997.

26. *York Gazette,* 27 September 1853.

27. Ibid., 24 October 1854 and 17 and 24 April 1855; and *York Democratic Press,* 24 October 1854.

28. See, for example, *York Democratic Press,* 5 September 1854.

29. For these developments see William Welling, *Photography in America: The Formative Years, 1839–1900* (New York: Thomas Y. Crowell, 1978), 111; William C. Darrah, *Cartes de Visite in Nineteenth-Century Photography* (Gettysburg: W. C. Darrah, 1981), 1–3; Brian Coe and Mark Haworth-Booth, *A Guide to Early Photographic Processes* (London: Victoria and Albert Museum, 1983), 18; and Rinhart and Rinhart, *American Daguerreotype,* 147–48.

30. For the technical differences between the collodian negative and positive see Coe and Haworth-Booth, *Early Photographic Processes,* 18; and Robert A. Weinstein and Larry Booth, *Collection, Use, and Care of Historical Photographs* (Nashville: American Association for State and Local History, 1977), 159–62. On Cutting and Simons, see Welling, *Photography in America,* 111.

31. Welling, *Photography in America,* 111; and Coe and Haworth-Booth, *Early Photographic Processes,* 18.

32. *York Gazette,* 30 October 1855.

33. Welling, *Photography in America,* 110, figure 3.

34. *York City Directory for 1856,* 70.

35. *York Democratic Press,* 14 October 1856.

36. Prowell, *History of York County,* 2:490, 512; and Anna Margaret Suppes Hay, *Geneaological [sic] Sketches of the Hay, Suppes, and Allied Families* (Johnstown, Pa.: William H. Raab & Son, n.d.), 113–15.

37. "John A. and Georgianna Weizer to Glenalvin Goodridge," 11 December 1854, 3Z, 260–61, and "Emanuel R. Ziegler and Wife to Glenalvin Goodridge," 11 December 1854, 3Z, 261–62, Register of Deeds, York County; and *York Democratic Press,* 8 March 1859.

38. *York Democratic Press,* 8 March 1859; and "Appearance and/or Common Pleas Dockets," Docket No. 9, p. 576, and Docket No. 11, pp. 122, 311, 312, Records of York County Prothonotary Office.

39. *York Democratic Press,* 14 October 1856. For use of the term "view" at this time see Peter Bacon Hales, "American Views and the Romance of Modernization," in *Photography in Nineteenth-Century America,* ed. Sandweiss, 205–9; and William C. Darrah, *The World of Stereographs* (Gettysburg: W. C. Darrah, 1977), 1.

40. Darrah, *World of Stereographs,* 1, 15–16.

41. Welling, *Photography in America,* 117; and Darrah, *Cartes de Visite,* 1–8.

42. *York Gazette,* 4 August 1857 and 30 November 1858; and Rinhart and Rinhart, *American Daguerreotype,* 381, 390.

43. Sarah Greenough, "'Of Charming Glens, Graceful Glades, and Frowning Cliffs': The Economic Incentives, Social Inducements, and Aesthetic Issues of American Pictorial Photography, 1880–1902," in *Photography in Nineteenth-Century America,* ed. Sandweiss, 260.

44. *York Gazette,* 11 October 1858; and *York Democratic Press,* 2 November 1859.

45. Trachtenberg, *Reading American Photographs,* 18.

46. *Gopsill's York Directory, 1863–4,* 335.

47. *Weekly Anglo-African,* 20 August and 17 September 1859.

48. Ibid., 17 September 1859; and Pennsylvania, Manuscript Census Schedules, 1860, York County, North Ward, York Borough.

49. *York Gazette,* 9 July 1861.

50. William C. Darrah, letter to author, 5 April 1985. Notes of a conversation between Mr. Darrah and Mr. Tex Treadwell of the National Stereoscopic Association Information Service provide additional information. Treadwell wrote: "My info on what was produced in York is solely from talking with Bill Darrah; . . . I dug out my notebook of discussions with him on PA photographers in 1986, and found the following (verbatim transcript): 'Vy. [very] unusual—father black businessman, moved to Mich. after war, think G.J.G. stayed—dropped out of sight, may have gone west also. Seen views by Goodridge Bros. in Mich (check this out). Worked early (50s), var. of formats—st [stereos], ambros, tts [tintypes], dags [daguerreotypes] incl. st. Vy rare, had 4 stereos, 2 stolen, city sts., farm. Saw a cab. port. in fam. album, prob. also made CDVs [cartes de visite].'" Treadwell added that "I remember him [Darrah] showing me these [farm stereos]. They were on cream or ivory mts. [mounts] of a family in front of a farmhouse." Tex (T. K.) Treadwell to author, 15 February 1992.

51. *Columbia Spy,* 30 March 1861.

52. Ibid.

53. The grand jury indictment in "Commonwealth vs. Glenalvin J. Goodridge," No. 24, August Term 1862, is in Record Group 26, Records of the Department of State, Clemency File, December 1864, Pennsylvania State Archives.

54. See ibid. for the trial transcript.

55. The verdict and list of jurors are in Record Group 15, Records of the Department of Justice, Bureau of Correction, Eastern State Penitentiary, Commitments, 1863, Pennsylvania State Archives. See also *York Gazette,* 18 November 1862 and 24 February 1863.

56. Prowell, *History of York County,* 1:485, 496.

57. The motions for a new trial are in "Copy of Record in the Court of Oyer & Terminor & General Jail Delivery for the County of York in the Case of Commonwealth vs Glenalvin J. Goodridge," Record Group 26, Records of the Department of State, Clemency File, December 1864, Pennsylvania State Archives. See also *York Gazette,* 11 November 1862.

58. See Record Group 15, Records of the Department of Justice, Bureau of Corrections, Eastern State Penitentiary, Commitments, 1863, Pennsylvania State Archives.

59. *York Democratic Press,* 9 May 1862; and Descriptive Register, 1858–1875, Record Group 15, Records of the Department of Justice, Bureau of Corrections, Eastern State Penitentiary, Pennsylvania State Archives.

60. See Record Group 15, Records of the Department of the Justice, Bureau of Correction, Eastern State Penitentiary, Admission and Discharge Book, 1844–1865, and Descriptive Register, 1858–1875, Pennsylvania State Archives. See also Kenneth N. Anderson, Lois E. Anderson, and Walter D. Glanze, eds., *Mosby's Medical, Nursing, and Allied Health Dictionary,* 4th ed. (St. Louis: Mosby, 1994), 570.

61. The petition is in Record Group 26, Records of the Department of State, Clemency File, December 1864, Pennsylvania State Archives.

62. V. K. Keesey and John Gibson to Andrew G. Curtin, n.d., David Fahs to Curtin, n.d., William Chapman to Curtin, 1 February 1864, Thomas K. White to Curtin, 3 February 1864, and D. E. Small to Curtin, 8 February 1864, all ibid.

63. Robert J. Fisher to Curtin, 17 February 1864, ibid.

64. William Hay to Curtin, 7 June 1864, ibid.

65. C. H. Bressler to Curtin, 21 November 1864, ibid.

66. Fisher to Curtin, 10 December 1864, ibid.

67. See ibid. for the pardon.

68. James McClure, "No Small Matter: Politics and a Small-

Town Editor" (master's thesis, Penn State University, Harrisburg, 1994), 55, 67–68, 66.

69. Quoted in ibid., 67.

70. For example, not even a hint that Glenalvin had been tried, convicted, and imprisoned for rape appears in any of the public or private accounts of the Goodridge family's history in York that are cited in note 2, chapter 1.

71. For an analysis of the subsequent meaning of the June 1863 Confederate occupation of York for Yorkers see McClure, "No Small Matter," 82–100.

72. York "Cartridge Box," 7 May 1865.

73. A record of Glenalvin's death is contained in "Rhoda C. Goodrich v. The Massachusetts Life Insurance Company," 1869, Circuit Court for the County of Saginaw, Michigan, Case No. 2571. William C. Goodridge's death is recorded in Certificate of Death Record 1873, p. 35, line 22, City of Minneapolis, County of Hennepin, State of Minnesota.

74. For Rhoda and Glen Goodridge following Glenalvin's death, see the appropriate city directory listings for both East Saginaw and York; the York Dispatch, 18 December 1903; and Roosevelt Samuel Ruffin, Black Presence in Saginaw, Mich., 1855–1900 (Saginaw: n.p., 1978), 40–53.

Chapter 3

1. Harpole, ed., "Black Community in St. Anthony," 42–53; and Saginaw Weekly Enterprise, 6 and 27 August 1863.

2. This information is derived from Ruffin, Black Presence in Saginaw, 40–56. At least one African American family from York, the Washington Foote family, may have followed the Goodridges to East Saginaw. The Footes' youngest son, Lincoln, was born in Pennsylvania in 1864, while youngest daughter Emma was born in Michigan in 1868. Ibid., 47; Pennsylvania, Manuscript Census Schedules, 1860, York County, York Borough, First Division; Michigan, Manuscript Census Schedules, 1860, Saginaw County, East Saginaw; and Michigan, Manuscript Census Schedules, 1870, Saginaw County, City of Saginaw, Second Ward.

3. This conclusion is based on information derived from the Saginaw Weekly Enterprise of 6 August, 10 September, and 22 October 1863 and the East Saginaw and Saginaw City directories for the period.

4. Leslie E. Arndt, The Bay County Story: From Footpaths to Freeways (Bay City, Mich.: Leslie E. Arndt, 1982), 61–71. Oblinger, in "New Freedoms, Old Miseries," 146, wrote that "William Goodridge of York developed an affinity for vacationing and visiting friends and family in the Bay City, Michigan, area" and that "In 1863, William Goodridge moved his family to Bay City, Michigan, moments before the Confederate army captured York." This author and the staffs of The Historical Society of York County and the Chester County (Pa.) Historical Society have not been successful in their attempts to locate the sources Oblinger cited to substantiate his conjecture regarding Goodridge connections with Bay City in 1863 or before.

5. For Tocqueville's visit to Saginaw see George Lawrence, trans., and J. P. Mayer, ed., Journey to America: Alexis de Tocqueville (New York: Doubleday, 1971), 399, 391, 390. For the historical development of Saginaw see Michael A. Leeson, History of Saginaw County, Michigan (Chicago: Chas. C. Chapman & Co., 1881; reprint, Evansville: Unigraphic, Inc., 1975), 493–96, 457, 593–608; and James Cooke Mills, History of Saginaw County, Michigan: Historical, Commercial, Biographical, 2 vols. (Saginaw: Seeman & Peters, 1918; reprint, Mt. Vernon, Ind.: Windmill Publications, 1992), 1:117–159.

6. Leeson, History of Saginaw County, 457.

7. Ibid., 389–92. The development of the industry is described in detail in Jeremy W. Kilar, Michigan's Lumbertowns: Lumbermen and Laborers in Saginaw, Bay City, and Muskegon, 1870–1905 (Detroit: Wayne State University Press, 1990), 19–34, 50–75.

8. James Sutherland, comp., State of Michigan Gazetteer and Business Directory for 1856–7 (Detroit: H. Huntington Lee & Co., 1856), 108; and Charles F. Clark, comp., Michigan Gazetteer and Business Directory for 1863–4 (Detroit, 1863), 298–300.

9. Sutherland, comp., Michigan Gazetteer for 1856–7, 108, 187; Saginaw Weekly Enterprise, 28 April and 24 November 1859; and East Saginaw Courier, 4 August and 24 November 1859.

10. Michigan, Manuscript Census Schedules, 1860, Saginaw County, East Saginaw; East Saginaw Courier, 12 July and 8 November 1860; and Saginaw Weekly Enterprise, 25 October and 1 and 8 November 1860.

11. East Saginaw Courier, 6 June 1861.

12. Saginaw Weekly Enterprise, 2 January 1862.

13. Ibid., 8 January 1863. "Views" doubtless refers to stereoscopic photographs.

14. Ibid., 8 April 1864. Eastman may have remained in East Saginaw for a time, but he does not appear in the 1870 census, nor is he listed in any directory after 1864.

15. Ibid., 30 July 1863, 7 January 1864, and 5 January 1865; East Saginaw Courier, 30 September 1863 and 16 November 1864; and Clark, comp., Michigan Gazetteer for 1863–4, 544.

16. James M. Thomas and A. M. Galatian, comps., Indian and Pioneer History of the Saginaw Valley, with Histories of East Saginaw, Saginaw City and Bay City, from Their Earliest Settlements, also Pioneer Directory and Business Advertiser, for 1866 and 1867 (East Saginaw: Lewis A. Lyon, 1866), 137; and Michigan Manuscript Census Schedules, 1870, Saginaw County, City of East Saginaw, Second Ward.

17. Saginaw Evening News, 17 July 1902.

18. Darrah, Cartes de Visite, 87. Darrah also notes that "A two-cent tax was levied on photographs selling for less than twenty-five cents, a three-cent tax on those selling for twenty-six cents to fifty cents, and a five-cent tax on those selling for fifty cents to one dollar. I know of no cartes de visite that sold for more than seventy-five cents. In March 1865 the act was amended, including a reduction of the tax on cards selling for less than ten cents to

one cent." Ibid. For a more technical discussion of the tax and its implementation see Kathleen Fuller, "Civil War Stamp Duty; Photography as a Revenue Source," *History of Photography* 4 (October 1980): 263–82.

19. *Saginaw Weekly Enterprise,* 19 January and 9 February 1865; and *Saginaw Valley Herald,* 17 May 1866. For the Meade and Merrill connection to the Meade brothers of New York, see Rinhart and Rinhart, *American Daguerreotype,* 402.

20. *Saginaw Weekly Enterprise,* 2 February 1865; and Albert A. Blum, "Guns, Grain, and Iron Ore: Michigan's Economy during the Civil War," *Michigan History* 69 (May–June 1985): 13–20.

21. "Rhoda C. Goodridge v. The Massachusetts Life Insurance Company," 1869, Circuit Court for the County of Saginaw, Michigan, Case No. 2571.

22. Ibid.

23. Ibid.

24. Pennsylvania, Manuscript Census Schedules, 1860, York Borough, First Division; Saginaw County, Death Records, Book A, p. 18; and Michigan, Manuscript Census Schedules, 1870, Saginaw County, City of East Saginaw, Fourth Ward.

25. Thomas and Galatian, comps., *Indian and Pioneer History of the Saginaw Valley,* 135, 137; *East Saginaw Courier,* 11 October 1866; *Saginaw Daily Enterprise,* 4 and 8 October 1867; *Saginaw Weekly Enterprise,* 11 October 1866, 15 October 1868; *Holland's East Saginaw and Saginaw City Directory for 1868–9* (Chicago, 1868), 82; *East Saginaw and Saginaw City Directory, 1870–1* (East Saginaw: Robert L. Dudley, 1869), 53; *General Directory of East Saginaw & South Saginaw* (East Saginaw: Brown, Smythe & Nichols, 1872), 107–8, 288.

26. Record of Marriages, County of Saginaw, Michigan, Book A, Document 66, p. 5; Ruffin, *Black Presence in Saginaw,* 50; Michigan, Manuscript Census Schedules, 1870, Saginaw County, City of Saginaw, Third Ward; and *Saginaw Daily Courier,* 22 January 1874.

27. *Saginaw News,* 4 March 1922; Pennsylvania, Manuscript Census Schedules, 1850, York County, York Borough, North Ward; Pennsylvania, Manuscript Census Schedules, 1860, York County, York Borough, First Division; and *Saginaw Evening News,* 17 July 1902.

28. *Saginaw Daily Enterprise,* 11 May 1869.

29. Thomas and Galatian, comps., *Indian and Pioneer History of the Saginaw Valley,* 62.

30. Welling, *Photography in America,* 175–77.

31. Quoted in ibid., 131, emphasis added. For a photograph of Gurney's original New York City gallery, see Robert Taft, *Photography and the American Scene: A Social History, 1839–1939* (New York: Macmillan, 1938), 115.

32. Ben L. Bassham, *The Theatrical Photographs of Napoleon Sarony* (Kent, Ohio: Kent State University Press, 1978), 3–22.

33. Welling, *Photography in America,* 170–72.

34. *Saginaw Weekly Enterprise,* 2 February 1865.

35. Taft, *Photography and the American Scene,* 153–66.

36. See *Saginaw Weekly Enterprise,* 8 November 1860, for an ad by Eastman; and ibid., 19 January 1865, for a similar directive to mothers by the Goodridges.

37. For a detailed discussion of the opposition see Fuller, "Civil War Stamp Duty," 267–71.

38. Darrah, *Cartes de Visite,* 4.

39. Ibid., 6–8.

40. Approximately eight hundred Goodridge photographs of all types for the period 1847 to 1922 are extant. Of that total, ninety-nine, or 12 percent, are cartes de visite.

41. Darrah, *Cartes de Visite,* 29.

42. Ibid., 28–29.

43. Ibid., 31.

44. Ibid., 119. Approximately one-half, forty-eight of ninety-nine, of the extant Goodridge cartes de visite are non-portrait cartes.

45. Martha A. Sandweiss, "Undecisive Moments: The Narrative Tradition in Western Photography," in *Photography in Nineteenth-Century America,* ed. Sandweiss, 112.

46. Leeson, *History of Saginaw County,* 519–20; and Lloyd J. Cartwright, ed., *Our Little Brown Church* (Saginaw: Jefferson Avenue United Methodist Church, 1978), 27, 32, 34, 56–58.

47. Mills, *History of Saginaw County,* 1:285–290.

48. Ibid., 609.

49. Ibid., 186.

50. Ralph K. Roberts, letter to author, 28 March 1994.

51. Leeson, *History of Saginaw County,* 498.

52. Mills, *History of Saginaw County,* 1:709. According to Ralph K. Roberts, the *Buena Vista* did not look "much like that drawing. I think she may have resembled a small stern wheel Ohio or Mississippi River steamboat. She would of necessity have been of very shallow draft, and almost certainly had hogging chains (to support the ends of a shallow hull). It probably wasn't more than a powered barge." Ralph K. Roberts, letter to author, 15 March 1992. Mills confirms Roberts's suspicion by noting that the *Buena Vista* "had no cabin and only rows of benches for seats." *History of Saginaw County,* 1:710.

53. Ralph K. Roberts, letter to author, 15 March 1992.

54. Mills, *History of Saginaw County,* 1:147.

55. Anthony Bannon, *The Taking of Niagara: A History of the Falls in Photography* (Buffalo: Media Study, 1982), 14.

56. Sandweiss, "Undecisive Moments," 113.

57. *Saginaw News Courier,* [1925?], "Saginaw Schools Clipping File," Eddy Local History and Genealogical Collection, Hoyt Public Library.

58. *Saginaw Daily Courier,* 6 June 1876.

59. Darrah, *Cartes de Visite,* 10, 170.

60. Charles Hamilton and Lloyd Ostendorf, *Lincoln in Photographs: An Album of Every Known Pose* (Norman: University of Oklahoma Press, 1963), 270.

61. Darrah, *Cartes de Visite,* 172–75.

62. For the relationship between art and photography, see Rinhart and Rinhart, *American Daguerreotype,* 225–63; and Beaumont Newhall, *The History of Photography from 1839 to the Present,* rev. ed. (New York: Museum of Mod-

ern Art, 1982), 73–83. F. H. Wilson asked the question "Is Photography Art?" of those attending the June 1886 convention of the Photographers' Association of America in St. Louis, Missouri. *Anthony's Photographic Bulletin* published the address in two installments, 14 and 28 August 1886, pp. 463–65, 490–91.

63. Welling, *Photography in America,* 195–98; and Hales, "American Views," 213.

64. Taft, *Photography and the American Scene,* 323–24.

65. Darrah, *Cartes de Visite,* 10.

66. Darrah, *World of Stereographs,* 23.

67. Hales, "American Views," 209.

68. William Culp Darrah, *Stereo Views: A History of Stereographs in America and Their Collection* (Gettysburg: Times and News Publishing Co., 1964), 8–9.

69. *East Saginaw Courier,* 26 August 1863 and 25 January 1865; and *Saginaw Weekly Enterprise,* 18 May 1865.

70. *Saginaw Weekly Enterprise,* 9 February 1865; Thomas and Galatian, comps., *Indian and Pioneer History of the Saginaw Valley,* 62; *Saginaw Valley Herald,* 7 June 1866; and *Saginawian,* 1 July 1870.

71. Dave Tinder, letter to author, 26 June 1995. According to the Michigan Manuscript Census Schedules, 1870, Saginaw County, City of Saginaw, Second Ward, Leonard Gradt was a twenty-eight-year-old photographer who had been born in Prussia. He was married to Ularia Gradt, also born in Prussia. The couple owned $1,000 each of personal and real property and had lived in Michigan since at least 1867 because both daughter Louisa, age three, and son Charles, seven months, had been born in the state. Only three examples of Gradt's work are known.

72. Mills, *History of Saginaw County,* 1:193.

73. Leeson, *History of Saginaw County,* 523.

74. Darrah, *Stereo Views,* 6.

75. Jack Naylor, telephone conversation with author, 18 October 1995.

76. Darrah, *World of Stereographs,* 3.

77. Mills, *History of Saginaw County,* 1:65–69.

78. Compare the Goodridge stereo (figure 3.24b) with the portrait of James S. Webber included in ibid., 187. The stereo is mounted on card stock printed for the Goodridge studio by W. T. Rich, an East Saginaw printer, whose business operated for only a single year, 1876. James S. Webber's initials, numbering system, and notes also appear on other than Goodridge stereos. Webber had owned a view of the harbor at Belfast, Maine, by H. L. Kilgore, an anonymous view of two young women "Down by the Creek," and an unsigned stereograph of Lincoln's funeral parade on Broadway in New York City, possibly by Gurney. Included in the same collection, although without Webber's initials, were four views of the steamer *Quebec* by William Notman of Montreal, a hard-hat diver in Duluth harbor by Caswell and Davy of Duluth, and the steamer *Red Wing* at St. Paul, a view of Lake Como, and a series on Native Americans, all by C. A. Zimmermann of St. Paul. Douglas Doughty, conver-

sation with author, Saginaw, Michigan, 10 October 1995.

79. Darrah, *World of Stereographs,* 44.

80. *Saginaw Daily Courier,* 27 March 1871.

81. Ibid., 21 March 1871.

82. Leeson, *History of Saginaw County,* 446.

83. Darrah, *World of Stereographs,* 7.

84. *East Saginaw Courier,* 24 January and 3 May 1866; and *Saginaw Valley Herald,* 17 January 1867.

85. Thomas and Galatian, comps., *Indian and Pioneer History of the Saginaw Valley,* 62; and *Saginawian,* 1 July and 31 December 1870.

86. Darrah, *World of Stereographs,* 91; and Darrah, *Stereo Views,* 237.

87. The Saginaw photographers included W. A. Armstrong (1865), L. W. Gradt (1873), J. T. Randall (1865), William Roberts (1865), and Charles Schroeder (1869). An inventory of Michigan photographers who worked in Bay, Genesee, Saginaw, and Midland Counties between 1865 and 1870 includes an additional twelve names. Dave Tinder, letter to author, 21 August 1992. The only one of the twelve who was serious competition to the Goodridge stereo series, both before and after 1872, was James A. Jenney, who operated a studio in Flint between 1866 and 1875. For a more complete discussion of Jenney and the Goodridges see chapter 4.

88. *Saginaw Evening News,* 18 August 1890.

89. Glyndon G. Van Deusen, *Horace Greeley: Nineteenth-Century Crusader* (Philadelphia: University of Pennsylvania Press, 1953), 345–46.

90. *Saginaw Weekly Enterprise* 11 October 1866; and Darrah, *Cartes de Visite,* 48.

91. *Saginaw Weekly Enterprise,* 17 October 1872.

92. *East Saginaw Courier,* 11 October 1866; *Saginaw Daily Enterprise,* 4 and 8 October 1867; and *Saginaw Weekly Enterprise,* 11 October 1866 and 15 October 1868.

93. *Saginaw Daily Courier,* 1 and 17 October 1870; *Saginaw Daily Enterprise,* 18 August, 1 and 18 October. 1869; *Saginaw Weekly Enterprise,* 2 September, 14 October 1869 and 27 October 1870; and *Saginawian,* 21 August and 15 October 1869.

94. Rinhart and Rinhart, *American Daguerreotype,* 108.

95. *Saginaw Daily Courier,* 30 September 1871.

96. *Saginaw Weekly Enterprise,* 2 November 1871.

97. *Saginaw Daily Courier,* 11 December 1872.

98. *Saginaw Daily Enterprise,* 4 February 1869.

99. Ibid., 4 and 21 January and 4 February 1869.

100. *Saginaw Daily Courier,* 3 January 1872.

101. Ibid., 23 and 24 October 1872.

102. Ibid., 25 October and 10 November 1872.

103. Ibid., 27 and 30 July 1871; and William Gooderich [*sic*] v. T. Daily Mower, 1871, Circuit Court for the County of Saginaw, Michigan, Case No. 3149.

104. *Saginaw Daily Courier,* 30 July 1871.

105. Ruffin, *Black Presence in Saginaw,* 46–56.

106. Michigan, Manuscript Census Schedules, 1870, Saginaw County, East Saginaw, Fourth Ward.

107. Ruffin, *Black Presence in Saginaw*, 45–46; and Francis H. Warren, comp., *Michigan Manual of Freedmen's Progress* (1915; reprint, with a foreword by John M. Green, Detroit: John M. Green Publisher, 1968), 298.

108. Ruffin, *Black Presence in Saginaw*, 45–46.

109. Ibid., 46–56.

110. Thomas and Galatian, comps., *Indian and Pioneer History of the Saginaw Valley*, 29; and *Saginaw Daily Enterprise*, 4 January 1869.

111. Thomas and Galatian, comps., *Indian and Pioneer History of the Saginaw Valley*, 29; Record of Marriages, County of Saginaw, Michigan, Book A, Document 66, p. 5; and William Gooderich [sic] v. T. Daily Mower, 1871, Circuit Court for the County of Saginaw, Michigan, Case No. 3149.

112. Ruffin, *Black Presence in Saginaw*, 9; Sheets, *Children of the Circuit Riders*, 82; and *Detroit Plain Dealer*, 20 February 1891 and 27 May 1892.

113. Warren, comp., *Michigan Manual of Freedmen's Progress*, 21–22; *Saginaw Daily Republican*, 8 June 1878; and *Saginaw Daily Courier*, 23 April, 1881.

114. *Saginaw Daily Enterprise*, 4 February 1869; *Saginaw Weekly Enterprise*, 17 October 1872; and *Saginaw Daily Courier*, 20 May and 27 March 1871, 14 February, 14 September, and 24 and 27 October 1872, 2 August 1876, and 19 November 1885.

115. Ruffin, *Black Presence in Saginaw*, 14–15.

116. *Saginaw Daily Courier*, 30 September 1871.

117. Ruffin, *Black Presence in Saginaw*, 13.

118. *Saginaw Daily Enterprise*, 4 and 21 January and 4 February 1869.

119. *Saginaw Daily Courier*, 30 July 1871.

Chapter 4

1. Mills, *History of Saginaw County*, 1:241.

2. Kilar, *Michigan's Lumbertowns*, 176–87.

3. Ibid., 260–65; and Mills, *History of Saginaw County*, 1:403.

4. *Saginaw City Directory for 1890–91* (Saginaw, 1890), 96–97, 637–38, 658, 664, 671–75, 678–85, 708–10, 714–15, 717–22, 729–30, 735; Brown, Smythe, and Nichols, comps., *General Directory of East Saginaw and South Saginaw*, 281–85, 287, 289; and *Saginaw City Directory, 1872–3* (St. Louis, 1872), 69, 71–72.

5. Mills, *History of Saginaw County*, 1:715; *Saginaw City Directory for 1890–91*, 105–6; and Kilar, *Michigan's Lumbertowns*, 91–93.

6. On the price war see *Saginaw Morning Herald*, 10 and 15 April 1883; *Saginaw Evening Express*, 10 April 1883; and *Saginaw Evening News*, 11 October and 20 December 1884.

7. *Saginaw Evening News*, 21 September 1888.

8. Dave Tinder, letter to author, 21 August 1992; and Franck Geuder, "Index of Saginaw Photographers, 1865–1891," manuscript in possession of author. For information on the Armstrongs, see *Saginaw Daily Courier*, 11 February 1874 and 28 September 1878. Mrs. W. A. Armstrong may have been Helen A. Newton, who married William A. Armstrong in East Saginaw on July 5, 1866, when she was seventeen years old and the groom twenty-four years old. See entry for William A. Armstrong in "Biography File," Eddy Local History and Genealogical Collection, Hoyt Public Library, Saginaw, Michigan.

9. *Saginaw Daily Courier*, 23 and 25 October 1872.

10. Ibid., 27 October 1872.

11. Ibid., 10 November 1872.

12. My analysis of the history of the ownership of Lot 3, Block 33 of Hoyt's Plat is based on the abstract of the title to the property. I am grateful to Larry Coulouris of Saginaw for the opportunity to examine the abstract. I am grateful to Dawn I. Coates of the Superior Abstract & Title Co. of Saginaw for assistance in analyzing the abstract.

13. The chronology of the Goodridge studio's evolution is based on an analysis of city directories for East Saginaw for the years 1872 to 1890 and the abstract of the title to the property at 220 South Washington.

14. *Saginaw Evening Express*, 22 October 1881.

15. *Detroit Plain Dealer*, 9 May 1890.

16. *Saginaw Daily Courier*, 10 November 1872.

17. Bassham, *Theatrical Photographs of Napoleon Sarony*, 4.

18. Darrah, *Cartes de Visite*, 32–33.

19. *Cleveland Gazette*, 20 August 1887. The *Gazette* was an African American weekly published in Cleveland between 1883 and 1892. It regularly reported news from African American communities throughout the Midwest.

20. Warren, comp., *Michigan Manual of Freedmen's Progress*, 296; Walter Romig, *Michigan Place Names* (Grosse Pointe, Mich., n.d.), 609. I am indebted to Dave Tinder of Dearborn, Michigan, for calling my attention to Freeney's career with the Goodridge brothers. For Freeney in East Saginaw, see the appropriate city directories for the period and *Cleveland Gazette*, 20 August 1887.

21. Michigan, Manuscript Census Schedules, 1880, Saginaw County, City of East Saginaw, p. 49. For details of Arthur William Brown's tenure with the Goodridge studio I am indebted to Dave Tinder of Dearborn, Michigan. Information on Brown's career in Gaylord was provided by William H. Granlund of Gaylord, Michigan. Also see *East Saginaw and Saginaw City Directory, 1879–80* (East Saginaw, 1879), 85; *East Saginaw and Saginaw City Directory for 1881–82* (East Saginaw, 1881), 104, 306; and *East Saginaw and Saginaw City Directory for 1883* (Detroit, 1883), 112, 339.

22. *Cleveland Gazette*, 20 August 1887. For William Edwards, see *Directory of the City of East Saginaw and the City of Saginaw for 1886* (Detroit, 1886), 157. Dave Tinder of Dearborn, Michigan, supplied the information on Edwards in Baltimore. For George Watson see the *Detroit Plain Dealer*, 9 May 1890. Joseph H. Gray's biography appears in *Cleveland Gazette*, 2 July 1887. See also Ruffin,

Black Presence in Saginaw, 33, 39. For Glen J. Goodridge, see *Directory of the City of East Saginaw for 1884* (Detroit, 1884), 139; *Directory of Saginaw for 1886*, 183; *Directory of the City of East Saginaw for 1887* (Detroit, 1887), 201; *Directory of the City of East Saginaw for 1889* (Detroit, 1889), 201; and *Directory of the City of Saginaw for 1891–2* (Detroit, 1891), 365.

23. Joan L. Severa, *Dressed for the Photographer: Ordinary Americans and Fashion, 1840–1900* (Kent, Ohio: Kent State University Press, 1995). See especially chapter 5, "The 1880s," 372–454.

24. Darrah, *Cartes de Visite*, 10.

25. Ibid., 33.

26. During the mid-1870s the Goodridge studio used card stock for carte de visite, cabinet card, and stereograph mounts printed by "W. T. RICH, Book and Job Printer, East Saginaw." According to the East Saginaw directories, W. T. Rich operated in East Saginaw only during 1876. For Rich see *East Saginaw Directory, 1876* (Detroit, 1876), 148.

27. *Saginaw Morning Herald*, 25 June 1879. See Welling, *Photography in America*, 175–76, 257–58, 260, for the chronology of dry-plate film and use of artificial lighting in photography in the United States.

28. Burns, *Sleeping Beauty*, [ii].

29. Darrah, *Cartes de Visite*, 144–45.

30. Burns, in Updike, "Facing Death," illustration, p. 105.

31. Darrah, *Cartes de Visite*, 175.

32. Ibid., 10.

33. *Saginaw Daily Courier*, 10 November 1872.

34. Mills, *History of Saginaw County*, 1:664–70. According to Candace Main Rush, Information Specialist for the National Association of Letter Carriers, the NALC Branch 74 in East Saginaw was chartered on November 23, 1890. The low branch number indicates that an association of letter carriers was active in East Saginaw during the 1880s. In addition, the mailbag with hobnail bottom was common from the 1860s on. The headgear was not regulation, but Rush suggests that "each local tended to pick their own hat style and in climates like East Saginaw this may have been acceptable winter headgear." Candace Main Rush to author, 11 March 1993.

35. Darrah, *Cartes de Visite*, 120–21.

36. For Effie Ellsler's career and the details of her 1878 visit to East Saginaw see Edward T. James et al., eds., *Notable American Women, 1607–1950*, 3 vols. (Cambridge, Mass.: Belknap Press of Harvard University Press, 1971), 1:579–80; William Granson Rose, *Cleveland: The Making of a City* (Kent, Ohio: Kent State University Press, 1990), 216–17, 260–61; *Saginaw Daily Courier*, 10 March, 20, 24, 25, and 27 October, 13 November, 8, 14, 20, and 21 December 1878; and George C. D. Odell, *Annals of the New York Stage*, 15 vols. (New York: Columbia University Press, 1970), 11:16, 21–22. For Henrietta Chanfrau's career, see Allen Johnson and Dumas Malone, eds., *Dictionary of American Biography*, 13 vols. (New York: C. Scribner's Sons, 1931–37), 2, pt. 2:2.

37. Darrah, *Cartes de Visite*, 191–92. A notice in the 6 March 1882 *Saginaw Evening Express* stated that the Goodridge brothers had recently "completed arrangements to make some mammoth views, 20 by 25 inches, for some of the leading rail roads of Michigan." The technology to make a mammoth portrait of Ellsler, therefore, was available at the studio.

38. *Saginaw Weekly Enterprise*, 11 October 1866, 17 October 1867, 15 October 1868, and 18 October 1869; *Saginaw Daily Courier*, 17 October 1870, 30 September 1871, and 27 and 28 October 1875; *East Saginaw Courier*, 28 October 1875; and *Saginaw Morning Herald*, 1 October 1878.

39. *Saginaw Daily Courier*, 30 September 1871.

40. Reese Jenkins, *Images and Enterprise: Technology and the American Photographic Industry, 1839 to 1925* (Baltimore: Johns Hopkins University Press, 1975), 160–61.

41. Mills, *History of Saginaw County*, 1:584.

42. George M. Brown to William B. Mershon, 7 February 1920, quoted in William Butts Mershon, *Recollection of My Fifty Years of Hunting and Fishing* (Boston: The Stratford Co., 1923), 144–45. I am grateful to William Oberschmidt of Saginaw for bringing my attention to Mershon's book.

43. Ibid., 156–57. Mershon included the Goodridge photograph of "The Peggy" in his book, facing page 156.

44. G. Forsberg Macliver, *Days and Ways of Pioneer Michigan as Revealed in Buttonville to North Bradley* (Ann Arbor: Edwards Bros., 1962), 10–11.

45. *Cleveland Gazette*, 20 August 1887.

46. For the technical details of this process, see chapter 3.

47. *Saginaw Daily Courier*, 18 July 1878; *Saginaw Morning Herald*, 2 October 1878.

48. Mills, *History of Saginaw County*, 1:731. According to Mills, "It was originally planned" that the Flint & Pere Marquette

> enter East Saginaw from the southeast in the vicinity of Bristol Street. On the east side of the river there was to be a depot and a freight house about where the City Hall stands, and on the other side of the river another depot near the present residence of Clark L. Ring. At this central point was eventually to be built the main shipping yards to serve both cities and shops and supply station for the entire road. This plan, though a very feasible one, met with decided opposition of the citizens of Saginaw City who fought every improvement promoted by outsiders. Led by George W. Bullock, Peter C. Andre and other obstructionists, they exerted every influence to defeat the project, believing that since theirs was the older town it only was entitled to the road. In order, therefore, to cut off East Saginaw from any connection with the new road they insisted that it should come in further south and cross the river near Mackinaw Street. The plan provided for a depot, yards and shops near Gratiot and Mackinaw Streets.
>
> But their folly defeated their own object. East Saginaw, promoted by more enterprising and progressive men, was forging rapidly ahead and it was apparent to all was destined to be the railroad center of Eastern Michigan. Thoroughly disgusted by the tactics of the narrow men of

Saginaw City . . . the railroad projectors decided to shut them off entirely. They accordingly located the line to enter East Saginaw to the north instead of the south of the business section, and purchased a large tract of land near the river for a depot and terminals. (720–21)

49. *Saginaw Daily Courier,* 27 May 1873. William made a second view of the Jackson Hall ruins looking down on them from the roof of the Bancroft House.

50. Mills, *History of Saginaw County,* 1:670.

51. *Saginaw Daily Courier,* 28 May 1873.

52. Ibid., 21 June 1873.

53. Ibid., 26 June 1873.

54. Darrah, *World of Stereographs,* 44.

55. Mills, *History of Saginaw County,* 1:726; and Ralph W. Stroebel, "Sawmills of Saginaw County," *Saginaw County Historian* 1 (Winter 1983): 20–21.

56. *Saginaw Daily Courier,* 23 April 1876.

57. *Saginaw Evening Express,* 6 March 1882.

58. Mills, *History of Saginaw County,* 1:150, 408–9; and Ralph Roberts to author, 22 March 1993.

59. Stan Berriman, *Upper Tittabawassee River Boom Towns* (Midland, Mich.: Messersmith, 1970), 152–53.

60. *Saginaw Daily Courier,* 25 March 1881.

61. *Midland Republican,* 31 March 1881, quoted in Berriman, *Upper Tittabawassee River Boom Towns,* 155.

62. *Saginaw Daily Courier,* 16 December 1873. A report detailing the 1878 Goodridge entry at the Agricultural Society Fair noted that it included "a moonlight photo—a double print." *Saginaw Morning Herald,* 26 September 1878. Views titled "Moonlight Saginaw River" and "Tittabawassee River by Moonlight" also are listed as numbers 624 and 297, respectively, in the "Miscellaneous" section of "Picturesque Michigan" (see figure 4.37a). A second view, but in larger 8 x 10 format and also titled "Tittabawassee River by Moonlight," was made from the exact same vantage point as figure 4.29c. The larger view, however, is numbered 307 rather than 297. The location of the logs and pattern of the clouds, moreover, suggests that 307 was made shortly after 297.

63. Welling, *Photography in America,* 267. Darrah, in *World of Stereographs,* 90, notes that on the night of 12 January 1884, Charles E. Emery of Silver Cliff, Colorado, "photographed Silver Cliff by moonlight. . . . This stereo view was a genuine triumph, not a printed fake from composite negatives."

64. *Saginaw Morning Herald,* 16 April 1879.

65. Mills, *History of Saginaw County,* 1:260.

66. *Saginaw Morning Herald,* 3 October 1879.

67. Stroebel, "Sawmills of Saginaw County," 9–10. Mills, *History of Saginaw County,* 1:373, includes a photograph of Saylor that may have been made by the Goodridge studio.

68. Mills, *History of Saginaw County,* 1:719–25; Forrest B. Meek, *Michigan's Timber Battleground: A History of Clare County, 1674–1900* (Clare, Mich.: Forrest B. Meek in Conjunction with the Clare County Bicentennial Historical Committee, 1976), 129–38, contains an excellent account of the development of the Flint & Pere Marquette Railroad in Michigan.

69. *Cleveland Gazette,* 18 February 1888. Peter B. Hales, *William Henry Jackson and the Transformation of the American Landscape* (Philadelphia: Temple University Press, 1988), 141–50, contains an excellent account of the relationship between photography and the railroads during the second half of the nineteenth century.

70. For Patrick Glynn's biography, see the *Saginaw News Chronicle*'s article the day following his death, 16 December 1922.

71. State of Michigan, Midland County, *Deeds,* Book K, 212–13, Book O, 337–38, and Book T, 330–32.

72. Mills, *History of Saginaw County,* 1:158.

73. State of Michigan, Midland County, *Deeds,* Book T, 608–12, and Book G, 422.

74. *Saginaw Daily Courier,* 16 September and 28 October 1874.

75. Ibid., 23 March 1873. According to the records in the Office of the Register of Deeds for Midland County, Michigan, Henry Gamble of East Saginaw purchased 400 acres of pineland from H. Morley of East Saginaw and J. C. Greenough of Dansville in Ingham County, Michigan, in November 1869. The land was located in Sections 7 and 18, Township 17, North Range 2 East, or present-day Bentley Township in Gladwin County. The land, a very swampy section of the present Ogemaw State Forest, is drained by Gurnsey Creek, which flows into Wixom Lake across from the town of All Bright Shores above the dam at Edenville. The *Courier* account is inaccurate in that the camp was located twenty, not three, miles from Midland City. See State of Michigan, Midland County, *Deeds,* Book F, 562. No other holdings for Henry Gamble are listed.

76. Darrah, *World of Stereographs,* 164. The Jenney stereo views of "L. B. Curtis & Co's Camp, Midland Co." in the collection of the Historical Society of Saginaw County bear the notation on the verso of each view that it was made "At L. B. Curtis Camp on Sturgeon River Winter 1871–2."

77. *Anthony's Photographic Bulletin* (May 15, 1875): 160.

78. It is possible to date the view precisely because the verso lists "Harry Shaw" as "Printer" of the stock, and Shaw is listed only in the 1877–78 Saginaw City directory as a printer living with his widowed mother on Webster between Millard and Thompson, within blocks of the Goodridge studio.

79. Darrah, *World of Stereographs,* 169.

80. *Saginaw Morning Herald,* 7 March 1880.

81. Darrah, *World of Stereographs,* 45–48.

82. *Saginaw Morning Herald,* 12 August 1880. Emphasis added.

83. New York Industrial Recorder, *An Illustrated and Commercial Review of Saginaw, Michigan* (New York, 1906), 20; and *Cleveland Gazette,* 14 April 1888.

84. The steam propeller vessel *Depere* was built of oak at Manitowoc, Wisconsin, in 1873 by Rand and Burger. It was 165 feet long, had a beam of 29 feet, and a depth of hold of 10 feet. Renamed the *State of Michigan* in 1893,

the vessel foundered off White Lake, Michigan, in Lake Michigan on 18 October 1901 when a connecting rod broke and punctured a hold in the bottom of the vessel. The boat sank three miles out in the lake in fifty feet of water. She was bound for Manistee from Muskegon on the last trip of the season. Ralph K. Roberts to author, 22 March 1993.

85. Meek, *Michigan's Timber Battleground*, 119, 378–80; and Forrest B. Meek, *Michigan's Heartland, 1900–1918* (Clare, Mich.: Edgewood Press, 1979), 150.

86. *Saginaw Daily Courier*, 31 July 1889.

87. Mircea Eliade, editor in chief, *The Encyclopedia of Religion*, 16 vols. (New York: Macmillan, 1987), 14:192–93, emphasis added.

88. Ibid., 193; and *Saginaw Morning Herald*, 14 March 1879. For information on Ingersoll and Sunderland see Johnson and Malone, eds., *Dictionary of American Biography*, 5:469–70 and 9:221–22.

89. *Saginaw Daily Courier*, 20 February 1876. Carrie Bliss was the daughter of Solomon and Frances Bliss, who had moved to East Saginaw in 1854 from Massachusetts and Ohio. Bliss rapidly established himself as a successful merchant, banker, and lumberman. In 1863–64 he was elected to the state legislature and was later appointed postmaster and treasurer of East Saginaw. He was founder of the Saginaw Valley Bank and built the Bliss Block at the southeast corner of Washington and Genesee Avenues. For a photograph and biography of Solomon Bliss, see Mills, *History of Saginaw County*, 1:198–99.

90. *Saginaw Morning Herald*, 23 May 1880.

91. Mills, *History of Saginaw County*, 2:271–72.

92. *Saginaw Morning Herald*, 29 February 1880.

93. John Cumming, *Little Jake of Saginaw* (Mount Pleasant, Mich.: Rivercrest House, 1978), 39–40 and passim.

94. *Saginaw Evening News*, 28 September 1884.

95. Mills, *History of Saginaw County*, 1:700; F. W. Beers & Co., *Atlas of Saginaw Co., Michigan* (New York, 1877; reprint, Evansville, Ind.: Unigraphic Inc., 1976), Section S, 58–59; Matthew Greenough, "Saginaw Improvement Company," *Saginaw County Historian* 1 (Spring 1983): 56.

96. *By-Laws and Rules of the East Saginaw Driving Park, also Articles of Association* (East Saginaw, 1873), 11–12.

97. Gross, *Saginaw*, 45.

98. Cumming, *Little Jake*, 27.

99. *Saginaw Daily Courier*, 5 September 1870 and 26 September 1873; and *East Saginaw Courier*, 11 October 1866.

100. *Cleveland Gazette*, 27 August 1887.

101. *Detroit Plain Dealer*, 9 May 1890; and *Saginaw Weekly Enterprise*, 5 October 1871.

102. Federal Writers' Project, *Connecticut: A Guide to Its Roads, Lore, and People* (Boston: Houghton Mifflin, 1938), 170–71, 181.

103. David J. Corrigan to author, November 17, 1993. For the iconography of the Charter Oak, see Robert F. Trent, "The Charter Oak Artifacts," and Christopher P. Bickford, "Connecticut and Its Charter," both in *Connecticut Historical Society Bulletin* 49 (Summer 1984).

Chapter 5

1. Welling, *Photography in America*, 122–23.

2. Quoted in ibid., 192.

3. *Saginaw Weekly Enterprise*, 19 January 1865.

4. Brown, Smythe, and Nichols, comps., *General Directory of East Saginaw and South Saginaw*, xlvii.

5. *Saginaw Evening Express*, 6 March 1882.

6. Welling, *Photography in America*, 326. The *Saginaw Morning Herald* for 23 May 1880 reported that "Having just received a new camera they [the Goodridge brothers] now have the largest collection of photographic instruments for portraits and views in the state."

7. *Detroit Plain Dealer*, 29 December 1889.

8. It is impossible to determine with any precision the number of large-format portrait and landscape photographs created by the more than two dozen photographers who worked in East Saginaw and Saginaw City between 1872 and 1890. The total certainly is in the thousands. What percentage of that total has survived and why some photographs did and others did not survive also is impossible to determine. My research during the past decade in both public depositories and private collections that contain large-format photographs created by Saginaw Valley photographers reveals that approximately one in three of these extant photographs can be attributed to an identifiable source. One-half of that one-third were made by the Goodridge brothers. Given the number of studios operating in the Saginaws at the time, that figure represents both a large number and a large percentage of the photographs. Why so many large-format Goodridge photographs have survived cannot be determined precisely. Perhaps it was purely by chance. Or it may have been that Saginaw residents early recognized the value of a "Photograph by Goodridge" and actively preserved them. Each is possible. But more likely the high Goodridge survival rate may simply have been due to the fact that the studio created many more large-format photographs than any other studio in the Saginaw Valley at the time.

9. Mills, *History of Saginaw County*, 1:308–9, 2:112–14. The Goodridge studio was chosen to make the portrait because of the Buckhout's satisfaction with an earlier commission. Under the headline "Fine Portrait," the *Saginaw Daily Courier* reported on 12 September 1874 that "We noticed last evening in the studio of Goodridge & Bros., a portrait of a lady, a relative of B. B. Buckhout, Esq. The work is very life like and finely executed."

10. *Saginaw Evening Express*, 28 August 1882. That same day, the *Saginaw Evening News* reported that "Goodridge Bros. took a photograph of the Cinderella troupe, but it did not 'pan out' very well because somebody moved the camera. Another picture will be taken tomorrow, when better results may be expected." On *Cinderella* as popu-

lar children's theater at the time, see Odell, *Annals of the New York Stage,* 11:206, 405.

11. Mills, *History of Saginaw County,* 1:671.

12. Roselynn Ederer, "The Academy of Music," *Courier of the Historical Society of Saginaw County,* 28 (November 1993): 4.

13. Mills, *History of Saginaw County,* 1:304–5. For a discussion of the design competition, see Thomas F. Trombley, "Invitation to Architects: The Competition to Design the Hoyt Library," *Saginaw County Historian* 1 (Summer 1983): 128–35.

14. *Saginaw Evening News,* 11 October 1890.

15. *Saginaw Daily Courier,* 9 June 1878.

16. Mills, *History of Saginaw County,* 1:208–19.

17. Ibid., 222.

18. Ibid., 231–35.

19. Ephriam Katz, *The Film Encyclopedia* (New York: Crowell, 1979), 750.

20. *East Saginaw Directory, 1877–8* (East Saginaw, 1877), 97; *East Saginaw and Saginaw Directory, 1879–80* (Detroit, 1879), 166, 325, 368; *East Saginaw and Saginaw Directory, 1881–82* (Detroit, 1881), 83, 211, 482; *East Saginaw and Saginaw Directory for 1883* (Detroit, 1883), 88, 233, 536; and *Directory of the City of East Saginaw and the City of Saginaw for 1886* (Detroit, 1886), which has no listing for Beals Photographers.

21. *Saginaw Morning Herald,* 23 May 1880.

22. *Saginaw Daily News,* 11 April 1914 and 11 January 1944. The verso of figure 5.6b is inscribed "George Boyd residence, 1617 S. Washington, Saginaw, Michigan."

23. Mills, *History of Saginaw County,* 1:109–10; and Leeson, *History of Saginaw County,* 304.

24. Leeson, *History of Saginaw County,* 314.

25. *Saginaw News,* 17 June 1934.

26. Mills, *History of Saginaw County,* 1:325; and William E. Richardson, George C. Ryan, and Anthony F. Brogger, *Seventy-fifth Anniversary, St. Andrew's Parish, Saginaw, Michigan, 1862–1937* (Saginaw: n.p., 1937), 10–16, 34.

27. *Saginaw Evening News,* 29 August 1887.

28. Don H. Scheuerlein, "'LIKE A SEED THAT IS SOWN': An abridged history of Michigan Lutheran Seminary—1885–1982" (1982), 1–8; and "A Brief History of the Evangelical Lutheran Synod of Michigan and Other States, 1860–1909" (n.d.), 16–17. Both manuscripts located in the Library of Michigan Lutheran Seminary, Saginaw, Michigan.

29. *Saginaw Courier-Herald,* 30 April 1889; and Thomas F. Trombley to author, 23 December 1997.

30. Mills, *History of Saginaw County,* 1:317, 334–36, 319.

31. *Cleveland Gazette,* 20 August 1887.

32. *Saginaw Morning Herald,* 29 July 1882.

33. Mills, *History of Saginaw County,* 1:721, 730.

34. Beers & Co., *Atlas of Saginaw Co.,* 58–59.

35. Thomas Mudd, telephone conversation with author, 5 February 1994.

36. The verso of figure 5.10b contains the following caption:

    The building at the right corner of the picture and just to the right of the park is the store supply building. The small building to the right of the roundhouse is the caller's office. The building behind the water tank is the store department office and oil room. The building behind the store department office is the mill. The building directly behind the roundhouse is the blacksmith shop and wheel shop. The building behind the blacksmith shop is the casting shed. The building behind the casting shed is the boiler shop. The building to the right of the boiler shop is the power plant. The long buildings to the left of the roundhouse is the machine shop and back shop. To the extreme left of the picture is the old Washington Avenue water tank.

37. New York Industrial Recorder, *Illustrated and Commercial Review of Saginaw,* 20.

38. *Saginaw Evening Express,* 11 April 1883; and *Saginaw Morning Herald,* 11 April 1883.

39. Darrah, *Stereo Views,* 9.

40. Darrah, *World of Stereographs,* 45–47. After 1872 no Saginaw photographer except the Goodridge brothers advertised stereographs in the local newssheets or entered them in the "Arts" competition of the annual Agricultural Society Fair. James A. Jenney of Flint was the lone exception.

41. *Saginaw Morning Herald,* 23 May 1880. Through the 1860s and 1870s the term "view" generally was applied to the "stereo view" or "stereograph." By the 1880s, however, the term "view" had been expanded to include large-format photographs, especially those made outside of a studio setting. The Goodridge studio generally followed this usage. See Darrah, *Stereo Views,* 3, and Hales, "American Views," 204–57.

42. *Saginaw Evening Express,* 6 March 1882. For a discussion of the relationship between technological changes in photography and the expanding influence of the railroad during the second half of the nineteenth century, see Trachtenberg, *Reading American Photographs,* especially chapter 2, "Albums of War," and chapter 3, "Naming the View."

43. Hudson Keenan, "America's First Successful Logging Railroad," *Michigan History* 44 (1960): 296–301; Meek, *Michigan's Timber Battleground,* 112–14, 136; and Forrest B. Meek and Carl Jay Bajema, *Michigan's Logging Railroad Era, 1850–1963: A Selected and Annotated Bibliography* (Clare, Mich.: Edgewood Press, 1991), 90–106.

44. Keenan, "America's First Successful Logging Railroad, 301–2.

45. Mills, *History of Saginaw County,* 1:403.

46. Hales, "American Views," 206. Hales's essay is concerned with this important transformation in the role of photography at the end of the nineteenth century.

47. For the technological impact of the railroad generally, see David E. Nye, *American Technological Sublime* (Cambridge: MIT Press, 1994), especially chapter 3, "The Railroad: The Dynamic Sublime," 45–76. For the perception of the impact of the railroad, see S. Danly and L. Marx, eds., *The Railroad in American Art: Representations of Technological Change* (Cambridge: MIT Press, 1988).

48. The concept of nature as commodity is developed at length in William Cronon, *Changes in the Land: Indians, Colonists, and the Ecology of New England* (New York: Hill & Wang, 1983), and applied more specifically to the timber industry in Cronon's *Nature's Metropolis: Chicago and the Great West* (New York: Norton, 1991), especially chapter 4, "The Wealth of Nature: Lumber," 148–206. For the concept's specific representation in photography, see Brian Black, "Recasting the Unalterable Order of Nature: Photography and the First Oil Boom," *Pennsylvania History* 64 (Spring 1997): 275–99.

49. Meek, *Michigan's Timber Battleground,* 55.

50. Mills, *History of Saginaw County,* 2:2.

51. For Wright's biography and the extent of his business interests, see ibid., 1–4; and Meek, *Michigan's Timber Battleground,* 52–53, 55.

52. For Ketcham's biography, see *Portrait and Biographical Album of Midland County* (Chicago, 1884), 367.

53. My estimate of Wright and Ketcham Lumber Company's holdings is based upon the following documents: State of Michigan, Midland County, *Deeds,* Book XXIV, 155; XXVII, 9; XXIX, 290; XXX, 148–50, 295–97, 391, 503–4, 587; XXII, 121, 406; and XXXV, 114, 213, 635.

54. Meek and Bajema, *Michigan's Logging Railroad Era,* 175–76, 191.

55. William A. Falkenberg, interview by author, Saginaw, Michigan, 18 February 1994. For a photograph of the "Sampson," see Meek, *Michigan's Timber Battleground,* 113.

56. Berriman, *Upper Tittabawassee River Boom Towns,* 155.

57. Thomas W. Dixon, Jr., *Pere Marquette Power* (Alderson, W.Va.: Chesapeake and Ohio Historical Society, Inc., 1984), 243.

58. Ralph W. Stroebel, "Bryant's Trip," *Saginaw County Historian* 1 (Winter 1983): 32–33.

59. Mills, *History of Saginaw County,* 1:400; Meek, *Michigan's Timber Battleground,* 125; and Ralph W. Stroebel, "Log Boom Companies Operating on the Tittabawassee River between 1856–1904," *Saginaw County Historian* 1 (Winter 1983): 30, which notes that "In addition to the above listed Tittabawassee River boom organizations there also appeared the Huron Boom Company, which operated on the Cass River, and the Bad River Boom Company, which operated on the Bad River and the Shiawassee River."

60. Ralph W. Stroebel, "The Use of Wooden Log Rafting Pins on the Saginaw River," *Saginaw County Historian* 1 (Winter 1983): 31.

61. Stroebel, "Sawmills of Saginaw County," 19–21.

62. Meek, *Michigan's Timber Battleground,* 53.

63. Stroebel, "Sawmills of Saginaw County," 19; and Beers & Co., *Atlas of Saginaw Co.,* 58.

64. Meek and Bajema, *Michigan's Logging Railroad Era,* 43.

65. Ibid.; and *Saginaw Daily Courier,* 25 May 1888.

66. Meek and Bajema, *Michigan's Logging Railroad Era,* 37, 75.

67. Calculation of board feet was accomplished using a measuring device known as a log scale but sometimes referred to as a "cheat stick." By combining the length of the log and its diameter as measured with the rule, the total board feet in the log was determined. For example, a twelve-foot log forty-six inches in diameter contained 1,190 board feet; a sixteen-foot log forty-eight inches in diameter contained 1,728 board feet. A board foot was a piece of lumber one inch thick and one foot square. Harold M. Foehl and Irene M. Hargreaves, *The Story of Logging the White Pine in the Saginaw Valley* (Bay City, Mich.: Red Keg Press, 1964), 36; and Michael F. Slasinski, telephone conversation with author, 30 December 1997.

68. *Saginaw Courier,* 26 January 1888; and Meek and Bajema, *Michigan's Logging Railroad Era,* 75.

69. In 1883, for example, the *Lumberman's Gazette,* April 11, 1883, p. 3, listed seventy-one men killed in Michigan forests by "falling limbs, trees, logs, or in other ways."

70. *Saginaw Courier,* 21 March 1888.

71. Ibid., 24 and 25 January 1889.

72. Berriman, *Upper Tittabawassee River Boom Towns,* 162.

73. *Saginaw Evening News,* 18 August 1890; *Saginaw Courier-Herald,* 18 and 19 August 1890; City of Saginaw, Forest Lawn Cemetery, Section 12, North 1/2, Lot 186.

74. County of Saginaw, Record of Deaths, Book C, No. 873.

75. County of Saginaw, Record of Marriages, Book A, Document 66, p. 5; *Saginaw Daily Courier,* 22 January 1874.

76. Alta (or Altena) Goodridge's vital statistics present a challenging research problem. All of the sources agree that she died on June 4, 1966. The details of her birth, however, are less certain. An obituary and the death certificate list her birthday as February 12, 1891. Her birth certificate records it as September 12, 1891. The 1890 census, however, states that she was born in March 1888 and was twelve years old in 1900. Each of the above documents except the census specifies that the photographer William O. Goodridge was her father and that he had died in August 1890. Each of the documents, with the exception of the birth certificate, also identifies Gertrude Watson Goodridge as her mother. The birth certificate simply records the mother as "Agnes." See *Saginaw News,* 15 March 1952 and 5 June 1966; County of Saginaw, Record of Births, Book H, No. 102; and Michigan, Manuscript Census Schedules, 1900, Saginaw County, City of Saginaw, Third Ward, p. 3.

77. Information on the residence, occupation, and death of Goodridge family members is contained in the published directories for Saginaw for the period.

78. *Saginaw Evening News,* 18 August 1890; *Saginaw Courier-Herald,* 19 and 20 August 1890; *Detroit Plain Dealer,* 22 August and 5 September 1890; and *Anthony's Photographic Bulletin,* 27 September 1890, p. 576.

79. *Saginaw Evening Express,* 22 October 1881. According to a notice in the 9 May 1890 *Detroit Plain Dealer,* the "Goodridge Bro's will break ground for their new store building next week."

80. *Saginaw Evening Express,* 22 October 1881; and *Cleveland Gazette,* 20 August 1887.

81. *Cleveland Gazette,* 20 August 1887. Emphasis added.

82. *Detroit Plain Dealer,* 27 December 1889.

83. Abstract of the title, Lot 3, Block 33 of Hoyt's Plat, East Saginaw.

84. *Saginaw Morning Herald,* 15 April 1883.

85. *Saginaw Evening News,* 2 November 1884.

86. According to Kilar, for example, the "Average Daily Wages of Common Sawmill Labor" varied from $1.21 to $1.75 per day for 11.5 hours of labor between 1876 and 1884. Kilar, *Michigan's Lumbertowns,* "Table 16," p. 215.

87. *Saginaw Morning Herald,* 26 September 1878.

88. *Saginaw Daily Courier,* 27 and 28 October 1874.

89. *East Saginaw Courier,* 28 October 1875.

90. Throughout the second half of the nineteenth century, *Leslie's, Harper's,* and the *Graphic* were the most popular and influential national publications in the United States. Each regularly printed illustrations using woodblock, lithographic, and halftone methods to reproduce photographs purchased from "special artists" worldwide. See Frank Luther Mott, *A History of American Magazines, 1741–1930,* 5 vols. (Cambridge, Mass: Belknap Press of Harvard University Press, 1966–68), 2:453–87.

91. *New York Daily Graphic,* 14 and 21 November and 17 December 1878.

92. *Saginaw Daily Courier,* 31 July and 6 December 1878; and *Saginaw Morning Herald,* 6 December 1878.

93. *New York Daily Graphic,* 3 December 1878.

94. *Saginaw Daily Courier,* 23 April 1876.

95. As early as 1844, Friedrich von Martens, a photographer-engraver living in Paris, designed and built a panoramic camera that could photograph an arc of 150 degrees. The system was based upon a "swiveling lens, which swept around a scene, 'wiping' a continuous image across a daguerreotype plate five inches high and 17½ inches long." Time-Life Books, eds., *The Camera: Life Library of Photography* (New York: Time-Life Books, 1970), 36–37. After Martens, several innovators introduced "banquet" cameras, which were simply view cameras that made photographs 7 x 17 inches and 12 x 20 inches on plates or flat sheet film. By 1900, however, both the Panoram Kodak and Cirkut cameras were available to make true panoramas. Eastman Kodak Company, ed., *Encyclopedia of Practical Photography,* 14 vols. (Garden City, NY: Amphoto, 1977–1979), 10:1843–45.

96. *New York Daily Graphic,* 5 December 1878.

97. "Chronological Roster of Bay City Photographers, 1866–1960, as Listed in Polk Directories," manuscript copy in Library of Bay County Historical Society-Museum, Bay City, Michigan.

98. *New York Daily Graphic,* 5 December 1878.

99. *Saginaw Evening Express,* 16 December 1881.

100. Ibid., 19 December 1881 and 9, 17, and 23 January 1882.

101. Mills, *History of Saginaw County,* 1:403.

102. Ibid., 398, 408–9, and 2:57–58.

103. *New York Daily Graphic,* 4 January 1882. Emphasis added.

104. Ibid., 5 September 1882; and *Lumberman's Gazette,* 20 September 1882.

105. *Saginaw Evening Express,* 6 March 1882. An earlier report in the 26 February 1882 *Saginaw Morning Herald* stated that "Goodridge Brothers, the photographers, have received a proposition from some New York parties to go out to Colorado and take stereoscopic views on the opening of spring." A search of the photographic archives of the Colorado Historical Society in Denver failed to locate any photographs by the Goodridge brothers there.

106. See, for example, *Saginaw Morning Herald,* 29 July 1882; and *Cleveland Gazette,* 20 August 1887.

107. *Saginaw Evening News,* 4 January and 21 September 1888.

108. In August 1879, Mr. Joseph Warner and a Professor Ruger sold a lithographed bird's-eye view of the city to subscribers in East Saginaw. See *Saginaw Daily Courier,* 22 August 1879. In 1885 A. W. Morse & Co. did the same with a fine bird's-eye view of both East Saginaw and Saginaw City. Copy of latter in possession of author.

109. *Saginaw Evening News,* 29 October 1888. The Goodridge views included in *Saginaw Illustrated* are part of a larger collection of Goodridge negatives that were discovered by photographer James Bosch in the basement of 115 N. Hamilton Street, Saginaw, West Side, when he established his studio in that building in 1947. Since its construction the building had been continuously occupied by Commercial National Bank and then Michigan National Bank. Mr. Bosch printed the negatives, which are no longer extant. I am grateful to his nephew, James Devers of Flint, Michigan, for this information and the opportunity to examine the prints created by Mr. Bosch.

110. Mills, *History of Saginaw County,* 1:524.

111. *Saginaw Evening News,* 29 October 1888.

112. *Saginaw Courier,* 21 March 1888.

113. Bernhard E. Fernow to Goodridge Bros., 11 November 1888, "Letters received by the Division," Record Group 95, No. 1, National Archives, Washington, D.C.

114. *Le Temps* (Paris), 5 December 1889. For the nineteenth-century expositions see Robert W. Rydell, *All the World's a Fair: Visions of Empire at American International Expositions, 1876–1916* (Chicago: University of Chicago Press, 1984); and Robert Muccigrosso, *Celebrating the New World: Chicago's Columbian Exposition of 1893* (Chicago: I. R. Dee, 1993).

115. Henri Loyrette, *Gustave Eiffel* (New York: Rizzoli, 1985), 103–68; and Paul A. Gagnon, *France since 1789* (New York: Harper & Row, 1964), 247.

116. On this relationship see, for example, H. Barbara Weinberg, "Cosmopolitan Attitudes: The Coming of Age of American Art," in Annette Blaugrund, ed., *Paris 1889: American Artists at the Universal Exposition* (Philadelphia and New York: Pennsylvania Academy of the Fine Arts and Harry N. Abrams, 1989), 33–52.

117. William M. Kern's correspondence with the Forestry Division is contained in Division of Forestry, "In Letters,"

Record Group 95, National Archives.

118. Fernow to Goodridge Bros., 28 December 1888 and 7 and 31 January and 8 February 1889, "Letters received by the Division," Record Group 95, No. 1, National Archives.

119. *Saginaw Morning Herald,* 31 January 1889. Emphasis added.

120. *Saginaw Evening News,* 22 July 1889.

121. Ibid., 6 August, 3 and 12 September, and 28 October 1889.

122. According to a report in the *Saginaw Courier-Herald,* 13 September 1889, the Goodridge lumber views were accompanied to Paris by "a large exhibit in the forestry department" from Morley Brothers.

123. *Le Temps* (Paris), 20 July 1889.

124. *Michigan Farmer,* 2 November 1889, p. 8.

Chapter 6

1. Ruffin, *Black Presence in Saginaw,* 46–56, contains a list of African American residents of East Saginaw and Saginaw City for 1870 derived from the manuscript census schedules. Subsequently Ruffin published a list of African American residents from the 1900 manuscript census in *Saginaw Valley Documents II: A Collection for the History and Social Science Student,* ed. John V. Jezierski and G. Alexander Ross (University Center, Mich.: n.p., 1990), 261–84.

2. For the development of this pattern at the national level, see C. Vann Woodward, *The Strange Career of Jim Crow* (New York: Oxford University Press, 1957), especially chapter 1, "Forgotten Alternatives," and for Michigan, David M. Katzman, *Before the Ghetto: Black Detroit in the Nineteenth Century* (Urbana: University of Illinois Press, 1973), especially chapter 2, "Patterns."

3. Katzman, *Before the Ghetto,* 115–16, found similar circumstances for African American barbers in Detroit between 1870 and 1910.

4. These figures are based on an analysis of Ruffin, *Black Presence in Saginaw,* 46–56, and Ruffin in *Saginaw Valley Documents II,* ed. Jezierski and Ross, 261–84, as well as occupational lists in *Holland's East Saginaw and Saginaw City Directory for 1868–9,* 159, 277; *Saginaw City Directory for 1897* (Detroit, 1897), 848–50; and *Saginaw City Directory for 1890–91* (Detroit, 1890), 638–39.

5. Ruffin, *Black Presence in Saginaw,* 47, 55–56, 59, 72; and Ruffin in *Saginaw Valley Documents II,* ed. Jezierski and Ross, 263, 282.

6. *Saginaw Daily News,* 21 December 1910.

7. Ruffin, *Black Presence in Saginaw,* 3–4. For a photograph of Atwood see ibid., 34. See also the biographical sketch included in Warren, comp., *Michigan Manual of Freedmen's Progress,* 109–11. For Atwood's lumber mill see Stroebel, "Sawmills of Saginaw County," 15. Before his death, Roosevelt S. Ruffin, who planned to write a biography of Atwood, discussed with the author his belief that Atwood had received a legacy from his slave-owner

father in Alabama that had enabled Atwood to establish himself in the Saginaw Valley.

8. *Saginaw Daily Courier,* 20 May 1871; and *Saginaw Evening News,* 14 September 1886 and 30 June 1890.

9. See, for example, *Saginaw Daily Courier,* 2 August 1876, 19 November 1885, and 31 July 1889; and *Detroit Plain Dealer,* 6 December 1889 and 10 January 1890.

10. Warren, comp., *Michigan Manual of Freedmen's Progress,* 111; and *Saginaw Evening News,* 16 May and 15 June 1888. An indication of Atwood's standing in the state Republican Party appears in a notice published in ibid., 8 August 1888, which stated that the "Hon. C. S. Draper, W. Q. Atwood, Representative W. S. Linton and others from this city (East Saginaw) are expected to give short, pointed addresses at the Detroit ratification (Republican Party Platform) meeting this evening."

11. Warren, comp., *Michigan Manual of Freedmen's Progress,* 111; and Ruffin in *Saginaw Valley Documents II,* ed. Jezierski and Ross, 268. Atwood's will and an inventory of his estate are contained in Saginaw County, Probate Court Records, Roll 120, No. 9672.

12. Ruffin, *Black Presence in Saginaw,* 44, 53; *Saginaw Daily Courier,* 14 May 1876; *Cleveland Gazette,* 18 February 1888; and *Detroit Plain Dealer,* 16 January 1891. Charles W. Ellis died intestate. The inventory of his estate is contained in Saginaw County, Probate Court Records, Roll 53, No. 4990.

13. *East Saginaw Directory for 1884* (Detroit, 1884), 113; and *Saginaw Evening News,* 18 April 1908. Olivet College records indicate that Charles W. Ellis, Jr., was a student at the college from 1881 to 1883. An appendix to the 1889–90 Olivet College catalogue lists all graduates from 1863 through 1889, but Charles W. Ellis, Jr., does not appear on that list as a graduate. Mary Jo Blackport, Assistant Director of Public Services, Olivet College, letter to author, 9 November 1994.

14. *Saginaw Morning Herald,* 30 March 1889.

15. *Saginaw Evening News,* 26 July 1893; and Anita M. Fisk, *The History of Saginaw County Medicine* (Midland, Mich.: Pendell Printing Co., 1986), 40–43.

16. For Dr. Ellis's European trip see *Detroit Plain Dealer,* 3 October and 14 November 1890 and 20 March, 17 April, and 8 May 1891. For the professional relationship between Drs. Ross and Ellis see *Saginaw Evening News,* 26 July 1893; *Saginaw City Directory for 1890–91* (Detroit, 1890), 256; and *Saginaw City Directory for 1897* (Detroit, 1897), 298.

17. *Saginaw Evening News,* 18, 20, and 21 April 1908. For Dr. Ellis's service as city health officer see *Detroit Plain Dealer,* 22 April 1892; *Proceedings of the Common Council of the City of Saginaw, Michigan, for the Years 1892–93* (Saginaw, 1893), 21–22; *Proceedings of the Common Council of the City of Saginaw, Michigan, for the Years 1893–94* (Saginaw, 1894), 17–18; *Proceedings of the Common Council of the City of Saginaw, Michigan, for the Years 1895–96* (Saginaw, 1896) 26; and *Proceedings of the Common Council of the City of Saginaw, Michigan, for the Years*

1896–97 (Saginaw, 1897), 12. Dr. Ellis's will, an inventory of his estate, and a list of his patients at the time of his death are contained in Saginaw County, Probate Court Records, Roll 104, No. 8568.

18. For the development of this pattern in Michigan see Katzman, *Before the Ghetto,* especially chapter 3, "Caste."

19. Saginaw County election results for 1833 to 1881 are contained in Leeson, *History of Saginaw County,* 327–37.

20. For antebellum and Civil War–era politics in Saginaw County see ibid., 338–49.

21. Ibid., 328; and Arendt, *Bay County Story,* 61–68.

22. Positive references to race appear during the 1870s in, for example, *Saginaw Daily Courier,* 23 January, 24 February, and 5 September 1874, 3 February, 1 March, and 9 May 1875, 2 August 1876, and 4 October 1878; *Saginaw Daily Republican,* 27 and 29 March 1878; and *Saginaw Morning Herald,* 8 September 1878, 5 February, 14 March, 10 and 24 June, and 7 August 1879. For the report of Sojourner Truth's visit, see *Saginaw Daily Courier,* 18 October 1877.

23. *Saginaw Daily Courier,* 2 April 1876.

24. Ibid., 27 October 1876.

25. *Saginaw Evening News,* 10 May 1881. For examples of positive racial references during the 1880s see ibid., 3 July 1885, 8 September 1886, 16 April, 16 and 25 August 1887, and 12 January 1888.

26. Ibid., 23 November 1883.

27. Ibid., 21 May 1885.

28. Ibid., 2 December 1884 and 27 January and 1 February 1890; and *Saginaw Daily Courier,* 6 January 1887. In 1885 William F. Goldie, assistant editor of the *Saginaw Evening News,* published *Sunshine and Shadow of Slave Life: Reminiscences as Told by Isaac D. Williams to "Tege"* (East Saginaw, 1885; reprint, New York: AMS Press, 1975), which purported to be a "true" account of the life of Isaac D. Williams but which actually became a caricature of "Uncle Ike" Williams.

29. *Saginaw Courier-Herald,* 11 January 1890. Emphasis added.

30. These figures were obtained by locating residential addresses for the African Americans listed in Ruffin, *Black Presence in Saginaw,* 46–56, and Ruffin in *Saginaw Valley Documents II,* ed. Jezierski and Ross, 261–84, in the East Saginaw and Saginaw City directories for the period and then plotting the locations of the residences on city ward maps for 1870 and 1900.

31. For African American political activity in Detroit during the second half of the nineteenth century, see Katzman, *Before the Ghetto,* especially chapter 6, "Politics."

32. Thomas and Galatian, comps., *Indian and Pioneer History of the Saginaw Valley,* 29; and *Saginaw Daily Courier,* 30 April 1870 and 14 February 1872.

33. The Saginaw African American community, like its counterparts throughout the nation, celebrated both the abolition of slavery by the British in the West Indies each August 1st and the 1863 U.S. Emancipation Proclamation each January 1st, although in Saginaw, perhaps because of the season, the former received much more attention than the latter. See, for example, *Saginaw Daily Enterprise,* 26 July 1869; *Saginaw Daily Courier,* 2 August 1874, 4 August 1875, 21 July and 1 August 1876, 22 December 1877, and 3 January and 2 August 1878; and *Saginaw Morning Herald,* 1 and 7 August 1879.

34. *Saginaw Morning Herald,* 10 August and 29 September 1880; and *Saginaw Daily Courier,* 1 November 1880. The election results are contained in Leeson, *History of Saginaw County,* 336. Notice that Hancock's winning margin in the county was only twenty-six votes. William Quincy Atwood estimated that the number of active African American voters in Saginaw County was at least 150, almost six times Hancock's winning margin. *Detroit Tribune,* 30 April 1888.

35. For a discussion of post–Civil War Michigan politics see Bruce A. Rubenstein and Lawrence E. Ziewacz, "Michigan in the Gilded Age: Politics and Society," in Richard J. Hathaway, ed., *Michigan: Visions of Our Past* (East Lansing: Michigan State University Press 1989), 133–47; Katzman, *Before the Ghetto,* 197–206; and Melvin G. Holli, *Reform in Detroit: Hazen S. Pingree and Urban Politics* (New York: Oxford University Press, 1969), 18–29. Atwood estimated Michigan's African American voters at seven thousand in *Detroit Tribune,* 30 April 1888. For Atwood and Dr. Samuel C. Watson at the Chicago conventions, see *Detroit Post and Tribune,* 25 April 1884, and *Detroit Tribune,* 9 May 1888.

36. *Detroit Post and Tribune,* 25 April 1884; and Warren, comp., *Michigan Manual of Freedmen's Progress,* 35.

37. Katzman, *Before the Ghetto,* 201.

38. *Saginaw Evening News,* 4 March 1884; *Saginaw Evening Express,* 8 March 1884; and *Detroit Post and Tribune,* 26 March 1884.

39. *Saginaw Evening News,* 17, 25, and 27 September 1884.

40. *Detroit Post and Tribune,* 25 April 1884. For Republican political activity in the Saginaw Valley during the fall of 1884 and the failure to include African American Republicans, see the *Saginaw Evening News,* 6 August, 18 and 19 September, 1, 2, 4, 11, 16, 17, and 31 October, and 1 and 3 November 1884.

41. For the gubernatorial and presidential election results for the state and Saginaw County, see John W. Jochim, Secretary of State, *Official Directory and Legislative Manual of the State of Michigan for the Years 1893–4* (Lansing, 1893), 288–91, 370–73.

42. Herbert Fairall, *The World's Industrial and Cotton Centennial Exposition* (Iowa City: Republican Publishing Co., 1885), 19; and *Saginaw Evening News,* 3 September 1884.

43. Rydell, *All the World's a Fair,* 73.

44. C. Vann Woodward, *Origins of the New South, 1877–1913* (Baton Rouge: Louisiana State University Press, 1951), 124–25.

45. Fairall, *World's Industrial and Cotton Centennial Exposition,* 379–80, 175; and Rydell, *All the World's a Fair,* figure 21, p. 82. For a more complete account of the exposition itself see Donald Clive Hardy, "The World's Industrial and

Cotton Centennial Exposition" (master's thesis, Tulane University, 1964).

46. Fairall, *World's Industrial and Cotton Centennial Exposition,* 380. Emphasis added.

47. Quoted in Rydell, *All the World's a Fair,* 81.

48. Quoted in ibid.

49. Kilar, *Michigan's Lumbertowns,* 242.

50. *Saginaw Evening News,* 7 August 1885.

51. Ruffin, *Black Presence in Saginaw,* 56–73.

52. Quoted in Katzman, *Before the Ghetto,* 124. For the relationship between the Knights of Labor and African Americans see Sidney H. Kessler, "The Negro in the Knights of Labor" (master's thesis, Columbia University, 1950).

53. Knights of Labor, *Proceedings of the First Regular Session of the Michigan State Assembly of the Knights of Labor, Held at Detroit January 11–12, 1884* (Detroit, 1884), 4–12. I am indebted to Professor Richard Oestreicher for calling my attention to this information.

54. Knights of Labor, *Report of the Second Annual Convention of the Michigan State Assembly of the Knights of Labor, Held at East Saginaw, June 3–4, 1885* (Detroit, 1885), 4–5; *Saginaw Evening Express,* 29 February 1884; and *Saginaw Evening News,* 3 June 1885. Jonathan Garlock, comp., *Guide to the Local Assemblies of the Knights of Labor* (Westport, Conn.: Greenwood Press, 1982), 208–28, 670, identifies a single fifteen-member "Black" assembly of Knights in Bay County in 1885 among the more than five hundred assemblies in Michigan. Saginaw County had twenty-six assemblies and Detroit fifty-nine, but none is designated as "Black."

55. *Saginaw Evening Express,* 5 April 1885. Emphasis added.

56. For the details of Douglass's visit see *Saginaw Evening News,* 22 May, 17 June, and 3–7 August 1885.

57. For the complete text of Douglass's address see ibid., 5 August 1885.

58. Ibid., 7 August 1885.

59. Ibid., 17 March and 19 October 1886, 13 and 18 January, and 14 and 22 September 1887.

60. Ibid., 15 and 16 November 1887. For a discussion of an earlier form of "Protective League" formed by African American freedmen in southeastern Pennsylvania during the 1850s, of which the Goodridge family may have been members, and the Reconstruction-era convention movement that may have served as the model for the Saginaw and then the Michigan Protective League, see Slaughter, *Bloody Dawn,* chapter 2; and Philip S. Foner and George E. Walker, eds., *Proceedings of the Black National and State Conventions, 1865–1900* (Philadelphia: Temple University Press, 1986), xiii–xxiii.

61. *Cleveland Gazette,* 18 February 1888; and *Saginaw Evening News,* 29 March 1888.

62. *Saginaw Evening News,* 7 and 18 April 1888; and *Cleveland Gazette,* 28 April 1888.

63. *Detroit Tribune,* 30 April 1888.

64. Ibid., 9 May 1888; and *Saginaw Evening News,* 14 June 1888.

65. For Atwood's political activity that summer see *Saginaw Evening News,* 14 and 16 May, 14 June, 24 July, 8 August, and 8 September 1888.

66. Ibid., 11 and 18 September and 2, 4, and 5 October 1888; and Jochim, *Official Directory and Legislative Manual,* 289, 371.

67. *Saginaw Evening News,* 13 and 28 February 1889; and *Saginaw Morning Herald,* 28 February 1889.

68. On April 11, 1890, shortly before the convention, Atwood addressed Bay City African Americans and argued that all leagues "should be free to take part in politics if they choose." *Saginaw Evening News,* 11 April 1890.

69. *Detroit Plain Dealer,* 25 April 1890. The composition of the delegation is interesting in that it included businessmen like Atwood and Robinson, professionals like Goodridge and Cotman, but also laborers like Brown and Gray. Most members, however—five of the fourteen—were barbers. See *Saginaw Directory for 1891–92,* 226, 263, 270, 371, 385, 402, 637, 691, 754.

70. *Detroit Plain Dealer,* 16 May 1890.

71. Ibid.

72. Ibid.

73. Ibid., 27 June 1890.

74. Ibid., 28 November 1890.

75. Ibid., 4 and 18 March 1892.

76. Ibid., 1 and 8 April 1892. The *Cleveland Gazette* reported on 12 March 1892 that the "Afro-Americans of Michigan will hold a state convention in Lansing April 5 for the purpose of securing a better organization of their political forces. Such well known and able men as W. Q. Atwood, Wallace L. Goodridge, W. H. Anderson and J. H. Gray are interested and will make it a success."

77. *Detroit Plain Dealer,* 22 April 1892.

78. For African American politics in Michigan at the turn of the century see Katzman, *Before the Ghetto,* 198–211.

79. *Detroit Plain Dealer,* 25 April 1890.

80. *Cleveland Gazette,* 27 August 1887 and 27 July and 3 August 1889; and *Detroit Plain Dealer,* 6 December 1889.

81. *Detroit Plain Dealer,* 11 July 1890, 20 February, 4 September, and 18 December 1891, and 1 January and 27 May 1892.

82. *Saginaw News,* 4 March 1922; Michigan, Manuscript Census Schedules, 1900, Saginaw County, City of Saginaw, Ward 3; Michigan, Manuscript Census Schedules, 1910, Saginaw County, City of Saginaw, Ward 3; and County of Saginaw, Record of Deaths, Book F, No. 5329, p. 243.

Chapter 7

1. Mills, *History of Saginaw County,* 1:403.

2. For population figures see Leeson, *History of Saginaw County,* 457; Daniel E. Soper, *Official Directory and Legislative Manual of the State of Michigan for the Years 1891–1892* (Lansing, 1891), 649; Fred M. Warren, *Michigan Official Directory and Legislative Manual for the Years 1901–1902* (Lansing, 1901), 512; Frederick C.

Martindale, *Michigan Official Directory and Legislative Manual for the Years 1911–1912* (Lansing, 1911), 225; and Charles J. DeLand, *Michigan Official Directory and Legislative Manual for the Years 1921–1922* (Lansing, 1921), 259.

3. The best account of the end of the pine lumber boom in the Saginaw Valley is Kilar, *Michigan's Lumbertowns,* 260–96.

4. Jenkins, *Images and Enterprise,* 112.

5. Ibid., 115.

6. These figures are based on an analysis of Geuder's "Index of Saginaw Photographers, 1865–1971."

7. *Saginaw Courier,* 20 January 1888.

8. *Saginaw Evening News,* 1 July 1887.

9. *Saginaw Courier,* 21 March 1888.

10. *Saginaw Evening News,* 21 September 1888.

11. New York Industrial Recorder, *Illustrated and Commercial Review of Saginaw,* 20.

12. *Detroit Plain Dealer,* 9 May 1890.

13. New York Industrial Recorder, *Illustrated and Commercial Review of Saginaw,* 20.

14. Biographical and occupational information on Glen J. Goodridge was compiled from the Saginaw and York city directories for the period.

15. Michigan, Manuscript Census Schedules, 1900, Saginaw County, City of Saginaw, Ward 3, lists William O. Goodridge, Jr., as a single, seventeen-year-old photographer who had been born in Michigan in July 1882. There is some confusion as to William O., Jr's., exact birth date in that notations on family photographs indicate that he may have been born as late as March 1883. An exact date of death also is unknown. Saginaw County death records do not include a listing for William O. Goodridge, Jr. The inventory of the family burial plot, however (see City of Saginaw, Forest Lawn Cemetery, Section 12, N 1/2, Lot 186), records his burial there on November 19, 1904.

16. Biographical and occupational information on Mary Goodridge Nichols (Nicholas), Gertrude Nichols, Gertrude Goodridge, and Alta Goodridge was compiled from Saginaw city directories for the period. For an account of Madame Nichols's success, see W. W. Hunt, *Saginaw, 1905–06* (Saginaw, 1905), 13. The likelihood of Alta Goodridge as a student at St. Frances Academy is considered in Sister M. Reparata Clarke, OSP, to author, 3 May 1995.

17. For the location of the Nichols salon at this time see the Saginaw city directories. A brief history of the John Johnson family appears in Gail Verplank, "The Highgate, Johnson, and Farmer Families," *Midland Log* (Spring 1986): 1–42.

18. Biographical and occupation information on John F. Goodridge was compiled from Saginaw city directories for the period.

19. *Saginaw Directory for 1894–1895,* 306.

20. *Saginaw Evening News,* 21 June 1900; and Michigan, Manuscript Census, 1900, City of Saginaw, Ward 3.

21. *Saginaw Courier-Herald,* 30 August 1906.

22. Eugene F. Schreyer, interview by author, 4 December 1991; and Michigan, Manuscript Census Schedules, Saginaw County, City of Saginaw, Ward 3.

23. *Saginaw Evening News,* 4 May 1908.

24. Abstract of Title, Lot 3, Block 33 of Hoyt's Plat, City of Saginaw.

25. Schreyer interview, 4 December 1991.

26. Karen Rousseau, U.S. Trotting Association, Columbus, Ohio, telephone conversation with author, 20 July 1995.

27. S. H. Knox & Co., *Views of Saginaw and Vicinity* (Portland, Maine: L. H. Nelson Co., 1904), 11; and Mills, *History of Saginaw County,* 1:78, 136, 141, 157, 184, 191, 196, 206, 209, 228, 287, 328, 334, 335, 337, 353, 406, 418, 613.

28. For the Nason family see the "Nason Family Clipping File" in the Chesaning Public Library, Chesaning, Michigan.

29. The location of the Nason mill is in *The County of Saginaw, Michigan. Topography, History, Art Folio* (Saginaw, Mich.: Imperial Publishing Co., 1896), 32.

30. Ibid.

31. Harold Seymour, *Baseball: The People's Game* (New York: Oxford University Press, 1990), 214. For an account of the popularity of the Flint & Pere Marquette team see *Saginaw News,* 17 June 1934.

32. *Saginaw News,* 17 June 1934.

33. Mills, *History of Saginaw County,* 1:727. For Spencer Goseline's obituary see the *Saginaw Evening News,* 12 October 1905.

34. Cumming, *Little Jake,* 112–15.

35. *Saginaw News,* 17 June 1934; and Jeremy W. Kilar, *Saginaw's Changeable Past: An Illustrated History* (St. Louis: G. Bradley, 1994), 125.

36. Mills, *History of Saginaw County,* 2:78–80, 1:731.

37. Ibid., 1:245–46.

38. For the daily development of the flood and its aftermath see *Saginaw Evening News,* 26 March to 4 April 1904.

39. Photographs of the extent of floodwaters are reproduced in ibid., 1 and 2 April 1904; and Appleby Brothers, *Souvenir Views of Saginaw's Greatest Flood* (Saginaw, 1904).

40. This data is derived from the published Saginaw city directories for the period.

41. *Saginaw News,* 20 February 1976.

42. Ibid.; and Mills, *History of Saginaw County,* 1:150–52, 706.

43. Roselynn Ederer, "The Semi-Centennial," *Newsletter of the Historical Society of Saginaw County* 30 (November 1995): 4; and *Saginaw Evening News,* 17 August 1907.

44. *Saginaw Evening News,* 19 August 1907.

45. Ibid., 22 August 1907.

46. "Herzog Time Line," Herzog Collection, Frankenmuth Historical Museum, Frankenmuth, Michigan; and Mills, *History of Saginaw County,* 1:568.

47. Tom McDonald, "John L. Jackson," *A Parade of Saginaw Folks I Wish I Had Known, Part III, 1990* (Saginaw: n.p., 1990), 24; and Mills, *History of Saginaw County,* 1:568.

48. Mills, *History of Saginaw County,* 1:570–72; and "Herzog

Time Line," Frankenmuth Historical Museum. I am in-debted to Clara Herzog of Ann Arbor, Michigan, William R. Voigt of Essexville, Michigan, Allen Koenigsberg of Brooklyn, New York, and Martin F. Bryan of the New Amberola Phonograph Company in St. Johnsbury, Vermont, for assistance with identifying the individuals and fixing the dates of the Herzog photographs. According to Mr. Bryan: "Herzog would not have been making the phonograph cabinets at this time, as all models were relatively small and could be set on a table. What they *were* making was the various record cabinets the machines are sitting on. The one under the Edison [in figure 7.28a] is probably their most elaborate cylinder cabinet. It had two doors which opened away from the center post, exposing six discs which each had about 25 pegs. The records themselves would be slipped over the pegs, and someone using the machine would have virtually the entire record collection exposed at one time for easy use. The Columbia and Zonophone cabinets are of a more modest design, having a single door. The Victor cabinet is the most elaborate of all. It was made to house a Victor Talking Machine, horn and all, in the top section. The sound would come through the elaborate grille at the end. There were two shelves underneath for storing records. This cabinet could not have been on the market too long, as Victor introduced their own enclosed horn model in 1906." Martin F. Bryan, letter to author, 28 December 1995.

49. *Saginaw News,* 9 July 1955.

50. Mills, *History of Saginaw County,* 1:572.

51. Ibid., 570–72; and "Herzog Time Line," Frankenmuth Historical Museum.

52. Sergeant First Class Arthur Windt, Unit Operations, Company B, 125th Infantry, Michigan National Guard, interview by author, Saginaw, Michigan, 11 January 1995; and Department of the Army, "Lineage and Honors, 125th Infantry (Third Michigan)," and Anonymous, "Military Companies of Early Days [Saginaw]," typescript, copies in possession of Sergeant Windt.

53. "Military Companies of Early Days,"

54. Welling, *Photography in America,* 175; and Naomi Rosenblum, *A World History of Photography* (New York: Abbeville Press, 1984), 248.

55. *Cleveland Gazette,* 18 February 1888.

56. Rosenblum, *World History of Photography,* 248; and Welling, *Photography in America,* 376.

57. Carroll Smith-Rosenberg, "The Female World of Love and Ritual: Relations between Women in Nineteenth-Century America," in *Disorderly Conduct: Visions of Gender in Victorian America* (New York: Knopf, 1985), 58–59, 61–62, 68. See also John D'Emilio and Estelle B. Freedman, *Intimate Matters: A History of Sexuality in America* (New York: Harper & Row, 1988), especially chapter 6, "Outside the Family"; and Lisa M. Fine, The Souls of the Skyscraper: Female Clerical Workers in Chicago, 1870–1930 (Philadelphia: Temple University Press, 1990), 151–65. I am indebted to Mary Hedberg

and Maria Quinlan Leiby for the above references.

58. Anonymous, interview by author, Saginaw, Michigan, 20 June 1985.

59. Rosenblum, *World History of Photography,* 451; and Welling, *Photography in America,* 202.

60. Dorothy B. Ryan, *Picture Postcards in the United States, 1893–1918,* updated edition (New York: Clarkson N. Potter, 1982), 157–59.

61. *Saginaw Evening News,* 17 July 1902.

62. *Goodridge's Art Souvenir of Saginaw, Michigan, U.S.A.* (New York and Saginaw: The Albertype Co., 1902), 2.

63. Ibid.

64. *Saginaw Evening News,* 17 July 1902.

65. Ryan, *Picture Postcards,* 1–3; Martin Willoughby, *A History of Postcards: A Pictorial Record from the Turn of the Century to the Present Day* (Secaucus, N.J.: Wellfleet Press, 1992), 22–43; and "Development of the Modern Postcard," in Library of Congress, *Detroit Photos Home Page* (http://lcweb2.loc.gov/detroit/detpstcd.html).

66. "Development of the Modern Postcard"; and Ryan, *Picture Postcards,* 145–46.

67. "Versions" refers to the fact that the same Goodridge photograph was sold and often resold to several postcard publishers who used the photograph to produce essentially identical postcards but with variations in printing technique, color, cropping, and perspective (see figures 7.32d–f).

68. Ryan, *Picture Postcards,* 146.

69. See the appropriate Saginaw city directories for the locations of these postcard "publishers."

70. Dave Tinder, letter to author, 5 March 1996.

71. Ryan, *Picture Postcards,* 146.

72. Knox & Co., *Views of Saginaw and Vicinity,* 1.

73. See the appropriate Saginaw city directories for the location of Booth & Boyd Lumber Company.

74. For a detailed account of the campaign to introduce sugar beet agriculture to the Saginaw Valley see Mills, *History of Saginaw County,* 1:466–87.

75. *Report of the Board of Park and Cemetery Commissioners of the City of Saginaw, Michigan* (Saginaw, 1908), 55–56. The *Report* is illustrated with Goodridge photographs of the Saginaw park system.

76. Information on John Goodridge's employment was obtained from the Saginaw city directories for the period.

77. New York Industrial Recorder, *Illustrated and Commercial Review of Saginaw,* 20.

78. Rosenblum, *World History of Photography,* 249.

79. Welling, *Photography in America,* 324.

80. Nancy Knight, Special Research Consultant, American College of Radiology and American Roentgen Ray Society, telephone conversation with author, 21 February 1996.

81. Ibid.

82. For the development of panoramic cameras, see Time-Life Books, eds., *The Camera,* 150–51; George Gilbert, *Collecting Photographica: The Images and Equipment of the First Hundred Years of Photography* (New York: Hawthorn

Books, 1976), 46–48; and Rosenblum, *World History of Photography,* 198. The description of the 1876 Goodridge panorama is printed in the *Saginaw Daily Courier,* 23 April 1876.

83. Tom Hoepf, "Cirkut Was Top Gun among Panoramic Cameras," *Antique Week,* 7 January 1991.

84. *Saginaw Courier-Herald,* 11 May 1913.

85. Ibid.

86. "Contents of Herzog Furniture Time Capsule," Herzog Collection, Frankenmuth Historical Museum.

87. *Saginaw Courier-Herald,* 9 April 1914.

88. *Saginaw Daily News,* 9 April 1914.

89. *Saginaw News,* 8 August 1948.

90. David H. Wallace, *John Rogers: The People's Sculptor* (Middletown, Conn.: Wesleyan University Press, 1967), 244–45, 97–121.

91. This information is based on an analysis of the Saginaw city directories for the period.

92. *Gratiot County Herald,* 16 and 30 May, 6 and 13 June 1918. Arnold Bransdorfer of St. Louis, Michigan, called my attention to these references.

93. *Saginaw Courier-Herald,* 3, 10, 11, and 12 June 1913.

94. Ibid., 12 June 1913. A notice in the 10 May 1913 *Saginaw Daily News* described Kinemacolor as the "'eighth wonder of the world' . . . [the] instantaneous photography of moving objects in their natural colors."

95. Tom McDonald, "Photo Play Men Meet," *Looking Back . . .* (Saginaw: n.p., 1993), 43; and *Saginaw Daily News,* 18 April and 3, 6, 7, 8, and 9 May 1913.

96. Quoted from the opening credits of *Saginaw in Action* (1913), video copy in author's possession. I am grateful to Earle D. DeGuise, a retired Saginaw fireman, for a copy of the film.

97. Quoted in McDonald, "Photo Play Men Meet," 43.

98. *Saginaw Courier-Herald,* 13 December 1900.

99. This information is derived from the Saginaw city directories for the period.

100. *Saginaw News Courier,* 27 August 1920.

101. See Katzman, *Before the Ghetto,* especially chapter 6, "Politics," 175–206, for a detailed discussion of these developments in Michigan and nationally.

102. Ibid., 203.

103. *Saginaw Evening News,* 17 September 1900.

104. Ibid., 1 August 1901; and *Saginaw News,* 31 August 1951.

105. See, for example, the reports in *Saginaw Daily Courier,* 27 July 1876 and 28 and 31 July 1889; and *Saginaw Evening News,* 3, 4, and 5 August 1885.

106. *Saginaw News,* 15 September 1950; and M. W. Prince Hall Grand Lodge, "The Life of Prince Hall" (Detroit: n.p., n.d.), 4 pp.

107. *Saginaw Daily Courier,* 31 July 1889; and Saginaw city directories for the years 1903 (p. 138), 1905 (p. 124), 1907 (p. 129), 1910 (p. 138), and 1912 (p. 143).

108. Saginaw city directories for the years 1903 (p. 138), 1905 (p. 124), 1907 (p. 129), 1910 (p. 138), and 1912 (p. 143); and Gary Reynolds, telephone conversation

109. with author, Saginaw, Michigan, 19 July 1996.

109. This analysis is based on the information available on these individuals in the Saginaw city directories for 1903 through 1912 and Ruffin, "Listing of Blacks in Saginaw, 1860–1900," in *Saginaw Valley Documents II,* ed. Jezierski and Ross, 231–84.

110. Warren, comp., *Michigan Manual of Freedmen's Progress,* 19–20, i–iii, 136.

111. Ibid., 362, 359, 360.

112. Ibid., 4.

113. Ibid., 6–10, 19–20, 30–31, 45, 162, 168, 175, 186, 209, 256, 297–98.

114. *Detroit Plain Dealer,* 11 July 1890, 20 February, 4 September, and 18 December 1891, and 1 January and 27 May 1892. For Margaret Goodridge's employment record see Saginaw city directories for the years 1897 to 1902.

115. *Detroit Plain Dealer,* 6 December 1889. For subsequent Goodridge residences see Saginaw city directories for the years 1890–1922. The mortgages are recorded in James B. Peter et al. to Wallace L. Goodridge and William O. Goodridge, October 26, 1889, Liber 151, p. 384; Ganshow to Goodridge, November 26, 1889, Liber 106, p. 355; Ganshow to Ganshow, February 20, 1907, Liber 151, p. 596; Peoples Savings Bank to Wallace L. and Margaret H. Goodridge, November 6, 1908, Liber 151, p. 280; Wallace L. Goodridge to Peoples Savings Bank, April 3, 1916, Liber 196, p. 76; and Peoples Savings Bank to Wallace L. Goodridge, November 29, 1922, Liber 221, p. 39, State of Michigan, County of Saginaw, Register of Deeds.

116. Michigan, Manuscript Census Schedules, 1900, County of Saginaw, City of Saginaw, Ward 3; Michigan, Manuscript Census Schedules, 1910, County of Saginaw, City of Saginaw, Ward 3; *Saginaw News,* 4 March 1922; and "Last Will and Testament of Wallace L. Goodridge," 28 January 1922, State of Michigan, County of Saginaw, Probate Court, Box 217, File No. 15963. For Wallace L. Goodridge, Jr., see Pennsylvania, Manuscript Census Schedules, 1900, County of Philadelphia, City of Philadelphia, Ward 7, District 147, Sheet 4; Pennsylvania, Manuscript Census Schedules, 1910, County of Philadelphia, City of Philadelphia, Ward 7, District 114, Sheet 3; Pennsylvania, Manuscript Census Schedules, 1920, County of Philadelphia, City of Philadelphia, Ward 46, District 1759, Sheet 8; John F. Goodridge et al. to Frederick R. Strutz and wife, 24 August 1923, Liber 380, p. 85, State of Michigan, County of Saginaw, Register of Deeds; and *Chicago City Directory* (Chicago, 1923), 1433.

117. This information is based on the 1870, 1880, and 1900 manuscript census schedules for Saginaw and the Saginaw city directories for the period.

118. "Last Will and Testament of Wallace L. Goodridge."

119. Death Certificate for Margaret Goodridge, 31 May 1914, State of Michigan, County of Saginaw, Record of Deaths, Book F, p. 243, No. 5329; *Saginaw News Courier,* 3 March 1922; and Saginaw city directories for the period 1889–1923.

120. Death Certificate for Wallace L. Goodridge, 3 March 1922, State of Michigan, County of Saginaw, Record of Deaths, Book H, p. 39, No. 9286; and Goodridge Family Grave, City of Saginaw, Forest Lawn Cemetery, Section 12, North 1/2, Lot 186.

121. *Saginaw News Courier,* 3 March 1922.

122. Ibid., 4 March 1922.

123. "Last Will and Testament of Wallace L. Goodridge"; Probate Court to George L. Henry, 10 October 1922, Liber 367, p. 181, State of Michigan, County of Saginaw, Register of Deeds; and Goodridge to Strutz, 24 August 1923, Liber 380, p. 85.

124. "Abstract of Property," Lot 3, Block 33 of Hoyt's Plat, City of Saginaw; and *Saginaw News,* 9 March 1952.

Index

Titles in the Great Lakes Book Series

Titles in the Great Lakes Book Series